WORD
BIBLICAL
COMMENTARY

General Editors
David A. Hubbard
Glenn W. Barker †

Old Testament Editor
John D. W. Watts

New Testament Editor
Ralph P. Martin

WORD

BIBLICAL

COMMENTARY

VOLUME 29

Ezekiel 20-48

LESLIE C. ALLEN

WORD BOOKS, PUBLISHER • DALLAS, TEXAS

Word Biblical Commentary
Ezekiel 20-48
Copyright © 1990 by Word, Incorporated

Library of Congress Cataloging-in-Publication Data
Main entry under title:

Word biblical commentary.

    Includes bibliographies.
    1. Bible—Commentaries—Collected works.
BS491.2.W67   220.7'7   81-71768
ISBN 0-8499-0228-2 (vol. 29) AACR2

Printed in the United States of America

The author's own translation of the text appears in italic type under the heading "Translation," as well as in brief Scripture quotations in the body of the commentary, except where otherwise indicated.

The illustrations reproduced on p. 231 (figures 1 and 2) are used by permission of E. J. Brill from *Der Temple von Jerusalem,* vol 2 (1980), by Th. A. Busink. The illustrations reproduced on pp. 233, 234, and 258 (figures 3, 4, and 5) are used by permission of J. C. B. Mohr (Paul Siebeck) from *Der Verfassungsentwurf des Ezechiel* (1957) by H. Gese in the first instance, and from *Ezechiel* (1955) by G. Fohrer and K. Galling in the other two instances.

5 6 7 8 9 9 AGF 9 8 7 6 5 4

Dedicated to the memory
of H. L. Ellison
whose torch as an Old Testament teacher
I proudly strive to bear

Contents

Editorial Preface

The launching of the *Word Biblical Commentary* brings to fulfillment an enterprise of several years' planning. The publishers and the members of the editorial board met in 1977 to explore the possibility of a new commentary on the books of the Bible that would incorporate several distinctive features. Prospective readers of these volumes are entitled to know what such features were intended to be; whether the aims of the commentary have been fully achieved time alone will tell.

First, we have tried to cast a wide net to include as contributors a number of scholars from around the world who not only share our aims, but are in the main engaged in the ministry of teaching in university, college, and seminary. They represent a rich diversity of denominational allegiance. The broad stance of our contributors can rightly be called evangelical, and this term is to be understood in its positive, historic sense of a commitment to Scripture as divine revelation, and to the truth and power of the Christian gospel.

Then, the commentaries in our series are all commissioned and written for the purpose of inclusion in the *Word Biblical Commentary*. Unlike several of our distinguished counterparts in the field of commentary writing, there are no translated works, originally written in a non-English language. Also, our commentators were asked to prepare their own rendering of the original biblical text and to use those languages as the basis of their own comments and exegesis. What may be claimed as distinctive with this series is that it is based on the biblical languages, yet it seeks to make the technical and scholarly approach to a theological understanding of Scripture understandable by—and useful to—the fledgling student, the working minister, and colleagues in the guild of professional scholars and teachers as well.

Finally, a word must be said about the format of the series. The layout, in clearly defined sections, has been consciously devised to assist readers at different levels. Those wishing to learn about the textual witnesses on which the translation is offered are invited to consult the section headed *Notes*. If the readers' concern is with the state of modern scholarship on any given portion of Scripture, they should turn to the sections of *Bibliography* and *Form/Structure/Setting*. For a clear exposition of the passage's meaning and its relevance to the ongoing biblical revelation, the *Comment* and concluding *Explanation* are designed expressly to meet that need. There is therefore something for everyone who may pick up and use these volumes.

If these aims come anywhere near realization, the intention of the editors will have been met, and the labor of our team of contributors rewarded.

General Editors: *David A. Hubbard*
Glenn W.Barker †
Old Testament: *John D. W. Watts*
New Testament: *Ralph P. Martin*

Author's Preface

The kind invitation to write this commentary came as a sad consequence of the untimely death of William H. Brownlee, to whom it had been assigned. I am most grateful to his widow, Mrs. Louise Brownlee, for the use of his papers relating to Ezekiel and for the generous loan of commentaries and other books from his library. In some respects this volume takes a rather different tack from *Ezekiel 1-19*, which may be seen as evidence of the diversity which the editors have graciously allowed the contributors to this series. The line which the intended author would have followed may be discerned from his numerous learned articles relating to these chapt rs and from his commentary in *The Interpreter's One Volume Commentary on the Bible*.

As always, I am indebted to my wife Elizabeth for her patient reading of the manuscript and constant improvement of its style and readability. I owe thanks to the National Endowment for the Humanities for a travel grant that permitted a sabbatical term's research into these chapters in the British Library, London, and in the libraries of London University, Cambridge University and Tyndale House. Not least I am grateful to Fuller Theological Seminary for time and encouragement to write and for library and word processing facilities.

LESLIE C. ALLEN
Fuller Theological Seminary
Pasadena

December 1989

Abbreviations

DOTT	*Documents from Old Testament Times*, ed. D. W. Thomas (London: Nelson, 1958)
EncJud	*Encyclopedia Judaica*
EstBib	*Estudios Biblicos*
ETL	*Ephemerides Theologicae Lovanienses*
EvQ	*Evangelical Quarterly*
EVV	English versions
ExpTim	*Expository Times*
FRLANT	Forschungen zur Religion und Literatur des Alten und Neuen Testaments
FzB	Forschungen zur Bibel
GB	*Gesenius' Hebräisches und aramäisches Handwörterbuch*, ed. F. P. W. Buhl (Berlin: Springer Verlag, 1949)
GKC	*Gesenius' Hebrew Grammar*, ed. E. Kautsch, tr. A. E. Cowley. 2nd ed. (Oxford: Clarendon, 1910)
GTTOT	J. J. Simons, *The Geographical and Topographical Texts of the Old Testament* (Leiden: Brill, 1959)
HALAT	W. Baumgartner, *Hebräisches und aramäisches Lexikon zum Alten Testament*, rev. 3rd ed. of KB (Leiden: Brill, 1967-83)
HAT	Handbuch zum Alten Testament
HKAT	Handkommentar zum Alten Testament
HSMS	Harvard Semitic Monograph Series
HTR	*Harvard Theological Review*
HUCA	*Hebrew Union College Annual*
IB	*Interpreter's Bible*
IDB	*Interpreter's Dictionary of the Bible*, ed. G. A. Buttrick, 4 vols. (Nashville: Abingdon, 1962)
IDBSup	Supplementary volume to *IDB*, ed. K. Crim (Nashville: Abingdon, 1976)
IEJ	*Israel Exploration Journal*
Int	*Interpretation*
ISBE	*International Standard Bible Encyclopedia*, ed. G. W. Bromiley, 4 vols (Grand Rapids: Eerdmans, 1979-88)
JAOS	*Journal of the American Oriental Society*
JBL	*Journal of Biblical Literature*
JETS	*Journal of the Evangelical Theological Society*
JJS	*Journal of Jewish Studies*
JNES	*Journal of Near Eastern Studies*
JNWSL	*Journal of Northwest Semitic Languages*
Joüon	P. Joüon, *Grammaire de l'Hébreu Biblique* (Rome: Pontifical Biblical Institute, 1947)
JQR	*Jewish Quarterly Review*
JRAS	*Journal of the Royal Asiatic Society*
JSOT	*Journal for the Study of the Old Testament*
JSOTSup	*JSOT* Supplement
JSS	*Journal of Semitic Studies*
JTS	*Journal of Theological Studies*

KAT	Kommentar zum Alten Testament
KB	L. Koehler and W. Baumgartner, *Lexicon in veteris testamenti libros* (Leiden: Brill, 1953)
KeH	Kurzgefasstes exegetisches Handbuch zum Alten Testament
LD	Lectio divina
Leš	*Lešonenu*
NCBC	New Century Bible Commentary
NICOT	New International Commentary on the Old Testament
NTS	*New Testament Studies*
OLZ	*Orientalische Literaturzeitung*
OTL	Old Testament Library
PEQ	*Palestinian Exploration Quarterly*
POS	Pretoria Oriental Studies
RB	*Revue Biblique*
SBFLA	*Studii biblici franciscani liber annuus*
SBLMS	Society of Biblical Literature Monograph Series
SBS	Stuttgarter Bibelstudien
SBT	Studies in Biblical Theology
SCS	Septuagint and Cognate Studies
SEA	*Svensk exegetisk arsbok*
Sem	*Semitica*
TDNT	*Theological Dictionary of the New Testament*, ed. G. Kittel and G. Friedrich, tr. G. W. Bromiley, 10 vols. (Grand Rapids: Eerdmans, 1964-74)
TDOT	*Theological Dictionary of the Old Testament*, ed. G. Botterweck and H. Ringgren; tr. D. E. Green. 4 vols (incomplete) (Grand Rapids: Eerdmans, 1974-)
ThB	Theologische Bücherei
TLZ	*Theologische Literaturzeitung*
TOTC	Tyndale Old Testament Commentaries
TRu	*Theologische Rundschau*
TynBul	*Tyndale Bulletin*
TZ	*Theologische Zeitschrift*
UF	*Ugaritische Forschungen*
UUÅ	Uppsala universitetsårsskrift
VT	*Vetus Testamentum*
VTSup	*VT* Supplements
WBC	Word Biblical Commentary
WC	Westminster Commentaries
WMANT	Wissenschaftliche Monographien zum Alten und Neuen Testament
ZAW	*Zeitschrift für die alttestamentliche Wissenschaft*
ZDPV	*Zeitschrift des deutschen Palästina-Vereins*

HEBREW GRAMMAR

abs	absolute
acc	accusative
adj	adjective
adv acc	adverbial accusative

art	article
c	common
coh	cohortative
consec	consecutive
constr	construct
fem	feminine
fut	future
hiph	hiphil
hith	hithpael
hoph	hophal
impf	imperfect
impv	imperative
ind	indicative
inf	infinitive
juss	jussive
masc	masculine
niph	niphal
pass	passive
pf	perfect
pilp	pilpel
pl	plural
ptcp	participle
sg	singular
subj	subject

Textual Notes

'A	Aquila
Akk.	Akkadian
Arab.	Arabic
Aram.	Aramaic
B	MT MS, edited by Jacob ben Chayim, Venice (1524/25)
C	MT MS, Cairo Codex of the Prophets
Eth.	Ethiopic
Gr.	Greek
Heb.	Hebrew
K	Kethib
K^{Occ}	Occidental (western) Kethib
K^{Or}	Oriental (eastern) Kethib
L	MT MS, Leningrad Codex
LXX	The Septuagint
LXX*	LXX in its prehexaplaric form
LXX^A	LXX MS, Alexandrian Codex
LXX^B	LXX MS, Vatican Codex
LXX^L	LXX MSS of the Lucianic recension
LXX^Q	LXX MS, Marchalian Codex
MS^G	Heb. MS edited by C. D. Ginsburg (1908)
MS^K	Heb. MS edited by B. Kennicott (1776-1780)

MS^R	Heb. MS edited by J. B. de Rossi (1784-1788)
MT	Masoretic Text
OL	Old Latin
Q	Qere
Q^{Or}	Oriental (eastern) Qere
4QEz^a	MS of Ezekiel from Qumran Cave 4
Syh	Syrohexaplaric text
Syr	Syriac Peshitta
Tg	Targum
Ug.	Ugaritic
Vg	Vulgate
Θ	Theodotion
Σ	Symmachus

BIBLICAL BOOKS AND APOCRYPHAL BOOKS

Old Testament

Gen	Exod	Lev		
Num	Deut	Josh		
Judg	Ruth	1, 2 Sam		
1, 2 Kgs	1, 2 Chr	Ezra		
Neh	Esth	Job		
Ps(s)	Prov	Eccl		
Cant	Isa	Jer		
Lam	Ezek	Dan		
Hos	Joel	Amos		
Obad	Jonah	Mic		
Nah	Hab	Zeph		
Hag	Zech	Mal		

New Testament

Matt	Mark
Luke	John
Acts	Rom
1, 2 Cor	Gal
Eph	Phil
Col	1, 2 Thess
1, 2 Tim	Titus
Phlm	Heb
Jas	1,2 Pet
1,2,3 John	Jude
Rev	

Apocrypha

1,2,3,4 Kgdms	1,2,3,4 Kingdoms	1,2,3,4 Macc	1,2,3,4 Maccabees
Add Esth	Additions to Esther	Pr Azar	Prayer of Azariah
Bar	Baruch	Pr Man	Prayer of Manasseh
Bel	Bel and the Dragon	Sir	Sirach
1,2 Esdr	1,2 Esdras	Sus	Susanna
4 Ezra	4 Ezra	Tob	Tobit
Jud	Judith	Wis	Wisdom
Ep Jer	Epistle of Jeremy		

MAIN BIBLIOGRAPHY

1. Commentaries *(in chronological order; cited by name hereafter)*

Hitzig, F. *Der Prophet Ezechiel.* KeH. Leipzig: Weidmann, 1847. **Fairbairn, P.** *Ezekiel and the Book of His Prophecy: An Exposition.* Edinburgh: T. & T. Clark, 1863. **Smend, R.** *Der Prophet Ezechiel.* KeH². Leipzig: Hirzel, 1880. **Cornill, C. H.** *Das Buch des Propheten Ezechiel.* Leipzig: Hinrichs, 1886. **Davidson, A. B.** *The Book of the Prophet Ezekiel.* CBSC. Cambridge: CUP, 1892. **Toy, C. H.** *The Book of the Prophet Ezekiel.* Sacred Books of the Old and New Testaments. New York: Dodd, Mead, 1899. **Kraetzschmar, R.** *Das Buch Ezechiel.* HKAT. Göttingen: Vandenhoeck und Ruprecht, 1900. **Skinner, J.** *The Book of Ezekiel.* Expositor's Bible. New York: Armstrong, 1901. **Jahn, G.** *Das Buch Ezechiel auf Grund der Septuaginta hergestellt.* Leipzig: Pfeiffer, 1905. **Redpath, H. A.** *The Book of the Prophet Ezekiel.* WC. London: Methuen, 1907. **Gaebelein, A. C.** *The Prophet Ezekiel: An Analytical Exposition.* New York: Our Hope, 1918. **Rothstein, J. W.** "Das Buch Ezechiel." *Die Heilige Schrift des Alten Testaments, Bd. 1.* Tübingen: Mohr, 1922. **Herrmann, J.** *Ezechiel.* KAT. Leipzig: Deichert, 1924. **Cooke, G. A.** *The Book of Ezekiel.* 2 vols. ICC. New York: Scribners, 1936. **Bertholet, A., and Galling, K.** *Hesekiel.* HAT. Tübingen: Mohr (Siebeck), 1936. **Keil, C. F.** *Biblical Commentary on the Prophecies of Ezekiel.* Tr. J. Martin from 1882 German edition. 2 vols. Grand Rapids: Eerdmans, 1950. **Steinmann, J.** *Le Prophète Ezéchiel.* LD 13. Paris: Cerf, 1953. **Fohrer, G., and Galling, K.** *Ezechiel.* HAT². Tübingen: Mohr (Siebeck), 1955. **Born, A. van den.** *Ezechiël uit de grondtekst vertaald en uitgelegd.* Roermond: Romen & Zonen, 1954. **May, H. G.** "Ezekiel." *IB.* New York: Abingdon, 1956. **Ellison, H. L.** *Ezekiel: The Man and His Message.* Grand Rapids: Eerdmans, 1956. **Auvray, P.** *Ezéchiel.* La Sainte Bible. Paris: Cerf, 1957. **Ziegler, J.** *Ezechiel.* Echter Bibel. Würzburg: Echter Verlag, 1963. **Wevers, J. W.** *Ezekiel.* NCBC. Grand Rapids: Eerdmans, 1969. **Feinberg, C. L.** *The Prophecy of Ezekiel.* Chicago: Moody Press, 1969. **Taylor, J. B.** *Ezekiel: An Introduction and Commentary.* TOTC. Downers Grove: Inter-Varsity Press, 1969. **Eichrodt, W.** *Ezekiel. A Commentary.* Tr. C. Quin from 1966 German edition. OTL. Philadelphia: Westminster, 1970. **Brownlee, W. H.** "Ezekiel." *Interpreter's One Volume Commentary on the Bible.* Ed. C. M. Laymon. Nashville: Abingdon, 1971, revised 1973. **Carley, K. W.** *The Book of the Prophet Ezekiel.* CBC. Cambridge: 1974. **Zimmerli, W.** *Ezekiel 1: A Commentary on the Book of the Prophet Ezekiel Chapters 1-24.* Hermeneia. Tr. R. E. Clements from 1969 German edition. Philadelphia: Fortress, 1979. _____. *Ezekiel 2: A Commentary on the Book of the Prophet Ezekiel Chapters 25-48.* Hermeneia. Tr. J. D. Martin from 1969 German edition. Philadelphia: Fortress, 1983. **Craigie, P. C.** *Ezekiel.* Daily Study Bible. Philadelphia: Westminster, 1983. **Greenberg, M.** *Ezekiel 1-20.* AB. Garden City, NY: Doubleday, 1983. **Gowan, D. E.** *Ezekiel.* Knox Preaching Guides. Atlanta: John Knox, 1985. **Lane, D.** *The Cloud and the Silver Lining.* Welwyn: Evangelical Press, 1985. **Brownlee, W. H.** *Ezekiel 1-19.* WBC. Waco, TX: Word, 1986. **Stuart, D.** *Ezekiel.* Communicator's Commentary. Dallas: Word, 1989.

2. Texts, Versions and Textual Studies

Barthélemy, D., et al. *Preliminary and Interim Report on the Hebrew Old Testament Text Project.* Vol. 5. New York: United Bible Societies, 1980. **Bewer, J. A.** "Textual and Exegetical Notes on the Book of Ezekiel." *JBL* 72 (1954) 158-68. **Boadt, L.** *Ezekiel's Oracles Against Egypt. A Literary and Philological Study of Ezekiel 29-32.* BibOr 37. Rome: Biblical Institute, 1980. **Brockington, L. H.** *The Hebrew Text of the Old Testament: The Readings Adopted by the Transla-*

tors of the New English Bible. Oxford: Oxford University Press, 1973. **Driver, G. R.** "Linguistic and Textual Problems: Ezekiel." *Bib* 19 (1938) 60-69, 175-87. _____. "Hebrew Notes on Prophets and Proverbs." *JTS* 41 (1940) 162-75. _____. "Ezekiel: Linguistic and Textual Problems." *Bib* 35 (1954) 145-59, 299-312. _____. "Abbreviations in the Massoretic Text." *Textus* 1 (1960) 112-31. **Ehrlich, A. B.** *Randglossen zur Hebräischen Bibel.* Vol. 5. Leipzig: Hinrich, 1912. **Elliger, K.** "Liber Ezechiel." *Biblia Hebraica Stuttgartensia.* Ed. K. Elliger et W. Rudolph. Stuttgart: Würtembergische Bibelstiftung, 1967/77. **Fohrer, G.** "Die Glossen im Buche Ezechiel." *ZAW* 63 (1951) 33-53. **Freedy, K. S.** "The Glosses in Ezekiel 1-24." *VT* 20 (1970) 129-52. **Herrmann, J.** "Stichwortglossen im Buche Ezechiel." *OLZ* 11 (1908) 280-82. **Jastrow, M.** *A Dictionary of the Tragumim, the Talmud Babli and Yerushalmi and the Midrashic Literature.* London, New York: Trübner, 1903. **Joüon, P.** "Notes philologiques sur le texte hébreu d'Ezékiel." *Bib* 10 (1929) 304-12. **Levey, S. H.** "The Targum to Ezekiel." *HUCA* 46 (1975) 139-58. _____. *The Aramaic Bible (The Targums): Ezekiel.* Wilmington, DE: M. Glazier, 1987. **Lust, J.** "Ezekiel 36-40 in the Oldest Greek Manuscript." *CBQ* 43 (1981) 517-33. _____. "Exegesis and Theology in the Septuagint of Ezekiel. The Longer 'Pluses' and Ezek. 43:1-9." *VIth Congress of the International Organization for Septuagint and Cognate Studies.* SCS 23. Atlanta: Scholars Press, 1987, 201-32. **McGregor, L. J.** *The Greek Text of Ezekiel: An Examination of Its Homogeneity.* Atlanta: Scholars Press, 1985. **Reider, J.** "Contributions to the Scriptural Text." *HUCA* 24 (1952/53) 85-106. **Sperber, A.** *The Bible in Aramaic.* Vol. 3 *The Latter Prophets.* Leiden: Brill, 1962. **Tov, E.** "Recensional Differences Between the MT and LXX of Ezekiel." *ETL* 62 (1986) 89-101. **Van Dijk, H. J.** *Ezekiel's Prophecy on Tyre: A New Approach.* BibOr 20. Rome: Pontifical Biblical Institute, 1968. **Ziegler, J.** *Septuaginta vol. XVI, 1. Ezechiel (2nd ed.) mit einem Nachtrag von D. Fraenkel.* Göttingen: Vandenhoeck & Ruprecht, 1977. **Zorell, F.** *Lexicon Hebraicum et Aramaicum veteris Testamenti.* Rome: Pontificum Institutum Biblicum, 1954.

3. Major Monographs and Articles

Bettenzoli, G. *Geist der Heiligkeit. Traditionsgeschichtliche Untersuchung des QDŠ-Begriffes im Buch Ezechiel.* Quaderni di Semistica 8. Florence: Instituto di Linguistica e di Lingue Orientali, Universita di Firenze, 1979. **Busink, Th. A.** *Der Tempel von Jerusalem von Salomo bis Herodes. 2. Von Ezechiel bis Middot.* Leiden: Brill, 1980. **Carley, K. W.** *Ezekiel Among the Prophets. A Study of Ezekiel's Place in Prophetic Tradition.* SBT 2:31. London: SCM, 1975. **Davis, E. F.** *Swallowing the Scroll. Textuality and the Dynamics of Discourse in Ezekiel's Prophecy.* JSOTSup 78. Sheffield: Almond Press, 1989. **Fishbane, M.** "Sin and Judgment in the Prophecies of Ezekiel." *Int* 38 (1984) 131-50. **Fishbane, M., and Talmon, S.** "The Structuring of Biblical Books. Studies in the Book of Ezekiel." *ASTI* 10 (1976) 129-57. **Fohrer, G.** *Die Hauptprobleme des Buches Ezechiel.* BZAW 72. Berlin: Töpelmann, 1952. **Garscha, J.** *Studien zum Ezechielbuch: Eine redaktionkritische Untersuchung von Ez 1-39.* Bern: Lang, 1974. **Gese, H.** *Der Verfassungsentwurf des Ezechiel (Kap. 40-48) traditionsgeschichtlich untersucht.* Tübingen: Mohr, 1957. **Graffy, A.** *A Prophet Confronts His People.* AnBib 104. Rome: Biblical Institute Press, 1984. **Haran, M.** "The Law Code of Ezekiel xl-xlviii and Its Relation to the Priestly School." *HUCA* 50 (1979) 45-71. **Herrmann, S.** *Die prophetischen Heilswartungen im Alten Testament.* BWANT 5. Stuttgart: Kohlhammer, 1965. **Hossfeld, F.-L.** *Untersuchungen zu Komposition und Theologie des Ezechielbuches.* FzB 20. Würzburg: Echter Verlag, 1977. **Hölscher, G.** *Hesekiel: Der Dichter und das Buch. Eine literarkritische Untersuchung.* BZAW 39. Giessen: Töpelmann, 1924. **Johnson, B.** *Hebräisches Perfekt und Imperfekt mit vorangehendem wᵉ.* ConB OT 13. Lund: Gleerup, 1979. **Joyce, P.** *Divine Initiative and Human Response in Ezekiel.* JSOTSup 51. Sheffield: JSOT Press, 1989. **Klein, R. W.** *Ezekiel. The Prophet and His Message.* Columbia, SC: University of South Carolina, 1988. **Krüger, T.** *Geschichtskonzepte im Ezechielbuch.* BZAW 180. Berlin: de Gruyter, 1989. **Kutsch, E.** *Die chronologischen Daten des Ezechielbuches.* Orbis Biblicus et Orientalis 62. Freiburg: Universitätsverlag, 1985. **Lang, B.** *Kein Aufstand in Jerusalem. Die Politik des Propheten*

Ezechiel. SBS 7. 2nd ed. Stuttgart: Katholisches Bibelwerk, 1981. _____. *Ezechiel. Der Prophet und das Buch.* Erträge der Forschung 153. Darmstadt: Wissenschaftliche Buchgesellschaft, 1981. **Levenson, J. D.** *Theology of the Program of Restoration of Ezekiel 40-48.* HSMS 10. Missoula, MT: Scholars Press, 1976. **Lust, J.** (ed.) *Ezekiel and His Book Textual and Literary Criticism and Their Interrelation.* BETL 74. Leuven: Leuven University Press, 1986. **Miller, J. W.** *Das Verhältnis Jeremias und Hesekiels sprachlich und theologisch untersucht.* Assen: Van Gorcum, 1955. **Mullo Weir, C. J.** "Aspects of the Book of Ezekiel." *VT* 2 (1952) 97-112. **Parker, R. A., and Dubberstein, W. H.** *Babylonian Chronology 626 B.C.—A.D. 75.* Providence: Brown University Press, 1956. **Parunak, H. V. D.** *Structural Studies in Ezekiel.* Ph.D. Dissertation, Harvard, 1978. **Rabenau, K. von.** "Die Entstehung des Buches Ezechiel in formgeschichtlicher Sicht." *Wissenschaftliche Zeitschrift des Martin Luther Universität (Halle)* 4 (1955/56) 659-94. **Raitt, T. M.** *A Theology of Exile: Judgment/Deliverance in Jeremiah and Ezekiel.* Philadelphia: Fortress, 1977. **Reventlow, H.** *Wächter über Israel. Ezechiel und seine Tradition.* BZAW 82. Berlin: Töpelmann, 1962. **Schmidt, M. A.** "Zu Komposition des Buches Hesekiel." *TZ* 6 (1950) 81-98. **Simian, H.** *Die theologische Nachgeschichte der Prophetie Ezechiels. Form- und traditionskritische Untersuchung zu Ez. 6; 35; 36.* FzB 14. Würzburg: Echter Verlag, 1974. **Vogt, E.** *Untersuchungen zum Buch Ezechiel.* AnBib 95. Rome: Biblical Institute Press, 1981. **Westermann, C.** *Prophetische Heilsworte im Alten Testament.* FRLANT 145. Göttingen: Vandenhoeck und Ruprecht, 1987. **Willmes, B.** *Die sogenannte Hirtenallegorie Ez 34: Studien zum Bild des Hirten im Alten Testament.* Beiträge zur biblischen Exegese und Theologie 19. Frankfurt: Lang, 1984. **Wilson, R. R.** "An Interpretation of Ezekiel's Dumbness." *VT* 22 (1972) 91-104. **Woudstra, M. H.** "Edom and Israel in Ezekiel." *Calvin Theological Journal* 3 (1968) 21-35. **Zimmerli, W.** "Das Phänomenon der 'Fortschreibung' im Buche Ezechiel." *Prophecy.* FS G. Fohrer, ed. J. A. Emerton. BZAW 150. Berlin: de Gruyter, 1980. _____. *I Am Yahweh.* Tr. D. W. Stott, ed. W. Brueggemann. Atlanta: John Knox, 1982.

Introduction

Bibliography

Ackroyd, P. R. *Exile and Restoration.* London: SCM, 1968. **Boadt, L.** "Rhetorical Strategies in Ezekiel's Oracles of Judgment." *Ezekiel and His Book.* Ed. J. Lust. Leuven: Leuven University Press, 1986, 182-200. **Carley, K. W.** *Ezekiel Among the Prophets.* SBT 2:31. London: SCM, 1975. **Cassuto, U.** "The Arrangement of the Book of Ezekiel." *Biblical and Oriental Studies.* Vol. 1. Tr. I. Abrahams. Jerusalem: Magnes Press, 1973, 227-40. **Childs, B. S.** *Introduction to the Old Testament as Scripture.* Philadelphia: Fortress Press, 1979. **Clements, R. E.** "The Ezekiel Tradition: Prophecy in a Time of Crisis." *Israel's Prophetic Tradition.* FS P. R. Ackroyd. Ed. R. J. Coggins, et al. Cambridge: CUP, 1982, 119-36. _____. "The Chronology of Redaction in Ezekiel 1-24." *Ezekiel and His Book.* Ed. J. Lust. 283-94. **Davis, E. F.** *Swallowing the Scroll.* JSOTSup 78. Sheffield: Almond Press, 1989. **Gosse, B.** "Le recueil d'oracles contre les nations d'Ezéchiel xxv-xxxii dans la rédaction du livre d'Ezéchiel." *RB* 93 (1986) 535-62. **Greenberg, M.** "The Citations in the Book of Ezekiel as a Background for the Prophecies" (Heb.). *BMik* 50 (1972) 273-78. **Hammershaimb, E.** *Some Aspects of Old Testament Prophecy from Isaiah to Malachi.* Copenhagen: Rosenkinde og Bagger, 1966. **Joyce, P.** *Divine Initiative and Human Response in Ezekiel.* JSOTSup 51. Sheffield: JSOT Press, 1989. **Klein, R. W.** *Ezekiel, The Prophet and His Message.* Columbia, SC: University of South Carolina Press, 1988. **Luc, A.** "A Theology of Ezekiel: God's Name and Israel's History." *JETS* 26 (1983) 137-43. **Lust, J.** "Ezekiel 36-40 in the Oldest Greek Manuscript." *CBQ* 43 (1981) 517-33. **Newsom, C. A.** "A Maker of Metaphors—Ezekiel's Oracles Against Tyre." *Int* 38 (1984) 151-64. **Rendtorff, R.** "Ez 20 und 36,16ff im Rahmen der Komposition des Ezechielbuches." *Ezekiel and His Book.* Ed. J. Lust. 260-65. **Robinson, H. W.** *Two Hebrew Prophets: Studies in Hosea and Ezekiel.* London: Lutterworth, 1948. **Tov, E.** "Recensional Differences Between the MT and LXX of Ezekiel." *ETL* 62 (1986) 89-101. **Zimmerli, W.** "The Special Form- and Traditio-Historical Character of Ezekiel's Prophecy." *VT* 15 (1965) 515-27. _____. "The Message of the Prophet Ezekiel." *Int* 23 (1969) 131-57.

In Ezek 21:26 (21) Nebuchadnezzar is pictured as standing at a fork in the road, wondering which way forward to take. For many, biblical scholarship is faced with a similar choice. On the one hand, there is a literary path, which urges the reader to take the text as it is. This is the approach of the new literary critic under the influence of a modern perspective on literature in general. It is espoused by James A. Sanders and Brevard S. Childs in their canonical approaches to the Old Testament and, in the case of Ezekiel, by Greenberg with his "holistic" attitude to the text. The rhetorical critic and the structuralist are also adherents to this literary approach. It is consciously opposed to the older, historical approach which endeavors to elucidate the text by getting behind it, whether by way of textual criticism, form criticism, source criticism or redaction criticism. Walther Zimmerli is largely wedded to this approach. Thus two important recent commentaries on Ezekiel represent the polarization within the field of Old Testament scholarship. Of course, not all scholars take radically opposing sides. There are many who adopt a mediating approach. They are grateful for the older approach in its various manifestations and are not convinced that it has had its day or proved grossly unfruitful, as its critics allege. They are also happy to learn from the newer so-called post-critical approach and acknowledge that it nicely supplements the older perspectives.

I count myself among this number, a "scribe" who is "like a householder who brings out of his store things new and old" (Matt 13:52). Ezekiel still warrants a thorough study of the total witness to the text. It also requires investigation of literary forms and the way they are used in the book. Not least it necessitates a tentative reconstruction of how the spoken oracles reached their present shape in a literary edition. Yet it must never be forgotten that the book is the proper focus of study, the goal of exegesis, and the end to which all other perspectives are the various means. Ideally the various scholarly approaches should not be pursued in isolation but allowed to bounce off each other in an ongoing team debate toward harmony and truth. The redaction critic needs to listen respectfully to the rhetorical critic, and vice versa. The latter has to appreciate that in the light of other evidence literary artistry may attest redactional unity, while the former must grasp that repetition may be an authentic stylistic device rather than evidence of a secondary accretion.

Ezekiel the Prophet

Ezekiel was a Zadokite priest of the Jerusalem temple, who was swept up in the deportation of leading citizens, including the young king Jehoiachin, to a settlement in Babylonia, after Nebuchadnezzar's conquest of the rebellious vassal state of Judah in 597 B.C. There he received a prophetic call in 593 to minister to these Judean hostages and later to the first generation of exiles after the fall of Jerusalem in 587; his ministry lasted at least to 571 (29:17). It has indeed been urged, since the 1930s, that Ezekiel prophesied partly in Judah. In 1936 Bertholet (xii-xvii), developing Herntrich's earlier proposal, so argued; later the view was popularized for English readers by H. W. Robinson (*Two Hebrew Prophets* 70-79). This view has largely been displaced by a more straightforward acceptance of the book's own insistence that Ezekiel was a prophet to the exiles. But it is not free of problems; hence P. R. Ackroyd, for one, has judged that Bertholet's view is "the more coherent" (*Exile and Restoration* 106 note 20). Moreover, W. H. Brownlee in *Ezekiel 1-19*, never a timid follower of academic fashion, endeavored to argue afresh for Ezekiel's prophetic labors in the west. This commentary, perhaps because it has not had to deal with the evidence of chaps. 1-19, finds Ezekiel firmly in the eastern sector of the Babylonian empire. When westerners are addressed, it judges the address to be rhetorical. Brownlee's stand has impelled a serious focus on the issue of provenance in each pericope.

Ezekiel was an unusual prophet. His priestly background is everywhere apparent: in the vocabulary he uses, in his emphasis on the holy and—since priests had a teaching role—in his didactic approach and echoing of priestly moral and cultic traditions. He is the most sophisticated of the prophets, undoubtedly because the early years of his ministry were devoted to sophisticated people, the elite of Jerusalem. Thus, with communicatory skill, he presents himself in turn as an expert in silver smelting (chapter 22) and in shipbuilding (chapter 27), and harks back to lore of paradise (chapter 28) and to the myths of the chaos monster (chapter 29; 32) and the cosmic tree (chapter 31). His use of extended metaphors or verbal cartoons may have been a device to penetrate into the minds and hearts of shellshocked folk, who had lost everything worth living for. It did not always work: sometimes the message was lost in the medium, and he was asked to speak plainly (21:5 [20:49]).

Since it is a feature of extreme disorientation to cling obstinately to the past and to wish the crisis away, Ezekiel enticed his hearers' assent with barbed, Achilles' heel metaphors. For example, he compared Judah's hoped for ally, Egypt, with the chaos monster—which was destroyed—and powerful Tyre resisting a Babylonian siege with an ocean-going ship, which was fraught with risk for land-locked Judeans, and with the glorious primeval specimen of humanity, who of course fell (cf. Newsom, *Int* 38 [1984] 157). The technique could work the other way: in 37:1-14 the prophet answers the despair of the exiles as to the future by dramatizing the well-known cultic saying that Yahweh kills *and* makes alive.

Another way of penetrating the dulled consciousness of the disoriented exiles was Ezekiel's engaging in representative drama, in perpetuation of a prophetic tradition of symbolic acts. His culturally alien lack of mourning on the occasion of his wife's death and his holding two sticks together, so that they looked like a staff, in each case stimulated interested questions (24:19; 37:18) that led on to the divine message as the decoding of the drama.

In exile Ezekiel's hearers lived in a religious desert, far removed from their world of religious tradition. It may have been for this reason that he presents himself as an old-world prophet, harking back to pre-classical prophetic traditions well known to his audience from their cultic literature (cf. Zimmerli, *VT* 15 [1965] 515-27; Carley, *Ezekiel* 13-47). Thereby he was turned into a living religious institution, an effective vehicle for the nurturing of faith and the communication of divine truth. The mystic pressure of Yahweh's "hand" grips him and transports him hither and thither, like an Elijah reborn (1 Kgs 18:46; 2 Kgs 2:16; Ezek 37:1; 40:1). Like Balaam of old, Ezekiel ritually and ominously turns in the direction of his prophetic target ("set your face," 21:3 [20:47], etc.; cf. Num 22:41, etc.). From the ninth century prophet mentioned in 1 Kgs 20:13, 28 he resurrects the proof saying that culminated in the recognition formula "and you shall know that I am Yahweh" and makes it the keynote of his prophesying. He spoke to the exiles as a prophetic figure from the venerable past. In a landscape devoid of traditional religious forms, he stood out as a religious landmark.

Ezekiel deliberately borrowed and built upon the messages of more recent prophets and doubtless thus enhanced his religious authority. In 22:17-22 the smelting metaphor that Isaiah had earlier used of Jerusalem (Isa 1:22) is developed. In 29:6-7 and 35:12-13 use is made of an element from prophetic narratives concerning Isaiah (Isa 36:6; 37:23-24, 34), while 32:17-32 reflects Isa 14:15-20. The negative marriage metaphor of 23:2-27 is a development of Jer 3:6-11, while the watchman figure of 33:7 picks up Jer 6:17, and the sheep imagery of 34:2-16 is based on Jer 23:1-2. Prophetic truth evidently came to Ezekiel through meditating on earlier prophetic revelation and reactivating it for his own time, just as Jeremiah regarded himself as the Hosea of the southern kingdom. Moreover, this updating of accepted prophetic teaching in a contemporary context was a subtle way of commending his own message, doubtless unpopular in the pre-587 period, which of itself might have been dismissed.

Till the fall of Jerusalem Ezekiel's message had to be one of judgment. Skinner (59) insightfully described his judgment oracles as having one or more of three intentions: to indicate its moral necessity, its credibility over against the people's optimistic illusions, and its certainty. These purposes are clearly at work in the heterogeneous oracles of judgment in chaps. 20-24.

With the news of the fall of Jerusalem, the tenor of the prophet's message changed from judgment to salvation. God's punitive work had been done; now his saving work could be unleashed into the future. As 36:36 later reflected, it was the very double message of Jeremiah, that Yahweh would first destroy and overthrow and then build and plant (Jer 1:10; 31:28). Yet Ezekiel was not transformed overnight into a prophet of pure salvation. Chaps. 33-34 (and 20:32-44) attest that warnings of judgment were still relevant for the heirs of salvation (cf. Rom 11:21; 1 Pet 4:17!). Ezekiel demonstrated a "fine balance between gift and demand in his future program" (Klein, *Ezekiel* 145). The foreign oracles of chaps. 25-32 form a bridge over to the following salvation chapters, and they too mix assurance (25:1-26:6) with a warning note that Tyre's resistance to the Babylonian siege must not revive old hopes (27:1-28:19).

Ezekiel's positive ministry reveals a pastoral concern, not in von Rad's sense of the care of individuals (*Old Testament Theology*, vol. 2 [New York: Harper, 1965] 231-32; cf. Eichrodt 449-51), but as one who took seriously the people's pain (cf. Greenberg, *BMik* 50 [1972] 276-78). He listened with God's ear to their bitterness over their plight (18:2), their dismayed confession (33:10) and their blank despair (37:11). In his oracles he echoed their sense of tragic loss and poured divine balm into their emotional wounds (25:6; 35:10, 12).

Yet Ezekiel was no prophet of mere self-realization. Essentially he was "grounding the necessity for redemption in the divine nature" (Skinner 365; see 36:17-23; cf. Luc, *JETS* 26 [1983] 137-43). He has been called the John Calvin of the Old Testament. (What a pity it is that Calvin never got beyond chapter 20 in his lectures on Ezekiel!) The people of Israel were Yahweh's clients clinging to his coattails, a hindrance rather than a help in representing him in the world. Yet he would prove himself sovereign by pushing them into a sphere of salvation and blessing, and so vindicate his shattered honor. Scholars have spoken of the radical theocentricity of Ezekiel. It dominates the book in Yahweh's constant term of address to the prophet, בֶּן אָדָם "human one, mortal," which emphasizes his own transcendent role, and in the double title אֲדֹנָי יְהוִה "Lord Yahweh" in the messenger formula and the divine saying formula, which begin and end oracles. It is especially reflected in the overall form of the book, which portrays the prophet as enveloped in a divinely woven cocoon, as it were. It is as if he mulled over events and in communion with God listened to their echo in the very voice of God, before delivering messages to the people. For example, even the exiles' remarks are refracted through a divine oracle (33:17, 30-32). Ezekiel lived in a period when Yahweh had lost face through the exile (36:20), when his authority had been impugned through the rebelliousness of his covenant people (24:3; cf. 44:6), and when his holiness had been profaned through an impure cult (20:39; cf. 22:26). Ezekiel's relation to God is offered as a model of what should be, and of what would be when Yahweh was revealed as all in all (20:44; 36:22). "Where men bow their knees before this God and acknowledge that in his just action he is on the move, there Ezekiel's proclamation achieves its proper goal" (Zimmerli, *Int* 23 [1969] 148).

The Book of Ezekiel: Thematic Structures

A key to major themes is provided by their repeated mention over a series of literary units, which thus comprise a redactional block. What follows is a study of such themes that emerge within particular blocks. Ezek 1-24, which relates to Ezekiel's ministry of judgment before the fall of Jerusalem, is commonly regarded as the first division of the book. If Boadt is correct in describing chaps. 15-19 as a self-contained block (*Ezekiel and His Book* 194-96), the way is open to considering chaps. 20-24 as a further block. Indeed, the accumulation of repeated motifs within these chapters points to an intentional juxtaposition. The proliferation of the stem שפט "judge" indicates the main theme. Ezekiel is portrayed as a prophet of judgment, whom Yahweh invites to pass a verdict of judgment upon a sinful people (20:4; 22:2; 23:36). Nebuchadnezzar and his troops are to be Yahweh's agents of judgment (21:32[27]; 23:24 [cf. 45]; 24:14 [cf. the wordplay in the Hebrew of vv 3, 7]). Yet eventually this agent of judgment would become its victim (21:35 [30]). Surprisingly even the new Exodus from exile would confront God's people with the possibility of judgment (20:35, 36).

If Yahweh is judge of his people, what are the charges against them? First, an offense against his divine holiness, consisting of תועבות "abominations" (20:4; 22:2; 23:36). Second, the denial of human rights, exemplified in (the shedding of) blood: 22:2-4, 9, 12, 13; 23:45; 24:6 (cf. 21:37 [32]). Cassuto (*Biblical and Oriental Studies* 234-35) noted this latter link. Yahweh's judgment is described in terms of "indignation" (21:36; 22:24, 31), or "fury" that must be "satisfied" (21: 22 [17]; 24:13) or in a passionate gesture (21:22 [17]; 22:13).

The second generally acknowledged part of the book is the group of judgment oracles against foreign nations in chaps. 25-32. A stylistic link with the preceding set of chapters is afforded by the hinge in 24:21 and 25:3 (Cassuto, *Biblical and Oriental Studies* 235): the profaned sanctuary becomes a theme of mockery, against which Yahweh would strike out on behalf of his people and of himself. A new positive note, at which 24:27 hints, is evident in the oracles against Palestinian states in chapter 25 and also in the first oracle against Tyre in 26:2-6. Indeed, the mocking exclamations of Judah's neighbors, האח "Aha" in 25:3 and 26:2, form an overarching framework. The three literary units made up of oracles against Tyre in chaps. 26 and 27 and in 28:1-19 each conclude with a sinister refrain, ". . . a victim of terror and you will be no more" (26:21; 27:36b; 28:19b). The oracles against Tyre and the final one against Egypt are characterized as קינה "lament," which anticipates the coming destruction of these great powers (26:17; 27:2, 32; 28:12; 32:2, 16). The downfall of Tyre and Egypt would provoke universal lamentation and shock (26:15-18; 27:35-36a; 28:19a; 31:15; 32:9-10). Tyre's sin is described as (גבה לב (ב "highness of heart" or hubris in 28:2, 5, 17. The stem גבה "be high" is used of Egypt with similar intent in 31:3, 5, 10. The doom of Tyre and Egypt is grimly portrayed in terms of Sheol in 26:19-21; 28:8; 31:14, 15-18; 32:18-32. Especially in the final instance it functions as a negative foil to the positive message of life for Israel in chaps. 33-48.

The next block consists of chaps. 33-37. It may be noted that Parunak (*Structural Studies* 158) envisages chaps. 24-33 as a block, with the first and last chapters forming an inclusion, while Joyce (*Divine Initiative* 143 note 82, 144 note 87) takes

33:1-20 as a recapitulation of the themes of chaps. 1-24, and the two watchman passages in chaps. 3 and 33 as "bookends around the pre-587 ministry of Ezekiel." Chap. 33 might be regarded as a self-contained chiastic introduction to chaps. 34-37. The radical announcement of the fall of Jerusalem forms its dynamic center. The warning of judgment at the beginning (vv 1-11, cf. שפט "judge," v 20) is echoed by the concluding v 33. Vv 24-29 serve to apply to the exiles the moral dimension relating to undeported Judeans in vv 12-20. Yet chapter 33 is already looking ahead, even as it looks back to the prospect of judgment on the verge of the promised land declared in 20:33-38: the similarly oriented 34:17-22 picks up the motif of judgment (see 34:17, 22). Moreover, an inclusion for chaps. 33-37 is formed by the promise of life, using the stem חיה "live." The despairing cry of 33:10, "How will we experience life?," receives a gracious response in v 11, which is explained in the conditional offer of vv 12, 13, 15, 16, 19. The word cluster finds an echo in the Death Valley vision and oracle of chapter 37, specifically in 37:3-10, 14.

Life is repeatedly defined in terms of returning to the land (34:13a; 36:24; 37:12, 14, 21) in literary echoing of 20:32, and of receiving Yahweh's blessing in the land (34:13b-15, 25-29; 36:8-15, 29-30, 33-38; 37:25-28). The emphasis on the land reflects the covenant triangle of Yahweh/Israel/land that pervades the Old Testament. So it is not surprising that covenant formulas or mention of the covenant feature in promises of renewal at 34:30-31; 36:28b; 37:23b, 26a, 27; comparable is the use of עמי "my people" at 36:8, 12 (cf. 20). The Davidic king or ruler is assigned a key role in Israel's future at 34:23-24; 37:22, 24. Perhaps the most dominant note that runs through these chapters is the pastoral assurance contained in the recurring promise "Never again . . ." (לא עוד). It faces up to the worries of God's people concerning their future and assures them that God already has solutions in hand. There were worries of royal or foreign oppression (34:10, 22, 28) and of famine and failure in the land and of consequent loss of face among other nations (34:29; 36:12, 14, 15, 30). Moreover, the meeting of Yahweh's own hitherto frustrated desires, the ideals of a united kingdom (37:22) and of pure worship and way of life (37:23), would characterize Israel's future.

The recurring themes of chaps. 38-39 will be treated in the next section. Consideration of chaps. 40-48 will be reserved for their own introduction later in the commentary.

Apart from clusters of themes in the different literary blocks of the book, there are also headline motifs that delineate its overall structure. The dumbness of Ezekiel features in chaps. 3, 24 and 33 in an A. . . A/. . ./A. . . outline. Similarly the watchman motif appears in chaps. 3 and 33 in a B. . ./. . ./B. . . pattern. Israel's realization of Ezekiel's prophetic worth (". . . know that there has been a prophet among them") characterizes 2:5 and 33:33 in a C. . ./. . ./C. . . structure.

The predominant feature of chaps. 20-39 and indeed of the whole book is the use of the recognition formula וידעו כי אני יהוה "and they will know that I am Yahweh" (and variations). Joyce (*Divine Initiative* 91) has compiled a useful table of its occurrences, categorizing it with the nations as subject in contexts of Yahweh's punishing them or (rarely) Israel, and with Israel as subject in contexts of Yahweh's punishing the nations (rarely) or Israel, or of Yahweh's delivering Israel. It demonstrates a pervasive concern for the vindication of Yahweh in the historical context of his people's political calamity. This concern will surface again in material to be discussed in the following section.

The Book of Ezekiel: Redaction

Oral tradition credits H. L. Ellison, to whose memory this volume is appreciatively dedicated, with a statement that certainly accords with his trenchant style: "No doctrine of inspiration is worth its salt that does not take the work of editors into account." The student of the book of Ezekiel has to reckon with the fact that, although it bears clear witness to the oral ministry of the prophet and to his involvement with contemporary concerns, it is marked by a distinctly literary stamp. The evidence seems to suggest that Ezekiel himself cannot be excluded from the process of ordering his oracles in a literary medium. In the discerning of literary layers, in case after case there exists a closeness of perspective to the basic oracle that suggests the same inspired mind at work. Moreover, Davis has observed the significance of the oracle of 29:17-21, dated in the 27th year of exile, which is an update of messages in chaps. 26-28 dated in the first instance in the 11th year:

> Within only sixteen years Ezekiel's words had ceased to be malleable, even by himself; they had entered into . . . the prophetic canon. The speed with which this fixity was achieved doubtless reflects Ezekiel's work in instituting the text as a primary vehicle of prophecy (*Swallowing the Scroll* 63).

Yet the evidence drives us further. Often general literary continuity is accompanied by jumps, generalizations and other discontinuities that go far beyond the specificity and immediacy of the basic oracle(s). It seems best to ascribe this hiatus to the work of other inspired hands.

At this point three observations are appropriate. First, the guiding principle followed in this commentary has been the general one applied to the book of Micah by Hammershaimb (*Some Aspects* 29): "to accept the tradition for those parts of the book where no compelling reason can be urged against their authenticity." American scholarship rightly tends to look askance at the excesses of some German redaction critics, such as Garscha. Second, the later redactional work discernible in chaps. 20-48 reflects a profound sympathy with the prophet's own work and in no way conflicts with it. It seems to have followed closely on the heels of Ezekiel's own ministry, and there is no clear evidence of its extension beyond the fall of Babylon. Third, of itself redaction poses no threat to the authority of the Bible. The discipline can be regarded as seeking to discern the divine means by which a book of scripture was written. Indeed, the same prophetic formulas as elsewhere in the book consistently appear in late redactional material. There is the same claim to divine authority and prophetic inspiration, and a sense of carrying on the work of Ezekiel.

It is conventional to refer to a "school" of Ezekiel or to his "disciples," as Zimmerli (*Ezekiel 1* 70-71) has done. The labeling is only an endeavor to clothe the evidence of redaction with a minimum of flesh and blood. Developing a suggestion of Zimmerli's, Clements has proposed to identify this "school" with those responsible for editing or developing the Holiness Code (H) of Lev 17-26 (*Israel's Prophetic Tradition* 128-33). The suggestion takes seriously the literary links between H and the book. Certainly one must think in terms of a priestly circle of exiles to which Ezekiel himself had belonged in the previous generation.

There are two main redactional thrusts evident in the book. Interestingly, they correspond to the two main streams of contemporary biblical scholarship, historical and literary, or diachronic and synchronic. The first is an endeavor to relate the oracles of Ezekiel to a chronological framework. Dates relating to the year of deportation (597 B.C.) occur in our chapters at 20:1; 26:1; 29:1, 17; 30:20; 31:1; 32:1, 17; 33:21; 40:1. (There are grounds for thinking that the date in 24:1 reflects a separate redactional activity.) Alongside this diachronic approach, which in most cases ties the prophetic ministry of Ezekiel into crucial phases of Judah's last years and may reasonably be credited to his own pen, there is a quite different, synchronic perspective. The book is a series of literary units in which characteristically clusters of oracles trail behind a basic oracle, like a flotilla of ships sailing in the wake of their flagship. Lest we polarize the two approaches overmuch, it should be noted that in the case of 29:17-20 both are at work together. However, there is generally some tension between the two approaches in that presumably the initial date applies strictly to the first oracle in the series. Again, the hand of Ezekiel himself may not be excluded from this second redactional process, as regards its earlier manifestations.

Within our chapters there is at least one example of a negative oracle being capped by an echoing positive one, in chapter 20. The phenomenon, which is similar to the one at work in Hos 2, gives the impression that here is a book produced for exiles for whom the fall of Jerusalem in 587 was already a generation ago, so that Ezekiel's old messages of judgment have lost their historical immediacy. Sometimes a thematic topic governs the selection of oracles within a literary unit. Thus in chapter 34 the covenant motif of Yahweh's role as shepherd to his covenant flock is worked out in two initial oracles (vv 2-16, 17-22) that appear to have different historical references; then vv 23-24 seem to have been borrowed from 37:24-25, relating to Yahweh's messianic undershepherd. The oracle in vv 25-30 gradually moves from sheep imagery to the underlying covenant reality. The metaphorical "wild beasts" of v 7 are translated first into literal terms at v 25 and then into the "nations" at v 28. The section is shot through with close quotation of Lev 26:4-13. Finally, v 30 is a literary conclusion that ties up the unit with a clear statement of the function of the shepherd/sheep imagery as covenant metaphor. One may discern from the distance in tone between the earlier and later parts of the chapter how two of Ezekiel's oracles have been woven into a larger editorial whole. Indeed, the intent of the exilic redactors was obviously to amplify and explain theologically the positive messages of Ezekiel for a second generation who now primarily needed a divine message of hope and assurance (see Clements, *Ezekiel and His Book* 292-94) and yet still needed to take seriously Ezekiel's burden of judgment. Nor is this task performed crudely. The sensitivity of the redactors will be observed time and time again in the stylistic symmetry with which they have lovingly endowed the whole literary unit.

There is no need to anticipate here what can better be done in detail in the course of the commentary. Attention may be drawn to an overall editorial composition running at least from 36:24 to 37:28. In it 36:27 functions as a key two-part verse worthy of grounding in two of Ezekiel's oracles: in 37:1-13 (v 14a echoes 36:27a) and in 37:15-24a (v 24b echoes 36:27b). The prophetic oracles have been woven into an explanatory framework concerning the role of Yahweh's spirit and the means whereby Israel's obedience to Yahweh may be secured.

At two points in the middle of the block of foreign oracles in chaps. 25-32 an opportunity is taken to highlight the positive implications of the oracles for the people of God. One is in 29:21, which has its own part to play in vv 17-21 but within its larger setting fulfills a further agenda. The other is in 28:25-26, which builds on an oracle against Sidon (vv 20-23) and its amplification (v 24) to supply a key to unlock this whole group of foreign oracles. The passage portrays in summarizing fashion Israel's future in its own land, and lays emphasis on its security (לבטח "securely" twice in v 26), an emphasis shared with 34:25-30 (see vv 25, 27, 28) and ultimately derived from Lev 26:5. The passage is comparable in vocabulary and intent with a similar summary in 39:23-29. Now the reference to security (v 26) recapitulates a recurring motif in the Gog unit (38:8, 11, 14; 39:6). Whereas the former passage stressed Israel's security in a context of threat from neighboring nations, now it is reaffirmed in relation to attack from a powerful bloc outside the land. Alongside this assurance, both passages emphasize the vindication of Yahweh as a God of holiness or transcendent power in the eyes of the nations (28:25; 39:27). In the latter case the motif again picks up a repeated emphasis of the Gog unit, in 38:16, 23; 39:7, 13, 31.

This latter emphasis serves to recapitulate a major motif in the book. In our chapters it is an issue, problematic or resolved, in 20:9, 14, 22, 41; 22:16; 36:20-23 (cf. Rendtorff, *Ezekiel and His Book* 261-65). Rendtorff, among others, has claimed that the nations function here as sharers in the salvation promised to Israel (*ZAW* 71 [1959] 33-43). Rather, they function as observers, with their noses pressed against the window from the outside, convinced against their will of Yahweh's supremacy (cf. Darr, *VT* 37 [1987] 271-72; Joyce, *Divine Initiative* 95-96). To this theological theme belongs also the use of the recognition formula recapitulated in 28:26; 38:22-23, 28. The being of Yahweh, in all its specialness, would finally be revealed to both Israel and the nations. Thus both summaries want to pinpoint as significant for the whole book the value of proclaiming Israel's positive future, as a means of providing pastoral assurance for those whose hearts failed them. At the same time, even more importantly, Yahweh's lordship over human history is unhesitatingly affirmed.

The Text

Divergence between biblical scholars as to the role of text criticism is a particular dimension of the general diachronic/synchronic diversity mentioned earlier. It may be seen in a nutshell in two works sponsored by the United Bible Societies. The *Good News Bible*, in its translation of Ezekiel as elsewhere, establishes an eclectic text based on both the Masoretic Text and the ancient versions, and occasionally resorts to conjectural emendation. On the other hand, the *Preliminary and Interim Report on the Hebrew Old Testament Text Project* (vol. 5), edited by D. Barthélemy et al., sticks rigidly to MT and only occasionally feels it justifiable to depart from it. In the present commentary textual study has been treated as a priority, both because of the problematic nature of the text in much of chaps. 20-48 (extremely so in 32:17-32 and chaps. 40-42) and because of my own conviction that one should press rigorously back to the earliest possible form of the text. By this is meant the redacted book of Ezekiel: an endeavor should be made to draw a firm distinction between text criticism and redaction criticism in this respect, a distinction which Fohrer failed to draw in his deletion of "redactional glosses" (*ZAW* 63 [1951] 44).

In the quest for an eclectic text MT is of such importance that very strong grounds are needed to substitute other readings or, as is more often the case, to delete words or short phrases. This principle has not always been foremost in the textual study of Ezekiel. Jahn's textual commentary is a notorious example of a perverse predilection for the LXX and a presupposition that MT was usually wrong. The principle of the harder reading will often induce the retention of MT; so will the appreciation of elements created at the level of translation or versional transmission. When MT is judged inferior to another reading, it deserves the courtesy of a convincing attempt to show how the present form of the Hebrew text may have arisen. As Greenberg has acknowledged with regard to MT in chaps. 1-20, "its soundness cannot always be maintained" (24). We may not return to a pre-critical assumption of *hebraica veritas*, such as Fairbairn advocated: "We abide, then, by the Hebrew text as the true handwriting of the prophet, the very difficulties of which are a proof of their correctness" (470, with reference to 42:15-20). Such a judgment carries inordinately far the principle of the harder reading. To this pre-critical stand the post-critical comes close, as evidenced in Childs' ideological strictures against Zimmerli's textual work (*Introduction* 369-70). Tov has taken a more explicitly sophisticated position in urging that one should regard the different texts of MT and LXX as reflecting two redactional stages (*ETL* 62 [1986] 89-101). Thereby the whole issue is transferred at a sweep into the sphere of redaction, so that two separate, inviolate texts are created. It is questionable, however, whether the principle of purposeful intentionality, which governs redactional work, can be extended to cover most textual variants. Very many of the differences represent the perpetuation of blunders (in both MT and LXX), both by way of the normal errors of confusion of consonants, metathesis and so on, and of the incorporation of random marginal comments into the text, often in the wrong place. The serious student of the early text of the book will seek to penetrate behind such mistakes and obiter dicta to as pristine a form of the text as may be achieved.

As for the ancient versions, we are fortunate to have good editions, such as Ziegler's (second edition) for the LXX, Sperber's for the Targum and Mulder's for the Peshitta. Textual conclusions ever need refining in the light of further study of the versions themselves. The Hebrew text critic is dangerously prone to an atomistic use of the versions that fails to appreciate first their value in their own right. Awareness of this failing must ever induce caution in, though not aversion to, the responsible, if tentative, taking of textual decisions. In the study of the LXX mention may be made of the importance of the second or early third century papyrus 967, the oldest witness to the pre-hexaplaric text, which has fine-tuned our knowledge of the LXX. Its re-ordering of the later chapters, so that chapter 37 is put after chaps. 38-39, has been championed as superior to the traditional order by Lust (*CBQ* 43 [1981] 517-18, 529-33). However, it may rather be judged to reflect a secondary attempt to put 37:24-28 next to its literary supplementation in chaps. 40-48, a well-intentioned change that unfortunately destroys the manifest continuity of chaps. 34-37.

Exodus, Old and New (20:1-44)

Bibliography

Baltzer, D. *Ezechiel und Deuterojesaja.* BZAW 121. Berlin: de Gruyter, 1971, 2-11. **Bettenzoli, G.** *Geist der Heiligkeit. Traditionsgeschichtliche Untersuchung des QDŠ-Begriffes im Buch Ezechiel.* Florence: Istituto di Linguistica, Universita di Firenze, 1979, 195-205. **Blank, S. H.** "Isaiah 52:5 and the Profanation of the Name." *HUCA* 25 (1954) 1-8. **Bligh, J.** *Galatians: A Discussion of St Paul's Epistle.* London: St Paul Publications, 1969. **Coats, G. W.** *Rebellion in the Wilderness.* Nashville: Abingdon, 1968, 231-41. **Falk, Z. W.** "Gestures Expressing Affirmation." *JSS* 4 (1959) 268-69. **Fishbane, M.** *Text and Texture. Close Readings of Selected Biblical Texts.* New York: Schocken Books, 1979, 131-32. **Freedy, K. S.**, and **Redford, D. B.** "The Dates in Ezekiel in Relation to Biblical, Babylonian and Egyptian Sources." *JAOS* 90 (1970) 462-85. **Galbiati, E.** *La struttura litteraria dell'Esodo.* Rome: Edizione Paoline, 1956. **Gese, H.** "Ezechiel 20,25f und die Erstgeburtsopfer." *Beiträge zur alttestamentlichen Theologie.* FS W. Zimmerli. Göttingen: Vandenhoeck & Ruprecht, 1977, 140-51. **Graffy, A.** *A Prophet Confronts His People: The Disputation Speech in the Prophets.* AnBib 104. Rome: Biblical Institute Press, 1984. **Greenberg, M.** "MSRT HBRYT, 'The Obligation of the Covenant' in Ezekiel 20:37." *The Word of the Lord Shall Go Forth.* FS D. N. Freedman, ed. C. L. Meyers and M. O'Connor. Winona Lake: Eisenbrauns, 1983, 37-46. **Heider, G. C.** *The Cult of Molek: A Reassessment.* JSOTSup 43. Sheffield: JSOT, 1985. _____. "A Further Turn on Ezekiel's Baroque Twist in Ezek 20:25-26." *JBL* 107 (1988) 721-24. **Hoffmann, Y.** "Ezekiel 20—Its Structure and Meaning." *BMik* 63 (1975) 473-89 (Heb.). **van Hoonacker, A.** "Ezéchiël xx 25-26." *Le Muséon* 12 (1893) 126-54. **Krüger, T.** *Geschichtskonzepte im Ezechielbuch.* BZAW 180. Berlin: de Gruyter, 1989, 199-281. **Lust, J.** "Ez. XX,4-26 une parodie de l'histoire religieuse d'Israël." *ETL* 43 (1967) 487-527. **Malamat, A.** "The Twilight of Judah: In the Egyptian-Babylonian Maelstrom." *Congress Volume, Edinburgh, 1974.* VTSup 28. Leiden: Brill, 1975, 123-45. **Mulder, M. J.** "Ezekiel xx 39 and the Pešitta Version." *VT* 25 (1975) 233-37. **Murray, D. F.** "The Rhetoric of Disputation: Re-examination of a Prophetic Genre." *JSOT* 38 (1987) 95-121. **Neher, A.** "A Reflection on the Silence of God: 'I Will Not Be Inquired of by You.'" *Judaism* 16 (1967) 434-42. **Pons, J.** "Le vocabulaire d'Ez 20. Le prophète s'oppose à la vision deutéronomiste de l'histoire." *Ezekiel and His Book.* Ed. J. Lust. Leuven: University Press, 1986, 214-33. **Reventlow, H.** *Wächter über Israel. Ezechiel und seine Tradition.* BZAW 82. Berlin: Töpelmann, 1962, 75-78. **Tsevat, M.** "The Basic Meaning of the Biblical Sabbath." *The Meaning of the Book of Job and Other Biblical Studies.* New York: Ktav, 1980, 39-52. **Zimmerli, W.** "Le nouvel 'exode' dans la message des deux grands prophètes de l'Exil." *Maqqél shâqqédh.* FS W. Fischer. Montpellier: Cause Graille Castelnau, 1960, 216-27. _____. "Das Phänomenon der 'Fortschreibung' im Buche Ezechiel." *Prophecy.* FS G. Fohrer, ed. J. A. Emerton. BZAW 150, Berlin: de Gruyter, 1980, 174-91.

Translation

[1] *In the seventh year, on the tenth day of the fifth month, some of Israel's elders came to consult Yahweh, and they sat down in front of me.* [2] *I received a communication from Yahweh:* [3] *"Human one, speak with Israel's elders and tell them: This is the message of the Lord Yahweh.*[a] *Have you come with the intent of consulting me? Upon my life, I am not going to let myself be consulted*[b] *by you—so runs the Lord Yahweh's*[a] *oracle.* [4] *Would you pass judgment on them, would you pass judgment, please,*[a] *human one? Inform them of the shocking history of their ancestors,* [5] *tell them: This is the message of the Lord Yahweh.*

*At the time I chose Israel, I raised my hand in an affirmation to the descendants of Jacob's family. I made myself known to them in Egypt and I raised my hand, affirming to them: 'I am your God Yahweh.' *⁶Then it was that I raised my hand with a promise to them of an exodus from Egypt to a country I had searched out for them—flowing with milk and honey, it was the most beautiful country in the world. ⁷I told them, 'Throw away, every one of you, the detestable objects of worship your eyes gloat over, and stop contaminating yourselves with Egyptian idols: I am your God Yahweh.' ⁸But they defied me and refused to listen to me. They did not throw away*ᵃ *those detestable objects they gloated over nor did they abandon the Egyptian idols. I had a mind to drench them with my fury, to give full vent to my anger against them, while they were still in Egypt. ⁹But I acted in the interests of my name, not wanting the nations they lived among to take a debased view of it, after they had witnessed my making myself known to Israel with promise of an exodus from Egypt. ¹⁰I did bring about their exodus from Egypt, and I provided entry into the wilderness. ¹¹I gave them my rules, I made known to them my standards, upon whose performance human life depends. ¹²I also gave to them my sabbaths, as a symbol of our relationship, wanting them to appreciate that I am Yahweh, the one who sets them apart as holy. ¹³However, the community of Israel defied me in the wilderness. They did not meet my standards, and they rejected my rules upon whose performance human life depends, and they utterly desecrated my sabbaths. I had a mind to finish them off in the wilderness, drenching them with my fury. ¹⁴But I acted in the interests of my name, not wanting a debased view of it to be taken by the nations who had witnessed their exodus I had brought about. ¹⁵However, I did raise my hand in the wilderness, affirming to them that I would not give them entry into the country I had given them*ᵃ—*flowing with milk and honey, it was the most beautiful country in the world. ¹⁶The reason was that they had rejected my rules and not met my standards, and they had desecrated my sabbaths; instead, their bent was to give allegiance to their idols. ¹⁷Yet I turned a compassionate eye on them rather than annihilate them; I did not finish them off in the wilderness.*

¹⁸*"I told their children in the wilderness: 'Don't take over your parents' standards, don't adopt their rules and don't contaminate yourselves with their idols. ¹⁹I am your God Yahweh. Meet my standards, keep my rules and put them into practice. ²⁰Set aside my sabbaths as holy and let them serve as a symbol of our relationship. These are the ways to appreciate that I am your God Yahweh.' ²¹The children defied me, however. They did not meet my standards, they did not put into practice my rules on whose performance human life depends, and*ᵃ *they desecrated my sabbaths. So I had a mind to drench them with my fury, to give full vent to my anger in the wilderness. ²²But I held back my hand,*ᵃ *acting in the interests of my name, not wanting the other nations to take a debased view of it after witnessing their exodus I had brought about. ²³However, I did raise my hand in the wilderness, affirming to them that I would scatter them among other nations, I would disperse them in foreign countries, ²⁴because they had not complied with my standards, they had rejected my rules, desecrated my sabbaths and could not keep their gloating eyes off their parents' idols. ²⁵Also I gave them no-good rules, standards that did not nourish life. ²⁶I made their gifts a means of contaminating themselves, when they*ᵃ *surrendered every firstborn son. I wanted to devastate them—and I wanted them to appreciate that I am Yahweh.*ᵇ

²⁷*"Speak then to the community of Israel, human one, and tell them: This is the message of the Lord Yahweh. Here is another way your ancestors showed contempt for me, breaking faith with me. ²⁸I gave them entry into the country which I had raised my hand in affirmation that I should give them. Yet whenever they saw a high hill or a leafy*

tree, they chose those places to slaughter their sacrifices, make their infuriating offerings,[a] *give their fragrant oblations and pour their libations!* [29]*I said to them, 'What is the high place you are resorting to?' It has been given the name 'high place' ever since.*[a]

[30]*"So tell the community of Israel: This is the message of the Lord Yahweh. Are you contaminating yourselves the same way your ancestors did! Are you giving adulterous allegiance to their detestable objects of worship!*[a] [31]*When you offer your gifts,*[a] *when you surrender your children to the flames,*[b] *all the while you have been contaminating yourselves for the sake of*[c] *all your idols. So should I let myself be consulted by you, community of Israel? Upon my life, runs the oracle of the Lord Yahweh, I will not let myself be consulted by you.*

[32]*"The thought that is in your minds will never happen, the prospect of your being like other nations, like the communities of foreign countries, worshiping wood and stone.* [33]*Upon my life, runs the oracle of the Lord Yahweh, I will use a strong hand, a brandished arm and drenching fury to demonstrate my royal rule over you.* [34]*I will use my strong hand, brandishing arm and drenching fury to bring about your exodus from other peoples, to gather you from the foreign countries you are scattered in.* [35]*I will give you entry into a nations-related wilderness.*[a] *There I will confront you with judgment.* [36]*Just as I passed judgment on your ancestors in the Egypt-related wilderness, so I will on you, runs the oracle of the Lord Yahweh.* [37]*I will make you file under my crook, imposing upon you the obligation*[a] *of the covenant.*[b] [38]*I will purge you of the rebels, those who are disloyal to me. I will bring about their exodus from the country they reside in, but they*[a] *will not obtain entry onto Israelite soil. Then you will appreciate that I am Yahweh.*

[39]*"As for you, community of Israel, this is the message of the Lord Yahweh. Go on worshiping your idols, every one of you, but afterwards, if you do not listen to me . . . !*[a] *You will no longer desecrate my holy name with your gifts and idols:* [40]*rather, my holy mountain, Israel's high mountain—runs the oracle of the Lord Yahweh—is where all the community of Israel in its entirety will worship me, back in that country.*[a] *That is where I will give them acceptance and where I will expect your contributions and your choicest gifts, along with your holy dues.* [41]*I will accept you with your fragrant offerings,*[a] *when I have brought about your exodus from other peoples, gathered you from the foreign countries you are scattered in and so used you to demonstrate my holiness to other nations.* [42]*Then you will appreciate that I am Yahweh, when I give you entry onto Israelite soil, into the country I promised with raised hand to give to your ancestors.* [43]*There you will remember what you did, all the ways you have been contaminating yourselves. You will regard yourselves with disgust after all the evil things you have been doing.* [44]*You will appreciate that I am Yahweh when I have used my name as the criterion for my treatment of you, rather than the deserts of your evil, corrupt ways, community of Israel—so runs the oracle of the Lord Yahweh."*

Notes

3.a. Contra *BHS* et al. the double designation יהוה אדני "the Lord Yahweh" is to be retained as an original standard element in the two messenger formulas: see Appendix 1 in Zimmerli, *Ezekiel 2* 556-62, and L. J. McGregor, *The Greek Text of Ezekiel* (SCS 18. Atlanta: Scholars Press, 1985) 75-93, 195-96.

3.b. As in 14:3, the verbal form is a niph tolerativum, for which see GKC 51c.

4.a. The impf in a question here seems to have the force of a polite request (cf. Wevers, *Ezekiel* 116).

8.a. MT adds איש "each, everyone" by assimilation to v 7. LXX* Syr rightly omit; otherwise the sg suffix with "eyes" would be expected.

15. a. MT lacks להם "them" and reads awkwardly. It is one of those little words easily overlooked in copying Hebrew. A few Heb. MSS and LXX Syr Vg attest it.

21. a. MT lacks the copula, probably by oversight: there is no reason for a staccato clause. Many Heb. MSS and the ancient versions represent it, in line with v 13.

22. a. LXX* Syr lack this clause, which does not occur in the parallel vv 9, 14. Greenberg (368) has drawn attention to the variations in similar parts of the chapter, at vv 6b and 15b, 8b and 13b, 12b and 20b, 16b and 24b. Here the clause is a stylistic variant of v 17a. For the pf see Greenberg.

26. a. For the implicit pl subj see Heider, *JBL* 107 (1988) 721 note 1.

26. b. LXX* lacks the recognition formula, which is certainly suspect since uniquely in Ezekiel it uses the form למען אשר "in order that" (but outside the formula its usage in 31:14; 36:30; 46:18 is significant) and also uses אשר for the usual כי "that." Elsewhere a *waw* consec construction is used or *lamed* with inf (20:12, 20) or once (38:16) למען with inf. However, it does fit neatly into the complex chiastic jigsaw of 3–31 (see *Form/Structure/Setting*), corresponding to the self-identification formula of v 7b. This may well suggest that it belongs to an early stage of the redacted text. The omission in LXX* may have been due to the overlooking of a Heb. line of twenty-one letters (see my *The Greek Chronicles*, vol. 2 [VTSup 27, 1974] 133-37).

28. a. This clause is not represented in LXX*. Its negative tone differentiates it from the objective listing of the offerings and may indicate that it is a later element.

29. a. There appears to be wordplay between הבמה "the high place" and הבאים "resort," which accounts for the strange use of the art with the verb. Moffatt tried to capture the paronomasia by rendering "what is the high place you hie to?" Eichrodt (261), following Rothstein, read בַּמָּה "with what?" for מה הבמה "what is the high place?" Brownlee in a private paper attempted to justify this reading textually via Qumran orthography אליהמה במה.

30. a. Joüon 161b refers to an exclamatory nuance for Heb. questions ("What, . . . !") and this appears to be the force here.

31. a. LXX, cited in *BHS* (τᾶς there is an error for τοῖς), presupposes ובראשית מתנותיכם במשאת "and with choicest gifts, with contributions," seemingly double variants for מה ובשאת under the influence of v 40.

31. b. LXX* omits this clause. It may be an interpretative addition (Zimmerli 402, et al.), but the textual confusion earlier may have caused it to be overlooked, perhaps as a Heb. fourteen-letter line.

31. c. Heb. ל(כל) appears to mean "for (the benefit of), in honor of" on the analogy of זבח ל "sacrifice to," etc. (cf. BDB 515a). Greenberg's interpretation of the phrase as having a summarizing force (371) labors under the difficulty that "idols" is not parallel to the earlier sacrificial expressions.

35. a. Lit. "the wilderness of the peoples," a typological expression corresponding to "the wilderness of Egypt" (v 36), reached after the Exodus from Egypt.

37. a. The claim that LXX ἐν ἀριθμῷ "in number" implies במספר (Zimmerli 403, *BHS* et al.) is unlikely: cf. the verb ἐξαριθμέω used to render the stem מסר in Num 31:5 LXX under Aram. influence (cf. Jer 33:13). Heb. מסרת appears to be an orthographical variant for מאסרת "bond (NEB), obligation": see GKC 23f, Cooke 225, Greenberg 372-73 and Krüger, *Geschichtskonzepte* 268.

37. b. The omission of הברית "the covenant" in LXX* is as likely to be due to haplography as to dittography in MT (cf. *BHS* et al.). NEB rightly retained MT. For the wordplay וברותי/הברית "and I will purge" compare the stem שפט "judge" in v 36 followed by שבט "crook" in v 37 (Greenberg 373).

38. a. MT has a sg verb by a mechanical error: see *BHS*, GKC 145n and cf. note 3.a. to chap. 10.

39. a. The text of v 39a is not very clear: see *BHS*. To delete portions of the text as unexplained glosses (Fohrer 115; Zimmerli 403) is a counsel of despair. The impv verbs appear to be ironical and the conditional clause has a suppressed apodosis (cf. GKC 159dd), expressing a frighteningly vague threat (Cooke 222, 226, Greenberg 374). Mulder (*VT* 25 [1975] 233-37), with some support from Syr, ignoring the MT punctuation, rendered "Let every one of you go and worship his idols, but after that, if you do not want to listen to me, you shall no longer defile . . ." He explained the final verb as "you will no longer have opportunity to defile." Seemingly independently Brownlee rendered in an unpublished translation "Go and serve your idols, each one of you, but later on, even though you are now unwilling to listen to me, you will never again profane . . ." Both renderings are slightly forced. LXX ἐξάρατε "destroy" may imply a rendering העברו "remove" (cf. Zech 13:2 LXX) or בערו "destroy" for עבדו "worship" (Zimmerli 403 et al.). However, the motif of service plays a key role in vv 32-44: cf. vv 32, 40. Moreover, the stylistic trick of repeating nouns or verbs in adjacent sentences (מדבר "wilderness," vv 35, 36; ארצה/ארצם "I will accept," vv 40, 41) suggests that עבדו corresponds to יעבדני "they will worship me" in v 40.

40. a. Heb. בארץ "in the land" is to be retained with *BHS* rather than deleted as a gloss since LXX* Syr omit (Fohrer 115, Zimmerli 403). It conveys a contextually fitting emphasis. Its apparent redundancy evidently encouraged its omission.

41. a. RSV "as a fragrant odor" (cf. Eichrodt 260) implies not an emendation כריח (*BHK,* Fohrer 115), as Wevers (121) claimed, but a comparative use of *beth essentiae*, as GKC 119i explains (cf. BDB 89a). It is a less likely interpretation: the literal use of cult-related terms in v 40 suggests the same here.

Form/Structure/Setting

Structurally and form-critically this chapter falls into two distinct parts, vv 1-31 and 32-44. In literary terms at least the second part functions as the continuation of the first, so that the chapter comprises a single redactional unit. Initially, however, the parts have to be considered separately before they can be reunited meaningfully.

Vv 2-31 represent the prophet's sermon-like transmission of a divine refusal to provide an oracle in response to the elders' request in v 1. This vehement "no," broached in v 3 and clinched in v 31b, employs a variation of a standard oracle of judgment, as v 4a shows. The refusal constitutes the judgment, and a reason for it in terms of accusation is furnished in vv 30, 31a (cf. Lust, *ETL* [1967] 502, 508-9). This reprimand is the climax of a long historical preamble in vv 5-29, which is described in v 4b as "the shocking history of their ancestors." That negative historical survey leads up to the precise accusation of vv 30, 31a. In form and also in spirit this pattern is close to Ps 81:6b-17 (5b-16), a cultic oracle which seems to have belonged to a liturgical service of covenant reaffirmation involving citation of the covenant stipulations. Ps 95:7b-11 is similar (cf. "my ways," Pss 81:14 [13]; 95:10). Both psalm passages, which are not necessarily post-exilic (cf. A. R. Johnson, *The Cultic Prophet and Israel's Psalmody* [Cardiff: University of Wales Press, 1979] esp. 19; by contrast J. Jeremias, *Kultprophetie und Gerichtsverkündigung in der späten Königszeit Israels* [WMANT 35, Neukirchen-Vluyn: Neukirchener Verlag, 1970] 125-27, attributes both psalms to post-exilic Levites), combine contemporary challenge with historical examples of Israel's infidelity in the wilderness period, with the message "Stop being like your ancestors." Here the questions of v 30 convey a similar sense of negative challenge as well as accusation. This type of cultic oracle appears to have been a development of the covenant formulation, which has the twofold pattern of a recital of Yahweh's activity on his people's behalf and a positive call to obey God (Exod 19:3-6; Josh 24:2-24; 1 Sam 12:1-15; cf. J. Muilenburg, "The Form and Structure of the Covenantal Formulations," *VT* 9 [1959] 347-65). A related development is an element in the so-called covenant lawsuit which recalls both Yahweh's benefits in past history and Israel's ingratitude (esp. Deut 32:7-18; Jer 2:5-8; cf. J. Harvey, "Le 'rîb-pattern,' réquisitoire prophétique sur la rupture de l'alliance," *Bib* 43 [1962] 172-96, esp. 178). Those covenant-oriented forms are strikingly akin to this oracle, which has its own covenant emphases, for instance on the covenant stipulations. The form-critical explanation given by Zimmerli (*Ezekiel 1* 405), in terms of a negative antithesis to credo-like summaries of Yahweh's benefits, is unnecessarily vague and betrays his dependence on von Rad's credo hypothesis (cf. Lust, *ETL* 43 [1967] 514).

The main structuring of vv 1-31 consists of a framework of five roughly parallel units, vv 5-9, 10-14, 15-17, 18-22 and 23-26, which are prefaced with vv 1-4 and to which vv 27-29 and 30-31 are appended. Bettenzoli (*Geist der Heiligkeit* 196-97, 203) has correctly analyzed the text in terms of these five units; he characterizes each as beginning with a movement of history, and the first two and the fourth as concluding with a refrain (vv 8-9, 13-14, 21-22). J. Bligh (*Galatians* 372) espied a chiastic scheme in vv 1-16, while E. Galbiati (*La struttura litteraria dell'Esodo* 57) claimed such a structure for vv 6-24. Their evidence is adequately explained by the repetitions in the parallel units, of which they were seemingly unaware. The constituent elements of the units in the framework are (a) a divine oath (vv 5-6, 15, 23), divine revelation (vv 5, 11) and the formula of self-introduction, "I am Yahweh" (vv 5, 19), and the same clause as a concluding formula (vv 7, 12, 20, 26); (b) human sin in terms of rebellion against Yahweh (vv 7-8a, 13a, 16, 21a, 24); (c) Yahweh's resolve to punish (vv 8b, 13b, 21b); and (d) his relenting (vv 9, 14, 17, 22), in three cases "in the interests of my name" (vv 9, 14, 22).

The symmetry of the five units is by no means exact, doubtless in illustration of the "symmetriphobia" of Hebrew literature, to use the term coined by G. A. Smith. For instance, the divine oath is positive in v 5, but negative in vv 15 and 23—and replaced by a divine appeal in vv 18-20. This variation is logical and true to Yahweh's nature: mercy and judgment were tussling in the heart of God. His relenting for his name's sake (שמי למען, vv 9, 14, 22) is ultimately capped by a statement of divine purpose, "I wanted to devastate them" (אשמם למען, v 26), with a striking wordplay which enhances the eventual turning from repeated demonstrations of mercy to final punishment. Lust (*ETL* 43 [1967] 496-502), after a useful discussion of the evidence, has analyzed vv 5-26 in terms of three rigorously symmetrical sections, (a) vv 5, 7-9a, (b) vv 6, 10-14, (c) vv 15, 16, 18-21, 22aβ-b, and also a final partial section, vv 23-26. He pays a price for consistent parallelism, which some may consider too heavy: he has to transpose v 6 and delete as glosses v 17 and also material in vv 9 and 22.

Generally historical periodization, with a glance toward repeated terminology, is made the basis of dividing the text into three sections, vv 5-9, 10-17, 18-26 (e.g., Wevers 115; Zimmerli 407; cf. J. Krašovec, *Antithetic Structure in Biblical Hebrew Poetry* [VTSup 35, Leiden: Brill, 1984] 103-4, who finds an antithetic core in the first section, which is differently expanded in the second and third) or into four sections, vv 5-9, 10-14, 15-22, 23-26 (e.g., Cooke 213; cf. Fohrer 107). Close to the latter is Parunak's scheme of four sections, vv 5-9, 10-14, 15-22 and 23-44 (*Structural Studies* 291-300), who finds three motifs, revelation, rebellion and wrath/reputation represented in the first three sections and expanded in the last (vv 5-7 + 8a + 8b-9, 10-12 + 13a + 13b-14, 15-20 + 21a + 21b-22, 23-26 + 29-32 + 33-44). The two main schemes reflect uncertainty over whether a break occurs after v 14 or after v 18, which a fivefold division resolves.

There is historical development between the five parts. Vv 5-9 begin the story in Egypt, and vv 10-17 move on to the first wilderness generation in a sequence of two parts, vv 10-14 and 15-17, while vv 18-26 progress to the second wilderness generation, again in two parts, vv 18-22 and 23-26. This structuring in an A/B1/B2/C1/C2 pattern cries out for a climax D. It is to be found in vv 30-31; it establishes a movement from Israel past in Egypt and the wilderness to Israel present in the land. The climax smoothly echoes the terminology of v 26 and concludes well by accusing the present generation of their ancestors' crimes. Subsequently but early in the history of the text (see below), vv 27-29 seem to have been inserted. They fill the historical gap of Israel's ancient experience in the land, but make no pretense to follow the parallelism of the five earlier units.

The whole passage, vv 3-31, with the notable incorporation of vv 27-29 into the framework material, has been woven into a chiasmus. The phenomenon of dual structuring in some of the Psalms, such as Pss 73 (see my article "Ps 73: An Analysis," *TynBul* 33 [1982] 93-107), 111, 137 and 140 (see my *Psalms 101-150* [WBC 21] 91, 241, 267) makes it not implausible here. The chiasmus develops the obvious inclusion in vv 3 and 31 and much of the parallelism of the separate units into a remarkable symphony of terms and motifs: A/A', vv 3, 31; B/B', vv 4, 30; C/C', vv 6, 28; D/D', vv 7a, 27b (vocabulary from the same semantic field); E/E', vv 7b-8a, 26-27a; F/F', vv 8b-11, 21b-25; G/G', vv 12-13, 20-21; H/H', vv 16, 18aβ-b; I/I', vv 17b, 18aα. The two halves of the chiastic composition are vv 3-17 and 18-31. With the incorporation of vv 3, 4 and 27-29 the overall development has been altered slightly. There is a movement from the present generation back to Egypt and the first wilderness generation (vv 3-17) and onwards to the second wilderness generation and Israel's past experience in the land and finally to Israel's present behavior there (vv 18-31). The hinge is the double phrase במדבר "in the wilderness" (vv 17, 18). A detailed study of this chiastic structure would reveal that a number of motifs are pushed to the fore. Most significant perhaps is the matching of God's life-affirming gift of his covenant terms and another, fatal, set at the end of F/F', vv 11, 25. Israel's shrugging off Yahweh's sovereign claims in favor of pagan religion is also highlighted (H/H', vv 16, 18). So too is their slighting of the distinctive role of the sabbath in the course of G/G' (vv 12, 20). Another impressive pair of correspondents is the ignored appeal from God to "stop contaminating yourselves" and his providential punishment whereby his unwanted gifts became "a means of contaminating themselves" (E/E', vv 7, 26).

The chronological setting of vv 1-31 is given in v 1 as 591 B.C. The dating in terms of King Jehoiachin's period of exile (cf. the explicit 1:2 and also 8:1) suggests that Babylon is the geographical setting rather than Palestine *pace* Brownlee (*Ezekiel 1-19* 127). The only obstacle to this locale is the mention of child sacrifice in v 31, which Cooke (220), Zimmerli (402, 412) et al., doubtless partly for this reason, removed as a gloss. Heider (*The Cult of Molek* 272-74) has reminded us that, unlike Jer 24, Ezekiel did not sharply distinguish between the exiles of 597 B.C. and the Judeans left in the land: "rather, Ezekiel's attention constantly alternates between Palestine and Mesopotamia, and 'house of Israel' includes the Israelites in both places." Thus mention of cultic aberrations in Jerusalem can be envisaged, even as the prophet addressed members of the covenant community who lived hundreds of miles away from there.

And what of vv 32-44? Their form is generally recognized as that of a disputation speech. The form is used here as the vehicle of a proclamation of salvation, a not infrequent combination of forms (cf. C. Westermann, *Isaiah 40-46* [ET Philadelphia: Westminster, 1969] 14). Here, however, the positive message of the proclamation is interwoven with an announcement of (partial) judgment (vv 33-38). Comparable is Mic 4:9, 10, although there the balance is tilted more toward the negative (cf. my *The Books of Joel, Obadiah, Jonah and Micah* [NICOT. Grand Rapids: Eerdmans, 1976] 332-34). Graffy (*A Prophet Confronts*, 65-72) has analyzed the passage in detail. The disputation speech contains (a) an introduction in v 32a, (b) a quotation of the people in v 32b, (c) a "programmatic refutation" or brief rebuttal (cf. 18:3, 4; 33:11; Isa 49:15; Hag 1:4) in v 33, which contains an oath formula (cf. 18:3, 4; 13:3, 11), and (d) a main refutation in three parts, vv 34-38, 39-42 and 43-44 (cf. Zimmerli 414). This analysis needs to be refined in the light of Murray's study (*JSOT* 38 [1987] 95-121), as introduction, thesis, dispute and counterthesis. Graffy has seen in his three parts of vv 34-44 a counterbalance to the three stages of Israel's history portrayed in vv 1-33 (vv 5-9, 10-17, 18-26); he compares the three stages of the disputation speech in 18:1-20. However, rhetorical analysis of the passage supports the medial break after v 38 envisaged by D. Baltzer (*Ezechiel und Deuterojesaja* 2). Yet Baltzer's division into two parts, vv 33-38 and 39-44, on grounds of form and conduct, requires refinement. Vv 32, 33 function as an introduction and vv 43, 44 as a conclusion, while the main part, vv 34-42, splits into vv 34-38 and 39-42. Evidence for this structuring is as follows. There is a prominent inclusion in vv 34 and 41, featuring ten Hebrew words (cf. Parunak, *Structural Studies* 798-99). The climactic recognition formula used in vv 38 and 42 is employed in contexts of non-entry and entry into the land respectively, whereas the one in v 44 has a different rationale in view. Each of the four parts, vv 32-33, 34-38, 39-42 and 43-44, contains an instance of the appended messenger formula, at vv 33, 36, 40 and 44. Each half of the main portion contains a reference to אבותיכם "your ancestors" (vv 36, 42).

The situation is obviously exilic in view of the content of the oracle. The rank despair of the quotation, however, appears not to presuppose a 591 B.C. dating, like the first oracle (v 1), but to envisage the total collapse of Judah rather than the first deportation of 597 B.C. Accordingly it must have originated after 587 B.C. (Fohrer 114; Zimmerli 414; Wevers 119). Zimmerli, who finds no good grounds to deny the oracle to Ezekiel, has drawn attention to the allusions to a new temple in vv 40, 41 as a harbinger of material in chaps. 40-48, which are dated 573 B.C. (40:1).

The separate oracles in vv 1-31 and 32-44 comprise a redactional unit. The second message has a host of verbal echoes of the first: the oath formula rendered "upon my life" (vv 3, 31, 33), God's raising of his hand (vv 5, 6, 15, 23, 28, 42), "idols" (vv 7, 8, 16, 18, 31, 39), "gifts" (vv 31, 39), the references to God's drenching fury (vv 8, 13, 21, 33, 34), the climactic second plural references to self-contamination (vv 31, 43) and the motif of the divine name as a positive motivation (vv 9, 14, 22, 44). Moreover, vv 33-35 and 42 develop the earlier use of Exod 6:6-8 (Fishbane, *Text and Texture* 132). Thus the second oracle has an impressive rapport with motifs used in the framework and conclusion of the first one. Graffy (*A Prophet Confronts* 65), noting the lack of a full introduction to the disputation speech, in contrast to 12:26, 27 and 18:1, 2, feasibly explains it as evidence that the oracle was intended to be regarded as closely related to what precedes. The brevity of the introduction and the linking with the conjunction *waw* (cf. Isa 49:14) may suggest that Ezekiel himself meant it as a sequel to the earlier oracle (cf. Zimmerli, *Prophecy* 187). The new conclusion tempered the previous refusal with a fresh message that blended negative with positive elements. Brownlee (243-44) suggested a similar development in the case of the negative 16:2-43 and the positive 16:44-63 (cf. Baltzer, *Ezechiel und Deuterojesaja* 11 n. 50).

Comment

In vv 1-31 a consultation with the prophet to ascertain the divine will meets with a negative response. His refusal is grounded in an accusation of wrongdoing which in turn is backed by a review of Israel's early history. History was repeating itself, it is implied, and spores of doom sown long ago were now spawning their terrible harvest.

1 The date is given as August 591 B.C., August 14th, according to R. A. Parker and W. H. Dubberstein's reconstruction (*Babylonian Chronology, 626 B.C.-A.D. 75* [Providence: Brown University Press, 1956] 28). The "seventh year" is that of Jehoiachin's exile, which took place in Nebuchadnezzar's seventh year, in our reckoning in 597 B.C. The previous dating in the book was in 8:1, referring to 592 B.C. Time was passing between the first Judean deportation in 597 B.C. and the second in 587 B.C. It was punctuated by a desire of the first group of exiles to ascertain Yahweh's will for them, in anxious hope of restoration. There have been endeavors to relate the dating to happenings in Palestine. Malamat (*Congress Volume* 138-39) has drawn attention to the prediction of Hananiah in August 593 B.C. that the exile would last only two years longer (Jer 28:1-4). He inferred that the elders hoped for Ezekiel's confirmation that return to the land was imminent. Nothing in the text, however, supports this hypothesis (B. Lang, *Ezechiel: der Prophet und das Buch* [Darmstadt: Wissenschaftliche Gesellschaft, 1981] 35). Freedy and Redford (*JAOS* 90 [1970] 480) have found in the mention of Egypt (vv 5-10) an oblique reference to Judean expectations that Egypt would support rebellion against Babylon after the recent festal visit Psammetichus II had paid to Syria and Palestine in 591 B.C. However, the reign of the Pharaoh is to be dated 595-589 (Malamat, *Congress Volume* 141; cf. K. A. Kitchen, *The Third Intermediate Period in Egypt* [Warminster: Aris and Phillips, 1973] 406-7), so that the fourth year in which the visit occurred was 592, and thus less relevant. All that we can infer is that the exiled leaders looked for good news about return to the land, which Ezekiel was unable to transmit to them. The supposition that the exiles were enquiring about instituting a sacrificial system of worship (Fohrer 108; cf. v 32) runs into the obstacle that v 32 begins a separate unit.

3 The characteristic address of the prophet as "human one" draws attention to his creaturely role and so by contrast to the transcendent nature of Yahweh as arbiter of his people's destiny (cf. Zimmerli 131). The habitual use of the title "Lord" in the two adjacent messenger formulas underlines this concept. The divine oath sworn "upon my life" stresses that the request ran counter to Yahweh's very being and will.

4 The indictment in contemporary terms is to appear in vv 30, 31. The intervening historical review plays an important part in establishing that present sins were symptomatic of radical willfulness and the climax of a trend that made the exile inevitable.

5, 6 Only here does Ezekiel use the deuteronomic concept of election (cf. Deut 7:7; 14:2). It is the first of a series of indications of Yahweh's concern for his people, a concern that was to be sorely tried by rebellion. From priestly tradition concerning Israel's experience in Egypt the prophet borrows the motifs of God's self-disclosure by name and of his sworn promise of the land (cf. Exod 6:3, 6-8). The reference to the physical gesture generally associated with swearing an oath, current still in modern courts of law, enhances an impression of divine commitment to his people's welfare. In v 5, however, raising the hand relates not simply to an oath but to the making of a covenant (cf. Falk, *JSS* 4 [1959] 268-69; Ehrlich, *Randglossen* 73). Yahweh's promise of salvation lay at the basis of his relationship with Israel; it was reinforced by promise of subsequent blessing. The lovegift of the land was the result of Yahweh's careful searching: only the best was good enough for his people. The reference to searching takes up a term used in Num 13-14 of the spies' reconnoitering the land, and strikingly reapplies it to Yahweh. The description of the land as "flowing with milk and honey" is a fixed phrase that belongs to general tradition. The term צבי "beautiful" may reflect Jeremiah's usage (cf. Jer 3:19). Ezekiel has ransacked earlier vocabulary to express the significance of the land and so the lengths to which Yahweh's care had gone.

7 Divine-human commitment ("your God," v 5) called for the breaking of other religious ties. Yahweh's claim on his people was an exclusive one. This summons is formulated in the priestly style of the Holiness Code (cf. Lev 18:2-5; 19:3, 4), which affirms that relationship with Yahweh creates for Israel an intrinsic lifestyle. The remaining vocabulary is firmly characteristic of Ezekiel. The pentateuchal narratives know nothing of idolatry in Egypt nor of an injunction against it at that period, but in Josh 24:14 Israel in Canaan is urged to "put away the gods your parents served in Egypt" (cf. the tradition of Israelite sin in Egypt at Ps 106:7). Here Ezekiel might be fusing this challenge with its own reference to worship of Egyptian gods, and backdating it.

8, 9 Israel's defiance (וימרו) echoes the label Ezekiel consistently used of the contemporary people, בית המרי "rebellious community" (2:5-7, etc.). It is also a term that belongs to the tradition of murmuring in the wilderness (Coats, *Rebellion* 78, 234). No wonder then that he saw lurking behind this recent tendency long shadows stretching back to Israel's earliest history (cf. 23:3). The sequence of Israel's rebellion and Yahweh's wrathful resolve and subsequent relenting establishes a pattern which is to be echoed in vv 13, 14 and 21, 22 as a litany of long-suffering grace. The constraint of Yahweh's "name" echoes a sentiment whose original habitat was probably cultic (e.g., Ps 79:9; cf. Jer 14:7, 21; cf. J. W. Miller, *Das Verhältnis Jeremias und Hesekiels sprachlich und theologisch untersucht* [Assen: Van Gorcum, 1955] 109). Yahweh's commitment to Israel could not be broken without a slur being cast on his reputation. Sensitive to the prospect of misrepresentation, Yahweh continued the relationship, remaining constant to his self-revelation and promises. He persisted in his commitment to those who had disowned their own commitment (vv 5, 7). In this oracle Ezekiel uses the notion of profaning Yahweh's name to describe not disobedience of his express will (cf. v 39; Lev 18:21, etc.), but the lowering of his prestige outside Israel so as "to retard the process by which he achieves recognition, to put off the day on which it shall be known that he is God" (Blank, *HUCA* 25 [1954] 8).

10-14 The pattern is repeated beyond Egypt's frontiers. Ezekiel now follows traditional strands of the pentateuchal narratives in his depiction of the Exodus and of lawgiving and lawbreaking in the wilderness. In this context, however, the grace demonstrated in the Exodus is enhanced as an amazing response to human sinfulness rather than being due simply to divine initiative (Exod 20:2). Now for the second time the message is sounded that God's patronage creates a specific call for allegiance. The statement that "human life depends on" performing Yahweh's covenant stipulations agrees strikingly with the Holiness Code (Lev 18:5). Each stipulation was "a commandment that promised life," as Paul was to confirm (Rom 7:10; cf. Ezek 33:15). Compliance with God's moral and religious terms meant "life and good fortune," while contravention spelled "death and disaster" (Deut 30:15). A blessed life flowed from "loving Yahweh your God, obeying him and cleaving to him" (Deut 30:20)—so far from legalism was the connotation of the laws of Sinai. They too were God's gift, along with the land.

Singled out for special mention is the sabbath ruling because of its function as a distinctive badge of the covenant (cf. Exod 31:13-17), which it has been for Judaism down the centuries. To observe the sabbath meant to stand apart from those who did not confess Israel's faith—and to stand with God and his declared will. It was intended to express the truth that on "every sabbath day the Israelite renounces his autonomy" as master of time "and affirms God's domain over his life" by abstaining from work and his own concerns (Tsevat, *Meaning* 48). Again Israel said no to God's covenant terms (cf. Exod 16:23-29; Num 15:32-36; Ps 81:12 [11]). And again Yahweh overruled the fatal reprisal they deserved, for his name's sake.

15-17 In an interim conclusion the narrative takes a sinister turn, all the more striking because it roughly follows the earlier pattern of vv 6-9, a divine oath about the promised land, human rejection and divine relenting. The first wilderness generation survived—but only to live out their lifespan within the confines of the wilderness (cf. Num 14:30-35; Ps 95:11). For them the promise of v 6 turned into a tantalizing mirage. It was a consequence of their rebelling against God, not only by breaking his rulings, including the crucial sabbath law, but also by reverting to paganism and so denying him the exclusive worship he claimed. The incident of the golden calf seems to be in view (cf. Exod 32:31). After this second provocation his mercy takes the form not of impunity but of mitigation of punishment in that they had a longer lease on life and their children were to inherit what they had forfeited.

18-22 The narrative begins a further installment, the story of the second wilderness generation. It is, however, a depressing rerun of the earlier phases, especially of that of vv 11-14. It echoes the exhortation of v 7, but makes positive additions to the negative injunctions. In both respects the expressions are remarkably similar to Lev 18:2-5, 24. There may be a reference to the tradition of Deuteronomy as a reaffirmation of the law of Sinai. Yahweh's terms are contrasted with an alternative program adopted by the first generation, a do-it-themselves approach to human existence. Failure though it had been, it proved a case of "like fathers, like sons." They too turned their backs on God's blessing of fulfilled lives. He stayed his "hand" from instant punishment, guarding against the misrepresentation that he had failed to fulfill his obligations.

23-26 Matching vv 15-16, a suspended sentence is passed on the rebellious children, as on their parents. Zimmerli (407) has noted the gradation of punishment: lacking in v 9, it appears in a single form in v 15 and now doubly in vv 23-25. The unspoken implication of v 23 is that Israel would have their possession of the land curtailed. Probably Ezekiel was leaning on the tradition preserved in Exod 32:34, where permission to enter the land is followed by the sinister, non-specific statement "But on the day when I punish, I will punish them for their sin" (Fohrer 112; Zimmerli 411). Evidently Ezekiel interpreted the ominous pronouncement in terms of fresh idolatry and related it to a particular future fate with the aid of two comparatively late texts, conditional covenant curses represented in Lev 26:33a (אזרה "I will disperse," cf. לזרות "to disperse") and Deut 28:64a (והפיצך "and he will scatter you," cf. להפיץ "to scatter"). The post-exilic Ps 106:27 echoed Ezekiel's interpretation in terms of God's justice chasing Israel down the corridors of time until it overtook Judah in 597 and 587 B.C. (and earlier the Northern Kingdom in 721 B.C.). The divine landlord gave only a limited lease to his tenants' families. It marked a final reversal of the promise of v 6, after an adumbration in v 15. There is a predestinarian note here which reflects the concept of vertical solidarity woven into the Ten Commandments (Exod 20:5, 6).

The people's fate is sealed by a new and harmful gift, which in the concentric structuring of vv 1-31 and also in the development of thought is the counterpart of the good gift of v 11. Ezekiel seems to have put back the reference from Canaan to the wilderness in line with his theme of Israel's early rebellion (Heider, *The Cult of Molek* 373 note 740). A new set of legislation forced them into a track that was to culminate in death, after their refusal of Yahweh's life-affirming terms. Elsewhere in the Old Testament חקות and חקים "rulings" are used interchangeably, and חקים is used of divine rulings in Ezek 11:12; 36:27. However, a careful reading of the present oracle discloses that while elsewhere in it חקות is used alongside משפטים "standards" with first singular suffixes relating to Yahweh, here not only is חקים used but both terms lack such a suffix. It seems to be significant too that חוקי has been used in v 18 concerning self-made rulings that Israel had substituted for Yahweh's and persisted in observing (van Hoonacker, *Le Muséon* 12 [1893] 150-54; Lust, *ETL* 43 [1967] 511; cf. Zimmerli 411). Here was a comparable set of rulings independent of Yahweh's positive will and yet enclosed within the purview of his punitive will. Not of God, they were given by God! Theologically the divine policy is akin to the role of prophecy in Isa 6:9–10, where the prophetic word is given to seal the people's fate by giving them an opportunity to add to their sin by rejecting that word. Judgment had already been passed and the gateway to life was locked by his providential judgment. The covenant goal of recognition of Yahweh, unreached by positive means (vv 5, 7, 12, 19, 20), had finally to be attained by a life-denying encounter with his judgment.

But what does v 25 mean in historical terms? Part of the vocabulary of v 26, כל פטר רחם (lit. "every opening of the womb") and העביר (lit. "make over"), echoes the law of the redemption of the firstborn particularly as represented in Exod 13:12, 13. It ruled that, whereas firstborn male sacrificial animals were to be sacrificed, firstborn sons were to be redeemed with money paid to the sanctuary. The combination of the motifs of giving and making over (v 26, cf. v 31) reminds the alert reader of 16:20, 21 (cf. Lev 18:21), where they were used in a description of child sacrifice. There seems, then, to be a double entendre in that the verb העביר suggests the fuller phrase העביר באש "make over by fire" or "surrender to the flames," which actually occurs in v 31. It is a formula for a pagan rite widely practiced in seventh-century Judah (cf. 2 Kgs 21:6; 23:10; Heider, *The Cult of Molek, passim*; J. W. McKay, *Religion in Judah Under the Assyrians* [SBT 2:26, Naperville: A. R. Allenson, 1973] 40-41). Accordingly v 25 seems to represent Ezekiel's retort to popular claims that in the law of the firstborn Yahweh had authorized the child sacrifice offered in the syncretistic cult: "In a baroque twist worthy of the prophet Ezekiel turns the theological tables on the practitioners: very well, Yahweh did give the law they were citing, but it was given so that obedience would not bring life but would 'devastate' them" (Heider, *The Cult of Molek* 372).

27, 28 This oracle, along with v 29, breaks the pattern of the preceding units and so shows itself to be a supplement to their carefully constructed framework.

The use of לכן "then, therefore" is strange. It fits rather the development of vv 30, 31 where it occurs at the outset ("so"). Perhaps the introductory v 27a originally prefaced the message of vv 30aβ-31 and, after the insertion of vv 27b-28 or 29, was loosely repeated in v 30aα. Repetitive resumption of this type is well attested in post-exilic prose (see S. Talmon, *IDBSup* 322; H. G. M. Williamson, *1 and 2 Chronicles* [NCBC, Eerdmans: Grand Rapids, 1982] 122-23, 179, 248, 272). This supplementary oracle, which has been woven into the chiastic jigsaw of vv 3-31, takes further the negative history of Israel. It accuses the people of the deuteronomistic charge of adopting Canaanite fertility sanctuaries. This infidelity was a shocking return for the faithfulness of God in giving the land.

29 This verse appears to be a prophetic fragment, slipped in because of the implicit references to high places in vv 27, 28. It uses the culturally popular device of wordplay in a propagandist attack on unorthodox religion.

30, 31 Here is the climax of the overall message, which originally continued v 26 and in fact echoes its vocabulary. The present generation were no better than their forebears. They had been traveling the same downward path away from Yahweh's revealed will. Repentance and efforts toward a better lifestyle were conspicuously absent. Accordingly Yahweh's refusal to give a favorable word in response to consultation (vv 1-3) was justified. They had forfeited any claim they might have had to the land.

There is a radical difference between the divine treatment of Israel in 20:1-31 and in chap. 18. Each generation's responsibility and repentance, prized there, are ignored in vv 9, 10, where deliverance comes despite human sinning, and in vv 23-26, where the punishment of the sins of the second generation is deferred to their descendants (cf. M. Fishbane, *Int* 38 [1984] 141-43, who speaks of "intense contradictions" between the two chapters). The differences are eased by the observation that Ezekiel thought in terms of two eras in Yahweh's dealings with his people: an old era dogged by a deuteronomistic type of theology featuring the eventual wearing down of divine grace by human disobedience and a burden of human liability carried over from the past, and a new era of grace renewed and bondage to the past removed (cf. T. M. Raitt, *A Theology of Exile* [Philadelphia: Fortress Press, 1977] 212-22). Ezek 18 had already pushed ahead to a vision of the new age, but 20:1-31 honor the overall pre-587 B.C. framework of chaps. 1-24 in preaching the bad news of God's past and present dealings with his people. Vv 32-44, like chap. 18, are to be a further indication that Ezekiel was eventually given another, relatively positive, word to transmit.

32, 33 Form-critically v 32 belongs to the disputation speech as introduction and thesis. Accordingly it does not align with vv 1-31, as Fohrer (107-8, 131) and Wevers (119) urged. Does willful challenge or hopeless despair underlie the mention of idolatry? Heb. נהיה could literally be rendered either as a defiant "We *will* be, let us be" (RSV; cf. 1 Sam 8:19, 20) or as a despairing "we shall be" (cf. 33:10; 37:11). In favor of the former possibility is the emphasis on judgment in vv 33-38 and the virtual accusation of v 39. The alternative view is suggested by the overall leaning of vv 33-44 toward promise: even the announcement of punishment relates only to a partial judgment. Elements of both facets appear to be present (Zimmerli, "Le nouvel 'exode'" 217) insofar as the exiles' resignation to their fate had already made them embrace idolatry (v 39). The ridicule with which idolatry is described, "worshiping wood and stone," reflects the prophetic tendency to recast popular attitudes in interpretative terms (cf. H. W. Wolff, "Das Zitat im Prophetenspruch," *Gesammelte Studien zum AT* [ThB 22, München: Chr Kaiser Verlag, 1964] esp. 72-84). One may not take it at face value, as Y. Kaufmann attempted to do (*The Religion of Israel* [ET Chicago: University of Chicago Press, 1960] 441).

Historically the total catastrophe of 587 B.C. prompted the despair; in literary terms there is a looking back to the certainty of exile pronounced in v 23, with which v 32 has language in common. Both the exiles and Ezekiel assumed that territorial residence and religion went hand in hand and that Yahwistic religion required return to Jerusalem, if assimilation to a pagan faith was not to ensue. In vehement protest Yahweh lays claim to his people's allegiance (cf. Exod 12:12; Num 33:4). The motif of kingship, which occurs only here in the book and seems to echo Exod 15:18 (cf. too 1 Sam 8:5, 7, 8), is a retort to popular resignation to the worship or service of other gods. Yahweh's powerful intervention would resemble that of the Exodus: cf. Exod 6:6 and the deuteronomic phrases of Deut 5:15, etc. The addition of "drenching fury," however, especially after the usage in vv 8, 13 and 21, indicates a typical prophetic reversal whereby the language of salvation became the vehicle of judgment, and Israel became the victim of divine power (cf. Jer 21:5). Here salvation and judgment are mingled in the one event.

34-38 There is thus a typological contrast between the old Exodus and the new version by which Yahweh was to inaugurate a new era of salvation. It is followed here by a comparison between the wilderness experience after the Egyptian Exodus and a parallel one after an "Exodus" from the Diaspora. The confrontation, literally "face to face" (v 35b), echoes Yahweh's self-revelation at Sinai (Deut 5:4). Another echo of the Sinai revelation is the reimposition of covenant "obligation" (v 37b), which the process of selection motivated by covenant principles would serve to accomplish. The images of judge and shepherd both had strong royal overtones in the ancient Near East and so represent a reassertion of Yahweh's kingly authority (cf. 34:17-24). The shepherd's role of sorting out his flock (cf. Lev 27:32) is a powerful metaphor for inexorable selection. Historically the tradition of Dathan and Abiram's rebellion appears to be in view (cf. Num 16; Deut 11:6; Zimmerli 416; Coats, *Rebellion* 241). This announcement of a partial judgment was meant as a powerful warning to the exiles not to exclude themselves from restoration to the land (cf. Fohrer 116). Only such a radical sifting process could rectify Israel's deficient understanding of Yahweh.

39-42 This second main part of the oracle, whose importance is indicated by a separate messenger formula, begins with an appeal for repentance strongly couched in ironic and threatening terms. Idolatrous worship among the exiles is implied (cf. Isa 48:4, 5; cf. A. Schoors, *I Am God Your Saviour* [VTSup 24, Leiden: Brill, 1973] 287; P. R. Ackroyd, *Exile and Restoration* [London: SCM, 1968] 42-43). Yahweh's reassertion of his authority, in reaction to their worshiping or serving (שרת, v 32) other deities, was demonstrated in vv 33-38 in terms of royal judgment. Now it is expressed in religious terms: Israel will serve or worship (עבד, vv 39, 40) only Yahweh. The general concept of service runs all through the oracle. A related keynote of vv 39-42 is Yahweh's holiness or transcendent supremacy. It would be reacknowledged via proper religious worship, legitimate as to both place and procedure. It would involve (a) a return to his "holy mountain," a phrase borrowed from Zion theology and used only here in Ezekiel, and (b) "holy dues" (v 40) as part of Israel's acceptable worship. And Israel's restoration to the land would spell the vindication of Yahweh's holiness on the international scene (v 41). This latter reference serves to resolve a problem left unanswered in vv 1-31. Yahweh's reluctance to damage his reputation by renouncing his people (vv 9, 14, 22) had to be set aside in the exile, which accordingly compromised his standing. The restoration of his people would resolve this anomaly (cf. 36:20-24; Ps 126:2b).

43, 44 Yahweh's remaking of a worshiping people would effect a spiritual work in their hearts. From their new vantage point they would be able to survey both the depths to which they had earlier sunk and the heights to which Yahweh's redeeming grace had lifted them (cf. 36:31). Over against the bankruptcy of Israel's own covenant claims, their patron's free determination to honor his ancient promises would gloriously come to light.

Explanation

The prophet Ezekiel straddled two eras, the grim era of the past and present which culminated in double exile and—in prospect at least—a glorious era to be inaugurated by a new work of God. In this chapter both these aspects are set side by side so that it presents an epitome of his total message.

Israel's theology placed a high value on the events of the Exodus, the trek through the wilderness and settlement in the land. This complex of events constituted a once-for-all divine intervention in human history which revealed ongoing positive purposes for Israel. For Ezekiel, however, these archetypal saving events were cancelled out by a counter-determination on Yahweh's part. A step behind each stage of his saving work there loomed a shadow of divine threat in reaction to Israel's rejection of their God. Here indeed was theological time which presented Israel with a warranty—but it was negative in its import. Yahweh was characteristically no longer one who saved and blessed but one who deprived and destroyed. Yet he took on this negative role not willingly but under the ever growing constraint of the perversity of his covenant partner. Commitment and justice tussled in the mind of God; eventually not even a possible slur of capriciousness could stay his hand, so blatant was Israel's lack of commitment. Singled out for special mention are their breaking of what in the Decalog is the first commandment, to have no other gods before Yahweh, and the profaning of the sabbath, which was regarded as a hallmark of Israel's faith.

This is perhaps the most striking example of ideological reversal so characteristic of the prophets. Ezekiel searched out and amplified negative traditions available to him. Thus he associated the wilderness not with a high level of human commitment, as in Hos 2:17 (15) and Jer 2:2, but with sin and judgment, as in Exod 16 and 32 and Num 14 and 16. The present had to be interpreted in terms of this theological past. Ezekiel had no positive reply from God to give to the exilic leaders. Exile was Yahweh's inevitable word for that hour. To this truth he brought a veritable sledgehammer of theological argument. The perversity of the present generation who had suffered the first deportation of 597 B.C. constituted a symptom of a chronic and terminal illness which had afflicted Israel from the beginning. Recent idolatry and sabbath-breaking had for Ezekiel deep roots in the people's past. There was "a hard bed-rock of unbelief and superstition in the national character which had never yielded to the influence of revelation" (Skinner 186). The radical tone which marks much of Ezekiel's prophesying finds illustration in this feature, which corresponds to the Christian tenet of original sin.

He regarded pagan rites introduced into Israelite religion as a destructive course into which the people had locked themselves—and even been locked by God in the playing out of his negative role (vv 25, 26). The Christian is reminded of the refrain in Rom 1:24, 26, 28 that "God gave them up" to self-chosen perversity. Rejected laws that were the key to a blessed life were replaced with death-dealing laws. Paul in his attitude to the Jewish law went further than Ezekiel: he linked a basically life-giving and good entity (Rom 7:10, 12) with its tragic effects inasmuch as human nature was unable to live up to it (Rom 8:3). However, he built on a foundation laid by Ezekiel in that he too envisaged a radically new work of God as the only way forward from failure.

Eventually the theological tide was to turn, and to this welcome change vv 32-44 are addressed. The Exodus is reinvested with promise, but only as an omen pointing to God's new activity. Its value, one might say, was that of "a shadow of good things to come" (Heb 10:1). The old Exodus was a model for a new one, which would this time fulfill its potential. There is a down-to-earth realism in the development, in that a selective judgment was to purge the exiles of their renegade members. In this respect Ezekiel differs from Second Isaiah who represented the new Exodus in purely positive terms. Supremely there would be a demonstration of Yahweh's sovereignty over his people in reaction to the threat of pagan religion. As Israel's king—and so judge and shepherd—he would resume his rightful place at their head. And as divine Lord he would receive their pure worship at—it is implied—a reconstituted temple. Is there a further echo of the Song of the Sea, which celebrated Yahweh's role as king along with worship at his appointed sanctuary (Exod 15:17, 18)?

The certainty of God's new work came not simply from its oracular attestation but also from its typological quality. Yahweh was to be true to his earlier revelation by reverting to a positive means of attaining his covenant will (v 42). There would be an authenticating consistency and development whereby the old was transmuted into the new, with a degree of promise that transcended the old. Realistically there was a call for individual response from the hearers as they adjusted to the new era, on the lines of chap. 18, but it is implied that this time Yahweh would not let human sinfulness stand in his way. Confronted by God's gracious achievement, his people would be shamed into deep contrition and true appreciation of his being. Grace would be the effectual means of God's positive will and of redemption from human failure (cf. Rom 5:21). His "purpose in election" (Rom 9:11) would find fulfillment.

The Sword of Damocles (21:1-37 [EVV 20:45-21:32])

Bibliography

Allen, L. C. "The Rejected Sceptre in Ezekiel 21:15b, 18a." *VT* 39 (1989) 67-71. **Boecker, H. J.** "Erwägungen zum Amt des Mazkir." *TZ* 17 (1961) 212-16. **Brownlee, W. H.** " 'Son of Man, Set Your Face'. Ezekiel the Refugee Prophet." *HUCA* 54 (1983) 83-110. **Carley, K. W.** *Ezekiel among the Prophets.* SBT 2:31. London: SCM, 1975, 40-42. **Delitzsch, F.** "Das Schwertlied Ezech. 21:13-22." *Zeitschrift für Keilschriftforschung* 2 (1885) 385-98. **Guthrie, H. H., Jr.** "Ezekiel 21." *ZAW* 74 (1962) 268-81. **Hillers, D. R.** "A Convention in Hebrew Literature: The Reaction to Bad News." *ZAW* 77 (1965) 86-90. **Lang, B.** *Kein Aufstand in Jerusalem.* SBS 7. 2nd ed. Stuttgart: Katholisches Bibelwerk, 1981, 115-69. _____. "A Neglected Method in Ezekiel Research: Editorial Criticism." *VT* 29 (1979) 39-44. **Long, B. O.** "Two Question and Answer Schemata in the Prophets." *JBL* 90 (1971) 129-39. **Maarsingh, B.** "Das Schwertlied in Ezek 21:13-22 und das Erra-Gedicht." *Ezekiel and His Book.* Ed. J. Lust. BETL 74 (Leuven: University Press, 1986) 350-58. **Moran, W.** "Gen 49:10 and Its Use in Ez 21:32." *Bib* 39 (1958) 405-25. **Seitz, C. R.** *Theology in Conflict. Reactions to the Exile in the Book of Jeremiah.* BZAW 176. Berlin: de Gruyter, 1989, 148-58.

Translation

[1]*I received the following communication from Yahweh:* [2] *"Human one, turn and face southwards and preach against the south, with a prophecy against the forest land in the south.*[a] [3]*Tell the southern forest: Hear Yahweh's word. This is a message from the Lord*[a] *Yahweh: I am about to light a fire in you, which will consume every green tree in you as well as every dry tree. The blazing flames will not be extinguished, and every face from south to north will feel their heat.* [4]*Everybody will see that I, Yahweh, have set the fire inextinguishably alight."* [5]*I protested, "Alas, Lord Yahweh, people are complaining that I am always*[a] *using figurative language."* [6]*I received the following communication from Yahweh:* [7]*"Human one, turn and face Jerusalem and preach against their sanctuary*[a] *with a prophecy against the land of Israel.* [8]*Tell the land of Israel: This is a message from Yahweh: I am your adversary, I am about to draw my sword from its scabbard and execute the innocent among you as well as the guilty.* [9]*Inasmuch as I mean to execute*[a] *the innocent among you as well as the guilty, my sword will be drawn from its scabbard against all people from south to north.*[b] [10]*Then everybody will realize that I, Yahweh, have drawn my sword from its scabbard, never to be put away.* [11]*As for you, human one, groan with sagging limbs,*[a] *groan with bitter grief while they look on.* [12]*When they ask you why you are groaning, tell them it is because of what you have heard. When it happens, every heart will melt, all hands will hang limp, all morale will flag and everyone will have water running down their knees.*[a] *It is about to happen and will become fact. So runs the Lord Yahweh's oracle."*

[13]*I received the following communication from Yahweh:* [14]*"Human one, prophesy and say, This is a message from the Lord. Say:*[a]

A sword, a sword is sharpened
and polished[b] *too,*

^{15}*sharpened for slaying,*
polished to shine like lightning.[a]
^{16}*It is presented for polishing,*[a]
for grasping in the palm.
It is sharpened, this sword,[b]
and it is polished
to be placed in the hand of a killer.
^{17}*Shout and wail, human one,*
because it is directed against my people,
against all Israel's rulers—
they are delivered[a] *to the sword with my people.*
So slap your thigh.
^{18}*So runs the Lord Yahweh's oracle.*[a]
^{19}*You, human one, are to prophesy*
and clap your hands.
Let the sword strike twice, thrice,[a]
the sword intended for those to be killed.
The great[b] *sword for those to be killed*[c]
will be surrounding them,
^{20}*so that hearts may melt*[a]
and the fallen[b] *be many.*
At all their gates I have set
the slaying[c] *sword.*
Ah,[d] *it is made to flash like lightning,*
it is drawn[e] *to slay.*
^{21}*Lunge to the rear,*[a] *to the right,*[b] *to the left,*
and wherever your front[c] *is situated.*
^{22}*I too will clap my hands*
and satisfy my fury.
I, Yahweh, have spoken."

^{23}I received the following communication from Yahweh: ^{24}"You, human one, are to represent two routes for the sword of the king of Babylon to approach by. They are both to begin in the same[a] region. And a signpost at the head of each route[b] ^{25}you are to represent, with a view to the sword's approach—referring to[a] Rabbah in Ammon and to Judah, whose stronghold[b] is in Jerusalem. ^{26}The explanation is that the king of Babylon has halted at the forking of the road, at the beginning of two routes, in order to practice divination. He has shaken arrows,[a] consulted teraphim and observed livers. ^{27}Into his right hand has come the divining device indicating Jerusalem,[a] which means that[b] a shout[c] must issue from his mouth, the loud command of a war cry, for[d] battering rams to be installed against the gates, earthworks to be piled up and siege structures to be built. ^{28}To them it seems like a false divination,[a] whereas it is evidence of their guilt, leading to their apprehension. ^{29}This therefore is the message of the Lord Yahweh: Because you have presented evidence of your guilt, in that your rebellious ways are exposed to view and your sins are conspicuous in everything you do—because this evidence against you has been presented—you will be apprehended by force.[a] ^{30}As for you, impious[a] villain, Israel's head of state, whose day of reckoning has come at a time of terminal guilt, ^{31}this is the message of the Lord Yahweh: Take off[a] the royal turban, remove the crown! The present state of affairs is not to continue.[b] Up with the low[c] and down with the high!

[32] *Ruin,*[a] *ruin, ruin is what I will reduce it to. Moreover, the present state of affairs is not to persist*[b] *during the time when*[c] *the person comes to whom the task of judgment belongs and to whom I assign it.*
[33] *"As for you, human one, prophesy with the words, This is a message from the Lord Yahweh against*[a] *the Ammonites and their insults. Say: Sword, sword, drawn for slaughter, polished in order to flash*[b] *in destruction*[c]—[34]*even while they see false visions about you, while they produce deceitful divinations about you—you are to be applied*[a] *to the necks of impious villains whose day of reckoning has come, at the time of terminal guilt.* [35]*Put it back in its scabbard.*[a] *In the place of your creation, in the land of your origin I will judge you.* [36]*I will vent my anger on you, I will blast you with the fire of my wrath, handing you over to brutal men, experts in destruction.* [37]*You will be consigned*[a] *to the fire as fuel, your blood will flow through the land, you will leave no memory behind. Surely I, Yahweh, have spoken."*

Notes

2. a. In MT נגב "south" functions appositionally. The Eastern reading נגבה "to the south" (cf. *BHS*) clarifies this role. The shorter phrase in v 3 has been interpreted as supporting a reading ליער הנגב "to the forest of the south" here, but stylistic shortening of a longer phrase is not impossible. Yet the syntactical oddity and the parallel terms of v 2 do favor the view that שדה "region, land" originated as a gloss on יער, which was inserted into הנגב (*BHS*, Fohrer 117, Zimmerli 420 et al.). Cf. the parallelism of השדה and היערים in 39:10, to which attention may have been drawn by the common phraseology of 21:12 and 39:8.

3. a. For the formulaic אדני "Lord" here and in vv 5, 12, 29, 31 and 33 see the note on 20:3. There is also unusual variation in this chapter, v 8 lacking אדני and v 14 lacking יהוה "Yahweh."

5. a. The piel, in distinction from the qal in 17:2, seems to have an intensive force (Fohrer 119; A. R. Johnson, VTSup 3 [1969] 169).

7. a. MT's indefinite form מקדשים "sanctuaries" is suspect, and מקדשׁם "their sanctuary," supported by a few MSS and Syr, is preferable. LXX τὰ ἅγια (αὐτῶν) "(their) holy place(s)" is used to render the sg as well as the pl noun and more probably gives further support than reflects the consonantally divergent מקדשיהם "their sanctuaries," as Wevers (123) supposes. The pl suffix refers to the people of Jerusalem.

9. a. The pf appears to be prophetic (cf. Cooke 228).

9. b. Contra *BHS* et al. it is not necessary to harmonize with צפונה in v 3: stylistic variation is feasible.

11. a. Lit. "breaking of loins," with reference to the psychosomatic effect of shock: the legs cease to give support. For Ug. examples see Hillers, *ZAW* 77 (1965) 86-87.

12. a. G. R. Driver, *ZAW* 65 (1953) 260, suggested that here and in 7:17 "knees" was a euphemism for penis.

14. a. Heb אמר "say" is seemingly redundant after ואמרת "and say" earlier. This may be why LXX* Syr omitted it. The well-attested form ואמרת in v 33 appears to be a paraphrase that presupposes it in a passage that echoes elements earlier in the chapter (cf. Zimmerli 449).

14. b. The parallelism suggests a pointing as a pual pf מרפה, as in vv 15, 16 (*BHS* et al.). MT has been assimilated to the form in v 33.

15. a. MT היה is unparalleled as inf constr "to be"; already LXX seems to have so understood it, although it rendered לה ברק "to it lightning" as though it were לברק "for lightning," perhaps by translator's license. The conjecture לְהָהֵלָּה "so that it might shine" from הלל (F. Zorell apud *Bib* 19 [1938] 67 n. 4; NEB [cf. Brockington, *Hebrew Text* 126]; cf. הָהֵל suggested by Cornill 300) commends itself. Then ברק "lightning" functions as a loose adv acc (cf. GKC 118m, q, v).

For vv 15b and 18a see *VT* 39 (1989) 67-71. V 15b appears to have originated as a marginal comment on כל־עץ "every tree" in v 3, relating it to the demise of the Davidic monarchy: cf. the note on v 18. It has the sense "Every tree: or the ruler(s) of Israel, the rejected scepter." In both cases שבט נמאסת "the rejected scepter" is to be read as the text underlying MT's divergent שבט בני מאסת "a scepter, my son, rejecting" and שבט מאסת "a rejecting scepter." For או "or" in the sense "that is to say" cf. H. C. Brichto's claim (*HUCA* 46 [1975] 62 note u) that it has this function in Mal 2:17 and probably in Gen 24:55; 1 Sam 29:3.

16. a. Seemingly an indefinite pf and a long form of the inf. In place of the latter the conjecture לְמָרְצֵחַ "to a slayer" (Cooke 237, following Bertholet) is attractive, as improving the sense and increasing the external parallelism of vv 16a, 16b; then assimilation to the consonants of the form in v 15 was suffered. Or was Ehrlich (*Randglossen*) 79) right in postulating מֹרְטָה "the one who polished it (gave it)," with ל intruding as an anticipation of (תפס)ל?

16. b. MT חרב "sword" is syntactically otiose, but not unparalleled as epexegetical in relation to the pronoun (cf. e.g., Exod 7:11; Ps 87:5 [4] and perhaps Ezek 3:21). To take היא as explanatory ("that is") with Cooke, ibid., awkwardly differentiates היא from והיא "and it." *BHS*, substantially following Ehrlich, ibid., attractively suggests הוּא הֶחַד הַחֶרֶב וְהוּא מְרָטָה "he sharpened the sword and he polished it." K. S. Freedy, *VT* 20 (1970) 142, took חרב as a rubrical gloss indicating the theme of the passage.

17. a. MT מגורי derives from מגר "overthrow," but Aram. usage suggests that the qal was intransitive, which rules out a pass ptcp. A hoph pointing מֻגְרֵי from נגר (hiph "throw down") is lexicographically a more feasible vocalization (Zimmerli 428, *BHS*, following J. Herrmann 129).

18. a. MT has in v 18a a comment related to the one in v 15b: it explains גם־זאת לא היה "also this will not continue" in v 32 with the tentative remark "For investigation has been made and what if (it means that) the rejected scepter will not continue?"

19. a. MT שלישתה "its third" (cf. GKC 91e) requires emendation to a verbal form (וְ)שֻׁלְּשָׁה "(and) let it be moved thrice," attested by Vg (*BHS* et al., following Kraetzschmar 179). Ehrlich's emendation (*Randglossen* 80) חרב וְשֻׁלֵּשְׁתָּה (cf. LXX) וְתִכְפֹּל "and you are to wield the sword twice, thrice," does more justice to the consonantal text, but Ezekiel's role is to order the slaying rather than carry it out.

19. b. The masc adj (הַחרב) הגדול needs to be fem (חרב) הַגְּדוֹלָה by redivision (cf. *BHS* et al.).

19. c. Heb. חלל is a collective sg, as in 11:6 after a pl, unless it represents an abbreviated form חלל/ = חללים "the killed."

20. a. MT למוג presupposes a pleonastic *lamed* and a qal with the metaphorical meaning "melt" elsewhere found in the niph. The *paseq* indicates masoretic uneasiness. The conjectured niph inf המוג (*BHS* et al.) may be correct, if a careless writing of initial *lamed*, as in the adjacent words, can be assumed.

20. b. In place of MT's rather stilted "the stumblings" LXX Syr render in personal terms, viz. הַמֻּכְשָׁלִים "those who are made to stumble" (cf. Jer 18:23), and Cornill (306) et al. are probably correct in so repointing.

20. c. The meaning of אבחת is unknown. LXX Tg presuppose טבחת "slaughter."

20. d. Heb. אח may be an exclamation like האח in the light of LXX (εὖγε, cf. Ziegler, *LXX* 183, with reference to P. Katz, *TLZ* 61 [1936] 280) Tg. Or it may represent abbreviated אבחת = אח/חרב, implying repetition of the earlier phrase (NEB[Brockington, *Hebrew Text* 226]; cf. Ehrlich, *Randglossen* 81), in which case a 2 + 2 + 2 tricolon is to be found in place of a 3 + 2 bicolon.

20. e. MT מעטה appears to be pointed to mean "wrapped, covered" from עטה, although M. Dahood, *Bib* 43 (1962) 226, claimed a privative meaning "unsheathed." A contextually better rendering is achieved by relating to Arab. *ma ʿata* "draw (a sword)," with the vocalization מֹעֶטָה (=מְעוּטָה) (Cooke 238; Driver, *Bib* 19 [1938] 68, comparing פתוחה "drawn" in v 33; NEB [Brockington, *Hebrew Text*, ibid.]).

21. a. MT התאחדי "be sharpened (?)" from אחד, perhaps here a by-form of חדד (Driver, *Bib* 19 [1938] 68), seems to have suffered a ד/ר error under the influence of (רת) (ה)חד in v 19. The reading of a few MSS, התאחרי "go behind," is contextually better (Hitzig 147-48; Delitzsch, *Zeitschrift für Keilschriftforschung* 2 [1885] 396; Zorell, *Lexicon* 30). LXX διαπορεύου ὀξύνου "come, be sharpened" seems already to presuppose MT, in the disjointed form חדי התא (לטבח).

21. b. MT prefaces with השימי, a hiph form of שום which is questionable. It appears to be an uncorrected erroneous start of השמילי (Cornill 307): cf. אח in 18:10.

21. c. Heb. פניך is usually interpreted as "your edge" (cf. Eccl 10:10), but there appears to be a directional chiasmus "rear, left, right, front." The fem gender accords with Mishnaic Heb. and also Syr. and Mandean counterparts (cf. H. Rosenberg, *ZAW* 25 [1905] 336; Zimmerli 431). For a discussion of the verb see W. McKane, *Jeremiah 1-25* (Edinburgh: T. & T. Clark, 1986) 605-6.

24. a. The masc אחד "one" appears to be original, and the expected אחת read by 2 MSS and preferred by *BHS* is the easier and so inferior reading. Driver, *Bib* 35 (1954) 145, suggested a colloquialism here, comparing cases in 1:6 and 2 Sam 23:8.

24. b. The MT of v 24 appears to be in a confused state, which has led to a false break with v 25. The first (pre-LXX) mistake was the intrusion of עיר "city," intended as a marginal comment on the difficult בצורה in v 25, understanding it in terms of the standard phrase "fortified city." It was taken as

a correction of the similar-looking יד "signpost": for this "cuckoo in the nest" cf. my articles in *JTS* 22 (1971) 143-50; 24 (1973) 69-73. The second (post-LXX) mistake was that the second ברא, meant as a simple abbreviation of a repeated בראש "at the head," attested by LXX, was annotated ברא בראש, indicating "for ברא read בראש"; but the note was taken as a correction of the first בראש, again attested by LXX, and displaced it. Then the repeated ברא was taken as an imperative "cut." The repeated יד בראש דרך "a signpost at the start of a road" is a distributive idiom (Ehrlich, *Randglossen* 82; Zimmerli 436; cf. GKC 123c, d). The verb תשים "you are to make" in v 25 governs the nominal phrase of v 24b.

25. a. Heb. את is the object sign. The following nouns are in loose apposition to יד "signpost."

25. b. Zimmerli 437 defends the Heb. well as a chiastic (ABB'A'), triple-accented pair of phrases relating to city and people. Heb. בצורה functions as a neuter noun: cf. GKC 122q with a reference to הנשמה "the desolate place" in 36:36. LXX reflects an easier reading בתוכה "in its midst": appeal to an underlying צור = Akk. *ṣurru* "heart" (Driver, *JTS* 41 [1940] 169; NEB [Brockington, *Hebrew Text*, ibid.]) is doubtful.

26. a. For *beth* introducing the object see GKC 119q. Here the usage is stylistic, matching the next two clauses.

27. a. L. Boadt, *VT* 25 (1975) 698, has defended MT לשום כרים "to install rams" as part of a chiastic chain (ABB'A) of four verbal phrases, but then a three-beat phrase is expected. It is generally deleted as an anticipation of v 27b (cf. *BHS*). It doubtless arose because a copyist's eye slipped a 24-letter line, from (פתח)ל to (שום)ל and the mistake was left uncorrected.

27. b. *Lamed* in the first two phrases loosely indicates the series of actions which follow the momentous initial act.

27. c. MT ברצח is a classic case of metathesis for בצרח "with a cry," attested by LXX and required by the parallel phrase.

27. d. The switch from a pair of parallel phrases to a triple parallel group implies that the latter is not coordinated but supplies the content of the earlier command.

28. a. MT adds שבעי שבעות להם, which is syntactically difficult and, in line with its omission in LXX* Syr, best explained as originally a marginal comment on להם earlier, with citation of the text as a cue, "to them: those who have sworn oaths." The gloss was referring to the broken oath and covenant of 17:13-19. The pass qal form seemingly stands for the normal niph.

29. a. LXX ἐν τούτοις seems to imply an inferior reading בכה "in this way" rather than בהם, as generally reconstructed (cf. *BHS*).

30. a. Heb. חלל, like the pl in v 34, means "profane" rather than "killed." In accord with the phrase there it is more idiomatically pointed חֲלַל, taking רשע as a genitive collective: "a profane person among the wicked" (*BHS* et al.; cf. GKC 128l).

31. a. The first two and final verbs of v 31 are seemingly intended in MT not as pf (Wevers 127) but as inf constr forms doing duty for inf abs (Boadt, *VT* 25 [1975] 695), which is required with the sense of emphatic impv. The vowel letter may have been meant simply as a *plene* writing for הָסֵר, etc. (GKC 113bb note 3).

31. b. For the idiom Ehrlich (*Randglossen* 83) compared 2 Kgs 9:37.

31. c. MT השפלה "the low" is pointed and accented with an otiose ה. ending (cf. GKC 90f), evidently to maintain a masc form in accord with the parallel הגבה "the high." Were the forms originally both masc, ה(השפל) being a dittograph, or fem, ה(הגבה) being lost by haplography?

32. a. Heb. עוה is apparently used in the sense of עי "ruin."

32. b. For היה after a fem subj separated by לא "not" see Driver, *JRAS* 75 (1948) 164-76. The pf is seemingly prophetic. An emendation אות "sign" for זאת "this" (Ehrlich, *Randglossen* 83, following Hitzig; RSV "trace") is not necessary. Nor is Cornill's אוי לה (309) with the sense "woe to it."

32. c. In view of the negative עד must here refer to a period rather than a temporal goal (Zimmerli 439).

33. a. Heb. אל is used in the sense of על "against" (*BHS*).

33. b. MT ברק is better pointed as a verb בְּרֹק after למען, which with a noun means "on account of." For the verb cf. Ps 144:6.

33. c. MT להכיל "to contain" (cf. 23:32) or "to feed" (short for להאכיל) is problematic. A developed meaning "as much as it can hold, to full capacity, as much as possible" (Smend 147, following Schnurr) seems strained. LXX Vg Tg may imply לכְלָה "for destruction" (Bertholet 76 et al.), but more probably represent an attempt to get some sense out of the present text. The parallelism does not require it, and its position in the clause is strange. RSV "to glitter" adopts Cornill's emendation לְהָהֵל (ibid.).

34. a. This rambling sentence lacks a main verb; perhaps לתת has this role (cf. GKC 114i, k, l; BDB 518a; *HALAT* 485b).

35. a. Contra Zimmerli (440) LXX μὴ καταλύσῃς "do not destroy" supports the consonants of MT, taken as אַל־תְּעָרֶה "do not pour out, slay." Cf. this rendering for another verb of destruction at 26:13.

37. a. Heb. תהיה more probably reflects a dislike of the fem form (cf. GKC 145t) than a change of person which indicates a gloss (Zimmerli, ibid.; Wevers 128).

Form/Structure/Setting

Chap. 21 is made up of four units, vv 1-12, 13-22, 23-32 and 33-37. The first has two message reception formulas, at vv 1 and 6, but the two pieces, vv 1-4 and 6-12, are closely linked by v 5 in terms of metaphor and meaning (cf. 17:2-10, 11-21). Vv 2-4 are a judgment oracle developed into a proof saying by the recognition formula of v 4. The variation of the normal "know" with "see" (וראו) is obviously due to the metaphorical nature of the passage: a forest fire is visually observed. After the prophet's plea in v 5 the oracle is reissued in vv 6-10 in a plainer version which substitutes the simpler imagery of the sword. It is then capped by a fresh call to Ezekiel in vv 11, 12. A command to engage in a symbolic action is combined with another command characterized by a question and answer schema, as in 37:18, 19 (cf. 12:9-11; 24:19-21). For this schema and its varied usage especially in Jer (e.g., 15:1-4) and Ezek see B. O. Long, *JBL* 90 (1971) 129-39. V 12 makes impressive use of the widespread convention describing the reaction to bad news, for which see D. R. Hillers, *ZAW* 77 (1965) 86-90.

This overall oracle, like the rest of the chapter, is not dated. The threat to Jerusalem and the temple (v 7) is significant. 20:1 cited a date in 591B.C. and 24:1 refers to 588, the beginning of the siege of Jerusalem. In line with this literary placement the present oracle feasibly falls between these dates, sometime before the Babylonian invasion. The reference to Judah as the "south" (v 2, cf. v 7) indicates that the oracle was spoken in Babylonia at the other end of the Fertile Crescent which stretched northwards from Judah to Syria. Editorial reworking has been suspected (cf. Zimmerli 422; Wevers 122-23), but the evidence adduced is hardly compelling.

Vv 2-4 and 6-10 are marked by remarkably detailed parallelism, noted by Fohrer (118-19), as far as his deletions of presumed glosses (vv 3b, 9, 10b) allow him. It was not a feature of 15:2-5/6-8 nor of 17:2-10/11-21. The difference is because 21:2-4 already take the clear form of a judgment oracle and proof saying, and what the interpretation requires is a recapitulation with recasting of the fire metaphor. Elements in the first section are repeated or rephrased—often in an alternating sequence—in the second; only the summons to hear (v 3aβ) has no counterpart. Assonance plays a part in the parallelism, a צא sequence marking v 3bβ (מצית) and v 8aδ (והוצאתי) and a ער sequence in v 4 (בערתיה) and v 10 (מתערה). The statement in v 3bδ intensifies v 3bγ; correspondingly v 8b intensifies v 8a by repetition. The latter phenomenon is part of a chiastic scheme which tightly interlocks vv 8-10 in an ABBACCA structure, as Boadt, *VT* 25 (1975) 697, observed. At the end of v 10 the addition of עוד "any more" adds an appropriate climactic force in comparison with v 4.

Vv 2-10 are caught up in another, larger scheme embracing further material, vv 11-12, rather as we noticed in chap. 20. There is a rhetorical structure marked by the speech of prophet and people in vv 3//8//12a (וְאָמַרְתָּ "and you are to say") and vv 5//12b (אֹמְרִים, יֹאמְרוּ "they say") with an ABABA rhythm. Moreover, הִנֵּה "behold" follows each A element. The passage highlights a verbal interchange between the prophet and people, in which the prophet's words are directed by Yahweh. There is an inclusion, שְׁמַע "hear" in v 3 and שְׁמוּעָה "what you have heard" in v 12b, which stresses the news of the disaster that Yahweh is to bring about. V 12b has a climactic role, with its four instances of כֹּל "all" echoing the two in v 3a and the two parallel ones at the end of vv 3, 9.

A poem, the song of the sword (vv 14bβ-22a), is set within a judgment oracle that Ezekiel is to report (vv 13-22; cf. v 18b), and indeed the oracular formula of prophetic address is included at the beginning of its second strophe (v 19a), while the prophet is also addressed at v 17aα . It may have been based on an existing song that Ezekiel used and amplified or it may represent a subsequent elaboration of an earlier poem he composed (cf. Fohrer 120; Zimmerli 431-32; cf. B. Maarsingh's comparison with an Akkadian poem, probably of the ninth century B.C., in *Ezekiel and His Book* 350-58). However, attempts to isolate additions on grounds of meter or repetition are not convincing, apart from the glaring glosses in v 15b and v 18a.

The oracle clearly antedates the fall of Jerusalem in 587 B.C. Reference is made to Jerusalem in respect of its administration (v 17) and gates (v 20). V 17 need not be regarded as a post-587 supplement (Zimmerli 432, 434-35; contrast Eichrodt 295). It fits structurally and its perfect verbs may be regarded as prophetic, relating to the divine purpose.

The poem divides into strophes, vv 14bγ -17, 19-22a. The first consists of six lines, three pairs marked by external parallelism. There are two tricola, in vv 16b and 17a. In the first pair the verb נָתַן "give" acts as an inclusion, while in the third (v 17) there is a chiasmus in an ABBA pattern. The second strophe, consisting of eight lines, breaks evenly into two halves, vv 19-20aα and 20aβ-22a. In the second half divine activity provides an inclusion (vv 20aβ, 22). The strophe as a whole has a double inclusion, the polarization of pronouns together with the clapping of hands (vv 19a, 22a) and the multiple strokes of the sword (vv 19bα, 21). The address to the "human one" functions as a hinge for the strophes (vv 17aα, 19aα). There is a loose overall inclusion, בָּרָק "flashing" and טֶבַח "slaughter" in vv 15a and 20b. The two strophes match in other repetitions: a multiple use of חֶרֶב "sword," including two cases in the first lines of each, the verb נָתַן "give," the preposition of purpose לְמַעַן "in order to" (vv 15a, 20aα) and the inclusive כֹּל "all" (vv 17aβ, 20aβ); while the reference to the people and their leaders in v 17 is paralleled by the plural pronouns in vv 19b and 20aβ. Zimmerli (431) has observed that כַּף "palm, hand" functions as a key term: apart from vv 16a, 19a and 22a, it occurs in a wordplay in וְתִכָּפֵל "and let it be doubled" in v 19bα. Outside the poem there is a stress on the divine word at its beginning, middle and end (vv 13-14a, 18b, 22b).

The third oracle of judgment, vv 23-32, consists of two parts. Vv 24-28 represent Yahweh's command to the prophet to perform a symbolic action concerning the threat to Jerusalem (vv 24, 25), together with its interpretation (vv 26-28). In vv 29-32 appears an accompanying double message to the people (v 29) and to Zedekiah (vv 30-32); each is introduced by the messenger formula. The second part develops the language at the end of the first (v 28b), with repetition of its verbs in v 29, repetition of עָוֹן "guilt" in v 30b and allusion to it in a wordplay, the triple עוה "ruin" in v 32a.

The addressees are to be taken as rhetorical rather than literal, as if the prophet were in Jerusalem (Zimmerli 441, contrast Brownlee xxvii). The reference to Nebuchadnezzar's campaign march against Judah (and Ammon) applies to 589 B.C., after Zedekiah's rebellion (cf. 17:15; 2 Kgs 24:20). Lang (*Kein Aufstand* 158-66) has feasibly grounded this oracle in a denial of the political hopes of a pro-rebellion party among the exiles (cf. Jer 29:21-32).

A fourth oracle of judgment occurs in vv 33-37. Because of its lack of a message reception formula it reads at first like a continuation of the preceding oracle. However, its contents mark it out as separate. It is directed against the Ammonites and clearly presupposes a post-587 B.C. phenomenon, their malicious enjoyment of Judah's downfall (v 33aβ). It leaves the reader with a distinctly literary impression, for it consists largely of material adapted from the three earlier oracles, from the first in v 35a and v 37aα and from the second in vv 33b, 34b and 36b and, despite different vocabulary, in the wrath of v 36. Most closely echoed is the third, especially in the vocabulary of opening (לפתוח, v 27a; פתוחה, v 33b), judgment (vv 32b, 35b) and pouring (לשפך, v 27b; ושפכתי, v 36a). Because of these marked borrowings and also because of recourse to prophetic motifs not clearly used by Ezekiel, it is generally judged to be later, although its claim to prophetic authority (vv 33a, 37bβ) must be taken seriously. It was presumably written before 539 B.C., when Babylon fell. It is unique in that only here in the book does Babylon feature as the object of judgment.

It is clear that the oracles in chap. 21 are intended as an overall redactional unit. All of them relate to the sword of judgment, whether Yahweh's (vv 8, 9), acting virtually under its own power (vv 14-22) or Nebuchadnezzar's (v 24). The calls to the prophet to lament (vv 11, 17) bind together the first and second oracles. Noteworthy too is the apparent echo of the "gates" and "hand" featured in the second oracle, in the course of the third (vv 27b and 29b ["by force"]); and also in the second oracle the echo of the remorseless כל "all" from the first. The song of the sword functions as the centerpiece, bounded on either side by a prose oracle, while the fourth, with its strong echoes of all three, has a supplementary role. The fourth supplies an overall inclusion: the devouring fire of v 37 matches that of v 3.

Comment

1-4 The oracle is introduced with a prophetic formula "set your face toward" that has already occurred in 6:2 and 13:17, and will recur in the interpretation of v 7, with reference to Jerusalem, in the foreign oracles at 25:2 (relating to Ammon); 28:21 (Sidon) and 29:2 (Pharaoh), and again in 35:2 (Seir) and 38:2 (Gog). The preposition "toward" is usually אל, but it is varied with על in 29:2; 35:2 and with דרך here. The formula is an archaism used of Balaam in Num 24:1 and of Elisha in 2 Kgs 8:11. In the former case it clearly refers to visual contact, but in Ezekiel it appears rather to be a symbolic action of staring in a certain direction, to indicate the target of an oracle (cf. "direct [הכין] your face toward," 4:3). Brownlee insisted on a literal sense of the formula as a travel idiom. It was one part of his package presentation of the prophet as exercising a Palestinian ministry (*HUCA*

54 [1983] 83-110; *Ezekiel 1-19* 96, 195). Others have found no difficulty in attributing a weakened meaning (cf. Zimmerli, *Ezekiel 1* 29-30, 182-83; Carley, *Ezekiel among the Prophets* 40-42). Here the use of the preposition דרך invites comparison with the directional turning toward Jerusalem in 1 Kgs 8:44 (cf. Dan 6:11). A symbolic interpretation accords with the phenomenon that foreign oracles in the prophetic books have rhetorical audiences, while the real audiences were the prophet's own constituency.

The "south," for which the Hebrew language can lavishly use three different words, stands for Judah, as v 8 is to clarify. Thus a geographical reference to the "Negeb" (RSV, NEB), south of Judah, is not to be seen; it has never been wooded anyway. In the background there seems to be the sinister motif of the "foe from the north" (Zimmerli 424; cf. Jer 6:22; Ezek 38-39). The prophetic image of fire for judgment is as old as Amos (1:4, etc.) and has already been used by Ezekiel in connection with the covenant metaphor of the vine (15:4-7; cf. 19:12, 14). Now the metaphor is extended to a forest fire (cf. Jer 21:14), which during dry summers must have been as fearful a phenomenon as it is in the brush of southern California. So intense was the conflagration to be that it would blaze unchecked, while all people nearby would have their faces scorched. The dire fierceness of the fire would force them to see Yahweh's hand in the incident.

5 The prophet, sensitive about the effectiveness of such an oracle, implicitly appeals for plainer speech, so that its message may not be blunted. His protest is born of painful experience ("alas") of contemptuous dismissal of his oracles among his contemporaries. Heb. משל refers to "a composition which offers in . . . colourful and . . . elaborate allegorical language a forecast of some impending event which is envisaged . . . in terms of Yahweh's purposeful action" (A. R. Johnson, VTSup 3 [1969] 168).

6-10 As a concession the oracle is reissued, admittedly dominated by another metaphor, that of the sword, but now speaking plainly of the people of Judah and their total fate. The homeland and its capital—temple and all—would be the target of Yahweh's weapon of judgment. Mention of the sword seems to echo the covenant curse of Lev 26:25, which thus provides an implicit reason for the onslaught. All would be caught up in a solidarity of judgment for the broken covenant. Vv 8-10 with their chiastic structuring stand out as tremendously forceful. The divine sword would be wielded until it had done its grisly work. So radical would be the onslaught upon Judah that others to the north would be included, like the seeping contamination of a neighborhood after a nuclear attack. In a culture prone to religious explanations of overwhelming crisis (cf. Jonah 1:4, 5), the message would be inescapable and no natural explanation could satisfy. It must be Yahweh's work.

The moral dimension of vv 8-9, accentuated by repetition, serves to underline the radical nature of the catastrophe expected by Ezekiel. Taken at its face value, it seems to rule out the survival of any, even in exile, over against such passages as 6:8-10; 12:16; 14:22, 23. Moreover, 14:12-20 had envisaged survival of the righteous—although so venerable are the grudging examples of righteousness cited there that doubt is implicitly cast on the existence of contemporary equivalents. Chap. 18 looks forward to a new era of divine dealing after the corporate experiences of 597 and 587 B.C. However, 9:4-6 seems clearly enough to exempt the repentant from destruction. Essentially Ezekiel speaks here as a pastoral theologian and in his use of overkill is evidently responding to a contemporary need to rule out any hope of reprieve, any optimism that life could by some means go on in Judah.

11, 12 If in the development of the oracle vv 1-4 present a parable and vv 6-10 its interpretation, this section serves to reinforce the message. The prophet is to engage in a symbolic action, in order to stimulate inquiry which will afford an opportunity to emphasize the severity and inevitability of the coming crisis. The literary schema used in v 12 deals with the symbolic action in a direct movement from omen to full communication of its meaning. Severity is indicated obliquely in the conventional terms of a reaction to bad news (cf. e.g., Isa 13:7, 8; Jer 6:24). The extreme nature of the reaction mirrors its grimness. The prophet is ordered to act out this reaction in advance and to reflect the ghastly shock in his own experience. No lesser reaction could match the coming catastrophe.

13-17 The next oracle, the song of the sword, owes its dynamic not so much to logic as to the aesthetic factors of poetry and a sustained imagery. In this first strophe preparation and purpose are the keynotes. A sword, a veritable Excalibur with a life of its own, is made ready for its grim destiny. There is a dwelling upon the necessary sharpening and burnishing, as unseen hands tenderly ensure that it will do its very worst. Focus passes from the sword to the hand that is to wield it to mete out death. But who is to die? None other than Yahweh's people and the members of their government: they are the destined victims. Again the prophet is ordered in his own person to act out a shocked reaction with the language of mouth and body. Once more his behavior is to be a measure of the tragedy (cf. Jer 47:2). It does not function as expression of sympathy (contra Zimmerli 435 et al.). The repeated "my people" represents not divine pathos and patronage, as it often does in the prophets, including Ezekiel (e.g., 13:10), but notes the discordant lengths to which Yahweh has to go in his estrangement from his erstwhile partner (cf. Isa 2:6).

19-22 The second strophe focuses upon the sword at work. Now the prophet's role is not merely to reflect the catastrophe but to initiate it with a prophetic gesture of command (cf. Hos 6:5; Jer 1:10). The sword was to hem in Jerusalem on every side, cutting off all escape. Fear and carnage would be rife as the drawn sword did its destined work. Behind this gruesome prospect stands the terrifying figure of Yahweh, stresses the second half of the strophe at its start and finish: the prophet was but the servant of his master in signaling that battle should begin (vv 19a, 22a). The savagery of the sword was to give vent to the passionate fury of Yahweh. In the whole scenario the hands of three persons have their part to play: the human wielder, the prophetic intermediary and the divine figure whose moral will was to be done.

23-25 In its present context the next oracle serves to identify the swordsman as the king of Babylon (v 24). Ezekiel is ordered to engage in a symbolic action depicting the campaigning king at the crossroads, confronted with two possible routes, to Ammon in the southeast and to Jerusalem in the southwest. The form the representation was to take is not specified: so presumably it was to be engraved with a stylus on a brick, as in 4:1. In light of 1 Sam 15:12; 2 Sam 18:18 and Isa 56:5 יד "signpost" seems to refer to an inscribed stone monument. Perhaps we are meant to think of Damascus as the junction—Nebuchadnezzar's military headquarters were at Riblah to the north (2 Kgs 25:6)—and the choice of the two great trade routes, the King's Highway down the Transjordan or the Sea Road which at a lower point ran along the coast. Or are we to envisage a junction to the south, a turning off the King's Highway in Bashan, which followed the watershed of central Palestine down to Jerusalem? The text implies that Ammon too had rebelled against Babylonian rule.

26, 27 The divine command to represent the routes has already mingled with the symbolic action a number of interpretative elements. The formal explana⸗tion (כִּי "for") that begins in v 26 abandons the general catchword "sword" and concentrates on details of military campaigning, initially the testing of the divine will by the taking of omens. Three types of divination are given. The third, the examination of animal livers, was a characteristic and highly developed feature of Babylonian religion. The first one, selection from marked arrows, was an Arabian practice, while the second was Israelite (cf. 1 Sam 15:23; Hos 3:4), but how the religious figurines were used is not known. Conceivably Nebuchadnezzar would have employed a mixture of oracular methods (under the influence of vassal kings under his command?). Alternatively the variety is intended in the account as cultural translation to communicate the king's intent with all clarity. The result of the inquiry indicates that Jerusalem was to be the first of the national capitals to be attacked. The element of choice presumably reflects hopes among the exiles that a campaign against Jerusalem would be deferred, allowing better prospects of defensive measures including the arrival and deployment of Egyptian troops. These hopes are dashed. The processes of siege warfare lay inevitably in Jerusalem's future and would soon be the explicit theme of Babylonian military orders. For the siege tactics mentioned here see Y. Yadin, *The Art of Warfare in Biblical Lands* (New York: McGraw-Hill, 1963) 313-17, 388-93.

28 Of course, Jerusalem's citizens, like Ezekiel's hearers, would not be disposed to take seriously Nebuchadnezzar's divinatory games. Yet ironically this non-Yahwist was taking a path marked out for him by Yahweh. His religious actions could not be ignored, for they were of a piece with other incriminating evidence against Jerusalem. Legal language is used which carries the discussion beyond controversial religious matters to a formal and decisive level. The "arrest" of the people of Jerusalem was clearly imminent. For מזכיר עון (lit. "causing guilt to be remembered") see H. J. Boecker, *TZ* 17 (1961) 212-16; for combination with תפש "apprehend" cf. Num 5:13, 15; for the latter verb cf. Jer 37:14.

29 The divine communication now takes on the form of a judgment oracle, introduced by the messenger formula and consisting of the standard two parts of accusation and punishment. Weight is laid on the element of accusation. There was further and more compelling evidence against Jerusalem: it is summed up in general terms as rebellion and sin. This internal evidence was warrant enough for the strong arm of the divine law to act. Nebuchadnezzar was Yahweh's policeman, providentially upholding law and order.

30-31 Zedekiah is singled out in a personal oracle. He is introduced not by name but by office (cf. 12:10, 12) and moral invective. There is a sinister allusion to the coming of the day of Yahweh in all its finality (cf. 7:2, 3, 6, 10, 12 and Brownlee, *Ezekiel 1-19* 114, 117, 119). Judah's mounting history of sinfulness had reached a level that forced Yahweh to intervene (cf. Gen 15:16; 2 Kgs 21:11). Zedekiah's own behavior had been "the last straw that breaks the camel's back" (Ehrlich, *Randglossen* 83, cf. 17:11-21). He is to lose his royal status: Yahweh's staccato orders already ring out, stripping his vassal of power. The social order was to be overthrown in the coming crisis, along with the regime of king and government.

32 The oracle reverts more generally to the fate of Jerusalem, which is the basic theme of the overall message (for the pronoun "it" cf. "them" in v 28). The unusual term עוה "ruin" seems to have been used deliberately for a play on עון "guilt" earlier. Its triple mention echoes the three instances of עון in vv 28-30. The punishment was to fit the crime, stresses the rhetoric. Yahweh would execute his sentence: his involvement in the situation is now disclosed by way of climax. The absolute climax is reserved for a damning echo of Gen 49:10 (cf. W. Moran, *Bib* 39 [1958] 416-25). The traditional promise of prosperity for Judah is subjected to prophetic reversal. The prophets typically gave sinister reinterpretation to motifs of hope (cf. Amos 5:18-20; Isa 28:21). V 32b has been understood by some in terms of restoration (e.g., RSV; Smend 147; Eichrodt 302-4), perhaps envisaging the replacement of Jehoiachin as king (Fohrer 125-26; Carley 143-44). However, the use of the same phrase ונתתי משפט "and I shall assign the judgment" in 23:24b in terms of the Babylonians points inexorably to "judgment" as the rendering of the noun rather than "right" (RSV), as Moran (*Bib* 39 (1958) 422-25) and Zimmerli (447) have emphasized (cf. M. Fishbane, *Biblical Interpretation in Ancient Israel* [Oxford: Clarendon, 1985] 502-3; Seitz, *Theology in Conflict* 151-54). By his parody Ezekiel indicated that this was no time for claiming royal promises (cf. the seeming parody of Isa 2:4 and Mic 4:3 in Joel 4[3]:10). Doubtless he was countering a claim currently being made by his contemporaries in exile. Instead, Yahweh's agent was the one who had been presented as his virtual policeman in vv 28-29, none other than Nebuchadnezzar. The oracle ends as it began, with the Babylonian king in the limelight.

33, 34 The final oracle weaves together threads drawn from the three previous ones. Lang has contended that "the Ammonites" is a subsequent insertion and that the oracle originally applied to Judah and was reapplied as too shocking by subsequent insertion of new addressees (*Kein Aufstand*, 120-125; *VT* 29 [1979] 40-41). However, in a literary sense the oracle as it stands fits the context. As for his argument that the second ואמרת "and say" is a case of resumptive repetition after intervening material was inserted, see *Note* 14.a. above. The oracle begins by taking up the unfinished business of v 25 and promises that Ammon's fate was merely deferred, in reprisal for exultation over the downfall of Jerusalem, which is described in 25:3, 6. The sinister sword of vv 13-22 is summoned for a fresh mission, which will make short shrift of the religious optimism of the Ammonites and at last get justice done.

35-37 Was Babylonian hegemony—for such the sword implies in the light of v 24 (Zimmerli 448-49)—to be Yahweh's last word? By no means. A voice offstage, as it were, gives an order for the sword to be replaced in its scabbard. Then the sword is addressed afresh, now as Yahweh's victim. Its work done, it is destined for destruction in its sheath, the place it came from, just as the Assyrian rod of Yahweh's anger had at length been broken (Isa 10:5-19; 37:23-38; cf. Mic 5:4, 5 [5, 6]). Babylon too was doomed to fall (cf. Isa 13-14; 47; Hab 1:6-2:20; Jer 50:1-51:58).

Explanation

The chapter is dominated by the image of the sword of judgment. In the powerful poem that stands at its heart the sword functions as a destructive force unleashed by Yahweh and so an instrument of his providential will. In the first oracle it is described more precisely as Yahweh's sword, seemingly wielded for breach of covenant, while in the third it is Nebuchadnezzar's, who functions as Yahweh's agent in punishing an immoral community. Divine and human factors are intertwined in Ezekiel's representation of Judah's grim future.

The prophet's agenda is to interact convincingly with his fellow exiles. They are not allowed to concentrate pettily on the medium at the expense of the message (v 5). It is too late for the theologically inclined to barter with God, as if a righteous remnant could preserve the city (cf. Gen 18:22-33). A symbolic action concerning reaction to crisis serves to reinforce the message, which far from being fabricated by Ezekiel was an expression of divine truth ("hear," "heard" in vv 3, 12). The dynamic centerpiece of the chapter intends to sway Ezekiel's fellow exiles by its emotive poetry, as they are permitted to overhear Yahweh's commissioning of sword and prophet to execute his terrible will. In the third oracle any flickering hopes of the exiles are firmly quenched. Jerusalem would not be allowed more time to repel the invader. Pagan religion would not lose the day against an external structure of Yahwistic faith. Above all, appeal to an ancient word of salvation could not be allowed to nullify Yahweh's present word of judgment. The catastrophe, eventually to materialize in 587 B.C., was inevitable. The prophet tells them naught for their comfort.

As in chap. 20, the final, supplementary oracle wants to peep around the corner of its pre-587 context. It seeks to consider more widely the issues raised earlier. Both by its rhetorical techniques and its content it endeavors to draw two matters to a satisfactory conclusion. First, Ammon was not to go scot free, despite Nebuchadnezzar's choice to attack Judah instead. Its turn would come, as 25:1-7 was to amplify. If Judah's guilt had to be punished (v 30), so too had Ammon's (v 34). Second, in vv 35-37 an issue is broached of passionate concern to other prophets. Was Babylon to rule unchecked, as Yahweh's favorite? Or, in theological terms, was Yahweh wedded to the sword? The negative answer turns judgment into a means, not an end, and so implicitly lets a chink of light into the dark early messages of Ezekiel. Beyond hopelessness there might yet be hope. If Yahweh was eventually to take up cudgels on behalf of his impugned people (v 33), it was a hint that, though temporarily enemies of God (v 8), their election was veiled rather than revoked (cf. Rom 11:28, 29).

Jerusalem: The Inside Story (22:1-31)

Bibliography

Allen, L. C. "A Textual Torso in Ezek 22:20." *JSS* 31 (1986) 131-33. **Fishbane, M.** *Biblical Interpretation in Ancient Israel.* Oxford: Clarendon, 1985, 461-63. **Forbes, R. J.** *Studies in Ancient Technology.* Leiden: Brill, 1964, vol. 8. **Greenberg, M.** "What Are Valid Criteria for Determining Inauthentic Material in Ezekiel?" *Ezekiel and His Book.* Ed. J. Lust. Leuven: University Press, 1986, 123-35. **Hossfeld, F.-L.** *Untersuchungen zu Komposition und Theologie des Ezechielbuches.* FzB 20. Würzburg: Echter Verlag, 1977, 99-152. **Reventlow, H.** *Wächter über Israel.* BZAW 82. Berlin: Töpelmann, 1962, 101-8. **Schulz, H.** *Das Todesrecht im Alten Testament.* BZAW 114. Berlin: Töpelmann, 1969, 181-87. **Zimmerli, W.** "Deutero-Ezechiel?" *ZAW* 84 (1972) 501-16.

Translation

[1]*I received the following communication from Yahweh:* [2] *"Human one, would you pass judgment, would you pass judgment, please,[a] on the bloodstained city? Inform it of all its shocking behavior,* [3]*saying, This is a message from the Lord[a] Yahweh: City[b] spilling blood inside yourself[c] to bring closer your time of reckoning and making yourself[d] idols to pollute yourself with,* [4]*you have incurred guilt from the blood you have spilled and pollution from the idols you have made, and so you have brought your period of reckoning[a] closer and your years of retribution nearer.[b] That is why I have made you the object of other nations' insults, the scorn of every country.* [5]*Countries nearby and far from you scorn you, famed as you are for pollution and eminent as you are for your social disorder.* [6]*For instance, you have had present in you Israel's heads of state who used their respective powers to spill blood.* [7]*Present in you are persons who dishonor fathers and mothers, treat resident aliens oppressively and abuse orphans and widows.* [8]*You have despised what is sacred to me and desecrated my sabbaths.* [9]*Present in you are informers who are responsible for blood being spilled. Present in you are people who eat on the mountains. Present in you are people who practice lasciviousness.* [10]*Present in you are those who go to bed with their stepmothers,[a] and others who force themselves on women suffering from menstrual pollution.* [11]*One man shockingly carries on with his neighbor's wife, another lasciviously sullies his daughter-in-law, while yet another man present in you forces himself on his half sister.* [12]*Present in you are people who take bribes to get blood spilled. You charge interest and usury and oppressively extort money from your neighbors. You have forgotten me!" So runs the oracle of the Lord Yahweh.*

[13] *"Accordingly I clench[a] my fist at the extortionate profit you have made and at the spilling of blood[b] that has taken place inside your walls.* [14]*Will your courage last, will you have any strength in your hands during the period I am dealing with you? I, Yahweh, have spoken and I will act.* [15]*I will scatter you among the nations, dispersing you throughout other countries, and I will remove your pollution from you completely.* [16a]*I will let the other nations[b] take a debased view of me[a] on your account, but you will realize that I am Yahweh."*

[17] *I received the following communication from Yahweh:* [18] *"Human one, the community of Israel has turned into dross*[a] *in their relations with me.*[b] *All of them are copper, tin, iron and lead in the furnace: they have turned into dross.*[c] [19] *So this is the message of the Lord Yahweh. Inasmuch as you have all turned into dross, for that reason I am going to put you together inside Jerusalem.* [20] *In the same way as*[a] *silver, copper, iron, lead and tin are put together inside a furnace, ready for the metal ore*[b] *to be blasted with fire in order to melt it down,*[c] *that is how I in my anger and fury am going to put you together*[d] *and melt you down.* [21] *I will blast you*[a] *with the fire of my wrath and you will be melted down inside Jerusalem.*[b] [22] *In the same way that silver is melted in a furnace, so will you be melted down inside it. Then you will realize that I, Yahweh, have vented my fury on you."*

[23] *I received the following communication from Yahweh:* [24] *"Human one, tell Jerusalem,*[a] *You are a region that has received no rain,*[b] *upon which no shower has fallen*[c] *at a time of indignation.*[d] [25] *Its heads of state*[a] *were reminiscent of a roaring lion tearing its prey: they devoured lives, seized*[b] *wealth and riches and widowed many women inside its walls.* [26] *Its priests did despite to my law and desecrated what is sacred to me. They made no distinction between what is holy and what is not, they did not teach the difference between what is impure*[a] *and pure, while they turned a blind eye to my sabbaths. The result is that I have been besmirched among them.* [27] *Inside its walls were officials like wolves who tore their prey—spilling blood and destroying lives for extortionate profit.* [29] *On the people of the land they practiced oppression and committed*[a] *robbery. The poor and needy they abused, and resident aliens they treated*[b] *unjustly.*[c] [28] *Its prophets whitewashed them by seeing false visions and making lying divinations for them, while claiming 'This is a message from the Lord Yahweh' when Yahweh had not spoken at all.* [30] *I looked for a person from their number who would build a barricade and on the land's behalf stand in the breach in front of me, to stop me destroying it; but I could not find anyone.* [31] *So I vented my indignation on them, I consumed them with the fire of my wrath, I held them responsible for their behavior." So runs the oracle of the Lord Yahweh.*

Notes

2. a. See the note on 20:4. The omission of the second verb in a few MSS LXX* Syr is a shortening of Ezekiel's idiomatic repetition (Zimmerli 452; cf. 20:4) rather than original (cf. *BHS*). In support of the Heb. may be cited J. S. Kselman's observation of a semantic-sonant chiasmus in an ABBA pattern (*Bib* 58 [1957] 221). The repeated verbs form the B/B elements, and the דם play of אדם "human being" and הדמים "blood" the A/A elements.

3. a. For the authenticity of אדני "Lord" in this formula here and in vv 19 and 28 and in the formula of v 12 see the first note on 20:3.

3. b. LXX ὦ "O" implies a vocative (עיר)ה lost by haplography after יהוה (Zimmerli, ibid.; Eichrodt 308; cf. v 5 and GKC 126e).

3. c. For the change from second to third person after a vocative in the Heb. of the rest of the verse see GKC 144p and cf. Isa. 22:16; 2 Kgs 9:31.

3. d. Heb. עליה means "on behalf of herself": cf. BDB 754a, b and על עשה "do for" in Neh 5:19.

4. a. Tg's sg form for ימיך "your days" would be easier (cf. 21:30 [25]), but 12:23 provides a parallel.

4. b. MT עד ותבוא "and you (masc) have come to (your years)" is generally emended in line with the parallel clause to עת וַתָּבִאי "and you (fem) have advanced the time." The verbal form is attested by LXX Vg, and the noun by 2 MSS Q^Or and the ancient versions. Hossfeld (*Untersuchungen* 115) has noted the association of עת "time" and יום or ימים "day(s)" in 7:7, 12; 12:27; 21:30, 34; 30:3. Probably MT arose via an intermediate reading עת ותבוא "and the time has come," as Syr Tg rendered.

10. a. Lit. "uncover the nakedness of a father." The sg verb of MT may be a mechanical assimilation to the verbs of v 11 from an original גלו, seemingly attested by the ancient versions.

13. a. The pf functions as performative, indicating instantaneous action (cf. Joüon 112f).

13. b. The following pl verb suggests a reading דמיך for MT דמך "your blood," with a few MSS and LXX. The sg דם in v 12, etc, has influenced MT.

16. a-a. For MT's second person verb ונחלתי "and I will be profaned" is generally read; it is attested by one MS and the ancient versions. This is supported by בך "on your account," while לעיני הגוים "in the eyes of the nations" commonly accompanies mention of Yahweh's profanation (20:9, 14, 22; cf. 36:20). MT may simply represent a wrong interpretation of תי- as an archaism for תְּ- (cf. GKC 44h), under the influence of the following verb.

16. b. MT גוים "nations" seems to be a slip for הגוים "the nations," attested by many MSS.

18. a. For K לסוג ("to backslide"?) the usual form לְסִגִים "to dross" is expected, as in v 19a (cf. v 18b). Probably *mem* was dropped by pseudohaplography before *kaph* (cf. v 20). Q לסיג appears to be an intermediate form.

18. b. For this sense of לי "to me" cf. the idiomatic usage of *lamed* of reference with a *lamed* of new condition, illustrated in BDB 512b (4b).

18. c. MT כסף adds "silver," a gloss mistakenly intended to supply the metal missing from the list in comparison with v 20 (see *Comment* and Zimmerli 463). LXX indirectly attests its secondary nature: in its underlying Heb. text כסף evidently stood in place of כור "furnace" because a marginal כסף had been wrongly taken as a correction for כור and displaced it. Accordingly LXX* does not represent it where MT does.

20. a. MT קבצת "gathering" has lost an initial *kaph* by pseudohaplography after *mem* (cf. v 18); it is attested by LXX Syr Tg. The cognate construction "gather with the like of a gathering" is matched by that of v 22a (cf. GKC 117p-q, 118s).

20. b. Heb. "it."

20. c. For להנתך "to smelt" LXX Syr attest niph לְהִנָּתֵך, but the hiph accords with the hoph form in v 22 (Cooke 247). In pausal forms of *pe-nun* verbs there is a tendency not to assimilate the *nun* (GKC 66f; Bauer-Leander 151).

20. d. MT adds והנחתי "and I will deposit," absent from Syr perhaps as incomprehensible. It was evidently an attempt to make sense of an abandoned error (י) והנתך miswritten for (כתי) והתך under the influence of להנתיך earlier: see *JSS* 31 (1986) 131-33 for elaboration of this and the next notes.

21. a. MT prefaces with וכנסתי אתכם, intended as a qal with the meaning "and I will bring you in" and meant as an explanatory gloss on והנחתי in v 20. In the Heb. MS. underlying LXX (καὶ συνάξω) the same gloss, without the pronominal object, had displaced והנחתי.

21. b. Heb. "it."

24. a. Heb. "her/it."

24. b. MT מטהרה "cleansed" hardly fits the term in the parallel clause. LXX βρεχομένη "rained on" attests an original מְמֻטָרָה, a pual ptcp lacking the preformative *mem* (cf. GKC 52s; cf. *BHS*) or, better, since this verb occurs in the hiph but not piel, a hoph pf הָמְטָרָה, assuming haplography of *he* (NEB [Brockington, *Hebrew Text* 227]). There is then a relative clause with ellipse of אשר "which"; for the resumptive pronoun cf. 2 Kgs 22:13.

24. c. MT גשמה appears to be a mixed form, combining a pual ptcp גֻּשָּׁמָה (cf. *BHS* et al.) "showered upon" with a suffixed noun "its showers" (from גֶּשֶׁם?).

24. d. An emendation זרם "storm," suggested by Ehrlich (*Randglossen* 88; cf. *BHK*) is prohibited by the structural role of זעם "indignation" (Zimmerli 465).

25. a. MT "conspiracy of its prophets" is generally judged inferior to אשר נשיאיה "whose rulers," attested by LXX. MT here and in v 24 may have originated in a pair of rubrical terms, placed in the margin to indicate the theme of v 26, טהר "pure" and קדש "holy" (cf. in principle Freedy, *VT* 20 [1970] 141-44). Cf. the confusion of קדש and קשר in Isa 8:12-14 (see H. Wildberger, *Jesaja 1-12* [BKAT², 1980] 334-35; J. D. W. Watts, *Isaiah 1-33* [WBC, 1985] 119). MT נביאה "its prophets" has been assimilated to the term in v 28. In favor of נשיאיה "its rulers," apart from LXX, is the use of the term in Zeph 3:4, which underlies the passage, and the same imagery in 19:3, 6 used of נשיאי ישראל "rulers of Israel" (M. Fishbane, *Biblical Interpretation* 462 n. 9).

25. b. For יקחו "they seize" a pf לקחו, read by 2 MSS, is often preferred, in line with the adjacent verbs (cf. *BHS*). However, Zimmerli (465) has compared the tense changes in 18:5-9, 10-13. Was there a desire for assonance (ויקר יקחו)?

26. a. MT הטמא "the impure" does not align with anarthrous לטהור. C and a few MSS read the expected טמא, as in 44:23. MT may have arisen from a comparative gloss citing הטמא in Lev 10:10; 11:47.

29. a. For the verbal continuation, indicating synonymous parallelism, see B. Johnson, *Hebräisches Perfekt und Imperfekt mit vergehendem* wᵉ (Lund: Gleerup, 1979) 79.

29. b. In place of עשקו "they oppressed," עשו "they dealt," attested by LXX, is generally regarded

as preferable: cf. v 7. Mechanical assimilation to עשׂק earlier was responsible for MT. Heb. את is then the preposition "with."

29. c. Cornill (316) transposed vv 28 and 29, taking עם הארץ "the people of the land" as object with LXX Syr. He noted that the section concerning the officials is then about as long as the one relating to the rulers in vv 25-26 and that v 30 more naturally refers to a prophetic obligation, as in 13:5. V 28 could easily have dropped out by a slip of the eye from בלא משפט (v 29) to ויהוה לא דבר (v 28). Then it was reinserted too soon on the assumption that (a) עם הארץ was the subject and so (b) a reference to prophets should go earlier alongside specific leadership groups rather than after a general statement. The structure of clauses in v 29 suggests that עם הארץ functions as object (cf. v 25). Then מהם "from them" in v 30 relates to the prophets, while עליהם "upon them" in v 31 refers to the Judeans generally, after the references to the land and its destruction in v 30b.

Form/Structure/Setting

Chap. 22 is composed of three prophetic units, vv 1-16, 17-22 and 23-31, each introduced by the message reception formula and focusing upon Jerusalem. The first is a proof saying, as the recognition formula of v 16b shows. It is basically a judgment oracle addressed to Jerusalem, with accusations leveled in general terms in vv 3aβ-4a and in detail in vv 6-12, while sentence is passed in vv 13-15. Interim judgment, which lies in the past, is cited in vv 4b-5. Vocatives begin and end vv 3aβ-5, which are thus characterized as having an introductory role in relation to the oracle as a whole. The divine saying formula in v 12 provides a caesura for the first half of the main oracle. An affirmation formula occurs near the end, in v 14b.

Like very many of Ezekiel's prose oracles, this oracle is marked by an elevated style. It is especially evident in the introductory section, which consists of two parts, each with its own parallelism, vv 3aβ-4a and 4b-5. The ABCD/ACDB repetitive scheme in the former highlights both the shedding of blood and the attraction of doom. To delete v 4a as "needlessly repetitive" (Freedy, *VT* 20 [1970] 145 n. 2) is to overlook the powerful role of repetition in the book. Vv 6-12 present accusations that develop those of the introduction. Like chap. 18, this section draws freely from traditional listings of obligations that have been infringed (cf. Reventlow, *Wächter über Israel*, 104-5). It falls into two parts, vv 6-8 and 9-12. Each concludes with statements that have Jerusalem as their subject (vv 8, 12), the second being climactically longer. The phrase למען שפך־דם "in order to shed blood" in vv 6, 9 and 12 functions as a double inclusion, for vv 6-12 and also for vv 9-12. Another inclusion is בעשׁק "in oppression" in vv 7 and 12. The phrase היו בך "they have been in you" significantly occurs in vv 6a and 9a. In fact the term בך "in you" is a persistent element, occurring three times in vv 6-7 and six in vv 9-12. Once in each part it is stylistically varied by בתוכך "in your midst" (vv 7, 9). There are close rhetorical links with the introduction, which twice uses שׁפך דם and specifies בתוכה "in her midst" and בך. Moreover, the stem טמא "be unclean," twice used in vv 3-4, is formally echoed by its presence in vv 10, 11.

In the final section, vv 13-16, והנה "and behold" is used to introduce divine reprisal for the accusations prefaced with הנה "behold" in v 6. The stem בצע "extort" is used as an intersectional hinge (vv 12, 13). The reference to Jerusalem's activity (עשׂית, v 13) picks up the use of the verb in vv 7, 9, and 11, and also in the first section at v 4. It meets its match in the divine activity of v 14 (ועשׂיתי, עשׂה). The drumbeats of the prepositional terms בתוכך and בך sound here too (vv 13, 16), while the reference to "blood" (דמיך, v 13) brings to a climax a concern of the whole oracle. So too does mention of "uncleanness" (טמאתך) in v 15. Specific throwbacks to the introductory section, by way of inclusion, are to be found in the international references (ארצות "countries" and גוים "nations") in vv 4b-5 and 15-16 and the sinister references to coming "days" (ימיך, לימים) in vv 4a and 14. There are thus strong rhetorical features which both characterize the three sections of the oracle and bind it together into a compact whole. Together with form-critical factors the tight bonding gives the impression of compositional—rather than redactional—unity, which hardly comports with suggestions that vv 13-16 are secondary (Zimmerli 455, 459; Wevers 128) or that only vv 1-5 and 14 are original (Fohrer 128). Greenberg has discussed the authenticity of 22:1-16 in *Ezekiel and His Book* 128-31, with reference to Hossfeld's arguments that a basic oracle, vv 1-6, 9a, 12, has been expanded with insertions and supplemented first with vv 13-14 and then with vv 15-16 (*Untersuchungen* 148-152). Schulz (*Das Todesrecht*) has argued that a number of passages, including 22:1-16, which depend on established sets of laws, are to be attributed to a post-exilic Deutero-Ezekiel. However, Zimmerli, *ZAW* 84 (1972) 501-16, has observed that many of these passages reflect the historical situation of Ezekiel's own period.

This first oracle reflects particularly well the midpoint historical position peculiar to Ezekiel's first period of prophesying. It looks back to the catastrophe of 597 B.C. and forward to the further, final one of 587. It has a geographical setting in Babylonia. Rhetorical address, here of Jerusalem, is a common prophetic phenomenon and against Brownlee (*Ezekiel 1-19* xxiv, 58, 220) there is no need to suppose the prophet's presence in the city. Certainly the use of traditional material as a basis for the detailed accusations strikes a different note from the immediacy of the denunciations of an Isaiah or a Jeremiah.

The second oracle in vv 17-22 is a proof saying developed from a judgment oracle. Working with a consistent metallurgical image, it presents accusation in v 18 and predicts punishment in vv 19-22, at the beginning of which the accusation of v 18 is briefly resumed, while the list of metals resumed from v 18 in v 20 provides a further link. The accusatory part is defined by a chiastic inclusion, היו . . . לסגים "they have become dross" and סגים . . . היו. In turn vv 20-22a are marked by an inclusion כ . . . כן "as . . . so," in vv 20 and 22a; in logical terms a simile is presented at length in vv 20-21 and summarized in v 22a. An inclusion for the whole oracle is provided by בתוך כור "in the midst of a furnace" at vv 18 and 22. In fact, the oracle is dominated by a wordplay תוך and נתך "smelt" (Parunak, *Structural Studies* 330), which gives rhetorical point to the imagery. Six times תוך is used concerning the furnace and Jerusalem in an alternating arrangement (ABABAB). The three verbs of the simile in v 20a, קבץ "gather," נפח "blast" and נתך, are picked up in turn in vv 20b-22a so as to create an ABC/AC/BC/CC pattern, with the element of smelting occurring emphatically at the end of four consecutive statements. There is a further rhetorical scheme that again runs from v 20 but now includes v 22b. The sequence of אש "fire," אפי "my anger" and חמתי "my fury" (v 20) is resumed with one variant in אש, עברתי "my wrath" and חמתי (vv 21, 22) in an ABCAB'C distribution. As in the first oracle, there is tight rhetorical structuring here in the second.

In its historical setting this one too looks forward to the final catastrophe, specifically to the successful siege begun early in 588 B.C. The introductory third person references to the people who were to be gathered in Jerusalem reflect the prophet's position in exile, while the subsequent second person address has a rhetorical function.

The third oracle, in vv 23-31, is an unusual type of judgment oracle in that, like Isa 1:2-9, it looks back to the past in its description of punishment (see esp. v 31). The note of judgment envelops the oracle in vv 24 and 31, while the accusations are presented in four sections in vv 25-29. In line with the content an expression of divine displeasure, זעמי/זעם "(my) indignation," functions as an inclusion in vv 24 and 31 (cf. Zimmerli 467). The four sections accusing civil and religious leaders are presented in an ABA'B' order. The similes of predation link the A/A' sections (vv 25, 27), while the topics of taking life and property from the under-privileged pervade both (vv 25, 27, 29). In the B/B' sections a series of short-comings is capped by a statement with a divine subject (vv 26, 28). Verbal repetition is a feature of most of the sections: cognate phrases in the first and third (vv 25, 27, 29) and also in v 30; triple use of a stem in the second (יחללו "and they profaned," לחל "and the profane" and ואחל "and I was profaned" in v 26); and double usage in the fourth (אמרים "they say," אמר "he has said" in v 28).

Historically the oracle seems to presuppose the fall of Jerusalem in 587 B.C. As to authorship, there is a strong scholarly consensus that its composition is to be credited to Ezekiel's "school" (cf. Fohrer 130; Zimmerli 467; Wevers 131; Eichrodt 316). First, there seems to be literary dependence on Zeph 3:3-4, 8 (cf. Fishbane, *Biblical Interpretation* 461-63), where a fourfold sequence of Jerusalem's civil and religious authorities occurs (but in an AA'BB' order). Apart from structure, the language is remarkably close in places: קדש חללו "they profaned the holy" and חמסו תורה "they did despite to the law" in Zeph 3:4 (cf. v 26 here), זאבי "wolves" in 3:3 (cf. v 27) and לשפך עליהם זעמי "to pour out on them my indignation" in 3:8 (cf. v 31). The oracle seems to have been composed with consultation of a scroll of Zephaniah. The material cited seems to date from the end of the seventh century B.C. (cf. W. Rudolph, *Micha, Nahum, Habakuk, Zephanja* [KAT, 1975] 256, 287-90) and so there is no intrinsic reason why Ezekiel himself did not make use of it, assuming that he had a hand in the literary adaptation of his oral oracles.

There are also clear verbal leanings on Ezek 13:2-16 in vv 28 and 30. More-over, it is significant that the oracle starts in midstream, making mention of Jerusalem only with pronouns. This is quite comprehensible if the oracle was composed as a literary continuation of the previous two. Links with them are not lacking. As to the first oracle, v 25 harks back to v 6; v 26 is closely linked in vocabulary to v 8, and v 29 to v 7. V 27 echoes not only the double mention of extortion (בצע) of vv 12-13, but also the refrain למען שפך־דם "in order to spill blood" in vv 6, 9 and 12, by the phrase לשפך־דם "to spill blood." As to the second oracle, the references to divine anger in vv 21 and 22 are echoed in v 31.

What provides the closest overall link between the oracles is the presence of (ב)תוך "(in) the midst" with direct or indirect reference to Jerusalem. Not only is it found in the first two oracles, but the third has it three times in vv 25 and 26. A second common feature is the stem שפך "pour out": human spilling of blood (vv 6, 9, 12, 27) finds reprisal in the outpouring of divine wrath (vv 21, 31): it is the third oracle that contains both. The combination of the three oracles is a result of devoted editorial labors that sought to highlight the deserved fate of Jerusalem.

Comment

1-5 In terms close to those of 20:4, Ezekiel is invited to transmit a message of crime and punishment; but now the perspective is contemporary or recent rather than historical, and it is Jerusalem's behavior that comes under scrutiny. It is characterized initially as "city of bloodshed," a phrase used of Nineveh in Nah 3:1! In the ensuing exposition two offenses are specified, not only holding human life cheap (cf. 11:6), but also abandoning Israel's traditionally aniconic faith. An implicit link between the two finds expression in the priestly perspective of Gen 9:5-6: humanity is precious as the image of God, and humanity is his only image. The state of moral guilt and religious impurity that resulted from the capital's behavior could not go unchecked by Yahweh as upholder of the social and sacred obligations he had laid on his people. Their wrongdoing would catch up with them; in fact they were inviting the onset of retribution (cf. Amos 6:3b). Already evidence was not lacking of such reprisal from Yahweh's hand (cf. Hos. 4:3. Heb. עַל־כֵּן "that is why" introduces "the statement of a fact rather than a declaration" [BDB 487a]). The fall of Jerusalem in 597 B.C. had been his handiwork. Yet it is only the start of "years" of punishment. Loss of face was dreaded in Israelite culture, yet this had been what Jerusalem had incurred (cf. 16:57). Jerusalem the golden, "she that was great among the nations" (Lam 1:1; cf. Ezek 16:14), had to learn to live with the consequences of a new reputation, for religious and social shortcomings.

6-8 In vv 6-12 the accusations of vv 3-4a are developed. It is a roll call of infamy. First place is given to the royal house who over a number of generations had abused their political power, staining their hands with blood. Jeremiah's strictures against Jehoiakim in Jer 22:13-19 for causing human suffering and death come readily to mind.

Commoners too followed in the kings' steps, in their lack of respect for persons. Aged parents and other underprivileged groups such as resident aliens and orphans and widows had suffered a similar abuse of power, directed at those low in society's pecking order. "The real test of any society is . . . how it treats the people with no voice and no power" (D. Lane, *The Cloud and the Silver Lining* [Welwyn: Evangelical Press, 1985] 88). It is clear that Ezekiel is echoing Israel's sacred lawcodes, for instance Exod 20:12; 22:20-26 (21-27), and implicitly claiming that their threat of retribution (e.g., Exod 22:22, 23 [23, 24]) was to be unleashed. This phase of the accusation is capped with cultic sins, with which the prophet confronted the city. Breaking the sabbath (cf. 20:12-13, 16, 21, 24) and infringing the cultic traditions of worship were a supreme affront to God in that they related to his revelation of himself (cf. Lev 19:30).

9-12 The second block of accusations is a catalog of three types of social disorder. The first recalls Lev 19:16, a prohibition of slander that could become the basis of false accusation at a trial for a capital offense. A religious wrong follows, mentioned earlier at 18:6, 11, 15, the eating of sacred meals at illicit shrines (cf. Hos 4:13). V 9bβ provides a headline (Zimmerli 458) for a series of five sexual crimes detailed in vv 10-11. They implicitly appeal to such traditions as are concentrated in Lev 20:10-18 (cf. Fishbane, *Biblical Interpretation* 293). In Israelite thinking they stood on the borderline between social and sacred wrongs and partook of both: accordingly the term "unclean" is used of two of them. Three cases relate to incest, one to adultery and one, no less real a taboo in Israel's culture, to intercourse during a wife's period, while she was ritually unclean.

The third type of wrongdoing is mercenary. Bribery with a view to the fatal miscarriage of justice and capitalizing on another's misfortune had featured in Israel's legal traditions (see especially Exod 22:24 [25]; 23:8). Here it is accompanied with a general charge of racketeering. The switch to direct address paves the way for the final charge (to be repeated in 23:35) of forgetting Yahweh (cf. Hos 2:15 [13]). Here too Yahweh's revelation of his comprehensive will in Israel's lawcodes is presupposed.

13-15 The previous scenario of vv 6-12 triggers another, one of judgment (הנה "behold," v 6; והנה "and behold," v 13). Hand clapping, to which the text literally refers, seems here to be the gesture of a hostile reaction (cf. 21:22 [17]) to the profiteering and murder, examples that span the foregoing, from v 12 back to v 3. The provocative question of v 14 intends to stimulate a sense of foreboding. Human activity (v 13; cf. v 4) was to give way to the activity of Yahweh, guaranteed by his solemn promise (cf. 12:25, 28; 17:24). In plain terms, those spared exile in the first deportation of 597 B.C. would now encounter it (cf. 12:15; 20:23), and so by implication Jerusalem was to fall again. Such drastic action was the only way to get rid of the rank pollution (cf. 24:11, 13).

16 The corollary was a mixed one. In the conquest of the capital and exile of its people Yahweh would himself suffer, as 36:20 will explain. At last he had to come to a point earlier avoided (cf. 20:9, 14, 22). It was the lesser of two evils that he was prepared to endure as the price to pay for making his forgetful people remember who and what he was.

17, 18 If the first oracle devotes more space to accusation, the second in vv 17-22 concentrates on judgment. Brief as it is, the accusatory element here tellingly conveys its message by the metaphor of dross. Ezekiel can evidently assume that the negative meaning of the metaphor is intelligible to his audience as a condemnation of the people left in Judah. This is not only because a smattering of the silversmith's art would be common knowledge, but also because its prophetic application could be presupposed. The prophet Ezekiel appears to be making fresh use of Isaiah's illustration of Jerusalem's political degeneration and coming punishment (Isa 1:22a [היה לסיגים], 25). Jer 6:27-30 also seems dependent on Isaiah, but makes a different point, that Jeremiah with his prophetic message functions as the refiner (cf. J. W. Miller, *Verhältnis* 2 note 2, 113). Unlike Isaiah and Jeremiah, Ezekiel refers not to the whole process of refining but only to the preliminary stage of smelting, thereby ruling out any optimism such as Isa 1:21-26 offers. In v 18 there is reference to the raw material, lead ore, which is galena or lead sulfide, a mixture of lead and small quantities of other metals. Hopefully it would contain silver, the extraction of which was the object of the metallurgical exercise, although in practice the silver content would be less than 0.5%. But here Yahweh pronounces that it is all mere slag, devoid of silver. He speaks as one who stands at the end of the smelting process. Dross was one of the products of the smelting stage itself, as it is in Isa 1:22a. Here, as there, it represents an accusation. The Hebrew etymological association of "dross" with deviation appears to be presupposed.

19-22 Isa 1:25, after speaking earlier of the smelting process that produced dross, refers logically to the second stage of refining. Here, however, there is a return to the first stage. What in v 18 was a prophetic metaphor for worthlessness is re-used in a different way. The metaphor now stands not simply for the divine evaluation but for divine event. There is to be a gruesome acting out of the metaphor, with Jerusalem as victim. There is a theological parallel for the double usage in the Gospel of John, where the unbeliever is condemned already but still has to undergo the last judgment (John 3:18; 5:24; 12:48). Jerusalem was to be put through the fires of judgment in a physical approximation to the smelting process. The capital under siege would be the furnace to which heat was to be applied. Those gathered for protection would find destruction instead. There is a sinister play on smelting (נתך) and the midst (תוך) of the furnace or Jerusalem.

The smelting process consisted of two stages, the first of which was desulfurization, in which the galena was heated gently in a hearth furnace to release most of the sulfur in the form of sulfur dioxide, leaving a mixture of galena and lead oxide or litharge. The second stage took advantage of the fact that lead has a lower melting point than most of the other metals contained in the metallic mass. The furnace was heated enough to melt the lead and silver, leaving behind the dross. The concentrated silver-lead alloy was then subjected to a further stage, refining (Heb. צרף) to isolate the silver, but that seems to be beyond the purview of the text. In the smelting the temperature was controlled by blasts of air, provided by bellows according to Jer 6:29. A brief description of the smelting and refining techniques has been supplied by W. L. Holladay, *Jeremiah 1-25* (Philadelphia: Fortress, 1986) 231. A fuller description may be found in Forbes, *Studies in Ancient Technology*, vol. 8, 228-39. The three steps of inserting the crude metal, heating it with the aid of bellows and smelting it, are recounted as metallurgical facts in v 20a, then rhetorically the prophet gives the interpretation, taking each of the first two steps in turn and combining it with the third. In the summary of simile and explanation at v 22 two mentions of the final step occur side by side. The result is a sinister emphasis on smelting down the raw material and so on subjecting the people cowering in Jerusalem to enormous stress. This would be Yahweh's way of teaching his people that unfaithful deviance from him (v 18) must end in tragic consequences, an experience of his wrath.

23, 24 The final oracle in this series of three, vv 23-31, reasons back from consequence to cause. The catastrophe of 587 B.C. was an outworking of divine indignation (vv 24, 31). The tradition of covenant curse or blessing whereby rain was the reward of loyalty to Yahweh and drought was a reprisal for unfaithfulness (cf. Lev 26:4, 19: Deut 11:14, 17; Amos 4:7) is here taken up by way of metaphor. Fallen Jerusalem is rhetorically bidden to reflect on the fact that its experience had been nothing less than divine judgment.

25-31 In a flashback the social history of the last period of Jerusalem is traced in terms of accusations that give warrant for the interpretation of v 24. The testimony of the prophet Zephaniah, who was contemporary with that period, is employed (Zeph 3:3, 4) and in fact the terms "day" and "indignation" in v 24 already drew on that source (Zeph 3:8). Jerusalem, viewed as administrative capital and religious center of the people of God, had proved to be a failure and so had to be obliterated (cf. Mic 3:9-12). The secular authorities, the priests and the prophets, are treated in an alternating scheme that looks from one authority to another and despairingly finds no cause for optimism anywhere.

By a terrible Jekyll and Hyde transformation the civil authorities who should have been shepherds with the welfare of their flock at heart changed into wild beasts preying on the sheep (cf. 34:8). Neither private property nor personal life had been immune to their ravages. While the royals had concentrated on such wrongdoing in Jerusalem, their officials who represented them in the provincial towns of Judah had illtreated people at large and especially the underprivileged. The priests, properly custodians of Israel's sacred traditions and both practitioners and teachers of the vital norms of purity and holiness, belied their calling. They contravened the ideology of separation that lay at the heart of Israel's cult in terms of calendar, food and many other aspects of religious life. Yahweh himself had been affected by these lapses, which allowed the impure and the unholy to infiltrate both a holy temple and a holy people. The tirade against the prophets is based on Ezekiel's metaphor of whitewashing and accusation of erroneous predictions in 13:2-16. The canonical pre-exilic prophets regularly complained of professional colleagues who ignored glaring moral factors and preached a comfortable message of blessing and salvation (cf. e.g., Mic 3:1-8).

The climax of the accusation against the prophets comes in v 30, a reprise of 13:5. Prophetic intercession against the coming catastrophe had been conspicuous by its absence. It could have averted or at least postponed the end (cf. Amos 7:1-9; Jer 5:1). Yahweh had no alternative but to do his worst, in moral retribution for the authorities' reneging on their duties, and to destroy Jerusalem, bastion of perversity as it had become.

Explanation

Chap. 21 with its symbolism of the sword painted a picture of ruthless destruction. This chapter provides a rationale for such ruthlessness, telling the inside story of Jerusalem's fate. Its keyword is תוך "midst," a term that binds together its three separate oracles. Its association with Jerusalem seems to reflect traditional Zion theology, with its stress on the glory and security of God's own city—but here in ironic denial (cf. v 5b in the light of Lam 1:1). The proud claims of worshipers in the temple courts was that they were able to praise Yahweh "in your midst (בתוככי), Jerusalem" (Ps 116:19). In the first oracle בתוך "in the midst" appears in stylistic variation with בך "in you." One cannot help recalling the happy sentiments of a Song of Zion, Ps 87: "Glorious things are spoken of you (בך), city of God" (v 3, cf. vv 5, 7), and the wish expressed in a pilgrim song, שלום בך "May peace be in you" (Ps 122:8). But Ezekiel found less happy ways of describing Jerusalem in vv 6-12. Its once valid claims proved hollow and pretentious. Jerusalem was destroyed from within; Yahweh's work of destruction only endorsed what Jerusalem had already done to itself.

The emphasis on moral irresponsibility in the first and third oracles is a vindication of other traditions in Judah's history. If Zion theology proved a mirage, there were other traditions that triumphed. The taking of human life and the misrepresentation of divine reality by means of images were particularly repugnant to priestly thinking. And the sacred lawcodes laid down wider standards for living in the presence of God. For Ezekiel recent history had already shown the priority of such criteria in Yahweh's providential ordering of Jerusalem's experience (vv 4b, 5). Respect for persons and their property, for religious traditions and for justice was ignored at Jerusalem's peril. A right regard for sexuality stands at the heart of human relations, proclaims this oracle by setting at its center a series of examples of perverse sexuality. The climax of its second part comes at the end of v 12: Yahweh's will was enshrined in such traditions, and to ignore them was to forget him.

If God's ancient word had gone unheard (cf. 20:13), so too had his contemporary, prophetic word, states the third oracle, which no longer anticipates the final tragedy of 587 B.C. but looks back at it. Zephaniah's denunciations of Jerusalem's civil and religious administration had been fulfilled in its experience of divine curse. Moreover, Ezekiel's own charges in chap. 13 had found verification. In the fall of Jerusalem the divine word in the law and the prophets stood all the more firm. For all its failure, the crisis of 587 B.C. paid tribute to Yahweh's revealed will and to the seriousness of his moral and religious claims upon his people. With similar challenge and in seeming echo of terms used in this chapter (cf. vv 2-4, 10, 11, 15, 28), the seer of Patmos spoke of the new Jerusalem, affirming that "nothing unclean shall enter it nor any one who practices abomination or falsehood" (Rev 21:27).

Chronic Nymphomania (23:1-49)

Bibliography

DeVries, S. J. "Remembrance in Ezekiel. A Study of an Old Testament Theme." *Int* 16 (1962) 58-64. **Gottwald, N. K.** *All the Kingdoms of the Earth.* New York: Harper and Row, 1964, 302-6. **Krüger, T.** *Geschichtskonzepte im Ezechielbuch.* BZAW 180. Berlin: de Gruyter, 1989, 139-98. **Zadok, W.** "West Semitic Toponyms in Assyrian and Babylonian Sources." *Studies in the Bible and the Ancient Near East.* FS S. E. Loewenstamm, ed. Y. Avishur. Jerusalem: E. Rubinstein, 1978, 163-79.

Translation

[1] *I received the following communication from Yahweh:* [2] *"Human one, there were once two women, daughters of the same mother.* [3] *They became loose women in Egypt; while still girls, they became loose women.[a] There it was their breasts were squeezed, there they had their virgin bosoms fondled.[b]* [4] *The older one's name was Oholah and her sister's name was Oholibah. I married them[a] and they gave birth to sons and daughters.[b]* [5] *Oholah continued her loose behavior while she was under my authority: she had affairs with her lovers.[a] They were soldiers[b]* [6] *in purple[a] uniforms, officers and men of rank;[b] all of them were handsome young cavalrymen, riding on horseback.* [7] *She bestowed her loose favors on them, all of them the pick of the Assyrians, and with all those with whom she had love affairs, with all their idols, she sullied herself.* [8] *Nor did she abandon her loose ways practiced back in the days of the Egyptians[a] who had slept with her as a girl, fondling her virgin bosom and wantonly ejaculating[b] upon her.* [9] *That is why I handed her over to her lovers, the Assyrians she had affairs with.* [10] *They it was who exposed her naked body, took away her sons and daughters, and used a sword to kill her. She became notorious to other women, after sentence had been carried out upon her.*

[11] *"Her sister Oholibah observed all this, only to become even more corrupt in her affairs and loose ways, which were worse than her sister's.* [12] *She engaged in love affairs with the Assyrians, who were officers and men of rank, soldiers in magnificent[a] uniforms, cavalrymen riding on horseback, all of them handsome young men.* [13] *I observed that she sullied herself—now both had gone the same way.* [14] *But she carried her loose ways even further. She saw on a wall reliefs of male figures, engraved representations of Chaldeans outlined in vermilion:* [15] *they had sashes round their waists and flowing turbans on their heads. The reliefs were wholly of officers, illustrating Babylonians whose native country was Chaldea.* [16] *When her eyes caught sight of them, she wanted love affairs[a] and sent envoys to Chaldea for them.* [17] *The Babylonians came and shared her love bed, sullying her with their loose ways. Once sullied by them, she reacted against them with disgust.[a]* [18] *That was the reaction I had to her for flaunting her loose ways and exploiting her naked body, just as I had reacted against her sister.* [19] *She took her loose living further, remembering her girlhood when she had lived so loosely in the country of the Egyptians.* [20] *She had love affairs[a] with Egyptian[b] paramours,[c] who rivaled asses in the size of their penises and horses in the amount of sperm they produced.[d]* [21] *You missed the lascivious ways of your girlhood, when the Egyptians fondled[a] your breasts, squeezing[b] your young bosom.*

^{22} "So, Oholibah, this message comes from the Lord Yahweh:^{a} I mean to influence against you the lovers you turned from with disgust. I will get them to invade you from all quarters—^{23} the Babylonians and all the Chaldeans, Pekod, Shoa and Koa, all the Assyrians with them, handsome young men, all officers and men of rank, adjutants and heroes,^{a} all riding on horseback. ^{24} They will invade you . . .^{a} with chariots and wagons and with an international army. From all quarters they will confront you with body protectors, shields and helmets. I will give them the right of judgment and they will carry out the sentence they have passed in accord with their own standards. ^{25} I will make you the object of my jealous anger, and they will deal with you in fury. They will sever your nose and ears, and your posterity will fall victim to the sword.^{a} ^{26} They will take off your clothes and remove your jewelry. ^{27} And so I will bring to an end your lasciviousness and your loose living^a which started in the country of the Egyptians. You will not make eyes at them nor will you remember the Egyptians any more."

^{28} The following message from the Lord Yahweh supplies the reason why: "I mean to hand you over to people you hate, to people you turned away from in disgust. ^{29} They will deal with you in hatred, taking away your hardwon earnings and leaving you stark naked, with the nakedness typical of your loose living exposed to view.^{a} That is where your lasciviousness and loose ways^b ^{30} will get you,^{a} in view of the fact that you chased after other nations, loose woman as you are, and let yourself be sullied with their idols. ^{31} You went the same way as your sister and I will hand to you the cup she drank from.

^{32} "This message comes from the Lord Yahweh:
You will drink your sister's cup,
a cup deep and wide,^{a}
brimming^b with contents.
^{33} You^a will be filled with drunkenness^b and depression:
A cup of devastation^c
is the cup your sister Samaria^d drank from.
^{34} You will drink it to the last drop,
consuming its dregs,^{a}
and you will tear at your breasts.^{b}
I have indeed spoken. So runs the Lord Yahweh's oracle.

^{35} "This then is the message of the Lord Yahweh: Because you have forgotten me and tossed me behind your back, you in turn are to bear the consequences of your lasciviousness and loose ways."

^{36} Yahweh said to me: "Human one, would you judge Oholah and Oholibah, please?^{a} Declare to them their shocking ways. ^{37} They have committed adultery and there is blood on their hands. It is their idols they have committed adultery with; they have even devoted to them for food their sons they bore me. ^{38} This too they have done to me: they have contaminated my sanctuary^a and desecrated my sabbaths. ^{39} When they^a slaughtered their sons to their idols, on the same day^b they came into my sanctuary to desecrate it—they have actually done this in my own house. ^{40} Furthermore they would send for men to come^a from a great distance after a messenger had been sent to them, and they did come—the men for whom you^b bathed, painted your eyes and put on your jewelry. ^{41} You sat on a magnificent^a couch, with a table set in front of it, on which^b you put my incense and oil. ^{42} She enjoyed^a the noise of a carefree crowd^b of men from all over the world^c—Sabeans^d had been brought^e from the desert. They gave bracelets for them to wear on their wrists and fine garlands for them to put on their heads.

[43] "Then I asked myself about this woman who was worn out[a] by adultery, whether they would there and then fornicate[b] with her.[c] [44]They paid calls[a] on her as if resorting to a prostitute: that was just how they visited Oholah and Oholibah, those lascivious women.[b] [45]But other people will rightly judge them to be guilty of adultery and bloodshed, because they have indeed practiced adultery and their hands do have blood on them.

[46]"This[a] message comes from the Lord Yahweh: An army is to be ordered to invade[b] them[c] and submit them to terror and looting. [47]They are to stone[a] them and cut them to pieces with their swords. Let them kill their[b] sons and daughters and burn down their homes. [48]I will finally remove lasciviousness from the land as a warning[a] to every woman not to commit adultery as you have. [49]Your lasciviousness will receive punishment[a] and you will bear the penalty for your sin of idols. Then you[b] will come to realize that I am Yahweh."[c]

Notes

3. a. The omission of זנו "they fornicated" in LXX Syr is a case of stylistic abbreviation (Zimmerli 471). L. Boadt, VT 25 (1975) 699, has drawn attention to the ABB'A chiasmus.

3. b. Heb. עשו "they squeezed" has an indefinite subj.

4. a. Cf. BDB 226b.

4. b. MT and the ancient versions add "and their names: Oholah is Samaria and Oholibah is Jerusalem." The addition is widely recognized as an early marginal gloss on v 4aα. The clues are the odd positioning and the presence of the cue word ושמותן "and their names," for which cf. in principle Freedy, VT 20 (1970) 131-36. The interpretation was inspired by v 33.

5. a. MT and the ancient versions add אל־אשור "concerning Assyria," which seems to be an early gloss anticipating v 7aβ .

5. b. Heb. קרובים is related to קרב "battle" (HALAT 1063b, following Ewald and Fohrer). The term is to be taken closely with v 6.

6. a. Strictly blue-purple: see the note on 27:7.

6. b. Heb. פחות וסגנים "governors and prefects" here and in vv 12 and 23 seems to be used loosely of highranking officials. For the vagueness of פחה see HALAT 872b with reference to A. Alt.

8. a. Heb. מ(מצרים) "from (Egypt[ians])" is used in a temporal sense, "since the time."

8. b. Heb. זנונת "fornication" seems to be an euphemism in view of the verb.

12. a. Heb. מכלול "perfection" is a case of stylistic variation: Syr assimilated to תכלת "purple" in v 6.

16. a. Qותעגבה coordinates with the form in v 20.

17. a. In this chapter the impf is derived from the stem יקע (vv 17, 18) and the pf from נקע (vv 22, 28).

20. a. For the ending, influenced by the coh form in the first person consec impf, see GKC 48d.

20. b. Lit. "their."

20. c. Heb. פלגשים is elsewhere fem and means "concubines." Is it used ironically here in the sense of gigolos (cf. 16:31-34)?

20. d. The stem זרם, primarily relating to a downpour of rain, here has a developed meaning (BDB 281a). KB 267b and HALAT 270b find metathesis and link with זמורה "twig," in the sense of penis. Support may come from LXX Syr, which render "private parts."

21. a. For MT בעשות "when (you) acted" the following דדיך "your breasts" and the phraseology in vv 3, 8 suggest the piel of the second stem, בעשׂות "when you pressed." Then מצרים "the Egyptians" (cf. vv 19, 20, 27) is best read with 2 MSS as subj in place of MT ממצרים "since (the) Egypt(ians)," which seems to have resulted from a misunderstanding of the verb and from comparing v 8.

21. b. MT למען "in view of" seems to be a copyist's error for למעך "to squeeze," attested by Syr Vg, in the light of v 3. There a pass qal is evidently used (cf. Lev 22:24; 1 Sam 26:7), which suggests a qal form here. For the ך/ן error cf. the minority reading וילן in Josh 8:13 for וילך.

22. a. For the formulaic use of אדני יהוה "Lord Yahweh" here and in vv 28, 32, 34, 35, 46 see the note on 20:3.

23. a. Heb. קרואים "famous" is a stylistic variant for קרובים "soldiers" in vv 5, 12 (contra BHS, RSV, NEB

24. a. Heb. הצן is of unknown meaning, although a number of guesses have been made. LXX renders "from the north," which implies הצפן (cf. RSV), an attempt to obtain meaning inspired perhaps by 26:7 (cf. 26:10).

25. a. MT and the ancient versions add the contextually unexpected "They: your sons and daughters they will take away," probably originally an early marginal gloss with המה "they" functioning as a cue word (cf. v 4). The gloss related to v 10 and supplied either a variant reading or an explanation for בניה ובנותיה לקחו "her sons and daughters they took away" there and became incorporated in the column on the wrong side of the margin (cf. my *The Greek Chronicles* [Leiden: Brill, 1974], vol. 2, 90-104). Perhaps fresh suffixes were introduced after the displacement. The textual tradition also adds "and your posterity: it shall be consumed with fire," evidently an early comparative gloss referring to v 37 (cf. the frequent phrase העביר באש "cause to pass through the fire," 20:31 etc.) and introduced by a cue word relating to v 25ay. The repetition of אחרית "posterity" in MT is very awkward.

27. a. Heb. זנות "fornication" deviates from the normal form תזנות found in chaps. 16 and 23. Like זנונים in v 29, it may be a stylistic variant: it occurs in 43:7, 9. Many prefer to regularize the form (cf. *BHS*).

29. a. Heb. נגלה "exposed," a fem ptcp, indicates a circumstantial clause. Emendation to a pf (Bertholet 83, cf. *BHS*) is unnecessary.

29. b. The verse division in MT is incorrect.

30. a. Heb. עשה is grammatically feasible (Cooke 261-62). In the light of Jer 4:18 it is not necessarily an adaptation of an original עשו (*BHS* et al.) after wrong sentence division.

32. a. MT adds "She becomes an object of laughter and mocking," which ill fits the present context in language and position. LXX* omits. It probably originated as a marginal comment on material in the adjacent column, שם ותהי "and she became a byword," where שם exhibits a rare usage (v 10; cf. BDB 1028a). Cf. Ps 44:14, 15 and the first note on v 25 above.

32. b. MT's unique noun מרבה "abundance" is more naturally pointed as a fem hiph ptcp מַרְבָּה in the light of the context and with the support of LXX Σ Vg Tg (BDB 916a et al.).

33. a. A change to תמלא "it will be filled," proposed by Cornill (323), is attractive, but the second persons of all the other finite verbs in the song militate against it.

33. b. The minority Heb. reading שברון "breaking," advocated by many since Cornill (ibid.; see *BHS*) is rightly rejected by Zimmerli (477) and Wevers (137-38). Cf. Isa 51:21; Jer 51:7.

33. c. LXX* has only one term for the synonymous pair of MT שמה ושממה "waste and destruction." Ezekiel's standard pair is שממה ומשמה (6:14; 33:28, 29; 35:3): שמה is characteristic of Jeremiah. Moreover, the secondary presence of שמה is explicable in terms of the first note on v 34.

33. d. The idiosyncratic absence of a rendering of שמרון "Samaria" in LXX^B* is irrelevant for MT (cf. Ziegler, *LXX* 197) contra Fohrer 135, Freedy, *VT* 20 (1970) 138, et al. It can be explained easily as an inner-Greek error, mechanical assimilation to the sequence in v 32.

34. a. MT has ואת-חרשיה תגרמי "and you will break its shards," but the stem גרם properly means "break bones." Ehrlich's emendation ואת-שְׁמָרֶיהָ תִגְמְרִי "and you will (complete =) consume its dregs" (*Randglossen* 91) is irresistible. The verbal form is graphically preferable to Cornill's proposal תגמאי "and you will swallow" (323-24). The interpretation of MT's verb as "gnaw" (RV) or "chew" (NEB), to get at every trace of the wine, following Vg *devorabis*, seems hardly permissible. Was a marginal correction שמריה misread as שמה (or שמה ו), assuming a ר/ו error) and wrongly inserted into v 33? RSV "and pluck out your hair" follows Syr (cf. *BHK*), which appears rather to give "a free rendering from the general context of mourning" (Zimmerli 477).

34. b. Structurally a third colon is expected (see *Form/Structure/Setting*) and so its omission in LXX* is a false track contra the scholarly consensus (cf. Zimmerli, ibid., *BHS*).

36. a. See the note on 20:4.

38. a. MT adds ביום ההוא "on that day," a wrong anticipation of the phrase in v 39 caused by a slip of the eye and not corrected. LXX omits.

39. a. The suffixes are masc throughout v 39.

39. b. Heb. ביום ההוא "on that day" is to be retained despite its omission in LXX (Cornill 324-25; Ehrlich, *Randglossen* 92) contra Zimmerli 478, *BHS* et al. See *Comment*.

40. a. For the use of a ptcp in place of an inf cf. Driver, *Bib* 35 (1954) 155.

40. b. The second person verbs are sg in vv 40, 41.

41. a. Heb. כבודה "glorious" is often emended to רבודה "covered" on the basis of LXX (ἐστρωμένης) Syr (see, e.g., Zimmerli, ibid.), but LXX more probably presupposes כבורה "covered with netting" (Cornill 325 with reference to LXX^L στρῶμα for מכבר in 4 Kgdms [2 Kgs] 8:15).

41. b. Heb. עליה with a fem suffix referring to the masc שלחן "table" is a case of careless writing,

perhaps original, under the influence of לפניה "in front of it" earlier.

42. a. The text of v 42a is very uncertain. Heb. בה is literally "in/with her."

42. b. MT and the ancient versions add (ו) אל־אנשים "(and) to men," possibly originally a variant of לאנשים "to men" in v 40.

42. c. Lit. "from a multitude of humanity."

42. d. K סובאים, assimilated to מובאים, presumably stands for סבואים "drunkards."

42. e. The ancient versions imply באים "coming."

43. a. The text of the whole verse is uncertain, not least in its switch to the sg. For בלה "worn out" cf. Gen 18:12. LXX (and in part Syr) presupposes ולא באלה נאפים "and do they not with these commit adultery?"

43. b. K עת יזנה "now (?) he will fornicate" becomes in Q עתה יזנו "now they will fornicate."

43. c. Lit. "(fornicate) her fornication and she": apparently the suffix is emphatically resumed by the pronoun (Smend 168). MT is already presupposed by LXX, where ἔργα πόρνης "works of a prostitute" is a loose rendering for תזנותיה inspired by 16:30. Cornill (327) et al. (cf. *BHS*) postulated מעשי זנה, but graphically it is improbable.

44. a. MT ויבא "and he/one came" is to be corrected to ויבאו "and they came" with 2 MSS and the ancient versions: see the notes on 14:1 and 20:38. The Qumran MS 4QEzᵃ is a further witness (J. Lust, *Ezekiel and His Book*, 98, 99).

44. b. Heb. אשה "women" accords with the Akk. pl aššati (Driver, *Bib* 19 [1938] 175).

46. a. MT prefaces with כי "for," omitted by one MS and LXX*: it probably arose by dittography. Freedy, *VT* 20 (1970) 152, regards it as an editorial gloss.

46. b. The following inf abs suggests that העלה is one also, rather than an impv: cf. 16:40.

46. c. The suffix is masc.

47. a. The following inf abs suggest a reading ורגום for MT ורגמו, which probably arose by parallel assimilation to 16:40. MT adds קהל "army" in an awkward position as subj and yet difficult as genitive, as LXX construed it. It is generally taken as an early gloss clarifying the subj of MT's pl verb.

47. b. The suffixes on the two nouns are masc.

48. a. For the form of the verb see GKC 55k.

49. a. Heb. ונתנו "and they will put" has an indefinite subj. LXX Tg fittingly render as a passive.

49. b. The verb is masc pl.

49. c. MT prefaces with אדני "Lord," which occurs only five times out of 87 in the recognition formula (Zimmerli, *Ezekiel 2* 556; see the note on 13:9). It may have come in under the influence of v 46. Zimmerli justifies it here as set in a passage not from Ezekiel's hand.

Form/Structure/Setting

From a redactional perspective the message reception formula of v 1 is obviously intended to identify the chapter as an overall unit. It is made up of a number of smaller oracles. The first in vv 2-27 constitutes the backbone of the unit. There follows a redactional complex, with vv 32-34 at its center, bordered by vv 28-31 and v 35. The third and last element consists of vv 36-45, to which vv 46-49 have been joined. Introductory messenger formulas occur at vv 28, 32, 35 and 46; at v 22 the second half of an oracle is so prefaced. In v 36 a piece is introduced by a formula uncommon in Ezekiel, ויאמר יהוה אלי "And Yahweh said to me" (cf. 9:4; 44:2, 5 and the shorter form in 4:13): elsewhere it belongs to consecutive narrative.

The main oracle in vv 2-27 is composed in elevated prose frequently marked by parallelism. Fundamentally it is a judgment oracle with two basic parts, accusation (vv 2-21) and prediction of punishment (vv 22-27). The latter part is introduced by a typical לכן "therefore." The whole has been cast in an allegorical framework of gross marital infidelity, while into the accusation has been woven an account of the shortcomings and judgment of the northern kingdom (vv 5-8, 9-10 [note לכן "therefore" in v 9]) in order to emphasize the certainty of the coming punishment of the south (cf. מאהביה "her lovers," v 9, מאהביך "your lovers," v 22).

The judgment section in vv 22-27 is also accentuated by a switch from third person citations of the accused to the second person, as well as by its own messenger formula at v 22. The direct address is anticipated at the end of the accusatory section, in v 21.

The motif of "the Egyptian affair" is broached in v 3. It plays a strong structural role: it recurs in the climactic v 27, and thus provides an inclusion that binds the piece together. Furthermore, it marks the ends of accusatory sections, at vv 8 and 21. The main sections of accusation and judgment end on a parallel note with זמה "lasciviousness" at vv 21 and 27, and on a contrasting note with memory (זכר) first stimulated (v 19) and then frustrated (v 27). Another unifying element in the oracle is the stylistically varied descriptions of the Assyrian lovers within the accusatory sections, at vv 5bβ-6 and 12. The repetition exhibits a not uncommon literary pattern of chiastic inversion (ABCD/BADC; cf. E. F. Davis, *Swallowing the Scroll* [Sheffield: Almond Press, 1989] 63, with reference to R. Weiss). The recurrence of this element at the start of the judgment passage (v 23b) provides an ironic reprise, which is not to be branded as secondary contra Cooke (253), Zimmerli (488) et al. The structural equivalent of this refrain occurs in the equally striking descriptions of the Babylonians in vv 14b-15 and of the Egyptians in v 20.

In historical terms the accusations of vv 11-21 fall into three parts, relating to Assyria (vv 11-13), Babylonia (vv 14-18) and Egypt (vv 19-21). The first two come to a peak with subjective statements of Yahweh's reactions in vv 13 and 18b, while in v 21 their counterpart is the direct address of the guilty party. The personal references to Yahweh are prefaced with mention of his initial involvement in v 4 and capped by his resolves to punish in vv 22, 24b-25aα and 27a, at the beginning, middle and end of the judgment section. Form critics have tended to brand a number of elements in this oracle as secondary (see, e.g., Zimmerli 418, Wevers 133-34), but rhetorical criticism urges the retention of most of them as stylistic highlights. Apart from the glosses in vv 4b, 5bβ and 25b, the only intrusive element appears to be the seemingly redactional reference to idols in v 7b (see *Comment* on v 30).

The passion of the piece comes out in the repetition of key sexual terms. Apart from those already mentioned, there is the dominant usage of the stem זנה "fornicate, be sexually loose" to describe Israel's pre-Canaanite history (v 3, twice), northern politics in vv 5, 7, 8 and southern politics in the three sections of vv 11-21, at v 11 (twice), vv 14, 17, 18 and v 19 (twice). The term is recapitulated at the end of the judgment portion in v 27, in such a way as to leap back to v 3 and to encompass the ensuing references up to v 19. Is אזניך "your ears" in v 25 intended to sound an ironic echo of the crime in the punishment? Another strong term is עגב "lust, have an affair." It marks the accusation and judgment of the north at the start of sections (vv 5, 9). It also punctuates the accusations of the south, at beginning (vv 11, 12), middle (v 16) and end (v 20), and so appears in each of the three sections of accusation. A vehement term characteristic of Ezekiel, טמא "be/make unclean," which itself has sexual overtones (cf. 22:10, 11), is found in the accusation of the north at v 7 and in the first two of the three accusatory sections relating to the south, at v 13 and 17. In v 21 it is replaced in its emotional tone by זמה "lasciviousness" in order to fulfill another structural agenda.

The historical setting of the oracle is clear from its emphasis on Judah's political dependence on Egypt. It must have been uttered between Zedekiah's breaking of his treaty of vassalage to Babylon (cf. 17:15) and Nebuchadnezzar's campaign against Judah which culminated in the fall of Jerusalem in 587 B.C. The strongly worded language of v 20 more probably refers to the dynamic Hophra who came to the Egyptian throne early in 589 B.C. than to his less ambitious predecessor Psammetichus II. If so, the oracle fits well between the last chronological reference in 20:1 (591 B.C.) and the next in 24:1 (588 B.C.).

The next passage, vv 28-35, is a redactional complex made up of three messages, each introduced by a messenger formula (vv 28, 32, 35), while a closing divine saying formula occurs after an affirmation formula, in v 34b. Its throbbing heart is the poem of the cup of wrath in vv 32aβ-34a, which is a judgment oracle directed evidently to Jerusalem in view of the mention of Samaria in v 33. The poem with its dominant prophetic motif of the cup divides into three strophes, each of which consists of a tricolon (3+2+2, 3+2+3, 3+3+2). The first speaks of drinking the contents of the large cup and the second of its baleful effects, while the third seems to combine both features by way of climax. The second strophe is marked by a series of assonances. The final שמרון "Samaria" is echoed by the נ- endings of שכרון ויגון "drunkenness and depression," by the *shin-mem* alliteration of תמלאי ... שכרון "you will be filled with ... drunkenness" and by the wordplay שממה "devastation." The alliteration and wordplay are continued in the first colon of the next strophe, שתית ... ומצית ... שמריה "and you will drink ... and drain ... its dregs." The poem is probably an independent oracle of Ezekiel's, placed here because of its similarity to the first one, with reference to sisterhood with Samaria and a common fate (cf. 16:46, 52).

The poem is introduced by vv 28-31, a judgment oracle with accusatory notes struck in vv 30-31a. It both looks back to the preceding oracle, in vv 28-31a, and forward to the next, in v 31b. It therefore has a bridging function. It has its own inclusion, a double handing over in punishment (נתן ביד "put into the hand," vv 28, 31), which seems to brand it as a unit and conflicts with the frequently found notion of units dividing into vv 28-30 and 31-34 (cf., e.g., Zimmerli 490). It is clearly redactional, although it may be the product of Ezekiel's later hand (Fohrer 136).

The cup oracle is supplemented with a short judgment oracle in v 35, which moves succinctly from accusation to verdict. Again it is dependent on vv 2-27. The echo of v 29b gives the impression that both vv 28-31 and v 35 were composed to cement the cup oracle to the preceding one. The direct address that runs through vv 28-35 serves to continue that of vv 21-27, as does the first person speech in vv 28-31 and 35.

Vv 36-49 are clearly meant to round off the chapter. They read as a judgment oracle and mostly revert to the motif of the two sisters of vv 2-4. The effect is that of an overall inclusion, especially as the sisters are mentioned in the third person, as in vv 2-4 (and 5-20). Vv 36-45 consist of two types of accusation, religious (vv 36-39, 45) and political (vv 40-44). The arrangement provides an inclusion, the issues of adultery and loss of life (vv 37a, 45). Vv 36-45 have been supplemented in vv 46-49 with a prediction of punishment that is also a proof saying (cf. v 49b). Both sisters are addressed in vv 48b-49, while throughout vv 36-49 feminine plural references are interspersed with masculine ones. The former phenomenon provides a vivid conclusion, while the latter exhibits simply a dropping of the imagery. What is very strange is the direct address of Oholibah in vv 40b-41 and third person references to her in vv 42a, 43-44a, both of which want to concentrate on Jerusalem alone. The variety of perspectives in vv 36-49 is evidence of a process of redaction: more than one hand has been at work.

Comment

The message of vv 1-27 re-uses the sexual allegory of chap. 16. However, the enhancement of human inconstancy by reference to initial divine grace is lacking here. Moreover, the pagan origins of Jerusalem are deliberately replaced by the nation's beginnings in Egypt, in line with the intent to decry Judah's current political involvement with Egypt. Accordingly, while chap. 16 has a cultic emphasis, here political issues are in view.

2-4 Israelite history is described by hindsight from the perspective of the divided kingdom of Judah and Israel, which are portrayed as sisters, probably on the model of Jer 3:6-11 (cf. Ezek 16:46). Even more starkly than in Hosea's imagery (Hos 1:2; cf. Ezek 16:3), the people are described as deviant from the start. So ingrained is their sin in Ezekiel's eyes that it is traced back to the sinners' very beginnings, just as in 20:7 idolatry is ascribed to Israel even in Egypt. Here, however, the basic development of the metaphor points to political sin. As vv 19-21 will make clear, Ezekiel has in mind a contemporary Judah that was aligning itself politically with Egypt in the hope of throwing off Babylon's yoke. In his mind too was doubtless Hosea's usage of wrong sexuality as a metaphor for political alliance (Hos 8:9; 9:10), which he had used also in Ezek 16:26-29, and he portrays Israel's ancient political dependence on Egypt in similar terms. Thereby he dashes contemporary hopes of Egypt as Judah's savior from Babylon, suffusing them with a negative image of pre-Exodus oppression in Egypt. He makes that image even blacker by attaching to it willfulness that he saw in Judah's present pro-Egyptian policy.

The metaphor of the covenant relationship as a marriage is here extended along bigamous lines, a development already implicit in Jer 3:6-11 (note especially v 8). The patriarch Jacob married sisters, but the tradition represented in Lev 18:18 prohibits it. Christian apologists tend to play down references to polygamy in the Old Testament, under the constraint of their own theological ethics, but the echo of this practice in a divine context discloses how unobjectionable it generally was in Israelite culture.

The names given to the two communities have a matching quality, like Tweedledum and Tweedledee, used to describe individuals or groups that are practically indistinguishable. "It was common in the East to give sisters or brothers names almost the same, as Hasan and Husein (little Hasan), the two sons of ᶜAli, the son-in-law of Mohammed" (Davidson 181). The names are compounded with אהל "tent" ("Tent" with a feminine ending and "My-tent-in-her"), perhaps with reference to the marriage tent (cf. 2 Sam 16:22) or, less likely, to the priestly term for the sanctuary, "the tent of meeting." Does it reflect the nomadism of the patriarchal period, since in v 2 the sisters are represented as alive before involvement with Egypt? Attempts to distinguish between the names as disparaging to Israel (as if Oholah means "her (own) tent") but complimentary to Judah are contextually out of place.

5-10 The political involvement of the northern kingdom with Assyria in the eighth century B.C. is interpreted negatively, as it was by Hosea. For Hosea it spelled a fundamental lack of faith in Yahweh—deserting him in favor of "lovers" (Hos 8:9; cf. 5:13; 14:3). Ezekiel develops this imagery in terms of the sexual attractiveness of macho Assyria, a veritable world power with all its impressive trappings. He categorizes Israel's subsequent overtures to Egypt, made in order to secure liberation from Assyria (cf. 2 Kgs 17:4; Hos 7:11; 12:2[1]), as a further manifestation of a deep urge toward inconstancy. This urge met its providential nemesis in the fall of Samaria and the end of the northern kingdom. The victors' indulgence in their fruits of victory, the rape and killing of women and the selling of children, is woven into the allegory, as is Israel's loss of face in the sight of other nations. For the reference to idols in v 7 see the exegesis of v 30.

11-13 The political sin of the northern kingdom in tangling with Assyria now gets a rerun in the case of the south. The phenomenon is intended to create an impression that in turn Judah's nemesis must eventually come. Ezekiel is here leaning on earlier Judean prophecy, Isaiah's isolationism and Jeremiah's language concerning Judah's religious sins (Jer 3:7). From Jer 3:11 comes the notion of Judah's greater guilt (cf. Krüger, *Geschichtskonzepte* 156-57). Her guilt was greater (v 11) in that she not only took over her sister's lovers but added the Babylonians to the list, as v 14 will explain. The northern kingdom had a bad image in Judean eyes (cf. 2 Kgs 17), but Judah had even more skeletons in her closet.

14-18 The second phase of Judah's political involvement was with Babylonia, Assyria's successor as the eastern world power. The glamor of Babylon is described in terms of architectural ornamentation. Doubtless Ezekiel and his audience had seen such painted bas-reliefs on Babylonian buildings, and the account is embroidered by the contemporary reference in the interests of communication with his hearers. Hab 1:6-11 reflects the tremendous impression the Babylonian army made on Judah. Underlying v 16 may be a tradition of secret negotiations with Babylon, whether in Hezekiah's reign (cf. 2 Kgs 20:12-15) or in Jehoiakim's (cf. 2 Kgs 23:34-24:1). Judah's subsequent disenchantment is clothed in the psychological phenomenon of sexual revulsion (cf. Gottwald, *All the Kingdoms of the Earth* 305-6), which for the prophet illustrates the restlessness of those who refuse to find their rest in Yahweh. The narration of this second phase of Judah's infidelity is drawn to a close by mention of Yahweh's abhorrence. The partner who sadly "observed" at the end of the first phase (v 13) is now stung to a stronger reaction, which with its reference back to the northern kingdom bodes ill for Judah.

19-21 The third phase, hinted at in v 17, relates to Egypt and brings the account down to the present. Judah's overtures to the ambitious Hophra, which Judeans at home and doubtless abroad viewed positively as the answer to all their problems, are invested with a negative aura, as a return to Egyptian bondage (v 3) and also as the history of the northern kingdom disastrously repeating itself (v 8). The coarseness of the description in v 20 leaves no doubt that for Ezekiel and his God the political alliance stank. The direct address of v 21, which continues in the next section, is both rhetorical and real in that Ezekiel was speaking to exiled Judeans. It creates a passionate conclusion.

22-27 Accusation gives way to pronouncement of punishment. The mounting reactions of Yahweh (vv 13, 18) now rise to a crescendo after the final provocation: v 22a ominously picks up v 9 (לכן "therefore" and מאהביך "your lovers"), as well as v 17bβ, while vv 9-10 are echoed in vv 24 and 25 (ונתתי "and I will give," the stem שפט "judge" and בחרב "with the sword"). How can Judah avoid Israel's fate after playing the same political game of brinkmanship? With the fury of the scorned lover the military machismo once so attractive (cf. vv 12, 15) was ironically to be turned against Judah (cf. 16:37). The invincibility of the army is indicated by the list of names in v 23. "Chaldeans" refers to dominant, tribal groups in Babylonia, and "Assyrians" presumably to a vassal contingent in the Babylonian army. The rhyming פְּקוֹד וְשׁוֹעַ וְקוֹעַ seem to refer to outlying tribes, the Aramean Puqudu east of the Tigris and probably to the Sutu and Qutu, other tribes in the area which are often coupled in Assyrian records (for discussion of the groupings see Zadok, *Studies in the Bible* 178-79). The trio of names also express a sinister wordplay, suggesting "punish," "cry for help" and "shriek" (cf. Jud. Aram. קְעַם "cackle"; Eichrodt 328), which has necessitated the distortion of the latter two names. The catalog of military equipment in v 24 gives another overwhelming impression. "Body protectors," carried by riot police today, are distinct from the small round "shields." The gruesome mention of mutilation and the killing of children in v 25 lends horror to the description. V 26, unless it is an addition from 16:39, intends to bring the account back to the basic imagery, to which v 27 more explicitly reverts.

Overshadowing this whole operation would be the figure of Yahweh, Ezekiel discloses in vv 22, 24b-25aα and 27a, at the beginning, middle and end of the pronouncement. It would be the reprisal of a cuckolded husband (cf. v 4) provoked to jealousy. The human enemies would be given free rein to put their own cruel standards into operation. Such was the noose into which Judah had rashly put its head by dallying with the Egyptians. The ghost of Egypt (cf. v 19) had to be laid to rest once and for all. Judah's dream was to turn into a waking nightmare.

28-35 The song of the cup that eventually follows in vv 32-34 serves to reinforce the message of the first oracle: the fate of the northern kingdom, Judah's "sister," was to be shared by Judah. Strictly Jerusalem is now in view, as in chap. 16, rather than Judah. The poem uses a prophetic motif concerning the manifestation of divine wrath, the consumption of an intoxicating drink (cf. Hab 2:15, 16; Jer 25:15, 17, 28). It would be an overwhelming experience, so large and full was the cup. Its effects would be both devastating and distressing; the draining of the cup would result in laceration of the breasts. Beating of the breasts, part of the body language of reaction to crisis (cf. Isa 32:12; Nah 2:7), is here seemingly heightened. In the redactional context the mention of breasts becomes an ironic echo of the earlier refrain of accusation (vv 3, 21).

The song is introduced by vv 28-31 and supplemented with v 35. Both passages seek to bond it to the previous oracle. The first is a summary of its accusation and even more of its prediction of punishment. V 28 uses the language of vv 9 and 22. V 29aα is a variation of v 25aβ, while v 29b echoes v 10aα and key terms of the previous earlier oracle, especially v 27a. V 31 adapts v 13. Especially interesting is the link between v 30bβ and v 7b. Not political fornication is in view, but a cultic variety. It is probable that the mention of idols in v 7 is redactional. Both there and in vv 28-31 there is a desire to ponder on the oracle and to note the short distance between political association with other, polytheistic communities and religious syncretism. The switch in perspective seems to reflect the influence of chap. 16 (cf. Zimmerli 490). As for v 35, it too is dependent on the first oracle, echoing its key language especially as used in v 27a, while the wrongful memories of vv 19 and 27 are developed. Jerusalem had "forgotten what she should have remembered and remembered what she should have forgotten" (S. DeVries, *Int* 16 [1962] 64). Ahijah's striking language in 1 Kgs 14:9 (cf. Neh 9:26; Ps 50:17) is reused to describe the situation, which was nothing less than blatant rejection of Yahweh himself.

36-39 Vv 36-49 also want to take the whole issue further in certain directions. They are mainly marked by unexpected references to both sisters as contemporary. The northern kingdom now falls into the background and the sisters stand simply for Judah as the covenant nation (note v 38). Vv 36-39 use the expressions of 22:2 (cf. 20:4) to introduce cultic accusations, which develop v 30 (and v 7b). Association with idols is explained not only as adultery—a sexual metaphor new to this chapter—but also in terms of child sacrifice to pagan gods (see 20:26 and *Comment*): chap. 16 seems to underlie these charges, especially 16:20, 38. Defiling, part of the sexual imagery of political fraternizing in the first oracle, is now used with reference to the temple and is linked with the worship of practitioners of child sacrifice.

40-44 There is a return to the political accusations of the first oracle. This section develops vv 16b-17, particularly in vv 40a-ba, 42b and 44. The intervening material imaginatively speaks of Judah in the singular, as an unfaithful wife. She prepares herself for the assignation—a borrowing from 16:18—and misuses her husband's provisions for the celebration, which is attended by such exotic foreigners as Sabeans from the Arabian desert.

45-49 This passage seems to carry on from v 39. V 45 crowns the accusations of vv 36-39 with forensic terminology taken from 16:38. A pronouncement of punishment follows in vv 46-49, investing vv 36-49 with the form of a two-part judgment oracle. Vv 46-48ba are a recapitulation of 16:40-41ba. In v 48b the reference to women is figurative, as in v 10, and signifies other nations (Keil 338, Eichrodt 333; contra Zimmerli 492; B. S. Childs, *Introduction* 368-69; cf. 31:14). Mention of the deterrent value of the punishment is meant to reflect its appalling severity. V 49a picks up the key term of the first oracle and of the chapter, "lasciviousness," and links it with the pervading redactional term "idols." The closing recognition formula looks forward to a convincing disclosure of divine reality and so to a response of respect, perhaps with special reference to v 35a.

The intent of vv 36-39 and 45-49 is to stress cultic sins connected with idolatry and to widen the perspective from political infidelity to Yahweh to religious unfaithfulness, on the lines of v 30. The emphatic inclusion in the accusatory section links infidelity with the taking of life, which is spelled out as child sacrifice. V 45 is clearly a crucial verse from a redactional perspective: its vocabulary of judgment underlines that of v 25 (cf. v 10). Overall there is a desire to enlarge the concerns of the chapter to include those of earlier chapters, the bloodshed of chap. 22—although now in terms of human sacrifice, as in 16:20, 21—and the divinely ordained punishment at Babylonian hands announced in chap. 21 (especially v 32). To these ends material has been borrowed from chap. 16.

Explanation

Ezekiel preaches in vv 1-27 a political sermon as inflammatory as any that Pastor Niemöller preached against the German government. The links that Judah forged with Egypt in a last, desperate attempt to avert Babylonian doom are denounced in the strongest of terms. Sexuality, about which Israel could be as coy as any Victorian, is used as a blatant weapon of communication, to convey the emotional distaste of Yahweh to this expedient. Its "potential to offend is, of course, its very point" (Stuart 220). Significantly the most repulsive sexual language is reserved for associations with Egypt. It is a vehement effort to convince a constituency who did not want to believe the truth the prophet brought.

Along with sexuality, theological history is used to interpret contemporary politics, in a culture where politics and religion were regarded as two sides of one coin. First, the Exodus traditions are used to remind the Judean exiles that Egypt is the enemy of God and that the purpose of the Exodus was to get his people out of Egypt's clutches and safe within the covenant relationship. By the present political link-up the Judeans in the homeland were not only trespassing outside that relationship, but putting the clock back to pre-Exodus times in an involvement that was not of God and constituted an act of infidelity to him. The temptation to harness Judah's wagon to Egyptian power was an illicit one.

The second lesson the prophet draws from history is the experience of the northern kingdom, which too had flirted with Egypt, only to meet its end at the hands of the power of the east. The parallel is no random one: it moves in a theological orbit already familiar to Judah. Ezekiel adopts the prophetic and deuteronomistic interpretation of the fall of Israel, that behind the thrust and parry of that phase of international politics lay the sovereign will of the covenant God. He does not hesitate to reapply this interpretation to contemporary politics and to predict in Yahweh's name reprisal against a people whose policies time and time again revealed not only a lack of allegiance to him but an espousal of human power. It was to be—and this is Ezekiel's third lesson—the end of the long road of two centuries of sordid Judean history, as first Assyria, then Babylon and now Egypt had been the pin-ups of the moment, to whom Judah had given her heart. But to fall away from the living God was to fall into the hands of that living God, a fearful thing (Heb 3:12; 10:31).

The message is a reminder that there is no seal between religious faith and the actualities of human life. The covenant relationship shines its searchlight into every corner and ruthlessly confronts that which is not compatible. And it is nobody's fault but our own that experience is not a better teacher of this truth.

The oracle of the cup of wrath reinforces the second lesson from history which the first message taught, that Judah was to drink the same bitter medicine as Israel. In using this imagery Ezekiel belongs to a long prophetic chain that was to culminate in Jesus, who absorbed in his own person the horror of God's judgment, accepting it from his hand not without a shudder (Mark 14:36). This oracle is set within a wider framework, which wants to underline the truth of the first message. Judah is indeed guilty of infidelity. The people in the homeland—and those exiles who mentally align themselves with them—have thrown God away and walked off without him. By way of further illustration, religious syncretism is cited. To worship the nations' gods was a violation of covenant faith.

Further developments follow. In vv 36-39 and 45 more light is shed on the charge of infidelity by specifying the horrible practice of child sacrifice, while in vv 40-44 Judah's political entanglements are portrayed in gaudy and vulgar hues. There was no alternative for Judah but to face the grim ordeal of invasion already forecast in chap. 16. There was no other way to get the cancer of infidelity out of Judah's system. To others, and so to us, the tragedy must function as a warning (v 48; cf. Heb 3:12; 4:1, 2).

Two Fateful Days (24:1-27)

Bibliography

Allen, L. C. "Ezekiel 24:3-14: A Rhetorical Perspective." *CBQ* 49 (1987) 404-14. **Brownlee, W. H.** "Ezekiel's Copper Caldron and Blood on the Rock (chap. 24:1-14)." *For Me to Live.* FS. J. L. Kelso. Ed. R. A. Coughenour. Cleveland: Liederbach, 1972, 21-43. **Christ, H.** *Blutvergiessen im Alten Testament. Der gewaltsame Tod des Menschen untersucht am hebräischen dām.* Basel: Friedrich Reinhardt, 1977. **Fuhs, H. F.** "Ez 24—Überlegungen zu Tradition und Redaktion des Ezechielbuches." *Ezekiel and His Book.* Ed. J. Lust. 266-82. **Kelso, J. L.** "Ezekiel's Parable of the Corroded Copper Caldron." *JBL* 64 (1945) 391-93. **McHardy, W. D.** "Ezekiel 24:10." *JJS* 2 (1949) 155. **Sherlock, C.** "Ezekiel's Dumbness." *ExpTim* 94 (1982/83) 296-98. **te Stroete, G. A.** "Ezekiel 24:15-27. The Meaning of a Symbolic Act." *Bijdragen* 38 (1977) 163-75. **Vogt, E.** *Untersuchungen zum Buch Ezechiel.* AnBib 95. Rome: Pontifical Biblical Institute, 1981, 92-106. **Wilson, R. R.** "An Interpretation of Ezekiel's Dumbness." *VT* 22 (1972) 91-104.

Translation

[1]*I received the following communication from Yahweh—in the ninth year, on the tenth of the tenth month:* [2]*"Human one, write down today's date:*[a] *this very day the king of Babylon has laid siege to*[b] *Jerusalem.* [3]*Tell a parable to that community of rebels, saying to them, Here is a message from the Lord*[a] *Yahweh.*

Set on the caldron, set it on[b]
and pour water into it[c] *too.*
[4]*Collect it into cuts of meat,*[a]
all the best cuts, shank and shoulder,
fill it with the choicest bones.
[5]*Take the choicest of the flock*
and pile the logs underneath it[a] *too.*
Boil its cuts,[b]
let there be cooked[c] *also*
its bones inside it.

[6]*The meaning is found*[a] *in this message from the Lord Yahweh. Woe to the bloodstained city, the caldron that has in it corrosion,*[b] *corrosion that does not come off. Cut by cut take out its contents.*[c] *Retribution*[d] *has not fallen on her,* [7]*although*[a] *the blood shed by her remains within her. The bare rock was where she put it: she did not pour it out on the ground where the dust would cover it.* [8]*I have permitted*[a] *the blood she has shed to be left uncovered on the bare rock, with a view to wrath being aroused and vengeance being exacted."*

[9]*Here therefore is the Lord Yahweh's message.*[a] *"I myself am going to make the pile larger.* [10]*Put on*[a] *an abundance of logs, keep the fire burning, finish cooking the meat and remove the broth*[b] *and let the bones be burned.*[c] [11]*Then let it stand empty on its coals in order that it may be heated and its copper may become red-hot and its uncleanness inside it may be melted and its corrosion consumed.* [12]*It has frustrated all efforts (?)*[a] *and its abundance of corrosion does not come off.*[b] [13]*In view of your unclean vileness,*[a]

because I have tried to purify you but you did not stay purified from your uncleanness, you will never be pure again until I have sated my wrath against you. [14]*I, Yahweh, have spoken—it is about to happen*[a]*—and I will act. I will not refrain nor spare nor relent.*[b] *Your own behavior is the measure of the judgment they have been meting out*[c] *to you. So runs the Lord Yahweh's oracle."* [d]

[15]*I received the following communication from Yahweh:* [16]*"Human one, I am going to take from you the delight of your eyes in a fatal blow, but you must not wail or weep.*[a] [17]*Groan in silence*[a]*—you may not engage in ritual mourning for the dead.*[b] *Bind your turban round your head and put sandals on your feet. You are not to cover your upper lip nor eat the bread of despair."* [c] [18]*That evening my wife died.*[a] *Next morning I carried out my instructions.* [19]*The people asked me to tell them the meaning of my conduct.*[a] [20]*I replied to the people that morning*[a] *with the statement that I had received the following message from Yahweh:* [21]*Tell the community of Israel I am going to desecrate my sanctuary, your source of pride and power, the delight of your eyes and desire*[a] *of your hearts, while the sons and daughters you've left behind will fall victims to the sword.* [22]*But you are to copy me: you must not cover your upper lips nor eat the bread of despair.* [23]*Your turbans are to stay on your heads and your sandals on your feet. You must not wail or weep, but be mortified over your iniquities and whimper among yourselves.* [24]*Ezekiel is to be your prophetic example, you are to copy him exactly. When it happens, you will realize that I am Yahweh.*[a]

[25]*"As for you, human one, on the very day I take away from them their refuge, their pride and joy, the delight of their eyes and the desire of their hearts, and*[a] *their sons and daughters,* [27]*on that very day*[a] *your mouth will be opened*[b] *and you will speak, dumb no longer. You are to be a prophetic sign to them and they will realize that I am Yahweh."*

Notes

2. a. MT's "the name of this day, this selfsame day" appears to be conflated. Probably the second phrase, missing from Syr Vg, was written by faulty anticipation of v 2b and a supralinear correction has been incorporated into the text. Wevers (140) suggests that עצם "selfsame" was intended as an explanation of שם "name," here unusually in the sense of date as in an Arad ostracon (see *ANET*, supplementary note 569 note 28).

2. b. Lit. "put pressure on."

3. a. For the formulaic use of אדני "Lord" here and in vv 6, 9, 14 see the note on 20:3.

3. b. The omission of the repeated verb in LXX* Syr is probably stylistic, removing a feature common in Ezekiel (Zimmerli 493).

3. c. MT בו originally was probably בָּה via בֹּה (cf. 31:18): elsewhere in the poem סיר "caldron" is treated as fem.

4. a. For MT נתחיה "its cuts" LXX Syr imply a suffixless נתחים. For the origin of MT see the second note on v 5.

5. a. The consonants of MT העצמים תחתיה "the bones under it" are to be redivided as העצים מתחתיה "the logs underneath it" (Driver, *Bib* 19 [1938] 175; cf. Ezek 1:8, etc.). The term in v 4 led a copyist astray.

5. b. MT רתחיה "its boiled things" is generally regarded as having suffered mechanical assimilation to רתח; נתחיה "its cuts" is to be read with 2 MSS. The parallelism of v 4 so suggests. Heb. נתחיה in v 4 probably originated in a marginal correction of the term here, which subsequently was taken as a correction of the form there.

5. c. The pf בשלו "they were cooked" is probably a slip for a juss יבשלו "let them be cooked," as Tg implies. The common emendation to a piel impv בַּשֵּׁל "cook" suits the context, but the ancient versions represent the *waw*.

6. a. Lit. "therefore."

6. b. MT חלאתה "its corrosion" (cf. GKC 91e) is probably to be accented חֶלְאָתה, a euphonic form

of חלאה, to avoid a final accented syllable before בה: cf. GKC 29e, f, 90f and Ezek 28:15; Ps 3:3 (contrast v 8).

6. c. Heb. הוציאה is lit. "take it out": the suffix seems to refer to its contents (Smend 172).

6. d. For this developed meaning see BDB 174b. The usual meaning "lot" does not fit.

7. a. Lit. "for," here in the sense "as one might expect in view of the fact that" (cf. BDB 473b, 474a).

8. a. Cf. BDB 679a and especially Deut 18:14. An emendation to נָתְנָה "she has put" (Ehrlich, *Randglossen* 95; Fohrer 139; Eichrodt 335) is ruled out by the resumption of the stem כסה "cover" in the passive (Christ, *Blutvergiessen* 77).

9. a. MT adds "woe to the bloodstained city," lacking in LXX* and probably added by mechanical assimilation to v 6. Zimmerli (494) notes that it fits the beginning of the accusation there better than that of an announcement of judgment here.

10. a. For another interpretation of this and adjacent verbs, which take Yahweh as subject, see *Form/Structure/Setting*. Redactionally, however, impv forms seem to be intended.

10. b. MT והרקח המרקחה "and season the seasoning," contextually illfitting, seems to have suffered metathesis and mutual assimilation from an original והרחק המרק "and remove the broth." A few MSS read הרק, which is graphically closer to MT than הָרֵק "empty," proposed by Kraetzschmar (196). LXX καὶ ἐλαττωθῇ ὁ ζωμός "and let the broth be diminished" seems to imply והדקה המרק. Its verb (hoph of דקק, cf. דק "small, fine") is a misreading of MT; its phrase attests a stage between the original and MT.

10. c. The omission in LXX* is probably a case of homoeoarcton (Parunak, *Structural Studies* 348). Brownlee in an unpublished paper suggested that עצמות meant the now meatless bones (cf. Zimmerli 495) as distinct from עצמים, the meat-covered bones of v 4. The verb יחרו "let ... be burned" fits the rhetorical structuring of the passage (see *Form/Structure/Setting*). McHardy's emendation of the verb to יחדו "together" (*JJS* 2 [1949] 155), accepted by NEB, imports a term not used in Ezekiel and loses the rhetorical value of the present text.

12. a. Heb. הלאת תאנים "she wearied toils" is most uncertain. LXX* lacks the phrase, and it is often regarded as a dittograph of חלאתה תחם at the end of v 11 (see *BHS*). Is it another case of an incorporated correction of a corrupted text (cf. v 2)? RSV "in vain I wearied myself" adopts the proposal of *BHK*, followed by Ziegler, *Ezechiel* 79, נלאתי חנם.

12. b. MT and the ancient versions add חלאתה באש, which may have been an early gloss on the end of v 11, with the sense of "its corrosion: (consumed) by fire" (P. Rost, *OLZ* 6 [1903] 443). For the cue element see the second note on 23:4.

13. a. For the construction cf. GKC 132r and 16:27 (Zimmerli 496).

14. a. For this variation of a standard formula (cf. 17:24; 36:36; 37:14) see *Comment*.

14. b. LXX* omits the last clause, but in favor of its retention (contra Zimmerli 496 et al.) see *Form/Structure/Setting*.

14. c. For שפטוך "they judged you" some MSS read שפטתיך "I judged you" and the ancient versions render as first sg, representing either that or אשפטך "I judge you." MT has the merit of being the harder reading; the variant is probably a case of assimilation to 7:3, 8. See *Form/Structure/Setting*.

14. d. LXX has an addition which seems to go back to a Heb. Vorlage in the form לכן אני שפטתיך כדמיך וכעלילותיך שפטתיך סמאת השם רבת המרי "Therefore I judge you according to your bloodshed and according to your deeds I judge you, unclean in name and great in rebellion." Apart from the initial word the addition seems to be a pastiche of comparative glosses. The first is from 7:3, with כדמיך corrupted from כדרכיך "according to your ways" via a כ/ד error; it was intended to qualify v 14ba. The second is from 36:19 with a change of suffixes and with the same intention. The third cites the vocative phrase in 22:5: רבת המרי appears to be a compression, via parablepsis, of רבת מהומה בית המרי, "great in disorder, house of rebellion." So there was a fourth reference, which evidently sought to identify the addressee in v 14bα with that of v 3. The third gloss cited a parallel for the uncleanness of Jerusalem (v 13abβ).

16. a. MT adds ולוא תבוא דמעתך "nor may your tears come," lacking in LXX*. It appears to have no place in the tight structuring of vv 16-23 (see *Form/Structure/Setting*). Was it an effort to make sense of an illegible דם האנק תבכה ולא "and you must not weep. Groan in silence," with which it shares a number of consonants (... דם ... א ... חב ולא)? Then the correct text was restored, but the aberration was preserved in a conflated reading. The unusual verb, as well as the spelling ולוא (cf. Zimmerli 502), arouses suspicion.

17. a. This sense seems to be corroborated by the parallel v 23b. For the coordination of the verbs in which the principal idea precedes cf. GKC 120h, with reference to Jer 4:5.

17. b. MT אבל מתים "dead, mourning" is best transposed with Fohrer (141) and Eichrodt (340). The massoretic accentuation includes מתים "dead" with what follows.

17. c. Here and in v 22 MT אנשׁים "(bread of) men" is best repointed as אֲנָשִׁים "despair" (Wellhausen apud Smend 176; Driver, *JTS* 41 [1940] 169; NEB). Vg Tg imply אונים "sorrow" (cf. Hos 9:4), read by many, including Zimmerli (503), and adopted by RSV.

18. a. MT and the ancient versions begin v 18 with "and I spoke to the people in the morning," which in terms of content seems to link with vv 18aβ-20a, but of itself is tantalizingly incomplete. Ehrlich (*Randglossen* 97) suggested that the main verbs of v 20aβ-b function as pluperfects ("now my wife had died . . . and I had done . . ."), but to relegate the fulfillment of v 16 to a flashback seems incongruous, and so does an initial mention of an address from the prophet, in the absence of a prior command so to do. To delete (Fohrer, ibid.; Zimmerli, ibid., et al.; cf. *BHS*) is a counsel of despair. The clause is best moved to a position between vv 19 and 20. Was it overlooked by homoeoarcton (וא/'ואי), restored in the margin and misplaced in the text under the assumption that the "morning" was on the same day as the evening of v 18aβ?

19. a. MT adds לנו "for us" superfluously. It is generally taken as an erroneous repetition of לנו earlier. LXX* Syr Vg omit.

20. a. See the first note on v 18.

21. a. MT מחמל used to be taken as "object of compassion," but the parallelism with משׂא (v 25) suggests that it is a synonym, "that to which one lifts (one's desire)," deriving from another stem cognate with Arab. *hamala* "carry" and evidenced in Talmudic חמילה "wrapper" (Ehrlich, *Randglossen* 98; Zimmerli, ibid.; *BHS*). Ehrlich suggested that a desire for assonance with the earlier מחמד prompted the usage.

24. a. MT adds אדני "Lord," which does not correspond to Ezekiel's formulaic usage (cf. v 27bβ). See the third note on 23:49.

25. a. The Heb. loosely appends with asyndeton. There hardly seems to be reason to delete the next phrase as secondary (cf. Zimmerli 508).

27. a. V 26 "On that day a refugee will come to you to give information" intrudes between the evident correlation of the fall of Jerusalem and the ending of Ezekiel's dumbness. Moreover, the verse creates a chronological problem in that it equates the day of Jerusalem's fall with the day when the news reached the exiles. It seems to have been a marginal exegetical note coordinating with 33:21-22, as the Aram. inf להשמעות "to cause to hear" suggests (Fohrer 143; cf. Zimmerli, ibid.; te Stroete *Bijdragen* 38 [1977] 169). It wants to suggest that the date in question was not when Jerusalem fell but rather later, when Ezekiel received the news. Heb. ביום ההוא "on that day" functions as a cue, citing the phrase in v 27. Perhaps the comment referred to Ezekiel in the third person and incorporation into the text caused a change to אליך "to you."

27. b. MT and the ancient versions add את־הפליט "with the refugee," which semantically aligns with ותדבר "and you will speak" (cf. 20:3): the misplacement suggests that it was a marginal comment occasioned by the intrusion of v 26 (cf. Zimmerli 504, 508; *BHS*).

Form/Structure/Setting

The message reception formula of v 1, which recurs at v 15, identifies vv 1-14 as an overall unit. A personal command to the prophet to record the date as a day of tragedy is followed by another to deliver publicly a parable that gives instructions for cooking meat. The addressee is not named in the poem of vv 3b-5 nor subsequently, but the structure of vv 3b-14 sheds light on his identity. They are marked by a punning inclusion, שפה "set on" and שפטוך "they have judged you." There is also a midpoint echo of both terms in the accusatory שפכתהו "she did (not) pour it" at v 7. The punitive inclusion seems to refer to the king of Babylon and his army (cf. 23:24; 24:2) and thus to identify him as the unnamed addressee for the imperatives of vv 3b-5 (and also of vv 10, 11). Accordingly the poem recites a parable rather than instructing the prophet to engage in a symbolic action, against Fohrer (138) and Brownlee (*For Me to Live* 30; *Ezekiel 1-19* 61). Whether the poem was originally a work song that Ezekiel re-used (van den Born 154; Zimmerli 496 et al.) can hardly be established.

Subsequent interpretation of the parable is expected, and an extended one follows in vv 6-14. It functions as a judgment oracle with two parts, accusation (vv

6-8) and pronouncement of punishment (vv 9-14), each part being introduced by a messenger formula. The role of לכן "therefore" in v 9 is the standard one of linking fault and fate, whereas that of לכן in v 6 is rather to introduce the interpretation, as in 15:6. By way of interpretation the caldron is identified with Jerusalem, "the city of blood" (v 6aβ), whose blood is as yet unpunished (vv 6bβ-8). However, the main intent of the judgment oracle is not to supply an interpretation of the parable but to develop it on allegorical lines as the prelude to further calamity at Yahweh's hands through his foreign agent (vv 6aγ-ba, 9b-11).

The complicated nature of vv 3b-14 with their double message of cooking meat in a caldron and removing corrosion from it raises the question whether a redactor has been at work, perhaps combining two separate messages. Bertholet (85, 87) divided simply into vv 1-5 and 6-14, but a prophetic parable does demand an interpretation (Zimmerli 497). Zimmerli himself has made a threefold division of vv 3b-14 into (a) vv 3b-5 and their original interpretation in vv 9-10a, (b) an expansion in which vv 6-8 was interpreted in v 10b-13a, and (c) a further addition in vv 13b-14, marked by a new keyword, טהר "be/make pure." Similarly Wevers (140) has split the passage into vv 3b-5 + 9-10 and vv 6-8 + 11-14 (cf. Freedy's redactional analysis in *VT* 20 [1970] 139 note 2). Both distinguish vv 9-10 (or 10a) from vv 11 (or 10b)-14 (or 13a) as relating to divine and human actions respectively, by interpreting the verbs of v 10a or 10a-ba (both delete v 10bβ) as infinitives absolute with Yahweh as subject. The LXX and Syriac provide ancient support for this interpretation. Then the interpretative role of vv 9-10(a) is to identify Yahweh as stoker and cook.

The form-critical coherence of vv 6-8 with what follows is indeed not a proof of unity. The distinction between vv 9-10(a) and its present sequel is a little wooden: Yahweh can be both collaborator with and cause behind his human intermediary (cf. the interlocked polarity of 23:22-27, even when pruned by Zimmerli [481]). Yet this observation may only attest the intelligibility of a skillfully redacted text. The division of vv 3b-14 into two parts is plausible: it manages to separate a complex passage into two straightforward strands. Zimmerli's third part is less convincing: v 14 seems to be required as a conclusion and Zimmerli's new catchword is actually confined to v 13b and follows naturally as a foil to טמאה "uncleanness" in vv 11-13a. How necessary is it to split the text into two parts? The fate of both citizens and city is hardly different than the message of 12:19, 20 and 15:6-8. Here, however, the allegorical text seems to bombard a hearer with too much material to assimilate at once. If vv 6-8 together with vv 11-14 did subsequently build on vv 3b-5 and 9-10, they could not have been uttered much later than the basic part: they must be Ezekiel's elaboration of a recent oracle (cf. Stuart 237). As vv 1, 3 indicate, the historical setting of the piece is the siege of Jerusalem begun in 588 B.C. The command to write down a date that was not yet significant for Ezekiel's audience points to an exilic location.

For full stylistic details of vv 1-14 the reader may be directed to *CBQ* 49 (1987) 404-14. Vv 3b-5 consist of two strophes, interlocked by מבחר "choicest" (Brownlee, *For Me to Live* 24). They go through the stages of preparation and cooking on separate and roughly parallel lines. The elevated prose of vv 6-8 also falls into two halves, each of which moves from accusation ("blood/corrosion") to the necessity for judgment. The third section, vv 9-14, is demarcated by its own inclusion, אני "I" in vv 9 and 14. It falls into three parts. The first two, vv 9-10 and 11-12, match an abundance of punishment (הרבה "multiply," v 10) with an "abundance" (רבת) of corrosion or reason for punishment. They are marked by a triple use of repetition or wordplay in an ABC/BCA order: התם "finish" and תתם "be consumed," הרחק "remove" and רקה "empty," and יחרו "be burned" and וחרה "and be red-hot." The third part, vv 13-14, with its direct address represents a climax. Vv 9-14 throb with their own somber wordplay: תחם "be heated," חמתי "my wrath" and אנחם "I will (not) relent." This wordplay serves to reinforce חמה "wrath" in v 8.

Vv 15-24 comprise (a) a divine command to the prophet to engage in a symbolic action (vv 16, 17); and (b) a report of the prophet's compliance (v 18); (c) the people's request for an explanation (v 19); and (d) the sequel, a proof saying that applies the symbolic action to the people in a message of judgment (vv 21-24). A further proof saying in vv 25-27 continues the foregoing; it is a personal message to the prophet. The continuing role of these verses is evident from the reverting in vv 25 to the event of v 21, and in 27bα to the motif of v 24, while מהם "from them" in v 25 presupposes the earlier reference to the people. Accordingly vv 15-27 make up an overall unit, as the single message reception formula in v 15 suggests: the unusual inclusion of the one in v 20 within an oracle serves to emphasize the continuity of the message. The mention of younger family members left behind (v 21) is a clear pointer to an exilic audience. The occasion seems to be later than the onset of siege in vv 1-2, but it is still within the period of siege that was to reach its climax in the summer of 587 B.C. with the fall of the city.

Structurally vv 16-24 are controlled by a quite rigid parallelism. The announcement of Yahweh's removal of Ezekiel's wife (v 16a) coordinates verbally with the parallel announcement of the loss of the temple in v 21a, and thematically with the loss of family members in v 21b. Three pairs of instructions to the prophet in vv 16b-17 are echoed chiastically in vv 22b-23a. An extra pair in v 27aαβ expands the first; so does a verbally nonparallel but thematically related pair in v 23b. Accordingly the structure is ABCD/ADCB. The effect is to highlight the instructions of vv 16bα-17 and vv 23aγ-b. There does not seem to be room in the structure for v 16bβ (see *Note* on v 16). On the other hand, the assessment of vv 22-23 as secondary, made by Zimmerli (508), Wevers (142), and te Stroete, *Bijdragen* 38 (1977) 169, 175, overlooks the important role that repetition has in Hebrew literature. The switch from the divine "I" to a prophetic "I" and back again in vv 21-24, at which they look askance, is not unparalleled in oracles. Another scheme is superimposed on the commands of vv 22b-23 and serves to extend them. The extra commands in vv 22a and 24a are wrapped round vv 22b-23 as an emphatic inclusion. It echoes an earlier scheme evident in vv 18 and 19, where the prophet's actions (ואעש "and I did," אתה עשה "you are doing") are a hinge linking the symbolic action with the truth to which it points.

As for vv 25 and 27, the A/A material of vv 16a and 21 is resumed in v 25 with vocabulary drawn from both, and Ezekiel's role modeling from v 24a is recalled in v 27bα. The parallelism of vv 24 and 27 is increased by the recognition formulas of vv 24b and 27bα. The rhetorical bonding of vv 15-27 confirms that it functions as a unit. However, one must think in terms of the whole chapter as a redactional unit. Just as the oracles of chap. 21 were linked by the term חרב "sword," so here יום "day" is the catchword: a special "day" in v 2 is echoed in "on the day when" in v 25 and "on that day" in v 27. The catchword operates as an inclusion linking two fateful days in the Jewish calendar.

Comment

1, 2 According to Parker and Dubberstein (*Babylonian Chronology* 28) this date represents January 15, 588 B.C. by our reckoning (see 20:1 *Comment*). This precision bears witness to the interacting of divine revelation and human history, so that neither can be understood apart from the other. On the human plane what happened on this day was a momentous event, like the arrival of the Russians at Berlin in World War II: it spelled the beginning of the end. On the theological plane it meant vindication for Ezekiel and for his insistence that the first fall of Jerusalem in 597 B.C. would not be reversed but worse was yet to come. Micawber-like hopes in Judah and doubtless among the exiles that the situation would improve were unjustified. The same date is attested in terms of Zedekiah's reign in 2 Kgs 25:1 (cf. Zech 8:19). Here it is intended as a specification concerning the event in v 2. However, there are variations from the normal ways in which the date is cited in Ezekiel (see Zimmerli 498; cf. Freedy and Redford, *JAOS* 90 [1970] 468), which tend to suggest that it has been borrowed from 2 Kgs, to identify the reference in v 2 for a later readership.

The prophet's insight was to be written down, for verification later when news came overland to Babylonia, as evidence that Ezekiel was an inspired prophet of Yahweh (cf. Isa 8:1-4; 30:8; Hab 2:2, 3).

3-5 The prophet is to deliver a parable about the siege to "the community of rebels" (בית המרי), which in the book of Ezekiel is the sardonic version of the title for the covenant nation, בית ישראל "house of Israel." The "house" or family is an unrepentant family of prodigal sons and daughters. The exilic representatives of Israel, who shared the rebellious spirit of the Judeans in the homeland, are meant. Fittingly such a people is to be the object of Yahweh's retribution, which is to strike at its heart. The context makes clear (see *Form/Structure/Setting*) that the parable addresses Nebuchadnezzar and orders him to make things hot for Jerusalem. The meaning of the imagery is relatively clear from Ezekiel's earlier usage in 11:7, where the meat in the caldron of Jerusalem represents those slain there. A "caldron" (סיר) was a large, two-handled cooking pot with a round base and a wide mouth (A. M. Honeyman, *PEQ* for 1939, 85). The point of the parable is that Yahweh is in charge of the military operations and that the king of Babylon functions as a servant or vassal carrying out his orders to besiege the city and threaten the lives of its citizens and refugees. There is irony in the rhetorical stress on "the choicest" (vv 4, 5): the most distinguished were by no means exempt from his culinary exercise, which is commissioned in two series of commands, in vv 3b-4 and 5.

6-8 The interpretation that follows identifies the caldron as "the city of blood," which recalls the charges in 22:2-5. Now, however, the imagery is developed on different lines, in terms of dealing with damage of the caldron. The word חלאה "corrosion" is to be related to the reference to copper in v 11. It occurs with copper in a verbal form (יחליא "corrode") at Sir 12:10. Semantically it is probably a development of the stem חלא/חלה "be sick." Driver's hypothesis of another stem meaning "be green, gangrenous" (*Hommages à André Dupont-Sommer*, ed. A. Caquot, Paris: Adrien-Maisonneuve, 1971, 283-84) is not convincing (cf. H. G. M. Williamson, *1 & 2 Chronicles* [Grand Rapids: Eerdmans, 1982] 276; *HALAT* 302a, b).

So blemished was the city that extremely harsh measures had to be taken to remove the blemishes. Accordingly the cooking process was to be only stage one of Jerusalem's experience of nemesis. The capital had undergone nothing yet by comparison with its eventual doom. In the second part of the section the inevitability of this fate is explained with fresh reference to the blood of v 6. The blatant taking of life in the capital was a crying shame. Like Abel's blood in Gen 4:10 (cf. Job 16:18), it cried out for vengeance. Yahweh himself had seen to it that the powerful moral process of retribution took its course and that no cover-up was possible to impede Jerusalem's exposure to vengeance. Retribution is expressed as an inexorable process at work in society, triggered by wrongdoing (cf. Wevers 141). Here that impersonal process is helped along by Yahweh's personal intervention.

9-12 Vv 6-8 represented the element of accusation in a judgment oracle. Now follows the pronouncement of punishment, emphatically confirmed by its own messenger formula. Yahweh's nudging (v 8) grows into a major part of the action. He stands behind Nebuchadnezzar, aiding him in his sinister focus on Jerusalem so that the second stage of punishment takes place. V 11 develops the imagery introduced in v 6. Not only would the inhabitants of Jerusalem suffer—and be removed in exile?—but the city would be engulfed in an inferno of destruction. Only thus could its ingrown blemishes be eradicated (cf. Mic 3:12). V 11 introduces the notion of religious uncleanness before God as an explanatory variant of corrosion: again it belongs within the orbit of 22:2-5. Indeed, v 11b recalls 22:15, the purpose of God to eradicate Jerusalem's uncleanness, while the imagery is not far from the smelting motif of 22:17-22. Here, however, the reference is not to the melting down of the metal pot into scrap, against Kelso, *JBL* 64 (1945) 391-92, and Brownlee, *For Me to Live* 26, but to the burning off of the blemishes on the metal.

13, 14 The close of the message dramatically shifts to the direct address of Jerusalem. Uncleanness is now equated with זמה "vileness," which in the sexual terms of chap. 23 was "lasciviousness." The series of references to wrath that began with the impersonal reference of v 8 and which wordplay has echoed in the heating of the caldron (v 11) and will echo again in Yahweh's relentlessness in v 14, now comes to a head as "my wrath." Yahweh identifies himself with the moral process that made Jerusalem its victim. The identification is of a piece with the emphatic pronoun "I" that occurs at the start and finish of the last section (vv 9, 14). The identification is reinforced in v 14 in terms of the fusion of the divine word and work with the arrival of a quasi-independent event. Yahweh's will was by no means vindictive: it was the materializing of a force activated by Jerusalem's wrong behavior. The Babylonian invaders stood as the final link in a moral chain of cause and effect. Does v 14 envisage positive purification, so that the pot may be re-used (Fohrer 140; Fuhs, *Ezekiel and His Book* 270-71)? The context and the parallel of the smelting furnace in 22:17-22 suggest rather that cleansing is an ironic metaphor for destruction.

16, 17 Perhaps nowhere does the radical significance of a prophet's surrender to the divine will emerge more clearly than here. Ezekiel is called to sacrifice his wife on the altar of his prophetic vocation. The pain of this bereavement is utilized as a reflection of his people's imminent catastrophe. The pain is intensified in that it must remain bottled up instead of trickling away in the reassuring routine of cultural behavior, which to this day makes Jewish reaction to bereavement psychologically superior to that of the Gentile. Disorientation of this type had its own customary conduct: loud wailing, neglect of one's appearance, the covering of the lower part of the face and the funeral meal (cf. R. de Vaux, *Ancient Israel: Its Life and Institutions* [New York: McGraw-Hill, 1961] 59-61). It all ministered to the expression of grief and so promoted a return to normal life. Here the norms of disorientation are suspended, so stunning is the experience of which it is meant to be the symbol (cf. Jer 16:5).

18-24 Ezekiel's submission to the divine command is dispassionately recounted. It stimulates the questioning of the exiles when the interment takes place on the morning of the next day. From experience of his symbolic actions they recognize the prophetic nature of the absence of mourning rites but not yet its significance. Ezekiel has the opportunity to give the divine interpretation and so to carry out his prophetic task, functioning as Yahweh's witness. A double blow is to befall the exiles. First, the temple is to be desecrated as a consequence of the coming fall of Jerusalem. The temple had immense significance in Judah's religion-based culture as the visible guarantee of divine goodwill. The formal Songs of Zion celebrated the aura of inviolability the temple gave to Jerusalem (Pss 46, 76, 87; cf. 78:68, 69), and their informal versions attested the people's devotion to it (Pss 84, 122). It stood as the bastion of the community's present life and future hopes. Now, however, this visible link between Yahweh and his people ("my . . . your") was to be severed. Second, just as Ezekiel had lost his wife, so the fall of Jerusalem was to mean the deaths of members of the exiles' families. In 597 B.C. people of significance had been deported as hostages to insure Judah's loyalty; evidently their children had been left behind. Hopes of fond reunion were dashed by the forecast. Ahead lay only the total breakdown of society, attested in the loosing of its religious moorings and in the damning of its hopes vested in the next generation.

So overwhelming a double calamity would force the exiles to take over Ezekiel's precedent. Not only would it be too stunning for tears but the inevitable "why?" of anguish would bring the appalling answer that the people's deviation from the divine will had been the ultimate cause of the catastrophe. There was no less cruel way for Yahweh to be appreciated for what he was.

25-27 However, the destruction of the temple and the killing of children would bring about a positive change in Ezekiel's prophetic role. Ironically such devastating disaster—indicated by the piling up of terms old and new—would mark a turning point in the people's fortunes. It would find its first focus in the prophet's symbolic experience. The dumbness with which Yahweh had earlier afflicted him would be removed. He would be given new words that revealed Yahweh's being from a different perspective. "In 24:24 he is a sign of God's *judgment* and its consequences; in 24:27 he is a sign of God's *grace* and its consequences" (R. W. Klein, *Ezekiel* 39-40).

The event has been preserved in two versions, here and in 33:21-22; a later attempt to bridge them is attested in 24:26. However, they must be left as independent witnesses to the spiritual watershed represented by the fall of Jerusalem. The double recording of the removal of the prophet's dumbness, which clearly has an important role in the structuring of the book, is not so problematic as their relation to the record of its imposition in 3:24-27, as a survey of some representative interpretations will show. Zimmerli (508-9) and Wevers (143) feel no need to relate the dumbness to chap. 24 since for them vv 25-27 are a secondary insertion based on 33:21, 22. At the other extreme, Eichrodt (348-50) holds that 3:24-26 (and 4:4-8) originally belonged with 24:15-27, so that the dumbness lasted for a period linked with the siege and fall of Jerusalem (cf. Cooke 44, 46). Vogt (*Untersuchungen* 95-101) has developed this hypothesis. Similarly, Brownlee associated the phenomena with the death of Ezekiel's wife and regarded 3:26-27 as relating to this period (*Ezekiel 1-19* 56-58, 209). Greenberg has developed the traditional understanding of 3:24-27, in terms of intermittent dumbness—as a sign of Yahweh's displeasure with his people—interrupted only by periodic messages of judgment from him (*Ezekiel 1-20* 102-21). Sherlock has taken this view further by noting how little of chaps. 4-24 is presented as public oracles (*ExpTim* 94 [1982/83] 296-98). Wilson has adopted the same longterm approach but understands מוכיח in 3:26 as "arbitrator" and so in a prophetic context "intercessor." He relates it to a prohibition of Ezekiel's prophetic role of positive intercession till Jerusalem fell (*VT* 22 [1972] 91-104). He is able to undergird his interpretation with reference to passages that appear to have in common the motif of intercession denied: 8:1-4; 20:1-31 (contrast 36:37-38). The complex problem has no incontrovertible solution, but on balance Wilson's seems the most impressive.

Explanation

Judaism was to single out a number of days in its calendar as fast days, including the 9th of Ab to commemorate the destruction of the temple (and also the second temple) and the 10th of Tebet, when Nebuchadnezzar began the siege of Jerusalem (cf. Zech 7:5; 8:19). In this chapter we find contemporary reactions to these two fatal days.

Human hopes are shattered in the messages of vv 1-14. Ezekiel's ministry was later to manifest a radically new, divinely based optimism, but that time was not yet. God's no to a sinful people had to be heard and accepted with despair before good news could take its place. Here the fire of warfare threatens the peace of Jerusalem. As yet only Ezekiel knew the ominous facts, by prophetic inspiration. For those who were ready or eventually compelled to accept the prediction, this black day was the moment of truth. Yahweh stood on the side of the enemy, issuing orders for the siege. The citizens of Jerusalem, swollen by Judean refugees, were so many joints of meat tossed into a boiling caldron. Their goose was well and truly cooked.

Yet even worse news must be communicated. Perhaps in a later message, which followed on the heels of the first and has been redactionally blended with it, the metaphor of the cooking pot is taken further. Attention turns from the fate of Jerusalem's inhabitants to that of the city itself. It was to suffer devastating damage. Jerusalem was infected with life-destroying social corruption, which must lead to its own demise. The capital was attracting to itself the outworking of a self-incurred curse. It was to become no mere ghost city, waiting quietly for a kinder turn of events, but a Dresden, an inferno of destruction (cf. Lam 2:8, 9, 15; Neh 1:3, 17). Such was its inevitable destiny—in which Yahweh too was mysteriously involved (vv 8, 11, 13). There was no less severe way for him to deal with the stain of spiritual impurity that contaminated the scene. The city was locked into a triangular situation. On the horizontal plane the Babylonian siege and its destructive outcome were the doom that the city had attracted to itself. Above both, however, towered the divine will, endorsing the nemesis triggered by the capital's wrongdoing and even using a foreign army to this end. Those exiles who perversely continued to put their faith and hope in something other than God had to grasp that outside God there was no hope.

For Ezekiel years of loving turned in an instant into history, when his wife passed away. He was not permitted, however, to let his first reaction of numb shock be channeled into the cultural modes of expressing grief, which would have brought eventual healing to the hurt and helped to make him whole again. By this ban he was to model the overwhelming shock of a communal bereavement caused by the destruction of the temple and the killing of children left in the capital. These two tragedies stole all the meaning from life then and thereafter, and turned the whole future into a chaotic void. The first was theologically more crucial than the second: it not only slammed the door on centuries of worship, but removed the ground of Israel's spiritual being. The fall of the temple exposed it as an outer shell corroded from within by national sinfulness. Yet in the removal of Ezekiel's dumbness the text drops a clue that the debris of a false foundation was cleared away in order that an authentic relationship might be inaugurated, as later chapters will make plain. The second day held out hope to the hopeless.

The two days of this chapter find a double antitype in the letter to the Romans. In the Christian gospel the wrath of God is revealed against Jewish and Gentile sinfulness—and every mouth is stopped!—as the prelude to the manifestation of his saving righteousness (Rom 1:18; 3:19, 21). Furthermore, Paul interpreted Jewish rejection of Jesus in terms of their being pruned out from the tree of God's people, with a view to their eventually being grafted back, which would mean nothing less than "life from the dead" (Rom 11:12-32; cf. Ezek 37). And he did not scruple to warn Gentile Christians that God's severity could strike again, to their own loss (Rom 11:22).

Palestinian Scores to Be Settled (25:1-17)

Bibliography

Clements, R. E. *Prophecy and Tradition.* Atlanta: John Knox, 1975, chap. 5. **Geyer, J. B.** "Mythology and Culture in the Oracles Against the Nations." *VT* 36 (1986) 129-45. **Gosse, B.** "Le recueil d'oracles contre les nations d'Ezéchiel xxv-xxxii dans la rédaction du livre d'Ezéchiel." *RB* 93 (1986) 535-62. **Lindsay, J.** "The Babylonian Kings and Edom, 605-550 B.C." *PEQ* 108 (1976) 23-39. **Mendenhall, G. E.** "The 'Vengeance' of Yahweh." *The Tenth Generation.* Baltimore: Johns Hopkins University, 1973, 69-104. **Reventlow, H.** *Wächter über Israel.* BZAW 82. Berlin: Töpelmann, 1962, 139-43. **de Vaux, R.** "Téman, ville ou région d'Édom?" *RB* 76 (1969) 379-85. **Woudstra, M. H.** "Edom and Israel in Ezekiel." *Calvin Theological Journal* 3 (1968) 21-35. **van Zyl, A. H.** *The Moabites.* POS 3. Leiden: Brill, 1960.

Translation

[1] *I received the following communication from Yahweh:* [2] *"Human one, look in the direction of the Ammonites and issue a prophecy against them.* [3] *Tell the Ammonites: Listen to Yahweh's[a] communication. Here is a message from the Lord Yahweh.[b] Inasmuch as you, Ammon,[c] jeered at the desecration of my sanctuary, the desolation of Israel's land and the deportation of Judah's community,* [4] *for that reason I mean to give the easterners the right to own your land. They will set up[a] their encampments in your country, making their homes there. They will eat the fruit and drink the wine that belong to you.* [5] *I will turn Rabbah into a camel corral and Ammon into a sheepfold. Then you Ammonites[a] will realize that I am Yahweh.*

[6] *"Here is a confirmatory[a] message from the Lord Yahweh: Inasmuch as you[b] clapped your hands, stamped your feet and laughed with passionate and utter scorn[c], over Israel's land,* [7] *for that reason I have determined[a] to deal you a blow. I will get other nations to plunder[b] you. I will eliminate you as a people, I will efface you as a country. I will destroy you[c]—then you will realize that I am Yahweh.*

[8] *"Here is a message from the Lord Yahweh: Inasmuch as Moab[a] declared that the community of Judah is no different from any other nation,* [9] *for that reason I mean to expose Moab's flank, depriving it[a] of cities, its cities[b] throughout its territory,[c] the showpieces of the country, Beth-jeshimoth, Baal-meon and Kiriathaim.* [10] *I will give[a] the easterners the right to own its land, as well as that of the Ammonites, so that its[b] national status[c] may not be remembered,* [11] *and I will carry out judgment on Moab. Then they will realize that I am Yahweh.*

[12] *"Here is a message from the Lord Yahweh: Inasmuch as Edom has treated Judah's community with vindictive revenge and incurred serious guilt by persisting[a] in revenge against them,[b]* [13] *this is the consequent message of the Lord Yahweh. I will deal[a] Edom a blow. I will eliminate from it humans and animals alike and turn it into a waste area: from Teman as far as Dedan[b] they will fall victims to the sword.* [14] *I will use my people Israel to avenge myself on Edom: their dealings with Edom will match my anger and fury. Then they will experience my vengeance. So runs the oracle of the Lord Yahweh.*

[15] *"Here is a message from the Lord Yahweh: Inasmuch as the Philistines have acted vengefully, and vindictively revenged themselves with passionate scorn, making destruc-*

tion an outlet for their undying enmity, *16this is the consequent message of the Lord Yahweh. I mean to deal the Philistines a blow. I will eliminate the Cherethites and efface the rest of the people along the coast. 17I will forcefully avenge myself on them by punishing them furiously. Then they will appreciate that I am Yahweh, when I have avenged myself on them."*

Notes

3. a. MT adds אדני "Lord," violating normal usage: cf. the next note. The addition anticipates the next clause.

3. b. For the presence of אדני "Lord" in this formula here and in vv 6, 8, 12, 13, 15, 16 and in the formula of v 14, see the note on 20:3.

3. c. The vocative has been added to the translation to express a switch from pl to fem sg (vv 3b-4).

4. a. For the piel of ישב cf. post-biblical Heb. usage (Jastrow 599a).

5. a. The noun has been added to the translation to show that the verb is pl.

6. a. Heb. כי "for."

6. b. The pronouns in vv 6-8 and the final verb are masc sg.

6. c. For the form see GKC 23c. The omission of בכל־שאט "with all your scorn" in LXX Syr is due to failure to understand the noun. The correct rendering in 28:24, 26; 36:5 comes from a different translator (Zimmerli, *Ezekiel 2* 7; cf. L. J. McGregor, *The Greek Text of Ezekiel* 197-99).

7. a. The pf is prophetic (Cooke 286). MT prefaces with הנני "behold I," unusual with a pf verb (cf. 36:6): it may be a case of mechanical assimilation to vv 4, 9.

7. b. K לבנ is meaningless; Q לבז "to plunder" is correct (cf. 7:21; 23:46). K is due to confusion with a marginal alternative בגוים for the following לגוים "to the nations" (cf. Cornill 336; *BHS*).

7. c. Heb. אשמידך "I will destroy you" is often regarded as a gloss, but it is well attested and a reason or source for such a gloss is difficult to detect. For a climactic single word preceding the recognition formula cf. 24:24b. However, the emphasis on destruction does appear to be excessive. Ehrlich's hypothesis (*Randglossen* 99) is worth considering, that והאבדתיך "and I will efface you" is a variant of והכרתיך "and I will eliminate you," that ומן "and from" once stood in the place of מן², and that אשמידך goes with the preceding phrase. More precisely, והאבדתיך could have originated as a comparative gloss, from v 16.

8. a. MT adds ושעיר "and Seir," absent from LXX* and from consideration in vv 9-11. Evidently a marginal note שעיר intended to note the parallels between the oracle against Edom in vv 12-14 and that against Mount Seir in 35:2-9, but the common beginning of vv 8 and 12 caused the note to be put too high and it was incorporated into the text at this point.

9. a. For the privative מן "from" see BDB 583b.

9. b. LXX does not represent מעריו "of its cities," perhaps by oversight, unless מעריו מהערים "of the cities, of its cities" reflects a conflated text.

9. c. See BDB 892a; *HALAT* 1046b.

10. a. The order of words may require changing: cf. Zimmerli 9; *BHS.*

10. b. MT בני עמון "Ammonites" is difficult with the fem sg verb, although the phrase may be used with the sense of Ammon (cf. v 5 and J. Reider, *HUCA* 24 [1952/53] 91-92). Even so, the context requires that Moab be the subject (see *Comment*). The phrase may have originated as a marginal note comparing the similar statement in 21:37 (32), which is often (erroneously) understood to refer to the Ammonites.

10. c. LXX* does not represent בגוים "among the nations," which could thus be an addition in MT, perhaps linked with the variant in v 7. It may, however, have been overlooked before ובמואב. It seems to have a structural role in the oracle (see *Comment*).

12. a. The consec pf has a frequentative force: cf. GKC 112f; Joüon 119v. However, B. Johnson (*Hebräisches Perfekt* 79) credits it with a pluperfect or specifying sense.

12. b. For בהם "against them" LXX reflects נקם "vengeance" under the influence of the phrase in v 15bא.

13. a. For the construction cf. 35:11.

13. b. MT wrongly links the phrase with what precedes. For ודדנה a pointing ודדנה is expected (cf. Driver, *Bib* 35 [1954] 156).

Form/Structure/Setting

The tradition of issuing oracles against foreign countries or cities is an ancient one in Israelite prophecy (cf. Clements, *Prophecy and Tradition*, 58-61). The tradition was well maintained in the prophetic books, each of the major books having a distinct and lengthy section devoted to this genre (cf. Amos 1-2). The present collection in chaps. 25-32 begins with a cluster of five short oracles directed against four of Judah's neighbors, Ammon, Moab, Edom and Philistia. Form-critically they are all proof sayings developed from judgment oracles by the addition of the recognition formula. Each is introduced by the messenger formula and proceeds from reasoned accusation (יען "because") to a logical verdict (לכן "therefore") and the closing recognition formula. The fourth and fifth oracles introduce the verdict with a second messenger formula (vv 13, 16), and the fourth ends with the final divine saying formula (v 14bβ). The first oracle has its own introduction, the message reception formula and the call to the prophet to symbolically confront Ammon and deliver an oracle. The structural rigidity of the oracles attests the antiquity of the foreign oracle form used here (cf. Clements, *Prophecy and Tradition* 60; Zimmerli 11).

The presence of a second oracle against Ammon (vv 6, 7) is thought-provoking. The use of second masculine singular forms, after the feminine singular and masculine plural forms earlier, suggests that, while the first oracle is presupposed, this one is a subsequent expansion (Zimmerli, ibid., et al., following G. Hölscher, *Hesekiel* 133 note 1). The third person references of the third, fourth and fifth oracles flow naturally from v 2, where Ammon is the object of direct address. The second oracle borrows freely from the language of the fourth and fifth oracles, besides echoing that of the first and third.

The four original oracles fall into two pairs: the first and third go together and so do the fourth and fifth. The last two, apart from their formal structure, are united by their extensive use of the vocabulary of vengeance (נקם) along with the motif of fury (חמה), the use of wordplay (חרבה "desolation," חרב "sword," v 13; והכרתי את־כרתים "and I will eliminate the Cherethites," v 16) and the sequence of action and reaction (עשה "do," vv 12a, 14aβ, 15a, 17a). The first and third oracles share the motifs of presumptuous speech (אמר "say") and transfer of land (מורשה) to the easterners. Apart from their common form, the third and fourth oracles are linked by their references to "the community of Judah."

The chronological setting of the oracles is clearly post-587 B.C.: the reactions of Judah's neighbors to the disaster are their explicit occasion, apart from the fifth, where it is implicit. The Ammon and Moab oracles seem to antedate 582 B.C. (see *Comment*). Whether they originated at the same time is a separate issue. To credit them all to the school of Ezekiel (Wevers 144) on the grounds that בית יהודה "community of Judah" is not a phrase of Ezekiel's, since he uses בית ישראל "community of Israel," is hardly compelling (cf. Zimmerli 13). The authenticity of the fourth has been doubted on the grounds that uniquely in Ezekiel's foreign oracles, divine reprisal is mediated through Israel (v 14), unlike the parallel oracle against Edom in chap. 35. To delete v 14a as a later expansion (cf. Zimmerli 18) would spoil the symmetry of the fourth and fifth oracles. To emend ביד "into the hand" to בעד "on behalf of" (Ehrlich, *Randglossen* 100) is too conjectural to carry conviction. Zimmerli, ibid., has noted too the variation in the recognition formula at v 14b. Accordingly it is possible that the two final oracles are a later composition. It is clear, anyway, that the two pairs of oracles arose independently and have been redactionally combined. Subsequently the second oracle was added, which addressed Ammon like the first but used the language of the last pair. The resultant composition comes over as a powerful fivefold statement of Yahweh's purpose to reveal himself on the side of his suffering people.

Comment

1-5 In 21: 33, 34 (28, 29) the book of Ezekiel has already demonstrated a concern that Ammon's crowing over Jerusalem's fall should not go unpunished. Here the prophet is bidden to direct his symbolic gaze upon Ammon (cf. 21:2, 7 [20:46; 21:2] and *Comment*) and in rhetorical address issue a formal oracle of denunciation to doom Judah's northeastern neighbor. Vv 2-5 form a unit, rounded by the inclusion of third person references to the Ammonites (vv 2-3a, 5b). Another inclusion is formed by the emphasis that Yahweh himself has been the victim of Ammonite jeers, and so needs to intervene in vindication of himself (vv 3b, 5b). But bound up with Yahweh's loss of face is that of his people. Hitherto punisher of a disobedient covenant people, Yahweh reveals himself as their patron, now that judgment has been carried out. The land was a third entity in the triangular covenant relationship and functioned as the gauge of its healthy or sorry state. Accordingly desolation of the land and expulsion from it featured in the punishment of his people. Now, with surprising grace, Yahweh proposes to leap to their defense. The oracle against Ammon clearly functions as an affirmation of support for the Judeans. The motifs of territorial desolation and deprivation were to boomerang into Ammon's experience. According to Josephus (*Ant.* 10.9.7) Nebuchadnezzar campaigned against Ammon and Moab in his twenty-third year, that is, 582 B.C. Ammon may have been deported, like Judah, and its land left as a vacuum for desert tribes to fill; certainly the area was largely depopulated before the middle of the sixth century B.C. until the third (G. M. Landes, *IDB*, vol. 1, 112-113).

6, 7 The previous message is reinforced by another, supplementary one. It reflects more emotion in its description of Ammon's insulting behavior: hand, foot and inner being had joined forces in a totality of opposition. In reprisal total extinction is threatened for the body politic. The harshness of the verdict corresponds to the depth of feeling aroused in the accusation.

8-11 The oracle against Moab, Ammon's southern neighbor, functions as a companion piece to the first Ammonite one. Their slighting of Yahweh, although only implicit in the accusation, is no less real than before, for their declaration is tantamount to a denial of his special relationship with Judah. Moab, in disparaging Judah (cf. Jer 48:27; Zeph 2:8), has Yahweh to answer to, in a double confrontation: the name rhetorically features three times (vv 8b, 9a, 11a). Again the punishment fits the crime, for national downgrading turns into national destruction (vv 8b, 10b). These generalities are interspersed with precise geographical references to the western side of the Moabite highland that towers above the Dead Sea and to three of Moab's many towns, Beth-jeshimoth (Tel el-ᶜAzieimeh) in the Jordan valley at the foot of the mountain slope, Baal-meon (Maᶜin), some thirteen miles to the south-east, and Kiriathaim, a city of uncertain location that van Zyl has placed near Medeba up on the plateau some five miles to the north-west of Maʿîn (*The Moabites* 83; cf. Y. Aharoni, *The Land of the Bible: A Historical Geography* [2nd ed. Philadelphia: Westminster, 1979] 381 note 52, who suggests a positive identification with Qaryat el-Mekhaiyet). The cities represent three of Moab's fortresses against western aggression, but they would prove of no avail against Yahweh's onslaught, while the eastern frontier too would be overrun, by the nomadic tribes of the desert.

12-14 The literary reactions to the tragedy of 587 B.C. in the Old Testament tend to highlight with peculiar passion the part played by Edom (e.g., Ps 137:7; Lam 5:21, 23; Joel 4 [3]:19; Obad). In the same vein especially strong language is used here to accuse Edom, in the first of a second pair of oracles against Judah's neighbors. Presumably such precise accusations as are mentioned in Obad 11-14 underlie the virulence of the complaint. As in the previous oracles, Yahweh makes himself responsible for punishing offenses against his people. Depopulation and desolation are to be his reprisal. The phrase "from Teman as far as Dedan" does not signify a north-south inclusiveness, as one might have expected. "Teman" seems to represent not the city of Tawilan, with which it used to be identified, but simply the southern region of Edom (de Vaux, *RB* 76 [1969] 383-84). Dedan (el-ʿUlā, cf. M. C. Astour, *IDBSup* 222) was south of Edom's territory. A "greater Edom" seems to be reflected here, with boundaries that stretched beyond Edom's traditional frontiers (Lindsay, *PEQ* 108 [1976] 38). Once more the punishment is to be a fitting one, in the light of the crime of v 12, as often in Old Testament oracles of judgment (cf. in principle P. D. Miller, *Sin and Judgment in the Prophets* [Chico: Scholars Press, 1982] passim). Here a deed triggers another deed done by its victims (עשה), and Edomite vengeance provokes divine vengeance (נקם). In this dire activity Israel is assigned a role, as in Obad 17b-21 in recapturing the Negeb from Edomite occupation. The stem נקם, when used in an accusation of base human conduct (v 12) implies vindictive excess, but in a divine context (v 14) refers to punitive vindication, "the executive exercise of power by the highest legitimate political authority for the protection of his own subjects" (Mendenhall, *The Tenth Generation* 78).

15-17 The companion message to the oracle against Edom is directed against the Philistines. The redactional unit represented by chap. 25 has by now moved around in a circular direction, from Ammon in the northeast to Moab in the east, to Edom in the southeast and eventually to Philistia in the west. That Judah had been their victim is not stated, but seems to be implied by the context. The oracle aligns with Joel 4 (3):4-8 in attacking the Philistines for capitalizing on Judah's downfall; there looting and slave trading are specified. Here the same high level of emotional language is used as against Edom, and they too are threatened with destruction at Yahweh's hands, which was to represent a boomerang of vengeance and an outbreak of fury. Only thus could Yahweh assert himself in self-vindication, after violation of his sovereignty.

Explanation

The end of chap. 24 gave a hint that the tide of Yahweh's dealings with his people was to turn. That hint is taken up in this chapter, the first part of a series of foreign oracles. Its role is to bring reassurance to the Judeans, in a round-about way. The chapter virtually takes up a host of communal laments for Yahweh to intervene on his people's behalf. Israel has been overwhelmed by crisis, and their enemies have taken advantage of the situation and derided them—and thereby done despite to Yahweh's own concerns (cf. Pss 74:7, 10, 18, 22; 79:1, 4, 10, 12).

Politics and religion were interlocked in the ancient world. In political terms these nations were expediently climbing onto the Babylonian bandwagon and expressing their allegiance to the victorious world power in opposing Judah. However, such a political move struck at the heart of the victimized nation and triggered religious reactions. Loss of face seems to have been an excruciating experience in Israelite culture—and Israel's God took tender notice of such deep feelings (cf. Joel 2:26b, 27b). Woudstra's denial that Judean emotions play an essential part here (*Calvin Theological Journal* 3 [1968] 23, 24) cannot be upheld. He was overreacting to liberal reductionism. The divine and the human are here inextricably intermingled, as passion-filled grievances find a hearing and promise of vindication at the lawcourt of their patron (cf. Luke 18:1-8). Throbbing beneath the surface of the text and surprisingly never verbalized is the Ezekielian motif of the profanation of Yahweh's name involved in the fate of the covenant nation (cf. 20:9; 36:20-23). Part of the clearing of that name was the repeated declaration of this chapter that he would intervene in Judah's world and make human experience a witness to divine justice and truth.

Reassurances that Tyre Would Fall (26:1-21)

Bibliography

Albright, W. F. "The Seal of Eliakim and the Latest Preëxilic History of Judah, with Some Observations on Ezekiel." *JBL* 51 (1932) 77-106. **Goldman, M. D.** "The Meaning of רצע." *Australian Biblical Review* 4 (1954-55) 7-16. **Jenni, E.** "Das Wort ʿōlām im Alten Testament." *ZAW* 65 (1953) 1-35. **Lohfink, N.** "Enthielten die im Alten Testament bezeugten Klageriten eine Phase des Schweigens?" *VT* 12 (1962) 260-77. **Parunak, H. V. D.** "Oral Typesetting: Some Uses in Biblical Structure." *Bib* 62 (1981) 153-68. **Tromp, N.** *Primitive Conceptions of Death and the Nether World in the Old Testament.* BibOr 21. Rome: Pontifical Biblical Institute, 1969. **Van Dijk, H. J.** *Ezekiel's Prophecy on Tyre: A New Approach.* BibOr 20. Rome: Pontifical Biblical Institute, 1968. **Yadin, Y.** *The Art of Warfare in Biblical Lands in the Light of Archeological Study.* 2 vols. New York: McGraw-Hill, 1963.

Translation

[1]*In the twelfth year, on the first of the month,*[a] *I received the following communication from Yahweh:* [2]*"Human one, inasmuch as Tyre has shouted about Jerusalem,*
'Hurray! Smashed is
that international meeting place.[a]
It has been turned over[b] *to me!*
I will be filled[c]—*it has been destroyed,'*
[3]*for that reason here is the Lord*[a] *Yahweh's message: I am your opponent, Tyre. I will get many nations to surge against you, like sea waves at high tide.*[b] [4]*They will destroy Tyre's walls and demolish its towers. I will clear away its rubble*[a] *and turn it into bare rock.* [5]*It will be a sea-girt area for spreading nets. I have given my word thereto. So runs the Lord Yahweh's oracle. Tyre will become plunder for other nations,* [6]*while the members of her satellite communities*[a] *on the mainland will be casualties of the sword. Then they will appreciate that I am Yahweh.*
[7]*"Here is a confirmatory message from the Lord Yahweh: I mean to make Tyre the target of invasion by Nebuchadnezzar,*[a] *Babylon's king in the north, the king of kings. He will bring horses, chariots, cavalry, and an army of large numbers of troops.*[b] [8]*The members of your satellite communities on the mainland he will make casualties of the sword. He will set up siege structures against you, pile up earthworks against you and raise a barrage of shields against you.* [9]*He will make your walls feel the brunt of his battering rams, and break down your towers with his iron bars.*[a] [10]*Dust raised by his hordes of horses will cover you, while the noise of his cavalry,*[a] *wagons and chariots will shake your walls, when he enters your gates with the triumphant air of one entering*[b] *a city whose walls he has breached.* [11]*He will trample all your streets with his horses' hooves, he will make your troops*[a] *casualties of the sword, and your stout pillars will be thrown down*[b] *to the ground.* [12]*His soldiers*[a] *will loot your wealth and plunder your commercial assets. They will demolish your walls and destroy your elegant houses. Your stones, timber and rubble they will consign to the waters'*[b] *depths.* [13]*I will put a stop to the sound of your songs, while the music of your lyres will never be heard again.* [14]*I will turn you into bare rock: 'it will be*[a] *an area for spreading nets,' never*

rebuilt. *I, Yahweh,*[b] *have given my word thereto. So runs the Lord Yahweh's oracle.*

[15]*"Here is a message from the Lord Yahweh to Tyre: The coastlands will certainly quake at the sound of your downfall, when the fatally wounded groan, when slaughter takes its toll*[a] *within you.* [16]*All the sealords will step down from their thrones. They will divest themselves of their robes and embroidered clothing, and trembling*[a] *will be their attire. Sitting on the ground, they will tremble in agitation,*[b] *appalled by your fate.* [17]*They will raise this dirge over you:*

'How distressing it is that you have perished[a] *from the seas,*
city once renowned,[b]
once potentate of the sea,
you and your citizens,[c]
once a source of terror[d]
that all your citizens inspired.[e]
[18]*Now the coastlands*[a] *tremble*
on the day[b] *of your downfall.*
Yes, the coastlands by the sea
are overwhelmed by your passing.[c]

[19]*"Here is a confirmatory message from the Lord Yahweh: When I turn you into a ruined city, as desolate as any unpeopled city can be, when I get the deep to surge*[a] *over you so that the ocean covers you,* [20]*then I will send you down to be with*[a] *those who have descended*[b] *to the Pit, to people of the distant past. I will give you a home in the nether world,*[c] *which is like*[d] *ancient ruins, along with those who have descended to the Pit. Your fate will be to cease to be peopled*[e] *or to maintain your position*[f] *in the world of the living.* [21]*I will make you the victim of a terrible end, and you will be no more. You will be sought, but never found*[a] *again.*[b] *So runs the Lord Yahweh's oracle."*

Notes

1. a. The date in MT, -/1/11, is problematic, apart from the absence of a month. If the first month is presupposed (cf. 32:17), it corresponds to April 23, 587 B.C. according to Parker and Dubberstein's reconstruction (*Babylonian Chronology* 28). However, v 2 mentions Tyre's reaction to the fall of Jerusalem, which probably took place in the summer of 587. Not only does that event need to be taken into account but also the time it took for news of it to reach the exiles. According to 33:21 that occurred in 10/5/12, another problematic date, which may originally have been 10/5/11. If so, here a dating (1)/1/12 (= April 13, 586) would be feasible. Some support for this may be derived from the unusual Heb. numeral for the eleventh year, עשרה עשתי, which elsewhere in Ezek is עשרה אחת (30:20; 31:1). A corruption from the similar עשרה שתי "twelfth" may have taken place, a slip which did occur in 40:49 (Zimmerli 26, following C. Steuernagel). In fact LXX[A] has a date 1/1/12, although the indication of the month appears to be secondary (cf. Zimmerli, ibid.). *BHS* follows a popular expedient in postulating a date 11/1/11, presumably on the assumption that the month numeral fell out, being the same as that of the year (cf. Cooke 294; Albright, *JBL* 51 [1932] 93; Fohrer 149). A third expedient is to relate the date in MT to vv 7-14 and to regard the oracle as a subsequent insertion (Freedy and Redford, *JAOS* 90 [1970] 469; Wevers 147).

2. a. Heb. דלתות "doors" here refers to the two doors of a gate (Zimmerli 27) and so a single entity: hence the sg verbs.

2. b. Cf. Jer 6:12 for the use of the verb.

2. c. LXX Tg imply הַמְּלֵאָה "she who was full (is destroyed)," preferred by some, such as Cornill (339) and Zimmerli, ibid., and adopted by NEB. But the contrast in MT provides four statements that make up an impressive ABB'A' structure.

3. a. For the formulaic use of אדני "Lord" here and in vv 5, 7, 15, 19, 21 see the note on 20:3.

3. b. MT כהעלות "like (Yahweh's) causing (the sea) to rise" has probably been assimilated to the previous verb (and cf. v 19). The ancient versions imply כעלות "like (the sea's) rising." The following לגליו provides a closer definition of the subj, "in respect of its waves" (BDB 514b). For Smend (189) and Fohrer (149) the sea is subj and, as in Aramaic, (גלי)ל introduces the object: "like the sea's raising its waves."

4. a. The preceding reference to destruction suggests that עפר so means, as in v 12; Ps 102:15(14) (Smend 189; Ehrlich, *Randglossen* 101).

6. a. Lit. "daughters" of a metropolis, here with reference to the inhabitants of daughter towns.

7. a. Heb. נבוכדראצר here preserves the form of the Bab. *nabû-kudurri-uṣur* "May Nabu protect the son," as elsewhere in Ezek and usually in Jer. Elsewhere in the OT the *resh* is changed to *nun* by consonantal dissimilation; hence the English form Nebuchadnezzar.

7. b. Heb. וקהל ועם "and army and people" is probably a case of hendiadys, as LXX implies. The earlier preposition ב "with" does double duty (Van Dijk, *Ezekiel's Prophecy* 15).

9. a. Heb. חרב, usually "sword," here refers to an iron tool: cf. Exod 20:25.

10. a. For the vocalization see GKC 130b.

10. b. Lit. "as (at) the acts of entrance."

11. a. For this meaning of עם "people" cf. v 7; 30:11.

11. b. For תרד "will come down" LXX Syr Tg imply יורד "he will bring down," maintaining the same subj. MT is to be kept as the less obvious reading (cf. Zimmerli 29). For the change of subj cf. v 13a,

b. For the sg verb cf. GKC 145k.

12. a. Lit. "they." LXX has sg verbs in v 12a, probably a harmonization. The interpretative role of vv 7-14 can explain the pl forms: they correspond to the invading nations in v 5.

12. b. For מים "water" LXX Syr Tg^MSS imply הים "the sea," preferred by many. But cf. 27:34. Van Dijk (*Ezekiel's Prophecy* 24-26), finding an enclitic *mem*, redivides as ים ס-בתוך "in the midst of (the) sea." However, H. Hummel, *JBL* 76 (1957) 107, and L. Boadt, *Ezekiel's Oracles against Egypt* 135 note 31, doubt whether the book contains convincing examples of the usage.

14. a. Heb. תהיה and תבנה are straightforward third person forms: "it will be," "it will be rebuilt." V 14 aβ seems to function as a quotation of v 5aα.

14. b. Some massoretic evidence (cf. *BHS*) and that of the ancient versions favor the omission of the divine name: cf. v 5; 28:10.

15. a. MT's vocalization of (הרג) בהרג implies an anomalous extension of the cognate acc construction in the passive: "when slaughter is slaughtered." A pointing as a qal בַּהֲרֹג is preferable (GKC 51l); then the subj is indefinite, "when one slaughters with a slaughter." For LXX see Zimmerli 29-30.

16. a. The pl חרדות is strange (cf. BDB 353b). Cornill (342) suggested a pointing חַרְדוּת, noting the sg rendering of the ancient versions.

16. b. Heb. לרגעים signifies "with movements" and so "in agitation" (cf. Goldman, *Australian Biblical Review* 4 [1954-55] 7-16).

17. a. MT has אבדת נושבת "you are destroyed, O inhabited one." LXX* lacks אבדת and takes the second word as נִשְׁבַּתְּ "you are brought to an end" (cf. NEB), finding a form of the stem שבת, as in v 13. Probably אבדת originated as an explanatory gloss clarifying a vowelless נשבת, which later, however, was vocalized as if from ישב under the influence of v 19.

17. b. MT ההללה is accented as pf with a relative use of the article. It is better taken as a pual ptcp without a preformative *mem* (Smend 192; Fohrer 151).

17. c. LXX* lacks the line v 17bβ; it may well have fallen out by homoeoarcton. For the third person references in v 17by see GKC 144p.

17. d. LXX implies נָתְנָה חִתִּיתָהּ "(who) produced terror of herself," with Tyre as subj rather than the citizens (MT): the subsequent specification of "citizens" so suggests.

17. e. Heb. ל further specifies the object of terror: cf. the sense "in reaction to" sometimes found after intransitive verbs connoting fear. To avoid repetition *BHK*, Bertholet (54) et al., with a little support from Syr, emend to לכל-היבשה "to all the mainland," which is adopted by RSV, NEB, and NJB.

18. a. MT איין "the coastlands" exhibits an Aram. pl. For a suggested differentiation between this term and the regular form האיים in the next line see Lohfink, *VT* 12 (1962) 272 n. 3.

18. b. MT יום "day" is syntactically difficult: cf. the discussion in Van Dijk, *Ezekiel's Prophecy* 38. It may reflect an acc of time: cf. GKC 118 i.

18. c. Heb. צאת implies exit or departure and so here evidently destruction. LXX* lacks v 18b. It is often taken as a variant or interpretation of v 18a, and so it may be. However, it could have fallen out in LXX* or its Vorlage because of its similarity to v 18a. It does have a recognizable poetic form 2 + 3, a respectable variant of 3 + 2. Heb. צאת is a distinctive term and not a trite equivalent for מפלת "overthrow."

19. a. Heb. בהעלות "when (I) cause to rise" depends on the double duty suffix of בתתי earlier (Van Dijk, *Ezekiel's Prophecy* 40).

20. a. Heb. את is used in a pregnant sense (cf. Cooke 295).

20. b. The ptcp relates to the past (Van Dijk, *Ezekiel's Prophecy* 42; Tromp, *Primitive Conceptions* 68 note 213).

20. c. The usual form is ארץ תחתיות "depths of the earth"; in this inversion here and in 32:18, 24 ארץ itself has the sense underworld, which the genitive reinforces. However, Tromp (*Primitive Conceptions* 181-82) understands in terms of a separate region within Sheol, to which it certainly seems to refer in 32:18 (see *Comment* there).

20. d. Many MSS B Syr read בחרבות "in the ruins" for כחרבות "like the ruins."

20. e. Ehrlich's proposal (*Randglossen* 103) to repoint תשבי "you will be populated" as תֵּשְׁבִי and take it adverbially, "and you will (not) again . . . , "has proved popular (cf. Zimmerli 32; *BHS*). Tromp (*Primitive Conceptions* 68, n. 215) also repoints, but takes as independent, "you will (not) return." However, these expedients ignore the structural value of the stem ישב (see *Form/Structure/Setting*).

20. f. MT ונתתי צבי "nor will I put glory" yields little sense. LXX implies ותתיצבי "nor will you stand" (cf. Num 22:22 for the rendering), which is generally read. For the structural role of the term see *Form/Structure/Setting*. MT probably suffered mechanical assimilation to נתתי in v 4 and/or to ונתתיך in v 14.

21. a. LXX* does not represent ותבקשי ולא־תמצאי "and you will be sought and not found," and in view of the parallel unit endings at 27:36; 28:19 its shorter text is often preferred (cf. Zimmerli 32; *BHS*). However, the material is distinctive and its source, if a gloss, is difficult to ascertain. See *Form/Structure/Setting*.

21. b. For עוד לעולם "again for ever" an emendation עד־עולם "for ever" is often postulated (Cornill 344 et al.), in line with 27:36; 28:19. But עוד has its own structural symmetry: it is matched in vv 13, 14.

Form/Structure/Setting

Chap. 26 is the first of three redactional units that forecast the fall of Tyre, all of which end with a refrain, in 26:21; 27:36b and 28:19b. The message reception formula and initial address to the prophet in vv 1-2aα serve to introduce the unit. It is made up of four oracles, which fall into two pairs, as the linking conjunction כי "for" in vv 7 and 19, the final divine saying formulas of vv 14bβ and 21bβ, and the climactic לא . . . עוד "never again" of vv 13b, 14aγ and 21bα suggest. The first oracle in vv 2-6 is a three-part reasoned proof saying, in which a messenger formula introduces the second part and an affirmation formula closes it, while supplementary material in vv 5b-6 paves the way for the recognition formula. The second oracle of vv 7-14, introduced by כי "for" and a messenger formula, gives careful interpretation of the message of judgment in the first oracle. It concludes with an affirmation formula before its final messenger formula. The third oracle in vv 15-18, which opens with a messenger formula, functions as an implicit judgment oracle: it looks forward to a funeral lament over Tyre. The fourth oracle in vv 19-21, like the second, opens with כי "for" and the messenger formula, and closes with a divine saying formula. It is a judgment oracle that announces the sending of Tyre down to Sheol.

The rhetorical structuring of the initial oracle is more impressive than a first reading might suggest. There are a number of correspondences between the accusation and the ensuing announcement of punishment. The prepositional על "about, against" with Jerusalem as object is picked up in the double עליך "against you" and echoed in the double use of the verb עלה "go/bring up" (v 3). The prepositional term probably also counters אלי "to me" in v 2. The breaking of Jerusalem's doors turns into the destruction of Tyre's defenses (v 4a). The ending of Jerusalem's international influence (העמים "the peoples") is matched by

Tyre's international victimization (גוים "nations," vv 3, 5). The prospect of Tyre's fullness finds correspondence in its emptiness in vv 4b-5a and 5b. Finally, the destruction (החרבה) of Jerusalem is echoed in the wordplay of חרב "sword" at v 6.

The second oracle falls into two parts, vv 7-9 and 10-13: so suggests the resumption of "horses" and "cavalry" from v 7 in vv 10-11a. It is framed by a double inclusion, the divine word and the divine "I" in v 7a and vv 13-14. But its most obvious feature is the careful echoing of material from the first oracle. Thus הנני עליך "behold I am against you" (v 3) becomes הנני ... אל "behold I ... against" in v 7, while גוים רבים "many nations" becomes עם־רב "much people." A whole set of terms are repeated in turn: three near the beginning of the earlier oracle, in vv 8b-9a ("against you," "walls," "towers," vv 3-4aβ) and three at the end, in vv 12b and 14 ("rubble," "bare rock," "it will be an area for spreading nets," from vv 4aγ-5aα). Indeed, the first two terms, "against you" and "walls," are emphasized, the first by repetition within v 8b and the second by further repetition in vv 10b and 12aβ. Correspondingly, the two final components in the first oracle, "plunder" and the killing of daughters on the mainland "with the sword" (vv 5b, 6a), are given pride of place at the beginning and center of the second oracle (vv 8a, 12aα). Outside this scheme stands v 13, which by way of climax means to hark back to the derisive poem of v 2. The dependence of the complex second oracle on the first appears so marked that it is difficult to understand Wevers' contention (200) that vv 2-6 are secondary and based on vv 7-14.

The third oracle has been helpfully analyzed by Parunak in terms of an extended inclusion (*Bib* 62 [1981] 158). Three words at the outset are repeated at the end: מפלתך "your fall," האיים "the coastlands" and יחרדו/וחרדו "(and) they will tremble" in vv 15-16 and 18. A narrative of mourning rites dominates the first half of the oracle, in preparation for the lament of the second. Parunak has also defined the fourth oracle rhetorically, as a chiasmus (*Bib* 62 [1981] 158-59), although one of his terms, the stem נתן "give" in vv 19 and 20b, must be abandoned (see *Notes*). Three components, the negated stem ישב "inhabit," את־יורדי בור "those who have gone down to the Pit" and עולם (מ) "(from) of old," occur twice in an ABC/CBA pattern. They demarcate the two main parts of the oracle, vv 19-20aα and 20aβ–b, with inverted parallelism. It may be noted that there is also evidence of a scheme of consecutive parallelism: the stem חרב "ruin" and כ "like" in vv 19aβ and 20aβ. The second part poses its own contrast with בארץ תחתיות "in the land of the nether places" and בארץ חיים "in the land of the living": this parallel contrast explains the form of the first phrase. The fourth oracle has a conclusion, v 21, which, as well as supplying the refrain of the redactional unit, caps the middle component of the chiasmus with לעולם "forever."

Just as there is an organic relationship between the first two oracles, so there is between the last two, although it is not so rigidly structured. The relationship consists of repeated words and motifs and wordplays. The "famed city" turns into the "ruined city" (vv 17, 19) and the references to Tyre's "inhabitants" are replaced by one to "uninhabited" cities (vv 17, 19). The "fall" of vv 15, 18 is echoed in the failure to "stand" in the emended v 20b, while in vv 18 and 21 being "overwhelmed" (ונבהלו) at the "passing" (מצאתך) of Tyre finds echoes in its "terror" (בלהות) and not being "found" (תמצאי). V 21 has organic, if redactional, links with its present context, which counter attempts to prune it in line with the other refrains (see *Notes*).

There is also a network of links between the oracles. The most obvious ones are the references to killing (הרג) in the first three, which are capped by the descent to Sheol in the fourth, and the motif of descent that marks the second, third, and fourth. Two lesser ones are the covering sea in the first and fourth, and the shaking/quaking (רעש) of the second and third.

The historical setting of the oracles is a post-587 B.C. situation (v 2), and a relatively short time seems to lie between the fall of Jerusalem and the first oracle, while the explanatory oracle was presumably delivered a little later. Nebuchadnezzar's thirteen-year siege of Tyre mentioned by Josephus from an earlier source, perhaps Menander of Ephesus (*Ant.* 10.11.1; *Contra Ap.* 1.21), is generally dated 586-573 B.C. The second oracle still seems to look forward to its inception, rather than merely to its success. The third and fourth oracles appear to depend on other material, the third on the lament over Tyre in 27:28-36, and the fourth on the descent of Egypt to Sheol in 32:17-32. They must antedate the somewhat disappointing outcome of the siege on which Ezekiel commented in 571 B.C. (cf. 29:17-20). The presence of literary echoes by no means precludes that in the course of the long siege Ezekiel himself reaffirmed its eventual result in these oracles.

Comment

1-6 The Phoenician city-state of Tyre was situated on the Mediterranean coast some 100 miles northwest of Jerusalem. An island with mainland suburbs, it was renowned for its maritime trade. Tyre had taken part in the anti-Babylonian conference of western states organized by Zedekiah at Jerusalem in 594 B.C. The subsequent siege of Tyre undertaken by Nebuchadnezzar indicates that this powerful maritime state persisted in its desire for independence. Presumably it took no warning from Jerusalem's fall, convinced that in its natural fortress it had no need to fear Babylonian attacks. Rather, it derived selfish relish from the event. It is not clear what precise advantage is envisaged. It may be economic, the "doors" or gate of Jerusalem standing for a market, as the Targum paraphrased. However, whether Jerusalem's trade was so extensive (cf. Eichrodt 369) and whether any benefit would be transferred to Tyre are moot points. Accordingly the reference is generally taken as political. The gate of the city, where the elders sat, was the controlling center of its affairs, and it functions here as a political rallying point. Tyre expects a shift of power as new leader of the western states. In Yahweh's name the prophet dashes such hopes, countering its attitude with corresponding reprisals point by point (see *Form/Structure/Setting*). Tyre would become victim of a relentless sea of foes, at Yahweh's behest. The predicted reversal of its proud claims would bring proof of Yahweh's power. In principle it would also reveal him as a patron of his covenant people, their new ally after his previous enmity.

7-14 The second oracle in relation to the first is like 21:6-10 (EVV 1-5) over against 21:1-5 (20:45-49), in that it invests the details of the first oracle with a new clarity (see *Form/Structure/Setting*). Here the clarity consists in the identification of Nebuchadnezzar as the foreign aggressor and in the references to successful siege warfare (cf. 21:27[22] and *Comment*) as the tactics of aggression. The latter reflects standard military procedure in attacking a city: presumably there was little or no vocabulary for a naval bombardment. In 332 B.C. Alexander the Great conquered Tyre by building a causeway between the mainland and the island. The title "king of kings" is striking: politically it echoes Assyrian royal usage, while in terms of the first oracle it expresses his role as ruler of its "(many) nations" (vv 3, 5). The mention of a barrage of shields in v 8 refers to a siege tactic called by the Romans testudo or tortoise, whereby troops in close formation advanced under the cover of their raised shields (cf. Y. Yadin, *The Art of Warfare* 316, 420-21). The silencing of music in v 13 harks back to the poem of v 2: there may be a slight reminiscence of the language of Amos 5:23, although the quite different context makes the possibility doubtful. The forceful language of v 14aβ-b also reacts to v 2. It provides an emotion-laden response to Judean resentment of Tyre's statement and attitude.

15-18 In the first of a second pair of oracles that presuppose the earlier pair, Tyre's downfall is viewed from another aspect, that of a funeral lament put in the mouths of Tyre's maritime partners. It has the effect of sealing the city's doom: its fall is irrevocable. The prose report specifies the elements of the mourning ritual (cf. 24:16b-17 and *Comment*; and Lohfink, *VT* 12 [1962] 269-72). An unusual component of the description, which in fact pervades it, is a reaction of fear, which envelops the mourners like a garment (v 16). It is an awed reflection of the unexpected reversal of great Tyre's fortunes. In the light of the foregoing oracles it implicitly evokes the power of Yahweh. The reaction of fear is an aftershock following the divinely caused quake of v 10 (רעש, v 15). The lament is shot through with an appropriate maritime emphasis. True to its form, it begins with a typical exclamation (איך "how [distressing it is that]") and counterposes past fame and present fate. The redactional juxtaposition of two poems reacting to a city's fall (vv 2, 17-18) points up the absence of malicious joy in this instance: the speakers now have a sober intuition that a power greater than themselves has been at work in their midst (cf. 32:10).

19-21 The companion piece now makes explicit the truth that Yahweh will have been at work in the fall of Tyre. It points overtly and constantly to Yahweh's activity. In so doing it means to shed light on the previous oracle. If the rehearsal of mourning rites served to seal Tyre's doom, even more does this portrayal of a descent to Sheol in premature death. The crumbling of the war-ravaged island into the sea would be both fact and symbol. The sea was a powerful image of chaos and death (cf. Tromp, *Primitive Conceptions* 59-61). Tyre was to join the dead in Sheol, becoming a nonentity as they were, and to exchange the land of the living for the land of the nether places. The once virile city would leave behind an uninhabited ruin (vv 19a-20aγ). Fallen, it would not stand (v 20b, cf. vv 15, 18). The "never again" of v 21b echoes and intensifies the close of the first half of the overall unit (v 14). This sealing of Tyre's fate in irrevocable finality (cf. Jenni, *ZAW* 65 [1953] 14) is meant to assuage the passionate feelings of Ezekiel's fellow exiles.

Explanation

Chap. 26 follows the agenda of the previous chapter. It functions as a response to shattered nerves, to people who cry out in poignant despair and raise impotent fists against cruel taunts. The prophet brings Yahweh's response to the sobs of the exiles, coming to them where they are and ministering to their immediate needs. As the laments of the Psalms abundantly testify, God takes into account each stage of human disorientation, even the feelings of angry frustration, ignoble as they may seem to the detached observer. The stops and starts of these oracles and their evident linking in a redactional chain illustrate how often the prophet had to revert to the one theme with repeated assurance to hearts that needed to hear it over again. Only as Ezekiel's readers appreciate the emotion-ridden setting of these oracles, can they put into focus their vehemence as that of a pastoral message of comfort.

Yahweh did not retract the necessity of Jerusalem's fall, but it was a private matter between him and his people. If others reacted thereto, a seemly response was in terms of uneasy awe (cf. vv 15-18). There was no place for the raucous triumphalism that brought agony to the exiles' raw and sensitive spirits, adding insult to injury and exposing them to utter loss of face. Yahweh's retaliatory threat rings out from different perspectives. Divine self-revelation (vv 1-6) and divine activity (vv 19-21) would bring reprisal, using human means to bring it about (vv 7-14) and getting human voices to testify in awe to its implementation (vv 15-18). The God who has chosen what is weak in the world also shames the strong by evidence of his power, so that no human being may boast in his presence (1 Cor 1:27-29).

Tyre In Terms of the Titanic (27:1-36)

Bibliography

Borger, R. "Die Waffenträger des Königs Darius." *VT* 22 (1972) 385-98. **Brenner, A.** *Colour Terms in the Old Testament.* JSOTS 21. Sheffield: JSOT Press, 1982. **Dahood, M.** "Accadian-Ugaritic *dmt* in Ezekiel 27:32." *Bib* 45 (1964) 83-84. **Durlesser, J. A.** "The Sinking of the Ship of Tyre (Ezek 27): A Study of Rhetoric in Hebrew Allegory." *Proceedings, Eastern Great Lakes and Midwest Biblical Societies* 7 (1987) 79-93. **Elat, M.** "The Iron Export from Uzal (Ezekiel 27:19)." *VT* 33 (1983) 323-30. **Good, E. M.** "Ezekiel's Ship: Some Extended Metaphors in the Old Testament." *Semitics* 1 (1970) 79-103. **Harden, D.** *The Phoenicians.* Harmondsworth: Penguin, 1971. **Jahnow, H.** *Das hebräische Leichenlied im Rahmen der Völkerdichtung.* BZAW 36. Giessen: Töpelmann, 1923, 212-18. **Katzenstein, H. J.** *The History of Tyre.* Jerusalem: Schocken Institute, 1973. **Krantz, E. S.** *Des Schiffes Weg mitten im Meer.* ConB OT 19. Lund: Gleerup, 1982. **Krinetzki, G.** "Tiefenpsychologie im Dienste der alttestamentlichen Exegese. Zu Stil und Metaphorik von Ezechiel 27." *Tübinger Theologische Quartalschrift* 155 (1975) 132-43. **van Lerberghe, K.** "An Enigmatic Cylinder Seal Mentioning the Ušûm-Tree in the Royal Museum of Art and History, Brussels." M. Stol, *On Trees, Mountains and Millstones in the Ancient Near East.* Leiden: Ex Oriente Lux, 1979, 31-49. **Millard, A.** "Ezekiel 27:19: The Wine Trade of Damascus." *JSS* 7 (1962) 201-3. **Miller, P. D.** *Sin and Judgment in the Prophets.* SBLMS 27. Chico: Scholars Press, 1982. **Moriarty, F. L.** "The Lament over Tyre (Ez. 27)." *Greg* 46 (1965) 83-88. **Newsom, C. A.** "A Maker of Metaphors—Ezekiel's Oracles against Tyre." *Int* 38 (1984) 151-64. **Petrie, G.** "Metaphor and Learning." *Metaphor and Thought,* ed. A. Ortony. Cambridge: CUP, 1969, 438-61. **Rabin, C.** "Rice in the Bible." *JSS* 11 (1966) 2-9. **Smith, S.** "The Ship Tyre." *PEQ* 85 (1953) 97-110. **Soskice, J. M.** *Metaphor and Religious Language.* Oxford: OUP, 1987. **Stol, M.** "Hebrew *pannag.*" *On Trees, Mountains and Millstones in the Ancient Near East.* Leiden: Ex Oriente Lux, 1979, 68-71. **Zohary, M.** *Plants of the Bible.* Cambridge: CUP, 1982.

Translation

[1] *I received the following communication from Yahweh:* [2] *"You, human one, are to raise a lament over Tyre* [3] *and to tell Tyre, dweller* [a] *at the entrances* [b] *to the sea and international merchant traveling to many coasts: Here is a message from the Lord* [c] *Yahweh:*

O Tyre, you were called a ship [d]
perfect in beauty.
[4] *In the heart of the seas was your range* [a]:
your builders brought your beauty to perfection.
[5] *With junipers* [a] *from Senir they built for you*
every part of your pair of decks. [b]
A fir [c] *from Lebanon they took*
to make a mast for you. [d]
[6] *With oaks from Bashan*
they made your oars.
Your planking [a] *they made* [b]
with cypresses [c] *from the coasts of Cyprus.* [d]
[7] *Fine, embroidered* [a] *linen from Egypt*

was your sail,
serving as your ensign.[b]
Purple[c] *and puce*[d] *cloth from the coast of Elishah*
was your awning.
[8]*Sidon's and Arvad's elders*[a]
were your oarsmen.
Your experts, Tyre,[b] *were on board:*
they were your sailors.
[9]*Elders of Gebal*[a] *were on board*
as ship's carpenters.[b]
All the maritime ships and their sailors visited you to barter[c] *for your wares.*
[10]*Persia, Lud and Put*
served in your navy
as your marines.[a]
Hanging shield and helmet on you,
they invested you with splendor.
[11]*The men of Arvad and Cilicia*[a] *manned the walls around you; the Gammadites*[b] *were stationed in your turrets. Hanging their weapons*[c] *on the walls around you, they brought your beauty to perfection.*
[12]*Tarshish was your trader because of your*[a] *great wealth of every kind: for silver, iron, tin and lead they sold*[b] *your goods.*[c] [13]*Ionia, Tubal and Meshech were your merchants: for slaves and bronze articles they sold your wares.* [14]*From Beth-Togarmah for draft horses, war horses and mules they sold your goods.* [15]*The folk of Rhodes*[a] *were your merchants; many coasts were your trading agents.*[b] *Ivory tusks and ebony they brought as your payment.*[c] [16]*Edom*[a] *was your trader because of your many products: for garnets,*[b] *puce cloth, embroidered fabric, fine linen, black corals*[c] *and rubies*[d] *they sold your goods.* [17]*Judah and the territory of Israel were your merchants: for wheat of Minnith,*[a] *early figs (?),*[b] *honey, oil and storax*[c] *they sold your wares.* [18]*Damascus was your trader because of your many products and great wealth of every kind: for wine of Heshbon, wool of Zachar*[a] [19]*and casks of wine from Izal*[a] *they sold your goods. Wrought*[b] *iron, cassia and aromatic grass were delivered in return for your wares.* [20]*Dedan was your merchant in saddle cloths.*[a] [21]*Arabia and all the sheikhs of Kedar were your trading agents in lambs, rams and goats: these were the items they traded with you.* [22]*Merchants of Sheba, Asshur, Kilmad*[a] *and Raamah were your merchants: for the best of all types of perfumes, for precious stones of every kind and for gold they sold your goods.* [23]*Haran, Canneh and Eden*[a] [24]*were your merchants: for fine garments, purple clothes,*[a] *embroidered fabrics, cloth*[b] *of variegated material*[c] *and braided, strong ropes—for these items they were your merchants.*[d] [25]*The ships of Tarshish were your transporters for your wares.*[a]
So you were filled and heavily laden
in the heart of the seas.
[26]*Out to sea you were brought*
by your rowers.
An east wind wrecked you
in the heart of the seas.
[27]*Your wealth, your goods, your wares, your mariners and sailors, your ship's carpenters, the dealers in your wares, all the marines who were aboard, in fact all*[a] *your company*[b] *who were on board, sank into the heart of the seas at the time of your sinking.*
[28]*At the loud cries of your sailors*

the countryside[a] *quakes.*
[29]*From their ships disembark*
all the handlers of oars.[a]
All the sailors of the sea[b]
go ashore
[30]*and cry out*[a] *for you*
with bitter shouts.
They throw dust on their heads
and wallow[b] *in ashes.*
[31]*They shave off patches of their hair for you*
and tie sackcloth around themselves.
They weep for you with bitter emotions,
in bitter mourning.
[32]*They raise a lament for you in their dirge,*[a]
lamenting over you in these words:
'Who was like Tyre,
like the fortress[b] *in the middle of the sea?'*
[33]*By the unloading*[a] *of your goods from the seas you brought plenty to so many peoples.*
By your great wealth and your wares you enriched kings the world over.
[34]*Now you are wrecked*[a] *by*[b] *the seas,*
in the watery depth.
Your wares and all your company on board have sunk.
[35]*All who dwell at the coasts*
are appalled at your fate.
The hair of their kings stands on end,
their[a] *faces are downcast.*[b]
[36]*Among the peoples the traders*
whistle at you.
You have become a victim of terror
and will be no more for ever."

Notes

3. a. For K see GKC 90 l-n.

3. b. The Heb. lacks an article with the genitive and is pl. LXX Syr Vg have been regarded as implying a sg מבוא הים "entrance to the sea" which was corrupted via a ה/ח error and wrong division (Zimmerli 42). But the versions' rendering may be free and the reference to the island's two harbors, on the north and south sides. Moriarty, *Greg* 46 (1965) 86, followed by Van Dijk, *Ezekiel's Prophecy* 56, postulated a Phoenician fem sg form.

3. c. For the formulaic אדני "Lord" see the note on 20:3.

3. d. MT אמרת אני "you said 'I (am)'" is doubtful: reference to a ship is expected and easily obtained by repointing אֳנִי: For the sense of a single ship (usually אָנִיה) rather than fleet there are Ug. and El Amarna parallels (cf. Zimmerli, ibid.; Dahood, *Bib* 45 [1964] 83 n. 2). Then the verb is to be repointed as pass qal אָמַרְתְּ (Dahood, ibid., followed by Van Dijk, *Ezekiel's Prophecy* 56-57): contra Ehrlich, *Randglossen* 103, the noun can be fem.

4. a. Lit. "borders," here in the sense of range or distance attainable by a well-made vessel (Ehrlich, *Randglossen* 104). Then the reference is not to the city and it is unnecessary to emend in order to relate to a ship (cf. Zimmerli 43, *BHS* et al.). The phrase בלב ימים "in the heart of the seas" refers not literally to the water round the island but metaphorically to the mid ocean, as in v 25 in the light of v 26 (Cornill 344). Smith, *PEQ* 85 (1953) 102, also interpreted in terms of a ship, finding a reference to its hull as "(defending) limits."

5. a. A reference to *Juniperus excelsa*, which still grows in the area (Zohary, *Plants of the Bible*, 106-7).

5. b. The dual form לחתם is better taken as referring to a double deck than to the wooden sides: see Krantz, *Des Schiffes Weg* 85-91, who observes in support the sequence decks, masts and oars. An emendation to לחתיך "your decks" on the evidence of Tg (*BHS* following J. Olshausen et al.) is unnecessary after לך "for you" (Krantz, *Des Schiffes Weg* 76; Zimmerli 43).

5. c. A reference to *Abies cilicica* (Zimmerli, *Ezek 1* 361).

5. d. A desire for metrical rigidity has dictated the popular emendation עליוני "the tallest of (the oaks)," taken with v 6 (*BHS* et al., following Bertholet 95). Van Dijk, *Ezekiel's Prophecy* 62, notes the parallelism of "for you" with לך "for you" in v 5a (cf. Krantz, *Des Schiffes Weg*, ibid.).

6. a. Heb. קרש is uncertain: cf. the discussions in Zimmerli 43-44 and Krantz, *Des Schiffes Weg* 78-83. The latter's interpretation is followed here. One factor is the meaning of the term in the account of the tabernacle in Exod 26:15, etc., where M. Haran, *HUCA* 36 (1965) 192 note 2, has argued for "planks": cf. B. S. Childs, *Exodus* (Philadelphia: Westminster, 1974) 525.

6. b. MT adds שן "ivory," an exotic item even in this magnificent context. RSV "(pines) inlaid with ivory," following Tg, hardly represents MT (Ehrlich, *Randglossen* 104), which is generally taken as an erroneous dittograph of the preceding שו(ע) (cf. *BHS*). The chiasmus in v 6 (Cooke 308; Krantz, *Des Schiffes Weg* 77) supports the omission.

6. c. Tg presupposes (ב)תאשורים, rendering as in Isa 41:19; 60:13. The tree cannot be identified with certainty: it may be *Cupressus sempervirens horizontalis*. See the discussion in Krantz, *Des Schiffes Weg* 160-62, 175.

6. d. The pun in the English is accidental.

7. a. Heb (ב)רקמה represents a *beth* of accompaniment; cf. GKC 119n; Van Dijk, *Ezekiel's Prophecy* 65; Krantz, *Des Schiffes Weg* 128.

7. b. Heb. נס may refer to a distinctive sail serving for identification of the vessel: see the discussion in Krantz, *Des Schiffes Weg* 122-26.

7. c. Heb. תכלת refers to a cloth dyed with a blue purple range of hues: cf. A. Brenner, *Colour Terms* 146, 148.

7. d. Heb. ארגמן refers to red purple shades: see Brenner, *Colour Terms* 147-48.

8. a. MT ישבי "inhabitants" does not accord with the special groups in vv 8b-9. Van Dijk, *Ezekiel's Prophecy* 66, translates "kings," hardly an obvious rendering. LXX has a doublet that is often held to represent נשיאי "rulers" (*BHS* et al. following Cornill 347). Zimmerli (45), noting the graphical difficulty, proposes שרי "leaders." An even better suggestion might be שבי "elders" from Heb. שיב "be gray, old" (cf. Aram. שבי in this sense in Ezra 5:5; 6:7, 8, 14), which may be presupposed by LXX.

8. b. The vocative relates to the city, as in v 3, and בך "in you" to the ship (Ehrlich, *Randglossen* 104). There is no need to change the text to חכמי צמר "experts of Zemer" (Kraetzschmar 209 et al., including RSV). Moriarty, *Greg* 46 (1965) 86, has noted that wisdom is associated with Tyre in 28:5, 7, 17.

9. a. The second term in MT, וחכמיה "and her experts," violates the structure of the listing. It may originally have been חכמי "experts of," a variant of חכמיך "your experts" in v 8bα, which was put into the next line and suffered dittography.

9. b. Lit. "those who strengthened your damaged parts." A repointing as piel מחזקי here and in v 27 accords with the phrasing in 2 Kgs 12:6, etc; 22:5 (*BHK*, Zimmerli, ibid.), but the hiph too is used of repairing (cf. BDB 305a).

9. c. Cognates of the verb ערב mean "give" in S. Arab. and Syr.: cf. Driver in *Studies in OT Prophecy* (Edinburgh: T. and T. Clark, 1957) 64-65, who pointed as a causative piel לערב "to cause to give, obtain." Other suggestions are to relate it to a stem meaning "take in pledge" and so "exchange in trade" (BDB 786b; *HALAT* 830a) or to another meaning "enter" with the sense of "import" (Dahood, *Bib* 45 [1964] 83 n. 2, following D. H. Müller).

10. a. The line functions as a tricolon.

11. a. Heb. חילך probably accords with Phoen. חלך and Akk. *Ḥilakku* "Cilicia" (BDB 299b; 319a). Cornill (348) considered it too far away.

11. b. The geographical location of this group is unknown. The N. Syrian *Kumidi* have been suggested (cf. Katzenstein, *History* 156 note 149).

11. c. The specific meaning of שלם is uncertain: see Borger, *VT* 22 (1972) 394-95.

12. a. The Heb. lacks a pronoun, but Tyre's wealth is in view: cf. vv 16, 27, 33 (Ehrlich, *Randglossen*, 105).

12. b. Heb. נתן "give" in commercial contexts refers to selling (BDB 679a). The places have the function of middlemen or agents (Van Dijk, *Ezekiel's Prophecy* 76). The construction is stylistically varied in this passage, together with the terminology for goods: sometimes a *beth* of price is used of the

object given in exchange or of that received or even (vv 16, 18-19) of both.

12. c. The precise meaning of עזבון is uncertain. Is it what caravans leave behind to be sold (*HALAT* 764a)? See the discussion in Van Dijk, *Ezekiel's Prophecy* 75-76.

15. a. MT רדן "Dedan" belongs geographically in v 20, not here. LXX implies רדן "Rhodes," which accords with איים "coastlands" in v 15aβ and is generally read.

15. b. Lit. "trading syndicate of your (hand =) agency": cf. Van Dijk, *Ezekiel's Prophecy* 78, with reference to Albright, *JBL* 71 (1952) 249. For the collective form סחרה see T. N. D. Mettinger, *JSS* 16 (1971) 11.

15. c. Heb. אשכר "gift, tribute" so signifies in this commercial context. It is a loanword from Sumerian via Akk. (*HALAT* 92a).

16. a. MT ארם "Syria" conflicts with the reference to Damascus in v 18. LXX presupposes אדם, which it took as אָדָם "human beings," but properly signifies אֱדוֹם "Edom," as Syr interprets. For the error in MT see 16:57. M. Haran (*IEJ* 18 [1968] 204) urged that some of the products cited apply better to Aram than to Edom. J. Lindsay (*PEQ* 108 [1976] 30) countered that Haran ignored the transit nature of the trade, which probably consisted of re-exports.

16. b. See the discussions in Driver, *Bib* 35 (1954) 156; H. Quiring, *Sudhofs Archiv* 38 (1954) 199-200; *HALAT* 670a.

16. c. Jewish tradition so interpreted. J. S. Harris, *ALUOS* 41 (1962/63) 60-61, prefers "red corals."

16. d. Cf. *HALAT* 439b.

17. a. Rabin, *JSS* 11 (1966) 2-7, saw here an Indian loanword for rice (cf. *HALAT* 570a).

17. b. The meaning of פנג, a hapax legomenon, is not known. 2 MSS read פנג "early figs." M. Stol, *On Trees* 68-71, explained פנג as a healing plant, cognate with Gk. πάνακες, a medicinal plant.

17. c. For the identification, which is controversial, see Zohary, *Plants of the Bible* 198.

18. a. Heb. צחר is either a place name (cf. Driver, *Bib* 35 [1954] 156-57) or a color, perhaps "white" (cf. Brenner, *Colour Terms*, 116-18).

19. a. MT ודן ויון מאוזל means "and Dan and Javan (= Ionia, cf. v 13) that which is spun" (cf. Aram. אזל "spin"). LXX implies וְיַיִן מֵאֻזָל "and wine from . . ." and accordingly Millard, *JSS* 7 (1962) 201-3, assuming three י/ו errors, proposed וְדַנֵּי יַיִן מֵאִיזֹל "and casks of wine from Izal," linking דני with Akk., Aram., Syr. Arab. and Ug. cognates signifying "cask." Izal, between Haran and the Tigris, was famous for its wine (Kraetzschmar 211; Millard, *JSS* 7 [1962] 201). Then v 19a is to be construed with v 18b. Elat, *VT* 33 (1983) 324, has objected that v 19b would then lack mention of a commercial source of the wares it enumerates: elsewhere in the trading list places and wares are linked. In fact, Damascus (v 18) appears to be the continuing source. MT has its own problems. Elat himself has noted the difficulty of the initial *waw* "and (Dan)," unique in the list. Moreover, a further mention of יון "Ionia" (cf. v 13) is anomalous. Elat's defense of MT in v 19 ignores the fact that v 18, as it stands, is incomplete (cf. Zimmerli 49).

19. b. The *hapax legomenon* עשות is so rendered in LXX Syr Vg.

20. a. The *hapax legomenon* חפש may be a loanword related to Akk. ḥib/pšu "woolen fabric" (*HALAT* 328a).

22. a. MT adds after v 23a an apparent gloss introduced by a cue phrase (cf. P. Rost, *OLZ* 7 [1904] 482): "merchants of Sheba: Asshur, Kilmad," which seems to indicate that two names have fallen out of v 22, Asshur, referring to the Arabian tribe אשורים "Asshurites" (cf. Gen. 25:3) and the now unknown Kilmad, which Tg rendered as if כל-מדי "all Media." For the tolerable repetition of "merchants" see Zimmerli 50.

23. a. See the note on v 22. MT also adds רכלתך "your group of merchants," for which see the final note on v 24. The authentic material in v 23 connects with v 24.

24. a. For גלומי "garments" see BDB 166a.

24. b Heb. גנזי is of uncertain meaning: see *HALAT* 191b.

24. c. Heb. ברמים is a loanword from Akk. birmu, variegated cloth woven from differently colored threads (Brenner, *Colour Terms*, 149-50).

24. d. MT במרכלתך "in your place of trade (?)" introduces a new term—a *hapax legomenon*—to the passage. V 21 suggests a division into בם רכלתך "for them your merchant group," to which the term רכלתך in v 23b may originally have referred, as a marginal note.

25. a. For the appositional construction cf. GKC 128d (Zimmerli 51).

27. a. MT ובכל "and with all" seems to be an error for וכל "and all," for which there is much ancient support (see *BHS*). The *beth* is a case of mechanical assimilation to בך "in you" (Cornill 355).

27. b. Rather than "crew" (Van Dijk, *Ezekiel's Prophecy* 83-84): see the discussion in Krantz, *Des Schiffes Weg* 193.

28. a. Heb. מגרשות may refer to open land associated with Tyre, i.e., territory under its control on the mainland. Driver, *Bib* 35 (1954) 157, rendered "driven waves," which is etymologically possible but hardly suits the context (cf. 26:15).

29. a. Or "rudders": see the discussion in Krantz, *Des Schiffes Weg* 110-22.

29. b. MT prefixes מלחים "mariners," which breaks the chiastic structure of vv 28-30a (cf. Krantz, *Des Schiffes Weg* 181). It was probably a marginal note explaining that this crew of other "ships" were so called in v 9b (cf. *BHS*).

30. a. For the construction see GKC 119q.

30. b. Or "sprinkle themselves (with)," as Driver, *Bib* 35 (1954) 157-58, argued (cf. Cooke 312).

32. a. Heb. בניהם is commonly regarded as an abbreviation for בנהיהם "in their lament" (= Vg; cf. GKC 23k). A pointing בְּנֵיהֶם "their sons," although it has ancient attestation (see *BHS*) makes little sense. The supposition of a gloss (Cornill 356) would get rid of the awkward and contextually redundant word, but no cogent explanation for such a gloss has been offered. Does בְּנַהֲם "in groaning" underlie MT? Cf. 24:23 and Ps 38:9(8).

32. b. For the rendering see Dahood, *Bib* 45 (1964) 83-84, who compared Akk. *dimtu* and Ug. *dmt* "tower, fortress." For less likely options see Zimmerli 52. A reading נדמה, often postulated for כדמה either in the sense "was likened" or "was destroyed," seems to have ancient support (cf. *BHS*), but is unlikely to be original. It was probably an attempt to make sense of an unrecognized word. The former alternative labors under the difficulty that the verb is never construed with כ "like," and the latter misunderstands the role of the verse, which praises the past glory of Tyre (cf. its elaboration in v 33 and the parallel at the start of a lament in 19:2).

33. a. Heb. יצא "go out" appears to refer here not to exporting (Van Dijk, *Ezekiel's Prophecy* 86) but to the unloading (NEB) of goods from the vessels.

34. a. MT עת נשברת "(at) the time of your being broken" (cf. GKC 116g note 1) is generally repointed עַתָּ (ה) נִשְׁבַּרְתְּ "now you are broken," with strong versional support (see *BHS*).

34. b. The preposition is instrumental (Driver, *Bib* 35 [1954] 158, with reference to Gen 9:11).

35. a. For the lack of suffix with parts of the body see the list of references in Van Dijk, *Ezekiel's Prophecy* 91.

35. b. Heb. רעם usually refers to (the sound of) thunder. KB 901a relates it to a separate stem "be disconcerted," cognate with Arab. *raghama* "be abased, humbled" here and in 1 Sam 1:6. LXX Syr imply ודמעו "and wept," but this would require "eyes" as subj (Zimmerli 53).

Form/Structure/Setting

Chap. 27 exhibits form-critical diversity in striking variance with its straightforward self-designation as a lament in v 2. On the other hand, in its present shape it bears clear marks of rhetorical unity, of which it is better to take note before discussing the diversity. The single message reception formula in v 1 brackets the contents of the chapter as an overall unit. V 36b is a refrain already encountered in 26:21 and to be met again in 28:19b: it labels chap. 27 as the second in a series of three explicit or implicit forecasts of disaster for Tyre. An inclusion for the unit is provided by רכלת העמים "merchant to the peoples" in v 3 and סחרים בעמים "traders among the peoples" in v 36; another is איים (רבים) "(many) coasts" in vv 3 and 35, which is echoed in v 15. From a rhetorical perspective the chapter falls into four sections. Vv 3-11, which describe the island-city of Tyre in terms of an ocean-going ship, are marked by the inclusion כללו יפיך "they perfected your beauty" in vv 4 and 11 (Parunak, *Structural Studies* 369-70; cf. כלילת יפי "perfect in beauty," v 3b). Vv 12-25a, which seem to describe the trading city's articles of commerce in terms of the ship's cargo (cf. v 25b), are framed at beginning and end by another inclusion, a double reference to Tarshish (Parunak, *Structural Studies* 370). Vv 25b-32a and vv 32b-36 are two parallel sections, which both portray a reversal from riches to ruin in terms of shipwreck and the shocked reactions of others to the catastrophe (see *Comment*). The parallel movement of the last two sections from past glory to destruction and then to present lament have a part to play within the lament of the whole chapter. Vv 3-11 and 12-25a are descriptions of past glory, which the final sections each resume before moving on to the grim sequel.

It is evident, however, that the present unit has been enlarged by elements which are both redactionally intrusive and formally diverse. Criteria for determining the primary material are (a) poetry rather than prose, (b) description of Tyre as a ship rather than as a city, and (c) the absence of mention of trading goods. A criterion of meter adopted by Zimmerli (64) and others is hardly valid (cf. Krantz, *Des Schiffes Weg* 29 note 14). The third criterion derives its force from the fact that vv 12-25a, which are in prose and relate to the city of Tyre, supply a catalog of commercial items and their places of origin. With the aid of these criteria a basic poetic composition can be isolated: vv 3-9a, 10, 25b, 26, 28-32, 34a, 35a, 36a (cf. substantially Krantz, *Des Schiffes Weg* 27-31; for a strong defense of v 25b, against Zimmerli 54-55, see P. D. Miller, *Sin and Judgment* 70 note 13). It functions as a lament (v 2, cf. v 32) and in keeping with that genre moves from past glory to present disaster. It does so in a double representation in which a long version flows into a much briefer one: vv 3b-9a, 10, 25b / 26, 28-32a and vv 32b / 34a, 35, 36a. There is a rhetorical and ironical fusing of the shift from prosperity to disaster in the repetition of בלב ימים "in the heart of the seas" at vv 4, 25b, 26b and in the alteration of בתוך הים "in the midst of the sea" to במעמקי מים "in the depths of the waters" (vv 32b, 34a). In the shorter version the accent shifts from splendor to humiliation, and the tone changes from sympathetic lament to horror that distances itself from the victim. "The lament genre . . . becomes an important factor in the creating of a rhetorical relationship between prophet and audience. [Its] limping . . . metre would have drummed into the minds of the hearers the belief that the subject of the oracle was doomed" (Durlesser, *Proceedings* 7 [1987] 80).

The intent behind the added material is both to enhance the reversal and to provide historical realism. The urban defense system of v 11 (after v 10) and the commercial catalog of vv 12-25a (before the implicit reference to cargo in v 25b) fulfill the latter purpose. Yet in both passages there is a concern for rhetorical style: v 11 with its reference to perfection rounds off a new sub-unit (vv 3b or 4-11) and so does v 25a with its mention of Tarshish. A further role of v 25a is to enhance the theme of reversal by anticipating the (negative) reference to ships in v 29; so does v 9b. Other verses that have this function are v 27, which echoes the terms used for crew and cargo in vv 8-10 and 12-22 respectively and is locked into its context by the repetition of בלב ימים "in the heart of the seas" from v 26; v 33, which aesthetically echoes in a positive context the sinister terms מים "from the waters" (v 34) and מלכיהם "their kings" (v 35); and v 34b, which briefly reiterates terms used in v 27 to accentuate the loss of former assets. These additions then are by no means crude and insensitive, but with a fresh display of stylistic skill seek to enhance the contrast of past prosperity and present adversity. The aspect of realism whereby the city takes the place of the ship seems to have been inspired by elements within the poem itself at vv 3b and 8bα (see *Notes*).

The effect of these expansions is to change the ABAB structure of the poem to a longer A A B B one, a composition of two parts, the first of which has a double celebration of the glory of Tyre (vv 4-11, 12-25a) and the second a double declaration of a fall from glory to disaster (vv 25b-32a, 32b-36). Greater weight to the glory of Tyre is given by the addition of the block of material in vv 12-25a. It does justice to a concern implied but not exploited by the poem, the commercial achievements of Tyre. It is generally and plausibly regarded as the writing up of an independent list of trading products and places. Its most dominant vocabulary, relating to traders, the stems רכל, which occurs some nine times, and סחר, which appears six times, is presumably derived from the introduction to the poem (v 3) and from the poem itself (v 36a); so too is the frequent המה ("these") formulation (cf. vv 8b, 10b). There is thus a concern to integrate the new material into its older context. There is also an attempt to make the list more readable by varying terms for products (עזבון "goods"; מערב "wares"), by mixing nominal and verbal sentences and by varying verbal constructions. The repetition of מרב כל־הון "because of great wealth of every kind" in vv 12, 18 may indicate a division into nearly equal halves, vv 12-17 and 18-24.

The chronological setting of the poem is within the period of the Babylonian siege of Tyre. As for the redactional insertion of the prose list and the terminologically related prose additions, the basic document obviously describes Tyre in its heyday, while v 17 suggests that it was written between 721 and 587 B.C.

Comment

1-3bα The divine command to utter a funeral dirge over Tyre accords well with the content of the chapter. However, the poem and the accompanying expansions are rigorously human in their perspective: theology is conspicuous by its sheer absence. The importance of the introduction is that it gives a divine orientation to the fall of the great city-state of Tyre. This was to be no mere human phenomenon whose repercussions would ripple through the consciousness of Tyre's neighbors and partners. The fate of Tyre was divinely ordained. The lament form essentially looks back to past glory from the perspective of present disaster. Here the usage is typically prophetic, serving the function of a prophetic announcement of doom by speaking as if that doom had already occurred. Tyre's present position of affluence as supplier of goods to the world around (v 3a), secure as it seemed, was destined not to last. Tyre had two harbors, a natural one on the north side of the island and an artificial one on the south (Katzenstein, *History* 11, 14, 154). From them its merchant ships traveled the Mediterranean.

3bβ-11 In a rhetorical address to Tyre the island city is described in terms of a magnificent ship. The metaphor appears to be regarded as a standard one, here re-used. In this case, however, the description, and by implication its magnificence, are set in the past in a sinister fashion (cf. Lam 2:15). The metaphor is a natural one in view of Tyre's island situation and the greatness it derived from maritime trading. The deeper significance of the metaphor will be revealed later in the chapter. After the introductory line of v 3bβγ, the metaphor is developed in vv 4-7 in terms of its construction and in vv 8-10 in terms of its crew. The initial phrase "in the heart of the seas" is to have a key structural role; here it refers to an ocean-going ship, superbly constructed for this task. Adjacent territories had yielded their best resources, to ensure the quality of the vessel that was to brave the seas. For each aspect of the ship the right lumber was selected, for the decking, mast, oars and sides. Only the best of cloth was chosen for sail and awning. Behind the metaphor lies the reality of Tyre's wealth as the result of trading with other states (cf. Newsom, *Int* 38 [1984] 156).

Likewise, the description of the crew expresses Tyre's political supremacy that came on the heels of success in trade (Newsom, ibid.). Sidon, a little higher up the coast, was to come to dominance after the completion of Nebuchadnezzar's siege (Harden, *The Phoenicians* 47), but till then it functioned as Tyre's subordinate, putting its best personnel at the disposal of Tyre. Other Phoenician coastal cities, Arvad and Gebal (or Byblos), were as eager as Tyre itself to use their manpower in Tyre's interests. The redactional v 9b seeks to explain the metaphor in terms of Tyre's role as a port for commercial ships from elsewhere, and finds a literal meaning in the reference to a maritime crew. It also wants to anticipate the reference to other ships in the description of the reversal of Tyre's fortunes at v 29, and so eventually to highlight that reversal. The military references in v 10 function in the metaphor as allusions to marines posted on board the merchant ship in case of piracy. Tyre's warships typically had a row of round shields hung along their sides (cf. *ANEP*, fig. 106), and conceivably a merchant ship would have done the same to deter pirates. The ethnic references in v 10 are not clear. Put seems to refer to Libyans (cf. *IDB*, vol. 3, 971). Lud is generally related to the Lydians, but conceivably may refer to an ethnic group in N. Africa (cf. Gen 10:13; Jer 46:9). Heb. פֿרס is most naturally to be taken as Persia (cf. Katzenstein, *History* 156 n. 146). Hence the far-flung sources of Tyre's mercenaries seem to be in view, from the east, west and south (cf. Keil 390; Cooke 300). Not unreasonably v 11 interprets in terms of Tyre's mercenary troops. Its walls and turrets are portrayed in Assyrian depictions (see, e.g., *ANEP*, fig. 356). The redactor sensitively rounds off the account of Tyre's glory by the stylistic device of inclusion *(see Form/Structure/Setting)*.

12-25a Between the description of the ship's construction and crew and the reference to its setting sail fully laden in v 25b has been inserted a bridging account of its cargo. For this purpose an extant commercial catalog of trading commodities and their sources has evidently been used. It has been written up into a prose account of Tyre's trade relations with other parts of the world. In this context it functions virtually as a cargo list, although strictly the trading city of Tyre is in view rather than the metaphorical ship. Again an eye for the aesthetic is evident in the inclusion referring to Tarshish, which was most probably in Spain and was renowned in ancient times as a source of metals. The material seems to be organized according to geographical groups (Simons, *GTTOT* 456-57, followed by Zimmerli 71 and Eichrodt 387-88): Mediterranean areas and Asia Minor, vv 12-15; Palestinian regions from south to north, vv 16-17; Syria, vv 18-19; Arabia, vv 20-22; and Mesopotamia, vv 23-24.

V 13 refers to the western (Ionia) and eastern ends of Asia Minor, and v 14 to Armenia according to Hittite and Assyrian parallel sources (cf. Zimmerli 66). Rhodes in v 15 (see *Notes*) points to an African source for the ivory and ebony rather than an Indian one implied by MT (cf. van Lerberghe, *On Trees* 44-45). The reference to merchants and many coasts picks up the introduction (v 3), and is eventually to be echoed in the anticlimax of v 35. The reference to Judah and Israel in this cosmopolitan list is intriguing. The existence of the monarchical state of Judah seems to be implied, while that of Israel was evidently no more, and only its territory is cited. Minnith may be the transjordanian place of Judg 11:33, which would be suitable in the context. Wheat, oil and honey were traditional Palestinian products (cf. Deut 8:8; Jer 41:8). The former reference would support an emendation of the unknown פנג in terms of figs (see *Notes*).

The second half of the list begins impressively with Damascus, the great center of caravan trade. Assyrian records mention in lists of regional wines Helbon to the north of Damascus and Izal in N.E. Syria. Vv 21-22 refer to various Arabian groups, and v 23 to cities in Mesopotamia. The list's varied range of goods and places presents an intricate web of trade relations throughout the ancient world, at the center of which sat Tyre, powerful and wealthy. This prose supplement has been artistically concluded in v 25a with a flashback to its opening reference to Tarshish. Here the reference to ships, like that in v 9b, paves the way for the reversal of v 29.

25b-32a The poem resumes, its implicit reference to cargo having been explained to the reader. Now, however, its glory, after a short two-line statement, is superseded by a report of the shipwreck. The key phrase "in the heart of the seas," as in v 4, refers to the mid-ocean in which the ship of Tyre proudly sails—and suffers shipwreck. "She who lived by the sea will fall by or into the sea. The means of her pride becomes the means of her destruction" (Miller, *Sin and Judgment* 72). The correlation is a dynamic dramatic expression of reversal. The supplement in v 27 reinforces the reversal by repeating the rich language of crew (vv 8-10) and cargo (vv 12-22) in a grim context of sinking, and by its own echo of the key phrase.

In v 28 the poem itself echoes previous terminology in "your sailors," used in a positive context at v 8. The neat chiastic grouping of four lines, vv 28-30 (Zimmerli 55, Krantz, *Des Schiffes Weg* 181) merges the loud cries of drowning men with those of their groaning colleagues from other ships. The bitterness of the latter cries is echoed in v 31 near the end of a listing of mourning rites, which culminates in a dirge. This final dirge is set within the larger dirge of the chapter and encapsulates its message.

32b-36 The content of the dirge, supplied in vv 32b-34, typically moves from past fortune to present fate. It has been sensitively expanded at two points, to enhance the reversal: v 33, with its echo of terms from the trading list and its anticipation of vv 35-36a ("kings," "peoples"), and v 34b with its resumption of terms relating to crew and cargo. More importantly the supplements develop the parallelism between vv 25b-32a and 32b-35—already present in v 34a ("wrecked," as in v 26)—by echoing the language of v 27 in v 33 ("your great wealth and your wares") and v 34b (passim). Furthermore, the poem's own correlation of fortune and failure, "in the heart of the seas," is supplemented by a new and similar one. Heb. מימים "from the seas" in v 33 functions as a foil to the sinister use of the term in v 34. In vv 35-36a the reaction of others involved in Tyre's enterprises, now stripped of metaphor and identified in plain terms, is no longer one of ritual mourning but is heightened to shock and horror. It serves as a commentary on the certainty and finality of Tyre's coming doom, as the refrain of v 36b explains.

Explanation

Chap. 27 is a brilliant exercise in communication. Tyre, queen of the sea with her merchant and naval fleets, and center of an advanced economic, political and artistic culture, was obviously there to stay. Its fall to the Babylonians was unthinkable. Ezekiel challenges this assumption by recourse to a type of lateral thinking, the use of analogy, in this case a metaphor. Metaphor can function as a pedagogical tool, as when the scientific educator describes the atom as a miniature solar system. It "can provide a rational bridge from the known to the radically unknown, to a changed context of understanding" by providing a new framework of reference (G. Petrie, *Metaphor and Thought* 440-441). By speaking of one thing in terms of another new horizons may be opened up. A "strong metaphor . . . suggests new categories of interpretation and hypothesizes new entities, states of affairs and causal relations" (Soskice, *Metaphor and Religious Language* 62). The initial material about the construction and crew of this magnificent ship is meant to prepare for the real point: Tyre is the Titanic, doomed to shipwreck. The poem's sudden switch to the motif of shipwreck in vv 25b-26 is eloquent evidence of this intent. The ship metaphor superimposes the powerful negative notion of shipwreck, especially for those like Ezekiel's audience who were landlubbers, having little to do with the sea. A new, emotive factor is introduced, which is able to dislodge the powerful positive images that Tyre suggested. From this perspective its glory only makes its fall heavier and more ignominious. A sense of doom is reinforced by clothing the poem in the form of a funeral lament.

The redactor seeks to provide an interpretation of the poem's metaphor. Writing in prose but by no means prosaic, he sensitively exploits the notion of reversal, while anchoring the metaphor in historical realities. He also provides literary continuity and theological depth for the poem. The poem itself does not theologize: it exercises restraint in developing a metaphor within its own dynamic boundaries (cf. Good, *Semitics* 1 [1970] 89). Yet, as a prophetic dirge, it obviously carries a message in keeping with Ezekiel's overall ministry at this period. The redactional refrain of v 36b serves to remind the reader that the chapter belongs with chaps. 26 and 28 and so has associations of sin and overweening pride, about which the poem is silent. Moreover, the redactor's word "fall" or "sink" (נפל, vv 27, 34) is deliberately reminiscent of 26:15, 18, in a context of lament over divine judgment. In such ways the role of the poem in Ezekiel's prophetic ministry could be made explicit. Miller (*Sin and Judgment* 72) has also noted the greater impact the literary contextualizing of chap. 27 provides: in chap. 26 the judgment of God is described consistently in terms of the sea and the waters, while in chap. 28 the key phrase בלב ימים "in the heart of the sea," as in chap. 27, correlates fortune with fate in the context of a judgment oracle (28:2, 8). The effect is to give chap. 27 a stronger, more explicit role as a judgment oracle.

Yahweh's purposes on earth were to be worked out inexorably, and not even Tyre could stand in his way. In opposing Babylon, Tyre stood against Yahweh, and so could not stand. With the certainty of prophetic revelation, the dirge form proclaims its inevitable doom. How are the mighty fallen! Inspired by this chapter, John the Seer was later to proclaim the fall of Rome, "who is seated upon many waters" (Rev 17:1), and the sure demise of its commerce-based empire. Human power, invincible as it seems in any given culture, meets its match in the Lord of history.

Tyre's Pretensions Shattered and Paradise Lost
(28:1-19)

Bibliography

Bogaert, P.-M. "Montaigne sainte, jardin d'Eden et sanctuaire (hiérosolymitain) dans un oracle d'Ezéchiel contre le prince de Tyre (Ez. 28:11-19)." *Homo Religiosus* 9 (1983) 131-53. **Dahood, M.** "Ugaritic Lexicography." *Mélanges E. Tisserant.* Citto del Vaticano: Biblioteca Apostolica Vaticana, vol. 1, 1964, 81-104. **Day, J.** "The Daniel of Ugarit and Ezekiel and the Hero of the Book of Daniel." *VT* 30 (1980) 174-84. **Garber, P. L., and Funk, R. W.** "Jewels." *IDB* vol. 2, 898a-905b. **Gowan, D. E.** *When Man Becomes God.* Pittsburgh: Pickwick Press, 1975. **Habel, N. C.** "Ezekiel 28 and the Fall of the First Man." *Concordia Theological Monthly* 38 (1967) 516-24. **Harris, J. S.** "An Introduction to the Study of Personal Ornaments, of Precious, Semi-precious and Imitation Stones Used throughout Biblical History." *ALUOS* 41 (1962/63) 49-83. **Hossfeld, F.-L.** *Untersuchungen zu Komposition und Theologie des Ezechielbuches.* FzB 20. Würzburg: Echter Verlag, 1977, 153-83. **Jahnow, H.** *Das Hebräische Leichenlied im Rahmen der Völkerdichtung.* BZAW 36. Giessen: Töpelmann, 1923. **Loretz, O.** "Der Sturz des Fürsten von Tyrus (Ez. 28:1-19)." *UF* 8 (1976) 455-58. **May, H.** "The King in the Garden of Eden. A Study of Ezekiel 28:12-19." *Israel's Prophetic Heritage.* Eds. B. W. Anderson and W. Harrelson. New York: Harper and Row, 1962, 166-76. **McKenzie, J. L.** "Mythological Allusions in Ezekiel 28:12-28." *JBL* 75 (1956) 322-27. **Quiring, H.** "Die Edelsteine im Amtsschild des jüdischen Hohenpriesters und die Herkunft ihrer Namen." *Sudhofs Archiv für Geschichte der Medizin und die Naturwissenschaften* 38 (1954) 193-213. **Strom, M. R.** "An Old Testament Background to Acts 12:20-23." *NTS* 32 (1986) 289-92. **de Vaux, R.** "Les chérubins et l'arche d'alliance. Les sphinx gardiens et les trônes divins dans l'ancien Orient." *Mélanges de l'Université Saint Joseph* 37 (1960/61) 93-124. **Widengren, G.** *The Ascension of the Apostle and the Heavenly Book.* UUÅ 1950. Uppsala: A. B. Lundequistka Bokhandeln, 1950. **Williams, A. J.** "The Mythological Background of Ezekiel 28:12-19?" *BTB* 6 (1976) 49-61. **Yaron, K.** "The Dirge over the King of Tyre." *ASTI* 3 (1964) 28-57.

Translation

[1]*I received the following communication from Yahweh:* [2] *"Human one, tell the ruler of Tyre that the message of the Lord[a] Yahweh is as follows: Inasmuch as you have displayed a proud attitude, supposing yourself to be a god[b] and to sit on a divine throne there in the middle of the sea, although you are really a human being rather than a god, and yet you have adopted[c] godlike pretensions—*[3]*obviously you are wiser than Daniel[a] and no mystery[b] is too obscure[c] for you!* [4]*You have used your wisdom and insight to get yourself wealth and to acquire silver and gold for your coffers,* [5]*You have used your considerable wisdom to augment your wealth through trading, and your wealth has given you a proud attitude.* [6]*That is why the message of the Lord Yahweh is as follows: Inasmuch as you have adopted godlike pretensions,* [7]*for that reason I intend to make you the victim of aliens, the most brutal nation in the world.[a] They will draw their swords against the beauty created by your wisdom[b] and they will sully your splendor.* [8]*They will send you down to the Pit and you will die a violent death,[a] there in the middle of the sea.* [9]*When your*

killers[a] *confront you, will you persist in your claim to be a god? In the clutches of those who wound you,*[b] *you will be a human being rather than a god.* [10]*You will die the death of the uncircumcised at the hands of aliens. I have given my word hereto. So runs the message of the Lord Yahweh.*"

[11]*I received the following communication from Yahweh:* [12]*"Human one, raise a dirge over the king of Tyre, informing him that the message of the Lord Yahweh is as follows: You were once a seal*[a] *of intricate design,*[b] *full of wisdom,*[c] *perfect in beauty.* [13]*You used to live in Eden, God's garden. You wore*[a] *precious stones of every kind—sard, topaz, moonstone(?), gold topaz, carnelian, jasper, lapis lazuli, garnet and emerald*[b]—*and the mounts and settings*[c] *you wore*[d] *were made of gold*[e] *and had been fashioned* [f] *on the day you were created.* [14]*With*[a] *a winged(?)*[b] *guardian*[c] *cherub I set you.*[d] *On God's sacred*[e] *mountain you lived, and amidst blazing gems you walked about.* [15]*Your conduct was blameless from the day you were created until wrongdoing was discovered in you.* [16]*Your extensive trading filled*[a] *your habitat*[b] *with violence and you committed sin. So I removed you in your sullied state from*[c] *the divine mountain, and the guardian*[d] *cherub banished you*[e] *from the habitat of the blazing gems.* [17]*Your beauty gave you a proud attitude. With your splendor in mind, you used your wisdom perversely. So I threw you down to the ground and exposed you to the gloating gaze of other kings.* [18]*Your serious wrongdoing*[a] *involved in your wicked trading led you to sully your sacred places. So I made fire issue from your habitat and it consumed you. I turned you into ashes before the gaze of all who saw you.* [19]*All who know you among the peoples are appalled at you. You have become a victim of terror and will be no more for ever.*"

Notes

2. a. For the formulaic אדני "Lord" here and in vv 6, 10, 12 see the note on 20:3.

2. b. Not "El": see Zimmerli 77-78.

2. c. For the syntax of v 2bβ see Hossfeld, *Untersuchungen* 158.

3. a. K lacks the vowel letter supplied by Q. The Semitic pronunciation was evidently Daniel: cf. Day, *VT* 30 (1980) 181 note 18, with reference to E. Lipinski.

3. b. LXX ἢ σοφοί presupposes a misreading of כל־סתום "every mystery" not as חכמי "wise" (BHS and most) but as if derived from the Aram. stem סכל "be wise."

3. c. The suffix is evidently datival (cf. GKC 117x). The form and meaning of the verb are uncertain. There appear to be two stems עמם meaning "be compared with" (31:8; cf. KB 715b) and "cover, darken" (Lam 4:1; cf. *HALAT* 800b, 801a). Driver, *Bib* 19 (1938) 177, followed the latter lexicographical option, but, deducing from cognate use of the stem that the verb is intransitive, changed slightly to a poel sg עוֹמֵמָךְ (= NEB [*Brockington*, Hebrew Text 229] "is too dark for you").

7. a. For the superlative expression see GKC 133k.

7. b. The expression is an unusual one. Joüon, *Bib* 10 (1929) 307, proposed פרי "fruit (of your wisdom)" for יפי "beauty" or that יפי is a false anticipation of יפעתך "your splendor" later. The phrase presumably means "the beautiful buildings and artifacts created by your wise skills," which is culturally appropriate.

8. a. Lit. "die the death of the slain." See *Comment.*

9. a. MT הרנך is defectively written for הרגיך "your killers," for which there is much Heb. and versional evidence (cf. *BHS*).

9. b. MT מחללך "those who profane you" is taken by most as a mispointing for מחלליך "those who wound you" (= MS[g] Syr Vg Tg), influenced by the verb in v 7.

12. a. MT חוֹתֵם "sealing, sealer" (= "completing, completer"? cf. NEB "you set the seal on perfection," following Driver, *Bib* 35 [1954] 159) is generally revocalized with the ancient versions and a Heb. variant tradition to חוֹתָם "seal." Ehrlich (*Randglossen* 107), comparing Arab. cognate terms, took MT as a byform of חוֹתָם "seal."

12. b. The ancient variant תבנית "construction, pattern" (cf. *BHS*) is less likely. Driver, *Bib* 35 (1954) 158-59, helpfully compared with Akk. taknû, taknîtu "careful preparation, correctness."

12. c. LXX omitted, perhaps as inappropriate for a seal. See *Comment.*

13. a. Either the jewels were worn or they feature in the topography. The echo of jewels worn by the high priest suggests the former. In that case מְסֻכָתֶךָ means "your covering" in the sense of a garment (= Vg *operimentum* "covering"; LXX "you bound on"; Syr "you girded yourself with"); otherwise it signifies a protective structure or enclosure (cf. Σ).

13. b. The identification of the stones is by no means certain or generally agreed, apart from the first, second, sixth, seventh and ninth terms. In the rest of the cases the detailed researches of Quiring, *Sudhofs Archiv* 38 (1954) 193-213, have been followed. Other treatments have been undertaken by Harris, *ALUOS* 4 (1962/63) 49-83, and by Garber and Funk, *IDB*, vol. 2, 900a-903b.

13. c. These two nouns are of uncertain meaning. A possibility for the second is metal cavities or setting for jewels: cf. נקב "bore out" and Vg *foramina* "holes" (cf. BDB 666a; Driver *JTS* 45 [1944] 14). If so, the earlier term has a similar sense (Cornill 360).

13. d. Heb. בָּךְ is literally "in/on/with you." Some delete as a dittograph of בְּיָד (נב) (cf. BHS).

13. e. Heb. וְזָהָב "and gold" is to be taken with v 13b (BHS)·

13. f. LXX* Syr lack כּוֹנָנוּ "they had been prepared," but it may function as a stylistic echo of תְכוּנַת "intricate design" in v 12.

14. a. MT has אַתְּ . . . וּנְתַתִּיךָ "you (were) . . . and I put you." If v 14a were an unpointed text, an interpretation - אֵת "with," as LXX Syr took it, would be a natural one. In the imagery the king represents the first man (cf. the stem ברא "create" used in vv 13, 15) in a tradition in which he was differentiated from the cherub, as in Gen 2-3. In ancient Near Eastern culture the cherub also has a subservient role. The form אַתְּ, usually fem, is rare for the masc sg pronoun (Num 11:15; Deut 5:24; cf. GKC 32g). MT subsequently prefixed the conjunction to the verb, which should be taken with v 14a, as in LXX Syr. The construction of clauses in v 14, in which the verb is put last in each case, favors this alignment (Yaron, ASTI 3 [1964] 31).

14. b. Heb. מִמְשַׁח is textually and semantically problematic. It is lacking in LXX*. It may mean "anointing" (משח "anoint"; thus Θ Syr), in which case Wevers' suggestion (217) that it is a gloss on הַסּוֹכֵךְ, relating it to סוּךְ "anoint," is worth considering. Aram. משׁח "measure, extend" underlies Σ Vg: this expedient yields a meaning "full-sized, colossal," like the *Akk. kurubu* guarding entrances to Mesopotamian palaces (Driver, JTS 41 [1940] 169-70) or "with outstretched wings" (Dahood, *Mélanges E. Tisserant*, vol. 1, 95). The last interpretation accords with the dominant ancient Near Eastern tradition of winged sphinxes (cf. de Vaux, *Mélanges de l'Université Saint Joseph* 3 [1960/61] 98-113).

14. c. Heb. הַסּוֹכֵךְ is also lacking in LXX*, but its probable corrupted representation in v 16 may well indicate that it was once represented here. The lack of the article with the accompanying noun seems almost to take it as a name. The verb, meaning "cover," is used of the cherubim covering the ark at Exod 25:20, etc., and here it may have the sense "protect," like the hiph in Pss 5:12(11); 91:4.

14. d. See note 14.a.

14. e. Heb. קֹדֶשׁ "holiness" has often been deleted as a variant of אֱלֹהִים "God" (e.g., Ehrlich, *Randglossen* 109; BHS) especially as it is not represented in v 16. The clause does correspond well in length to the parallel statement in v 13aα, הָיִיתָ בְּעֵדֶן גַּן־אֱלֹהִים "you were in Eden, God's garden," in relation to which it may have a resumptive role.

16. a. Heb. מָלוּ, vocalized in MT as a pl "they filled," perhaps under Aram. influence seems to stand for מָלְאוּ, read by a few MSS: cf. מלו for מלאו in 1QIsᵃ at Isa 14:21 (R. Meyer, *TLZ* 75 [1950] 721-22). It appears to take the subj as pl in sense: "those in your midst" (Zimmerli 86). Probably it should be repointed as inf abs מָלֹו (= מָלוֹא, cf. GKC 75n, aa, nn-rr) "(your midst) was full of," used as a finite verb (cf. Van Dijk, *Ezekiel's Prophecy* 121).

16. b. Lit. "your midst": the king appears to represent the city-state, and the perspective varies.

16. c. Heb. מִן "from" has a pregnant force which by implication lends action to the verb (cf. GKC 119z).

16. d. Whether LXX* omitted הַסּכֵךְ "protected" (BHS) is disputed. Probably the reading of MS 967 τὸ σεχ, supported by an OL MS (*sech*), corrupted from a transliteration, is authentic (Wevers, *TRu* 22 [1954] 124; Zimmerli 86).

16. e. MT vocalized as "and I banished you" and took the adjacent noun phrase as vocative. This construction is consistent with and dependent on MT's interpretation of v 14a. LXX seems to represent an earlier tradition in implying וְאָבַּדְךָ "and he banished you" with the cherub as subj. The Gr. rendering ἤγαγε "brought" is not unparalleled in the Gr. OT for אבד: see my *The Greek Chronicles*, vol. 1, 126. A Heb. variant וַיּוֹבִילְךָ (BHK; cf. Zimmerli 86) is not implied. The resultant Heb. form, a pf with weak *waw* after a pf or consec impf, accords with other cases in Ezek: cf. 22:29; 25:12; 37:10; 40:24 (cf. B. Johnson, *Hebräisches Perfekt und Imperfekt* 78-81). The preceding 1st person verb and the unusual construction helped to cause confusion in MT.

18. a. In place of the pl form in MT a sg is preferable, with much support within the Heb. tradition: see *BHS* and Zimmerli 86.

Form/Structure/Setting

Vv 1-19 fall into two prophetic units, vv 1-10 and 11-19, as the separate message reception formulas in vv 1, 11 and the concluding messenger formula in v 10 reveal. However, they comprise a single redactional piece, in the light of the refrain of v 19b, which repeats the refrains of 26:21 and 27:36b. The first of the combined units is a judgment oracle. It characteristically has two parts, presenting an accusation and a pronouncement of punishment that features divine intervention and its results, and is confirmed by a formula of asseveration (v 10bα). The two parts are tightly coordinated by logical statements of cause and consequence (vv 2aβ-b, 6-10), with the cause reiterated at the beginning of the statement of consequence (v 6b; cf. 22:19). However, the strict coordination is interrupted by a further statement of accusation introduced by הנה "behold" (vv 3-5). This expansion of the element of accusation has been regarded as redactional (see Zimmerli 75-76, 79-80; Wevers 213; Hossfeld, *Untersuchungen* 159) and linked with a later desire to import the motif of wisdom. Then the resumptive recapitulation of the basic accusation was needed, evidence of which has been found in the variants את-לבבך/לבך "your heart" at v 2bβ and v 6b. However, the perspective of rhetorical criticism tells another story. Stylistic variation occurs in אלהים אני/אל אני "I am a god" (vv 2, 9) and ממותי/מותי "death" in vv 8,10), and the variants לב and לבב may be similarly explained. The oracle has an overall inclusion in the rejected divine claim of vv 2 and 9, while the second part has its own inclusion in the reference to זרים "aliens" in vv 7 and 10 (cf. Parunak, *Structural Studies* 376, who plausibly envisages a chiastic structure for vv 7-10 [ABC/CBA], with the motifs of aliens and death surrounding a claim to deity that is denied). An inclusion for the first part may be sought and found in the proud heart of vv 2 and 5 (cf. Parunak, *Structural Studies* 374). Moreover, there appears to be a wordplay running through the piece: the accusation contains a threefold חיל(ך) "(your) wealth" in vv 4-5, and the pronouncement of punishment uses forms of חלל three times (וחללו "and they will sully," v 7; חלל "slain," v 8; and מחלליך "those who wound you," v 9). Vv 3-5 fit well into this rhetorical complex. A further stylistic feature is the coordination of present fortune and future fate in the ironic repetition of בלב ימים "in the heart of the seas" in vv 2 and 8 (Miller, *Sin and Judgment* 71-72). Moreover, in vv 6-10 a divine promise to intervene (v 7a) and a divine asseveration (v 10b) frame a series of human actions in vv 7b-10a (Hossfeld, *Untersuchungen* 161).

The second unit, vv 12-19, is described as a dirge. Unlike other prophetic laments, it seems to be composed in rhythmic prose rather than in poetry. Zimmerli's attempts to restore a lament meter (3 + 2) and strophes, as well as his deletions of what does not conform (87-89), are questionable. The composition does retain the contrast of then and now typical of the dirge, and the sinister displacement of the present into the past and of future ruin as an accomplished fact. Yet the form is somewhat overwhelmed by the imagery it is made to carry (Jahnow, *Leichenlied* 228). There is an emphatic triple mention of an intermediate stage, the committing of wrong (vv 15b-16a, 17a, 18a). The form functions therefore as a sophisticated kind of judgment oracle. A series of stylistic repetitions reinforces the message. By use of the same verb divine privilege (נתתיך "I set you," v 14) turns into divine reprisal (נתתיך "I set you," v 17; ואתנך "and I made you," v 18). The mountain of God features as a place of privilege in relation to access and expulsion (vv 13, 16); so does אש אבני תוך "the midst of fiery stones" in vv 14, 16 (cf. אש מתוכך "fire from your midst," v 18). The guardian cherub features in the idyllic stage and in its reversal (vv 14, 16), while the holy setting (קדש "holiness") of v 14 is shattered by the profanation of v 18 (מקדשיך "your sanctuaries").

The chronological setting of both oracles was evidently the long siege of Tyre, while the Babylonians were endeavoring to subdue the island fortress. The second oracle seems consciously to echo the first in places, a phenomenon that must have encouraged its redactional combination. The monarch's proud heart features in vv 2, 4, 17; his beauty in vv 7, 12, 17; his splendor (יפעתך) in vv 7, 17; his wisdom in vv 4, 5, 7, 17; and his trading in vv 5, 16, 18. Gold finds a place in both pieces (vv 4, 13).

Comment

1-2 The target of the judgment oracle is the ruler of Tyre, Ethbaal II. His claims centered in the impregnability of his island city and the survival of his power. These claims were doubtless echoed by or attributed to him by Tyrian exiles known to Ezekiel and his Jewish compatriots in Babylonia (cf. Katzenstein, *History of Tyre* 307). For Ezekiel they constituted a challenge to God and his ongoing purposes, which were bound up with the success of Babylonian interests. The self-confidence of the king, who functions also as a symbolic figure for the city-state of Tyre, was an attitude of proud defiance against Yahweh as well as against Nebuchadnezzar. The claim to divinity is a stronger expression of Isaiah's characterization of Judah's allies in an earlier confrontation between Mesopotamia and the west: "The Egyptians are men and not God" (Isa 31:3). Whether an ancient Near Eastern concept of divine kingship has contributed to the imagery (cf. Zimmerli 78; Eichrodt 390) is by no means certain.

3-5 The note of excess is sounded now in a claim (הנה "behold" has an ironic force, "obviously") to wisdom greater than that of most men. Daniel, as in 14:14, 20, functions as a figure from remote antiquity, who appears in Ugaritic literature, in the Aqhat epic (esp. *ANET* 153-54a), as a ruler who practiced magical wisdom (see Day, *VT* 30 [1980] 174-84). The pride of the Tyrian king is now linked with his commercial wealth, which in his own eyes makes him more than a match for Nebuchadnezzar.

6-10 The ruler has reckoned without Yahweh. His brazen challenge was to find a reprisal in Yahweh's punishment, to be meted by cruel "aliens," who for the reader, as for Ezekiel's hearers, stand for the Babylonian army (cf. 26:7). It would patently disprove Ethbaal's quasi-divine claims upon life and power by establishing his mere humanity—in death. Not only would the external evidences of human power be attacked, but its very heart, life itself, would pass away. The place where Tyre ruled the waves in commercial power would become the place of its downfall. This ironic reversal would be the final proof of the falsity of present claims. The event would overtake Tyre and its ruler with an unanswerable counter argument. As to the reality of such a future event, Ezekiel pledges God's own promise. In vv 8 and 10 an ignominious death is in view. Heb. חלל "slain" functions in the context as shorthand for חללי חרב "slain by the sword," an idiom for violent death whose victims forfeited proper burial and a normal resting place in Sheol (cf. Eissfeldt, *Studies in Prophecy* 81 n. 22), as did those who died uncircumcised (see 31:17, 18 and *Comment*).

11-14 On another occasion Ezekiel delivered a prophetic lament which with eloquent finality attested the reality of Tyre's downfall by projecting it into the past. Unfortunately the passage leaves the reader uncertain as to how to interpret some of its details. Basically it makes use of a version of the garden of Eden story that appears in Gen 2-3. The description of the garden as "the garden of God" accords with 31:8-9 and is comparable with the phrase "garden of Yahweh" in Gen 13:10 and Isa 51:3. Yet this version knows nothing of the serpent or the first woman; it credits the first man with wisdom and adorns him in bejeweled clothing and apparently leaves him dead (cf. May, *Israel's Prophetic Heritage* 168; McKenzie, *JBL* 75 [1956] 326). However, it does speak of the garden of Eden and expulsion from it, of moral perfection before a fall and of one cherub who is the agent of expulsion (cf. further Yaron, *ASTI* 3 [1964] 154). To what extent Ezekiel is retelling an oral tradition known to him we cannot know. He obviously adapts the tradition to the Tyrian situation (cf. Fohrer 162), but whether to this end he created other elements that do not belong to the Adam and Eve story in Genesis and/or whether he is fusing different creation myths known to him is tantalizingly uncertain (cf. Williams, *BTB* 6 [1976] 49-61, who seems, however, to go too far in seeing merely Ezekiel's imagination at work).

Does the first-man imagery begin with v 12b or with **v** 13? Is the seal or signet ring simply an object of artistic beauty or does it consciously have a royal reference, as in Jer 22:24; Hag 2:23? Does it characterize the king of Tyre as Yahweh's vassal or instrument of authority? And is kingship already associated with the traditional story used by Ezekiel (cf. e.g., Ps 8:6[5]b)? The metal settings, if such they are, in v 13b seem to echo the beautiful seal (תכנית "intricate design," v 12, כוננו "were prepared," v 13). The reference to wisdom seems to allude to the king rather than to the seal: it is to be resumed in the perversion of his wisdom at v 17. A wisdom motif is part of the creation and first man traditions in the Old Testament, e.g., in Job 15:7-8 (Habel, *Concordia Theological Monthly* 38 [1967] 519).

The role of the precious stones in v 13 is not clear. Are they worn by the king or do they feature in his topographical environment, as vv 14bβ and 16bβ more naturally suggest, if they are the equivalent of the fiery stones (אבני אש) mentioned there? Perhaps they are not meant to be the same, and we are to envisage a more complex picture involving stones of two kinds (cf. Yaron, *ASTI* 3 [1964] 38-39). The listing of nine jewels in a gold setting at v 13 is evidently borrowed from the catalog of twelve jewels mounted in gold which were attached to the high priest's breast piece according to Exod 28:17-20; 39:10-12. The order is slightly different. The LXX reinforces the reference by listing all twelve stones. The list has been regarded as redactional (e.g., Zimmerli 82; Wevers 217), although, if so, it is valuable early evidence of interpretation of the message. However, the frequent use of the language of P by Ezekiel (cf. here the stem ברא "create" in vv 13, 15) may indicate that the prophet borrowed the list (Gowan, *When Man Becomes God* 83) in order to express the privilege of wealth with which the king was endowed as Yahweh's creature and perhaps to indicate the role of the king of Tyre as priest-king, in line with the religious references elsewhere in the passage. The difference in the order and number of gems may indicate inexact reminiscence of a written text.

A threefold chain of divinely given endowments commences with a reference to the cherub or attendant sphinx-like creature of mixed animal and human appearance. In the second link of the chain the reference to the holy mountain of God (or the gods) complicates the picture. It sounds like Mount Zaphon in N. Syria, in Ugaritic mythology the abode of the gods, rather than a place for human habitation. It is likely that its polemical transfer to the sanctuary of Zion (cf. Ps 48:3[2]) was in Ezekiel's mind, and that he projected it onto Tyre, where the king traditionally was also a priest (cf. v 18; cf. Bogaert, *Homo Religiosus* 9 [1983] 139, who, however, believes that an oracle originally relating to Jerusalem has been amplified and reapplied to Tyre). Widengren usefully compared בכל־הר קדשׁי "in all my holy mountain" at Isa 11:9 in a description of the return of Paradise (*Ascension of the Apostle* 97).

The fiery stones have been compared with a divine garden in the Mesopotamian Gilgamesh epic, in which the fruit and leaves of the trees took the form of jewels (*ANET* 89), but other suggestions are not lacking (cf. Zimmerli 93).

15-19 The narrative takes a sinister turn, with a willful moral decline. Vv 16-18 present an emphatic threefold account of human sin and divine punishment. In each case a double sin meets a double reprisal. In the reference to commerce (vv 16, 18) contemporary reality mingles with the tradition. Commerce gave rise to oppression and to the arrogance (cf. vv 2, 5) that is the stepchild of privilege, and to perverse use of the gift of wisdom. The religious allusion in v 18aβ is not clear: it may be a reference to the pagan religion of the priest-king.

The punishment first keeps to the story line, expulsion from the garden—the place of privilege—at the hands of Yahweh and the attendant cherub. The ensuing descriptions of retribution speak more generally of social humiliation and of Yahweh's triggering the providential fate inherent in the human situation, although in the latter case the fiery stones appear to put their fire to new use (cf. v 14bβ), which may be linked with the "flaming sword" of Gen 3:24. In v 19a the motif of shock resumes a note struck in the two previous chapters (26:16; 27:35). As the refrain of v 19b implies, Tyre's fate was sealed.

The application of vv 11-19 to Satan by third and fourth century A.D. Church Fathers, Tertullian, Origen, John Cassian, Cyril of Jerusalem and Jerome, and thence in some modern popular conservative expositions, is based on MT's equation of the king and cherub and on comparison with Isa 14:12-15. It is a case of exegeting an element of Christian belief by means of Scripture and so endeavoring to provide it with extrabiblical warrant and to fit the passage into the framework of the Christian faith. However, it is guilty of detaching the passage from its literary setting (Ellison 108-9).

Explanation

Ezekiel's necessary task was to counter a mood of optimism among the Jewish exiles. Stunned as they were at Jerusalem's fall, they were evidently clutching at a straw offered to them by their fellow exiles from Tyre. With a shift of confidence, they imagined that Tyre's resistance to the besieging Babylonians might mean a turning of the tide for them. The prophet reacts to this chauvinist reading of current affairs with a divine no. Yahweh was working in a more radical way. The old order had to go completely before a new day of salvation and blessing could dawn. Vv 2-10 and 12-19, rhetorically addressed to one termed Tyre's ruler and king, respectively, are two striking attempts to communicate this political and theological truth.

The first puts Tyre firmly in its place as essentially a human, and therefore weak, entity whose commercial affluence had gone to its head and whose efforts at resistance were perilously tantamount to pretensions of divine power. Such lay only with Yahweh and with those whom he chose as his agents. Tyre was guilty of hubris, and in reprisal had to be horribly struck down. The prophet's coloring of the political map with these theological hues comes over with compelling persuasiveness. It is emotionally reinforced by wordplay, a technique that exerted much influence on the Hebrew ear. Tyre's wealth (חיל) had in it the seeds of profanation, wounding and slaying (חלל). Tyre's sense of security grounded in economic power and natural resources was to be rudely shattered by political events controlled by Yahweh himself.

The second message is much more dramatic. Rather like the ship metaphor of chap. 27, it superimposes negative imagery of ruined grandeur on Tyre's cultural success and self-confidence. Despite regrettable difficulties of interpretation in so many of its details, the general picture of Paradise lost shines through clearly. Tyre was not self-made, but as a created entity owed its prosperity and glory to divine endowment. Yet privilege had not been matched with moral responsibility. "Violence," ever a besetting sin in the prophetic vocabulary, had accompanied its rise to power. The tragic truth was that Tyre's wrongdoing contained the seeds of its own destruction, which Yahweh's intervention would encourage to germinate and grow into a baneful harvest. Three times it is stressed that moral failure must result in loss of fortune and in subjection to a terrible fate. Moreover, there is a religious theme that seems to run through the oracle. The monarch in his role as priest-king is evidently accused of misrepresenting true religion, despite the strong religious basis of his rule.

Ezekiel had two perceptions of reality, whereas his fellow exiles had only one. With prophetic insight and boldness he was able to judge one perception by the standards of the other, and to find it wanting. In a radical reinterpretation of current affairs he was enabled to grasp that the most solid and settled expression of human power was ephemeral, if it took issue with the moral and providential will of God. He was one with Paul the apostle: "We look not to the things that are seen, but to the things that are unseen; for the things that are seen are transient, but the things that are unseen are eternal" (2 Cor 4:18). Luke was aware of Ezekiel's message: by coloring the narrative of Acts 12:20-23 with tints derived from the palette of Ezekiel 28:2-10, if not 2-19 (cf. Strom, *NTS* 32 [1986] 289-92), he used the death of Herod to affirm the triumph of God's moral will in the interests of his covenant people.

Sidon's Fate and Judah's Fortune (28:20-26)

Bibliography

Reventlow, H. *Wächter über Israel.* BZAW 82. Berlin: Töpelmann, 1962, 153-56. **Westermann, C.** *Prophetische Heilsworte im Alten Testament.* FRLANT 145. Göttingen: Vandenhoeck und Ruprecht, 1987, 137-44.

Translation

[20] *I received the following communication from Yahweh:* [21] *"Human one, look in the direction of Sidon and prophesy against it,* [22] *informing it that the message of the Lord*[a] *Yahweh is as follows: I am your adversary, Sidon, and I will reveal my glory within you. People will realize*[b] *that I am Yahweh when I carry out acts of judgment against it and reveal my holy power therein.* [23] *I will send against it plague and bloodshed in its streets, and the slain will fall*[a] *within it, victims of the sword*[b] *raised on all sides against it. The people will realize that I am Yahweh.* [24] *No longer will the community of Israel feel briers tearing at them or thorns harming them, created by all their neighbors who have treated them with contempt. Thus they will come to appreciate that I am Yahweh."*[a]

[25] *The message of the Lord Yahweh is as follows: "When I gather the community of Israel from the peoples in whose territory they are scattered, I will reveal*[a] *my holiness among them in the sight of all other nations. Then they will live in their country, which I gave to my servant Jacob.* [26] *In it they will live securely, building houses and planting vineyards. They will live in security, once I have carried out acts of judgment on all their neighbors who have treated them with contempt. Thus they will come to appreciate that I am Yahweh their God."*

Notes

22. a. For the formulaic אדני "Lord," here and in v 25, see the note on 20:3.
22. b. LXX has a 2nd sg verb here and 2nd fem pronouns through v 23a, inferior readings that exhibit contextual assimilation.
23. a. MT ונפלל is a slip for ונפל "and ... will fall," read by a few MSS. The false doubling was occasioned by the following חלל (Cornill 363).
23. b. The proposal to read וחרב "and the sword" for בחרב "by the sword" (Ehrlich, *Randglossen* 110; cf. *BHK*) produces a smooth circumstantial clause. The phrasing of 32:22b, etc., supports the text.
24. a. MT prefaces with אדני "Lord," in violation of formulaic usage in Ezek (cf. Zimmerli 556): it is to be omitted with a few masoretic witnesses (cf. *BHS*).
25. a. The syntax of the clauses is uncertain: the main clause may begin with v 25b or even with v 26bβ.

Form/Structure/Setting

This passage is demarcated from the foregoing by its own message reception formula. Although it is capable of being divided into coherent smaller units, it is marked by an ongoing movement from unit to unit. Its flow eddies from bank to bank, as it were, with a contrasting mode, before it pushes forward in steady spate. It betrays consciousness of earlier material and gives the impression of being a literary tailpiece, although the widely held notion that it was added to bring the number of nations up to seven (e.g., Eichrodt 396) has little to commend it.

In form this epilogue consists of a collection of proof sayings. The recognition formula occurs four times, but the first two cases (vv 22b, 23b) belong together after a double statement of divine intervention; the third is set in a supplementary sentence (v 24b), while the fourth concludes its own oracle (v 26b). The two initial messenger formulas in vv 22 and 25 reinforce the impression of a two-part structuring. First, an oracle of judgment against Sidon is introduced by an address to the prophet to confront Sidon rhetorically and to deliver the oracle. It contains no specific accusation and simply announces punishment to come. In v 24 the oracle shades into an oracle of salvation for Israel. The rest of the material reverses these perspectives: an oracle of salvation veers into a subordinate threat of punishment for Israel's persecutors. The overall passage thus displays a loose ABBA pattern. Linguistically this pattern is reinforced by a double inclusion, consisting of the recognition formula and בעשותי שפטים "when I carry out acts of judgment" in vv 22b and 26b; and by the hinge-like phrase בית ישראל "community of Israel" in vv 24aα and 25aβ. There is not lacking, however, terminological evidence of a complementary structure, ABAB: the motif of Yahweh's vindication (ונקדשתי בה/בם "and I am sanctified in it/them") in vv 22bβ and 25aδ (A/A) and the combination of the recognition formula and mention of all the contemptuous neighbors of Israel in vv 24aγb and 26b (B/B). The two messages have been sensitively interwoven.

Signs of an interlacing of this epilogue with its immediate context, the related oracles against Tyre in vv 1-19, are also evident. An overall inclusion is provided by the stem ישב "sit, dwell" in a contrast between Tyre, temporary occupant of a pseudo-divine throne (מושב אלהים ישבתי "I sit on a divine throne," v 2) and Israel, prospective secure occupant of a God-given country (ישבו ["they will dwell"] x 3, vv 25, 26). The somber term חלל "slain" in v 23 not only echoes the fate of the king of Tyre in v 8 but prolongs the חלל wordplay that permeates the two previous oracles. The passage, then, functions as a literary finale to the chapter. It also reveals awareness of other local ethnic groups at whose hands Israel had suffered, and so awareness of chaps. 25-26. In fact the stem שאט "scorn" seems consciously to echo its use in 25:6, 15, while the formula of prophetic gazing in v 21 recalls 25:2; the formula of encounter in v 22 pairs Sidon with Tyre in 26:3. Moreover, the passage is marked by positive content and phraseology characteristic of the following section of the book, chaps. 33-39. Zimmerli (100; cf. Hossfeld, *Untersuchungen* 493) has noted the similarity of vv 25-26 in form and content to the closing verses of chap. 39, and Westermann (*Heilsworte* 144) the overlap with chaps. 36-37. Moreover, there are close parallels with 34:25-30. It is probable that a basic oracle against Sidon in vv 21-23 has been expanded to fulfill a literary function. Most likely one should envisage two stages of supplementation, first v 24 and then vv 25-26. Overall, 28:25-26 seems to belong to a series of late redactional supplements, which are continued in 34:25-30; 36:24-32; 37:24b-30 and 39:23-29, and serve to present summaries of important truths. As in chap. 39, the intent here is to relate the foregoing material to the general positive themes of the book as they pertained to the people of God. The assignment of third fem sg material in vv 22b-23 to a redactor (see, e.g., Cooke 321; Wevers 219) is less convincing: the switch to third person speech follows on naturally after a verb with a different subject.

Comment

21-24 The solemn old formula of turning a prophetic gaze upon Sidon (cf. the comment on 21:2) and the formula of encounter serve to remind the reader of 25:2 and 26:3, and to give the impression of reaching the end of a series of oracles against foreign nations. Sidon, a coastal city 25 miles north of Tyre, alternated with Tyre as the leading city of Phoenicia. Tyre was dominant in the period up to its siege, but thereafter Sidon gained supremacy. According to Jer 27:3, early in Zedekiah's reign Sidon took part in an anti-Babylonian conspiracy, a circumstance that fits the military opposition to Nebuchadnezzar underlying this oracle. No historical reason is given for Yahweh's intervention, which may therefore imply the triumph of his will in his sponsorship of Babylon's attacks. However, v 24 explains it in terms of Sidon's animosity against the Judeans, presumably in connection with the fall of Jerusalem (cf. 25:6, 15; 26:2).

Pride of place is given to the revelation of Yahweh's glory (cf. 39:13 and *Comment* thereon). There may be a deliberate echo of the priestly passage Exod 14:4, 17-18 and so the drawing of a typological parallel: as in the case of Pharaoh long ago, Yahweh's glory would be manifested by means of a negative demonstration of his will against Israel's and so his foes. The related motif of Yahweh's revelation of his transcendent power or holiness (cf. 36:23; 38:16, 23; 39:27) provides implicit contrast with his apparent humiliation in the fall of Jerusalem and the Judean exile. Klein (*Ezekiel* 130, 141) has found in v 22 a theological key to the oracles against the nations: only if the nations were judged could Yahweh's glory and holiness be maintained. The description of Sidon's downfall in v 23 uses a standard combination of pestilence, blood and sword (cf. 5:12; 6:12; 14:12-23). Since elsewhere in Ezek it is used in connection with the fall of Jerusalem, reprisal for an offense related to that event may be implied, in line with v 24.

The expansion of v 24 develops the term מסביב "on all sides" in v 23b into a quid pro quo reprisal for Judean harassment at the hands of their ethnic neighbors, which was treated in chaps. 25-26. From this perspective Sidon is regarded as typical of the total group of adjacent alien states. An implication of Yahweh's intervention is presented. One of Ezekiel's metaphors for hostility (סלון "briers," 2:6) is blended with a priestly or deuteronomistic one (קוץ "thorns," cf. Num 33:55; cf. Josh 23:13). One may compare the use of Num 33:50-54 in 47:13-23; probably in both cases we have to do with a relatively late redaction.

25-26 The second oracle develops in positive terms the note of relief sounded in v 24. There is a looking forward to the restoration of the Judeans to their own country, as frequently in chaps. 33-39 (e.g., 34:13). It is envisaged as a further stage in Yahweh's self-vindication (cf. 39:27). The motif of settling in the promised land is an anticipatory echo of 37:25. Such settlement would be Yahweh's checkmate against Tyre's presumptuous claims (v 2). There is an emphasis on security, borrowed from 34:25-28, but here developed in terms of building houses and planting vineyards (cf. 36:36), motifs common in the book of Jeremiah. Such welcome reorientation, incredible as it seemed, would be the aftermath of the reprisals of vv 22b and 24aβ, which are repeated in v 26bα. It was to be a sacramental sign pointing the Judeans beyond themselves to the praiseworthy reality of their covenant God.

Explanation

An implicit aim of many prophetic oracles against foreign nations was to bring reassurance to their Judean hearers. The oracles in chaps. 25-26 served this very purpose. Now the series of Palestinian and Phoenician oracles is rounded off with an expanded oracle against Sidon, before Egypt becomes the subject of the complex of foreign oracles. In this passage the pastoral role of the oracle of judgment against Sidon is spelled out loud and clear. A theological parallel is to be found in Paul's message to the persecuted Christians at Thessalonica. "At the revelation of the Lord Jesus from heaven" God would "repay with affliction those who afflict you" and also grant "rest to you who are afflicted" (2 Thess 1:6, 7). Then the focus of the passage moves from the relief of the church's suffering to the vindication of Jesus, who would be "glorified among his saints" and "admired among all believers" (2 Thess 1:10). Correspondingly, here the coming vindication of Yahweh is found both in the destruction of Sidon and in the rehabilitation of the covenant people. The latter were to be caught up in his purposes and to be participants in his triumph. The assurance is given that solid proof was forthcoming and human politics would surrender to the divine purpose. Till then faith and hope in the prophet's interpretation of the divine will were necessary. Bruised and insecure hearts were soothed with the promise that justice, peace and truth would prevail. A caring God would provide the cure for their ills.

False Faith in Egypt (29:1-16)

Bibliography

Boadt, L. *Ezekiel's Oracles against Egypt. A Literary and Philological Study of Ezekiel 29-32.* BibOr 37. Rome: Biblical Institute, 1980. **Day, J.** *God's Conflict with the Dragon and the Sea: Echoes of a Canaanite Myth in the Old Testament.* University of Cambridge Oriental Publications 35. Cambridge: CUP, 1985. **Höffken, P.** "Zu den Heilszusätzen in der Völkerorakelsammlung des Jeremiabuches." *VT* 27 (1977) 398-412. **van Rooy, H. F.** "Parallelism, Metre and Rhetoric in Ezekiel 29:1-6." *Semitics* 8 (1982) 90-105. **Vogels, W.** "Restauration de l'Égypte et universalisme en Ez. 29:3-16." *Bib* 53 (1972) 473-94. **Wakeman, M. K.** *God's Battle with the Monster. A Study in Biblical Imagery.* Leiden: Brill, 1973.

Translation

[1] *In the tenth year, on the twelfth[a] day of the tenth month, I received the following communication from Yahweh:* [2] *"Human one, look in the direction of Pharaoh, Egypt's king, and prophesy against him and the whole of Egypt.* [3] *You are to tell[a] him that the message of the Lord[b] Yahweh is as follows:*

> *I am your adversary, Pharaoh,*
> *king of Egypt,*
> *great monster[c] lying*
> *in your[d] Nile streams,*
> *thinking, 'My Nile[e] is mine,*
> *made for me by myself.'[f]*

[4] *I will put hooks in your jaws and make the fish in your streams stick to your scales. From your streams I will haul up both you and[a] all the fish in your streams that are sticking to your scales.*

> [5] *Then I will hurl[a] you into the wilderness,*
> *you and all the fish from your streams.*
> *you will lie fallen on the open ground,*
> *neglected and ignored.[b]*
> *To the wild animals on the earth and to the birds in the sky*
> *I am giving you for food.*
> [6] *Then all who live in Egypt will realize*
> *that I am Yahweh.*
> *"Inasmuch as you[a] have proved to be*
> *a reedy staff*
> *for the community of Israel to lean on—*
> [7] *when they grasped you,[a] you collapsed*
> *and badly wrenched their shoulders,[b]*
> *and when they leaned on you, you broke*
> *and left their hips quite unsteady[c]—*

[8] *That is why the following message comes from the Lord Yahweh: I intend to make a sword attack you, exterminating from you humans and animals alike,* [9] *while Egypt will turn into an area of desolate ruin. Then they will realize that I am Yahweh.*

"Inasmuch as you[a] *have been thinking, 'The Nile is mine, made by me,'* [10]*that is why I am an adversary of you and your Nile streams. I will turn Egypt into an area of desolate and waste ruins*[a] *from Migdol to Syene*[b] *and as far as the Egyptian border.* [11]*It will lie untrodden by any human foot and untraversed by any animal paw: it will stay uninhabited for forty years.* [12]*I will make Egypt as desolate as any country could be.*[a] *Its cities, as ruined as any city could ever be, will lie desolate for forty years. I will scatter the Egyptians among other nations, dispersing them into other countries.* [13]*What this means,*[a] *runs the message of the Lord Yahweh, is that at the end of forty years I will collect the Egyptians from the peoples they have been dispersed among* [14]*and change their fortunes,*[a] *bringing them back*[b] *to the area of Pathros, their native country. There they will comprise a paltry nation,* [15]*more paltry than any other realm and unable to dominate any other nation—I will keep them too small to exercise such control.* [16]*Never again will the community of Israel have*[a] *an object of trust to which they turn and which they follow mistakenly to their eventual regret,*[b] *but they will realize that I am Yahweh."*[c]

Notes

1. a. LXX μιᾷ "first" implies באחד. Probably בשנים עשר "on the twelfth" was lost by homoeoteleuton and then a filling out of the now incomplete date from 26:1 and/or 29:17 (cf. 45:20 LXX) occurred.

3. a. Heb. דבר "speak" is not represented in LXX* before ואמרת "and say," and is often deleted (cf. *BHS*). It is unusual in this formulaic context, but present in 14:4; 20:3. LXX may have omitted as otiose, like its omission of מלך מצרים "king of Egypt" later.

3. b. For the formulaic אדני "Lord" here and in vv 8, 13 see the note on 20:3.

3. c. Heb תנים is usually a plural "jackals," but the sg verb and adj demand a sg sense, and its watery habitat rules out a reference to jackals (Wakeman, *God's Battle* 75). It is either a slip for תנין (cf. Jer 51:34) or a variant form of it: it recurs in 32:2.

3. d. For the idiomatic third pl references in the Heb. of v 3a δ-b see the note on 22:3.

3. e. Heb. יארי "my stream" is more naturally pointed יארי "my streams" (cf. Zimmerli, ibid.) in view of the pl in v 3a, 4, 10. On the other hand, the versional evidence points in a different direction (cf. *BHS*) and in v 9 the term occurs in the sg without a suffix. Stylistic variation may have been intended (cf. Boadt, *Ezekiel's Oracles* 29).

3. f. The suffix on the verb appears to be datival: cf. Boadt, *Ezekiel's Oracles* 30, and GKC 117x. Emendation to עשיתם "I made them," if a pl is read earlier, or to עשיתיו "I made it" (cf. Zimmerli 106-7) is unnecessary.

4. a. Heb. את could be emphatic (Boadt, *Ezekiel's Oracles* 31), but is more probably the object sign, in which case v 4bγ functions as a short relative clause (Ehrlich, *Randglossen* 111). The omission of v 4bγ in LXX* is probably due to the translator's judging it to be superfluous after v 4aβ.

5. a. Heb. נטש normally means "leave," but here and in 31:12; 32:4 both the ancient versions and the adjacent verbs suggest a primary sense "throw" (Driver, *Bib* 35 [1954] 299; *HALAT* 657a).

5. b. The two Heb. verbs for "gather" here have the sense of care and concern (cf. BDB 62a). Since the first verb אסף can be used for gathering for burial, the second תקבץ is often emended to תקבר "be buried" with the support of some MSS, Tg and perhaps LXX (cf. Jer 8:2); but MT is to be retained (cf. Zimmerli 107). In v 13 אקבץ "I will gather" appears to be a conscious positive development of v 5.

6. a. MT היותם "(because of) their being" has suffered dittography of *mem* and wrongly takes as subj the pl entity in v 6aα. A new sentence appears to begin at v 6b: יען "because" looks forward to לכן "therefore" in v 8. In content too v 6b goes closely with v 7. LXX Syr Vg render with 2nd sg verbs and so probably היית "(because) you were" is to be read, assuming a י/ו error. This emendation is simpler than the common one of היותך "your being" (*BHS* et al.) and more feasible than Boadt's explanation of MT (*Ezekiel's Oracles* 36).

7. a. MT adds בכפך "in your hand" (K), corrected by Q to בכף "by the hand." The reading כף "hand" presupposed by LXX Syr for כתף "shoulder" later suggests that in MT a variant כף has been taken as a correction of בך "(grasped) you" to בכפך. The external parallelism of v 7aα and 7bα supports its omission.

7. b. Heb. כל "all" here and in v 7bβ means "the whole of" (GKC 127a) and implies extensive harm, here conveyed in the translation by "badly" and "quite." The reading כף "hand" presupposed by LXX Syr (see previous note) is probably a case of assimilation to 2 Kgs 18:21 (= Isa 36:6): the difference of accompanying verb is significant.

7. c. The stem עמד "stand" in MT is an error of metathesis for מעד "(to cause to) shake," as Syr Vg (cf. LXX) imply (*BHS* et al.): cf. Ps 69:24(23). Driver's appeal to Akk. and Arab. usage (*Bib* 35 [1954] 299) is a linguistic tour de force.

9. a. MT takes Pharaoh as the 3rd person subj of the verb (cf. אמר "he said," v 3). LXX Syr Vg imply אמרך "(because of) your saying," which seems to be required (*BHK* et al.). MT appears to have suffered assimilation to v 3.

10. a. Heb חרב "desolation" or "drought" is rendered as if חֶרֶב "sword" in LXX Vg and not represented in Syr. In its favor Boadt has noted the triad of sinister terms in Isa 61:4; Jer 49:13 (*Ezekiel's Oracles* 42): he takes them as parallel terms in asyndeton, pointing the first as abs לְחָרְבוֹת.

10. b. Here and in 30:6 MT סונה is uncoordinated: it is to be pointed סוֵנָה "to Syene" (Smend 231, following Michaelis; Zimmerli 108).

12. a. The two expressions with בתוך "among" appear to have a comparative force: cf. Ehrlich, *Randglossen* 112, who compared the superlative קדש קדשׁים "holy of holies."

13. a. Lit. "for." The implication of the limitation of forty years is spelled out. LXX* Syr do not represent, perhaps omitting because of the subtlety of usage.

14. a. For this idiom of reorientation see most recently J. M. Bracke, *ZAW* 97 (1985) 233-44.

14. b. LXX Syr Vg derived the Heb verb from ישׁב "inhabit," rather than from שׁוב "return."

16. a. MT יהיה "it will become (. . . an object of trust)" strangely speaks of Egypt as masc sg, in a context of masc pl and fem sg references. The ancient versions imply יהיו "they will be," which appears to be a simplistic correction that leaves the present reading unaccounted for. Ehrlich (*Randglossen* 112) interestingly suggested reading מבטח "object of trust" as subject, assuming dittography of *lamed*. Then the obviously intended parallelism with 28:24 is even more complete.

16. b. Lit. "reminding of iniquity."

16. c. MT prefaces with אדני "Lord": see the note on 28:24.

Form/Structure/Setting

29:1-16 falls into three proof sayings, vv 3-6a, 6b-9a and 9b-16. The distribution of the recognition formula in vv 6a, 9aβ and 16b so suggests, and this form-critical clue is generally so interpreted, even Keil so dividing vv 6 and 9 (vol. 2:5, 7). MT, however, in its division of verses and sections follows another arrangement, vv 3-7, 8-12 and 13-16. Van Rooy, *Semitics* 8 (1982) 90, has endeavored to justify this arrangement by regarding the messenger formula of vv 3, 8, 13 as an initial refrain. This argument is not convincing, since the messenger formula regularly occurs at the head of the second part of a judgment oracle or proof saying, as well as at the very beginning.

The proof saying of vv 3aβ-6a consists of the standard three parts of accusation, pronouncement of punishment and recognition formula, with the accusation introduced by the formula of confrontation, to which the accusation is related as appositional description. The second oracle, which lacks an oracular introduction, is a proof saying of the classic, logical type inasmuch as accusation and announcement of punishment are locked together with a "because-therefore" formulation, as in the oracles of chap. 25. The third proof saying, which also begins abruptly, closely follows the format of the second, except that the second component is lengthened by a modification of the punishment in vv 13-15, and by the spelling out of positive implications for Israel in v 16a.

The third oracle seems deliberately to echo the first two. Thus vv 9b-10a repeat clauses and terms from v 3, and in v 16 allusion is made to the motif of

Israel's trusting in Egypt that was used in vv 6b-7. Moreover, the verb of judgment ונתתי "and I will give" in v 4 (cf. נתתיך "I have given you" in v 5b) reappears in this role in vv 10b and 12, and the comprehensive reference to absence of human and animal life in v 8b reappears in a different formulation in v 11a, while the terms for desolation and ruin in v 9aα feature too in vv 10 and 12a. The impression given by these echoes is that vv 9b-16 comprise a literary expansion of the two former oracles, presenting their message in a less radical tone. The repetition of the stem קבץ "gather" at v 13 in a positive setting, after its negative usage in v 5, is striking. A *shin-beth* wordplay seems to run through the three oracles: ישבי "inhabitants" (v 6a), תשבר "you broke" (v 7b), תשב (לא) "you will (not) be inhabited" (v 11), and ושבתי את־שבות "and I will change the fortunes" and והשבתי "and I will restore" in v 14. The wordplay seems to carry a rationalizing message, which the third oracle claims to explain: the breaking of Egypt in the second oracle is not to be regarded as final, in view of the survival and presence of inhabitants in Egypt at the end of the first. Rather, the loss of habitation must be temporary and eventual restoration is to be envisaged. The statement in v 16a aligns closely with that in 28:24a, and each occurs before the recognition formula. It seems then that both may well come from the same redactional hand (cf. Höffken, *VT* 27 [1977] 409), which could easily have been Ezekiel's own at a later period.

As to the setting of the oracles, the dating of v 1 seems determinative for the first, which accordingly belongs to the period just before the fall of Jerusalem. The second, independent oracle appears to be a little later. In characterizing Egyptian help as vain, it presupposes the military support that Hophra sent to try to relieve besieged Jerusalem (Jer 37:5): Ezekiel and his contemporaries knew of its failure. The generalizations in both these oracles suggest Ezekiel's remoteness from the Palestinian scene and so an exilic provenance. The third oracle, which consciously develops the other two, is a meditation that builds upon the positive phase of the prophet's ministry, inaugurated by the fall of Jerusalem. It is associated with the written form of the previous oracles in a literary redaction.

Comment

1-6a The chapter opens with a solemn introduction, consisting of date, the message reception formula and the formula of prophetic gaze. Parallelism with 25:1 and 26:1 seems to be intended: here begins the third block of oracles against foreign nations, after those against the Palestinian states and against Tyre (Boadt, *Ezekiel's Oracles* 17). The date, reconstructed by Parker and Dubberstein as January 7, 587 B.C. (*Babylonian Chronology* 28), sets the first oracle half a year before the fall of Jerusalem, although of course it reflects events rather earlier than that, since Ezekiel is commenting on matters known to the Babylonian exiles. There seems to be an awareness of the willingness of the dynamic new Pharaoh Hophra, who came to the throne in 589 B.C., to become involved in the attempts of the Palestinian states to rebel against Babylon, and even of Zedekiah's negotiations to this end (cf. 17:15). Ezekiel firmly quenches such Judean hopes as not in accord with the divine will.

The metaphor of v 3aγ b obviously categorizes the Pharaoh as a malevolent despot, but the nature of the metaphor is not certain. Is the king portrayed as a crocodile or in terms of the sea monster, the mythological chaos god defeated at the creation of the world, called Leviathan or Rahab in the Old Testament? Day has argued strenuously in favor of the latter (*God's Conflict* 94-95). Indeed, Isaiah's nickname for Egypt, Rahab (Isa 30:7), which is called ˆynt (the term used here and rendered "monster") in the sense of sea monster in Isa 51:9, supports this hypothesis. However, the evident Nile setting, accentuated by the use of the Egyptian loanword ray "Nile, Nile stream," points rather to the crocodile. It is probable that both conceptions are in view, and that this particular crocodile is larger than life and invested with mythological overtones (Fohrer 166, Eichrodt 403, Boadt, *Ezekiel's Oracles* 27-28).

The arrogant claims of the Egyptian monster to be master and even maker of his Nile domain, made prosperous by its system of irrigation, conclude a scenario of secular power. Yahweh, however, would be more than a match for him. The intent of the last clause of v 3 is to trigger an awareness that Yahweh is the true and only creator and so to stimulate a shocked, negative reaction to Egyptian power. The account of his destruction imaginatively extends the metaphor by using terms of hunting and expulsion from his Nile habitat. The phrase בתוך יאריו "among his Nile streams" (v 3a) is deliberately countered with מתוך יאריך "from among your Nile streams" (v 4b). The fish clearly correspond to the royal subjects, who are to be caught up in this removal and destruction. Behind the sinister vignette lurks the implication of Babylonian defeat of Egypt, and even the exile of its citizens. It is regarded as the outworking of Yahweh's providential will: it would prove to Egypt his dynamic reality.

6b-9 The second oracle owes its force to its evocation of a metaphor used in a prophetic narrative that is set in an earlier period of history. In Isa 36:6 (= 2 Kgs 18:21) trusting in Pharaoh is described as leaning on a staff no stronger than a reed, that breaks and hurts the hand that holds it. Here the metaphor with its clever reference to the Nile bulrush, is re-used but associated with more serious physical harm. The oracle looks back on Hophra's abortive attempt to give military support during the siege of Jerusalem (cf. Jer 37:5, 7-8). It functions, however, as a theological comment, rather than as a political one: the later interpretation in v 16 is correct. Leaning is part of the Old Testament vocabulary of faith: God's people had once again turned elsewhere for the support they should have sought in him and his will (cf. Isa 36:6, 7). So nothing but ill could have come from this spiritual adventure. Divine reprisals were to be meted out on the Egyptian tempter and his realm, in the form of a devastating attack, which would bring home to the Judeans the truth taught in this oracle.

9b-12 The later message in vv 9b-16 wants to reflect on the two previous oracles against Egypt and to set them within a wider framework of revelation. To this end it repeats their form and echoes their vocabulary, both plainly and by way of significant wordplay (see *Form/Setting/Structure*). Yahweh's intent was still to counter the defiant claims of this world power. The punishment of the earlier oracles is endorsed in the double representation of vv 10b-11 and 12, both of which begin with the initial verb of v 4. Indeed, the totality of Egyptian destruction, indicated in v 10 by the geographical references to its northern and southern frontiers and even beyond, serves to underline the statement of v 9a. However, in each case a temporal limitation is set on the punishment, a span of "forty years." The exuberance of the preceding oracles is abandoned in a sober reappraisal, in the course of which the vivid statements of vv 5 and 8b are interpreted, not unreasonably, in terms of exile.

13-15 A third phase of punishment is now set out, reinforced by an emphatic messenger formula and a re-use of the key phrase "forty years," in order to prepare for the blatancy of affirming a gathering denied earlier (v 5). A generation (cf. Num 14:28-31) would serve the sentence imposed by the divine judge (cf. Ezek 4:6, of Judean exile), yet even their repatriated posterity would not enjoy the privileges of world power. Instead, they were to be demoted to a third-world country and confined territorially to Upper Egypt, with Lower Egypt in the north seemingly remaining a no man's land. The language of 17:14, set in a wider Egyptian context and so not unnaturally coming to the redactor's mind, is borrowed to help to describe the low political profile to which Egypt was to be reduced (cf. Vogels, *Bib* 63 [1972] 488-89).

16 This political shrinkage was to be Yahweh's way of preventing his people's backsliding. By delving into the context of Isa 36:6 the redactor is able to use the crucial term "trust" (Isa 36:4) to describe the point of the metaphor of vv 6b-7. Systematically Yahweh was to deal with the ills that beset his people (cf. 28:24), first by removing the threat that the other Palestinian states posed to them (28:24) and, second, by forestalling a perpetual temptation to sin posed by Egypt in putting it beyond their reach (cf. Höffken, *VT* 27 [1977] 409). Only thus could he get them to take him as seriously as his being warranted.

Explanation

The first oracle is an eloquent warning that for Judah to put its political eggs into Egypt's basket was a mistake. It is part of Ezekiel's crusade, to which chap. 23 notably belongs, against the Judeans' hopes that Egypt would get them out of Babylon's clutches. The truth of the matter, as the oracle proclaims at its opening, was that Yahweh's will lay in a contrary direction. For all its present greatness, Egypt was doomed, victim of its own hubristic arrogance. This super crocodile, this Egyptian Shelob, was to go the way of the fabled chaos monster of the sea who attempted to battle with the creator God! The metaphor, used because of its sinister finale, like the nautical one of chap. 27, could discount present power, however great. The Judeans at home, supported by their compatriots in exile, were totally failing to read the historical situation aright. By this imaginative oracle the prophet warned that a pro-Egyptian policy was out of alignment with Yahweh's providential—and destructively powerful—will. In New Testament terms, they were resisting the Holy Spirit (Acts 7:51).

The second oracle, evidently spoken after the failure of Hophra to make a lasting dent in Babylon's armor, draws a historical parallel with the events of the eighth century. Once more, Egypt's support had been shown to have all the strength of a Nile reed. Judah's hopes had been dashed—but what else could one have expected of such demonstrably false hopes, marked as they were by reliance on a human power rather than on Yahweh? Once more it is affirmed that Egypt was on the losing side in the battle between political giants. Yahweh was Babylon's champion, and Egypt was to be its, and his, victim. The future was to make quite clear that Judah had been backing a loser. To gain support for his message, Ezekiel is here consciously reflecting a conviction of eighth-century prophets, especially Isaiah, that spiritual faith had to be exercised in the political arena.

The third and strongest message, written sometime after the heat of religio-political controversy had cooled, wants in part to reaffirm the truths of the earlier oracles: the inevitable harvest of national arrogance and the need for a true faith in God that resists temptations to look elsewhere for salvation. However, evidently there was now a need to temper the message to one of a limited chastening of Egypt, rather than permanent destruction. This toning down is achieved by borrowing from the language of Judah's own past and prospective experience: a limited exile and reduction in power (cf. Vogels, *Bib* 53 [1972] 480-89). The reasons for this reappraisal are no longer discernible. It seeks to know the will of God in terms of a wider agenda. Perhaps there is a recognition that Yahweh may threaten, but eventually "relents of evil" (Joel 2:13; Jonah 4:2) and "has no pleasure in the death of the wicked" (Ezek 33:11; cf. 2 Pet 3:9). Or there may have been a desire to reckon with other, more positive, prophetic traditions concerning Egypt (cf. Jer 46:26): Isa 19:19-22 appears to bear some relation to this passage.

The Sealing of Egypt's Fate (29:17-21)

Bibliography

Carroll, R. P. *When Prophecy Failed: Reactions and Responses to Failure in the Prophetic Traditions.* London: SCM, 1979. **Roberts, J. J. M.** "A Christian Perspective on Prophetic Prediction." *Int* 33 (1979) 240-53. **Unger, E.** "Nebukadnezar II und sein Šandabakku (Oberkommissar) in Tyrus." *ZAW* 44 (1926) 314-17.

Translation

[17] *In the twenty-seventh year, on the first day of the first month, I received the following communication from Yahweh:* [18] *"Human one, Babylon's king Nebuchadnezzar has put his army to strenuous efforts in fighting Tyre. Every head is worn bald and every shoulder chafed, but neither he nor his army has had any remuneration for the efforts he has expended against it.* [19] *That is why the Lord*[a] *Yahweh's message is as follows: I am going to present Babylon's king Nebuchadnezzar with Egypt. He will carry off its troops*[b] *and plunder and loot it, and it will be his army's remuneration.* [20] *As compensation for his efforts*[a] *I give*[b] *him Egypt.*[c] *So runs the oracle of the Lord Yahweh.* [21] *When that happens, I will cause the community of Israel to grow a horn and I will permit you to speak freely. Then they will realize that I am Yahweh."*

Notes

19. a. For the formulaic אדני "Lord" here and in v 20 see the note on 20:3.

19. b. LXX* does not represent this clause. Heb. המון "troops" functions as a catchword in the oracles against Egypt, and it may have been added to enhance this feature (Zimmerli 117).

20. a. Lit. "(as) his wages for which he worked."

20. b. The pf is performative: see 22:13 *Note.*

20. c. MT adds אשר עשו לי "which they have made/done for me." The clause is not represented in LXX Syr and is difficult to relate to the context. Was it a marginal exegetical comment on the end of v 18 "(the work) that he did against it," supplying an expected pl verb (cf. Cornill 368)? If so, it may have slipped because of the similarity of v 18bβ and v 20aα. It is significant that in v 18bβ Vg inserted *mihi* "for me."

Form/Structure/Setting

Two oracles are to be found here, in vv 17-20 and 21. The first appears to be an oracle of judgment in the light of the announcement for punishment for Egypt in its second half (vv 19-20), which is emphatically prefaced with a messenger formula and concluded with a divine saying formula. However, the first element is not an accusation but a statement of the disappointing nature of Nebuchadnezzar's capture of Tyre. This introduction puts the focus on Nebuchadnezzar in vv 19-20, which are thus reminiscent of an oracle of holy war promising victory. In fact, v 20 includes the perfect verb נתתי "I have given" characteristic of such oracles (Zimmerli 118, referring to Josh 6:16). The second oracle is a supplementary double oracle of salvation for Israel and Ezekiel, to whom it is addressed; it concludes with a recognition formula. This positive type of proof saying occurred in 28:25-26. There seems to have been a redactional intent to conclude chap. 29 in a similar way to chap. 28. There is also evidence of redactional alignment within chap. 29: (a) the phrase כל־כתף "every shoulder" (v 18), which appeared earlier at v 7; (b) the role of נתתי(ו) "I have given/and I will give" as a key verb throughout the chapter (vv 4, 5, 10, 12, 20) and indeed the echo of the fuller ונתתי את־ארץ מצרים "and I will give the land of Egypt" (vv 10, 12) in vv 19 and 20; and (c) the initial similarity of vv 8a and 19a, which gives an air of continuity and explanation of the latter verse, just like 21:23-28 (18-23) after 21:13-22 (8-17). Vv 17-20, when read in the light of the foregoing, have their perspective shifted from Nebuchadnezzar to Egypt, and the role of the Babylonian king becomes that of the human agent through whom Yahweh is to do his destructive work against Egypt. Accordingly the redactional role of the oracle is one of judgment.

The historical setting assigned to the oracle of vv 17-20(21) places it sixteen years after that of vv 1-6a and out of sequence with the otherwise consecutive series of Egypt-related oracles in chaps. 29-32. It has been inserted here as a link between the Tyre oracles in chaps. 26-28 and the Egypt oracles of chaps. 29-32. As noted above, it fits well redactionally both in its role within chap. 29 and in its relationship to chap. 28. V 21, although supplementary to vv 17-20, seems to belong to the same period.

Comment

17-18 The date has been reconstructed by Parker and Dubberstein as April 26, 571 B.C. (*Babylonian Chronology* 28). The thirteen-year siege of Tyre (see *Form/ Structure/Setting* of chap. 26) must have lasted about 586-573 B.C. This date is the latest one attached to Ezekiel's oracles and gives some indication of the length of his prophetic ministry. The objective reason for the oracle is supplied in v 18. However, the more immediate agenda is implied by v 21ab: Ezekiel was being criticized by his Jewish contemporaries for the lack of precise fulfillment of his oracles against Tyre. It was to some extent a carping criticism: the siege was successful and Tyre did pass into Babylonian control. In a list of royal hostages at Nebuchadnezzar's court, to be dated about 570 B.C., the king of Tyre has the initial place (*ANET* 308a; Katzenstein, *History of Tyre* 326). About 564 B.C. Baal, Ethbaal's successor as king of Tyre, was replaced by a Babylonian High Commissioner (Katzenstein, *History* 332-33; cf. Unger, *ZAW* 44 [1926] 314-17). Any prophet might have been glad to chalk it up as a vindication of his or her prediction, despite Nebuchadnezzar's non-destruction of Tyre. Evidently Nebuchadnezzar's troops returned home disgruntled at the lack of loot: after so long a campaign they found Tyre's cupboard bare, used up over the years or salted away by its fleet to a safe place. Their expected perquisites and indeed perhaps their literal wages (cf. Cooke 329 with reference to Driver) had not been forthcoming. The disappointment, overheard by the exiles, was used as a weapon against Ezekiel, who had indeed spoken of spoils (26:5, 12). To him then was given this sympathetic word from Yahweh.

Most of v 18 is carefully constructed as a chiasmus, with an ABCD/DCBA structure. In sense its double center qualifies the first half. It relates to the carrying of loads on the head and shoulders during the siege. These may be simply conventional expressions for land siege warfare (cf. 26:8 and *Comment*) or perhaps efforts were made to construct a causeway between the mainland and the island, as Alexander was to do later. Essentially Yahweh takes over responsibility for the situation from Nebuchadnezzar, who functioned as Yahweh's agent. Pastorally, of course, Yahweh is lifting the blame from Ezekiel's head and shoulders.

19-20 The initial response to the situation described in v 18 corresponds to that verse at beginning and end (v 19aβ, bβ); the parallel clauses in the middle (v 19bα) have a qualifying function, like the center of v 18. V 20a echoes another component of v 18, עבד "do, work," and serves as a final restatement of v 19aβ and 19b. Promise of a victory over Egypt anticipates Nebuchadnezzar's campaign against Hophra's successor Ahmose II in 568 B.C., which may already have been in the air. The new oracle applies an adaptive principle to the old, not completely satisfying, oracle: a switch of position is offered as compensation for the exuberant claim with which Ezekiel's constituency found fault (Carroll, *When Prophecy Failed*, 172-77).

21 An accompanying disclosure spells out, again in terms of consolation, the advantages to accrue to both the Jewish community and to the prophet himself. The initial "on that day" seems to be simply an adverb of time, rather than having the specialized eschatological function it often does in oracles of salvation (Fohrer 170; cf. S. DeVries, *Yesterday, Today, Tomorrow* [Grand Rapids: Eerdmans, 1975] 306). Despite the royal usage of the phrase אצמיח קרן "I will cause a horn to grow" in Ps 132:17, to take it as messianic in this context would amount to eisegesis. The horn is a common metaphor for vigor and power (cf. Ps. 92:11[10]). Ezekiel's critics by implication cast doubt on the positive images that he delivered in the period after the fall of Jerusalem concerning renewal and restoration to the land. This promised resurgence here finds confirmation. Ezekiel too is encouraged by promise of vindication of his messages. The expression פתחון פה "opening of the mouth" occurs also in 16:63. The usage in these two passages is to be differentiated from the special circumstances encountered in 24:27, which historically lay in the past (cf. 33:22). Here it connotes confidence in speech. Greenberg (*Ezekiel 1-20* 121) by comparison with Mishnaic Hebrew has seen in the phrase the connotation "a claim to be heard" afforded by the fulfillment of Ezekiel's oracles. The pastoral encouragement comes to a head in the recognition formula. The prophet is reminded that he is a witness to Yahweh and that Yahweh's revelation of himself depends on his vindication of Ezekiel by fulfilling the oracles entrusted to him.

Explanation

These twin oracles, which historically mark the end of Ezekiel's recorded ministry to the exiles, reveal an all too human situation. The prophet is the victim of literalists who pass on to him the resentment of returning Babylonian veterans, in the form of blame that implicitly casts doubt on the positive oracles that flowed from Ezekiel in the latter part of his ministry. Readers must be careful not to share the woodenness of Ezekiel's contemporary critics and so distance themselves from the text itself. The prophet "does not find it necessary to defend or explain away his earlier prophecy; in effect he just admits that it didn't happen. The failure of a prediction in every detail thus does not appear to have been considered any great scandal . . . Prophecy [must have been understood] in a way different from those who believe it must involve one hundred percent predictions" (Gowan 103). An element of rhetorical exuberance was naturally involved in prophesying, the role of which was to persuade the audience of a basic theme, using both conventional and emotional language as supportive aids. Physical images may be used to convey emotional reality (Roberts, *Int* 33 [1977] 251). Language contains a legitimate element of hyperbole, and prophetic language is entitled to this feature. For Ezekiel the criticism was evidently a depressing experience, which warranted these two messages that dealt with the immediate complaint and also with the implication that Ezekiel's subsequent positive ministry was untrustworthy. It is pastorally reassuring to observe that Ezekiel's recorded oracles conclude with a divine concern for the prophet himself, so that he might share the spirit of Isa 49:4: "My cause is in Yahweh's hands and my recompense lies with my God" (cf. 1 Cor 4:1-5).

The redactional agenda of these verses is a different one. Their content functions as a supportive statement of the downfall of Egypt and so as a confirmation of the work of God in the world of political power, and as an assurance that his destructive work was a precursor of salvation for his people. Yahweh would effect his providential will, clearing obstacles from his people's and his own path (cf. v 16; 28:24) before he brought rehabilitation and honor (v 21; cf. 28:25-26). He was to use his lordship of history as a means of fulfilling his covenant purposes (cf. Rev 11:15-18).

Egypt's Day of the Lord (30:1-19)

Bibliography

Hossfeld, F.-L. *Untersuchungen zu Komposition und Theologie des Ezechielbuches.* FzB 20. Würzburg: Echter Verlag, 1977, 99-152.

Translation

[1]I received the following communication from Yahweh: [2]"Human one, prophesy and say that the message of the Lord[a] Yahweh is as follows:
Wail 'Alas, the day!'
[3]because Yahweh's day is nearly here.[a]
A day of clouds,
it will be a fateful time for the nations.
[4]A sword will invade Egypt
and anguish will befall Ethiopia,
when people drop dead in Egypt[a]
and its foundations are razed.
[5]Ethiopia, Put, Lud and all the various foreign troops, and Libya(?)[a] and the people of the covenant land will fall there,[b] victims of the sword along with them.
[6]Egypt's supporters will fall
and its vaunted power will collapse.
From Migdol to Syene[a]
people will fall there, victims of the sword.
So runs the Lord Yahweh's oracle.
[7]It[a] will be desolated, becoming as desolate as a country could be,[b] and its[c] cities will be as ruined as any city could ever be. [8]Then they will realize that I am Yahweh, when I set fire to Egypt and all its helpers are shattered. [9]At that time messengers will leave my presence[a] in ships[b] to alarm the heedless[c] Ethiopians, and anguish will befall them on Egypt's fateful day—indeed it is on its way.

[10]"The message of the Lord Yahweh is as follows: I will use the Babylonian king Nebuchadnezzar to make an end of Egypt's troops. [11]He and his army with him, the most terrible army in the world, will be brought in to ravage the country. They will draw their swords against Egypt and fill the country with their dead. [12]I will make the Nile streams dry, selling the country into the control of evil folk,[a] I will use foreigners to devastate the country and everything in it. I, Yahweh, have given my word.

[13]"The message of the Lord Yahweh is as follows: I will make an end of rulers[a] from Memphis and no leader will arise any more from Egypt. I will inflict fear on Egypt.[b] [14]I will devastate Pathros and set fire to Zoan. I will carry out acts of judgment on Thebes. [15]I will drench with my wrath Egypt's stronghold Pelusium and will make an end of Thebes'[a] troops. [16]I will set fire to Egypt. Pelusium will writhe in anguish[a] and Thebes will be breached. Memphis will be attacked in broad daylight (?).[b] [17]At On[a] and Pibeseth men in their prime will fall to the sword, while their communities[b] will leave as captives. [18]At Tahpanhes the day will turn dark[a] when I break Egypt's scepters[b] there and its vaunted power is brought to an end in it. It will be covered with a cloud, and its women

folk^c will leave as captives. ^19*I will carry out acts of judgment against the Egyptians^a—then they will realize that I am Yahweh.*"

Notes

2. a. For the formulaic אדני "Lord" here and in vv 6, 10 and 13 see the note on 20:3.

3. a. MT adds וקרוב יום "and near is the day" after v 3aα. It is not represented in LXX* and is taken by most as a dittograph. In MT the first, anarthrous יום "a day" is difficult. Hossfeld (*Untersuchungen* 192) has adduced in favor of the shorter text the chiastic inclusion of v 3: קרוב יום "near is the day"/יהיה עת־גוים "a time for the nations it will be."

4. a. MT adds ולקחו המונה "and they take away its troops," not represented in LXX* and probably reflecting a tendency in MT to increase the frequency of המון "army," a catchword in the Egyptian oracles (cf. 29:19 *Note*). The act verb with indefinite subj is awkward and the content does not accord with the death and destruction of the context.

5. a. MT כוב "Kub" is not known. It may be an error for לוב "Libya," which LXX Λίβυες "Libyans" at the end of the previous list may support, although elsewhere it stands for פום "Put."

5. b. MT begins v 6 with כה אמר יהוה "thus said Yahweh." In its place LXX* presupposes בָהּ "in it," taking it with v 5. In the light of the clause in v 6bβ, probably this was corrupted to כה by a not uncommon ב/כ error, and subsequently filled out in terms of the messenger formula under the influence of the final divine saying formula in v 6bβ. The lack of the normal אדני "Lord" suggests a secondary hand (Zimmerli 124).

6. a. MT סוֵנה should be pointed סוֵנה "to Syene": see 29:10 *Note*.

7. a. For MT נשמו "they will be desolated" we should read fem sg נשמה with reference to Egypt, as LXX presupposes and as 29:12 suggests. MT evidently suffered mechanical assimilation to ו(יפל) earlier and/or to נשמו(ת) later.

7. b. For the superlative idiom here and in v 7b see 29:12 *Note*.

7. c. MT עריו "its cities" has a masc suffix: עריה with fem suffix is expected, as in 29:12. To relate the suffix to Pharaoh (Smend 238) hardly seems possible.

9. a. LXX* does not represent מלפני "from before me," perhaps finding difficulty with it. The term seems to develop in 8bα "when I set fire to Egypt," which implies Yahweh's presence in Egypt.

9. b. The Heb. appears to echo the thought of Isa 18:2. LXX* Σ Syr may imply אצים "hastening" (cf. RSV, NEB), as Θ εσσιμ evidently does.

9. c. For the adjectival use of בטח "security" cf. Gen 34:25.

12. a. LXX* does not represent v 12aβ, which employs unusual language (see Zimmerli 125) and does not fit the adjacent topics of natural and military catastrophes. However, it is difficult to see why it was added. Does omission of a nineteen letter line underlie LXX?

13. a. LXX appears to presuppose אילים "rams, leaders" for אלילים "divine images" and does not represent the earlier clause in MT והאבדתי גלולים "and I will destroy idols." MT seems to reflect a later reference to Egyptian gods, perhaps encouraged by a miswriting of אילים (Hossfeld, *Untersuchungen* 198). It is significant that the term אלילים occurs in Ezekiel only here, whereas איל(ים) does occur in the sense of rulers (17:13; 31:11; 32:21; 34:17).

13. b. LXX* Syr lack v 13b, but with its mention of Egypt it seems to be required structurally: see *Form/Structure/Setting*.

15. a. LXX presupposes נף "Memphis" for MT נא "Thebes," and in v 16aβ סון "Syene" for MT סין "Sin," evidently seeking to vary the repeated terms. The structure of the passage supports MT (see *Form/Structure/Setting*).

16. a. The verbal forms are uncertain, as the K and Q variants attest. An inf abs form חול seems to be required. Q חָחוּל may represent vocalic assimilation (GKC 73d).

16. b. Lit. "and as for Memphis enemies (or besiegers) of daylight." Boadt (*Ezekiel's Oracles* 79) urges that the preceding verbal phrase does double duty: "and Memphis will be for (= serve as) daytime besiegers." LXX seems to presuppose ונפוצו מים "and water will spread" or ונפרצו מים "and water will burst forth." RSV "and its walls broken down" follows Cornill's imaginative emendation ונפרצו חומתיה (371).

17. a. LXX Vg rightly presuppose אן "On, Heliopolis" for MT's misvocalization אָוֶן "iniquity."

17. b. Lit. "they" (fem pl), referring to the (inhabitants of the) cities.

18. a. For חשׂך "withhold" MT has an alternative tradition חשׁך "grow dark," which the ancient versions support (see *BHS*). In the first case an ellipse of the natural object (sc. "its light" [cf. Cooke

334]) or an intransitive force "withdraw" (Driver, *JTS* 34 [1933] 380) is presupposed. Darkness is associated with day of Yahweh imagery (cf. e.g., Zeph 1:15).

18. b. The breaking of מֹטוֹת "yoke bars" (MT) suggests liberation (Cornill 372; Zimmerli 127). LXX Vg (cf. Syr) presuppose מַטּוֹת "scepters," which provides more obvious parallelism with v 18aγ (cf. Boadt, *Ezekiel's Oracles* 82-83).

18. c. Or "dependent towns."

19. a. Heb. מצרים signifies not "Egypt" but "Egyptians" here and in vv 23 and 26.

Form/Structure/Setting

Vv 1-19 are distinguished as a literary unit by the message reception formula and the formula of prophetic address in vv 1-2; the former does not reappear until v 20. The repeated messenger formulas in vv 2, 10 and 13 (for v 6 see *Note*), the recognition formulas of vv 8 and 19, and the confirmatory statement of v 13 serve to separate the piece into three smaller units, vv 1-9, 10-12 and 13-19. The divine saying formula that closes v 6 seems to have an intermediate role, here marking the conclusion of a subdivision. The first unit is a proof saying announcing judgment for Egypt and concluding in v 9 with a supplementary statement that serves to round off the unit. The second unit is an oracle of pure judgment, lacking (like the first) any note of accusation. The third is a proof saying that permutates conventional terms of divine aggression with mention of Egypt and its key cities.

As to structure, vv 2-9 are marked by a double, inverted inclusion (AB . . . BA) at vv 2b-4a and 8b-9, which features (ליהוה) יום "the day (of the Lord)" and a cluster of terms, "Ethiopia," "Egypt" and חלחלה "anguish" (cf. Boadt, *Ezekiel's Oracles* 71, who, however, thinks in terms of a larger chiastic structure). Vv 10-12 have their own inclusion ביד "by the agency of, into the hand of" in vv 10 and 12a, b. Its punning sequence חרבותם "their swords" (v 11) and חרבה "dryness" (v 12) reads like an echo of בחרב "by the sword" (vv 4-6) and נחרבות "desolated" (v 7).

Boadt has sensitively split vv 13-19 into three sections, vv 13-14a, 14b-16a and 16b-19 (*Ezekiel's Oracles* 74-75; Hossfeld offers a different threefold structure [*Untersuchungen* 201]). While each section mentions Egypt twice, the second also alternates two cities, Thebes and Pelusium, in a checkerboard sequence into which the two references to Egypt are integrated in an overall ABCACBA pattern. The other two sections both start their random lists of cities with Memphis.

The complex of small units has been supplied with a double inclusion, by echoing the "day" (יום) and the "clouds" (ענן) of vv 2b-3 in v 18. This is the only group of oracles in the Egyptian collection that lacks an initial dating. There is a scholarly tendency to use aesthetic appreciation as the bench mark of originality and so to credit Ezekiel with the first oracle, if any, because of its creative application of the "day of Yahweh" imagery to Egypt and because of its poetic form, at least in vv 2-4, 6 (cf. Eichrodt 415-18; Zimmerli 127-28). The oracle of vv 10-12, with its precise mention of Nebuchadnezzar, must antedate his attack on Egypt in 568 B.C. It is not close enough to the previous oracle to be regarded as originating in a literary expansion of it—the meaning of גוים "nations" in v 3, where it is explained by "Egypt" and "Cush" (v 4), and in v 11 is quite different—and yet its similarities, especially the wordplay of (ה)חרב as "sword" and "dryness," make it a fitting sequel. The verbal affinities with 28:7, 10 may indicate that language used concerning Tyre is deliberately being reapplied to Egypt.

The oracle in vv 13-19 seems consciously to be echoing at its close the earlier, distinctive "day of Yahweh" language, which suggests that it was written as a literary affirmation of the coming fall of Egypt. The recurrence of other phraseology from the first and second oracles (e.g., בחרב יפלו) "they will fall by the sword," vv 5, 6, 17; והשמתי "and I will devastate," vv 12, 14) points in the same direction. These criteria are more solidly grounded than Cooke's modern distaste for a "haphazard enumeration of . . . cities" (331). The listing of cities is a traditional prophetic technique in foreign and also domestic oracles (cf. Isa 15:1-9; Jer 48:1-5; Mic 1:10-16).

Comment

1-6 The concept of the day of Yahweh is well attested as a sinister prophetic figure of judgment against Israel or other nations. Ezekiel had made use of it in chap. 7 (see esp. 7:7), with Israel as its target. Yet what threatened Israel threatened the nations also, according to the prophetic pattern (cf. Lam 1:21, RSV; Zeph 1:3-4, 18; 2:3; Obad 11-14, 15). In vv 2b-3 the announcement of the day begins with a traditional call to communal lamentation: of its three standard elements of a plural imperative, a vocative and an explanatory clause, only the second is absent (cf. Joel 1:5-14; Isa 13:6; cf. H. W. Wolff, *Joel and Amos* [ET Philadelphia: Fortress Press, 1972] 21-22). It is here combined with a cry of lamentation similar to Joel 1:15, while there too, as also in Isa 13:6, the explanation features the nearness of the day, the earliest known instance of which occurs in Zeph 1:7, 14. As a time of Yahweh's intervention, his day was associated with motifs of theophany, attendant storm and "cloud" (cf. Zeph 1:15). The prophet seems to exploit older language and conceptions, which he applies to Egypt and to Ethiopia, its southern neighbor, in terms of death and devastation. The function of v 5 is to elaborate the reference to Ethiopia in v 4 as further victim of the coming destruction (cf. Eichrodt 414). Since it is in prose, it may have been added to the oral version of the oracle. It specifies auxiliary and mercenary troops in the Egyptian army and interestingly appears to include Jewish mercenaries (cf. B. Oded, *Israelite and Judean History*, ed. J. H. Hayes and J. M. Miller [Philadelphia: Westminster, 1977] 487). A mightier force would prove victor under Yahweh and bring about the subjection of Egypt, from south to north (cf. *Comment* on 29:10).

7-9 The superlatives for destruction, so telling that they were taken over in 29:12 (cf. Zimmerli 128, 130), describe a scenario that would be revelatory to its victims. The supplementary statement in v 9 imaginatively borrows from Isaiah's oracle against Ethiopia in Isa 18:1-2. The detail of ambassadors sailing the Nile is used to help to draw a word picture of apprehension and dread.

10-12 The originally independent little oracle that follows grounds the coming destruction of Egypt in political actualities. Nebuchadnezzar is named as Yahweh's agent and so, in this context, as the wielder of the sword of the previous oracle. The total devastation that was stated earlier in geographical terms (v 6b) is now expressed in the doubled reference to fullness (ומלאו "and they will fill," v 11; ומלאה "and its fullness," v 12). The explicit reference to Nebuchadnezzar prompts the reader to ask how it relates to historical fact. There has survived a Babylonian fragment that mentions Nebuchadnezzar's campaign against Egypt in his 37th year, in 586 B.C. (see *ANET* 308b; D. J. Wiseman, *Chronicles of Chaldean Kings*,

London: British Museum, 1956, 94-95; *CAH,* vol. 3, 215, 304; Katzenstein, *History of Tyre* 338), but it seems to have achieved Egyptian acceptance of Nebuchadnezzar's control of Palestine and Syria rather than his mastery of Egypt itself. The purpose of the early Egyptian oracles was to dash contemporary Judean hopes rather than to establish predictive parameters of future history (see *Explanation* of 29:17-21). The strong language of destruction (and of exile in vv 17, 18, etc.) characterizes Egypt as a political nonentity in the face of Yahweh's sovereign will.

13-19 By its re-use of earlier language this literary oracle wants to reaffirm the message of the fall of Egypt. The message is set in a new framework of lists of cities, interspersed with references to Egypt as a whole. They serve to break up the mention of the land and its cities (v 7) and of Egypt and "its fullness" (vv 11-12) in a detailed and specific manner. In the first section, vv 13-14a, pride of place is given to Memphis, an important city of Lower Egypt, as doomed to lose its civil authorities and in this respect a paradigm for Egypt as a whole. Upper Egypt ("Pathros") would not escape; Zoan in the eastern Delta would also suffer.

The second section, vv 14b-16a, selects two cities, northern and southern, as microcosms of fated Egypt, combining them in an artistic permutation. Thebes, a key city in Upper Egypt, is polarized with Pelusium in the N.E. Delta, a frontier city of military importance. In the last section, vv 16b-19, the singling out of specific targets begins with Memphis, as in the first section. It moves north to the adjacent city of On or Heliopolis and then further north to Pibeseth or Bubastis. It concludes with Tahpanhes in the N.E. Delta, and at the same time reverts to the opening theme of the first oracle, the day of Yahweh, first combining it with the traditional motif of darkness and then repeating the clouds of v 3. On a smaller scale, the smashing of Egypt's political power echoes thematically the oracle's own beginning (v 13a). By such means was Yahweh to break into the historical scene as a factor to be reckoned with.

Explanation

The prophet Joel, faced with a spiritually apathetic audience, stabbed it awake with the theme of the day of the Lord (Joel 1:15-2:11). It is reasonable to suppose that Ezekiel too made use of this ultimate weapon in the prophetic armory in order to add emotional vehemence to an unwelcome message. Did vv 1-9 originate in the Indian summer of 29:1, when expectations of Egyptian aid for a beleaguered Jerusalem ran high? If so, Ezekiel's realistic message was that the only deus ex machina intervention to await was one in which Egypt would be the victim. The sinister language and grim associations of the day of the Lord are used at the start and finish to communicate this unpalatable truth. For all its military power, reinforced by allied and mercenary contingents, Egypt was to be no match for Yahweh and the destructive forces at his disposal. The message is part of Ezekiel's larger agenda, that God's way forward for his people lay only by way of frustration and loss.

The role of vv 10-12 is to accentuate the human and divine agencies at work against Egypt, combining to nullify Judean hopes. At Yahweh's behest

Nebuchadnezzar was to continue his conquests down into Egypt. It was Ezekiel's way of emphasizing that the Judeans had put their political and providential eggs into the wrong basket. The final message means to underline the two earlier ones. By interweaving echoes of them into a recital of Egypt's urban centers, it states that none of its cities was so great or so impregnable as to escape the wrath of God against those who challenged his will (cf. Rev 6:12-17).

Egypt's Broken Arms (30:20-26)

Translation

²⁰*In the eleventh year, on the seventh of the first month, I received the following communication from Yahweh:* ²¹*"Human one, I have broken the arm of the Egyptian king Pharaoh. In fact it has not been bandaged to allow healing by applying a dressing,*ª *with the prospect of its getting strong enough to wield a sword.* ²²*Accordingly the message of the Lord*ª *Yahweh is as follows: I am an opponent of the Egyptian king Pharaoh. I intend to break both his arms, the strong one as well as the broken one,*ᵇ *and make the sword drop out of his hand.* ²³*I will scatter the Egyptians among other nations, dispersing them in foreign countries.* ²⁴*I will strengthen the arms of the Babylonian king and put my sword into his hand; but I will break Pharaoh's arms and he will face him with the groans of a dying person.*ª ²⁵*I will strengthen*ª *the arms of the Babylonian king, but Pharaoh's arms will fall useless to his side. Then people will realize that I am Yahweh, when I have put my sword into the hand of the Babylonian king and he brandishes it over Egypt, country wide,* ²⁶*and when*ª *I scatter the Egyptians among other nations, dispersing them in foreign countries—then they will realize that I am Yahweh."*

Notes

21. a. MT adds לחבשה "(or) bandaging it," not represented in LXX* and otiose after חבשה "it was bandaged" earlier. To define it as a gloss on לשום חתול "by applying a dressing" (Zimmerli 136) seems unlikely: theoretically the opposite would be more feasible. In MT the phrase לחבשה לחזקה "to bandage it, to strengthen it" probably represents a doublet, with the correct reading standing beside an erroneous term written under the influence of חבשה "it was bandaged" earlier.

22. a. For the formulaic אדני "Lord" see the note on 20:3.

22. b. Heb. את-החזקה ואת-הנשברת "the strong one and the broken one" is often deleted as a clumsy attempt to harmonize the arms yet to be broken with the broken one of v 21 (Cooke 337; Eichrodt 419; Wevers 233). The ancient versions found difficulty with the phrase, seemingly on rationalizing grounds (cf. Zimmerli, ibid.).

24. a. In place of v 24b LXX has "and he will bring it upon Egypt and he will plunder it and loot it" (cf. *BHS*). This material seems to go back to two Heb. explanatory glosses, first, מביא עליך חרב "(I am) about to bring a sword upon you" from 29:8, and, second, ושלל שללה ובזז בזה "and he will plunder it and loot it" from 29:19. The first gloss was meant to elucidate v 25bβγ ("when I put . . . Egypt") and the second v 25bγ ("and he has brandished . . . Egypt"). The glosses were incorporated into the text, with the wrongful application of the first statement to Nebuchadnezzar; in the process they displaced v 24b. *BHK* and *BHS* have reversed the looting clauses in their notes (contrast Zimmerli 137): the evidence for retroversion of the terms in the LXX is not crystal clear, but tends to support an order as in 29:19.

25. a. The Heb. hiph over against the piel in v 24 exhibits a type of variation found in poetic parallel clauses, the use of two different conjugations of the same verb (cf. M. Dahood, *Psalms 101-150* 414; Boadt, *Ezekiel's Oracles* 32-33).

26. a. For this syntactical interpretation see *Form/Structure/Setting*.

Form/Structure/Setting

This unit is initially similar to 29:17-21 in following a dated message reception formula with a prophetic address that lacks a commission to speak, and then citing an established fact that is made the logical basis of a divine assurance. The oracle is a proof saying in view of the recognition formula(s) of vv 25b-26. However, its initial part is not an accusation, as the use of לכן "therefore" in v 22 might suggest. Rather, in the context the conjunction has the looser sense of "accordingly," in arguing from the past to the future. The repetitions in vv 22-26 suggest to the redaction critic that the passage has been worked over and amplified (cf. Cooke 335-36; Zimmerli 137-39). The rhetorical critic, on the other hand, although not averse to the possibility of redactional unity, wants to ask whether or not repetition has been used deliberately for emphasis. From this perspective the pronouncement of judgment may be understood in terms of three sections: a fourfold statement of Pharaoh's overwhelming defeat (vv 22aγ-23), a fourfold statement of victory and defeat (v 24) and a double statement of victory and defeat (v 25a). Each section mentions royal arms, negatively in the first case and both positively and negatively in the other two. The recognition formula in v 25bα is followed by two resumptive elements (v 25bβ-26), which look back to the second and first sections, respectively. Their length not unreasonably warranted a repetition of the recognition formula (cf. Zimmerli, *Ezekiel 1* 39). Probably vv 25-26 together comprise a longer, climactic third section, which recapitulates the other two in a comprehensive summary. There seems to be no need to envisage v 21 as originally an independent oracle that was subsequently expanded (e.g., Fohrer 173-74; Zimmerli 137; contrast Eichrodt 420). Its motifs of Pharaoh's broken arm and unused sword prepare well for the triple sequel. Boadt's double chiastic scheme (*Ezekiel's Oracles* 86), with a break after v 22, suffers from the defect of highlighting the role of the sword in vv 21-22 but ignoring it in v 24 (v 25b is judged to be an addition).

As to setting, both date and content suggest that news of the Babylonians' repulse of the Egyptian attack had reached the exiles, in the period before the fall of Jerusalem.

Comment

20-21 Parker and Dubberstein's reconstruction of the date is April 29, 587 B.C. (*Babylonian Chronology* 28). The significance of the date in Judah's history is that it was about three months before the besieging Babylonians managed to break through the walls of Jerusalem (2 Kgs 25:3-4). The statement of v 21 implies that the Judean exiles had by now heard that Hophra's attempt to come to the aid of Judah, while initially successful in drawing away the invaders, had failed (cf. Jer 34:21-22; 37:5). The information is cast in a standard theological turn of phrase (cf. Job 38:15; Ps 10:16[15]; Jer 48:25), in order to claim that a higher agenda than human conflict had been pursued and that Hophra had suffered a decisive defeat, as v 21b underlines. In content v 21 could stand by itself, but in form it looks forward to the sequel in vv 22-26.

22-26 Hophra's military future is invested with even stronger negative language. It is stronger in intensity ("break arms," as in Ps 37:17; cf. Job 22:9), in its series of repeated motifs and in its polarization of the defeat of the Egyptian king and the victory of the Babylonian king. Freedy and Redford, *JAOS* 90 (1970) 471 note 39, 482, have plausibly seen in the breaking of two arms the defeat of a two-pronged attack by land and sea, of which the first had already been repulsed (cf. Boadt, *Ezekiel's Oracles* 85). The reference to breaking the broken arm strains the metaphor, but is probably a case of passionate rhetoric outrunning reason. The final section in vv 25-26 adds its own emphasis by using the recognition formula to recapitulate the most telling statements, that the Babylonian king was to be Yahweh's swordsman in attacking Egypt and that so utter would be Egypt's eventual defeat that deportation would occur. It may be that we are to see in the vehemence of this oracle a psychic presentiment of the Persian king Cambyses' brutal conquest of Egypt in 525 B.C.

Explanation

Like Jeremiah, Ezekiel had the difficult task of communicating to his Judean hearers an unpatriotic message. Elsewhere he established on moral grounds the prophetic truth that Yahweh's judgment was at work in the fall of Jerusalem. As a corollary he had to counter jingoistic hopes with theological cold comfort. His vehement language was a loud and repeated "no" to the nervous optimism of his compatriots. If Judah was doomed by divine decree, so too were all attempts to save it. The prophet's yearning was that not only his fellow exiles but all people would confess the lordship of Yahweh and assent to his sovereign will (cf. Isa 45:23-25; Phil 2:10-11). Before such a hope all lesser hopes had to wither.

The Felling of the Egyptian Cosmic Tree (31:1-18)

Bibliography

Eissfeldt, O. "Schwerterschlagene bei Hesekiel." *Studies in OT Prophecy.* FS T. H. Robinson, ed. H. H. Rowley. New York: Scribner, 1950, 73-81. **Eliade, M.** *Patterns in Comparative Religion.* E. T. London and New York: Sheed and Ward, 1958. **Fishbane, M.** *Biblical Interpretation in Ancient Israel.* Oxford: Clarendon, 1985, 46-48. **Gowan, D. E.** *When Man Becomes God: Humanism and Hybris in the OT.* Pittsburgh: Pickwick, 1975, 94-116. **Haag, E.** "Ez 31 und die alttestamentliche Paradiesvorstellung." *Wort, Lied und Gottesspruch.* FS J. Ziegler, ed. J. Schreiner. Würzburg: Echter Verlag, 1972, 171-78. **Lods, A.** "La mort des incirconcis." *Comptes rendus de l'Académie des Inscriptions et Belles-Lettres,* 1943, 271-83. **Solomon, A. M. V.** "Fable." *Saga, Legend, Tale, Novella, Fable,* ed. G. W. Coats. JSOTS 35. Sheffield: JSOT, 1985, 114-25. **Widengren, G.** *The King and the Tree of Life in Ancient Near Eastern Religion.* UUÅ 1951:4. Uppsala: Lundequistska Bokhandeln, 1951.

Translation

[1]*In the eleventh year, on the first of the third month, I received the following communication from Yahweh:* [2]*"Human one, address the Egyptian king Pharaoh and his entire army:*

With what[a] *do you compare in your magnificence?*
[3]*There was a cypress*[a]
or a cedar in Lebanon
with beautiful branches[b]
and lofty height,
whose top was up in the clouds.[c]
[4]*Water made it so magnificent,*
the deep made it grow so tall,
letting its currents flow[a]
round where it was planted,[b]
and sending its channels
to all the trees in the countryside (?).[c]
[5]*That is why its height became more lofty*
than all the other trees in the countryside.
Its branches grew large,
its boughs grew long
because of abundant water in its shoots.[a]
[6]*Every bird in the sky*
used its branches for nesting,
and every animal in the countryside
gave birth to its young beneath its boughs,
while every powerful nation
lived[a] *in its shade.*

> [7] *It was magnificently beautiful*
> *with its long limbs,*
> *because its root system*
> *had access to abundant water.*
> [8] *Other cedars could not rival*[a] *it*
> *in God's garden,*
> *junipers*[b] *could not match its branches*
> *nor could plane trees*[c] *compare*
> *with its boughs.*
> *No tree in God's garden*
> *was like it, such beauty did it have.*
> [9] *I made it a beautiful thing*[a]
> *with its abundant limbs,*
> *and it was the envy of all of Eden's trees,*
> *which were in God's garden.*

[10] *That is why the Lord*[a] *Yahweh's message is as follows: Inasmuch as it*[b] *was so lofty in height, putting its top up in the clouds, and its pride soared with its height,* [11] *I handed*[a] *it over to a leader of nations, to deal*[b] *with it as its wickedness warranted. I expelled it,*[c] [12] *and aliens, the most terrible in the world, cut it down. They hurled*[a] *it on the mountains. Its limbs fell into every valley, its boughs lay broken in every ravine on the earth. All the peoples in the world fled*[b] *from its shade, when it was hurled out.*[c] [13] *On its fallen trunk perched*[a] *every bird in the sky, while over its boughs prowled every animal in the countryside.* [14] *This happened to stop any watered trees gaining such lofty height and putting their tops up in the clouds,*[a] *or any irrigated trees reaching up to them by means of their height. In fact they have all been assigned to death, to the underworld, to share the human lot, to join those who descend to the Pit.*

[15] *The message of the Lord Yahweh is as follows: On the day it descended to Sheol, I caused the deep to mourn for it.*[a] *I restrained its currents—the abundant water was held back. I dressed Lebanon in black for it, and every tree in the countryside fainted*[b] *over it.* [16] *At the noise of its fall I made nations quake, when I brought it down to Sheol to be with*[a] *all who descend to the Pit. In the underworld every one of Eden's trees, the choicest*[b] *of Lebanon, every irrigated tree, was gratified.* [17] *They too descended with it to Sheol, to join victims of violent death, while those among the nations who once lived in its shade perished.*[a] [18] *With what do you compare in such*[a] *splendor and magnificence among Eden's trees? Yet you will be brought down with Eden's trees to the underworld, to live among the uncircumcised, along with victims of violent death. This is all about Pharaoh and his entire army. So runs the Lord Yahweh's oracle.*"

Notes

2. a. For the sense "what" for מִי (normally "who") see Driver, *Bib* 35 (1954) 300.

3. a. Heb. אַשּׁוּר is problematic. RSV "I will liken you to" adopts the emendation לְ(אֶרֶז) אֲשֻׁוְךָ (*BHK*). It may be a variant of תְּאַשּׁוּר "cypress" (27:6; for similar variants see Boadt, *Ezekiel's Oracles* 99) or a miswriting for it (cf. *BHS* et al.). If it means "Assyria," then vv 3-17 are a metaphorical description of the past power of Assyria (Ehrlich, *Randglossen* 115-16; Joüon, *Bib* 10 [1910] 309 note 1; van den Born 188; Haag, *Wort* 172-73; Fishbane, *Biblical Interpretation* 46-48; NEB). But v 18 implies that the question of v 2b is rhetorical rather than literally answered by reference to Assyria. Vv 3-8, rather than answering the initial question, draw a metaphorical parallel between Pharaoh or Egypt and an incomparable tree (cf. v 8; Smend 246). "When we follow the connection of ideas,

we cannot fail to see that Assyria is not in the prophet's thoughts at all" (Skinner 272)

3. b. MT adds וחרש מצל "(beautiful as to branches) and as to shade-giving growth" or "and over-shadowing the wood." LXX* does not represent the phrase, which does not accord with the parallel-ism of the accompanying phrases. Ehrlich (*Randglossen* 116) plausibly explained it, with the sense "shady growth," as a gloss on עבותים, understanding it as "interwoven foliage" (cf. BDB 721b).

3. c. Ezekiel consistently uses the form עבותים for עבות "clouds," in 19:11; 31:3, 10, 14. See the *Note* on 19:11.

4. a. MT הלך "going" seems somehow to have the tree as subject. LXX implies הלכה "(the deep) made to go," a good external parallel with שלחה "it sent" in the next line.

4. b. MT מטעה must be pointed with a masc suffix מטעו "its place of planting" since the tree is masc.

4. c. This reading is universally attested, but can hardly be right, since (i) it fails to explain the superiority of the special tree (v 5a) and (ii) external parallelism requires a reference to the tree itself. Early vertical dittography could account for the present text, but, if so, what originally stood there is irrecoverable (cf. *BHS*). Ehrlich (*Randglossen* 116) attempted to explain the text on the sup-position that תעלה "watercourse, channel" was much smaller than נהר "river," and so supplied less water.

5. a. V 5 has been regarded as a later addition because of its Aramaisms גבהא "it was high" and סרעפתיו "its branches" (contrast the form in vv 6, 8). Boadt (*Ezekiel's Oracles* 108) suggests stylistic variation. LXX* lacks one of the parallel clauses in v 5b, and the deletion of the second is sometimes counseled (Cornill 375; *BHS*), but v 12 seems to echo it in a contrast. Boadt (*Ezekiel's Oracles*, ibid.) has noted the parallelism of רב "great" and ארך "long" in the credal statement of Exod 34:6, etc. MT בשלחו "when it sent forth (branches?)" is difficult and perhaps for that reason not represented in LXX*. It may be a short writing for בשלחיו "in its shoots" (Cornill 375-76; RSV) or "in its channels" (Bewer, *The Book of Ezekiel*, vol. 2, 31; NEB).

6. a. For MT's impf ישבו a pointing as a pf ישבו "they lived," read by many MSS and implied by the ancient versions, seems to be required.

8. a. The parallelism suggests that the stem means "be comparable with": see 28:3 *Note*.

8. b. See 27:5 *Note*.

8. c. Heb. ערמון is the oriental plane, *Platanus orientalis* (Zohary, *Plants of the Bible* 129).

9. a. עשיתיו יפה "I made it beautiful," not represented in LXX*, is often regarded as a theological gloss. However, Cooke (341) noted that the motif of divine agency accords with vv 11, 15.

10. a. For the formulaic אדני "Lord" here and in vv 15, 18 see 20:3 *Note*.

10. b. MT "you," supported by LXX, accords with the direct address of vv 2b, 18, but conflicts with the present context. Syr Vg presuppose a third person form גבה which is generally read.

11. a. MT ואתנהו seems to mean "and I will give it," influenced by the later impf יעשה "he will deal." LXX Vg correctly imply ואתנהו "and I have given it".

11. b. The strange fut reference of יעשה "he will deal" has led to the suggestion that v 11b is a later addition (Zimmerli 144; Wevers 237). For עשו יעשה "he will surely deal," ויעש "and he dealt" is sometimes read (e.g., Fohrer 175; Eichrodt 424). MT's punctuation is rather unnatural ("he will surely deal with him; according to his wickedness I drove him out"), although Driver has endeavored to justify it by recourse to another stem גרש "expose to scorn," cognate with Arab. *jarasa* (*Bib* 19 [1938] 178; = NEB "I made an example of it as its wickedness deserved"). It was probably an attempt to accom-modate the otherwise staccato final verbal form.

11. c. The final verb is best taken with v 12, so that parallel statements are made in vv 11-12a: "I . . . and he . . . , I . . . and they . . ." (Boadt, *Ezekiel's Oracles* 114).

12. a. For this meaning of נטש see 29:5 *Note*.

12. b. MT וירדו "and they went down" is supported by the ancient versions, but is a strange verb. Hitzig's proposal וידדו "and they fled" (241), from נדד "retreat, flee" used of birds and beasts in Jer 4:25; 9:9, is graphically feasible. The use of the verb in Dan 4:11(14) may well be dependent on its original presence here. Conceivably וירדו מצלו "and they went down from its shade" in MT suffered assimilation to בצלו . . . ירדו "they went down . . . in its shade" in v 17.

12. c. Heb. ויטשהו "and they flung it" seems redundant. Driver, *Bib* 35 (1954) 301, took it to mean that all the others joined the aliens in their attack.

13. a. Heb. ישכנו "they will rest (?)" may be an error for שכנו "they rested" by pseudodittography, but it could be a frequentative impf.

14. a. MT אליהם "their leaders" seems to have been influenced by איל "leader" in v 11 and should be repointed אליהם "to them (= the clouds)" in line with a minority masoretic tradition and LXX Tg (Ehrlich, *Randglossen* 117).

15. a. MT "I inflicted mourning, I covered the deep over it" is difficult. V 15bα suggests that here the deep is made to mourn. LXX* does not represent כסתי "I covered," which may be a gloss linking with 26:19 (Cornill 379).

15. b. MT עֻלְפֶּה seems to be pointed as a noun or adj: it is generally repointed as a verb עֻלְפָּה "fainted."

16. a. Heb. את has a pregnant force "so as to be with" (Cooke 345), as in 26:20.

16. b. MT adds וטוב "and best" in a difficult double construction (cf. GKC 128a note 1). Its absence from LXX* may indicate a conflated text in MT.

17. a. MT "and his arm, they lived in his shade among the nations" makes no sense. LXX (cf. Syr) implies וזרעו ישבי "and his descendants who lived . . ." The most feasible of a number of emendations is (ישבי) וגועו "and (those who lived . . .) perished" (Bertholet 110; Fohrer 175; Zimmerli 145). LXX ἀπώλοντο "they perished" at the end of v 17 (see BHS) may represent an incorporated gloss to this effect. Driver repointed to וזרעו "and . . . were scattered" (= NEB) with appeal to Syr. zr ͨ (Bib 19 [1938] 179), but a reference to death seems to be required (cf. Boadt, Ezekiel's Oracles 121).

18. a. Heb. ככה "thus" is used strangely here, which may explain the variant בכח "with strength" underlying Θ (see BHS).

Form/Structure/Setting

Chap. 31 is distinguished as a literary unit by the dated oracular introduction of vv 1-2a. The initial messenger formulas in vv 10 and 15 and the final one in v 18 point to three smaller units, vv 2b-9, 10-14 and 15-18. There are structural indications that lend support to these divisions: an inclusion expressing incomparability marks the first (אל־מי דמית "with what do you compare?" in v 2b; לא דמה אליו "did not compare with it" in v 8b), and a triple inclusion marks the second (ABC . . . ABC: v 10, resumed in v 14a). The whole piece is bound together by a double, chiastic inclusion, relating to interpretation and to incomparability (AB . . . BA: vv 2a, b, 18a, by [Fishbane, Biblical Interpretation 48]). It functions as a judgment oracle, as the telltale לכן "therefore" in v 10 reveals. The oracle is explicitly directed against Pharaoh and his army. Accordingly, the poem of vv 2b-9 has the role of an implicit accusation, which becomes explicit in the rephrasing of v 10. After the direct rhetorical question of v 2b, the story is told of a magnificent tree, a mythological cosmic tree. From v 10 the story takes a sinister turn as the tree is accused of pride and wickedness, and Yahweh describes how he had it cut down and humiliated. In vv 15-17 the ritual mourning for the tree and its descent to Sheol are related, while v 18 returns to the present and to direct address in a threat of future punishment that echoes the language of Sheol used earlier. V 18 has a summarizing role, presenting the chapter in a nutshell and with greater clarity.

A striking phenomenon in vv 3-17 is the use of past tenses, which resembles the style of a קינה or funeral dirge that Ezekiel often uses elsewhere. The device, as it does in the formal dirge, serves to characterize the coming downfall of Egypt as a prophetic certainty, already decreed in the counsels of Yahweh (cf. Zimmerli 148). Moreover, the movement from glory to destruction and the reference in v 15 to mourning (cf. Parunak, Structural Studies 400) also fits the prophetic dirge as Ezekiel used it. It is therefore less likely that the verbs relate to the past and so to the Babylonian defeat of Egypt's military attempt to relieve besieged Jerusalem (Freedy and Redford, JAOS 90 [1970] 472), an interpretation that necessitates the omission of v 11b. The chapter is complex in form. It has the force of a judgment oracle, yet uses the past perspective of a lament. It relies heavily on allegory. However, the allegory wears thin as the chapter goes on and, with its mixture of real and unreal features, takes on more of the character of a political fable (cf. Solomon, "Fable" 119).

The chronological setting of the piece given in v 1, two months later than the previous indication in 30:20, accords with the contents and with historical events. Its lack of awareness of the actualities of the ongoing siege of Jerusalem suits its composition away in exile. The oracle probably contains little adaptation from its original form. V 5 has been regarded as an addition because of its Aramaisms, but it fits its context well. V 14 has greater claim to be considered redactional: its generalized warning makes use of information yet to be given in vv 17-18 (cf. Cooke 342). Stylistically, however, like the additions in chap. 27, it has been made to fit snugly by the use of inclusion.

Comment

1-2a The date in Parker and Dubberstein's reconstruction (*Babylonian Chronology* 28) corresponds to June 21, 587 B.C., while the siege of Jerusalem was still taking its relentless course. Ezekiel has yet again to deal with an obsession that gripped the minds of the exiles, a continuing obsession that Pharaoh would ride to the rescue of the beleaguered city.

2b-4 After the initial question the poem of vv 3-9 divides into three strophes, vv 3-4, 5-6 and 7-9, each of which begins with the size of the tree and moves to the supply of water (cf. Parunak, *Structural Studies* 401-2). The rhetorical question concerning Pharaoh in his military might gives way to an allegory of a cosmic tree. The parallel is a flattering one, and by it Ezekiel is empathizing with the dreams of his compatriots. The beauty and height of the tree and its unfailing water supply (cf. Gen 49:25; Deut 33:13) are admiringly described.

The motif of the cosmic tree is well attested in ancient mythology. It presents the living world as an enormous tree with its roots in the subterranean deep and its top in the clouds, a shelter for every living being. It is a separate motif from that of the tree of life, although the two were often linked, as later in this poem. The motif came to greatest prominence in Indian and Scandinavian mythology. There is some evidence of it in Sumerian and Mesopotamian literature (cf. Eliade, *Patterns in Comparative Literature* 271-73; Gowan, *When Man Becomes God* 103-5; Zimmerli 146), and it must have been from Mesopotamian culture that Ezekiel became aware of it and utilized it for the allegory. Whether the royal application he made depends on a previous association of the tree of life with royalty, as the embodiment of human life and power (cf. Widengren, *The King and the Tree of Life* 42-58) or whether this development was Ezekiel's own contribution from Israelite tradition in which monarchy and tree language were associated (Gowan, *When Man Becomes God* 111; cf. Isa 11:1; Jer 23:5; Ezek 17; 19:10-14) is uncertain. It may be that both sources come to a nice meeting point here.

5-6 The second strophe develops like the first, but moves to the tree's cosmic dimensions, alluding to the political power wielded by its Egyptian representative. The royal application of the tree imagery is evident in the reference to "nations."

7-9 The final strophe, after repeating the two parallel characterizations of the earlier two, returns to the note of incomparability struck at the beginning of the piece and also reiterates the beauty of the tree. In the statement of v 9a there appears to be a variant of the reference to water as the cause of the tree's beauty (cf. v 7a, b). The tree, for all its assets, is not self-made or self-perpetuating, but has a function within a larger scheme of creative force, to which it is subordinate. The expressions of incomparability blend the motifs of the cosmic tree and the tree of life by referring to the Israelite conceptions of Eden or the garden of God, traditionally a grove of trees (cf. Eichrodt's caution, however, against identifying the streams of the deep with the rivers of Paradise [427]. Haag [*Wort, Lied und Gottesspruch* 177-78] goes too far in seeking to harmonize the chapter with Gen 2-3).

10-14 The idyllic tone of the previous poem now takes a sinister turn with the use of language associated with pronouncement of divine judgment. The tree's height is associated with pride by means of a semantic twist not alien to Hebrew usage (רממתהו "made it tall," v 4; רם לבבו "its heart became high," v 10; cf. Isa 2:12). The cosmic tree myth is strikingly abandoned in the divine command to fell the tree. While vv 3-4 (or 5) are echoed in the accusation of v 10, in vv 12-13 the language of vv 5-8 is repeated in a shocking reversal. The tree's former power and protective role are mocked as beasts roam over the dead trunk.

V 14 stands aside from the narrative as an interlude. It extends the horizon of the judgment into a warning to all other nations who are tempted ambitiously to follow Egypt's lead and soar away from their roots. In so doing, they virtually forget their grounding in a source of life not inherently their own ("watered trees," "irrigated trees"), and so forget too that creaturely mortality is their lot (cf. v 17).

15-18 The allegory fades into a description of human bereavement, in a development of the human allusions introduced in vv 10-11. The falling of the tree (vv 13, 16) is equated with its descent to Sheol (vv 15-17). The mourning for the dead tree instigated by Yahweh is blended with the withdrawal of the life-giving waters of the deep, in a reversal of vv 4-5. Yahweh's positive control over the tree, unacknowledged, becomes a negative and destructive force. Lebanon's forest and the trees of the countryside (vv 3-4) now have a new role as mourners. The allegory lingers, however, since the mourning of nature was an established Hebrew concept (cf. Isa 24:7; 33:9; Joel 1:10, 12). The references to the trees of Eden and Lebanon in v 16 merge the natural and mythological concepts of vv 3 and 9. At this point they have become mere ciphers for other great powers who have already waned, but the note of reversal is still dominant: envy (v 9) gives way to consolation and satisfaction, now that their powerful survivor has in turn been toppled. The reference to "those slain by the sword" (חללי חרב) together with mention of the "uncircumcised" in v 18 suggests a grimmer experience in the shadowy afterlife than most underwent. Lods plausibly argued that here, as in 28:10 and in chap. 32, there is an echo of an Israelite custom, for which there are anthropological parallels in other cultures, that infants who died before they were circumcised were buried separately from other people's remains and that this difference gave rise to a belief in a difference of experience in Sheol itself (*Comptes rendus* [1943] 279-83). In turn Eissfeldt has urged that חללי חרב means murdered or executed persons and so victims of violent death, who were likewise treated differently in their burial and, by a natural extension of thought, in the underworld (cf. Isa 14:19-20; *Studies in OT Prophecy* 73-81).

V 18 provides a clear interpretation of the allegory in its developed form, pairing present magnificence and future doom in a shocking blend that is facilitated by the double role of "Eden's trees" (vv 9, 16).

Explanation

Outright denial does not necessarily change an opponent's mind. Here Ezekiel was faced with the task of persuading his fellow exiles to forget their optimistic hopes that Hophra's military forces would be a match for the Babylonians besieging Jerusalem. He shrewdly begins by sharing their positive assessment of Egypt. Pharaoh was indeed the embodiment of a world power, magnificent in its impression of permanence. As such, he corresponded to the cosmic tree of ancient lore, filling his observers' horizon with his fascinating prestige. Essentially, however, his continued vitality was derived from a source outside himself, like the subterranean water supply of the cosmic tree. This element of contingency struck a warning note for those with ears to hear. The virtual hymn to Pharaoh suddenly turns into an oracular pronouncement of punishment for his lofty pride. The scenario changes into woodcutters at work, leaving a fallen giant of a tree, like some California redwood, lying inert and powerless over an enormous expanse of ground.

The great embodiment of throbbing vitality is forced to take the low road to death and the underworld. As nearly as Ezekiel is able to express it culturally, it is a descent to hell. The question of v 2 is repeated ironically at the end. The incomparable finally meets his match in the one who has power of life and death. The greatest of trees in God's garden has the gardener to answer to.

V 14 is already aware that the piece speaks far beyond its own concerns of feasibility of Egyptian relief of Jerusalem. Secular power has its temporal and moral limits. In God's world ideological pride in human achievement is doomed to end in destruction. It was a lesson that the book of Daniel would need to proclaim afresh, finding literary inspiration for its fourth chapter in this very allegory. The Christian Church too, liable to be deceived by the empty promises of the world, needs to be ready to take this lesson to heart (cf. 1 Cor 1:28-31; 1 John 2:16-17).

The Slaying of the Egyptian Dragon (32:1-16)

Bibliography

Day, J. *God's Conflict with the Dragon and the Sea.* University of Cambridge Oriental Publications 35. Cambridge: CUP, 1985. **Gunkel, H.** *Schöpfung und Chaos in Urzeit und Endzeit.* Göttingen: Vandenhoeck und Ruprecht, 1895. **Jahnow, H.** *Das hebräische Leichenlied im Rahmen der Völkerdichtung.* BZAW 36. Giessen: Töpelmann, 1923, 232-36.

Translation

[1]*In the twelfth[a] year, on the first of the twelfth month, I received the following communication from Yahweh:* [2]*"Human one, utter a lament for the Egyptian king Pharaoh and tell him:*

You lion of the nations, you are undone![a]
Once you were like the monster[b] in the seas,
splashing in your rivers,[c]
disturbing the water with your feet
and fouling its rivers.
[3]*The message of the Lord[a] Yahweh is as follows:*
I will spread my net over you[b]
and bring[c] you up in my mesh.
[4]*Then I will throw[a] you on the land,*
hurling[b] you down to the ground.
I will invite all the birds in the sky to settle on you
and get all the beasts of the earth[c] to gorge on you.
[5]*I will put your flesh on the mountains*
and fill the valleys with your bulk.[a]
[6]*I will soak the land with your body fluid[a]*
and the ravines will be filled with your blood.[b]
[7]*When you are extinguished,[a] I will cover the sky*
and black out all its stars.
The sun I will cover with clouds,
and the moon will not bear its light.
[8]*All the light bearers in the sky*
I will black out on your account
and I will bring darkness over your land.
So runs the Lord Yahweh's oracle.
[9] *"I will distress many people's minds when I bring your broken parts[a] among the nations, to countries unknown to you.* [10]*I will fill many peoples with horror at your fate. The hair of their kings will stand on end because of you, when I wave[a] my sword in their faces. Each of them will tremble in agitation[b] for his own life on the day you fall.*
[11] *"The explanatory[a] message of the Lord Yahweh is as follows: The sword of the Babylonian king will reach you.*
[12]*I will make your army fall to the swords of warriors,*
all of them the cruelest in the world.

They will ravage Egypt's source of pride,
and all its army will perish.
[13] *I will destroy all its animals*
beside an abundance of water.
No more will it be disturbed by human foot
nor will animal hooves disturb it.
[14] *Then I will make their water clear*
and cause their rivers to flow smooth as oil.
So runs the Lord Yahweh's oracle.
[15] *"When I reduce Egypt*[a] *to a ruin*
and the land is ruinously stripped[b] *of all that fills it,*
when I strike down[c] *all who live there—*
then they will realize that I am Yahweh.
[16] *Such is the lament that will be chanted. Women among the nations will chant it. Over Egypt and all its army they will chant it. So runs the Lord Yahweh's oracle."*

Notes

1. a. The minority reading "eleventh" (see *BHS*) is an attempt to cope with the difficulties of the next date in v 17, in such a way as to ensure consecutive dating. See further v 17 *Note*.

2. a. There are two stems דמה. One occurs in the niph conjugation, as here, with the sense "be destroyed," while the other, meaning "be like," is not so used. Ehrlich (*Randglossen* 119) suggested that the niph, related to the latter stem, had a reflexive sense "you considered yourself" and that the next clause was adversative "but (you are only) . . ." (cf. RSV; Eichrodt 430, Boadt, *Ezekiel's Oracles*, 129). The series of echoes of v 2 in vv 13–14a suggests that destruction is here in view, as in v 13a.

2. b. For the Heb. form see 29:3 *Note.*

2. c. Since Ewald, בנהרותיך "in your rivers" has generally been emended to בנחירותיך "(you snorted) in your nostrils," but it should be retained with Gunkel (*Schöpfung* 72 note 4), Boadt (*Ezekiel's Oracles* 132) and Day (*God's Conflict* 94 note 25). It is a good parallel to בימים "in the seas"; see further *Form/Structure/Setting.*

3. a. For the formulaic אדני "Lord" here and in vv 8, 11, 14, 16 see 20:3 *Note*.

3. b. MT adds בקהל עמים רבים "with a company of many peoples," the first word of which is not represented in LXX*, which has "(nets of=רשתי) many nations." The genitive phrase is used at vv 9, 10 not in terms of the agents of the catastrophe, but in terms of reaction to it, and the metaphorical language of the context makes it unwelcome here. Moreover, the rest of the passage envisages Yahweh as agent. Cornill (382) plausibly saw the influence of 19:8 here. At a later stage בקהל (cf. 26:7) was inserted to ease the addition into the sentence (Jahn 220; Zimmerli 155).

3. c. MT והעלוך "and they will bring you up" appears to be an adaptation of והעליתיך "and I will bring you up," presupposed by LXX Vg: the overall context favors a verb with Yahweh as subject. MT is the consequence of the previous amplification.

4. a. For this rendering of the verb see 29:5 *Note* and cf. Boadt, *Ezekiel's Oracles* 136.

4. b. LXX πεδία πλησθήσεταί σου "plains will be full of you" appears to be a rendering of v 6b ואפיקים ימלאון ממך "and valleys will be full of you," which evidently slipped here and probably displaced the original Gr. rendering of v 4aβ because of the common factor of πεδίον, which is used to render both שדה "countryside" and אפיק "valley" in adjacent chapters of the LXX (see 31:12, 15; 34:27; 35:8).

4. c. For MT's anomalous חית כל־הארץ "beasts of all the earth" a few MSS and LXX* Syr attest הארץ כל־חית "all the beasts of the earth."

5. a. Heb. רמות apparently means "heap," although the form of the noun is strange. Σ Syr took as רמה "worms." LXX presupposes at this point two Heb. glosses, ἀπὸ τοῦ αἵματός σου "from your blood" representing מדמך which relates to v 6 and displaced the similar-looking רמותך; and πᾶσαν γῆ עלה "all the land," representing כל הארץ, which was intended as a reference to the variant חית כל־הארץ (= MT) "beasts of all the earth" in v 4, but it displaced הגאיות "the valleys."

6. a. MT adds מדמך "with, of your blood," which came into the text as a correction of ממך "from you" in v 6b (see *BHS*). MT also inserts אל־ההרים "to the mountains," originally intended as a variant for על־ההרים "on the mountains" in v 5 (Ehrlich, *Randglossen* 120).

6. b. MT מִמְּךָ "from, with you" seems to be an accidental miswriting for מִדָּמֵךְ "from, with your blood": see the previous note.

7. a. MT בְּכַבּוֹתְךָ implies "when (I) extinguish you" (cf. GKC 115e note 1). More naturally, however, one would point as a qal בְּכַבּוֹתְךָ "when you are extinguished," as LXX Syr Vg imply (Cornill 384 et al.). Cooke (356) and Wevers (242) regard MT as having an indefinite subj and so pass in sense.

9. a. LXX implies שְׁבִיךְ "your captivity," which appears to suit the context. However, Boadt (145) has observed that in Ezek שבי always occurs with הלך "go" and is not used in threats of exile. MT שברך "your breaking" may be used in the concrete sense "your broken army" (NEB; cf. Tg's paraphrase "your war-broken ones").

10. a. Heb בעופפי is probably to be derived from עוף "fly": cf. Zimmerli's discussion (156).

10. b. For the sense see M. D. Goldman, *Australian Biblical Review* 4 (1954/55) 13-15, and the note on 26:16.

11. a. Heb. כי "for."

15. a. MT אֶת־אֶרֶץ "the land of (Egypt)," not represented in LXX, is probably a comparative gloss, harmonizing with 29:12.

15. b. MT has a participial form וּנְשַׁמָּה "and ruined": it is more naturally pointed as a consec pf וְנָשַׁמָּה "and will be ruined," which the ancient versions imply. For the pregnant construction with מִן "from" cf. 12:19.

15. c. LXX renders in terms of scattering (cf. *BHS*), but it is interpretative rather than of textual significance (Boadt 149). For the Heb. verb cf. Deut 13:16.

Form/Structure/Setting

Verses 1-16 are clearly demarcated as a unit by their introductory dating and prophetic formulas, which vv 17-18 give all over again. Although the unit describes itself as a lament (vv 2, 16), in form-critical terms it is a very loose representation of the genre, which has little left of its characteristic elements (Jahnow, *Leichenlied* 229). The strict 3 + 2 meter is found only sporadically (vv 2bαβ, γδ, 3aβ-b, 8a). As regularly in the lament, the destruction is set in the past at v 2aγ (cf. 26:17a) and so is Pharaoh's power (v 2b). The composition is a lament-tinged oracle of (future) judgment and even, in view of the recognition formula of v 15, a three-part proof saying. The element of accusation is here represented by a metaphorical statement of power (v 2b), as in 31:2-9. The usage of the introductory messenger formulas and closing divine saying formulas suggests a series of smaller units, vv 3-8, 9-10, 11-14 and 15-16. Further examination suggests that v 2aγ-b goes closely with vv 3-8, the messenger formula in v 3 serving to introduce the pronouncement of punishment. The extended recognition formula of v 15 is strictly to be separated from v 16, whose role is to complement v 2aaβ with an inclusion that emphasizes the role of lament (Parunak, *Structural Studies* 398). This stylistic framework may be regarded as part of a loose chiastic structure in which metaphor is matched with interpretation. Thus vv 9a and 10 echo the cosmic mourning of vv 7-8 on a human scale, and v 9b echoes vv 5-6, while vv 11-12 echo v 4b and vv 13-14 echo v 2b. A key word of the whole unit is גוים "nations," which occurs in vv 2, 9, 12 and 16, and so in most of the small units. A feature of vv 2aγ-8 is the cosmic orientation: water (v 2b), earth (vv 4-6) and sky (vv 7-8a) come respectively to the fore as major terms used along with members of their semantic fields. This feature suggests that MT is correct in its reading בנהרותיך "in its rivers" in v 2bβ (cf. *Note*).

To what degree this literary unit has been built up by stages is difficult to assess. Certainly v 15, which has a form-critical role but shares no stylistic features with the rest of the piece, looks like a redactional addition, perhaps to clarify the theme of vv 13-14. The rest consists of metaphor, vv 2aγ-8, and interpretation of various kinds, vv 9-14. The careful hinging of vv 10 and 11-12 (חרב "sword" and נפל "fall") appears to be a blatant literary device. The echoing of motifs of earlier oracles against Tyre and Egypt in vv 9-10 (cf. Zimmerli 160) may suggest that this part too is redactional. The whole unit, however, has a coherent and artistic harmony, which may well reflect Ezekiel's own penmanship.

The setting of at least vv 2-8 depends on the dating of v 1. If MT is correct, Jerusalem's fall lies in the past even for the exiles. Vv 11-14, like 29:17-21, obviously look forward historically to Nebuchadnezzar's invasion of Egypt.

Comment

1-2 The major textual evidence supplies a date that corresponds to March 3, 585 B.C., according to Parker and Dubberstein (*Babylonian Chronology* 28). Earlier hopes that Egypt would rally to Jerusalem's support in its hour of need had been dashed, and for the exiles the fall of the capital was history (cf. 33:21). The oracle that follows is virtually a re-issue of 29:3-6. The description of the oracle as a lament strikes a more strident note than the previous one. It affirms the inevitability of Egypt's fall: a lament looked back on past tragedy, and the temporal perspective of v 2aγb aligns with this formal feature.

The double zoological description of Pharaoh is strange, even when it is granted that "lion" may have strong royal associations (cf. 19:3, 5-6). King of the international jungle though Pharaoh was, his defeat was assured. His power, sinisterly set in the past, is then described in terms of an aquatic beast, doubtless as in chap. 29 a fusion of the Nile crocodile and the mythological chaos monster. The former perspective is less pronounced here, although the muddying of shallow waters suggests the crocodile.

3-8 The mythological story line dictated the sequel of defeat at the hands of the creator God. The very metaphor spelled defeat. The form now used is the straightforward pronouncement of future punishment. The elements of water, earth and heaven introduce a cosmic dimension appropriate to the subject. The lord of the seas is wrenched from his habitat by the divine hunter, and the remains of this enormous being are strewn over the earth. To seal its death, heavenly mourning is ordered. The terms also evoke the grim motif of the day of Yahweh announced for Egypt in 30:3, 18 (cf. Joel 2:2, 10).

9-10 The interpretation of the extended metaphor begins here, in reverse order. The cosmic mourning of vv 7-8 is equated with universal lamentation and shock, as others who witness Pharaoh's downfall fear for their own safety. It is a motif that has run through the oracles against Tyre (cf. 26:15-18; 27:28-36; 28:19) and helps to bind together the section of foreign oracles. The reference to exile in v 9b explains vv 5-6, using a motif already employed in 29:12; 30:23, 26.

11-15 First, v 4b is interpreted in vv 11-12. The cosmic battle between Yahweh and the Egyptian monster is grounded in a historical perspective of Nebuchadnezzar and his ruthless swordsmen (cf. 30:11), who would get the better of Pharaoh's army. In v 13a the destruction of the lion and the crocodile monster (v 2aγ-bβ) is correlated with the killing of all the animals that drink from the Nile, as part of a program of desolating Egypt (cf. v 15; 29:9-12). Its extension to the human plane would bring back a reversal of the muddying of v 2bγδ. V 15 spells out even more clearly the divine agenda and its human consequences, before providing a closing recognition formula, as in 29:9.

16 The literary unit is tied together by these closing statements that revert to the lament of v 2aα. It stands, however, at a little distance from vv 2-8 in that it focuses not on Pharaoh but on Egypt, which has gradually come to the fore in recent verses (vv 12b-15). The reference to universal mourning, traditionally carried out by women (cf. Jer 9:16-17 [17-18]) echoes that of vv 9-10, while the reference to "Egypt and all its army" recapitulates v 12b and is also reminiscent of 31:18bγ.

Explanation

Although vv 2-8, and indeed vv 2-16, may only loosely be called a lament, sufficient elements are present in v 2aγb to regard the piece as an ironic obituary for an arrogant world power. The emphasis is not on Babylon's defeat of Egypt, but on Egypt's defeat at the hands of Yahweh. Did the exiles even now cling to a hope that Egypt would not tolerate Babylonian control of Palestine and Syria, but would retaliate in a counterthrust? As in earlier oracles, Ezekiel grants that Egypt is larger than life in its military and economic power and influence. However, a distinctive metaphor, used already in chap. 29, cuts it down to size. Just as the description of Tyre in terms of a veritable Titanic revealed the island fortress in a new and negative perspective, so here does the chaos monster metaphor for Egypt. If Egypt is a mighty dragon, one might say, Yahweh is cast in the role of St. George! Yahweh is quite capable of fighting and winning a cosmic battle against such a foe.

The series of interpretations that follow and complete the literary piece concentrate on the failure of Egyptian militarism, with their war-related language (cf. המון "army," vv 12a, b, 16b). They also pick up the initial גוים "nations" and mockingly turn it into a keyword for radical reversal. Pharaoh, the "lion" of other nations (v 2), was to lose his power. At Yahweh's behest the political tables were to be turned. Nations would provide new homes for the displaced (v 9), would victimize the defeated (v 12) and would lament the dead (v 16). The message is plain: "It is better to take refuge in Yahweh than to put confidence in princes" (Ps 118:9).

Egypt's Infernal Doom (32:17-32)

Bibliography

Bewer, J. A. "Beiträge zur Exegese des Buches Ezechiel." *ZAW* 63 (1951) 193-201. **McAlpine, T. H.** *Sleep, Human and Divine, in the Old Testament.* JSOTS 38. Sheffield: JSOT, 1987. **Rost, P.** "Schreibgebrauch bei den Sopherim und seine Bedeutung für die alttestamentliche Kritik." *OLZ* 6 (1903) 403-7, 443-46; 7 (1904) 390-93. **Tromp, N.** *Primitive Conceptions of Death and the Nether World in the Old Testament.* BibOr 21. Rome: Pontifical Biblical Institute, 1969.

Translation

In the twelfth year, on the fifteenth day,[a] *I received the following communication from Yahweh:* [18] *"Human one, wail over the Egyptian army and bid it go down among mighty nations,*[a] *to the lowest parts of the underworld, among those who have gone down to the Pit.*

[19]*Whom do you surpass in loveliness? Go down*
and be laid to rest with the uncircumcised.[a]
[20]*Among victims of violent death*[a]
they will lie fallen with him.[b]
[21]*To him will speak the leaders of the valiant*
from the middle of Sheol,[a] *(and) with his helpers.*[b]
[22]*Assyria is there and all its company around its grave,*[a] *all of them killed after falling*[b] *as victims of the sword,* [23]*those who*[a] *once inspired terror*[b] *in the land of the living.* [24]*Elam is there and all its army around its grave, all of them killed after falling as victims of the sword, who went down uncircumcised to the underworld, yet who once inspired terror in the land of the living. Now they bear their shame among those who have gone down to the Pit:* [25]*among the killed was placed a bier for it.*[a] [26]*Meshech-Tubal is there and all its army around its grave, all of them uncircumcised, killed*[a] *as victims of the sword, because although*[b] *they inspired terror in the land of the living,*[27] *they do not lie with the valiant ones who fell long ago,*[a] *who went down to Sheol with their weapons of war, their swords placed under their heads and their shields*[b] *over their bones because there was terror of the valiant ones in the land of the living.* [28]*But as for you, among the uncircumcised you will lie broken*[a] *and you will rest with those killed as victims of the sword.*

[29] *"Edom is there, its kings and all its leaders*[a] *who in spite of*[b] *their might are set with those killed as victims of the sword. They lie with the uncircumcised and with others who have gone down to the Pit.* [30]*The commanders of the north are all there, and all the Sidonians who*[a] *have gone down to join the killed despite the terror they inspired, let down by*[b] *their might. They rest uncircumcised with those killed as victims of the sword and bear their shame with others who have gone down to the Pit.* [31]*The sight of them will bring consolation to Pharaoh for the loss of all his army.*[a] [32]*For, although he inspired terror*[a] *while he was in the land of the living, Pharaoh and all his army will be laid to rest among the uncircumcised, with those killed as victims of the sword. So runs the oracle of the Lord*[a] *Yahweh."*

Notes

17. a. MT lacks a month (cf. 26:1). It may be that the month mentioned in v 1 is to be understood (Cooke 350; Boadt, *Ezekiel's Oracles* 152). LXX* refers to the first month, but it seems to be interpreting the present text, and its form is linguistically suspect (Zimmerli 163).

18. a. MT has אותה ובנות גוים "it (fem) and the daughters of (the) nations." The first word is often emended to אַתָּה "you" (Hitzig 248-49 et al.). The phrase seems to be an early (pre-LXX) variant for (וקוננו)ה בנות הגוים "(and) the daughters of the nations (will chant) it" in v 16, reading אותה for the suffix and a conjunction before בנות (cf. *BHS* note b in v 16) and writing גוים carelessly for הגוים. The marginal note evidently slipped down because of the similarity of ועל־כל־המונה "over Egypt and over all its army" in v 16 and על־המון מצרים "over the army of Egypt" in v 18. However, the second command is left unreasonably short and אדרים "mighty" requires explanation. It is probable that the gloss displaced the partially similar בתוך גוים "among (the) nations" (cf. Bewer, *ZAW* 63 [1951] 201, following Heinisch).

19. a. LXX places v 19 after שאול "Sheol" in v 21, in order to provide the direct speech implied there. For its secondary nature see Zimmerli 164.

20. a. See 31:17-18 and *Comment*.

20. b. LXX presupposes אתו "with him": in MT the corresponding term is אותה "here, it" in v 20bβ. In v 20bα חרב is unrepresented in LXX Syr: it may have been supplied as a subj for the following נתנה "it has been given, appointed." The phrases משכו "they drew away" and וכל־המוניה "and all its armies" are best explained as originally marginal variants related to כל־המונה "Meshech-Tubal and all its army" in v 26, while נתנה, lacking in LXX Syr, is a replacement for נתן in v 25bβ, whose subj is the fem חתית. Evidently the variants became attached to the column on the wrong side of the margin. In v 20 LXX for משכו implies והשכב "and it shall be laid to rest," which has probably suffered assimilation to the verb in v 19 (and v 32); it provides a closer rapport with משכב in v 25. It is likely that משכו is related to the minority reading משך ותובל "Meshech and Tubal" in v 26 (see *BHS*).

21. a. LXX implies בירכתי בור "in the furthest parts of the Pit" (cf. v 23), which is hardly correct here. Probably in its *Vorlage* a gloss from v 18b, which sought to clarify the infernal phraseology, displaced the original text which had similar meaning.

21. b. Heb. את־עזריו "with (?) his helpers" seems to function as a prepositional phrase corresponding to לו "to him" earlier: "(speak) with . . ." In v 21b MT adds ירדו שכבו הערלים חללי חרב "they went down, lay, the uncircumcised, victims of violent death." LXX lacks completely and Syr lacks the first three terms, which appear to be a variant of רדה והשכבה את־ערלים "go down and be laid to rest with the uncircumcised" in v 19: probably a jussive sense was intended, "let them go down and lie (ושכבו)," and הערלים "the uncircumcised" prosaically corrects the anarthrous ערלים. The last pair of words probably originated as a marginal correction of מחללי חרב "slain by the sword" in v 26, which became attached to the wrong column.

22. a. MT has various forms of this phrase in vv 22-26. (i) Sometimes it is construed as a circumstantial clause ("while its graves were around it") and sometimes as a prepositional phrase ("around its grave"). (ii) The noun is sometimes pointed from a sg קבורה and sometimes from a plural קברות. This second type of variant is closely linked with the first: if the army's burial place is around the ethnic entity, it is regarded as pl, but if the army is around the ethnic entity's burial place, the latter is treated as sg. (iii) The suffixes vary between masc and fem. One expects a masc suffix with סביבות, agreeing with קהל "company" or המון "army," and a fem suffix with the noun, referring to the ethnic entity. Here סביבותיו קברתיה "while its graves were around it" (cf. v 25aβ) or else סביבות קברתה "around its grave" (cf. v 23aγ) is expected. Are the two basic variations stylistic? The ethnic name appears to stand for its king (cf. v 29), and logically his troops or their graves would be ranged around his own. Accordingly סביבות קְבָרָתֶהָ "around its grave" must have been original, as in vv 23 and 24. So the rendering of LXX presupposes, although in v 22aβ the phrase is not represented, probably because in the Heb. *Vorlage* an erroneous reading has been deleted.

22. b. Here and in v 24bα the Heb. is הנפלים "the fallen," yet נפלים "fallen" in v 23. Driver, *Bib* 19 (1938) 179, viewing the article as resumptive, "who (fell)," urged that the form in v 23 should be corrected. LXX does not represent the phrase: probably in its Heb. text, as at v 22aβ, a rejected rendering had been deleted.

23. a. MT repeats אשר נתנו "those who inspired (terror)," with a different pointing of the verb. Between the repeated phrases are what appear to be a string of variants which have been incorporated into the text. The LXX attests a non-glossed text. The addition of ויהי "and . . . was" in v 23aβ gave a modicum of sense (cf. Rost, *OLZ* 6 [1903] 446). After the incorporation the interrupted אשר נתנו

was understandably repeated in the last line. (i) קברותיה "its graves" relates to קברתיו in v 22a, rightly supplying a fem suffix (Rost, ibid.). (ii) בירכתי בור "in the recesses of the Pit," has already appeared as a variant in the LXX of v 21. (iii) קברתה קהלה סביבות "its company around its grave," is a correction of the phrase in v 22β with a cue word קהלה. With its sg noun and fem suffix it supplies the authentic reading. (iv) כלם חללים נפלים בחרב "all of them killed, having fallen by the sword," is a variant for v 22b, which deletes the article with נפלים.

23. b. In place of חתיתם "terror of them(selves)," which appears in vv 24-26, MT has simply חתית "terror." See *BHS*.

25. a. MT continues with what seem to be two versions of the same text, up to the end of v 26. Significantly the LXX has only one version. The most plausible explanation is that v 25a-b has been heavily annotated with a mass of material, which has survived in the form of vv 25bδ-26 (cf. Rost, *OLZ* 7 [1904] 393). Most of the material takes the form of corrections of a poor text. (i) בתוך חללים נתנו "among the slain they set" and בתוך חללים נתן "among the slain was set" are variants, with a different form of the verb. (ii) שם משך־תובל "Meshech-Tubal is there" is supplied, having fallen out after the very similar-looking משכב לה "a bier for it." (iii) וכל־המונה "and all its army" is a correction of בכל־המונה "with all its army." (iv) סביבתיו קברתיה "with its graves around them" is a minor correction of קברתה סביבותיו, making clear that the noun is pl. (v) כלם ערלים מחללי־חרב "all of them uncircumcised, killed by the sword" is an incorrect variant of the line that rightly has חללי "killed." (vi) כי־נתנו התיתם בארץ חיים "for they inspired fear of themselves in the land of the living" provides a correction of נתנו for the sg verb נתן. Seemingly variants (i) and (vi) are double recordings of an originally single variant, probably (vi).

26. a. See the preceding note. MT arose by dittography of *mem*. The stylized phrase of vv 20 and 25 relates to the victims of violent death.

26. b. The first of the two syntactically coordinated clauses is logically subordinate to the second, to which כי "because" refers: cf. GKC 111d; BDB 474a.

27. a. For MT ערלים "from (the) uncircumcised" LXX correctly presupposes מעולם "from of old." The error arose from a ו/ר confusion and from assimilation to the frequent term ערלים. Support for the corrected text comes from 26:20. See further the next note.

27. b. MT with the support of all the ancient versions has עונתם "their iniquities," which is totally unfitting, both because a better class of dead is under consideration and because in the context a piece of military equipment is expected. Cornill's conjectural emendation צנותם "their shields" (390) is generally accepted. Cornill envisaged a ע/צ error. But why would it ever have occurred? Was an annotation ע, intended to correct מערלים earlier to מעולם, wrongly regarded as a correction of צ? In that case here is ancient Heb. evidence for a reading מעולם. One cannot discount, however, the possible influence of בעונו "in his iniquity" in the next column (33:6, 8, 9).

28. a. LXX* does not represent (ותשבר (ותשכב "you will be broken and (you will rest)." It is customary to omit it as a corrupt dittograph of תשכב (Cornill 391 et al.). However, the shorter text in LXX may represent parablepsis due to homoeoteleuton. In favor of MT is the alliteration of the verbs (Boadt, *Ezekiel's Oracles* 166), the chiastic structure of the sentence and the distinctiveness of the first verb.

29. a. LXX ἐδόθησαν οἱ ἄρχοντες Ασσουρ "the rulers of Assyria were given" seems to reflect a complex Gr. tradition. ἐδόθησαν probably originated as a marginal correction of οἱ δόντες "who gave" in line with the Heb. נתנו (אשר), which displaced the initially identical Εδωμ "Edom." The rest is a loose rendering of מלכיה וכל־נשיאיה אשר "her kings and all her rulers who," with אשר treated as אֲשֶׁר.

29. b. Cf. Cooke 358; Zimmerli 168 and Boadt, *Ezekiel's Oracles* 166, for this rendering of the preposition. It recurs in v 30.

30. a. In place of כל־צדני אשר "every Sidonian who" LXX has πάντες στρατηγοὶ Ασσουρ "all the generals of Assyria." It seems to be an alternative or supplementary rendering of כל־נשיאי(ה) אשר in v 29, which slipped to this place, probably dislodging the Gr. original.

30. b. For the construction see P. Haupt, *AJSL* 26 (1910) 228-30. The non-representation of בושים "let down, ashamed" in LXX* is a consequence of its misconstruing of מגבורתם "by, in spite of their might" and has no significance for the Heb. text (cf. Zimmerli 169).

31. a. MT חללי חרב פרעה וכל־חילו "killed by the sword, Pharaoh and all his host," not represented in LXX*, is a variant of חללי חרב פרעה וכל־המונה "killed by the sword, Pharaoh and all his army," which, using cue words, was intended to define המון in terms of the more military term חיל (cf. 17:17; 38:4). It is probable that the divine saying formula in v 31 was also in the variant as part of the cuing device.

32. a. MT נתתי "I inspired" is supported by LXX Syr Vg. LXX^L and Tg imply נתן "he inspired," which the wider context supports: v 32 is a restatement of v 24by (cf. v 26bβ) in terms of Pharaoh. A first person reference, if anywhere, would be expected in v 32ba, rather than here. Then Q חתיתי "terror

of myself" is a consequence of the change and is to be rejected in favor of K חתיתו "terror of him," which LXX Syr Tg imply.

Form/Structure/Setting

In essence this literary unit, distinguished by its separate dating and prophetic introduction, is an oracle of judgment against Egypt or Pharaoh, which lacks any clear element of accusation and only pronounces judgment. The term נהה "wail" (v 18), which belongs to the semantic field of mourning for the dead (cf. Jer 9:17-19; Amos 5:16), merely enhances the sinister nature of the message and anticipates its preoc-cupation with Sheol; it is reminiscent of the loose use of קינה "dirge" in the previous unit. Although there is no initial messenger formula, two divine saying formulas appear in vv 31 and 32 in MT (but see *Note* 31.a). Vv 29-32, which consist of pure prose rather than poetry, have the air of a literary epilogue. It is doubtful, however, whether one may envisage two additions, on the evidence of the double final formula (cf. e.g., Zimmerli 169): v 32 goes closely in content with v 31. The form שמה "there" in vv 29 and 30 does not accord with the triple שם of vv 22, 24 and 26; and the language of vv 29 and 30 is obviously intended to be merely a loose echo of the pre-ceding strophes. Moreover, v 28, with its direct address, forms an inclusion with v 19.

There are three stylized parallel strophes relating to Assyria, Elam and Meshech-Tubal, which are reminiscent of the parallel sections of chaps. 18 and 20. However, even when textual criticism has done with them what it can, they are not con-structed symmetrically. The Assyria strophe consists of three lines, the Elam one of six lines and the climactic Meshech-Tubal one, including its section of con-trast, of nine lines. The third strophe contains a wordplay that enhances the contrast, כלמתם "their shame" and כלי־מלחמתם "their weapons of war." At the beginning and end of v 27 גבורים "valiant ones" provides an inclusion for this contrasting section, while גבורים and שאול "Sheol" there supply an inclusion for the whole poem, echoing גבורים . . . שאול in v 21. The Elam strophe itself points forward to the final contrast: the relative clause relating to their shameful fate, אשר ירדו . . . "who went down . . ." (v 24bβ), is countered in v 27bα with a refer-ence to a nobler end, while the ignoble משכב "bier" provided in v 25aα contrasts with the negated resting (ישכבו) of v 27a. Indeed, שכב "lie" is the keyword of the whole poem, occurring at the beginning and end (vv 19, 28) and in the second and third strophes. It is then correspondingly echoed in vv 30-32.

The temporal setting of vv 18-28 seems to be close to that of vv 2-8. Egypt's military power is associated not with hope but with hopelessness, not with life but with death, a necessary message for the Judean exiles. The listing of Mesopotamian nations suits a Babylonian provenance.

Comment

17-18 According to Parker and Dubberstein's comparative scheme (*Babylonian Chronology* 28), if the same month is intended as in v 1, the date would be March 17, 585 B.C. Ezekiel is given the task of ironically bewailing the coming fate of Egypt's army. Defeat, not victory, was to be their lot— defeat resulting in a death that was the doorway to an ignominious fate in Sheol. Ezekiel has the role of inaugurating that fate with this oracle, for such is the power of the prophetic word (cf. Hos 6:5). The "mighty nations" are the three to be enumerated as the poem is developed. The phrase ארץ תחתיות "land of nether places" here and in v 24, with its intensive genitive plural and contextual distinction from Sheol proper (vv 21, 27) seems to refer to a deeper level, the lower regions (Tromp, *Primitive Conceptions* 181; cf. Isa 14:15). Egypt was to occupy a place that distinguished it from the generality of those who went down to the Pit or Sheol. Such a concept is found in Isa 14:15-20, and Ezekiel may be depending on that text and developing it. There are also traces of it in Mesopotamian literature: in the Akkadian Gilgamesh epic, concerning one who has died, it is said that "he lies upon the night couch and drinks pure water," while as for "him whose corpse was cast out upon the steppe," "his spirit finds no rest in the nether world" (12:148, 151-52; *ANET* 99). The characteristics of the grave are transferred to Sheol, so that the underworld reflects the burial status of the corpse (cf. Tromp, *Primitive Conceptions* 139, 183). This concept is especially noticeable in the reference to a bier in v 25. Although that and the related verb שכב "lie down, rest" are used in this passage, they do not imply a state of unconsciousness (cf. McAlpine, *Sleep* 147-49).

19-21 The question cuts Egypt down to size. In the end it has no special claims. Perhaps the thought is that they are (to be) forfeited in death (cf. Eichrodt 439; cf. 31:2-3, 18a). As in 31:17-18 (see *Comment* there), the uncircumcised and the victims of violent death represent classes that at death are not buried with their families, and so in Sheol are regarded as occupying a separate place in dishonor. The direct address is dropped from v 20 until the concluding v 28. In vv 20-21 Egypt stands virtually for Pharaoh its representative (cf. vv 31-32), like the other nations of vv 22-26. Accordingly it is spoken of in the masculine singular. The plural references appear to allude to the army, which, as in vv 22-26, is distinguished from the ethnic entity or figurehead. Over against the national symbol and its army are set certain inhabitants of the regular Sheol, who are called "valiant ones." They correspond to "the kings of the nations who lie in glory" in Isa 14:18, and they reappear here in v 27. The reference to their speaking suggests that their speech should follow. This is an old problem that the LXX tried to solve by placing v 19 after v 21a. It may be that vv 22-26 are to be understood as the speech of the valiant ones, who greet the newcomers and from their own more comfortable quarters point to the lower regions, where the Egyptians were to go, and somewhat like Virgil in Dante's *Divine Comedy*, describe the neighbors alongside whom Egypt is to exist.

22-23 The short Assyria strophe envisages the Assyrian figurehead and his once invincible army now lying in dishonor in a vast cemetery-like place where the troops are ranged around their leader. For the living the Assyrian empire was now only a bad memory. A contrast is posed between their present state and their former position of awesome power on earth. Now they are classed with the victims of violent death, to which the language of the second line refers.

24-25 The Elam strophe develops the theme of dishonor. As in 28:8, "the killed" seems to have the special sense of victims of a dishonorable death. Elam, east of Babylonia, enjoyed periods of power over southern Mesopotamia in ancient times. Its might was broken by Assyria.

26-27 The third example of fallen imperialism is Meshech-Tubal (cf. 38:2-3 and *Comment*), who occupied the area south-east of the Black Sea. Historically the nations known to the Assyrians as Mushki and Tabal are in view, who in the eighth century B.C. posed a threat to Assyria in the south. Here they too are classed with the hapless uncircumcised and victims of violent death. Their fate is contrasted with that of the valiant in the regular part of Sheol. There may be a link at this point with the heroes of Gen 6:4; but, if so, it is not a direct one, as there they have no military role. Whether we are to find a concept of world ages in this passage (cf. Zimmerli 176) is doubtful: historically the nations mentioned do not fall into a chronological sequence nor does there seem to have been such an intention. The valiant are conceived as lying in a veritable Valhalla of a cemetery, their earthly phase of awesome power finding a fitting sequel in their honorable state of rest.

28 The fortune of the valiant provides a foil for Egypt's coming ignominy. The Egyptians are assigned the same dishonorable fate as the nations previously listed.

29-30 The literary conclusion in vv 29-32 takes the opportunity to assign two further groups to the bitter fate of Assyria and the other two. Now the perspective is unambiguously future. Edom is to lose its present power. There was a lingering antagonism against Edom in the Judean heart, which this reference seeks to assuage (cf. 25:12-14; 35). The second group of references is much less straightforward. Its slightly shriller vehemence suggests that here too a chord of contemporary resentment is being struck. The Sidonians (cf. 28:20-23) may refer generally to the Phoenicians (Katzenstein, *History of Tyre* 324 n. 166). Doomed kings of the north appear in Jer 25:26 after an earlier reference to Elam, but a desire to round off a literary list is not appropriate here. The Phoenicians did in fact practice circumcision: as before, the reference is to sharing the special fate of the uncircumcised.

31-32 The literary unit is concluded with a final reference to Egypt, now in the form of Pharaoh and his army, which reverts to the language of v 18 and to the thought of vv 20-21. In a final statement that gathers up both v 19 and v 28 it firmly equates Pharaoh's fate with that of the doomed nations earlier, contrasting present awe and might with future shame.

Explanation

Ezekiel refused to be mesmerized by the spectacle of Egypt's military power or captivated by Judean dreams of the political renewal that might be served thereby. History's theatrical wardrobe was cluttered with the national costumes of those who had strutted across its stage for a while, until the curtain fell on their particular scene. They lived on only in popular infamy—or, in terms of contemporary beliefs about the underworld, in the deeper regions of Sheol. Such would be Egypt's fate, instead of a Valhalla of chivalrous warriors who rested in peace and honor.

The supplementary conclusion changes the tone by adding to the list of dishonored dead others at whose hands the Judeans had seemingly suffered (cf. 28:24). They too would pass away to an inglorious fate. But the climax reverts to Egypt, which once more is cast in the sinister role of a tragic has-been. The pronouncement is a warning to world powers in any age:

The tumult and the shouting dies;
The captains and the kings depart . . .
Lo, all our pomp of yesterday
Is one with Nineveh and Tyre!
Judge of the nations, spare us yet.
Lest we forget—lest we forget.
    (R. Kipling, *Recessional*)

The emphasis on the underworld brings to a climax a motif that has been running through the oracles against the nations (cf. 26:20-21; 28:8; 31:15-18). Its literary role is to be a counterpoint to the promise of life for God's people, which follows and is developed in the remaining chapters of the book.

The Goodness and Severity of God (33:1-20)

Bibliography

Auvray, P. "Le prophète comme guetteur. Ez 33, 1-20." *RB* 71 (1964) 191-205. **Brownlee, W. H.** "Ezekiel's Parable of the Watchman and the Editing of Ezekiel." *VT* 28 (1978) 392-408. **Graffy, A.** *A Prophet Confronts His People.* AnBib 104. Rome: Biblical Institute Press, 1984, 72-78. **Koch, K.** "Der Spruch 'Sein Blut bleibe auf seinem Haupt'." *VT* 12 (1962) 396-416. **Krüger, T.** *Geschichtskonzepte im Ezechielbuch.* BZAW 180. Berlin: de Gruyter, 1989, 341-50. **Murray, D. F.** "The Rhetoric of Disputation: Re-examination of a Prophetic Genre." *JSOT* 38 (1987) 95-121. **del Olmo Lete, G.** "Estructura literaria de Ez. 33:1-20." *EstBib* 22 (1963) 5-31. **Raitt, T. M.** "The Prophetic Summons to Repentance." *ZAW* 83 (1971) 30-49. **Schmidt, M. A.** "Zur Komposition des Buches Hesekiel." *TZ* 6 (1950) 81-98.

Translation

[1] *I received the following communication from Yahweh:* [2] *"Human one, speak to your fellow nationals and tell them: Suppose*[a] *I cause a sword to attack a particular country, and its people take an individual from their number*[b] *and make him their lookout,* [3] *and then he sees the sword attacking the country and blows on the horn to warn the people.* [4] *Now if anybody hears the horn without acting on the warning*[a] *and the*[b] *sword attacks and dispatches him,*[c] *the responsibility for his death rests on his own head.* [5] *He heard the horn but did not act on the warning. His death is his own fault. If he had acted on the warning,*[a] *he would have saved his life.* [6] *As for the lookout, if he sees the sword attacking but fails to blow on the horn, so that the people are not warned—and then the sword attacks and dispatches somebody, that person is dispatched for his wrongdoing, but I will hold the lookout responsible as agent of his death.*

[7] *"You it is, human one, whom I have appointed lookout for the community of Israel. Whenever you hear a message from my lips, you are to pass on to them a warning from me.*[a] [8] *If I tell someone who is wicked, 'You wicked person,*[a] *you are doomed to die,' and you have not given him an explicit warning about his behavior, he*[b] *will die for his wrongdoing, but I will hold you responsible as a party to his death.* [9] *If, on the other hand, you have warned him about his behavior, urging him to give it up, but he fails to do so, then he will die for his wrongdoing, but you will have saved your life.*

[10] *"You, human one, are to tell the community of Israel, Your complaint has been*[a] *'Our rebel ways and our sins are getting us down and they are sapping our vital energies. How are we going to experience life?'* [11] *Tell them that I swear by my own life—so runs the oracle of the Lord*[a] *Yahweh—that what I want is not the death of the wicked person but for him to win life by giving up his present behavior. Give up, do give up your bad behavior—why should you die, community of Israel?*

[12] *"You, human one, are to tell your fellow nationals: The virtue of the virtuous person will not keep him safe once he backslides, nor will the wickedness of the wicked person be his downfall once he gives up his behaving wickedly. Wickedness prevents the virtuous person from gaining life, when he sins:*[a] [13] *when I promise the virtuous person that he*[a] *will win life and then, relying on his earlier virtue, he does wrong, none of his virtuous actions*[b] *will be remembered. The wrong he does will be the cause of his death.* [14] *Again, when I tell the wicked person 'You are doomed to die' and he gives up his sins and does*

what is right and fair, [15]*such as*[a] *returning a pledge, giving back stolen property and generally behaving in line with the rules that make for life rather than doing wrong, he will win life, he will not die.* [16]*None of his past sins*[a] *will be remembered against*[b] *him. He is doing what is right and fair, he will certainly win life.*

[17] *"Your fellow nationals have been objecting 'The Lord's*[a] *attitude is not equitable,'* [b] *when it is their own*[c] *attitude that is not equitable.* [18]*If the virtuous person gives up his virtue and does wrong, he will die on those grounds.*[a] [19]*Correspondingly, if the wicked person gives up his wickedness and does what is right and fair, he will win life on that score.* [20]*You have objected 'The Lord's attitude is not equitable.' I mean to make individual behavior the measure of my judgment of you, community of Israel."*

Notes

2. a. In this long hypothetical sentence the apodosis comes in v 4b in the Heb. (Cooke 370).
2. b. For the meaning of the Heb. term see Zimmerli 179.
4. a. Heb. נזהר can have the positive sense "take warning" as well as "be warned" (BDB 264a). The switch to a pf here and in v 6aβ implies that an actual case is now envisaged (Cooke, ibid.).
4. b. The lack of an article with חרב "sword" here and in v 6aγ is a mark of idiomatic and/or slack composition; cf. the anarthrous רשע "wicked" in vv 8, 9, 11.
4. c. Attempts to translate this pericope with more inclusive language led to distortion of its meaning or clumsiness. Essentially the translation reflects ancient culture in a readable, fairly close form.
5. a. For the conditional use of the ptcp see GKC 116w, 159i; for the following hypothetical pf see GKC 106p. Wellhausen (*apud* Smend 268) proposed a widely adopted conjectural emendation הזהיר "(but he [= the lookout]) passed on the warning (and saved his life)," on the ground that the parallel statement in the interpretation (v 9bβ) so suggests. From the same standpoint Auvray, *RB* 71 (1964) 193, keeping MT, rendered "(but he) acted on the warning," urging that a conditional sense was tortuous after the series of narrative verbs. Zimmerli (180), impressed by the unanimity of the textual tradition, objected that the verb הציל "save" would have been used, as in v 9; 3:19, 21. In reply Auvray, ibid., rightly pointed out that in those texts the prophet is in view, but here the lookout, so that a different verb is permissible. However, the usage of והוא "and he" in v 13 suggests that the same subj is in view as in v 5a. The lookout has not been in view since v 3, so that he is not an obvious antecedent, while the initial והצפה "and the lookout" in v 6 suggests that a new subject is broached at that point. Auvray's interpretation labors under the difficulty that elsewhere the lookout/prophet is the channel of warning. In v 9bβ a new, climactic element appears to be added.
7. a. The force of ממני "(warn) from me," here and in 3:17, is not absolutely clear. Greenberg (*Ezekiel 1-20* 84) interprets the phrase as "advise of the danger . . . coming from someone" and so "warn against." Likewise, del Olmo Lete, *EstBib* 22 (1963) 14, who correlates with the coming of the sword in the parable.
8. a. Heb. רשע "O wicked one" may be a dittograph: it is lacking in the parallel 3:18 (cf. 33:14) and here in LXX* Syr.
8. b. Heb. הוא רשע "that wicked person" (cf. BDB 215b) is perhaps an Aramaism: cf. Dan 2:32 and J. A. Montgomery, *Daniel* (Edinburgh: T. & T. Clark, 1927) 166 (Brownlee in an unpublished note; cf. Greenberg, *Ezekiel 1-20* 85).
10. a. For the seemingly redundant לאמר "saying" cf. v 24; 35:12; 37:18 (Zimmerli 180-81).
11. a. For the formulaic אדני "Lord" see the note on 20:3.
12. a. V 12b, taken in the sense "and the righteous one cannot live thereby," is widely held to be not original: it is redundant after the parallelism of v 12aβ and בה "thereby" is too far away from צדקת "righteousness" to be the antecedent, and the clause represents a gloss on v 12aα (Cooke 365; Zimmerli 181 et al.). However, Ehrlich (*Randglossen* 124) argued that the antecedent was רשעה "wickedness" and that בה qualifies "cannot" rather than לחיות "live," with the sense given in the translation. He regarded (מ)רשעו not as a noun "wickedness" but as an inf constr "(from) acting wickedly," comparing especially 2 Chron 11:4 for the construction. Then the clause is evidently not a repetition of v 12aα but a restatement expressing a basic principle, which paves the way for v 13 (cf. del Olmo Lete, *EstBib* 22 [1963] 21 note 32).
13. a. LXX^MSS attest a 2nd person verb, which reflects harmonization with v 14 (Zimmerli, ibid.).
13. b. K צדקתו "his righteous acts" reflects an older spelling, for which Q attests the *plene* written

form (F. I. Andersen and A. D. Forbes, *Spelling in the Hebrew Bible* [BibOr 41. Rome: Biblical Institute Press, 1986] 325-26).

15. a. MT adds רשע "(the) wicked one," which reads awkwardly at this point. Since 2 MSS LXX* Syr do not represent it, it may well be a misplaced annotation relating to v 14, with reference either to ושב "and he turns" or to מות תמות "you will surely die" as a vocative to match v 8 (Hitzig 258).

16. a. Cf. the second note on v 13.

16. b. The *lamed* expresses a dative of disadvantage (BDB 515a).

17. a. For אדני "Lord" here and in v 20 many MSS have יהוה "Yahweh": cf. 18:25, 29 and *Note.* The divine name may have been replaced to avoid its association with an offensive charge.

17. b. Heb. תכן appears to mean here in the niph "be conformed to a standard, be right and fair" (cf. BDB 1067a). Greenberg (*Ezekiel 1-20* 333-34), working from the primary sense "determine," regards the niph as tolerative, with the sense "(not) determinable" and so "erratic, arbitrary." Fishbane (*Biblical Interpretation* 338 note 62), working from a basic meaning "measure," interprets with NEB "acts without principle."

17. c. Heb. המה "they" reinforces the suffix: see GKC 135f.

18. a. Heb. בהם "by them" seems to use the pl in a neuter sense (Cooke 370-71).

Form/Structure/Setting

The boundaries of the literary unit are set as vv 1-20 by the message reception formula of v 1 and by the beginning of a new, dated piece in v 21. The use of the prophetic address in vv 2, 7, 10 and 12 reveals four sections, vv 2-6, 7-9, 10-11 and 12-20. It is customary to split these sections into two larger units, vv 2-9 and 10-20, mainly because of the external links these verses have with chaps. 3 and 18 respectively. However, there are five internal factors that suggest otherwise. (i) The occurrences of בני עמך "your compatriots" in vv 2, 12, 17 (and 30) may indicate a significant break at v 12. (ii) In vv 2-20 there is an alternating sequence of divine address to Ezekiel and through the prophet to the people, in an ABA/ABA pattern, with the first group ending at v 11. (iii) In v 11 בית ישראל "house of Israel" seems to echo its occurrence in v 7, so that the force of vv 7-10a is that Ezekiel receives an order to speak in his role as watchman for the community, the role assigned to him in vv 7-9. (iv) Direct address to "the house of Israel" at vv 11 and 20 brings about parallel endings. (v) Disputations (vv 10-11, 17-20) end both sections, after double treatments of (a) the prophet's responsibility, in parable and interpretation (vv 2-9), and (b) the people's moral responsibility in relation to a shift from good to bad or from bad to good (vv 12-16).

The parable of the lookout uses a framework of legal language. Two "cases" are presented (כי "if, when," vv 2, 6), in accord with priestly casuistic formulation of offenses. The style of the Holiness Code is very similar, especially the combination of case and verdict in Lev 24:17, "If (כי) someone kills a human being, he will surely be put to death." V 9 in the course of the application is closer to this formulation: the parabolic illustration demanded its own terminology. The casuistic framework is developed with a loose narrative sequence of clauses, like Deuteronomy's homiletic development of the case-law style (cf. e.g., Deut 13:1-5). The polarized opposition of life or death is also derived from Deuteronomy, from a deuteronomistic portion (Deut 30:15-20). The legal framework is used to describe a non-legal set of circumstances, which comprised no legal offense and for which no legal penalty had been prescribed. The priestly style is used to convey an essentially prophetic concern. The application (vv 7-9) is addressed to the prophet, for it takes the form of a commissioning oracle (v 7), investing Ezekiel with the role of a lookout, and of exposition of that role (vv 8-9). The two cases of the parable are here inverted in a chiastic order (v 4 = v 9, v 6 = v 8; del Olmo Lete, *EstBib* 22 [1963] 15).

Vv 10-11 are a disputation, consisting of three basic elements, thesis, dispute and counterthesis (cf. in principle Murray, *JSOT* 38 [1987] 99; Graffy [*A Prophet Confronts* 72-78] has postulated an extended disputation, vv 10-16 or vv 10-20). The first element is also a lament, while the second and third elements (v 11) comprise a summons to repentance, with motivation mingled with appeal, in an overall combination of standard elements: the messenger formula, divine promise or assurance, accusation, admonition, threat and a vocative (cf. Raitt, *ZAW* 83 [1971] 35). An inclusion is formed by the phrase בית ישראל "house of Israel."

Vv 12-16 are a didactic discourse, summarized in a double formulation at the beginning (v 12a) and developed separately in vv 12b-13 and vv 14-16. There is a fourfold parallel structuring of points: (i) a divine pronouncement of life or death, (ii) apostasy or conversion, (iii) the irrelevance of past behavior, and (iv) a final pronouncement of death or life (del Olmo Lete, *EstBib* 22 [1963] 22). The parallelism is broken at two points, the introductory v 12b and the catalog and pronouncement of v 15, each of which strives to reinforce the stage of apostasy or conversion.

Vv 17-20 are a disputation, presented obliquely until the direct, recapitulating conclusion in v 20. V 17a, repeated in v 20a, is the thesis, and it is disputed in v 17b. A counterthesis occurs in vv 18-19 and is restated in v 20b. There is a chiastic structure ABBA in vv 17-20a, with vv 18-19 constructed in a parallel fashion and v 17 reiterated in v 20a. In sense, v 20b functions as a further B element, so that emphasis is laid on the counterthesis.

The primary setting of vv 1-9 is difficult to determine because of the fact that vv 7-9 are a virtual repetition of 3:17-19. The factor of literary structuring has undoubtedly played a role in this double placement: chap. 33 introduces a new section of the book, in which a positive message of judgment replaces the earlier proclamation of judgment. However, where the watchman passages originally belonged is disputed, and both literary and historical factors are involved in the question. Schmidt, *TZ* 6 (1950) 92, has claimed that different situations lie behind vv 1-6 and 7-9 respectively, in that first the people and then the prophet are addressed, and that, while the parable belongs to the second, post-587 B.C., phase of the prophet's ministry, the "application" has been borrowed from the chronologically earlier 3:16-21. By contrast, Kraetzschmar (35-36) argued that 33:1-9 all belong to the second phase and that the emphasis on the individual rather than on national solidarity is evidence of that setting. A number of scholars, including Eichrodt (75) and Zimmerli (189), have made similar claims. As to the unity of vv 1-9, Zimmerli has pointed to the close correspondence between vv 1-6 and 7-9 and the unlikelihood that vv 2-6 ever existed independently, although it is possible that they were subsequently inserted to amplify vv 7-9.

The issue is complicated by the extra material 3:20-21, which does not recur here, concerning the perseverance of the righteous and wicked. Auvray, *RB* 71 (1964) 197, has noted that the theme of this material does not logically belong to the watchman illustration, and concluded with some reason that it represents a desire to present a more comprehensive and systematized description of Ezekiel's prophetic task (cf. del Olmo Lete, *EstBib* 22 [1963] 29). There it serves to enhance the dual response of 2:5, 7; 3:11, 27 (cf. Zimmerli, *Ezekiel 1* 55). In that case, there is a concern in chap. 3 to give an introduction to the prophet's ministry as a whole, rather like the redactional role of Isa 1 in relation to the work of Isaiah (cf. Fohrer, *ZAW* 74 [1962] 251-68). If that is so, then 3:17-19 comprise a repetition of material already present in 33:7-9. It must be said, however, that other scholars have argued differently to a greater or lesser degree. For instance, Eichrodt (444) would place 3:20-21 after 33:9 (cf. Fohrer 23, 184). On the other hand, Brownlee, *VT* 28 (1978) 398, considered that 33:2-6 have been removed from an earlier position before 3:17. In harmonizing fashion Greenberg (*Ezekiel 1-20* 90-97) has urged that Ezekiel's role as a watchman belongs to both periods of his activity (cf. Reventlow, *Wächter über Israel* 130), although the claim of a new emphasis on individualism in the second phase is illfounded. Klein (*Ezekiel: The Prophet and His Message* 28-32) has limited Greenberg's view of a double delivery to a redactional concern that must be taken seriously within the present form of the book: difference in context indicates that the first watchman pericope in chap. 3 is a private message to Ezekiel, linked to the prophet's call, while the second in chap. 33 is part of the prophet's public message later on and is oriented toward forgiveness.

33:10-11 are related to portions of chap. 18, viz. 18:23 and, in general terms, 31b. This relationship is part of a larger one shared with vv 12-20. Chap. 18 does seem to belong to a post-587 B.C. period, and so to the second part of Ezekiel's twofold ministry (Zimmerli, *Ezekiel 1* 377). Hence parallels with it have a not unreasonable role in chap. 33, which serves to introduce the prophet's new words of hope. Vv 12-16 are close to 18:21-22 and 24. Here there is an emphasis on divine address, absent from chap. 18. The order of the propositions in vv 13 and 14-15a, 16 is reversed: they accord with 18:24 and 18:21-22 respectively (v 15a accords loosely with the series of positive and negative catalogs found in chap. 18; v 11a has a counterpart in 18:23). Auvray, *RB* 71 (1964) 202, has commented on the illogicality of the order here: the divine principle relating to conversion in chap. 18 (18:21-22, 23) is here separated from it and placed next to the statement of apostasy, on which it has no bearing. His comment holds good only if vv 10-11 belong with vv 12-16. Vv 17-20 are found at greater length in 18:25-30, with minor differences.

It is clear that similar material now exists in different recensions. Whether one can trace literary dependence is uncertain. Auvray, *RB* 71 (1964) 203, and del Olmo Lete, *EstBib* 22 (1963) 31, have argued for the priority of the material in chap. 33 rather than in chap. 18, while Wevers (176) has urged that chap. 33 is an editorial recapitulation of chap. 18. Zimmerli (189) leaves the relationship of vv 10-16 to chap. 18 open, while inclined to regard vv 17-20 as a secondary addition from chap. 18, in view of their extreme closeness.

Comment

1-5 Ezekiel is instructed to tell a parable to his exiled compatriots. It concerns providential warfare, whereby military invasion is instigated by the punitive will of Yahweh (cf. 21:13-22 [8-17]). As a defensive measure the people appoint a lookout to warn them with a trumpet signal when the attack is launched. If any do not heed the warning signal, presumably by running for shelter into the walled city, they have only themselves to blame when they become casualties of war, having failed to take the opportunity open to them. The statement "his blood is on his own head" originally related to the innocence of the human agent of death (Koch, *VT* 12 [1962] 413; cf. 2 Kgs 2:37). Here the implicit reference is not to the killing invaders but to the lookout who had discharged his responsibility in giving a signal. The purpose of v 5 is to underline this observation. The fault lay with the heedless—and so not with the lookout, whose trumpet blast had been clearly heard.

6 Next, the case of the lazy lookout is considered. When the sword strikes and lives are taken, justice is done from the divine standpoint, for the sword accomplishes Yahweh's punitive will (v 2a). Yet the case is a complex one: the lookout, having failed in his duty, is guilty of a capital offense, and from this perspective his life too is forfeit because of the bloodguilt resting on him. The task of a lookout is to pass on a warning, and woe betide him if he is remiss. Yahweh will act as a גֹּאֵל or avenging next of kin, claiming the lookout's life (del Olmo Lete, *EstBib* 22 [1963] 13; cf. Num 35:12-21).

7-9 This section, addressed to the prophet, looks back and forward. It interprets the parable in terms of Ezekiel's role and paves the way for vv 10-11 by clarifying in what capacity the prophet is to transmit Yahweh's message in v 11. This conception of the prophet as a lookout is a development of Jer 6:17 (cf. J. W. Miller, *Das Verhältnis Jeremias* 112-12). In the application the place of the citizens in appointing the lookout is strikingly taken by Yahweh. The phenomenon looks forward to v 11, to the role of Yahweh as would-be defender of his people and not their destroyer, the preserver and giver of life and not the taker. The two cases of vv 2-5 and v 6 are now considered in reverse, with reference to the prophet. His task is to pass on to his constituency verbal messages of Yahweh's moral judgment in order that they may act as a deterrent. This is a reapplication of a positive concept of prophecy as encouraging a change of heart and habit, in order that divine punishment might be averted (see 2 Kgs 17:13; Jer 23:14; Zech 1:4; cf. Ezek 13:22).

To a large extent the parable of the lookout had in view a pre-exilic type of situation, the invasion of Judah and destruction of its inhabitants as the outworking of a moral providence. In the interpretation, however, all such language falls away, as befits an exilic situation. Ezekiel prophesies to the community of exiles in order to win moral converts. The verdict "You will surely die" has its roots in a judicial setting, and the priests as the custodians of sacral law were cognizant of capital offenses. Here, however, such doom as the prophets traditionally threatened sinners with (v 21) is in view. Ezekiel's task was to warn, and if he failed to do so, the doom of which he warned sidestepped to include him in its path. Yahweh would again intervene as גֹּאֵל, as in v 6. The reason why Yahweh avenges the death in the first case but not now, is that then the prophet's silence deprived the sinner of the potential to begin anew and so sealed his liability to death. The prophetic warning was necessary as the first step in Yahweh's positive purpose for the exiles.

10-11 What this purpose was the disputation now makes clear. Ezekiel's constituency in its post-587 B.C. situation was well aware of the aura of death that had already invaded their life and impoverished its quality. They were aware too that their own sins were the cause. In terms of the context, the admission puts them in the category of the wicked person dying for his wrongdoing (vv 8, 9, cf. v 6). That we are so to understand it is suggested by the resumption of earlier vocabulary, "the death of the wicked person," in v 11aβ. The people's admission is expressed in the style of a communal lament, the first clause of which poignantly uses a series of three *-ēnû* sounds, as in Isa 53:5a; 59:12. It uses a distinctive lament motif in speaking of death as a power rampant in their lives (cf. Ps 116:3, 8), and in posing a despairing question (cf. Ps 137:4) they were expressing the conviction that a new lease on life seemed unattainable. Yahweh is the implicit agent of such disorientation, as Ps 22:16 (15) affirms: "You set me in the dust of death." Historically the lament gives expression to the aftermath of the catastrophe of 587 B.C. and to the social and religious disorientation that the crisis created (cf. Lam 3:42-47).

In a vehement protest Yahweh objects to being cast solely in the role of punitive destroyer. It does not express his ultimate will, which is to bestow life on those who turn from the bad lifestyle that occasioned the punishment. The judgment was a means to this very end. The divine principle here enunciated gathers up the message of the prophetic canon, that judgment was the precursor of salvation: Yahweh plucks up with a view to planting again (Jer 1:10). Also, life's present death is regarded as an omen of real, future death. The deuteronomistic alternatives of life or death on the basis of a radical choice are offered anew (Deut 30:15-20; cf. Jer 21:8). For Ezekiel there was an eschatological connotation, which his later chapters expand, the opportunity of a new life associated with return from exile (cf. 36:24-32; 37:11-14). Yahweh would honor a change of lifestyle, the fruit of repentance, and to this end the people are summoned (cf. 14:6, in an earlier message to the exiles). The divine question is a hope-laden challenge to the despairing question of the people. Such was Yahweh's gracious offer, to which the prophetic warning was the necessary precursor in order to expose the danger that loomed over the impenitent (cf. 2 Chron 24:19; 36:15-16). Does the offer of life link theologically with the divine life of the oath formula? If so, Ps 102: 12-13, 24-25 (11-12, 23-24) and John 14:19b provide significant parallels.

12-16 The ensuing discussion majors not in Yahweh's offer of life but in the necessity for a choice of life or death and pursuit of a God-honoring moral way of life, with which Yahweh's pronouncements are inextricably linked. The term "give up" or "return" (שוב) is now used not only in the sense of renouncing evil and embracing God's good way but also in the opposite sense. There is a refusal to think in conventional categories of sinner and saint. Or rather, these categories are regarded not as fixed but as flexible. A conditional element looms large. It is disconcertingly possible both for the apostate who has not taken Yahweh's moral will to heart and for the person whose way of life has been an outworking of that will to reverse their roles. Neither is locked into a previously made moral determination, nor is Yahweh's word of hope or doom irrevocable. The saint may abandon the lifestyle that is the fruit of his faith, while the apostate may return to the path of obedience that leads to life (cf. 20:11, 13, 21; Lev 18:5). Yahweh's word is an amen, a "So be it!" that affirms each deliberate choice to pursue good or evil. The onus for judgment or salvation is placed squarely on the shoulders of the people of God.

17-20 The disputation echoes and answers an objection voiced evidently by those whose pretensions of a comfortable, superior status and conventional religious categorizing had been shattered by this disconcerting message. It is not fair: is God so unjust as either to overlook earlier moral commitment (cf. Heb 6:10) or to welcome back diehard sinners? In reply the charge of unfairness is thrown back in the critics' faces. The alternatives set out in vv 12-16 are uncompromisingly restated and summed up in a principle of judgment addressed to the nominally sound members of the people of God. If the cap of v 18 fitted, they had to wear it! "Whoever rejects the redeemer finds himself face to face with the judge" (Eichrodt 456).

Explanation

The prophet is fighting on two pastoral fronts. On the one hand he has to counter despair and demoralization among the exiles; on the other, he has to do it in such a way as not to encourage moral indifference and a false sense of security. The complexity of his message is occasioned not only by his pastoral situation but also by a traditional tension in Yahweh's self-revelation, which the New Testament and Christianity also know, that he is both gracious savior and moral judge. The first is affirmed in the parable of the lookout and its application to the prophet, and also in the accompanying disputation that anchors the prophet's role to a specific exilic situation. Emphasis rests on the will of Yahweh and the communication of that will to the people. His will for the exiled community was life and restoration (cf. 37:1-14). Yet it was not an automatic, unconditioned hope: "whoever has this hope in [God] purifies himself as he is pure" (1 John 3:3). Ahead lay not merely a new Exodus that issued in a return to Yahweh's favor and land, but also a judgment scenario such as the generation of the old Exodus encountered in the wilderness: rebels would have no part in the return (20:35-38; 34:17-22; cf. C. J. Mullo Weir, *VT* 2 [1952] 109-11). It is in the light of this coming judgment which would split God's people that they are counseled to prepare themselves. Yahweh warns of judgment and the prospect of an eschatological death precisely because life and not death is his priority (cf. 2 Pet 3:9). The warning given through the prophet is itself evidence of Yahweh's grace, as the first step toward a desired goal achieved via reformed, godly lives, the goal of a life that was life indeed (cf. 2 Pet 3:11-12). The prophet thus had a vital role. A necessary task was laid on him, as in a later era on Paul, both as gospel preacher (1 Cor 9:16) and as church teacher (Col 1:28).

Yet divine grace is easily misunderstood as implying moral irresponsibility, and indeed it has always been difficult to find rational coherence between the righteousness and grace of God (cf. Rom 3:5-8; 6:1, 15). Accordingly, the second half of the total message has a human focus, an emphasis on a moral imperative. It is grounded in Yahweh's earlier revelation, in the provision of the Torah that with precise directions (v 15) pointed to the path of life. So Torah and prophecy alike spelled out Yahweh's will, and the role of the latter was to reinforce the former in the creation of a people who with integrity and steady commitment sought to walk in the path of life that was also a path of righteousness. There are New Testament parallels to this dynamic emphasis on conditionality, such as Col 1:23. Supremely, perhaps, Ezekiel's total message may be summed up in the words of Rom 11:22: "Take note of the goodness and severity of God: severity to those who fell and goodness to you, provided that you continue in his goodness; otherwise you too will be cut off."

This emphasis on Yahweh's gracious longing and moral demand is fittingly placed at the head of a new section of the book which will announce promises of hope. It reminds the Christian reader of Jesus' ironic allocation of divine judgment and grace in Matt 7:21-23; 20:1-16; Luke 15:11-32. Here it seems to serve as a corrective. Later chapters might be understood to imply that all the exiles had to do was to wait idly till Yahweh's gift of new life fell into their laps. Earlier in the book 18:30-31 provided an implicit rejoinder: the gift of a new heart had to be appropriated, and a change of heart and habit played a part in that appropriation. As noted above, 20:35-38 convey their own caution. Gospel and law do have a certain essential compatibility (cf. Rom 6:15-17).

Do the two halves of vv 1-20 reflect two separate messages concluded with divine disputations and subsequently united with the help of their common keyword שוב "return, give up"? The presence of elements from both halves in chap. 18, if that chapter reflects a single situation, may indicate that vv 1-20 were delivered on one occasion and sought to clarify a complex theological and pastoral issue. In any case, the material finds its unity in the nature of God and in the outworking of divine truth in the experience of his people.

Perspectives On The Fall of Jerusalem (33:21-33)

Bibliography

Brownlee, W. H. "The Aftermath of the Fall of Judah According to Ezekiel." *JBL* 89 (1970) 393-404. **Kutsch, E.** *Die chronologischen Daten des Ezechielbuches.* Orbis Biblicus et Orientalis 62. Freiburg: Universitätsverlag/Göttingen: Vandenhoeck und Ruprecht, 1985. **Malamat, A.** "The Last Kings of Judah and the Fall of Jerusalem." *IEJ* 18 (1968) 137-56. **Reventlow, H.** *Wächter über Israel.* BZAW 82. Berlin: Töpelmann, 1962, 99-101. **Roberts, J. J. M.** "The Hand of Yahweh." *VT* 21 (1971) 244-51. **Sanders, J. A.** "Hermeneutics in True and False Prophecy." *Canon and Authority.* Ed. G. W. Coates and B. O. Long. Philadelphia: Fortress, 1977, 21-41.

Translation

[21] *In the twelfth[a] year of our deportation, on the fifth of the tenth month, a person[b] who had survived the fall of Jerusalem came to me with the news that the city had been captured.* [22] *Now I had felt Yahweh's hand on me the evening before the survivor arrived, and he had opened my mouth by the time he came[a] in the morning. Yes, my mouth was opened and I was dumb no more.*

[23] *I received the following communication from Yahweh:* [24] *"Human one, the folk who live in those[a] desolated areas on Israelite soil are claiming that Abraham was just one individual and yet he took over the country. 'We are numerous,' they are saying. 'We have been given the country to take over.'* [25] *Tell them, then, the following message from the Lord[a] Yahweh.[b] You eat meat containing blood,[c] you look up[d] to your idols and you spill blood. Is it likely then that you will take over[e] the country?* [26] *You rely[a] on your swords, you engage[b] in shocking religious practices and you are one and all sullying your neighbors' wives. Is it likely that you will take over the country?* [27] *This is what you are to tell them. The message of the Lord Yahweh is as follows: I swear by my life that those who are in the desolate areas will fall as victims of the sword, and anyone in the open country is assigned by me to the wild animals as prey,[a] while those in hideouts and caves will die of plague.* [28] *I will reduce the country to wrack and ruin. Its celebrated assets will be destroyed and Israel's mountains will become untraveled ruins.* [29] *Then they will realize that I am Yahweh, when I reduce the country to wrack and ruin, in reprisal for all the shocking religious practices they have been engaging in.*

[30] *"Your fellow nationals, human one, who are talking about you in alleys and doorways, invite[a] each other[b] to come and hear what message Yahweh has sent.* [31] *They come to you in crowds[a] and sit down in front of you.[b] They listen to your messages without acting on them.[c]* [32] *To them you are just like a fine vocalist, some professional musician who sings[a] erotic songs. They listen to your messages without acting on them.* [33] *When it finally happens—and happen it will—then they will realize that they have had a prophet among them."*

Notes

21. a. There is some ancient support, a few MSS and LXX[L] Syr, for "eleventh": see *Comment.*
21. b. Heb. הפלים "the survivor" exhibits an idiomatic use of the article: see GKC 126r.

22. a. MT בוא "coming" may have suffered metathesis from an original באו "his coming": the phenomenon is not uncommon in Ezek with this verb (see Zimmerli 191).

24. a. Heb. "these," as mentally present to the speaker. LXX* probably omitted as inappropriate for an exilic setting.

25. a. For the formulaic אדני "Lord" here and in v 27 see 20:3 *Note.*

25. b. LXX* omits vv 25aβ-27a by parablepsis due to homoeoteleuton: a copyist's eye slipped to the next messenger formula. The missing material comprises the logically necessary accusation.

25. c. Cornill's fairly popular emendation על־ההרים "on the mountains" (396), aligning with 18:6, is not necessary. For the idiomatic use of על "together with" see BDB 755b.

25. d. MT ועינכם "and (you raise) your eyes" is written defectively.

25. e. For the interrogative sense after the conjunction here and in v 26b see GKC 150a.

26. a. Lit. "stand on": cf. English "stand by."

26. b. Heb. עשיתן "you have done," as if fem, is anomalous for the regular עשיתם, for which there is a little support (cf. *BHS*): see GKC 44k.

27. a. MT לאכלו "to eat him" is possible, but נתן לאכלה "give for food" is a regular phrase in Ezek, which suggests that an original לאכלה, for which there is some Heb. and versional support (see *BHS*), was misunderstood as לאכלה and modernized into the present form.

30. a. For the Heb. construction see Cooke 371 and GKC 112oo, 116w. A pl is expected: perhaps the Heb should be pointed as inf abs ודבר (Zimmerli 196).

30. b. MT may have a conflated text. If so, which is the intruder is hard to assess, although the first phrase חד את־אחד "one with one," not represented in LXX*, is often so regarded (Cornill 398 et al.). The doubling may intend to represent a plethora of gossiping (Zimmerli, ibid.). Heb. חד is a strange Aramaism alongside אחד, which is evidently so pointed for assonance (Cooke, ibid.).

31. a. Lit. "like the coming of people": cf. 26:10.

31. b. MT adds עמי "my people," which is difficult to fit into the sentence. LXX* Syr do not represent, and it may originally have been a marginal gloss on עם "people" earlier (Cornill, ibid., et al.). Ehrlich (*Randglossen* 125-26) regarded it as a true correction, rendering the earlier phrase "as a person to whom my people should come."

31. c. MT adds "for erotic talk [cf. Tg תולעבא "lascivious talk"] is on their lips, their minds pursue their illgotten gain." Zimmerli (196-97) and Wevers (256), following Hölscher, delete v 31aβ-b as an expansion linked with v 32, but at least the repetition of v 31aβγ in v 32b provides a fitting emphasis. As a whole v 31b seems to be saying too much. The focus of the content is on hearing without heeding Ezekiel's messages rather than on actual wrongdoing. V 32b reads like an anticlimax after it. Was כי־עגבים בפיהם "for erotic talk is on their lips" originally a comment on v 32a "you are to them like a love song (MT)," understanding the people to be the singers of disreputable songs—not the prophet? LXX Syr render עגבים as "lying," which is a better match with בצעם "their gain" in v 31bβ (cf. 22:27b-28a). It may represent an interpretative translation, supplying a general derogatory term suitable to the context. Many read כזבים "lies" (Cornill, ibid.; Fohrer 189, et al.), but it is graphically unlikely. LXX also represents בצעם as "defilements," perhaps reading עצבים "idols" (Cornill, ibid., cf. 11:21; 20:16). LXX* Syr do not represent המה עשים "they do," which does not easily relate to talking. The phrase probably originated as a marginal variant for, or clarification of, עשים "do" in v 32bβ. Was the staccato אחרי בצעם לבם הלך "their hearts pursue their gain" meant as a comment on the bad shepherds of chap. 34? If so, it was intended as a reminiscence of the greedy shepherds of Isa 56:11b. MT הלך "goes (after)" is not represented in LXX*. It was probably overlooked before the following והנך.

32. a. For MT כשיר "like a song" the following reference to a musician requires "like a singer." The consonantal text may be maintained if, instead of reading כשר (Fohrer, ibid., following Herrmann, et al.) one points כשיר (Driver, *Bib* 19 [1938] 180, following Ewald).

Form/Structure/Setting

The autobiographical narrative report in vv 21-22, prefaced with a chronological reference, serves as an introduction to an extended oracle that is introduced by a message reception formula, in vv 23-33. The separate addressing of the prophet in vv 24 and 30 splits the oracle into two parts, vv 24-29 and 30-33. The two prophetic messages—for such they are in their diverse content and targets—are both proof sayings ending in third-person recognition formulas (vv 29, 33). The first is a standard three-part proof saying, developed from an oracle of judgment that consists of both a second-person accusation and a third-person pronouncement of punishment (vv 25-26, 27-28). Each part is introduced with commissioning and messenger formulas (vv 25aα, 27aα) and in the second case a divine oath has a reinforcing intent (v 27aβ), while a typical לכן "therefore, then" interlocks charge and verdict. The piece is also a disputation that consists of thesis in v 24, dispute in vv 25-26, and counterthesis in vv 27-29 (Murray, *JSOT* 38 [1987] 103-4). The second divine communication also has elements of an oracle of judgment. An accusatory tone sounds loud and clear in the bittersweet narrative of vv 30-32, while there is a short, sinister reference to punishment in v 33a, as a qualification of the recognition formula.

The chronological setting of this prophetic unit is clearly post-587 B.C. and the geographical setting the place of exile, as the introductory message makes clear. The second message reflects the prophet's vindication, now that Jerusalem has fallen. The message concerning the survivors of Judah rhetorically addresses them directly in vv 25-27aα, before lapsing into a natural third-person reference (*contra* Brownlee, *JBL* 89 [1970] 393). It obviously reflects a period some time after the initial shock of destruction had passed and in which there was a turning to a brighter future (Cooke 367; Eichrodt 461). Wevers (254) has queried the relevance of vv 28-29 to a post-587 B.C. situation on the ground that threat of further devastation seems out of place, and so he has suggested a setting for vv 25-29 after 11:15. However, Zimmerli (199-200) has compared the presence of this very theme in Jer 52:30, while Graffy (*A Prophet Confronts* 82) has observed that the prophet uses strong stereotyped language of destruction in order to answer the positive claims of v 24.

In rhetorical terms the three phases of the disputation in vv 24-29 are highlighted by three expressions featuring a double use of אמר "say," in vv 24, 25 and 27. Running through the accusation, pronouncement of punishment and amplified recognition formula is the issue of giving the land (נתן, הארץ) in vv 24, 28 and 29: the positive sense of the first is ironically twisted to a negative one in the second and third cases. Stylistically, rather than form-critically, the disputation falls into two parts, vv 24-26 and 27-29. The first raises and disputes the question of the possession of the land (ירש and הארץ in vv 24, 25b, 26). The mention of "ruins" (חרבות) provides parallel beginnings in vv 24 and 27.

The second message is rhetorically paralleled with the first by different locations involving the verb ישב "sit, inhabit": the first target comprises "those who inhabit (ישבי) ruins" (v 24), and the second those who "sit (וישבו) before" the exilic prophet (v 31). This message is engrossed with hearing (שמע) and coming (בוא): the seemingly positive coming and hearing in v 30 turn into a heedless pair of activities in v 31 and into a heedless hearing in v 32—which is capped in v 33 by a reference to the coming of disaster.

Although chap. 33 falls into two distinct literary units, there are clear indications of a larger structuring for this introductory chapter. In a frightening inclusion the coming of the sword in vv 2-6 is echoed in the coming of an unnamed woe in v 33. The motif of hearing to no effect in vv 30-32 picks up the double statement in the parable at vv 4-5, while the mention of a "word . . . from Yahweh" in v 30 resumes "a word from my mouth" in v 7. Moreover, the styling of the exiles as בני עמך "your compatriots" takes the reader back to vv 2, 12 and 17, and especially to v 2 in view of the watchman terminology reiterated in vv 30-33. Perhaps one may envisage an ABBA structuring for the oracles of chap. 33, with vv 1-11 matched in vv 30-33 and then vv 12-20 finding a counterpart in vv 23-29 with their shared moral emphasis. The historical pivot of the chapter, C in an overall ABCBA pattern, is the sequence of events in vv 21-22.

There are also wider structural links with earlier material. The ending of Ezekiel's "dumbness" was adumbrated predictively in 24:27 and marks a reversal of its imposition in 3:26. Moreover, the divine assertion that Ezekiel's prophetic gifts would eventually be acknowledged by the exiles constitutes an echo of 2:5.

Comment

21-22 The dating corresponds in Parker and Dubberstein's reconstruction (*Babylonian Chronology* 28) to January 19, 585 B.C. It creates a problem in that it means that a year and a half had elapsed since the fall of Jerusalem, which seems an unreasonably long time for the news to reach Babylonia. So the minority tradition for the "eleventh" year is attractive, especially when it is supported by the suggestion that the present text is the result of an attempt to follow on from the dating of 32:17 (Zimmerli 192; Eichrodt 457-58). Then there is a more feasible six-month lapse between the fall and its communication (cf. the nearly four months' journey of Ezra's party from Babylonia to Jerusalem in Ezra 7:9; 8:31), especially if one envisages the פליט "survivor" not as a refugee making his own way eastwards, but a survivor of the fall who shared in one of the general and more time-consuming deportations to Babylonia (see Zimmerli, ibid.). However, one cannot help suspecting that the textual support for the earlier date is a secondary rationalization.

Kutsch (*Die chronologischen Daten*, esp. 41-45) has argued that the first year of Jehoachin's deportation, from which most dates in Ezekiel are reckoned (except 24:1) occurred in 598/7 B.C., while Zedekiah's first regnal year was not until 597/6 B.C. Accordingly, the dates relating to the deportation need to be set a year earlier, and here interpreted as January 19, 586 B.C., which again posits six months or so as the time for the news to travel east. Malamat, *IEJ* 18 (1968) 146-50, following Cooke (366), May (248) et al., has justified the present text on the supposition that, while the dates throughout Ezekiel rely on a calendar that began the new year in the spring, in the month Nisan, the regnal years of the Judean kings are based on an autumn calendar beginning in the month Tishri, while the months were reckoned from Nisan. Thus the fall of Jerusalem occurred in the summer between Nisan and Tishri, already in the twelfth year of Zedekiah according to the reckoning in Ezekiel, but still in Zedekiah's eleventh year that was going to end in Tishri. By this means too a six-month interval is achieved. It is clear that there are serious chronological problems connected with the fall of Jerusalem, and somehow the present text may be correct.

Judean confirmation of Jerusalem's fall (cf. 14:22) has repercussions for the prophet's ministry forecast earlier in 24:27. Whatever the precise significance of the dumbness (see *Comment* on 24:25-27), its termination, here mentioned twice for emphasis, clearly marked a turning point for the prophet and his people, and made possible a new message of national hope to replace that of judgment. The momentous release that Ezekiel underwent first in his own person was suitably anticipated by an uncanny presentiment that he recognized as the working or "hand" of Yahweh (cf. 1:3, etc.; see Roberts, *VT* 21 [1971] 244-51), which preceded important developments in the prophet's experience of God.

23-24 Yet exile was the necessary channel of true hope. Ezekiel somehow hears of a false hope that, theologically grounded as it was, had to be exposed as not of God. At an earlier period the prophet had to disabuse the non-exiled Judeans of the notion that, while the deportation of 597 B.C. spelled divine rejection, staying in the land was an earnest of God's providential favor (11:15). Such theological naivety was being used again, in a post-587 B.C. situation, to bolster a self-centered resilience that merely indicated that Yahweh's purpose had not yet been understood (cf. v 29; cf. Isa 9:8-10). Those still in the land saw themselves as religious pioneers, typologically reliving not the occupation achieved by Israel under Joshua, but Abraham's earlier occupation (cf. Gen 15:7, 8; Exod 6:8). This parallel, rather than the other, made their hopes seem more likely to be fulfilled. It is striking that in Isa 51:2 forty years or so later the same patriarchal tradition is claimed as relevant by the prophet of the exile (cf. Fishbane, *Biblical Interpretation* 375-76). In this case the timing was wrong. The people needed a fallow period for the lessons of the exile to sink in before they were ready for restoration (Sanders, *Canon and Authority* 31-33).

25-26 The prophet counters this optimistic bandying of theological language with a rhetorical disputation. He argues that its proponents have disqualified themselves from such a promise. Like the orthodox Jews who much later in history claimed that secular Zionists were flying in the face of heaven, he denies that their enthusiasm can be of God. His argument is a pragmatic one. "You shall know them by their fruits"! Here the fruit was not promising, for it violated traditional standards of religious and moral propriety. In 22:3-4, 6-12 this test had been applied to the yet unfallen Jerusalem, and its truth had not ceased to be valid, although the lesson of the capital's destruction had not been learned. Here both specific covenant rulings (cf. Lev 18:20; 19:26) and more general deviations are combined in a vehement double protest at the incompatibility of claims and way of life. The reference to the sword seems to relate to social unrest in which might was right.

27-29 Those who take the sword will perish by the sword! The punishment would fit the crime. The prophet's counterthesis invokes, instead of occupation of the promised land, covenant curses for these covenant-breakers (cf. Reventlow, *Wächter über Israel* 100; Fishbane, *Biblical Interpretation* 294, 420). The threefold bane of sword, wild animals and plague evokes Lev 26:22, 25, and the ruin and destruction of v 28a relates to Lev 26:19a, 33ba. An inexorable fate would remorselessly search out any survivors of the earlier destruction and deprive them of both hope and life. The land-giving of v 24 is ironically transformed into a giving of the land to ruin in v 28. The extended recognition formula of v 29 neatly recapitulates the ironic reversal along with its logical basis. Only thus could inconsistency with Yahweh's own nature be exposed for what it was.

30-33 The primary message of vv 24-29 must have been to reassure the exiles that the spiritual future, in terms of return to the land and to God's favor, lay with them rather than with those still in Judah. In this sense, along with the news of Jerusalem's fall in vv 21-22 and its implications for the prophet's ministry, it provides a fitting prelude to this next oracle. Ezekiel, long regarded with suspicion and distaste for his defeatism and scolding (cf. 2:6; 3:9), has been vindicated as a true prophet. In spirit he now seems to stand shoulder to shoulder with his compatriots in exile. Ezekiel's popularity knows no bounds, as the exiles crowd into his home (cf. 8:1; 14:1; 20:1) to hear what this sensational prophet will say next. Unfortunately, it was the popularity of an entertainer, a pop star, that Ezekiel enjoyed, and he was being taken no more seriously than before. His hearers functioned as a concert audience rather than a congregation. The extended simile of the singer refers not to the prophet's poetic eloquence, as Brownlee supposed (*JBL* 89 [1970] 396), but to the fact that his words were so welcome that they were music in the ears of those who thronged to hear them.

Yahweh gives his prophet an assurance, which in the publishing of the personal oracle became a warning, that a fresh vindication was on its way. The recognition formula is here strikingly reused to apply to the prophet: in this context Yahweh and prophet were inextricably linked. To those who came and heard without acting on the prophetic message, divine judgment (cf. 24:24) would come instead of salvation.

Explanation

This pericope has its own coherence as a triple statement of the effect of Jerusalem's fall: on the prophet and on those of the people who did not feature in the wave of deportations from Judah and on those who had been deported earlier. However, it fits well with the previous pericope as a continuation of material intended to be introductory to the new, positive messages of chaps. 34–48. Indeed, within chap. 33 as a whole the report of the downfall of Jerusalem and its prophetic implications has a central role, around which the surrounding oracles are set with the purpose of sounding notes of caution. From this perspective the final reference to the coming of doom in v 33 neatly echoes in an inclusion the warning the prophetic watchman was to give to the exiles. Divine grace is never cheap: Yahweh's new word of hope carried with it the responsibility for the exilic generation to appropriate it by turning from their wicked ways. In turn, the moral dimension of vv 12–20 is echoed in vv 24–29, so that the latter oracle is not only an insistence that basic immorality undercuts the happy theology of the non-deported Judeans, but in the light of its literary setting carries with it a corollary that the exiles too may not exempt themselves from Yahweh's moral will, if they are to obtain repossession of the promised land.

The New Testament in turn applies to theology the acid test of social and religious ethics and issues its own warning that those who fail the test "will not inherit the kingdom of God" (Gal 5:19-21; cf. 1 Cor 6:9-10; Eph 5:5). And the divine protest against hearing and not heeding, against stirring of emotions without a moving of the inner spirit, finds an echo in the parable Jesus directed against the destructive folly of "every one who hears my words and does not do them" (Matt 6:26; Luke 6:49).

The Good Shepherd (34:1-31)

Bibliography

Baltzer, D. *Ezechiel und Deuterojesaja.* BZAW 121. Berlin: de Gruyter, 1971. **Brownlee, W.H.** "Ezekiel's Poetic Indictment of the Shepherds." *HTR* 51 (1958) 191-203. **Hossfeld, F.-L.** *Untersuchungen zu Komposition und Theologie des Ezechielbuches.* FzB 20. Würzburg: Echter Verlag, 1977, 230-86. **Krüger, T.** *Geschichtskonzepte im Ezechielbuch.* BZAW 180. Berlin: de Gruyter, 1989, 449-61. **Levin, C.** *Die Verheissung des neuen Bundes: in ihrem theologiegeschichtlichen Zusammenhang ausgelegt.* FRLANT 137. Göttingen: Vandenhoeck und Ruprecht, 1985, 218-22. **Rembry, J.G.** "Le thème du berger dans l'oeuvre d'Ezéchiel." *SBFLA* 11 (1960/61) 113-44. **Reventlow, H.** *Wächter über Israel.* BZAW 82. Berlin: Töpelmann, 1962, 44-50. **Willmes, B.** *Die sogenannte Hirtenallegorie Ez 34. Studien zum Bild des Hirten im Alten Testament.* Beiträge zur biblischen Exegese und Theologie 19. Frankfurt: Peter Lang, 1984.

Translation

[1] *I received the following communication from Yahweh:* [2] *"Human one, prophesy against Israel's shepherds. Prophesy and tell them: You shepherds,[a] here is a message from the Lord[b] Yahweh. Alas for Israel's shepherds, who have been tending themselves.[c] Are not shepherds supposed[d] to tend the sheep?* [3] *You eat the curds,[a] wear the wool, slaughter the fatlings and fail to tend the sheep.* [4] *You have not strengthened the infirm,[a] cured the ailing, bandaged the fractured, brought back the strays nor searched out the lost, while you have dominated the strong in a brutal manner.[b]* [5] *My sheep[a] have been scattered for lack of a shepherd and eaten by all the wild animals.* [6] *On all the mountains, on every high hill and all over the country my sheep have been scattered, with nobody to look for them and go searching.* [7] *So, you shepherds,[a] listen to Yahweh's declaration:[b]* [8] *Upon my life, declares the Lord Yahweh, I swear an oath.[a] Because my sheep have become prey and my sheep have been eaten by all the wild animals for want of a shepherd, because they[b] have not looked for my sheep, but the shepherds have tended themselves rather than my sheep,* [9] *in view of all this, you shepherds, listen to Yahweh's declaration.* [10] *The message from the Lord Yahweh is as follows: I am the shepherds' adversary, I will hold them liable for my sheep and stop them tending my[a] sheep. No longer will the shepherds tend themselves: I will snatch my sheep from their mouths to stop them being eaten by them.* [11] *In explanation the Lord Yahweh has sent the following message: I will intervene[a] and look for my sheep and seek them out.* [12] *I will seek out my sheep just as a shepherd seeks[a] out his flock when his sheep have been dispersed.[b] I will rescue them from wherever they were scattered on a day of clouds and dark skies.* [13] *Taking them out from other peoples and gathering them from foreign countries, I will bring them home to their own soil and tend them on Israel's mountains, in the valleys and in all the habitable parts[a] of the country.* [14] *I will feed them with good pasture, and the mountain heights of Israel will be their grazing land. There they will rest on good grazing land, and on rich pasture will they feed on Israel's mountains.* [15] *I will tend my sheep myself and I myself will give them rest—so runs the oracle of the Lord Yahweh.* [16] *I will search out the lost, bring back the strays, bandage the fractured, strengthen the ailing; as for the strong,[a] I will tend[b] them justly.*

¹⁷ *"As for you, my sheep, this is the Lord Yahweh's message: I am going to adjudicate between this animal and that. You rams and male goats,*[a] ¹⁸ *are you not satisfied with*[a] *feeding on good pasture that you have to trample down the rest of the pasture with your hooves, and not only drink the clear water but have to foul with your hooves what is left?* ¹⁹ *And as for my sheep, they have to feed on what your hooves have trampled, and drink what your hooves have fouled.* ²⁰ *This then is the Lord Yahweh's message to them: I am going to intervene in adjudication between the fat animals and the thin ones,* ²¹ *because you have used flank and shoulder to push all the infirm, and your horns to butt them, until you made them run off.* ²² *I will come to the rescue of my sheep and they will no longer be prey, and so I will adjudicate between this animal and that.*

²³ *"I will appoint over them*[a] *a single*[b] *shepherd and he will tend them, namely my servant David.*[c] *He will be their shepherd,* ²⁴ *while I, Yahweh, will be their God;*[a] *and my servant David will be head of state among them—I, Yahweh, give my promise.*

²⁵ *"I will make with them a covenant of peace and I will rid the land of dangerous animals. They will sit in the wilderness with security*[a] *and go to sleep in the woods.* ²⁶ *I*[a] *will send down rain in its season: there will be the blessing of abundant rain.* ²⁷ *The trees in the countryside will yield their fruit, the ground will yield its crops, and they will live secure on their own soil. Then they will realize that I am Yahweh, when I break the poles of their yokes and release them from the control of their taskmasters,* ²⁸ *so that they will never again be the prey of other nations. Wild animals in the land will not eat them up, but they will live secure and fearless lives.* ²⁹ *I will provide them with prosperous*[a] *plantations, and they will never again be victims of starvation in the land. Nor will they anymore have to put up with humiliation from the other nations.* ³⁰ *Then they will realize that I am their God Yahweh*[a] *and that they, the community of Israel, are my people—so runs the oracle of the Lord Yahweh.* ³¹ *You are my flock, you are the flock I tend,*[a] *I am your God. So runs the oracle of the Lord Yahweh."*

Notes

2. a. In the sense "to the shepherds" לרעים does not fit after אליהם "to them," which is probably why LXX* Vg omitted the former term, nor is it likely to be a gloss explaining it. It has been understood as originating in a chapter heading "concerning the shepherds" (Zimmerli 204 et al.; cf. Jer 21:11; 23:9). However, taking the *lamed* as a vocative particle, as Syr seemingly did (contra *BHS*), has the merit of leaving the text as it stands (cf. v 17; Driver, *Bib* 35 [1954] 302; Eichrodt 469; NEB).

2. b. For the formulaic אדני "Lord" here and in vv 8, 10, 11, 15, 17, 20, 30, 31 see the note on 20:3.

2. c. For the reflexive usage see GKC 135k. The alternative reading of LXX in this clause (see *BHS*: "Should shepherds tend themselves?") suits the context, but its closeness to v 8 suggests assimilation. Zimmerli, ibid., aptly cites 13:3 in favor of MT.

2. d. For the modal impf in the sense of obligation cf. Joüon 113m.

3. a. LXX Vg presuppose a pointing הֶחָלָב "milk" and presumably here "curds" in view of the verb "eat," which is generally preferred to MT הַחֵלֶב "fat," since the necessary slaughter does not occur till later in the sequence.

4. a. For MT's pl הנחלות "sick ones" LXX Syr Vg imply sg הנחלה, which conforms to the sg terms hereafter. Possibly a comparative gloss from v 21 displaced the sg. Driver, *Bib* 19 (1938) 180, vocalized הַנֶּחֱלָה, relating to a stem *nhl* attested in Syr. and Arab. "be wasted from fatigue, sickness" (= NEB "the weary"), but Ezekiel's propensity to use the same stem in different conjugations is well attested (cf. vv 5, 6).

4. b. Both the object-verb order throughout v 4a and the reverse statement in v 16 suggest that LXX is correct in implying וּבְחָזְקָה "and (rule) over the strong" for MT "and with strength," and in omitting ו אֹתָם "(rule) them and." The verb is generally, though not always, construed with *beth*, as in 29:15; the misunderstanding required the addition of a copula before בפרך "with severity." For the different use of *beth* in the same clause cf. Lev 25:43, 46. Zimmerli (205) has plausibly explained אֹתָם "them" as arising by pseudodittography after רדיתם. Driver, ibid., followed by NEB (Brockington, *Text*

of the Hebrew Bible 232), proposed repointing to אַתֶּם "you," with reference to GKC 135b, with the function of emphasizing a change from negative to positive offenses.

5. a. MT lacks צֹאני "my sheep," presupposed by LXX Syr Vg: it doubtless fell out after צִינה (ותפוֹן) (Cornill 400). The change of subject warrants its inclusion (Willmes, *Hirtenallegorie* 46). Probably ותפוצינה צֹאני "and my sheep were scattered" in vv 5b-6a, which LXX takes together in v 6, leaving ישגו "they strayed" unrepresented, comprises a correcting gloss in which the verb functioned as a cue (Zimmerli 206, following J. Herrmann [219]; Hossfeld, *Untersuchungen* 237). The second verb ישגו was probably inserted after the wrong sentence division, since it is unexpectedly masc and, inasmuch as it is used only morally elsewhere in Heb., appears to be an Aramaism.

7. a. The anarthrous רעים "shepherds" seems to be simply a stylistic variant of הרעים "O shepherds" in v 9.

7. b. The object-sign את, unique in the summons to hear formula throughout the book (e.g., 6:3; 37:4), is unattested in 20 MSS and may be secondary.

8. a. Heb. אם־לא "surely," normally introducing an oath, functions as an anacoluthon (GKC 149c, 167b); it is logically resumed in v 10.

8. b. MT רעי "my shepherds" conflicts with the usage throughout the context. LXX Syr imply הרעים "the shepherds," which looks suspiciously like a harmonization. Was the subj delayed till v 8ba in order to enhance the רעה play ("shepherds/tend")? If so, MT arose from an abbreviated gloss 'רע (= רעים) "shepherds" clarifying a change of subj or from a comparative gloss relating to v 2, 'רע י' = רעי ישראל "shepherds of Israel."

10. a. For MT צאן "sheep" LXX Syr presuppose the expected צאני "my sheep." Pseudohaplography of *yod* before *waw* was doubtless responsible (Zimmerli, ibid.).

11. a. Lit. "Behold I myself," also in v 20.

12. a. For the Aram. type of inf or verbal noun cf. 16:52 and see GKC 84ᵇe.

12. b. ביום . . . נפרשות "on the day when he is among his flock, separated (?)" is corrupt. The verb means "separate" in later Heb. and in Aram.; generally the form is repointed נפרשות "dispersed" (cf. 17:21), as the synonymous נפצו "were scattered" in v 12b suggests. Driver's rendering "on the day when he is in the midst of his sheep, scattered as they are " (*Bib* 35 [1954] 302), followed in principle by NEB, is hardly intelligible. Apparently rightly one MS reads, and LXX presupposes, היות "(when) there is, they are" for MT היותו "(when) he is," but LXX fills up a seeming lacuna by a loose reference to v 12bβ: "darkness and cloud"; similarly Syr "on the day of storm." Cooke (380) et al., following Toy, delete בתוך "among" (so RSV): it may have intruded somehow from בתוכם (היה) in 33:33, adjacent in the previous column. For the construction of היה and participle cf. v 2.

13. a. Heb. מושב "inhabited place" elsewhere has a fem pl. Accordingly Driver, *Bib* 19 (1938) 181, related it to an Arab. stem *wasaba* "abound with grass," whence NEB "green fields."

16. a. In the light of the stylistic counterpointing with v 4 (see *Form/Structure/Setting*) there is no room for the preceding ואת־השמנה "and the fat"; moreover, the sg suffix on ארענה "I will tend it" presupposes a sg object. It may well have originated as a comparative gloss on בריה "fat" in v 20b: in Num 13:20 רזה "thin" is opposed to שמנה. If so, it became misplaced in the margin to a position near ושפטתי בין־שה לשה "judge sheep and sheep" (v 17) from a place adjacent to ובין . . . שה בין־שה "and I will judge between sheep . . . and sheep" (v 20) and was subsequently understood to qualify את־החזקה "the strong."

16. b. MT's negative understanding "And as for (the fat and) strong I will destroy, I will tend him in judgment" was encouraged not only by the previous gloss (cf. v 20) but also by relating במשפט "with justice" to שפט "judge" in v 17, with the sense "in judgment." For the negative usage of רעה "tend, feed on" in the sense of "destroy" cf. Mic 5:5(6). The intrusive אשמיד "I will destroy," omitted by one Heb. MS, was evidently a gloss intended to confirm the negative sense: the parallel v 4b leaves room for only one verb, and the רעה/רדה "dominate/tend" match is clearly deliberate. LXX Syr Vg imply a correction אשמר "I will keep," which sought to uphold a positive understanding; their rendering of the suffix on the next verb as pl, adopted by Cornill (403), *BHS* et al., is ruled out by the intended parallelism with v 4b.

17. a. A vocative particle *lamed*, as in v 2, and a different sentence division suit the overall context (Driver, *JTS* 35 [1954] 302; NEB). Then the male addressees of vv 18-21 are specified, as one would expect: שה "sheep" is fem. Ehrlich (*Randglossen* 128) noted that ל. . .בין "between . . . and" applies to two parties, so that the extra terms do not belong in v 17.

18. a. Heb. מעט "little" is usually followed by a כי ("that") clause; in Isa 7:13 by an inf constr. For the present construction see GKC 120c.

23. a. עליהם "over them," which is not represented in C, conflicts with the fem context of the verse. It betrays the influence of the underlying text in 37:24 (see *Form/Structure/Setting*).

23. b. For MT אחד "one" LXX presupposes אחר "another," with obvious reference to v 15.

23. c. The object sign is due to the influence of the initial verb (cf. T. Muraoka, *Emphasis in Biblical Hebrew* 121-23). MT adds "he will tend them," lacking in LXX* and an apparent alternative to v 23bβ. It may have been a gloss noting the tension with v 15a.

24. a. V 24aα functions as the counterpart of v 23bβ in a double formulation. The verse division in MT is insensitive here and also in v 28.

25. a. LXX omits לבטח "securely," which is stylistically required (see *Form/Structure/Setting*).

26. a. MT prefaces with "and I will make them and the areas round my hill (recipients of) blessing." The clause falls outside the fairly tight grouping of motifs (see *Form/Structure/Setting*). It appears to be a jumbled pair of glosses. "My hill" conceivably refers to the temple mount, but is a very unusual term (cf. Isa 31:4) and not at all obvious in this context (Cornill 404). It is probably a misunderstanding of בעתו (= נשם) נ "rain in its season," via a *waw/yod* error. The error was encouraged by גבעה "hill" in v 6. This part of the gloss attests an alternative reading "and I will give rain in its season (as a) blessing" that reflects assimilation to Lev 26:4. The LXX in v 26b attests a similar reading: "and I will give the rain to you, rain of blessing." The phrase סביבות אותם, omitting the copula with LXX, means "אותם in the context" and relates to אתהם in the previous column at v 12 (cf. vv 2, 8, 10, 14).

29. a. MT לשם "for a name, honorable" seems to have suffered metathesis. LXX Syr Tg presuppose שלם "peace, prosperity," which stylistically fits the context (see *Form/Structure/Setting*).

30. a. MT adds אתם "with them," which gilds the lily: it is formally intrusive in the covenant formula (Zimmerli 211): a few MSS LXX* Syr lack it. Probably it was meant to be אתם "you" (masc), a gloss relating to fem (ו)אתן "(and) you" and aligning it with אתם at the end of v 31a: cf. the reading ואתם "and you" in two MSS.

31. a. MT adds אדם "human," missing from LXX*. The annotation was inspired by 36:37-38 (Cornill 406).

Form/Structure/Setting

The message reception formula in v 1, which next occurs in 35:1, labels the chapter as a literary unit. The commission to prophesy in v 2 introduces an oracle that seems to run to v 16. It has an overall metaphorical theme of shepherding; Willmes (*Hirtenallegorie* 408-13) has rightly disputed its designation as allegory. In form it has the elements of both an oracle of judgment and an oracle of salvation. The two-part oracle of judgment introduces its first part of accusation with a short third-person "woe" statement that serves to identify the target of the oracle and to make a basic charge (v 2bβ). The accusation continues with second-person address (vv 2bγ-6), beginning with a rhetorical question, as in 13:18 (cf. Isa 10:1-3; Amos 5:18; 6:1-2). The pronouncement of punishment begins with a consequential (לכן "therefore") summons to hear (v 7) and, after a divine oath, recapitulates the charges (v 8). It proceeds to echo the earlier consequential summons and, with a formal messenger formula and a formula of encounter, threatens to deal with the "shepherds" (v 10a). Equally, however, Yahweh's intervention would bring salvation to his "flock" (v 10b). This positive message is developed in a further, explanatory (כי "for") section, after a messenger formula, by means of a series of promises (vv 11-16). This section has a grammatical peculiarity in that masculine suffixes are consistently used for the flock, while, as in vv 5-10, verbs with the flock as subject are feminine (vv 12, 14). The anomaly is probably to be explained in terms of looseness (cf. GKC 135o), which was not liable to misunderstanding, now that the shepherds were no longer in view. It hardly warrants finding a fresh oracle in vv 11-16 or 11-15 (Hossfeld, *Untersuchungen* 241-43). The double nature of vv 2-16 as both oracle of judgment and oracle of salvation is striking. Willmes (*Hirtenallegorie* 259-68) has called it a "differentiating" prophetic oracle and noted other examples in Isa 1:21-26; Zeph 3:11-13; 2 Kgs 22:14-20.

Vv 7-9 have been widely regarded as redactional on account of their repetitious nature (e.g., Zimmerli 212; Wevers 181; Hossfeld 237-38; cf. vv 2-6, 9; for the object sign in v 7 see *Notes*), but the forceful echoing of an accusation at the outset of a pronouncement of judgment is an attested modification of a judgment oracle (cf. v 21; 22:19; 28:6; see C. Westermann, *Basic Forms of Prophetic Speech* [London: Lutterworth, 1967] 175, 180-81. Parunak, *JBL* 102 [1983] 533-34, appealed to 5:5-11; 13:1-16, but the original unity of these passages is not beyond doubt [see, e.g., Zimmerli, *Ezekiel 1* 175-76, 295]). V 16 too has been viewed as supplementary (e.g., Zimmerli 212; Wevers 181-82; Hossfeld, *Untersuchungen* 265-66). However, the use of the formula for a divine saying in v 15 does not necessarily indicate the close of the oracle: its role here is to stress the certainty of divine action (cf. 38:21; 39:8). Moreover, the verse hardly introduces the next oracle (Hölscher, *Dichter* 170) or serves as a literary link between the previous oracle and the next (Hossfeld, *Untersuchungen* 244, 265-66). Although the motif of the strong sheep occurs in both v 16 and in vv 17-22, in the first case they are best understood as the object of care, while in the second they are the target of judgment. Admittedly the mention of justice/judging (vv 16, 17) is shared, but the phenomenon is no more than an instance of redactional linking in the arrangement of oracles (cf. e.g., Isa 1:9, 10).

The next unit is evidently vv 17-22. It shares the general metaphor of the previous oracle, but now its target is not irresponsible shepherds but domineering sheep. The initial יצאנה ואתנה "and you are my flock" may be redactional (cf. v 30), since the flock is not addressed in the oracle (cf. vv 19, 22). The parameters of the oracle are determined by the triple A . . . /A . . . A structure (vv 17bα, 20b, 22b), whereby, after the initial messenger formula, mention of judging between the sheep acts as an overall inclusion and also as an inclusion for the divine intervention of vv 20-22. Within this framework comes first an accusation, in the form of an extended rhetorical question (vv 18-19). Then after a second messenger formula introduced by a linking לכן "therefore," fresh charges are incorporated in a causal clause. The final element is not an expected pronouncement of punishment, but rather an announcement of salvation (v 22a). Thus this second oracle has the same double perspective as that in vv 2-16.

Vv 23-31 variously develop the two basic oracles in a series of three amplifications (cf. Zimmerli 219-20, 222; cf. Taylor 222: "If the chapter is taken as a whole, it will appear full of inconsistencies, but if each section is taken separately it will be obvious that new ideas are being added all along."). Vv 23-24 take further the shepherding theme of vv 2-16 and the covenantal concept of Israel as Yahweh's flock, shared by vv 2-16 and 17-22. They promise "a single shepherd" and spell out the nature of this triangular relationship, before closing with a formula of divine asseveration. The new motif appears to be borrowed from 37:24-25. The second amplification, in vv 25-30, reflects in turn on the motif of the covenant implicit in vv 2-22 and explicit in v 24, and defines it in a series of promises based on Lev 26:4-13. The pair of recognition formulas (vv 27b, 30) characterize it as two proof sayings. V 31 is the final amplification, which in Yahweh's name seeks to tie together the earlier metaphorical and literal references to the covenant relationship between Yahweh and Israel.

As to the setting of the various oracles, in their final arrangement they comprise a literary assurance to the Judean exiles that they are under Yahweh's care and heirs of a positive destiny. The first oracle sends conflicting signals concerning its background. Based on Jer 23:1-2, it at first sight has a pre-exilic setting insofar as it attacks the Judean monarchy, presumably in the person of its last representative, Zedekiah. However, a post-587 B.C. provenance is evident, probably in v 6 and certainly in v 12b. It is possible to envisage an original, pre-587 oracle in vv 1-10 (Brownlee, *HTR* 51 [1958] 190-203, who reconstructs a poetic original and interprets v 6 in terms of Judean high places) or in vv 1-2, 9-10 (Hossfeld, *Untersuchungen* 280), or to reconstruct two interwoven oracles, one pre-exilic and the other post-exilic (Willmes, *Hirtenallegorie* 255-58; Rembry, *SBFLA* 11 [1960] 119, by relating v 12b to the Exodus, regards the whole oracle as pre-exilic.). But the glance at the monarchy may well be a backward and rhetorical one (cf. Hölscher's designation of the oracle as a literary fiction [*Dichter* 169])— as to a certain extent at least it was in the basic Jer 23:1-2—which serves as a powerful prelude to promises of return from exile. Possibly the second oracle, in vv 17-22, seesaws on 587 B.C. in a similar way. Then the rams and male goats refer to the upper classes who exploited their economic power at the expense of the poor, and were the moral cause of the exile (v 21b). It is more likely, however, that we are to relate the oracle to the still future judgment of 20:35-38 and to envisage dissension among the exiles as the occasion.

The combination of the two oracles formed the nucleus for the literary unit, which has been rounded out with three supplements. The first, Zimmerli is prepared to ascribe to Ezekiel's pen (220), but its dependence on 37:24-25, which in part is a product of late redaction, witnesses against such an ascription. The second, in vv 25-30, has a very different perspective from what precedes and operates at a distance from it. Especially its literal interpretation of the wild beasts of vv 5 and 8, in vv 25 and 28—v 28 also relates them to the nations (cf. v 8)—seems to betray another hand. Moreover, in some of its content it has parallels with the evidently late 28:25-26. Yet it affirms its own prophetic authority (v 30bβ). The same is true of the concluding v 31 (cf. v 31bβ), which wraps up the literary unit in a comprehensive fashion.

A sophisticated inclusion for the chapter is provided by the reference to צאן מרעיתי "the sheep that I tend," an allusion to Jer 23:1-2, which was the starting point for the first unit (see *Comment*). The threefold mention of Israel being a prey (vv 8, 22, 28) is a further unifying factor. As to the first oracle, an inclusion is provided in vv 4 and 16 by chiastic repetition, in which the first two clauses of v 4 are telescoped in v 16, using the noun of one and verb of the other (see, e.g., Parunak, *Structural Studies* 447). The review in v 8 comprises a chiastic recapitulation, echoing first vv 5-6 and then vv 2-3. The echoes continue, of v 3 in v 10, and of the scattering of vv 5-6 in v 12, in a loose chiasmus. The verb דרש "look for, hold liable" functions as a keyword: there are four instances, in the indictment, pronouncement of punishment and announcement of salvation (vv 6, 8, 10, 11).

The stylistic structure of vv 17-22 has been mentioned earlier. Vv 23-24 present an overall chiastic formation: the central paired reference to David's and Yahweh's role vis-à-vis the people (vv 23bβ, 24aα) are surrounded respectively by mention of "my servant David" and by mention of his relationship to the people (v 23a, 24aβ). The framework of vv 25-30 is the "covenant" of v 25aα and the two-part covenant formula of v 30. Within these parameters is a double scheme, ABC/ABC, which twice mentions the motifs of wild animals (vv 25aβ, 28aβ), fertility (vv

26b-27aαβ, 29abα) and the nations (vv 28aα, 29bβ) respectively. Hossfeld (*Untersuchungen* 276) noted this doubling, but confined it to wild beasts and fertility. Attached to each of the first two motifs are references to the "land" (ארץ) and to mutually related concepts, לבטח "securely" in three cases (A/A', B; cf. Willmes, *Hirtenallegorie* 224) and שלום "peace, prosperity" in the last case (B'). There is also an interlocking between the inner pairing and the framework: שלום "peace" of v 25aα is repeated in v 29a, and the recognition formula of v 27b is repeated in v 30.

Comment

1-16 When Ezekiel used metaphor to communicate his divine message, he sometimes borrowed images from earlier prophets. Thus the metallurgical imagery of 22:17-22 was inspired by Isa 1:22, 25, while the sexual allegory of 23:2-27 may well be a development of Jer 3:6-11. Here Jer 23:1-2 is evidently the source of the shepherd metaphor, which Ezekiel characteristically embellished (J. W. Miller, *Verhältnis* 106; Fohrer 192; Wevers 182). Levin's inclusion of Jer 23:3-8 as source material for chap. 34 as a whole (*Verheissung* 218-19; cf. Zimmerli 214) is much less certain: the differences are such that probably we are to envisage independent developments of basic material in the two complex texts. The series of correspondences between Jer 23:1-2 and this oracle is striking: "against the shepherds" (על-רעי/רועים), "alas for the shepherds" (הוי רעי [ם]), "my flock" (צאני), "stray" (נדח), "lose" (אבד) and "scatter" (הפיץ). Moreover, פקד "care for, punish," used in positive and negative senses, seems to have been paraphrased as דרש "look for, hold liable." Jer 23:1-2, in referring to shepherds, appears to relate to the last major kings of Judah, Jehoiakim and Zedekiah, as responsible for the deportation of 597 B.C. and Judah's ensuing ills because of their negligence (cf. McKane, *Jeremiah 1-25* 555, 559). The term "shepherd" is standard for a king throughout the ancient Near East. In this context it is combined with the use of the metaphor to portray the covenant between Yahweh and Israel (cf. Pss 74:1; 79:13; 80:2[1]; cf. the individualization in Ps 23). Accordingly the shepherds were employees of the divine shepherd and responsible to him.

2-6 However, the Judean kings had failed in their responsibilities to Yahweh for their charges. Ezekiel dramatically repeats Jeremiah's ominous accusations, now vindicated by history. The self-centeredness of v 2bγ is elaborated in the direct address of v 3a. The taking of milk (cf. Deut 32:14) and wool from the flock appears unobjectionable in itself (cf. 1 Cor 9:7); yet the taking was unaccompanied by giving, and rights were unmatched by responsibilities. However, the climactically placed slaughter of the best sheep, in the light of v 10, is a grimmer charge, as something inherently wrong. The general challenge of v 2bδ is particularized in the accusation of v 3b, which in turn is elaborated in the failures of v 4. Behind the shepherd language lies the typical royal duty of welfare of society's weaklings (cf. Jer 21:12; 22:3; Ps 72:4, 12-14)—and its absence from the royal agenda in the last decades of the kingdom (cf. Jer 22:15-17; 34:8). Nor had only the weak suffered: the resources and rights of the strong too had been wantonly abused. Tragically the monarchy had been the bane of its subjects: it had brought about grim consequences for them, which are spelled out in vv 5-6. Responsibility for the deportation of 597 B.C. and for the flight of refugees from Judah to neighboring states is laid at the palace door. The end of v 6 returns to the charge of searching out the lost in v 4 and underlines the perverse neglect of royal responsibility. It also introduces a new key term of the oracle, דרש, the shepherd's duty to put himself out and "look for" the missing sheep in order to bring them home.

7-8 The emotional vehemence of Yahweh's reaction is expressed by the divine oath and emphasized by the abrupt change of construction in the Hebrew. The reprehensibility of the Judean kings is summed up in a sweeping review of vv 5-6 and 2-3.

9-10 Yahweh declares that he will take on the monarchy and—with a deft re-use of the keyword דרש—"hold it liable" for its negligence. Nothing less than their removal from their royal post would transpire in view of their general self-seeking (vv 2, 3, 8) and in particular the suffering and fatality of their subjects at their hands (cf. v 4). They are ironically portrayed as wild animals (cf. v 5)—a travesty of true shepherding (cf. 1 Sam 17:35; Amos 3:12). Only by removal of the monarchy could God's people be preserved. Although Yahweh's positive concern has resounded through the oracle thus far, especially in the outraged phrase "my sheep," it comes to the fore in the first and last verbs of divine action at v 10, as the focus gradually changes from punishment of one group to salvation of the other.

11-16 This positive note is now developed in a fresh section. Yahweh declares that he is to take over his negligent agents' responsibilities. Pride of place is given to the keyword דרש in a promise that the subjects' future is assured by his determination to "look for" them. Yet, by now, their situation was dire indeed. They needed to be saved not only from royal rapacity (v 10) but from homelessness. Ezekiel moves from reliving the past to describing the people's present lot. The horror of the fall of Jerusalem and its tragic consequences in 587 B.C. is summed up in the pregnant phrase "a day of clouds and dark skies." For those with ears to hear, it conveys overtones of the Day of Yahweh (cf. 13:5; 30:3; Zeph 1:15), the fulfillment of prophetic doom in a final catastrophe. Yet, marvelously, the divine enemy takes on the role of the shepherd, tending and retrieving his flock. In his hands shepherdly duties would be capably discharged. The alien places of exile were only temporary habitations for God's people, until they enjoyed a new exodus and a new settlement in the land of promise (cf. 20:34). Israel's mountainland—for Ezekiel an emotion-laden phrase—would be theirs once more. The prophet uses this phrase three times, along with a threefold use of the basic shepherding verb רעה "tend, feed," now with Yahweh as subject, in virtual echo of v 11. Good pasture is promised, at some length, as a metaphor of the blessings that would be theirs. Yahweh's provision would be a measure of his responsibility, as he devoted himself to caring for his own. The point is emphasized in a final contrast. The derelictions of the pre-exilic monarchy (v 4) would be no more. Now, in keeping with the exilic context, the retrieval of the lost and strayed is set at the head of the list. Justice—ever an ideal royal virtue, but denied by the overbearingness of v 4—was to be the hallmark of Israel's divine shepherd and king (cf. 20:33).

17-22 The final note of v 16 provides a neat carry-over to the theme of the next oracle, which was originally separate from, though not uninfluenced by, the former one. Infighting and competition among the flock, which in ancient times contained both sheep and goats, now replace the issue of rapacious and negligent shepherds. The promise of justice, which dominates the oracle at beginning, middle and end, has two connotations, retribution for the guilty and vindication for their victims. Here "the rams and male goats" are accused in a long, indignant question of unfair exploitation by dominating the flock. Both nouns are used elsewhere as metaphors for human leadership (cf. e.g., 17:13; 32:21; Isa 14:9; Zech 10:3). The setting is not divulged, but it is noteworthy that exile, if such it is, is now a minor theme (v 21b) and that the emphasis on judgment is reminiscent of 20:35-38 (cf. the conditional promise of life for the exiles in 33:1-20). These factors suggest that we are to envisage social exploitation not in pre-exilic Judah but among the exiles themselves, which Ezekiel endeavors to correct. It is striking that the phrase "my sheep" is reserved for the victims, rather like the pre-exilic prophets' use of "my people," as in Isa 3:12, 15; Mic 2:8, 9; 3:3, 5. The self-serving leaders, in distancing themselves from the rest of the community, had disqualified themselves from its membership—and divine ratification of their status was to be only a matter of time. The fresh charges in v 21 go beyond privation to a more penetrating accusation of outrageous abuse of superior power. Yet ironically the fat and sleek who shoved the weak away were themselves the outsiders in Yahweh's eyes. The point of the oracle comes in v 22. As in the Psalms, the verbs "save" and "judge" are used side by side with Yahweh as subject (Pss 54:3[2]; 72:2). Divine justice spelled vindication for God's suffering people, even and perhaps especially when the suffering was caused within the community.

23-24 In the first of three literary developments, a topic that is an important corollary of the two earlier oracles is broached. It is borrowed from chap. 37, where one shepherd-king is promised in the constitution of a new, now undivided, kingdom (37:24-25). In this context the oneness has its own point, as God's eventual solution for divisions among his people, in that a single authority would be put in charge, ensuring social unity. Yet the door would not thereby be opened to the pre-exilic abuses of the first oracle. The restoration of the Davidic monarchy would have new safeguards in the realization of a subordinate vassal status ("my servant") and in the constitutional nature of the ruler as "head of state among them" rather than as despotic overlord (see 37:25 *Comment*). Thus his shepherding role, resuming that of the pre-exilic kings (cf. v 2), would this time be compatible with Yahweh's covenant relationship with his people. Such is the message of the parallel formulations of v 23bβ and 24aα.

25-30 The covenant formula used in v 24aα triggers a fresh development, which is also meant as an interpretative unfolding of "my sheep," a key term in the first two oracles, and so as a reassuring delineation of Yahweh's commitment to them. The relationship is now set to a different tune, the blessings of Lev 26:4-13 (see the table in Baltzer, *Ezechiel* 156-157). It is not difficult to trace a very close connection with it, especially 26:4-6, 13. Yet the borrowing is not slavish but creative. The blessings are relayed via a double, parallel scheme of banished dangers relating to wild animals, famine and the nations respectively. The expanded recognition formula of vv 27b-28aα has been inspired by the self-introduction formula of Lev 26:13, with the old Exodus achievement reapplied to future liberation in a manner reminiscent of v 13a earlier. There is thus a sensitivity to the previous material in this chapter: the danger of being eaten by beasts corresponds to the metaphor of vv 5, 8 and the provision of fertility to the good pasture of vv 14, 18, while sheep imagery lingers in v 25b (cf. Mic 5:3[4]b). The accent on political and psychological inferiority to other nations, while in the first case echoing Lev 26 and interpreting the "prey" metaphor of vv 8, 22, also sympathetically responds to keenly felt exilic (and post-exilic) concerns. The prophetic assurance is that Yahweh was able and willing to resolve these and the other problems. The double presentation of promises of Yahweh's sufficiency is set in a covenantal framework, in vv 25aα and 30. As the latter verse implies, the realization of covenant blessings would bring with them a proof of the bond between Yahweh and his people.

31 In a summarizing climax to the unit, readers are warmly ("you," "your") reminded of the pervading metaphor by an echo of the phrase "the sheep that I tend" from Jer 23:1, part of the passage that underlies vv 2-16. They are reminded too of the precious reality behind the metaphor, the covenant bond between them and Yahweh, in a recapitulating echo of vv 24a and 30.

Explanation

This chapter is full of pastoral reassurance. The backward look at the last years of the Judean monarchy, through the eyeglasses of Jeremiah (Jer 23:1-2), answers the question as to why the bitter experience of exile was the people's lot. The blame is laid firmly on the policies of the last kings of Judah, and the catastrophe is interpreted in prophetic vein as the outworking of a moral providence. The monarchy had to go, divinely ordered as it was, after it degenerated into a self-serving institution that ignored the interests of its subjects, neglecting the weak and exploiting the strong. Yahweh's traditional covenant role as royal "shepherd" of his people, to whom the kings were responsible as under-shepherds, drove him to intervene against them. Yet this very role carried welcome promises that the ravages of destruction and deportation would be repaired. What Ezekiel typically has to say at length was expressed a generation later in distilled form: "He will tend his flock like a shepherd . . ." (Isa 40:11). Above all, combined with a land-based theology, Yahweh's covenant guaranteed return to the land.

However, even the exiles had not seen the end of internal oppression. A more immediate assurance is given that Yahweh in his very role as shepherd would not tolerate a contemporary trampling on others' rights and an abuse of power. Such behavior brought about in God's eyes self-excommunication from the covenant community and its future, which would be endorsed by Yahweh as judge. The threat aligns with that sounded earlier in the book, using shepherd language (20:37), and underlines the warnings of chap. 33. As in the Psalms and in the parable of the importunate widow (Luke 18:1-8), divine judgment carries with it an assurance for the victims of those to be judged. The promise "no longer" (v 22), which echoes a motif of the first oracle (v 10), was intended to bring psychological comfort to the exiles (Fishbane, *Biblical Interpretation in Ancient Israel* 374, note 141).

Matters are not left there. Further light could be shed on a place for the Davidic monarchy in the life of the community. Yahweh's promise (cf. v 15), properly understood, did not entail the abrogation of an older promise. The restored monarchy was to have a role under God, as a guarantee of social unity and as a means of working out their covenant relationship with Yahweh. What that outworking involved is spelled out in vv 25-30. The needs of the community would be met and their natural fears would be resolved, as the reiterated, double "no longer" of vv 28 and 29 underlines. The land-oriented theology of vv 13-14 is developed in physical promises for the renewed nation. The triangle of Yahweh, Israel and land, whereby life in the land was a measure of fellowship with Yahweh, would find full expression. Finally, with literary sensitivity, the sheep metaphor and its covenant meaning are reaffirmed.

It is not surprising that the New Testament took up this shepherd motif and echoed chap. 34 together with other texts that give expression to it. Jesus' self-proclaimed purpose "to seek and to save the lost" (Luke 19:10) attests the undertaking of a divine mission. The allegory of the "good shepherd" in John 10 betrays the influence of v 23 especially in the "one shepherd" of 10:16. The same verse is reflected in Rev 7:17 ("the Lamb . . . will feed [ποιμανεῖ] them"). The parable of the last judgment (Matt 25:32-46), with its segregation of sheep and goats, is indebted to vv 17-22, especially to v 17, and again envisages (the glorified) Jesus as discharger of a divine function, this time of judgment. The strictures of Jude include a reference to those "who feed [ποιμαίνοντες] themselves" (v 12), and thus update Ezekiel's warning (34:2, 8, 10) that leadership of God's people carries with it obligations of selfless service.

Whose Land? (35:1-36:15)

Bibliography

Reventlow, H. *Wächter über Israel.* BZAW 82. Berlin: Töpelmann, 1962, 60-65, 143-46. **Simian, H.** *Die theologische Nachgeschichte der Prophetie Ezechiels. Form- und traditionskritische Untersuchung zu Ez. 6; 35; 36.* FzB 14. Würzburg: Echter Verlag, 1974. **Woudstra, M. H.** "Edom and Israel in Ezekiel." *Calvin Theological Journal* 3 (1968) 21–35.

Translation

[1] *I received the following communication from Yahweh:* [2] *"Human one, look in the direction of Mount Seir and issue a prophecy against it.* [3] *Tell it that this is the message of the Lord* [a] *Yahweh:*

I am your opponent, Mount Seir,
and I will deal you a blow,
reducing you to wrack and ruin.
[4] *I will make your cities desolate*
and you will become a ruin—
then you will discover that I am Yahweh.

[5] *"Inasmuch as you discharged an ancient enmity by handing the Israelites over to the sword at their time of calamity, at the time of terminal guilt,* [6] *for that reason I swear by my life—so runs the Lord Yahweh's oracle* [a] *—that you have committed the sins of bloodshed,* [b] *and blood will pursue you.* [7] *I will reduce Mount Seir to wrack and ruin* [a] *and will eliminate every wayfarer* [b] *from it.* [8] *I will fill its mountains with its casualties* [a] *— on them will fall casualties of the sword.* [9] *I will reduce you to perpetual ruins, and your cities will remain unpopulated.* [a] *Then you will discover that I am Yahweh.*

[10] *"Inasmuch as you claimed the two nations,* [a] *the two countries, for yourself, boasting in Yahweh's presence, 'We will take possession of it,'* [b] *despite the fact that Yahweh was there,* [11] *for that reason I swear by my life—so runs the Lord Yahweh's oracle—that I will treat you in requital for your anger and passion with which you treated them because of your hatred* [a] *for them, and I will make myself known to them* [b] *when I judge you.* [12] *Then you will discover that I, Yahweh, have heard all the insults you leveled against the mountains of Israel, claiming 'Ruined as they are,* [a] *they have been given to us to devour.'* [13] *I was the one you opened your big mouths against, I was the one you bragged (?)* [a] *over, I heard.*

[14] *"The message of the Lord Yahweh is as follows:* [a] [15] *I will treat you in requital for your jubilation over the ruin of the heritage of Israel's community. You will be turned into a ruin, Mount Seir, and so will all Edom in its entirety,* [a] *and then they will discover that I am Yahweh.*

[36:1] *"You, human one, are to issue a prophecy to the mountains of Israel, saying, Mountains of Israel, hear Yahweh's pronouncement.* [2] *The message of the Lord Yahweh is as follows: Inasmuch as the enemy jeered over you 'The ancient high places* [a] *are* [b] *ours to possess,'* [3] *for that reason issue a prophecy, telling them this message from the Lord Yahweh: Forasmuch as* [a] *ruination and hounding* [b] *from all sides have resulted in your* *becoming the possession of the remainder of the nations, and tongues have wagged about you[c] and people have defamed you, [4]for that reason, mountains of Israel, hear Yahweh's[a] pronouncement.* The Lord Yahweh has the following message for the mountains and hills, ravines and valleys, for the desolate ruins[b] and abandoned cities that have been looted[c] and derided by the remainder of the nations round you. [5]For that reason here is the message of the Lord Yahweh: Assuredly I speak with fiery passion against the remainder of the nations and particularly against Edom—all[a] who have made[b] my country their possession with such heartfelt jubilation, such vehement scorn.[c] [6]For that reason issue a prophecy to the land of Israel and tell the mountains, hills, ravines and valleys that this is the message of the Lord Yahweh: I speak in my passion and anger because you have had to put up with other nations' humiliating you. [7]For that reason this is the message of the Lord Yahweh: I raise[a] my hand in a solemn promise that the nations round you will have to put up with humiliation themselves. [8]But you, mountains of Israel, will put forth your branches and produce your fruit for my people Israel, because they will soon be arriving, [9]because I am disposed toward you and will turn to you, and you will be tilled and sown. [10]I will put many human beings on you, all the community of Israel in its entirety, and the cities will be repopulated and the ruins rebuilt. [11]I will put many human beings and cattle on you,[a] and will make you as populous as you were in your past and do you more good than I ever did before; then you will realize that I am Yahweh. [12]I will get you trodden by human beings, namely my people Israel, and they will possess you,[a] and you[a] will be their heritage and will no longer take away their children.*

[13] *"The message of the Lord Yahweh is as follows: Inasmuch as it is said[a] of you[b] that you eat people up and take away your nation's[c] children, [14]consequently you will no longer eat people nor will you any longer take away[a] your nation's children—so runs the Lord Yahweh's oracle. [15]I will no longer let other nations' humiliating talk about you be heard nor will you have to put up any longer with the taunts of other peoples.[a] So runs the Lord Yahweh's oracle."*

Notes

3. a. For the formulaic אדני "Lord" see the note on 20:3. It recurs in vv 6, 11, 14; 36:2, 3, 4, 5, 6 ,7, 13, 14 and 15.

6. a. MT adds כי־לדם אעשך ודם ירדפך "because I will make you into blood and blood will pursue you." It is unattested in LXX and interrupts the oath formula of v 6aαβ from its continuation with אם־לא "surely" in v 6b. Basically לדם appears to be a variant for דם in v 6b, "(in)to, in respect of blood," which preserves the correct reading there. Heb. כי אעשך "because I will make you" seems to go back to an annotation of ועשיתי (לך) "and I will do (to you)" in v 11, paraphrasing the unusual construction and adding a prepositional form with LXX Syr, with the sense "surely I will do to you." The note slipped back to v 6 because of the similar beginnings of vv 6 and 11; adapted for a modicum of sense to כי אעשך it was taken as a variant of v 6b and was accordingly supplied with the wording of v 6bβ.

6. b. For MT's strange דם שנאת "you hated blood" LXX attests a seeming original לדם אשמת "in respect of blood you have incurred guilt" (for the verb cf. 25:12). Heb. שנאת appears originally to have been a gloss on the complex משנאתך "(because of) your hating" in v 11, which, as in the previous case, strayed to v 6 and was regarded as a correction of אשמת, with which it shares three out of four letters. To fit the new verb ל(דם) "in respect of (blood)" was dropped.

7. a. MT לשממה ושממה "to ruin and ruin" appears to be a slip for וּמְשַׁמָּה לש׳ "to wrack and ruin," as in v 3 and in Ezek generally and as some MSS read. MT לִשְׁמָמָה is a subsequent attempt to differentiate between the two nouns: the minority masoretic reading לִשְׁמָמָה (see *BHS*) is correct.

7. b. Lit. "him who passes by and returns."

8. a. MT adds "your hills and your valleys and all your ravines," an attempt to fill out the text in accord with the fourfold phrasing of 36:4, 6 (and 6:3). The order is different, גאות "valleys" is spelled differently and the 2nd masc suffixes accord with vv 3–6, 9a rather than with vv 7–8a. LXX attempted

to harmonize by deleting את־הריו "his mountains" and rendering חלליו "his slain" with a 2nd masc sg pronoun, but it thereby lost the first and original part of the chain of nouns (Zimmerli 225; Simian, *Nachgeschichte* 106).

9. a. For the abnormal scriptio plena of K תישבנה (= תֵּשַׁבְנָה "they will be inhabited"), for which Q substituted a form "they will be restored" from שוב "return," see GKC 69b note 1.

10. a. The object signs indicate that the nouns are perceived as objects, in anticipation of the later verb וירשנוה "and we will possess it" (T. Muraoka, *Emphasis in Biblical Hebrew* 123).

10. b. The ancient versions presuppose וירשתין "and I will possess them," an easier and so inferior reading (Kraetzschmar 246). Heb. וירשנוה "and we will possess it" has a 1st pl subject, as in v 12b, and presupposes the land as the object, with loose reference to the territory of the previous clause.

11. a. MT משנאתיך "because of your hatred" has an unexpected pl form, for which many MSS read משנאתך. MT may have been influenced by נאצותיך "your insults" in v 12.

11. b. Israel is in view: cf. 20:9 (Simian, *Nachgeschichte* 107). Many (cf. *BHS*) prefer בך "in you," implied by LXX, but it is an easier reading.

12. a. K שממה "she is ruined" links with the sg reference in v 10; Q שממו "they are ruined" aligns with the following pl reference.

13. a. This stem עתר is not otherwise known—hence presumably the omission of the clause in LXX*—but the general meaning here is assured from the parallelism. An emendation to והעתקתם "and you made bold" (cf. Cornill 408; *BHS*) is not methodologically sound. A link with Aram. עתר (= Heb. עשר) "be rich" is unlikely. N. S. Doniach's appeal to an Arab. cognate with the sense of "stumble" (*AJSL* 50 [1933/34] 178) is not convincing.

14. a. MT adds כל־הארץ שממה אעשה לך "as (you) rejoiced 'The whole land is ruined,' (so) I will do to you." Basically כל־הארץ was a gloss on שממה (K) in v 12a explaining the sg form. The gloss was evidently wrongly related to שממה (כשמחתך = כשמח) in v 15a; subsequently it was reinterpreted as an alternative to v 15a and so supplied with a framework of terms from there. Usually v 15a is regarded as secondary to (a corrupt) 14b (cf. *BHS* et al.) because it is unattested in LXX*, but parablepsis by homoeoteleuton may well be the cause (Parunak, *Structural Studies* 463).

15. a. For the idiom, which recurs in 36:10, see 20:40 and note. Misunderstanding the idiom, LXX implies וכלה "and ... will perish" for וכל "and all," which is adopted by *BHS* and NEB.

36:2. a. LXX presupposes ושממות or ושמות "and ruins" for Heb. ובמות "and high places," probably by assimilation to שממות עולם "perpetual ruins" in 35:9. For the copula see note 3. a.

2. b. Heb. היתה is a collective sg (Simian, *Nachgeschichte* 130; cf. GKC 145k).

3. a. For יען ביען "because, by the cause" compare יען וביען in 13:10; Lev 26:43. The unexpected copula with במות "high places" earlier may be due to the misunderstanding of a note וב', intended to compare the form found elsewhere.

3. b. For the two Heb. verbs see Zimmerli 228.

3. c. Lit. "and you have come up on the lip of tongue(s)." The verb וַתֵּעֲלוּ appears to be a mixed form for qal תַּעֲלוּ and niph תֵּעָלוּ (GKC 75y).

4. a. MT אדני יהוה "the Lord Yahweh" defies the formulaic practice in Ezek: see Zimmerli 556 and the first note on 25:3. Assimilation to the messenger formula in the next clause is probably to blame here.

4. b. Here and in v 10 NEB's "palaces" for חרבות "ruins" depends on Driver's equating the word with what he regarded as S. Arab. and Arab. counterparts (*ETL* 26 [1950] 349).

4. c. To obtain synonymous parallelism with the next verb Bertholet (123) proposed לְבָז "to despise," as Tg interpreted לְבַז "to plunder." But both verbal and physical persecution runs through the chapter.

5. a. MT כלא has been regarded as an (Aramaizing?) error for כֻּלָּה "all of it" (cf. 35:15), but dittography is the more likely culprit: for אשר כלא should be read כל־אשר "all who" (cf. Ehrlich, *Randglossen* 132–33; Fohrer 199).

5. b. Heb. נתן here, as often, has the sense "make, constitute."

5. c. MT adds למען מגרשה לבז "with a view to its (= ?) open land to plunder." Since מגרש means "open land around a city," a link with "cities" in v 4 is feasible. Probably the words were an early gloss in which ה' לבז was a cue phrase in a final position (cf. 21:28 and note) specifying that the note related to היו לבז "were subject to plunder" in v 4by. The note wanted to harmonize "cities" with the three rural terms that preceded by indicating that in the last case the cities' open land was exploited along with the rural areas, presumably by using it and them for grazing. When the *he* was understood as a fem sg suffix, it was evidently related to ארצי "my land" in v 5b and the gloss was incorporated into the text at the end of that verse.

7. a. For the performative pf see the note on 22:13.

11. a. MT adds ורבו ופרו "and they will increase and be fruitful," which is not represented in LXX* and interrupts the direct address in the context. Probably it was a loose comparative annotation, which sought to compare the command פרו ורבו "be fruitful and multiply" in Gen 1:22, 28; 9:1 with the occurrences of פריכם "your fruit" (v 8) and והרביתי "and I will increase" (vv 10, 11).

12. a. MT construes as masc, presumably as a counterpoint to Edom's claims (cf. 35:10, 15). It is more probable that fem forms were intended (וירשוך "and they will possess you," והיית "and you will be" and תוסיפי "you will add") with reference to the land (vv 6, 14–15). In the third case תוסיפי was doubtless adapted to תוסף after the reinterpretation. The pl verbal forms in LXX Syr are clearly secondary.

13. a. Heb. אמרים is an indefinite pl ptcp ("they say") after the conjunction (not preposition) יען "because" (cf. Driver, *Bib* 35 [1954] 302–3).

13. b. Heb. לכם "of you (pl)" relates to the mountains. In view of the following fem sg references Kraetzschmar's division לְךְ מֵאֲכֶלֶת "to you (fem sg) ... eat" (248) is attractive, although the lack of a piel elsewhere militates against it. The pl may simply be a redactional attempt to link the fresh saying more closely with the preceding context.

13. c. Q גוייך "your nations" here and in v 14 obviously harks back to the "two nations" of 35:10. K גויך "your nation" is supported by the ancient versions.

14. a. K תכשלי "you will cause to stumble" appears to be an error by metathesis for Q תשכלי "you will make childless," the verb in vv 12, 13.

15. a. V 15b appears to be a dittograph, copied from v 14. It is absent from one MS, LXX and Syr. A copyist's eye evidently strayed back to עוד "any longer" in v 14aα.

Form/Structure/Setting

35:1–36:15 comprises a literary unit in view of the single message reception formula in 35:1. 35:2 and 36:1 mark the separation of the unit into two halves, by the addressing of the prophet as בן־אדם "human one" and also by the commission to address הר שעיר "Mount Seir" and הרי ישראל "mountains of Israel." Chap. 35 contains two messenger formulas, in vv 3, 14, and four recognition formulas, in vv 4, 9, 12(–13), 15. Accordingly it falls into four oracles: vv (2)3–4, 5–9, 10–13, 14–15. They are all judgment oracles developed into proof sayings by the addition of the recognition formula. The first lacks an accusatory element. The second, third and fourth are tripartite. In vv 10–13 the last element is extended and reverts to accusation, as the conclusion of a judgment oracle sometimes does. In vv 14–15 the accusation is varied with a comparison (כ . . . . כן "as . . . so"). Apart from vv 7–8a, all the oracles are spoken to Mount Seir, which is identified with Edom in v 15, perhaps redactionally in view of the third person reference. After the first oracle there is no separate introduction specifying the addressee, so that the chapter reads consecutively as a tirade of judgment against a foreign nation.

36:1-15 falls into two sections, vv 1–7 together with the closely linked vv 8–12, and the concluding vv 13–15. Vv 8–11 are a positive proof saying in which a recognition formula caps an oracle of salvation; v 12 which falls outside this formal structure appears to be a redactional amplification (see *Comment*). Vv 13–15 are a two-part oracle of salvation that begins with a messenger formula and moves from a reasoned (יען "because") description of present adversity to a corresponding (לכן "therefore") reversal. Vv 1–7 are form-critically less coherent. They are essentially an oracle of judgment against the nations surrounding Judah and especially against Edom (v 5), which in the light of the sequel in vv 8–12 has the role of an oracle of salvation for "the mountains of Israel," which are the addressees from v 1 onwards. The oracle culminates in a pronouncement of punishment at v 7, which reverses the accusation in v 6. Its underlying structure is that of a reasoned oracle of judgment in which the accusation is resumed at the beginning of the pronouncement of punishment (cf.

34:1–10, 17–22). However, this structuring is developed in a most complex way: there is a series of stops and starts. After a call for attention in v 1 and a motivating accusation in v 2, לכן "therefore" inaugurates the pronouncement of punishment no less than five times before it finally emerges in v 7. In v 3 לכן is followed by a fresh commission to speak, a messenger formula and a motivating accusation; in v 4 it is followed by a call for attention, a messenger formula and an implicit accusation; in v 5 by a messenger formula and an oath threatening judgment against the nations, who are accused afresh; in v 6 by a commisssion to address the land of Israel and the mountains, a messenger formula, a threat of judgment against the nations and an accusation; and finally in v 7 by a messenger formula, an oath formula and the long awaited pronouncement of punishment. In order to explain this unwieldy structure, there is substantial, though by no means unanimous, agreement that at least vv 3 and 5 have been added to the basic oracle (Hölscher, *Hesekiel* 172–73; Zimmerli 237; Simian, *Nachgeschichte* 83–84). Another, not unattractive possibility is that two oracles have been b lended in vv 1–12: Bertholet (122) separated vv labα, 3aβb, 4b, 5aβb, 6ab, 9, 10, 12 from vv lbβγ, 2, 4a, 5aα, 6bβ, 7, 8, 11. Whatever the explanation, vv 1–7 in their present form are heavily weighted on the side of grievance. The continuation of vv 1–7 in vv 8–11 makes the combined piece a proof saying developed from an oracle of both judgment and salvation, the same complex type as appeared in 34:2–16, 17–22.

As to rhetorical structure, in chap. 35 the combination of הר שעיר "Mount Seir" (vv 2, 3, 15) and שממה "ruin" (vv 4, 15) forms a fitting overall inclusion (cf. P. D. Miller, *Sin and Judgment in the Prophets* 73). There seems to be extensive wordplay that emphasizes the total message: the ruin Mount Seir is to experience (שממה, משמה in vv 3, 4, 7, 9, 12, 15ab) is linked with the underlying guilt it has incurred (אשמת, v 6), Yahweh's presence as witness in Israel (שם "there," v 10) and the divine hearing of Edom's claims to the land (שמעתי, vv 12, 13). Within vv 5–8 חרב "sword" provides an inclusion of crime and punishment (vv 5, 8), while there appears to be implicit wordplay on אדום "Edom" in אידם "their calamity" (v 5; Kraetzschmar 246) and the repeated דם "blood" (v 6; Reventlow, *Wächter* 143–44). Within vv 10–13 the verbal claims of Mount Seir function as an inclusion: אמרך "your saying," v 10, and אמרת "you have said," v 12.

In 36:1–11 the motif of desolate places and abandoned cities is matched with an opposite one (vv 4, 10), while the mention of surrounding nations occurs in vv 3, 4, 7 (cf. v 5). V 12 provides a bridge between vv 1–11 and vv 13–15, amplifying the blessing of human repopulation for "my people Israel" (vv 8, 10, 11) and paving the way for the removal of a related curse on the land (vv 13–14). V 15 resumes the motif of כלמת הגוים "the humiliation of the nations" from vv 6, 7.

There are close links between chap. 35 and 36:1–15. A number of these are appropriately concentrated in 35:15, which thus has a transitional role in a literary complex: בית ישראל "house of Israel" (36:10), the counterpoint of the cursed כל־אדום כלה "all Edom in its entirety," namely the blessed כל־בית ישראל כלה "all the house of Israel in its entirety" (36:10), and Edom's rejoicing (שמח) that is resumed in 36:5. 36:12 builds on this linkage by using the verb ירש "possess" and נחלה "heritage." Of course, the keywords of the chapters, הר שעיר "Mount Seir" (35:1, 7) and הרי ישראל "mountains of Israel" (36:1, 4, 8) are set in antithesis. The latter phrase is anticipated in 35:12. The different meanings of הנני אליך "behold I am against you" (35:3) and הנני אליכם "behold I am disposed toward you"

(36:9) are blatant counterparts. The "enmity" (איבת) of 35:5 finds an echo in the "enemy" (האויב) of 36:2. Adverse quotations feature in both 35:10 and 36:2, 13. Mount Seir's passion in 35:11 meets its match in Yahweh's passion in 36:5, 6. Edom's predicted desolation (חרבה) of 35:4, a present fact for Israel in 36:4, is reversed for the latter in 36:10; Edom's prospect of uninhabited cities in 35:9 is the opposite of Israel's in 36:10. It is probable too that we are meant to see the occurrences of אדום "Edom" (36:5) and the repeated אדם "human beings" in 36:10, 11, 12 and in 36:13, 14 as intentional wordplays. They serve as a link between the three pieces of chap. 36 and also between them and the theme of chap. 35 (see especially 35:15). It is clear that the judgment of chap. 35 is intended as a foil for Israel's salvation in 36:1–15.

The charges against Mount Seir in chap. 35 represent a later historical setting than that of 25:12, where the Edomites' behavior at the fall of Jerusalem in 587 B.C. is the only point at issue. Here Edom's occupation of unpopulated Judean territory is an accompanying charge. Likewise, in 36:1–7 the claims of surrounding ethnic groups are disputed. These matters were obviously of concern for the exiles, just as the question of the rights of Judeans left in the homeland after 587 B.C. was in 33:24–29.

There seems to be no compelling reason for denying Ezekiel's voice and hand in most of this material, although the complexity of 36:1–7 does raise questions of redaction that have not yet been resolved. The use of stereotyped language in 35:1–4, 5–9 is not adequate ground for ascribing the material to the school of Ezekiel (Zimmerli 234–35 et al.). The proximity of return from exile (36:8) need not be taken too literally. However, the apparent echo of Lev 26:9 in 36:9-11 recalls the use of Lev 26 in 34:25-30 and anticipates its further use in 37:26-28. Baltzer (*Ezechiel* 156-57) noted the echoes in chaps. 34 and 37, but overlooked this evidence, which suggests that at least vv 9-11 are from the same redactional hand as the other passages. One has also to take into account the summarizing nature of v 12, which forms a literary bridge to vv 13-15.

Comment

At first sight chap. 35 belongs with chap. 25, where indeed an oracle against Edom appears (25:12–14). However, the function of the chapter is to serve as a dark backcloth to enhance the revelation of Israel's glorious salvation in 36:1–15, in a series of general and specific contrasts (cf. in principle Mal 1:2–5), and to highlight the question whether the land belonged to Edom or to Israel. There is a larger agenda here too. 35:1–36:15 functions in the group of positive messages for Israel as a counterpart to chap. 6, an oracle of judgment against the mountains of Israel. Parunak has noted the similar initial framework of the chapters (*Structural Studies* 455–56). In chap. 6 the commission to Ezekiel to "direct" his "gaze against the mountains of Israel and prophesy against them and say 'You mountains of Israel, hear the word of the Lord Yahweh,'" finds a counterpart in chap. 35, where the first two elements appear with Mount Seir as object, and in chap. 36, where the last two elements reappear in a positive sense. Moreover, the call to attention and messenger formula directed "to the mountains and hills, ravines and valleys" (6:3) are repeated in 36:4. There is surely a link intended between the במות "high places" of 36:2 and those under attack in 6:3, 6. The prediction of divine intervention in 6:14 is closely paralleled in 35:3, 4b, with

Mount Seir as the victim now. It could not have been made clearer that whereas before sin and judgment predominated, now grace and salvation were to succeed them as marks of the new era that awaited the people of God.

35:2–4 For the formula of v 2a see the comment on 21:2; it significantly recurs in oracles against foreign nations at 25:2; 28:20; 29:2. "Mount Seir" is the traditional description of the mountainous area to the south-east of Judah, on the other side of the rift valley, where Edom was situated (see Gen 36:8, 9). The formula of encounter in v 3a is used in a foreign oracle at 26:3; 28:22. The formula of Yahweh's stretching out his hand against his victim has a parallel in the Edom oracle in 25:12–14. This proof saying, rhetorically addressed to Edom in the dramatic convention of the oracles against the nations, lacks an accusation. It is a stark pronouncement of judgment that would serve to vindicate the true nature of Yahweh.

5–9 The remaining two oracles amplify the first one by giving reasons for its blunt language. In this one the Edomites' behavior at the fall of Jerusalem in 587 B.C. is the focus of accusation. Obad 10–14 serve as a commentary on these charges. There is a heightened sense of time: history comes to a head in the outworking of Seir's "ancient enmity" (cf. 25:15) and in the ultimate punishment of Judah for generations of sin (cf. 21:30, 34 [25, 29]). The mention of Israel's "calamity" (cf. Obad. 13) serves to trigger an uncanny nemesis: אידם is reminiscent of אדום "Edom." The ominous wordplay, so powerful to the Hebrew ear, is sustained in the references to דם "blood" in the impassioned threat of v 6. The reference to sinning (אשמת) is paralleled in the Edom oracle at 25:12. "The blood is personified as the gō'ēl who demands full retribution (cf. Gen 9:6)" (Wevers 187)—and pursues the sinner mercilessly (Deut 19:6; Josh 20:5; Christ, *Blutvergiessen* 94). The punishment of v 3 is reinforced in v 7, and the prophetic principle of reaping as one sows is expressed in the grisly work of the sword at v 8b. The same principle comes to the fore in v 9: the discharge of the age-old (עולם) enmity of v 5 was to find a fitting echo in the perpetual (עולם) ruins. Again it would be a demonstration to the Edomites of Yahweh's supremacy.

10–13 The framework for this piece, which again is grounded in explicit accusation, is the verbal claims made by Israel's aggressive neighbor. We are to see as the historical background Edom's incursion into Judean territory, to fill a vacuum left by exile. The extreme statement of v 10a (cf. 37:22), whereby even the territory of the old northern kingdom was under threat, seems to reflect the nightmares of the exiles who exaggerated the reports that reached them into a danger to the land as a whole (Zimmerli 235). The aggressor had reckoned without Yahweh, who as owner of the land was present in his people's absence and witnessed this outrage (cf. 36:5; Lev 25:23. The cultic presence of Yahweh in Jerusalem [cf. 11:23] was, of course, a separate concept.). His reaction would match Edom's hostile actions in all their vehemence. Yahweh's judgment of them would be his way of vindicating himself to Israel: the statement in v 11b gives expression to the aim of the chapter, to use the foreign oracle form as a means of ministering to Israel. The extended recognition formula in vv 12–13 reverts to the theme of accusation. There seem to be echoes of Isa 37 in the divine hearing of human insults (Isa 37:3-4 // 2 Kgs 19:3-4, including נאצה "insult") and in the divine self-understanding as victim of the aggressor (Isa 37:23, 24 // 2 Kgs 19:22, 23) against Israelite territory. The application of an old prophetic message to a new, parallel historical event serves to reinforce the pronouncement. The reference to devouring uses the imagery of beasts of prey (cf. 34:5, 8). The passive form נִתְּנוּ ("have been given") claims divine permission for taking over the land (cf. 33:24), which is firmly repudiated in the statement of v 13, where the plural verbal forms follow on naturally from לָנוּ "to us" in v 12 (contra Zimmerli 236; Wevers 186). The divine hearing develops the divine witnessing of v 10b.

14, 15 This short final oracle draws the chapter to a close by echoing vv 2 and 4, and looks ahead to motifs contained in chap. 36 (see *Form/Structure/Setting*). Edom's ruin would be a fitting return for its malicious involvement in the ruin of Judah (Miller, *Sin and Judgment* 73). Israel's right to the land is reaffirmed: Yahweh as owner had given it to "the community of Israel" as a "heritage." While the promise was in abeyance, it was not abrogated.

36:1–7 The "mountains of Israel," earlier the object of human aggressive claims (35:12), are now the rhetorical recipients of divine assurance. The exiles, who are the real recipients, had evidently heard disquieting news of usurpation of their land, which spelled the end of any hopes of return. The report is sympathetically taken up by the prophet in Yahweh's name (cf. 25:3, 8; 26:2). Although there might be justification for forfeiture in the religious sins of the pre-exilic community (cf. 6:4–6), in fact Yahweh wondrously declares himself on the side of the exiles. In view of 35:5 "the enemy" is primarily Edom, but v 3 suggests that Edom is the archfiend who represents and speaks for a multiplicity of ethnic groups in Palestine (cf. Amos 9:12a; Obad 15, 18). Political claim to the land, now that the old order had passed for Judeans and other groups alike ("remnant," cf. 25:16), was a matter of seizure and declaration that the absent, defeated owners had lost all rights. Yet Yahweh "acts by laws totally different to those taken for granted by political calculators" (Eichrodt 490). Devastation, dispossession and disgrace were heavy blows that rained down on the heads of the cringing exiles, but they failed to reckon with Yahweh's positive will and his determination to champion his land and so, by implication, his people. The catalogue of disjointed oracular formulas and accusations in the text serve to reflect the reverberations of doubt and despair in the hearts of the exiles—and to reassure them that Yahweh has something else to say (cf. Ps 118:6, 7). Yahweh can speak with a passion that challenges that of the enemy (vv 5, 6; cf. 35:11; 25:14). The malicious vehemence of the enemy (v 5; cf. 25:6, 15) not only struck at the Judeans' self-esteem but reached Yahweh's own heart, for it was his own country that was at stake. The humiliation they had experienced was both external and subjective, physical and psychological, and to ease its pain the promise is given that the tables will be turned (cf. Miller, *Sin and Judgment* 74).

8–11 The message opens out into a positive unfolding of blessing for the land and for its old-new owners, whose time for repatriation was imminent. The "mountains of Israel" and "my people Israel" belonged together, under Yahweh who in grace still acknowledged himself a party to the old trio of God, people and land, and promised a new manifestation of such grace. The blessings for the land in Lev 26, already appropriated in chap. 34, are now claimed afresh (vv 9-11; cf. Lev 26:9a). The grim present of abandoned cities and desolate ruins (v 4) would give way to a program of rebuilding and repopulation—unlike Edom's lot (35:9). The counterecho of Edom's fate is seemingly continued in a positive wordplay (אָדָם "human beings," vv 10, 11). In characteristic typological vein, the best of the past is promised again, in an even better form (cf. the elements of correspondence and contrast in the typology of Second Isaiah, for which see B. W. Anderson, *Israel's Prophetic Heritage* 185–92).

12 This transitional verse lingers on promises just given, gathers up fresh contrasts with Edom and anticipates the next passage. The covenant phraseology "my people Israel" (v 8) is savored anew and related to the promises of population growth given in vv 10–11. The last clause relates the promise to the cessation of the curse on the land to be presented in vv 13–14. The Edomite claim to the land (35:10) and malicious dismissal of Israel's claim (35:15) would both be overturned, for Israel would come into its inheritance once more. The underlying factor that binds together the material of v 12 is the enhancing of the play on אדם/אדום (Edom/human beings).

13–15 Here "the land of Israel" (v 6) is the implicit subject. An old slur is echoed, the charge of those who went to spy out the land before its first occupation, that "the land is a land that devours its inhabitants" (Num 13:32). In a sense it had proved tragically true. Would repatriation repeat the nation's history of failure and loss? Seemingly the fears of the exiles are crystalized in this pessimistic grievance—although strictly the criticism is credited to the nations, in the light of v 5—and countered in a promise that the past would not haunt their future. The implicit reverting to v 6 in the references to the land prompts a reversal of the grievance mooted there: the land would be free of humiliating criticism from Judah's neighbors. Yahweh was going to change its image and make the land a means of life instead of an instrument of death.

Explanation

This literary unit has a number of agendas to fulfill. It has its own internal agenda: Edom and Israel are polarized as negative and positive counterparts. Edom's involvement in Israel's fate meant that Edom's experience would echo that fate, while Israel's fate would give way to coming fortune. Both promises operate on the level of pastoral reassurance, as damaged self-respect is built up with recourse to faith in a powerful covenant God. The role of the destroyed Jerusalem in the oracles of Second Isaiah is that of the desolated land here. It stands as an objective image of the inner feelings of the exiles. Both prophets appealed to the land-centered theology of pre-exilic times and insisted that it still represented the divine intent. Another agenda of this unit is to provide a counterpart to chap. 6. The judgment on the land and people presented there was not Yahweh's last word: its task done, it was to give way to a new proclamation of salvation. In the two contrasting units the double message of Ezekiel finds its focus. A third agenda is to carry forward the message of salvation inaugurated in chap. 34. Apart from the form-critical parallels, a number of motifs find fresh expression here. Its psychological assurances that past and present grievances would be dealt with ("no longer," 34:10, 22, 28, 29) are underlined (36:12, 14, 15). In this connection the assurance about "the humiliation of the nations," which reflected so deep a wound in the Judean psyche, is given again (34:29; 36:15). The worth of "the community of Israel" in Yahweh's eyes is reaffirmed (34:30; 36:10; cf. 35:15), along with its role as "my people" (34:30; 36:8, 12). Moreover, the echoing of the blessings of Lev 26:4–13 and their grounding in the prophetic program for the future (cf. 34:26–29) continue in the use of Lev 26:9 at 36:9bα, 10a. There is continuity and development in the gospel of salvation for the shellshocked exiles. Those who had lost everything would find in God—and nowhere else—new resources for life and fulfillment.

Two Inner Constraints (36:16–38)

Bibliography

Brueggemann, W. *Hopeful Imagination. Prophetic Voices in Exile.* Philadelphia: Fortress, 1986, 69-87. **Filson, F. V.** "The Omission of Ezek. 12:26–28 and 36:23b–38 in Codex 967." *JBL* 62 (1943) 27–32. **Hossfeld, F.-L.** *Untersuchungen zu Komposition und Theologie des Ezechielbuches.* FzB 20. Würzburg: Echter Verlag, 1977, 287–340. **Krüger, T.** *Geschichtskonzepte im Ezechielbuch.* BZAW 180. Berlin: de Gruyter, 1989, 441-49. **Levin, C.** *Die Verheissung des neuen Bundes.* FRLANT 137. Göttingen: Vandenhoeck und Ruprecht, 1985, 209–14.**Lust, J.** "Ezekiel 36–40 in the Oldest Greek Manuscript." *CBQ* 43 (1981) 517–33.**Reventlow, H.** *Wächter über Israel.* BZAW 82. Berlin: Töpelmann, 1962, 69–75.**Simian, H.** *Die theologische Nachgeschichte der Prophetie Ezechiels.* FzB 14. Würzburg: Echter Verlag, 1974. **Spottorno, M. V.** "La omisión de Ez. 36. 23b-38 y la transposición de capitulos en el papiro 967." *Emerita* 50 (1981) 93-99.

Translation

[16]*I received the following communication from Yahweh:* [17]*"Human one, the community of Israel, when living in their own land,*[a] *defiled it with both their general behavior and their specific practices. I regarded their behavior as being in the same defiling category as menstruation.* [18]*So I drenched them with my fury*[a] [19]*and scattered them through the nations so that they were dispersed in foreign countries as a judgment on their behavior and practices.* [20]*But, whichever nation they came*[a] *to, they got my holy name desecrated, because people said about them, 'They are Yahweh's people, but they have left his country.'* [21]*I felt concerned about my holy name, which the community of Israel got desecrated, whatever nation they came to.* [22]*So tell the community of Israel that this is the message of the Lord*[a] *Yahweh: I am going to act not for your sakes, community of Israel, but on behalf of my holy name which you have gotten desecrated in each country you came to.* [23]*I will honor the holiness of my great name, now desecrated among the nations where you got it so treated. Then the nations will realize that I am Yahweh*[a] *when they see my holiness reflected in your experience.*[b] [24]*I will take you from the nations, gathering you out of every country, and bring you home to your own land.* [25]*I will sprinkle pure water on you so that you are purified from all that defiles you and from all your idols I will purify you.* [26]*I will give you new hearts,*[a] *putting a new spirit within you. I will remove the stony hearts from your bodies, giving you hearts soft as flesh.* [27]*I will put my own spirit within you and ensure*[a] *that you follow my rulings and maintain my standards by putting them into effect.* [28]*You will live in the country I gave your fathers, and you will be my people and I will be your God.* [29]*I will save you from everything that defiles you. I will summon the grain and make it plentiful, instead of sending you famine.* [30]*I will make the fruit of the trees plentiful and also the produce of the fields, so that you are no longer the object*[a] *of taunt from the other nations because of famine.* [31]*Then you will remember your evil ways and no-good practices, and loathe yourselves for your iniquities and shocking behavior.* [32]*You must realize that I am not going to do this for your sakes—so runs the Lord Yahweh's oracle. Feel ashamed and penitent for your ways, community of Israel.*

[33]*"This is the Lord Yahweh's message: At the same time as I purify you from the taint of all your iniquities, I will repopulate the cities and the ruins*[a] *will be rebuilt.* [34]*The*

*country now desolated will be tilled again, instead of being a scene of desolation for all
who pass by.* [35]*They will say, 'This desolated country has become a veritable garden of
Eden, and cities once ruined, desolated and destroyed have been repopulated and fortified.'*[a]
[36]*Then the nations left in your vicinity will realize that I, Yahweh, have rebuilt scenes of
destruction, I have replanted areas of desolation. I, Yahweh, have spoken, given my
promise and will keep it.*

   [37]*"This is the message from the Lord Yahweh: Furthermore I will encourage the community of Israel to ask me to grant them this petition, that in terms of people*[a] *I make them
as numerous as sheep.* [38]*The ruined cities will be filled with veritable flocks of people, as
many as the sheep for sacrifice, as many as the sheep in Jerusalem used to be at its public
services. Then they will discover that I am Yahweh."*

Notes

   17. a. For the construction of the ptcp see Cooke 395.
   18. a. MT adds material that is unrepresented by LXX*, "because of the blood that they shed on
the land and with their idols they defiled it." It reads awkwardly both in respect of the repetition of על
("upon/because of") in different senses and in the change of construction in the last clause. It appears to have originated as two explanatory comments on v 17aγ and v 17aβγ respectively. The first
appears to depend on Num 35:33, 34. LXX reflects in v 17aγ a similar need to define the vague terms:
"with their idols and their defilements." Both sets of clarifications depend on v 25.
   20. a. For MT ויבוא "and he/one came," an amply supported (cf. *BHS*) reading ויבאו "and they
came" is required. This particular error of metathesis is common in the book: see the note on 20:38.
The indefinite construction here has an intensive sense (Vriezen, cited by Zimmerli 241).
   22. a. For the formulaic אדני "Lord" here and in vv 23 (MT), 32, 33, 37 see the note on 20:3.
   23. a. MT adds a divine saying formula "so runs the oracle of the Lord Yahweh," lacking in two
Heb Mss and LXX[B]. It is here employed uniquely in the middle of an expanded recognition formula
(cf. 25:14). It may have originated as a comparative gloss on v 22a, noting that in place of a messenger
formula a divine saying formula occurs in v 32. For the omission of vv 23bβ–38 in LXX[967] see *Form/
Structure/Setting*.
   26. a. Lit. "heart": a sg is used where a part of the body is common to a number of persons (S. R.
Driver, *Hebrew Syntax* 17 remark 4).
   27. a. For the construction see GKC 157c and BDB 795a, with reference to Eccl 3:14.
   30. a. The Heb. stem לקח is here used not of taking but of receiving (Ehrlich, *Randglossen* 134).
   33. a. For NEB "palaces" see the note on v 4.
   35. a. For the Heb. construction see Cooke 396.
   37.a. Heb. אדם "human beings" seems to be used appositionally: see GKC 131d, k.

Form/Structure/Setting

   Ezek 36:16–38 constitutes the next literary unit, as the message reception formula of v 16 reveals. The three messenger formulas of vv 22, 33 and 37 indicate
three oracles: vv 22–32, 33–36 and 37–38. In content they are all oracles of salvation. The first is introduced with an address to the prophet and a historical explanation to him (vv 17–21) that provides the background for the ensuing public
oracle, as in 22:18 + 19–22; 23:2–21 + 22–27. The expanded recognition formula
in v 23b seems to mark a caesura in the oracle, as it does in 34:27b. The oracle
ends with an appeal in v 32. The second oracle is a positive proof saying. It
begins with a careful recapitulation of the first oracle (v 33aβγ) and closes with a
formula of affirmation (v 36b; for the form of v 36 cf. 17:24) after an expanded
recognition formula. Its conscious continuation of the first oracle is indicated by
its second person references without specification of the addressees. The third is

also a positive proof saying, but it speaks of its objects in the third person. The phrase עוד זאת "furthermore this" marks out the oracle as an amplification of the foregoing: cf. 20:27; 23:38.

As for the rhetorical structure of the first piece, a common inclusion is provided for the divine explanation and the prophetic oracle by בית ישראל "house of Israel," in vv 17, 21, 22 and 32; it is picked up in the final oracle at v 37. The public oracle has another inclusion, אני עשה לא למענכם "not for your sakes am I about to act" in vv 22 and 32. Thematically vv 17–32 appear to exhibit a chiastic structure ABBA, relating to uncleanness of people and land in vv 17–19, 24–32 and to profanation of Yahweh's name in vv 20–21, 22–23 (cf. Parunak, *Structural Studies* 472, 474). In vv 24–32 the phrase מכל־טמאותיכם "from all your uncleannesses" (vv 25, 29) acts as a headline for two sections, vv 25–28 and 29–32, after the introductory v 24. Parunak (*Structural Studies* 472) has noted the parallel sequence "I—you" in vv 24–27a/27b–28 and 29–30/31 (better 29–30a/30b–31). The second oracle majors in vocabulary for destruction and reversal. The third re-uses this motif on a minor scale and combines it with a triple sheep simile (כצאן "like sheep").

As with many literary units in the book, it is clear that a basic oracle has been subjected to a series of literary expansions. The issue of setting is complicated by the omission of vv 23bβ–38 in the oldest LXX manuscript, papyrus 967, and the significance of this omission for the Hebrew text. The extant Greek rendering is marked by elements out of accord with the translational block of chaps. 26–39 and was clearly supplied later to amplify the shorter text (Filson, *JBL* 62 [1943] 29–30, with reference to Thackeray's researches; McGregor, *The Greek Text of Ezekiel*, 190–91). Filson (*JBL* 62 [1943] 31), followed by Wevers (192), himself no mean septuagintalist, explained the omission as a case of inner-Greek parablepsis from the recognition formula in v 23 to the one in v 32, noting that the manuscript exhibited many errors of this type. However, Lust (*CBQ* 43 [1981] 517–33) has developed argumentation used by W. A. Irwin, in tracing the phenomenon back to the Hebrew tradition. He has noted that nowhere else in 967 does parablepsis feature so much material. Moreover, the Old Latin Codex Wirceburgensis shares the omission (cf. P.-M. Bogaert, *Bib* 59 [1978] 390–91). Significant too is the non-Ezekielian nature of the Hebrew, notably אנכי "I" (v 28), the longer form of the first person pronoun in place of אני, מעלל "deed" (v 31) for עלילה (used in vv 17, 19), תחת אשר "instead of the fact that" (v 34) and הלזו "this" (v 35). Lust considers the missing material a late redactional addition. Certainly the omission in 967 is of great significance for the history of the LXX text, as its reflection in the Old Latin codex and the alien nature of the extant Greek demonstrate. However, it may well go back to a mechanical accident, as the breaking off in the middle of the expanded recognition formula could indicate. Spottorno (*Emerita* 50 [1981] 96-97), who also notes that ordinary parablepsis of so much material would be unusual, has related the omission to a codex page of 1512 letters in the past history of the papyrus: a page was lost either through frequent use in the synagogue or through parablepsis. Moreover, one should take note of the structural importance of v 27 within the redactional framework of the ensuing chapter: seemingly v 27a is deliberately repeated in 37:14a, and v 27b in 37:24b. It is probable that we are to envisage two separate phenomena, redactional amplification within the Hebrew text and coincidental omission of a wider block of material in the Greek tradition. The unusual language in vv 28 and 31, which in both cases is characteristic of later elements in the book of Jeremiah (cf. the longer form אנכי "I" in Jer 11:4; 24:7; 30:22), may indicate that vv 24–32 are a redactional amplification to be ascribed to Ezekiel's school and yet to be regarded as fully prophetic in their authority (cf. v 32). The overlap of material in vv 24–32 with other parts of the book (see *Comment*) could certainly point in the direction of later redaction. The artistic coherence of the piece is then, as in chaps. 20 and 27, a mark of redactional sensitivity. Vv 33–36, which presuppose vv 25 and 31, and vv 37–38, which presuppose vv 33 and 35, are then likewise a product of later redaction. There seems to be no reason to put this literary activity beyond the period of the exile.

Comment

17–19 The first half of the divine introduction to the oracle characterizes the history of Israel in the land as a history of failure. The failure is put in cultic terms as uncleanness, in accord with the priestly theology of Ezekiel—an uncleanness that infects the land (cf. Num 35:34; Deut 21:23). Lev 18:24–30 is especially worth noting in its insistence that self-defilement has the effect of defiling the land, which is prone to vomit out its defilers. Here the taboo matter of menstruation (cf. Lev 15:19–30) is cited as an indication of the intensely abhorrent nature of Israel's offense against God. Thus his vehement reaction was to expel them in judgment. An emphatic framework for this section is provided by דרכם "their way" and עלילותם "their deeds" in vv 17 and 19; here the terms function as the measure of and justification for divine judgment.

20–21 The solution had an unfortunate corollary, which is also expressed in cult-based language, the profaning of Yahweh's holy name. It is a problem that Ezekiel described in chap. 20, unencountered in Israel's earlier history because Yahweh had refrained from the ultimate treatment that their blatant provocation deserved (20:9, 14, 22). The portrayal of their pre-exilic history in these terms was obviously occasioned by the exile and by the loss of prestige that Yahweh consequently suffered as Israel's patron, in view of the territorial nature of ancient religious and political thinking. A theological interpretation in terms of Yahweh's weakness was more obvious to "the nations" than the prophetic one of vv 17–19. To vindicate his "holy name" Yahweh would have to act again. The verb חמל "feel concern," used in v 21, implicitly evokes its standard negative use earlier in the book: in consigning his people to exile Yahweh showed no mercy (5:11; 7:4; 8:18; 9:5, 10). The new usage paves the way for the statement of v 22. An inclusion for vv 20–21 is formed by the repeated "the nations to whom they came": it represents the basic situation of exile that posed the intense theological problem. It is part of a chiastic structure whereby a sinister logic of "nations," "profaning" and "my holy name" is traced to and fro (Parunak, *Structural Studies* 473).

22–23 In the proclamation of the resolution of Yahweh's problem the language of vv 20–21 is echoed. What was implicit in the first verb of v 21 is now brought into the open. Israel had no claim on Yahweh, who had been entirely fair in rejecting them from his land and favor. No, his own honor was at stake (cf. 20:9 and *Comment*). From this perspective the exile was intolerable, and its ending was a theological necessity, in order that Yahweh's holiness or transcendent power might be vindicated in human history. The recognition formula fittingly caps the theme of the clearing of his name.

24–28 Vv 24–32 move from the "holy/profane" category of vv 20–21 and 22–23 back to the "unclean" category of vv 17–19, and provide its polar opposite "clean, pure" (v 25; cf. 22:26). If vv 22–23 show how the problem of vv 20–21 may be resolved, vv 24–28 indicate how Israel's history in the land may be prevented from repeating itself. V 24 puts vv 17aα and 19a into reverse, using the new Exodus language of 20:34 and 34:13 but borrowing from 37:21 the distinctive verb לקח "take." In order to reverse v 17abβ, v 25 employs the language of a purificatory rite as a metaphor for forgiveness and spiritual cleansing (cf. Num 19:13, 20; Ps 51:9 [7]); the terminology of 37:23 has been borrowed and enhanced. In fact the language is partly metaphorical and partly literal: moral, social and cultic ("idols") sins are all in view.

This fresh start, wonderful as it was, was not enough. How could Israel hope to maintain Yahweh's covenant standards, after their signal failure in pre-exilic times? The promise of 11:19–20 is echoed (cf. Hossfeld, *Untersuchungen* 336). The two statements of v 26a are unpacked in v 26b and v 27. Yahweh would creatively endow Israel with new wills that were to be sensitive rather than stony and hard in their reactions to Yahweh's will. Thanks to him, their lives would be governed by a new impulse that was to be an expression of Yahweh's own spirit. He would re-make their human natures, so that they marched to the music of the covenant terms that expressed Yahweh's nature and will. Only thus could the covenant relationship become a living actuality rather than a doctrinal truth. Only thus could the old ideal of Yahweh's people in Yahweh's land (cf. v 20) become a reality.

29–32 The role of vv 24–28 has been to cope with the defiling sins of vv 17, 19. But what of the defiled land of v 17? There too reversal had to take place, as the new headline of v 29a announces. Divine salvation from the consequences of uncleanness, a motif derived from 37:23, is a glorious counterpart to the divine judgment of v 19b. The produce of the land would be responsive to Yahweh's rich blessing (cf. v 8a; Hos 2:23–24a [22–23a]). Famine, associated with judgment earlier in the book (5:16, 17; 14:13, 21), would be a thing of the past in the new era of salvation (cf. 34:29). So too would be the old lifestyle of vv 17, 19. Far from being a temptation to revert to, it would be recalled with revulsion, as 20:43 had proclaimed. Far from having any claims on Yahweh, the exiles needed even now to share his view of their former lives by making an appropriate response of repentance (cf. 20:44).

33–36 The new oracle consciously supplements the previous one by echoing the language of vv 25 and 29 by way of summary. The homeland, now deprived of the exiles and reduced to ruins and to the curse of disuse, would be changed by Yahweh's work of renewal. The terminology of judgment used in 5:14 is significantly reversed (Simian, *Nachgeschichte* 232). A vignette of wonder at the miraculous change is presented in v 35. In its light v 36 serves the purpose of promising the vindication of God's people, which is accentuated by the straits of those who once crowed over Israel's downfall (cf. vv 3–6) and seized their land. The glory would go to Yahweh as, in Jeremiah's terms, not only the one who overthrows but also the one who builds and plants (cf. Jer 1:10; 18:9; 24:6).

37–38 If vv 33–36 focus upon the land, this message focuses on the people restored to the land. The exiles felt themselves to be a small, insignificant group (cf. 12:16; Isa 41:14a), whose lamenting prayer was to be restored to the dimensions of a sizable nation. Yahweh declares himself sensitive to their prayer. The transformed ruined cities of v 35 are reinvoked, as sheepfolds teeming with human flocks. The lively similes of v 38a, emanating from a priestly circle, reflect positive memories of pre-exilic Jerusalem.

Explanation

The unit speaks of two inner constraints. The first concerns the issue of theodicy. Transcendent though Yahweh ever is throughout the book, nevertheless even for him commitment to others meant personal pain and loss. The divine image that is presented is eventually to be reflected in New Testament teaching. A model is provided for a descent to weakness as the precursor of a demonstration of power and glory. Ezekiel's insight into a transcendent God, now veiled to others, would be revealed to all when Yahweh reversed his people's fortunes. The prophet's faith would be transformed to sight. In this way the absolute certainty of restoration was pastorally underlined, by defining it in terms of divine necessity. "All hope for the future rests in the very character of God, for their God will take seriously being God" (Brueggemann, *Hopeful Imagination* 79). Moreover, covenant Lord of Israel though Yahweh was, his people had exhausted every possibility of laying any claim or condition upon him, and Yahweh's new show of strength was to be a manifestation of sheer grace. Just deserts were a signpost to exile and to destruction (v 19). The road from exile to salvation was paved with mercy and forgiveness (vv 25, 29).

The second inner constraint relates to the people of God. Failure seemed inevitable. How could the self-forged chains of sin be broken? Only a "heart" transplant could achieve obedience to Yahweh's revelation of his will for his people. And only God could bestow sufficient inner resources. Lest the concept suggest the creation of clones and the loss of the free will that is the hallmark of humanity, we must be aware of the dire straits of destruction and deportation to which free will had led. We must also take into consideration that the Christian ideal, achieved fully only in the hereafter, is to do the will of God and therein find true personal fulfillment. Even now that ideal creates a moral challenge to live up to the grace of inaugurated eschatology (cf. 1 Thess. 4:8 in its context).

There is a beautiful sense of the achievement of human destiny in the pictures of land and work and communal life. There is also an awareness that only with the constructive help of God could this be achieved. Yet, before that era dawned, hope was able to foster a new attitude, a discerning regret that laid in the heart a foundation for the new work of God (v 31; cf. 2 Pet 3:11–14; 1 John 3:3).

A dominant concern in this literary unit is to carry forward the message of salvation begun in chap. 34. Certain notes already sounded are struck again. The weighty description of the exiles as "the community of Israel" (34:30; 35:15; 36:10) is echoed at significant points (vv 17, 21, 22, 32, 37), and their role as his "people" (34:30; 36:8, 12) is reaffirmed (vv 20, 28), while their description as "sheep" (vv 37, 38), though nuanced differently, evokes 34:30. Obviously the promise of return to the land is given afresh (36:24; cf. 34:13), since the presence of Yahweh's people in Yahweh's land (cf. v 20) was necessary for the glory of Yahweh. The psychological assurance that hurtful negative features would be blotted out (34:22, 28, 29; 36:12, 14, 15) is pastorally preached again (v 30), with relation to the human fear of famine and the equally deep dread of loss of self-respect (cf. 34:29; 36:15). The vindication of God was to bring with it the vindication of the people, who represented him, so that in his service they might walk tall.

The Promise of New Life (37:1-14)

Bibliography

Baltzer, D. *Ezechiel und Deuterojesaja.* BZAW 121. Berlin: de Gruyter, 1971, 100-118. **Bartelmus, R.** "Textkritik, Literaturkritik und Syntax. Anmerkungen zur neueren Diskussion um Ez 37, 11." *BN* 25 (1984) 55-64. _____. "Ez 37, 1-14, die Verbform w^{e}qatal und die Anfänge der Auferstehungshoffnung" *ZAW* 97 (1985) 366-89. **Baumann, E.** "Die Hauptvisionen Hesekiels." *ZAW* 67 (1955) 56-67. **Fox, M. V.** "The Rhetoric of Ezekiel's Vision of the Valley of the Bones." *HUCA* 51 (1980) 1-15. **Graffy, A.** *A Prophet Confronts His People.* AnBib 104. Rome: Biblical Institute Press, 1984, 83-86. **Grassi, J.** "Ezekiel xxxvii.1-14 and the New Testament." *NTS* 11 (1964/65) 162-64. **Greenspoon, L. J.** "The Origins of the Idea of Resurrection." *Traditions in Transformation: Turning Points in Biblical Faith.* Ed. B. Halpern and J. D. Levenson. Winona Lake, IN: Eisenbrauns, 1981, 247–321. **Höffken, P.** "Beobachtungen zu Ezechiel xxxvii. 1-10." *VT* 31 (1981) 305-17. **Hossfeld, F.-L.** *Untersuchungen zu Komposition und Theologie des Ezechielbuches.* FzB 20. Würzburg: Echter Verlag, 1977, 341-401. **Kilian, R.** *Ich bringe Leben in euch.* Stuttgart: Verlag Katholisches Bibelwerkes, 1975, 92-106. **Krüger, T.** *Geschichtskonzepte im Ezechielbuch.* BZAW 180. Berlin: de Gruyter, 1989, 426-38. **Lang, B.** "Street Theater, Raising the Dead and the Zoroastrian Connection in Ezekiel's Prophecy." *Ezekiel and His Book.* Ed. J. Lust. BETL 74. Leuven: University Press, 1986, 297-316. **Nobile, M.** "Ez 37,1-14 come costituvo di uno schema cultuale." *Bib* 65 (1984) 476-89. **Perles, F.** "נול = 'Gewebe' im Alten Testament." *OLZ* 12 (1909) 251-52. **Unger, M. F.** "Ezekiel's Vision of Israel's Restoration." *BSac* 106 (1949) 312-24, 432-45; 107 (1950) 51-63. **Wagner, S.** "Geist und Leben nach Ezechiel 37,1-14." *Theologische Versuche* 10 (1979) 53-65. **Westermann, C.** *Prophetische Heilsworte im Alten Testament.* FRLANT 145. Göttingen: Vandenhoeck und Ruprecht, 1987, 133-34.

Translation

[1]*I felt the pressure of Yahweh's hand, and he used his own[a] spirit to carry me off, eventually setting me down[b] in the middle of the plain, which was filled with bones.* [2]*He took[a] me on a complete tour of them,[b] and I noticed that there were a great many of them strewn over the plain and also that they were extremely dry.* [3]*He asked me, "Human one, can these bones come back to life?"[a] "Lord[b] Yahweh," I answered, "you must know that."* [4]*He told me to prophesy over the bones that were there and to tell them, "Dry bones, listen to Yahweh's pronouncement.* [5]*Here is the Lord Yahweh's message to these bones: I am going to imbue you with breath,[a] and you will come back to life.* [6]*I will put sinews upon you, I will make flesh form over you and then cover you with skin. Then I will imbue you with breath and you will come back to life and realize that I am Yahweh."* [7]*I prophesied as I had been ordered, and as I did so I heard a rattling[a] and the bones[b] joined[c] themselves together in their proper order.* [8]*Before my very eyes sinews appeared on them, flesh formed and a top layer of skin covered[a] them.* [9]*He told me to prophesy to the spirit[a] "Prophesy, human one, and tell the spirit[a] that the Lord Yahweh's bidding is to come from the four winds and to breathe into these corpses that are victims of carnage, enabling them to come back to life."* [10]*So I prophesied[a] as he ordered me, and the spirit entered them and they came back to life and got to their feet, an enormous army.*

[11]*Then he told me, "Human one, these bones represent the whole community of Israel,[a] who in fact[b] have been saying, 'Our bones are dried out, our hope has perished,[c] we are*

bereft of life.[d] ' [12]*So prophesy and tell them this message from the Lord Yahweh: I am going to open up your graves and raise you from those graves of yours,*[a] *and take you home to the land of Israel.* [13]*You will realize that I am Yahweh when I do open your graves and raise you from those graves of yours.*[a] [14]*I will imbue you with my spirit so that you come back to life, and I will settle you in your own land. Then you will realize that I, Yahweh, have made a promise that I will keep." So runs Yahweh's oracle.*

Notes

1. a. Lit. "the spirit of Yahweh," apparently used as a stereotyped term in this clause where Yahweh is subj (Zimmerli 254).

1. b. Here and in 40:2 the first hiph of נוח "rest" is used in the sense of the second form.

2. a. The consecutive pf forms here and in vv 7, 8, 10 may be employed under Aramaic influence (cf. GKC 112 pp; Hossfeld, *Untersuchungen* 347-49). B. Johnson (*Hebräisches Perfekt* 78, 80) took the present case as iterative, but listed v 10 among cases in the later chapters of the book where the usage deviated from general Hebrew practice. Bartelmus (*ZAW* 97 [1985] 385-89) interpreted the phenomena as evidence that vv 7a, 8b-10 belong to an insertion dating from the Maccabean era in terms of a literal resurrection. For a brief critique see Klein, *Ezekiel: The Prophet and His Message* 155 note 7.

2. b. Masc suffixes are consistently used in this section, to refer to fem עצמות "bones" and in v 7 to עצם "bone," either as a simpler form or because their humanity is in view (cf. v 9). The fem would have conveyed a neuter, inanimate connotation.

3. a. The verb has an ingressive sense in this pericope (BDB 311a; Hossfeld, *Untersuchungen* 376-77). The impf is modal (Hossfeld, *Untersuchungen* 150; cf. Joüon 1131).

3. b. For the formulaic usage of אדני "Lord" here and in vv 5, 12 see the note on 20:3. In v 14, however, it is uncharacteristically absent, probably because it occurs in a redactional addition (Hossfeld, *Untersuchungen* 387). Here the cry lacks a preceding interjection אההּ "alas": contrast 21:5.

5. a. In this section רוח variously means "spirit," "breath" and "wind." In v 6 the LXX interpreted as "my (= Yahweh's) spirit," under the influence of 36:27; 37:14.

7. a. MT anticipates רעש "rattling" with קול "noise," which takes away any sense of surprise in the narrative and is not represented in LXX* and one Heb. MS. It probably originated in a comparative gloss inspired by 3:12, 13, where the terms occur together (Cooke 399; Hossfeld, *Untersuchungen* 379, although he relates it on p. 357 to 1:25).

7. b. The anarthrous עצמות "bones" in MT is suspicious. Is it an uncorrected miswriting of the following עצם "bone" under the influence of the earlier pl forms? Or did it arise as a marginal indication of the subj (Driver, *Bib* 35 [1954] 303 note 9)? Two MSS lack it; the reading העצמות "the bones" in two other MSS is undoubtedly secondary. Whether the LXX so reads is impossible to determine (Cornill 416).

7. c. For the unusual verbal form see GKC 60a note 1 and Driver, *Bib* 35 [1954] 303.

8. a. The transitive use in v 6 leads us to expect here a niph form, וַיִּקְרְמוּ (*BHS* et al.). MT seems to understand as active with עור "skin" as object and Yahweh as implicit subj, corresponding to v 6.

9. a. Or "breath." The same uncertainty applies to v 10. See *Comment.*

10. a. The hith form replaces the niph used in v 7. Its rare and special usage elsewhere in Ezek (13:17) may suggest an error under the influence of the niph impv הנבא (Cornill 418; Zimmerli 255-56), but see *Comment.*

11. a. For המה "they" see GKC 141g, h. On the proposal of Baltzer (*Ezechiel* 102) and Hossfeld (*Untersuchungen* 361-62) to attach המה to v 11b see Bartelmus, *BN* 25 (1984) 55-64.

11. b. Heb הנה "behold" can stand without definition of subj (GKC 116s; Driver, *Bib* 35 [1954] 303). The subj seems to be "the whole community of Israel" (Keil 119). The supplying of a pronoun in LXX* Vg Tg is a natural clarification of the translators.

11. c. In view of the asyndeton of the next clause the copula in MT ואבדה "and ... has perished" is generally deleted as a dittograph with many MSS LXX Tg.

11. d. NEB "our thread of life is snapped, our web is severed from the loom" has adopted in the latter clause the interesting emendation of Perles (*OLZ* 12 [1909] 251-52; cf. *BHS*), נִגְזַר נוֹלֵנוּ "our web is cut off"; he appealed to post-biblical Hebrew. The suggestion was adopted by KB 602b, but cf. *HALAT* 643a. The lack of parallels in the rich imagery of the OT renders it unlikely (Zimmerli 256). In the earlier clause תקוה "hope" has been related to a homonym meaning "cord" (cf. Josh 2:18, 21). For לנו see GKC 119s.

12. a. MT adds עמי "my people," unrepresented in LXX Syr and, if authentic, expected earlier in the direct speech. It probably originated as a comparative gloss on לעם "to a people" in the verbal covenant formulation of v 27, citing עמי in the nominal clause of 34:30; it became attached to the wrong column.

13. a. MT עמי "my people" has been repeated by dittography from v 12; it is not represented in Syr. However, its presence in LXX may indicate that it was first incorporated into the text at this point and subsequently entered v 12 by assimilation.

Form/Structure/Setting

The message reception formula which usually begins a literary unit, and which will return in v 15, is here replaced by a formulaic introduction to a vision account (cf. 1:3; 40:1). The unit of vv 1-14 continues the vision account of vv 1-10 with an interpretative oracle of salvation in vv 11-14. This oracle is also a disputation consisting of a thesis of despair (v 11) and a counterthesis of hope (vv 12-14) (cf. Graffy, *A Prophet* 83-86). The latter element is a two-part proof saying concluded with an extended recognition formula (v 13) and amplified with a summarizing, seemingly redactional, statement (v 14). The vision narrative has its own two-part proof saying, vv 5-6, and a further oracle, a command, in v 9.

After the introduction in v 1a, the vision narrative falls into two parts unequal in size but largely symmetrical as to their motifs, vv 1b-8a and vv 8b-10. A negative description (vv 1b-2, 8b) is eventually countered with a positive one (vv 7b-8a, 10b). In between lies divine speech, introduced by ויאמר אלי "and he said to me" (vv 3, 4, 9) and its prophetic transmission (vv 7a, 10a). The divine speech begins with בן אדם "human one" (vv 3, 9) and continues with a commission to prophesy and a messenger formula (vv 4, including a summons to hear, 9). An extra element in the first part is the question and answer of v 3. The two parts of the vision account find a close structural parallel in vv 11-13. Here too a negative description (v 11) appears, but now set within a divine speech, which is once more introduced by ויאמר אלי "and he said to me" and begins with בן אדם "human one" (v 11) and continues with a prophetic commission and a messenger formula (v 12). Moreover, just as the first part of the vision story introduces the negative situation, the announcement of divine activity and the positive fulfillment with (ו)הנה "(and) behold" (vv 2 [twice], 5, 7, 8), so in the interpretation the negative description includes the term (v 11) and the announcement of divine intervention starts with it (v 12).

The double and triple structuring is in each case accompanied by an inclusion that serves to confirm its respective boundaries. The two separate instances of מאד "very" in v 2 are capped by its doubled presence at the end of v 10 (Baltzer, *Ezechiel* 109). The double והנה "and behold" in vv 2b, 7-8 supplies an inclusion for vv 1b-8a. Within two of the three divine speeches the bringing/ bestowing of רוח "breath" in vv 5b and 6aγ provides an inclusion (Höffken, *VT* 31 [1981] 306; similarly Parunak [*Structural Studies* 481] speaks of a chiasmus, ABA), and so do the divine promises to "open your graves" and "raise you up from your graves" in vv 12-13 (Parunak, *Structural Studies* 483) in an emphasis on the reversal of death. Overall inclusions are afforded by the mention of Yahweh's רוח "spirit" and the verbs of resting (נוח in two different hiphil forms) in vv 1 and 14. Fishbane (*Biblical Interpretation* 451-52) has viewed this inclusion as part of a chiasmus with v 11 at its center.

The overall form of the unit is similar to that of 36:16-32 in consisting of a private communication to the prophet and a public oracle. In content, although not in the order of its component parts, it is especially close to 11:1-13, where a vision and its divine interpretation are followed by a commission to deliver an oracle, an account of its effect and the prophet's question. There can be little doubt that this unit reflects a situation not long after 587 B.C., when sentiments of death-like hopelessness occasioned by the shock of Jerusalem's fall, the dissolution of Judah and the Babylonian exile must have been rife. An important issue is the relation of the oracle of disputation to the vision account, in view of their quite different representations of a field strewn with unburied bones and a cemetery of graves. Bertholet (126), Fohrer (209-10) and Wevers (194, 196) resolved the discord by regarding vv 12aβ-13 as a redactional intrusion. Hossfeld (*Untersuchungen*, esp. 369) has gone further in differentiating between vv 1-11a (up to ישראל "Israel") and vv 11b (from המה "they")-13a: he regards the latter as redactional and later than Ezekiel's own work in the former passage. The basic question is whether the tension in the imagery requires such a literary-critical conclusion (see *Comment*). A further issue relates to the closing verses. Garscha (*Studien zum Ezechielbuch* 222) and Hossfeld (*Untersuchungen,* esp. 400-401) have followed Jahn and J. Herrmann in regarding vv 13b-14 as redactional. Although Zimmerli (257) has regarded this expedient as unnecessary, there does seem to be sufficient ground for detaching v 14 (only) as a typical redactional conclusion to the unit (cf. 31:18; 34:31) which wants to connect it closely to the key promise of 36:27 (cf. Baltzer, *Ezechiel* 107-8).

Comment

1a The introduction to the vision impressively describes the psychic experience of being caught up by supernatural power and transported elsewhere. The language used evokes very ancient prophetic experiences and characterizes Ezekiel as an old-world prophet with authoritative credentials (cf. 1 Kgs 18:12, 46; 2 Kgs 2:16). Divine agency is indicated both by the pressure of Yahweh's "hand" (see 33:22 and *Comment*; cf. 1:3; 3:14, etc.) and by the participation of his "spirit" (cf. 8:3; 11:1, 24). The "plain" or broad valley appears to be that mentioned in 3:22-23 and 8:4, close to Ezekiel's residence in exile at Tel-abib. Whereas before it was the scene of a revelation of God's glory, now it has quite different visionary associations. The abrupt beginning of the account, softened in the LXX and Syriac by a copula, has led commentators to speculate whether at an earlier stage a date was prefixed, as in the case of other visions (cf. 8:1; 40:1). Brownlee considered that 1:1a, with its difficult reference to the thirtieth year, related to the exile (= 568 B.C.) and belonged here (xxxi-ii, 4), but the historical setting of the vision appears to be earlier than that.

1b-3 The visionary scene, a gruesome one, is gradually unfolded. First impressions of a grotesque mass of bones are reinforced as the prophet is taken round the site; he is made aware too that what were once corpses had long since rotted or been eaten away into fleshless bones. The divine question is a standard element in a vision, to wrest significance from the sight (cf. Jer 1:11, 13; Amos 7:8; 8:2; Zech 4:2, 5). It was a ridiculous question. A seeming corpse might be revived, but these pathetic piles of bones were hopelessly dead. Out of polite deference to his questioner the prophet leaves him to answer his own question. Yahweh knew the answer as well as he did (cf. Craigie 260)!

4-6 No, evidently Yahweh knew more than Ezekiel did, for he commands the prophet to address the defunct bones around him and to announce their imminent reanimation. Yahweh is to do the impossible (Wevers 278)! The promise of reanimation is given twice, as a framework for the reclothing of the bones with bodies made up of sinews, flesh and skin. Yahweh is portrayed as the creator of the individual, the giver of personal life (cf. Job 10:11-12; Ps 139:13-16), but now in a context of restoring life rather than initially bestowing it. The demonstration of such power would be proof indeed of Yahweh's being.

7-8a The prophetic oracle triggers a movement from disorientation to reorientation. Ezekiel discharges his strange commission, and the ensuing silence is broken by a rattling sound as the bones realign themselves into skeletons. Then before his wondering eyes they turn into bodies, in step with the stages of his oracle. First sound, then sight: Ezekiel's senses are bombarded with an overwhelming experience.

8b However, the narrative lapses into negative description. The process is halted without the emphasized reanimation of vv 5b and 6aγ having yet taken place. These bodies lack the essential element of "breath," and it requires a further oracle to achieve the renewal of life. Zimmerli (257) has referred to 3:1-2 as a precedent for a two-phased visionary process. It is also customary to compare the double manner of creation in Gen 2:7, whereby the human being was first given a shape, like some life-size doll, and then received from God himself animating breath, נשמת חיים "the breath of life," although רוח "breath, spirit" is the term used here. (It is seemingly in dependence on Gen 2:7 that the LXX has "the breath of life" at the end of v 5.) So here separate acts take place because two miracles were necessary, to reconstitute the bones into bodies and to reanimate the bodies. There is also an element of drama in the double process. "One is reminded of the magician who invariably 'fails' once or twice in attempting his grand finale in order to intensify suspense and to focus attention on the climactic success to follow" (Fox, *HUCA* 51 [1980] 11). The process accentuates the power of God even as it concedes the difficulty of the enterprise.

9 The prophetic commissioning follows the pattern of v 4, but this oracle is to be addressed to the רוח "breath, spirit" that is out there in the wide world. Moreover, the oracle is not a statement of Yahweh's imminent action but a command to the רוח, unleashed to the four points of the compass, to focus its attention on the corpses. The in-breathing echoes the verb of Gen 2:7 (נפח), when Yahweh "breathed" into the human being the breath of life. However, the conception seems to borrow too from the priestly account of creation, in which the רוח of God hovered over the raw elements of the world, waiting to transform them into a living cosmos (Gen 1:2). It was this pervading power that gave continued life to a finite world (Ps 104:29-30; Job 34:14-15). One may compare too the powerful creative word in Genesis 1 (Baltzer, *Ezechiel* 112).

10 Again the prophet functions as agent of the process, and at last the coming of the breath forecast in v 5b is achieved. The verb of prophesying used in v 7 (and in vv 4, 9) is slightly varied. The hithpael form is elsewhere used in the book only at 13:17, where it characterizes a misused psychic gift of mediating life or death (13:19). Here the prophetic word shares this powerful potential (cf. R.

Rendtorff, *TDNT* 6, 799; Baltzer, *Ezechiel* 113-14). The superlatives of the negative description in v 2b (מְאֹד "very," twice) are gathered together in a positive account of the dynamic sequel (מְאֹד מְאֹד), to enhance the transformation of bones on an old battlefield into a virile company standing up and so poised and purposeful. The contrast is accentuated by the consonantal wordplay between (ב) הַהֲרוּגִים הָאֵלֶּה "these slain ones" (v 9), referring to the inanimate bodies into which the bones had been transformed, and עַל־רַגְלֵיהֶם "on their feet." Moreover, the notion of new life (וַיִּחְיוּ "and they became alive") is carried forward in the term חַיִל "army, strength."

11 Once more the prophet hears the divine voice, as especially in v 3 and also in vv 4 and 9. Now tantalizing question and performative commissions are replaced by plain interpretation. The negative factors of vv 1b–2 and 8b are perpetuated in the explanation. The bones represented the exiles, and dramatized the evidence of their own mouths in a communal lament (cf. 33:10). The quotation is a poetic tricolon (2 + 2 + 2; cf. 33:10) that expresses pathos with *-ēnû* and *-ānû* syllables, as in 33:10. Their "bones" stand for the whole person, which has been sapped of vitality by the crisis of exile (cf. Ps 31:11 [10]; 32:3; 102:4-6 [3–5]; cf. A. R. Johnson, *The Vitality of the Individual* [Cardiff: University of Wales Press, 1964] 67–68). The second of the three clauses alludes to death, the death of hope (cf. Ps. 9:19 [18]). The third clause, literally "we have been cut off," refers to loss of life (cf. Isa 53:8), here in the sense of being reduced to a deathlike state (cf. Lam 3:54). The metaphor of death is typical of the psalms of lament and thanksgiving. It is used to described an abysmally low level of human existence that, crushed by crisis, lacked any of the quality that life ordinarily had. "The dangerously ill, the accused who face the court without any support, the persecuted who are hopelessly delivered over to their enemies—all these already belong to the world of the dead" (H. W. Wolff, *Anthropology of the Old Testament* [Philadelphia: Fortress, 1974] 111; cf., e.g., Ps 116:3, 8-9). Clearly the vision has grown out of the lament of the exiles: the dry bones of the first clause have been strikingly reinterpreted in terms of the explicit death language of the third. "Strange, shocking and bizarre images. . . are needed when one seeks to break down old frameworks of perception and to create new ones" (Fox, *HUCA* 51 [1980] 9).

12-13 The divine response to the lament is to commission an oracle of salvation, with opening formulas that deliberately echo those of vv 4-5. The three clauses of lament are answered with three divine statements of reversal. The inconsistency in the imagery of death between a cemetery and a battlefield is more real to the Western mind than it would have been to the ancient Hebrew one, which did not object to the mixing of metaphors (cf. G. B. Caird, *The Language and Imagery of the Bible* [Philadelphia: Westminster, 1980] 149-52). In the laments the aura of death that surrounds the sufferer may be described at one and the same time in terms of drowning and of being caught in a hunter's trap (Ps 18:5-6 [4-5]). Mention of the grave finds a parallel in Ps 88:6 (5), along with the verb "cut off," so that v 12 follows on naturally from the end of v 11 (cf. Baltzer, *Ezechiel* 104). At another level than the thematic there are ample reminiscences of the vision oracle of vv 4-5 especially with reference to Yahweh's dynamic acts: the repetition of the verb "and I shall raise" (וְהַעֲלֵיתִי, vv 6, 12) and of the divine bringing of vv 5 (מֵבִיא אֲנִי "I am going to bring") and 12 (וְהֵבֵאתִי "and I shall bring"), and the assonance between opening (פָּתַח) and breathing (פֻּחִי v 9) and of graves (קִבְרוֹתֵיכֶם) and the joining of the bones (וַתִּקְרְבוּ, v 7). The experience of exile is a veritable graveyard; to live again is to return to the land. The lament is countered with an oracle of salvation that proclaimed afresh the truth of a new Exodus, here expressed in contextually adapted terms, and of a return to the land that symbolized return to living fellowship with Yahweh. As ever in the book of Ezekiel, salvation is to be a means to a divine end. The redeeming act of God would bring with it the revelation of his true self.

14 The editorial rounding off of the unit wants also to tie it to the preceding piece. The vision and its interpretation were of a piece with the message of 36:27, "I will put my spirit within you." The following of the promise with an assurance of dwelling or settling in the land both in 36:28 and here confirms that an echo of 36:27 is intended. In fact, the placing of this whole unit in its present position seems to have been due to an intent to amplify 36:27: רוח "breath, spirit" is used no less than ten times. The metaphorical reviving breath given by Yahweh (v 6) is related to a new potential, the opportunity to comply with Yahweh's covenant terms and so to enjoy the life that is life indeed (cf. 20:21; 33:19). The pathway to this reinterpretation runs via v 1, where the רוח "breath, spirit" is that of Yahweh (cf. Wagner, *Theologische Versuche* 10 [1979] 62). There is another echo of v 1 in the verb "settle" (והנחתי, cf. ויניחני "he set me down," v 1). The prophetic experience itself contained seeds of hope for the people of God (cf. too v 10 with 2:1-2; 3:24). He was the harbinger of a new work of God, just as Joel's prophetic insight was the model of Israel's coming closeness of fellowship with Yahweh (Joel 3:1-2 [2:28-29]) and Isaiah's burning of purification prefigured that of the people (Isa 6:6-7, 13; cf. 4:4). The repeated recognition formula also harks back to v 6. It is followed by an affirmation that not only recalls 36:36b and links this oracle with the preceding one, but also has a role within this unit. The vision's sequence of divine word and action (vv 5-6/7, 9/10) would not fail to have its counterpart in coming reality.

Explanation

In terms of tradition history one must look back to Israel's hymnic language, doubtless derived from cultic use, which celebrated Yahweh as one who can "kill and make alive" (Deut 32:39; 1 Sam 2:6). As the immediate context in the former case ("I wound and heal") and the usage in 2 Kgs 5:7 with relation to healing make clear, the reference is to rescuing from the aura of death that surrounded the victim of crisis, especially at time of illness (see Johnson, *Vitality* 108-9). This credal statement seems to underlie the present message of vision and interpretation. The Judeans, suffering the fate of exile and estranged from both Yahweh and their land, were in the throes of disorientation. Yet Yahweh was able to deliver from so threatening a crisis. And, the prophet proclaims, Yahweh's own desire was to put the people back on their feet. The leitmotif of the vision, רוח וחייתם/ויחיו "breath, and you shall live/and they lived" loudly proclaims Yahweh to be the creator of new life. Before the exile the temple courts had echoed with personal testimonies of thanksgiving to Yahweh: "You have delivered my soul from death, my eyes from tears, my feet from stumbling. I walk before Yahweh in the land of the living" (Ps 116:8, 9). This cultic heritage was the fuel for an affirmative answer to the lament of the exiles. It provided the theological dynamic for the vision of miraculous renewal. Ezekiel has historicized the Psalms' gospel of reorientation and actualized "the land of the living" sought by the disoriented bringer of lament.

A recurring element in the vision, which is both resumed in the interpretation and reflected on in the supplement of v 14, is the prominent role played by Ezekiel as agent of renewal (cf. Hossfeld, *Untersuchungen* 399). He functions not merely as observer but as participant. As in 11:4-12, Ezekiel's prophetic word controls the development of the vision (cf. Zimmerli, *Ezekiel 1* 258). This role served both as an assurance to the prophet and as an assertion to his audience regarding the authority and authenticity that he possessed as prophet of salvation, as truly as when he had predicted judgment. The vision exposes an organic relationship between the two prophetic events, the wreaking of judgment and the bestowing of salvation. Salvation was to rise phoenix-like from the embers of judgment. The vision affirms the reality of divine judgment: Yahweh had indeed dealt a death blow to his covenant people (הרוגים "slain," v 9; the verb is used of Yahweh's judgment of Israel in 9:6; 21:16 [11]; 23:10, 47). However, even from this veritable Sheol the promise of deliverance could be given.

It would be surprising if the New Testament did not take up the vibrant terminology of this vision. In his own vision John the Seer described the resurrection of God's two prophetic witnesses after three and a half days of death in terms of vv 5 (LXX) and 10 (Rev 11:11), in a theological affirmation of the invincibility of the witness of the Church to God, which is undergirded by God's power. There are close parallels between vv 7 (σεισμός "earthquake," LXX) and 12 and the account of earthquake and raising of the saints in Matt 27:51-54 (Grassi, *NTS* 11 [1964/65] 163). Naturally Christian (and Jewish) development in the conception of salvation envisaged the literal re-use of Ezekiel's metaphor of death and revival, so that Matthew's narrative could recall the vision in an omen of the resurrection of the people of God. More true to the original intent of the passage is the seeming echo of v 9 at John 20:22, in the breathing of the risen Christ upon the disciples, bestowing the Holy Spirit (ἐνεφύσησεν "he breathed"; cf. LXX ἐμφύσησον "breathe"; Grassi, *NTS* 11 [1964/65] 164). In different ways both these references relate the passage to the inauguration of eschatological hope. Paul seems to relate it rather to eschatological consummation in discussing the anticipated final Jewish acceptance of God's further revelation in Christ. He vividly describes their re-incorporation into the community of faith as "life from the dead" (Rom 11:15). It is difficult to miss a Christian Jew's interpretation of Ezekiel's vision.

One King, One People (37:15-28)

Bibliography

Baltzer, D. *Ezechiel und Deuterojesaja.* BZAW 121. Berlin: de Gruyter, 1971, 156-61. **Barth, C.** "Ezechiel 37 als Einheit." *Beiträge zur alttestamentliche Theologie.* FS W. Zimmerli, ed. H. Donner et al. Göttingen: Vandenhoeck und Ruprecht, 1977, 39-52. **Caquot, A.** "Le messianisme d'Ézéchiel." *Sem* 14 (1964) 5-23. **Demson, D. E.** "Divine Power Politics. Reflections on Ezekiel 37." *Intergerini Parietis Septum (Eph 2:14)* FS M. Barth, ed. D. Y. Hadidian. Pittsburgh: Pickwick, 1980, 97-110. **Gottlieb, H.** "Die Tradition von David als Hirten." *VT* 17 (1967) 190-200. **Greenwood, D. C.** "On the Jewish Hope for a Restored Kingdom." *ZAW* 88 (1976) 376-85. **Kellermann, U.** *Messias und Gesetz.* BibS 61. Neukirchen-Vluyn: Neukirchener Verlag, 1971, 86-88. **Krüger, T.** *Geschichtskonzepte im Ezechielbuch.* BZAW 180. Berlin: de Gruyter, 1989, 438-41. **Levin, C.** *Die Verheissung des neuen Bundes.* FRLANT 137. Göttingen: Vandenhoeck und Ruprecht, 1985, 214-18. **Long, B. O.** "Two Question and Answer Schemata in the Prophets." *JBL* 90 (1971) 129-39. **Martin-Achard, R.** "Quelques remarques sur la réunification du peuple de Dieu d'après Ezechiel 37,15 ss." *Wort-Gebot-Glaube.* FS W. Eichrodt, ed. H. Stoebe et al. ATANT 59. Zürich: Zwingli Verlag, 1970, 67-76. **Seybold, K.** *Das davidische Königtum im Zeugnis der Propheten.* FRLANT 107. Göttingen: Vandenhoeck und Ruprecht, 1972, 145-52. **Speiser, E. A.** "Background and Function of the Biblical nāśîʾ" *CBQ* 25 (1963) 111-17.

Translation

[15] *I received the following communication from Yahweh:* [16] *"As for you, human one, take a stick and write on it 'Judah*[a] *and all of the Israelites associated*[b] *with it.' Then take*[c] *another*[d] *stick and write on it 'Joseph*[e] *and all of the community of Israel associated*[b] *with it.'* [17] *Then join*[a] *them to one another as one stick, so that they are united*[b] *in your hand.* [18] *When*[a] *your fellow nationals ask you to tell them what you mean by this,* [19] *inform them of the following message from the Lord*[a] *Yahweh: I am about to take the stick*[b] *representing Joseph*[c] *and the tribes of Israel associated with it and put*[d] *with it the stick representing Judah, and make them one stick so that they are one in my hand.*[e]

[20] *"With the sticks you write on clearly visible in your hand,* [21] *inform them of the following message from the Lord Yahweh: I am going to take the Israelites out of the nations they went to, gathering them from the surrounding areas, and I will bring them home to their own country.* [22] *I will make them one nation in the land,*[a] *on Israel's mountains, and one king*[b] *they will all have as king:*[c] *no longer will they be*[d] *two nations nor will they be divided into two kingdoms any longer.*[e] [23] *No longer will they sully themselves with their idols, their detestable objects of worship or any of their rebellious ways.*[a] *I will save them from all their deviations*[b] *in which they have sinfully engaged and purify them. Then they will be my people and I will be their God.*

[24] *"My servant David will be king over them: they will all have one shepherd. They will follow my standards and observe my rulings and carry them out.* [25] *They will live on the land I gave my servant Jacob, in which your*[a] *forebears lived. They, their children and their grandchildren will live on it for always.*[b]

"David my servant will be their head of state for ever. [26] *I will make with them a covenant of peace: there will be an everlasting covenant with them.*[a] *I will swell their numbers and put my sanctuary in their midst for ever.*

²⁷*My dwelling place will overlook*ᵃ *them, and I will be their God and they will be my people.* ²⁸*Then the other nations will realize that I, Yahweh, have set apart Israel as holy, when my sanctuary is set in their midst for evermore.*"

Notes

16. a. Heb. (ליהודה) ל is generally taken as *lamed inscriptionis*, introducing the wording of an inscription or title (GKC 119u), but it may indicate possession "for, belonging to" (Ehrlich, *Randglossen* 136; Zimmerli 267; RSV).

16. b. For the spelling in K here and in v 19a see the note on 40:6.

16. c. Heb. לקח (וֹ) "take" is a rare form of the impv: קח is expected, as in v 16a. Perhaps it should be pointed as inf abs (cf. Zimmerli 268).

16. d. Heb. אחד ... אחד in v 16a, b means "one ... another," as in v 17a. An emendation אחר "another" on the supposed basis of LXX Syr Vg is counterproductive, since אחד functions as a sectional key word (Zimmerli, ibid.).

16. e. MT and the ancient versions add עץ אפרים "Ephraim's stick," which spoils the parallelism. It is generally taken as an early gloss, explaining the uncommon "Joseph" as a designation for the northern tribes; "Ephraim" may have been influenced by the reunification promises of Jer 31:9, 18, 20. It also seems to interpret the *lamed* as one of possession.

17. a. For the vocalization see GKC 52n, 64h.

17. b. The pl אחדים seems to be a case of grammatical assimilation to the verb (Hölscher, *Hesekiel* 176 note 3; cf. Gen 11:1).

18. a. LXX represents here and at the beginning of v 19 a more idiomatic Heb. style: see *BHS*.

19. a. For the formulaic אדני "Lord" here and in v 21 see the note on 20:3.

19. b. LXX φυλήν "tribe" for עץ "stick" here and in v 19bα is due to the translator's wish to replace metaphor with reality in this statement of Yahweh's actions: cf. Tg עמא "people" for עץ in v 19bβ.

19. c. MT and the ancient versions add אשר ביד אפרים "which is in Ephraim's hand," which seems to be an early gloss on עץ "stick" in line with the one in v 16bβ. It may have been an amplification of the previous one, which has entered the text at this lower point. In that case its interest was primarily grammatical, ביד indicating possession.

19. d. MT adds אותם "them," which does not fit the clause. It was probably a variant or comparative gloss relating to ועשיתם "and I will make them": cf. in v 22 ועשיתי אתם "and I will make them." The LXX or its *Vorlage* appears to be secondary to MT: it represents אותם and then has to render עליו את־עץ "with it the stick" as if it were "with the stick" (cf. Zimmerli 269).

19. e. LXX renders בידי "in my hand" as if ביד יהודה (cf. *BHS*), which is interesting evidence for the practice of abbreviation in Heb. MSS.

22. a. LXX implies בארצי "in my land," which Cornill (420) et al. prefer. However, not only is it inappropriate here (see Zimmerli, ibid.), but it is significant that in the context the LXX reflects assimilation to other passages: to v 11 in rendering "house" for בני "sons" in v 21a; to 28:24 in translating "from all around them" for מסביב "around" in v 21b; and to v 12 in its translation "the country of Israel" for אדמתם "their country." Correspondingly, here the influence of 36:5 is probable.

22. b. LXX ἄρχων "ruler" here and in vv 24 and 25, as if reading נשיא "head of state" for מלך "king," seems to reflect the same assimilating tendency, in this case to 34:24. The same passage is echoed in v 23 in the addition of "Lord" after "I" and in v 24, implying נשיא בתוכם "leader in their midst." Zimmerli (269, 275) observed that the parallelism of גוי ... מלך ("nation ... king") with ממלכות ... גוים ("kingdoms ... nations") in v 22b favors MT.

22. c. Heb. למלך "for, as king" is not represented in LXX* Syr. Again Zimmerli, ibid., has noted in its favor a correspondence with the construction of v 22bα.

22. d. K יהיה retains the king as subj: "he will be (king for ...)." Q יהיו "they will be" is generally read with many MSS and in accord with the ancient versions, as the parallelism of v 22bαβ requires.

22. e. Unlike LXX Vg, MT repeats עוד "(no) longer." It reflects a conflated text: in Ezek עוד is usually placed immediately after the verb, while 19:9; 39:7 attest a later position.

23. a. LXX* does not represent the latter two noun phrases; it is difficult to decide whether parablepsis or secondary accretion in MT is the culprit. Levin (*Verheissung* 215 note 67) argues for the priority of MT, with reference to 14:11.

23. b. MT מושבתיהם "their dwelling places" reflects the incorrect insertion of a vowel letter into משבתיהם = משובתיהם (cf. *BHS*) "their deviations," implied by LXX Σ. MT was influenced by the triple

usage of (וישבו) (ו) "(and) they will dwell/dwelt" in v 25 and perhaps by the association of בכל מושבותיהם "in all their dwelling places" in 6:14 with כל גלוליהם "all their idols" in 6:13.

25. a. LXX Syr imply "their," an easier and so secondary reading. See *Form/Structure/Setting*.

25. b. For the omission in LXX* see Zimmerli 270.

26. a. MT adds ונתתים "and I will give them." An original אותם והרביתי אותם ונתתי "with them and I will increase them and give" seems to have suffered the loss of והרביתי אותם by parablepsis caused by homoeoteleuton: the LXX attests such an abbreviated text (cf. *BHS*). A marginal correction והרביתי אותם ונתתי "and I will increase them and give," in which the last term functioned as a cue word, was mistakenly inserted after the shortened text. Subsequently ונתתי[1] was slightly adapted for sense, by the addition of a pronominal object. Tg wrested sense out of ונתתים by rendering "and I will bless them," which RSV adopted. Herrmann (234) followed by Cooke (406) and Zimmerli, ibid., regarded the first אותם (= אתם "with them": cf. GKC 103b) as not original, but אתכם "with you" in a similar context at Lev 26:9b supports its presence here; moreover, it affords a reasonable explanation for the basic error.

27. a. Lit. "will be over, above." The temple's standing on a hill is in mind (cf. 40:2).

Form/Structure/Setting

This literary unit is demarcated by its own message reception formula (v 15) and by that which introduces chaps. 38-39 in 38:1. It begins with a command to perform a symbolic action (vv 16-17) and continues with a question and answer format that in Ezekiel is used to create a hinge between a symbolic action and its meaning (vv 18-19; see Long, *JBL* 90 [1971] 134-37, with references to 12:9-12; 21:12; 24:19-21). Vv 20-28, after an introductory reference to the symbolic action and a messenger formula (v 20), launch into a further oracle that eventually concludes with a recognition formula (v 28). However, one would hesitate to call vv 21-28 a proof saying, since the content of the formula does not relate to the theme of the earlier part of the oracle. This factor raises the question of literary development within vv 20-28. A further pertinent question concerns the relation of vv 20-28 to the earlier two parts of the unit. Zimmerli (272-73, 275) views these verses as a redactional addition to the basic text of vv 16-19, which emanated either from Ezekiel or from his school in the case of vv 20-23+24a and from the latter, in a late phase, in the case of vv 24b-28. Certainly the explanatory oracle of salvation in vv 16-19 could be complete in itself. Yet there is logic in what follows it, whether it is secondary or not. While vv 16-19 proceed from symbolic action to meaning, the "meaning" is simply a conversion of the prophetic sign into divine metaphor. It remains for the salvation oracle of vv 20-22 (at least) to move from metaphor to factual interpretation. What in Ezekiel is elsewhere separately attested as a pair, a symbolic action and its meaning on the one hand or a metaphorical statement or parable and its meaning on the other hand, appears here to be combined in a triad. Yet v 20 indicates continuity with what precedes: v 21 is still intended as an answer to the exiles' question concerning the symbolic action. This organic unity is to be taken seriously. In terms of content v 22 seems to be a necessary interpretation of the symbolic action, as Garscha recognized in his own way by regarding it as originally linked with v 19 (*Studien* 225), and as Bertholet (129) and Fohrer (210) acknowledged by continuing the basic unit till v 22. Certainly vv 16-22 have a structural flow, in moving from קח ... (ולקח) ... וקרב אתם ... לעץ אחד, "take ... (and take) ... and join them ... into one stick" (vv 16-17) to לקח ... ועשיתם לעץ אחד "(I will) take ... and make them into one stick" (v 19) and on to לקח ... ועשיתי אתם לגוי אחד "(I will) take ... and make them into one nation" (vv 21-22). Moreover, the flow seems to continue till v 24a, in that a key word אחד "one" dominates vv 16-24a, and ומלך אחד יהיה לכלם

"and they will all have one king" (v 22aβ) and ורועה אחד יהיה לכלם "and they will all have one shepherd" (v 24aβ) are an evident inclusion. The latter clause is closely related to 34:23a, but the borrowing is to be attributed there rather than here, since רעה "shepherd" is a common royal term, and אחד "one" clearly has its home in this context (cf. Baltzer, *Ezechiel* 138).

With v 24b one has to compare the redactional v 14a: both seem to be derived from 36:27. Nor can one overlook the similarity of v 25aβ to 36:28a, which includes אבותיכם "your fathers," less suited to the present context than to its original setting (cf. Levin, *Verheissung* 215, 216 note 69). Moreover, v 25 has a close relation with the late 28:25-26. The term נשיא "head of state" in v 25bβ differentiates from מלך "king" in vv 22, 24a in a seemingly corrective way (cf. 34:24). The change in order from עבדי דוד "my servant David" in v 24a to דוד עבדי "David my servant" in v 25bβ is a minor indication of a different hand. Vv 25-28 are united by their own key word, עולם "everlasting." This passage complements the late 34:25-30 in its use of Lev 26 (see *Comment*) and is a parallel piece.

The addition of vv 24b-30, an oracle of salvation in the form of a proof saying, brought changes to the overall structure, such as occurred in chap. 27 as a corollary of supplementation. The royal references in vv 22a, 24a and 25b function now as headlines in a series of three sections. The initial section with the key word עוד "(no) longer" (vv 22b, 23a) and the final one that has the key word לעולם "forever" (vv 25b, 26b, 28b) or עולם "everlastingness" (v 26a) are nicely bridged by the middle one, which ends with עד־עולם "forever" (v 25bα). It is clear that vv 15-28 represent a basic text that has been subsequently amplified, as is the case with very many of the literary units in the book. Its early part derives from Ezekiel, but seems to be later than vv 1-13, which still reflect the shock of the catastrophe in 587 B.C. It looks back at the crisis reflectively (Zimmerli 272) and ponders deeply on its reversal. Whether vv 23-24a belong to this early part or have already begun the process of literary growth is not easily decided. The term משובתיהם "their deviations" is unique in the book (cf. Jer 2:19; 3:6, etc). However, the sharing of the vocabulary of v 23 by the late 36:25, 29 is by way of echo. The double use of מלך "king" in vv 22a and 24a, and the persistence of the key term אחד "one" in v 24a appear to attest the integral nature of vv 22-24a in a seemingly original fashion (cf. Carley 251).

The echoes of 36:27a in 37:14a and of 36:27b in 37:24b suggest extensive compositional structuring. 37:1-13 seems to have been intended as a commentary on 36:27a, as we noted earlier, and likewise 37:15-24a as a commentary on 36:27b. Ezekiel's oracles have thus been artistically woven into an explanatory framework, which sought to illustrate the role of Yahweh's spirit and the means whereby obedience to Yahweh's moral will would be achieved in the new age.

Comment

15-17 Ezekiel is commanded to perform a symbolic act, such as occasionally preceded and reinforced his public oracles (cf. 24:15-24). It is a simple one, holding two sticks together end to end in his hand, with the adjacent ends concealed so that they looked a single long stick: v 20 makes clear that they were still really two. An essential part of the action was that these sticks were to have writing on them and so were openly representational. "Judah" and "Joseph" stand respectively for the people of the old southern and northern kingdoms. "Joseph" refers to the two leading tribes, Ephraim and Manasseh, while by implication "Judah" has a tribal flavor, the tribe of Judah being the main constituent of the state of Judah. The extra material in the labels identifies the two groups as joint members of a larger entity, the sons/community/tribes of Israel. Are the sticks simply convenient objects to convey a written message and feature in an enacted demonstration? The Targum interpreted in terms of wooden tablets, in view of the writing (cf. Isa 8:1). G. R. Driver (*JTS* 22 [1971] 549-50) developed this notion by envisaging two leaves of a folding tablet (=NEB; cf. Steinmann 188). He noted that such folding tablets had been found at Nineveh. However, the LXX rendered with ῥάβδος "staff," perhaps with Num 17:16-26 in mind, where "rods" (מטות; LXX ῥάβδοι) representing tribal leaders have names written on them. The present context leads us further along this direction with its mention of two kingdoms and a single nation and king in v 22: reasoning back from these data, the sticks stand for royal scepters (cf. the interpretation of עץ "tree, piece of wood" at 21:3[20:47] as שבט "scepter" in the gloss of 21:15b [10b]). It may be that the LXX was alluding to 19:11-14, where the מטה "rod, stem" that became a ruler's scepter is thrice rendered ῥάβδος, although the factor of a different Greek translator must be borne in mind. Here the ensuing emphasis on kingship in the inclusion of vv 22a and 24a and redactionally in the three royal headlines that included vv 25bβ so highlight the concept of kingship that it is difficult to avoid seeing such an implication in the stick symbolism. The sticks have a national significance insofar as they suggest the institution of monarchy that represents the nation.

18-19 The sign, performed in public, was intended to stimulate Ezekiel's audience of Judean exiles. The scenario of question and answer in v 18 leads into the oracular answer, which transforms the prophetic act into divine metaphor and thus affirms that the prophet was in advance enacting Yahweh's own intent.

20-23 The plain interpretation of the two hand-held sticks that follows adopts the same twofold sequence of the symbolic act and metaphor: "take . . . join/ make into one . . ." The homogeneity of the two groups is pushed to the fore rather more by the absence of the distinguishing terms "Judah" and "Joseph." Their repatriation and reunion would be a realization of a truth for long tragically hidden from view, the ideal of a united kingdom. The miracle Yahweh would perform for Judah (vv 1-14) he could also work for its northern partner. The theological triangle of God, people and land now seemingly becomes a square with the addition of a fourth component, the king. Really, however, the king represents both the people in their unity and the rule of Yahweh (cf. 20:33b), as the earthly guardian of the people's worship and way of life (cf. Seybold, *Königtum* 152) or, in terms of the British conception of monarchy, "defender of the faith." By such means pre-exilic failure in these areas would be prevented from recurring, and the covenant relationship would be brought to glorious fulfillment.

24-25bα The original conclusion to the previous oracle (v 24a) now becomes the redactional introduction to a new stanza. It gives expression to the role of the king as symbol of social unity under God. As "servant" or vassal of an overlord, he would be committed to Yahweh's will. His designation as "David" characterizes him not only as a scion of Davidic lineage but as an upholder of the united kingdom, such as David himself was as nominee of all the tribes of Israel (2 Sam 5:1-4; cf. 1 Kgs 3:28). The title "shepherd" "seeks to guard against a one-sidedly political understanding of the future ruler" (J. Jeremias, *TDNT* 5 488, with reference to K. Galling). It gives the king the role of an undershepherd of the covenant flock, fulfilling all of God's purposes for them (cf. Isa 44:28; Gottlieb, *VT* 17 [1967] 196). The addition of v 24b alludes to the fulfillment of 36:27, as surely as 37:14aα claimed the outworking of 36:27a. In this new context it draws on the deuteronomistic conception of the Davidic dynasty as model and monitor of the covenant law (cf. 1 Kgs 3:6, 14; 9:4; 18:6; 23:3, 24-25; Kellermann, *Messias und Gesetz* 87). The people's obedience would make possible continued occupation of the promised land envisaged in 28:25-26 and 36:28. The disobedience that had been the cause of the exile would haunt them no longer.

25bβ -28 The final stanza celebrates afresh the restoration of the united monarchy, but now in place of the traditional מלך "king" the modified term נשיא "head of state" appears. Ezekiel revived this archaic title for an elected tribal chieftain or intertribal president and used it often, although not to the exclusion of מלך, to differentiate minor kings in the ancient Near East from imperial kings (cf. 1 Kgs 11:34, 37; Speiser, *CBQ* 25 [1963] 111-17). In chaps. 40-48 it is the standard term for the royal leader of the new state. Here it seems to underline the monarch's subordination to Yahweh, the real king whose vicegerent he was, and to distinguish his rule from an expression of absolute, tyrannical power (B. Lang, *Kein Aufstand* 180). It also emphasizes the king's links with the people, as an old, democratic term. The old promise of the permanence of the Davidic dynasty (cf. 2 Sam 7:13, 15) is recalled and it provides the key word of the stanza. Like the people, the dynasty is to live on from generation to generation (Caquot, *Sem* 14 [1964] 20-21). The dynasty's deuteronomistic role as guarantor of the Mosaic covenant is the implicit link with what follows. In vv 26-27 there are deliberate echoes of Lev 26:4-13 that parallel those in 34:26-29 and 36:9-11. In fact a principle of filling in the gaps seems to underlie the present text: expressions left unused in the earlier pieces are now taken up (cf. Baltzer, *Ezechiel* 156-59). An overlapping framework is provided by the sentiment of making a covenant of peace (34:25aα; cf. Lev 26:6, 9b) and by the self-introduction formula (34:30; cf. Lev 26:13). In between, the motifs of population increase and Yahweh's making a covenant with Israel (Lev 26:9), his setting his dwelling place in their midst (Lev 26:11) and the double covenant formula (Lev 26:12) are taken up here. In the penultimate case the sentiment is expanded and integrated by the use of Ezekiel's characteristic term מקדש "sanctuary." Similarly the self-introduction formula both here and in 34:30 is woven into the typical recognition formula.

A new element, with respect to Lev 26, is ברית עולם "an everlasting covenant" (cf. 16:60), which happily marries a Davidic tradition (2 Sam 23:5) with the national tradition of the patriarchal covenant (Gen 17:7; cf. Ps 105:10). In keeping with the context, the conception that dominates this final stanza is the echoing of the historical period of the united monarchy, which under David and Solomon was closely connected with the centralization of worship in Jerusalem and especially with the building of the temple. That period is visualized as creating an ideal for the future. Emphasis is laid on the restored temple towering over the people as the capstone of the new divine-human constitution that time would not decay. It would be a material symbol to the world of the special relationship between God and the people consecrated to him (cf. Lev 20:26).

Explanation

This literary unit, like the previous one, functions as a commentary on 36:27. It wants to carry forward the earlier one in a dynamic development. The pair of units conforms to a pattern in the book: vision followed by symbolic act (cf. 1:1-3:15/3:22-5:17; 8:1-11:25/12:1-20; Barth, *Beiträge* 42-43). The repeated promise to bring the people home to their own country hinges the units, ending the former and introducing the interpretative oracle in the latter (vv 12, 21). In the first case the promise functions as a goal, and in the second as a starting point for a new work of God. The same figurative verb for uniting occurs in both, with reference to the joining of the bones in the vision and the joining of the sticks in the symbolic act (קרב, vv 7, 17). But now the first simile of coherent life has given way to one of greater unity. "All the house of Israel" (v 11), which in its context connotes the Judean exiles, is broadened to signify a larger grouping, together with the terms "Israelites" and "tribes of Israel" (vv 16, 19, 21, cf. v 28). There is a reaching back beyond the claims of a southern kingdom to represent the Yahwistic traditions, beyond the religious and political tensions of a divided nation. The deuteronomistic ideal of a united kingdom, under a monarchy that reflected and upheld Yahweh's purposes for lifestyle and worship, is held up as a model for the future. The Davidic heritage, represented by such terms as "king" and "my servant David" (cf. 2 Sam 7:5, 8; Ps 89:21[20]) is to be revived, although its future role is to be a constitutional symbol of national unity and a means whereby Yahweh may keep at bay abuses prevalent in Judah's pre-exilic history. The redactional supplement develops these concepts further, downplaying and limiting the royal function both by use of a lesser term and by highlighting the ends to which it was to be the means. Memories of an autocratic monarchy that served its subjects badly were so bitter, and the constraints of political realism were so compelling, that messianic exuberance was necessarily absent. The focus is on Yahweh and the fulfillment of his purposes in setting aside a people for himself. For all its symbolism, the palace must play second fiddle to the temple as a pointer to a fulfilled and lasting covenant of fellowship between God and the community of faith.

Ezekiel's prophetic dream of a reunited Israel (cf. 4:4-8; 16:53) had antecedents among the prophets. Jeremiah in his early ministry endorsed Joseph's aim of political reunion between Judah and the members of the northern kingdom left in the land after the exile of 721 B.C. (Jer 3:12, 14; 31:2-6; cf. Holladay, *Jeremiah 1* 65, 118, 120), and his redactors, if not he himself, extended the hope to the northern upper classes who were exiled to Assyria (3:8; 31:18, 27, 31). The hope cherished by Jeremiah went back to Hosea's expectation that one day the people of the northern kingdom would return to favor with Yahweh (e.g., Hos 11:11). We know comparatively little about the history of the exiled northerners, but there is no evidence of any return. There was Jewish awareness of northern tribes in Assyria: the apocryphal book of Tobit has such a setting. In Judah's early post-exilic period it is clear that barriers were erected from the southern side, and time seems to have done nothing to demolish them.

Greenwood called the predictions regarding a restored northern kingdom "perhaps the most conspicuous example in the [Old Testament] of patently false prophecy" (*ZAW* 88 [1976] 384). Should it not rather be regarded as a truly divine wish that became victim, in part at least, to human willfulness (cf. Luke

13:34)? The prophetic dream refused to bow totally to the intransigence of historical realities: it continued to surface in one form or another. The Chronicler, probably around 400 b.c., took seriously the prophetic ideal and tried to heal the breach among divided Yahwists in the land with a call to Judah to rediscover the principle of "all Israel" and to welcome northerners to worship at the Jerusalem temple. Eventually, however, a final schism took place, so that "the Jews" had "no dealings with Samaritans" (John 4:9). The New Testament proclaimed a new Christ-centered unity between Jew and Samaritan (John 4:7-42; Acts 1:8; 8:5-25) and indeed an overarching unity between Jew and Gentile that created a metaphorical "holy people" (Eph 2:11-22) and posited the ideal of "one flock, one shepherd" (John 10:16). The ideal, like that which Ezekiel set before his Judean audience, presents a challenge to work toward.

The unit in its closing verses clearly paves the way for the vision of chaps. 40-48. In its latter part it also wants to draw together positive strands from chaps. 34 and 36, as well as from chap. 28. The message of new life and of the fulfillment of covenant ideals is both repeated and developed along fresh lines.

Israel's Security Paradoxically Affirmed (38:1-39:29)

Bibliography

Ahroni, R. "The Gog Prophecy and the Book of Ezekiel." *Hebrew Annual Review* 1 (1977) 1-27. **Alexander, R.H.** "A Fresh Look at Ezekiel 38 and 39." *JETS* 17 (1974) 157-69. **Astour, M.C.** "Ezekiel's Prophecy of Gog and the Cuthean Legend of Naram-Sin." *JBL* 95 (1976) 567-79. **Balentine, S.E.** *The Hidden God: The Hiding of the Face of God in the Old Testament.* Oxford: OUP, 1983. **Block, D.I.** "Gog and the Pouring Out of the Spirit: Reflections on Ezekiel xxxix 21-9." *VT* 37 (1987) 257-70. **Erling, B.** "Ezekiel 38-39 and the Origins of Jewish Apocalyptic." *Ex Orbe Religionum.* Vol. 1. FS G. Widengren. Leiden: Brill, 1972, 104-14. **Grech, P.** "Interprophetic Re-interpretation and Old Testament Eschatology." *Augustinianum* 9 (1969) 235-65. **Grill, S.** "Der Schlachttag Jahwes." *BZ* N.F. 2 (1958) 278-83. **Hossfeld, F.-L.** *Untersuchungen zu Komposition und Theologie des Ezechielbuches.* FzB 20. Würzburg: Echter Verlag, 1977, 402-509. **Lust, J.** "The Final Text and Textual Criticism. Ez 39,28." *Ezekiel and His Book.* Ed. J. Lust. Leuven: University Press, 1986, 48-54. **Lutz, H.-M.** *Jahweh, Jerusalem und die Völker.* WMANT 27. Neukirchen: Neukirchener Verlag, 1968, 63-84, 125-30. **Müller, H.-P.** *Ursprünge und Strukturen alttestamentlicher Eschatologie.* BZAW 109. Berlin: Töpelmann, 1969, 86-101. **Price, J. D.** "Rosh: An Ancient Land Known to Ezekiel." *Grace Theological Journal* 6 (1985) 67-89. **Ribichini, S., and Xella, P.** " 'La valle dei passanti' (Ezechiele 39:11)." *UF* 12 (1980) 434-37.

Translation

[1]*I received the following communication from Yahweh:* [2]*"Human one, look in the direction of Gog,*[a] *the chief*[b] *officer of Meshech and Tubal, and issue a prophecy against him,* [3]*telling him that the following message comes from the Lord*[a] *Yahweh: I am your adversary, Gog, chief officer of Meshech and Tubal.* [4]*I*[a] *will summon to battle*[b] *you and your entire army of horses and riders, all of them fully armed, a huge company,*[c] [5]*with them Persia, Cush and Put,*[a] [6]*Gomer and all its hordes, northernmost Beth Togarmah and all*[a] *its hordes—many peoples with you.* [7]*Be ready, steady,*[a] *you and all your company that has been mobilized for you, and take good care of them.*[b] [8]*A long period of time will elapse before you are given your orders. When those years are past,*[a] *you will invade a country that has been rehabilitated from the sword's effects, which has been reconstituted from among many peoples on Israel's long ruined mountains, whose population*[b] *all live securely after being brought out from among other peoples.* [9]*You will advance like a storm, invading like a cloud to cover the country,*[a] *you and all your hordes and many peoples with you.*[b]

[10]*"Here is the Lord Yahweh's message: That will be the time when you start thinking up a scheme. Devising an evil plan,*[11] *you will decide 'I mean to attack a defenseless*[a] *country. I will invade*[b] *peaceable folk who all*[c] *live securely, who live without walls and have no bars or gates.'* [12]*Your motive will be to loot and plunder, to raise your*[a] *hand against ruins that have been repopulated and against a people who have been gathered from among other nations, who have now acquired livestock and other property and live at the center of the earth.* [13]*Sheba and Dedan and the merchants of Tarshish and all its*

traders[a] *will ask you: 'Is looting the reason you are invading? Is plunder the reason why you have mobilized your company? Is it to get gold and silver, to carry off livestock and other property and so to acquire a lot of loot?'* [14]*Prophesy therefore, human one, and tell Gog that here is the Lord Yahweh's message: At that coming time, when my people Israel are living securely, you will be prompted to make a move,*[a] *won't you?* [15]*You will leave your home in the farthest north, you and many peoples with you, all mounted on horseback, a huge company, an enormous army.* [16]*You will attack my people Israel, covering the country like a cloud. Yes, when the time comes, I will send you to invade my country, with the intent that the other nations may acknowledge me when they see me using you, Gog,*[a] *to reveal my transcendent holiness.*[b]

[17] *"The Lord Yahweh's message is as follows: You are*[a] *the one of whom I was speaking in past history through my servants, the prophets of Israel who prophesied in those days,*[b] *promising that I would induce you to invade them.*

[18] *"At that future time, when Gog invades the land of Israel—so runs the Lord Yahweh's oracle—my fury will be aroused, along with my anger* [19]*and my passion.*[a] *In my fiery rage I declare that a severe earthquake will befall the land of Israel at that time.* [20]*My presence will convulse the fish in the sea, the birds in the sky and the beasts of the countryside, all the reptiles that crawl on the ground and all the human beings on the earth. Mountains will be overthrown, steep places*[a] *will collapse and every wall will fall to the ground.* [21]*I will summon against him every sword,*[a] *runs the Lord Yahweh's oracle: every man's sword will be directed against his comrade.* [22]*I will enter into judgment with him, using plague and bloodshed. Drenching rain and hailstones, fire and brimstone will I pour down upon him and his hordes and the many peoples with him.* [23]*I will reveal myself in my greatness and in my transcendent holiness, and communicate my presence visibly to many nations, and they will learn that I am Yahweh.*

[39:1] *"Now you, human one, are to counter Gog with a prophecy, telling him that the message of the Lord Yahweh is as follows: I am your adversary, Gog, chief officer of Meshech and Tubal.* [2]*I will repel*[a] *you, having led you along*[b] *and brought you up from the farthest north to invade the mountains of Israel,* [3]*only to strike your bow out of your left hand and dash your arrows out of your right.* [4]*The mountains of Israel will be the place where you fall, you and all your hordes and the peoples*[a] *with you. I will*[b] *give orders for you to be eaten by birds of prey of every kind*[c] *and by*[d] *wild beasts.* [5]*You will fall on the battlefield, I promise (so runs the Lord Yahweh's oracle).* [6]*I will launch fire against Magog*[a] *and the secure denizens of the coastlands, and then they will learn that I am Yahweh.* [7]*My people Israel will be the setting for the revelation of my holy name. I will allow that holy name of mine to be desecrated no longer, and the nations will learn that I am Yahweh, the one who is holy in Israel.* [8]*It will come to pass and become actual fact (so runs the Lord Yahweh's oracle): that is the day I foretold.* [9]*The people who live in Israel's cities will come out and set fire to the weaponry and burn it, bows*[a] *and arrows, hand javelins and spears. They will take seven years to burn them up.* [10]*They will have no need to bring wood from the countryside or cut it down from the woods because they will use the weapons as fuel for fires. It will be the plunder they take from their plunderers, their loot from those who looted them. So runs the Lord Yahweh's oracle.* [11]*At that time I will provide Gog with a burial place there*[a] *in Israel, the valley of Abarim,*[b] *east of the (Dead) Sea. It will be blocked off*[c] *and Gog and his entire army will be buried there, and it will be given the name 'Gog's Army Valley.'* [12]*The community of Israel will take seven months to bury them, as a means of decontaminating the country.* [13]*Everybody in the land will be responsible for the burying and it will redound to their honor, on the day when I am revealed in my glory. So runs the Lord Yahweh's oracle.* [14] *A full-time group of people will be assigned to the respective tasks of touring the country and burying*[a] *any left lying on the ground, with a view to decontaminating the country. They are to carry on searching until seven months are up.* [15] *As the search party*[a] *tours the country, they are to erect a marker beside any human bones they see, for the burial party to bury them in Gog's Army Valley,* [16] *leaving*[a] *the country decontaminated.*

[17] *"Now you, human one—what follows is a message from the Lord Yahweh*[a]*—are to proclaim to every kind of bird and to every wild beast: Congregate and come, gather from everywhere around to my sacrificial feast that I am holding for you, a huge sacrifice on Israel's mountains. Eat flesh and drink blood.* [18] *The flesh of warriors is to be your food, and the blood of national leaders your drink, all of them so many rams, sheep and goats, bulls*[a] *and Bashan fatlings.* [19] *You are to eat fat till you are full and drink blood till you are sated, partaking of my sacrificial feast I have held for you.* [20] *You are to eat to the full at my table—horses and chargers,*[a] *officers and soldiers: so runs the Lord Yahweh's oracle.*

[21] *"I will manifest my glory to the nations: all nations will view my judgment that I will have carried out and the effects of my hand laid on them.* [22] *From that time onward the community of Israel will know that I am Yahweh their God.*

[23] *"The nations will become aware that iniquity was the reason for the exile of Israel's community, because they were so faithless to me that I hid my face from them and handed them over to their foes to be victims of the sword.* [24] *I treated them as their impurity and rebellious ways warranted, and so I hid my face from them.*

[25] *"This then is the message from the Lord Yahweh: Now I will restore Judah's fortunes*[a] *and show affection to all the community of Israel out of passionate concern for my holy name.* [26] *They will take seriously*[a] *their humiliation and their faithlessness to me, when they live securely on their own soil, free from care,* [27] *when I have brought them back from among other peoples, gathering them from the countries of their enemies, and have used them to reveal my transcendent holiness to the nations.*[a] [28] *They will realize that I am Yahweh their God when, after exiling*[a] *them to other nations, I bring them together on their own soil, not leaving behind any of them there.* [29] *No longer will I hide my face from them, once I have*[a] *poured out my spirit*[b] *on the community of Israel. So runs the oracle of the Lord Yahweh."*

Notes

2. a. MT adds ארץ המגוג "in/to (?) the land of Magog," which intrudes between "Gog" and the appositional phrase (contrast v 3; 39:1) and is to be regarded as an early gloss inspired by 39:6. The ancient versions attest it; the omission in the hexaplaric LXX[62] is probably a case of oversight due to homoeoteleuton. Driver's interpretation of MT as "Gog of the land of Magog" (*JBL* 73 [1954] 127) is unlikely: cf. M. Tsevat, *HUCA* 36 (1965) 54 note 36. The article is awkward: was the earlier form of the gloss ארצה מגוג "Magog is his land"?

2. b. So the masoretic accentuation interprets ראש: contrast the first accent in the listing of v 5a. For the double construct cf. GKC 127a(d). For the phrase cf. כהן הראש "chief priest" at 2 Kgs 25:18, etc. (cf. J. R. Bartlett, *VT* 19 [1969] 5-7). LXX Θ Σ transliterated as Ρως, regarding as the name of a country, "Rosh" (= NEB), while ΔA Syr Vg Tg took as "head, chief" (=KJV,RSV). "The only known ancient geographical name that would resemble the alleged Rōʹs is Rāšu (or Αραšι) of neo-Assyrian records, a district on the border of Babylonia and Elam . . ., which had nothing in common with Meshech and Tubal" (Astour, *JBL* 95 [1976] 567 note 4). Accordingly one has to accept a difficult, but not impossible, grammatical construction (cf. GKC 130f, note 4, 135n). Price (*Grace Theological Journal* 6 [1985] 67-89) made the construction unnecessarily difficult by regarding ראש as an adj rather than a noun.

3. a. For the formulaic אדני "Lord" here and in vv 10, 14, 17, 18, 21; 39:1, 5, 8, 10, 13, 17, 20, 25, 29 see the note on 20:3.

4. a. MT prefaces with "And I will repel you and put hooks in your jaws," most of which is not represented in LXX (see below) and is very probably a gloss (Fohrer 213; Zimmerli 284). It is significant that the first verb recurs in 39:2 in a similar context. Most probably a gloss intended for 39:2 was misplaced here because of the similarity of context. It was seemingly intended as an explanation of the hapax legomenon וְשֹׁבַבְתִּיךָ "and I will lead you along." The first verb functions as a cue word. The interpretation was borrowed from 29:4a; it was encouraged by the presence of וְהַעֲלִיתִיךָ "and I will bring you up" in 29:4bα and 39:2aβ and of עַל־פְּנֵי הַשָּׂדֶה תִּפּוֹל "on the ground you will fall" in 29:5aβ and 39:5aα, and also by the similarity of 29:5b and 39:4b. Here in LXX* καὶ συνάξω "and I will gather" stands for וְהוֹצֵאתִי ... וְשֹׁבַבְתִּיךָ "and I will repel you . . . and bring out." Cornill (422), citing 2 Sam 10:16 LXX, argued that LXX* lacked v 4a (cf. BHS). However, the use of συνάξω for וְשֹׁבַבְתִּי in 39:2 complicates matters (cf. Zimmerli, ibid.). Most probably at some stage in the LXX's Vorlage a full text like that of MT had been revised against a shorter text but carelessly a wrong run of words was struck out, viz. וְהוֹצֵאתִי ... וְנִתַתִּי "and I will put . . . and bring out."

4. b. The verb has a military connotation (Lutz, Yahweh 76; cf. BDB 424b).

4. c. MT adds without coordination "body shield and small shield, wielding swords, all of them." The first term is not suitable for cavalry (Cornill, ibid.; perhaps for this reason Syr Vg have "spears") and the change of number and construction in the last phrase is suspicious. The words appear to be an explanatory gloss on מִכְלוֹל "panoply" (Herrmann 238; Cooke 415-16 et al.), with כֻּלָּם "all of them" functioning as a cue word; תֹּפְשֵׂי "wielding," not represented in LXX, may be a separate comparative gloss: cf. Jer 46:9 כּוּשׁ וּפוּט תֹּפְשֵׂי מָגֵן "Cush and Put wielding small shield(s)." The last term may have been inspired by v 21. For the first two terms LXX appears to presuppose מָגֵן וְכוֹבַע "small shield and helmet," as in v 5b.

5. a. MT (cf. versions) adds ungrammatically כֻּלָּם מָגֵן וְכוֹבַע "all of them shield and helmet," which appears to be a variant of the weapons in v 4, with כֻּלָּם "all of them" functioning as an initial cue word (Herrmann 238 et al.). The variant is attested in v 4bβ by the LXX (see previous note).

6. a. Cf. the use of אֵת to introduce the second part of a subject in Samaritan Heb. (cf. J. Macdonald, VT 14 [1964] 268-76). The difference from v 6aα and the fact that the place name and first accompanying phrase balance v 6aα may indicate that the second phrase is a gloss (Zimmerli 285).

7. a. Heb. הָכֵן וְהָכֵן "prepare and make preparation" has assonance characteristic of Ezek: cf. the examples in Zimmerli (286).

7. b. Heb. לָהֶם לְמִשְׁמָר "(and be) on the watch for them." Driver (Bib 35 [1954] 303-4) took the noun as "something kept under observation" and so "rallying point." LXX implies לִי, with the apparent sense "Be on the watch for me, await my command," which fits well the command of v 7a (Zimmerli, ibid.) and is often adopted. But perhaps MT is to be preferred as the harder reading, with the sense of taking charge, as an example of readiness.

8. a. Heb. בְּאַחֲרִית הַשָּׁנִים "at the end of the years" is a variant of the more common בְּאַחֲרִית הַיָּמִים "at the end of the days," which replaces it in v 16. It refers not to an eschatological finale (cf. 39:22) but to a second phase of Israel's future after the first phase of return from exile and resettlement in the land (Hossfeld, Untersuchungen 440-41; cf. in general H. Kosmala, ASTI 2 [1963] 27-37).

8. b. Lit. "it," the country standing for the people. For the omission of the two clauses in Syr see Zimmerli, ibid.

9. a. In MT תָּבוֹא "you will come" and תִּהְיֶה "you will be" appear to be alternatives (Wevers 202): Syr Vg omit the second, which may be a comparative gloss from v 16, taking תִּהְיֶה there not as 3rd fem sg but as 2nd masc, as Vg (and Driver, Bib 19 [1938] 183) did.

9. b. Heb. אוֹתְךָ is a stylistic variant of אִתְּךָ "with you": cf. BDB 85b.

11. a. Lit. "a country of (unwalled) villages."

11. b. The verb בוֹא in the sense "attack" can take a direct object, elsewhere a suffix (e.g., 32:11). A more natural division would be שְׁקָטִים אָבוֹאָה, with a coh form following אֶעֱלֶה "I will invade" and an anarthrous object (Ehrlich, Randglossen 137).

11. c. Heb. כֻּלָּם "all of them" is perhaps better taken with v 11a. Then there is a metrical balance in the three clauses; for the order cf. vv 4, 8, 15 (Hossfeld 415).

12. a. LXX "my hand" continues the quotation.

13. a. MT כְּפִרֶיהָ "its lions, rulers" (cf. 32:2) is strange in this context. LXX Θ Syr interpreted as כְּפָרֶיהָ (= RSV) "its villages." An emendation רֹכְלֶיהָ "its traders" (Toy 67 et al.) is plausible, assuming an insertion of פ for sense after corruption to כֹּרֶיהָ (וְכֹל־), but a simpler suggestion would be כֹּרֶיהָ "its traders": since the stem is not used elsewhere in Ezek, it would be liable to adaptation.

14. a. MT תֵּדַע "you will know, be taught a lesson" is generally emended to תֵּעֹר "you will be aroused" with the support of LXX and assumption of a ר/ד error and metathesis. The sequence לָבֶטַח תֵּדַע may have been influenced by לָבֶטַח וְיָדְעוּ in the next column (39:6); or תֵּדַע may have originated as a

comparative gloss relating to the formula in 39:5b , with 5:13; 17:21 (cf. 6:10) in view, which subsequently displaced the similar-looking תער. Cf. usage of the niph verb in a "foe from the north" passage of Jer 6:22; cf. the hiph in Ezek 23:22.

16. a. The absence of the vocative from LXX* Syr and its seeming alternative representation within v 17 in LXX* (see *BHS*) may indicate that it was originally an explanatory gloss on אתה "you" in v 17.

16. b. For this non-Ezekielian version of an extended recognition formula see Zimmerli, *Ezekiel 1* 39.

17. a. MT האתה "are you?" is generally emended to a statement אתה "you are," assuming dittography of *he*, with the support of LXX Syr Vg. The change to a question had v 14 in view, but then הלא "are (you) not?" would be necessary (Cornill 425).

17. b. MT (cf. versions) adds שנים "years," presumably as an alternative to ימים "days" (Talmon, *Textus* 1 [1960] 171). It probably originated as an early gloss on באחרית הימים "at the end of the days" (v 16), comparing באחרית השנים "at the end of the years" in v 8, and was placed beside the wrong ימים.

19. a. Sentence re-division seems necessary with LXX (cf. *BHS*); cf. 35:11.

20. a. Perhaps terraces constructed on hillsides: see Zimmerli 289.

21. a. MT prefaces with הרי "my mountains." LXX* has φόβον "fear" for הרי חרב, which could presuppose חֲרָדָה, read by many but rightly doubted by Ehrlich (*Randglossen* 139) and Cooke (417). It is more likely that out of the sequence הרי חרב some sense was wrested by understanding as הרהב "frighten" (cf. KB 876a). Ehrlich's suggestion to delete הרי as a dittograph of חר(ב) may be refined: הרי appears to be an adapted torso, whereby הר was written for חר under the influence of ההרים ונהרסו in v 20, then abandoned and adapted to הרי for a modicum of sense.

39:2. a. The meaning of this polel form is disputed: see the summary of discussion in Hossfeld, *Untersuchungen* 462. The sense that the hiph may bear (BDB 999b) fits well here.

2. b. The verbs after the first one appear to have a parenthetic recapitulating force until v 3 (Hölscher, *Dichter* 184 note 6). The consec pf need not imply temporal sequence: see Joüon 119e, f (cf. 118h-j). The verb שׁשׁא is a *hapax legomenon*, related to Eth. *sosawa* "walk along" (KB 1013).

4. a. In 38:6, 9 the recurring phrase includes רבים "many," which many MSS and LXX^967 L Syr Tg insert; the shortening appears to be stylistic.

4. b. For the fut reference see GKC 106n.

4. c. For the idiom see GKC 130e.

4. d. The earlier preposition does double duty (cf. GKC 119hh; Hossfeld, *Untersuchungen* 421, contra *BHS*).

6. a. LXX* "Gog" for "Magog," read by Eichrodt (518), is an inferior reading: see Zimmerli 315. "Magog" occurs in Gen 10:2 along with Meshech and Tubal.

9. a. MT prefaces with ומגן וצנה "and small shield and big shield." The lack of preposition suggests that the phrase relating to defensive weapons is a gloss (cf. 38:4; Zimmerli 291; Wevers 204). LXX Syr Vg unaccountably render the second noun "spears."

11. a. C LXX Vg attest a variant שֵׁם "name" ("a famous" or "memorial place") for שָׁם "there," but MT is usually preferred, as a short relative clause: "a place where there is a grave in Israel" (cf. GKC 130c, d).

11. b. MT הָעֹבְרִים "(valley of) the travelers, passers by" has probably suffered assimilation to the term in v 15 and was originally הָעֲבָרִים "Abarim," a mountainous district in Moab, as the Coptic version interpreted and as J. D. Michaelis suggested (cf. BDB 717b, 720b). Although Moab was not in Israel, it did belong to the Davidic empire (2 Sam 8:2; cf. Josh 1:4). Ribichini and Xella (*UF* 12 [1980] 434-37) have claimed Ug. support for a reference to the dead as having passed away, so that the place fittingly describes a cemetery.

11. c. MT has את-העברים היא והסמת "and it will stop the passers by/ tourers," but LXX Syr imply את-הגיא והסמת "and they will stop up the valley," which is preferable (Hitzig 297 et al.). In MT את-העברים "the tourers" is to be explained as a gloss on בית ישראל "community of Israel" in v 12 (for את introducing a gloss see Driver, *L'Ancien Testament et l'Orient* 127, with reference to 4:1, unless it here means "together with"), in an attempt to square the two sets of burial descriptions (cf. v 15). It was wrongly set next to וקברו "and they will bury" rather than near וקברום "and they will bury them" in v 12. The 3rd pl verb והסמו suits the next two verbs. MT may have been corrupted after the gloss entered the text.

14. a. For the circumstantial use of the two ptcp forms see Cooke 424. The asyndeton may well refer to a subdivision into two groups (cf. v 15; Hossfeld, *Untersuchungen* 475). MT adds את-העברים "(with ?) the tourers," unrepresented in one MS and LXX* Syr. It is to be explained in the same way as in v 11. In this case it was meant to qualify כל-עם הארץ "all the people in the land" in v 13, but was linked with מקברים "bury" here rather than with וקברו "and they shall bury" there.

15. a. Lit. "the tourers."

16. a. MT prefaces with ‏וגם שם-עיר המונה‎ "and also the name of a city is Hamonah," generally acknowledged as a gloss, even by Barthélemy et al., *Preliminary and Interim Report on the Hebrew OT*, vol. 5, 130. Driver, *Bib* 19 (1938) 184, with typical rearrangement of consonants, suggested ‏וְנָמֵר שָׁמַע הָמוֹנֹה‎ "and the fame of his multitude will come to an end" (cf. NEB), developing earlier suggestions made by Hitzig and Cornill. But this, like MT, interrupts the context. MT seems to represent two glosses relating to v 11 and misplaced here due to the presence of ‏גיא המון גוג‎ "valley of Gog's army" in both vv 11b and 15b. The first two words "also name" were a comment on ‏שם‎ "there," indicating the variant (see note). The second pair of words was originally ‏המונה‎ (‏עמים רבים‎=) ‏ע/ר‎ "his army: many nations," indicating that earlier the phrase had accompanied a reference to Gog (cf. 38:15 and also 38:6, 9, 22; 39:4).

17. a. For the unusual placing of the messenger formula cf. 21:33.

18. a. For the accentuation see Zimmerli 294.

20. a. Heb. ‏רכב‎ usually means "chariots," an unlikely part of the menu. It appears to mean here "chariot horses," as in 2 Sam 8:4.

25. a. See the note on 29:14.

26. a. MT ‏ונשו‎ implies a short writing of ‏ונשאו‎ "and they will bear," read by a few MSS and implied by the ancient versions (cf. 28:16; GKC 75qq). Hitzig's proposal to read ‏ונשו‎ "and they will forget" (301) has been widely adopted (cf. BHS, RSV, NEB, NJB). Zimmerli (295), however, has noted that the verb never occurs in Ezek, while ‏נשא כלמה‎ with the sense of "bear shame" is common, and also that the sequence "change fortunes . . . bear shame" occurs in 16:54, with the latter phrase being evidently used as here.

27. a. MT adds ‏רבים‎ "many" ungrammatically; it is unexpected and unwanted in comparison with the stylistic counterpart in 38:23, and the nonrepresentation in LXX* suggests its secondary nature. The reading of a few MSS, ‏גוים רבים‎ "many nations," is a correction of MT. It appears to be a comparative gloss relating to 38:23.

28. a. For the variant vocalization underlying LXX see Zimmerli, ibid.

29. a. Lit. "(I) who will have . . ."; LXX Vg interpreted more specifically as causal, "because."

29. b. LXX τὸν θυμόν μου "my anger" is most probably an exegetical interpretation (pace Lust, *Ezekiel and His Book* 52-53; cf. the equivalence in Isa 59:19; Zech 6:8; Prov 18:14; 29:11). It relates v 29bα to the past experience of judgment in defeat and exile, in reminiscence of vv 23-24 and also 36:17-19 that in v 18 uses the phrase ‏ואשפך חמתי‎ "and I poured out my wrath" (cf. the motif of uncleanness in both v 24 and 36:17). However, as Cornill (433) observed, 36:27 and the whole context favor a positive sense.

Form/Structure/Setting

These two chapters form a single complex introduced by the message reception formula, with the single theme of a future invasion of the land of Israel and Yahweh's resounding victory. The complexity and size of the unit make an initial investigation of its structuring expedient. Taylor (242), followed by Stuart (352), has found in the repetition of the messenger formula a clue that the unit is made up of seven oracles so introduced in 38:3, 10, 14, 17; 39:1, 17, 25. However, 39:23-24 appear to belong with vv 25-29 in view of the recurring motif of Yahweh's hiding his face (vv 23, 24, 29), and so the messenger formula has an intermediate role within a larger subunit. Moreover, 38:17 hardly introduces a subunit vv 17-23: v 18, with its supplemental reference "on that day," appears to begin afresh. The repeated messenger formula functions as a stylistic drumbeat of divine control rather than as a strict structural marker.

Parunak (*Structural Studies* 490-91) has seen a fourfold structure, introduced in each case by the vocative ‏בן-אדם‎ "human one," in 38:2, 14; 39:1, 17. However, Hossfeld (*Untersuchungen* 406) has argued convincingly that the instance in 38:14 belongs to a subunit vv 10-16: he notes especially the initial ‏לכן‎ "therefore," which links with the foregoing. One might then envisage a threefold structure, signaled by the initial oracular introductions of 38:2; 39:1, 17. Zimmerli's position (296-99; so Garscha, *Studien* 237) is similar to this: in redactional terms he finds three original "strophes," which were subsequently amplified with further material. The basic text, 38:1-9; 39:1-5, 17-20, is characterized by individual repeated phrases relating respectively to Gog's forces (38:6, 9), Gog's falling "on Israel's mountains/on the ground" (39:4, 5) and Yahweh's "sacrifice" (vv 17, 19). Lutz (*Jahweh, Jerusalem* 65 note 10), however, has noted an inconsistency in Zimmerli's treatment, in that he also characterizes the second occurrence of the special phrase in the first strophe (38:9bβ) as a gloss (Zimmerli 287)! Closer examination discloses that the third strophe is of quite a different kind than the two earlier ones, which are marked initially by extensive parallelism (38:2; 39:1). Accordingly one might envisage a twofold scheme, as the chapter division evidently does. But there are two further pointers to a threefold division. The first is the presence of climactic references to the fulfillment of a prophesied event or day in 38:17 and 39:8, which appear to be capped in 39:22. A second is the reference to Yahweh's vindication in 38:16, 23; 39:7, 13 and 39:21, 27.

One cannot analyze structure without consideration of redaction. The overall unit looks like a kaleidoscope of facets of Gog's invasion and his defeat. Although superficially it moves from invasion to conquest, it lacks logical coherence: most obviously, the command to birds and beasts in 39:17-20 to devour the dead develops the statement in v 4b, but meanwhile they have been buried, in vv 11-16! The repatriated people lack walls in 38:11, but walls figure in the destruction of 38:20. The reference to Yahweh's destructive judgment in 38:18-23 anticipates Gog's downfall in 39:3-5. Taylor (247) denied redaction in these chapters (cf. Block, *VT* 37 [1987] 263), but it is not insignificant that a pattern of redactional growth has been detected in recent chapters, especially chaps. 34, 36 and 37, and this phenomenon suggests that the evidence of tension be so explained here. Indeed, Taylor's redactional characterization of chap. 34 admirably fits the Gog unit: "If the chapter is taken as a whole, it will appear full of inconsistencies, but if each section is taken separately, it will be obvious that new ideas are being added all along" (222). In this case, as Zimmerli has argued, a basic threefold unit has been successively amplified. There is emphasis throughout on the prophetic/ divine authority of the amplifications by means of the messenger formula and the divine saying formula.

As to the hypothetical basic core, Lutz (*Jahweh, Jerusalem* 65) has whittled down Zimmerli's three strophes to two, regarding 38:1-9 as a copy of 39:1-5 in form and content (cf. Wevers [201] who regards 39:1-4, 6 as the original core; earlier Herrmann [249] and Hölscher, *Hesekiel* 178, 186-87, had regarded 39:17-20 as secondary). Hossfeld (*Untersuchungen* 444, 481, 497, 499-504) considers 38:3b-9 and 39:17-20 as early expansions of an original 38:1-3a and 39:1b-5 respectively. He derives support for his hypothesis from the fact that together these passages exhibit the form of a foreign oracle very like Ezekiel's other oracles against the nations, especially 25:1-5; 26:1-5a; 28:1-10; 29:1-6, and in fact Hossfeld identifies it as a pre-587 B.C. oracle of his. Hossfeld's form-critical observation is striking and clearly gives him the edge over Lutz's assessment of the whole of 38:1-9 as secondary. However, there is danger in confusing form criticism and redaction criticism: development of a basic form does not necessarily imply separate literary accretion. It is safer to envisage a larger core of basic Gog material that is modeled on the form of a standard foreign oracle but manifesting a development of its own. As elsewhere in the prophets (see S. DeVries, *Yesterday* 297-310, esp. 306-7), a clue to supplementary material is the use of ביום ההוא "on that day" (38:10, 14, 18; 39:11, 21). Hossfeld (*Untersuchungen* 432, 469, 485, 505-7) shows interesting alignment of supplementary material, viz. 38:10-16; 39:6-7 and 21-22, as a parallel set of revisions that is concerned with Yahweh's vindication, and also 38:18-23 and 39:11-16, which both begin in the same way, mention Gog in the third person and also refer to the vindication of Yahweh. Hossfeld (*Untersuchungen* 506) has linked the latter sequence with the relatively late oracle against Sidon in 28:20-23 (compare 38:22 with 28:23; 39:13 with 28:22a [but compare also 38:16bβ with 28:22b]). He also parallels the independent 38:17 with 39:8-10 (ibid.), but 38:17 and 39:8 with their emphasis on prophecy fulfilled make a better match. 39:9-10, lacking an introduction, aligns with vv 6-7 and so with related units.

Most would agree with Hossfeld that 39:23-29 functions as a redactional epilogue (*Untersuchungen* 408, 429). The precise beginning of the final unit has been disputed, but a major break does seem to occur with v 23, while v 22 makes a climactic conclusion. As Block has clearly shown (*VT* 37 [1987] 266-70), the final unit serves to integrate the Gog unit with the message of chaps. 33-37. In terminology it is especially close to 28:25-26 (see Hossfeld, *Untersuchungen* 493, 508), which belongs to the final redactional layer of the book; both passages have the character of compendiums. It also uses language new to the book but familiar outside it: Yahweh's hiding his face (cf. 7:22), צריהם "their foes" (cf. the uncertain case in 30:16), רחם "show affection," (ה) גלה "go/send into exile" (cf. 3:3, on which see Hossfeld, *Untersuchungen* 485) and כנס "gather" (cf. the gloss in 22:21). The epilogue presumably serves to express what was already latent in the earlier compilation, the final security of God's people in the face of the worst of threats, as well as to reaffirm the fundamental promise of return to the land.

As to authorship, scholars tend to attribute the basic core, however they define it, to Ezekiel and the subsequent layers to his school. It is probable that some of the layers are to be assigned to Ezekiel's hand. It is not possible to find a historical occasion in the early exile that triggered the basic oracle, although clear links with Jeremiah's "foe from the north" oracles afford a parallel with Ezekiel's evident dependence on Jeremiah elsewhere.

Comment

38:1-6 Meshech and Tubal were two nations in Cappadocia, in the northeast sector of Asia Minor. They were characterized in 32:26 as a bygone power in the world, along with Assyria and Elam (and in 27:13 as engaged in metal trading). Here they are regarded as resurgent, an old menace come back to haunt their southern neighbors. Until they were destroyed by the Cimmerians, they were a threat to the Assyrians in the reign of Sargon toward the end of the eighth century, and probably this memory, current in Babylonia, had reached the Jewish exiles. Here they are under the authority of "Gog," who has been given preeminent power over his fellow leaders. The name seems to relate to one known to the Greeks as Gyges and to the Assyrians as Gugu, who was a powerful king of Lydia in west Asia Minor in the first half of the seventh century. As with the national names, so here a great figure of the past is evidently used to define a future threat, as we might speak fearfully of a new Hitler. The complementary influence of a popular Babylonian legend of invasion from Asia Minor has also been suggested (Astour, *JBL* 95 [1976] 567-79).

Dire though this mysterious threat is intended to be, it is firmly set in the comforting context of a judgment oracle against foreign nations. Although the enemy is a figure of the future, rather than a present entity as elsewhere, Ezekiel is to formally look in his geographical direction (cf. 21:2 *Comment*) and indicate Yahweh's hostility in a formula of encounter. The oracle does not continue in a standard message of destruction until the form is resumed and developed in 39:1-5 (cf. Zimmerli 307-8). Instead, the enveloping of threat with assurance is continued with a positive message that the hostile movements of Gog's enormous army are masterminded by Yahweh. Its great numbers are further augmented by mercenary troops from the east and far south (cf. 27:10; 30:5 *Comment*) and by local allies, the Cimmerians ("Gomer") who had been in earlier history a threat to Assyria, and the people of Armenia ("Beth Togarmah").

7-9 The theme of Yahweh's control stated in v 4, is here stylistically developed in a summons to make preparations for Yahweh's signal to mount a future campaign. With rhetorical generalization reference is made to God's people duly returned from exile and resettled in a land that had been ravaged by destruction. The area is identified by the phrase "mountains of Israel," which is Ezekiel's standard way of referring to the Judeans' homeland. The rather labored conglomeration of phrases and clauses in v 8 serves to lay emphasis on a new era of security and the welcome putting down of new roots after a period of homelessness. Living in security becomes a key phrase in the overall unit (cf. vv 11, 14; 39:6, 26). Here it is threatened by the prospect of post-exilic invasion, but the context both before and after makes it clear that Yahweh would prove an adequate protection. The figurative references to storm and advancing rainclouds deliberately echo older prophetic threats, Isa 10:3 and Jer 4:13, which function as prototypes for this final onslaught against the land of God's people. The latter reference is significant, for it indicates Ezekiel's dependence on Jeremiah's early oracles concerning a foe from the north (Jer 4-6; compare the cavalry of v 4 with Jer 4:26; 6:23 as well as Isa 5:28). The piece ends with a refrain (cf. v 4b) harking back to the gigantic forces at Gog's disposal. But the ironic truth is that Gog is carrying out Yahweh's orders and operates within limits that Yahweh has set.

10-16 A fresh, supplementary oracle reiterates and develops the themes of Gog's invasion and Yahweh's overwhelming control. The verbs of invasion in vv 8 and 9 (תבוא "you will invade," ועלית "and you will advance") are repeated in vv 11, 13, 15 and 16a, and in v 16b are capped by the causative verb with Yahweh as subject, והבאותיך "and I will cause you to invade" (cf. v 4). The oracle is a triad of verbal statements, using אמר "say" four times with relation to the speaking of Gog (v 11), of foreign traders (v 13) and of Yahweh through his prophet (v 14, twice); בן-אדם "human one" is used here to identify the third significant party after Gog and the Sheba group.

This oracle, with its repetition of earlier vocabulary, clearly functions as a commentary on the earlier one, but its series of short speeches give it dramatic liveliness. The first of the three sections, in vv 10-12, builds on the use of Isa 10:3 in v 9 by echoing Isa 10:7 ("mind," "devise," "loot," "plunder"). Here is a counterpart of Sennacherib, who set his self-centered ambition to work—yet, as Isaiah declared, he was Yahweh's unwitting tool and doomed to destruction (Isa 10: 5, 12, 15, 16; Jer 49:30-33 seems also to have colored the passage). Gog is given enough rope to be eventually hung by. With unprovoked, brutal aggression he intends to take advantage of a defenseless people who have been given a new lease on life (v 8; cf. 36:10) and are enjoying a new freedom and prosperity. The exceptional nature of this people is indicated by their habitat at "the center (lit. "navel") of the earth," which appears to indicate their role as God's elect (cf. 5:5 with reference to Jerusalem; contra D. Sperling, *IDB Sup* 622-23, and Talmon, *TDOT* 3, 437-38, who both overreact against an older mythological emphasis). The reference to lack of fortifications conflicts with 36:35. If harmonization is necessary, this passage may envisage a period before fortifications were built (Fohrer 216; Wevers 203).

In the short middle section the world's traders by land and sea (cf. 27:12, 20, 22) lend their voices, as would-be customers hoping to buy up the expected booty. Their question serves to reinforce Gog's military aims. These aims function as a ground of accusation, which triggers the prophet's judgment oracle of vv 14-16 ("therefore"). It repeats the message of the basic oracle, that Gog's momentous invasion after Israel's return from exile would be at Yahweh's behest. A fresh "foe from the north" allusion is added in the emphatic verb of v 14, תֵעוֹר "you will be stirred up": in Jer 6:22 it occurs in parallelism with בּוֹא "come" (cf. v 15) and together with "the land of the north" and "the farthest places of the earth." The reference to election in v 12 is now given further and clearer expression in "my people" and "my land" (for the latter cf. Isa 14:25). The genre of vv 14-16 as a judgment oracle indicates their sinister nature, which is also reflected implicitly by the accusing notes of Yahweh's personal grievance and by Gog's role as Yahweh's dupe, and explicitly by the final statement of Yahweh's aim to use Gog to win further world recognition of his own divine status (cf. 28:22, 25; 36:23).

17 The use of older prophecies prompts an explanatory oracle that makes explicit the reasoning that underlies the literary echoes (cf. Fishbane, *Biblical Interpretation* 477, 514; Grech, *Augustinianum* 9 [1969] 248; Erling, *Ex Orbe Religionum*, vol. 1, 111-13). There is a distance between the writer and the past prophets that suggests a period later than Ezekiel himself. Moreover, the phrase "my servants the prophets" has a deuteronomistic ring. There is a canonical assumption that, although the prophets spoke for their own times, their words were not exhausted in earlier fulfillments: there was an overplus of meaning, a typological pattern to be realized at a still later time. One may compare Joel's insistence that Obadiah's "day of Yahweh" was not consummated in the tragedy of 587 B.C. but found a comparable encore in a locust plague that threatened to wipe out the community. In such Old Testament antecedents lie the seeds of the New Testament's treatment of earlier scriptures.

18-23 A further supplementary oracle follows, which wants to build on vv 10-16. It subdivides into a divinely oriented framework consisting of vv 18-19a and 23, and a double center, vv 19b-20 and 21-22, in which Yahweh's instruments of judgment have as their targets "the land of Israel" and "Gog" respectively (cf. Hossfeld, *Untersuchungen* 418, 451-59). Gog's brazen proposal (דְּבָרִים "words," v 10) finds a response in Yahweh's own proposal (דִּבַּרְתִּי "I promise," v 19), while its "coming" to mind (יַעֲלוּ "will come," v 10) corresponds to the surge of Yahweh's anger (תַעֲלֶה "will be aroused," v 18). So the oracle presents Yahweh's vehement counter declaration. Gog's military destination, "the land of Israel" (vv 18, 19), would be the scene of a theophany of judgment that caused cataclysmic devastation (cf. esp. Jer 4:23-26, which appears to be in mind). In the context the sole victims of the theophany are Gog and his forces (vv 21, 22). Earthquake, self-destruction, plague and a gamut of celestial devices would be the versatile means of Gog's downfall and so of Yahweh's vindication. "Great" forces (v 15) would be met by a "great" earthquake (v 19) and by proof of Yahweh's greatness (v 23). The series of supplements to the basic oracle is drawn to a stylistic close by echoes of the refrain of vv 6 and 9 in v 22, and of the world recognition of v 16 in v 23.

39:1-5 The form of a foreign oracle is now resumed from 38:2-3 and brought to completion. In fact the content of vv 1-2 is a recapitulation of 38:2-4, while the reference to Gog's forces in v 4 picks up the refrain of 38:6 and 9. Now, however, the earlier material is associated explicitly with judgment. The divine encounter with Gog (v 1) would result in his weapons being dashed from his hands and in his military destination (38:8) becoming the scene of defeat and of dishonor for his corpse, like a second Pharaoh (29:5).

6-7 The previous oracle is supplemented with material that recalls 38:10-16 and may be from the same hand. The war is to be carried into the enemy country. The phrase "send fire" is an old expression for divine judgment (Amos 1:12; Hos 8:14; cf. Ezek 21:3). "Magog" is the people or country of Gog. The tables are to be turned: invasion of a people living in security is to be met with destruction of Gog's secure neighbors in the western coastlands of Asia Minor, as proof of the universal power of Yahweh (cf. 38:16). And Yahweh's coming to the aid of the nation allied to him in covenant (cf. 38:14) would bring about the vindication of his transcendent holiness anticipated in 38:16. The motif of clearing Yahweh's holy name from profanation is borrowed from the theological justification of the termination of exile (cf. 36:20-23). It serves to provide a cast-iron warranty of Israel's deliverance.

8 This appears to be a separate amplification akin to that in 38:17; it uses the terms of 21:12(7)bβ. Whereas 38:17 focused on Gog's invasion, now his defeat is celebrated as the long-range fulfillment of Yahweh's prophetic word. Like the motif used in v 7, the claim brings assurance that Israel had nothing to fear from the worst of foreign foes.

9-10 This self-contained unit, concluded by a divine saying formula, is appended without introduction, like vv 6-7; it may have been an addition from the same hand. But now Israel's work, rather than Yahweh's, is in view. The "fire" of v 6 becomes a catchword, used here twice, and the theme of turning the tables continues. Gog's intent to plunder (38:12, 13) would be reversed, as his troops' wooden weapons are seized and burned. Israel, hitherto safe in its cities, engages in mopping up operations. The motif of burning weapons, which represents the sealing of Gog's fate, was doubtless taken over from the Songs of Zion (Pss 46:10 [9]; 76:4 [3]; cf. B. C. Ollenburger, *Zion the City of the Great King*, JSOTS 41 [Sheffield: Sheffield Academic Press, 1987] 141-44; cf. the transference of the "navel" motif from Jerusalem [5:5] to the land in 38:12). The seven years' period of burning the firewood refers obliquely back to the overwhelming size of Gog's forces, now ironically with reference to the aftermath of their destruction.

11-16 This supplementary unit is parallel to 38:18-23, although its interests are priestly rather than prophetic. It falls into two halves, vv 11-13 and 14-16, with v 13b providing an interim climax. It flows from the foregoing material in that

Yahweh's provision for disposal of the human remains (v 4) is continued: the eating of flesh is followed by the burial of bones (v 4 נתתיך "I will give you"; v 11 אתן לגוג "I will give for Gog"). Moreover, the numeral "seven" becomes a catchword, seven months of burial linking with seven years of burning, in both cases with threat-free reference to Gog's immense army. The dominant concerns of the unit are not only the burial of remains—the stem קבר "bury" occurs seven times—but also the ritual cleanness of the land, which is mentioned three times, in vv 12, 14 and climactically in v 16. The motif may have been triggered by mention of Yahweh's "holy name" and of Yahweh as "holy in Israel." The motifs of purity of the land and divine holiness are associated in 36:17-21. As in 36:18, contamination, here by human remains (cf. Num 19:11-22; Deut 21:1-9), is associated with the land. The decontamination would be a fitting and necessary corollary to God's triumph and so bring credit to its executors (v 13). It underscores from a cultic perspective the vindication of Yahweh. The seven-month task by the general population is followed scrupulously by the commissioning of a work party divided into two groups, one to flag extant remains and another to collect and bury them in the designated cemetery.

17-20 This prophetic unit, closed by the divine saying formula in v 20, appears to be the original development of v 4b and so the continuation of 39:1-5. It has been separated by redactional layers that parallel those in 38:10-23. Despite a lack of chronological sequencing, the unit provides a dramatic climax as the penultimate piece, before the epilogue was eventually appended. The symbolism of Yahweh's sacrifice, which provides a double refrain, is probably derived from Jer 46:10 (cf. Zeph 1:7; cf. Grill's study of the motif in *BZ* N.F. 2 [1958] 278-83), where it is significantly linked with "the north country." Now, however, the devouring and blood-sated sword is replaced by birds and beasts of prey, in line with v 4 (cf. Hossfeld, *Untersuchungen* 479). The gruesome metaphor signifies the satisfying coup de grace for the army that had earlier posed such a threat to "the mountains of Israel" (38:8; cf. 39:3, 4).

21-22 Such a finale effectively discouraged a trail of expansions such as the earlier basic units attracted. However, it was deemed appropriate to append a short, final and emphatic drawing of the moral of Yahweh's vindication. He would be vindicated in the eyes of the pagan world by means of his act of judgment (cf. 38:22) and retaliatory blow (cf. 38:12) against Gog and his international forces. And a direct lesson is drawn for Israel, the real audience of these oracles, that by the events of "that day" (cf. 39:8 and also the repeated supplemental "on that day") the covenant relationship between them and Yahweh would be fully and finally endorsed. The threat would serve to tighten rather than cut the bond of fellowship, to enhance rather than disrupt the covenant union. The affirmation coincides happily with an assurance linked with resettlement in the land in 34:30, 31; 36:28; 37:23.

23-29 In the final stage of the book the Gog prophecy in its expanded form has been integrated with its preceding context, so that the overall positive message of return to the land in chaps. 33-37 may not be obscured. An inclusion for this epilogue is provided by the striking description of Judah's defeat and exile in terms of Yahweh's hiding his face (vv 23-24, 29). In the final case it is denied in assuring tones of pastoral psychology, with the same לא . . . עוד ("no longer") construction that marked earlier chapters (34:10, 22, 29; 36:12, 14, 15, 30; 37:22; cf. 39:7). The divine face-hiding, which occurs only here in the book, implies a break in communication that in this context is the opposite of covenant intimacy (vv 22, 28). In prophetic literature, which took over the expression from the cultic lament, it relates to God's punishment of sin and especially to his judgment meted out in 587 B.C. (Isa 54:7-8; 64:6; Jer 33:5; cf. Mic 3:4); yet mostly it has a temporary duration that promises future restoration (Isa 8:17; 54:8; Jer 33:6-9; cf. Balentine, *The Hidden God* 65-76). It is used fittingly here as the prelude to a permanent new covenant relationship such as Isa 54:7-8 (cf. 9-10) predicates in more polarized terms.

The epilogue falls into two sections, vv 23-24, with negative emphasis on Israel's sin and its divine consequences, and vv 25-29, which positively stress Israel's restoration in both human and divine terms. A relation between the two phases of Yahweh's deliverance of his people, from exile and from subsequent invasion, is drawn first in v 23: the final proof of Yahweh's power evinced in the latter would shed light back on the destructive episode of the exile and make clear that even then he was in control. The parallelism between the two phases becomes explicit in the "now" of v 25, which serves as a counterpoint to the later phase of the Gog affair (cf. 38:8, 16; Block, *VT* 37 [1987] 265). Ezekiel's constant message is repeated, that destruction and deportation were nothing less than divine punishment of a guilty people: terms for the people's sin that are characteristic of Ezekiel abound in vv 23-24. But it was to be the prelude to a divinely occasioned turn of events—return from exile—that would find motivation both in his affectionate love and in his zealous desire to clear his profaned name (cf. v 7; 36:20-23). There is a rhetorical exuberance about the use of כל "all" in vv 23 and 25 (echoed in different terms in v 28b) that is matched in spirit by Paul's "As in Adam all die, so in Christ shall all be made alive" (1 Cor 15:22).

In v 26 a phrase of Ezekiel's, "bear humiliation," is adapted, as in 16:54 (cf. esp. 34:29; 36:6-7), to a new meaning of remorse for former sins, which Yahweh's gift of secure resettlement in the land would provoke. The lengthened emphasis on security repeats 34:28, with the hint that even the invasion of Gog would constitute no real threat to its continuance. The language of 38:8 is resumed in a reminder that before the Gog crisis and its resolution there was to take place a more fundamental act of deliverance, which like the later event (38:16) would reveal Yahweh's transcendent power to the world. Like that later event too (39:22), restoration from exile would prove to Israel his covenant relationship with them. It would be the beginning of a new era of favor, with the door firmly shut on Yahweh's former break in communication. The new age would be characterized by the gift of Yahweh's enabling spirit, as 36:26 and 37:14 had proclaimed. The verb "pour out" seems to be used to point an implicit contrast. The old era of destruction and exile is characteristically in Ezekiel and especially in 36:18 described as the outpouring of his wrath. The new era would be marked by equally lavish dealings of a positive nature. Thus the phrase has a different nuance from the cases in Isa 44:3; Joel 3:1 (2:28); Zech 12:10.

In the renewal of covenant blessing for "the community of Israel" (vv 28-29), the epilogue has reverted to the older ending of the Gog unit in v 22. However, the readers' attention has been diverted to the more basic work of salvation Yahweh was to perform. The implication is that it would be a work that the worst onslaught of alien forces was powerless to undo. As 28:25-26 had affirmed the security of the resettled people of God in relation to neighboring nations, so the epilogue promises it in the face of a terrible onslaught from afar.

Explanation

The Gog unit is proto-apocalyptic in its forward look into a distant future. It is "an example of apocalyptic taking off but still touching the runway" (Grech, *BZ* N.F. 2 [1958] 249). A new period within human history is under consideration, rather than a transcendental age inaugurated by a decisive break with that history. Two phases of the new period are envisaged. The first is marked by the repatriation of the exiled people, to enjoy secure lives in their own land. The second, after a considerable interval of time, is characterized by the combating of a foreign invasion that seemed to threaten Israel's security, but provided an opportunity for a miraculous intervention that both glorified Yahweh and successfully put Israel's safety to the test. The invasion thus has the function of a fire drill to test the system and hopefully confirm its efficiency.

The re-use of motifs associated with Jerusalem (38:12; 39:9-10) suggests that behind this unit as a whole and in its basic form there stands the tradition of the Songs of Zion. Those poems celebrated the divine averting of a military threat to Jerusalem and drew from that victory the assurances of Yahweh's absolute power and Israel's permanent security (see Pss 46; 48; 76; esp. 46:2-4, 6 [1-3, 5] and 48:15 [14]; cf. Ollenburger, *Zion* 66-100; Levenson, *Theology* 15). These motifs coincided well with the theological emphases of Ezekiel and his school. Here such a foreign threat has been projected into the eschatological future and the "mountains of Israel" have been substituted for Zion as the target of invasion (cf. Ps 125). Seemingly in 39:9 "the cities of Israel" have replaced Jerusalem as a place of refuge. This re-use of Songs of Zion motifs has presumably been channeled through their prophetic echoes in Isa 17:12-14 (cf. עמים רבים "many peoples," Isa 17:12; cf. Isa 8:9-10; cf. in general Müller, *Ursprünge* 86-101). The door was thereby opened for material from Isa 10 (cf. "my mountains," Isa 14:25) and for Jeremiah's "foe from the north" oracles to be integrated into the Gog prophecy. Whereas this latter prophetic material was dominated by Yahweh's use of foreign nations to punish Israel, the underlying positive influence of the Songs of Zion and also of Isa 8:9-10; 17:12-14 has transformed the theological purpose. The emphasis in Isa 10 on Assyria's culpability, which manifestly underlies 38:10-16, undoubtedly aided this transformation. The resultant eschatological hope is presented as a warranty of faith in Yahweh's supremacy and Israel's permanent security. It is offered as an assurance to counteract the trauma of exile, with the pastoral message that "if God is for us, who is against us?" and "in all these (sufferings) we are more than conquerors" (Rom 8:31, 37).

The Gog revelation colored the prediction of the end of Antiochus Epiphanes in Dan 11:40-45. Thereafter it became a firm part of Jewish eschatology in rabbinic tradition. It is correspondingly reflected in Rev 20:7-10 as an event after the millenium and before the Last Judgment. In that event "Gog and Magog," the labels of "the nations at the four quarters of the earth," feature as dupes of Satan. The linking with Satan, who "must be loosed for a little while" but then is overthrown and suffers "for ever and ever" (Rev 20:3, 10), is significant: it reveals a comparable Christian pastoral emphasis that evil is destined to fail and so God's people are on the winning side.

There has been a Christian tendency to actualize biblical eschatology exclusively in terms of one's own generation and political circumstances. Thus Luther, true to the original geography, interpreted Gog's forces as the Turks. With the principle of wordplay replacing that of geography, modern dispensationalism, taking ראש "head" as a noun "Rosh," has seen communist Russia as the great threat to the faithful, further equating Meshech with Moscow and Tubal with Tobolsk (and earlier in this century Gomer with Germany [see Gaebelein 259]). Inconsistently, however, it has tended to locate the fulfillment primarily before the second advent as well as in a postmillennial period (Ellison, 133-34, who characterized a reference to Russia as "an excellent example of the wish being father to the thought"; cf. Alexander, *JETS* 17 [1974] 162-69).

The Sanctuary as Focus of the New Age (40:1-48:35)

Bibliography

Cooke, G. A. "Some Considerations on the Text and Teaching of Ezekiel 40-48." *ZAW* N.F. 1 (1924) 105-15. **Gese, H.** *Der Verfassungsentwurf des Ezechiel (Kap. 40-48), traditionsgeschichtlich untersucht.* BHT 25. Tübingen: Mohr, 1957. **Greenberg, M.** "The Design and Themes of Ezekiel's Program of Restoration." *Int* 38 (1984) 181-208 = *Interpreting the Prophets*, ed. J. L. Mays and P. J. Achtemeier (Philadelphia: Fortress, 1987) 215-36. **Haran, M.** *Temples and Temple Service in Ancient Israel.* Oxford: Clarendon, 1978. —. "The Law-Code of Ezekiel xl-xlviii and Its Relation to the Priestly School." *HUCA* 50 (1979) 45-71. **Levenson, J. D.** *Theology of the Program of Restoration of Ezekiel 40-48.* HSMS 10. Missoula, MT: Scholars Press, 1976. **Mackay, C.** "Why Study Ezekiel 40-48?" *EvQ* 37 (1965) 155-67. **Niditch, S.** "Ezekiel 40-48 in a Visionary Context." *CBQ* 48 (1986) 208-24. **Rautenberg, W.** "Zur Zukunftsthora des Hesekiel." *ZAW* 33 (1913) 92-115. **Rendtorff, R.** *Studien zur Geschichte des Opfers im Alten Israel.* WMANT 24. Neukirchen-Vluyn: Neukirchener Verlag, 1967. **Roberts, J. J. M.** "A Christian Perspective on Prophetic Prediction." *Int* 33 (1979) 240-53. **Tuell, S.** "The Temple Vision of Ezekiel 40-48: A Program for Restoration?" *Proceedings. Eastern Great Lakes Biblical Society* 2 (1982) 96-103. **Unger, M. F.** "The Temple Vision of Ezekiel." *BSac* 105 (1948) 418-432; 106 (1949) 48-64, 169-77. **Vogt, E.** *Untersuchungen zum Buch Ezechiel.* AnBib 95. Rome: Biblical Institute, 1981, 127-75. **Zimmerli, W.** "Plans for Rebuilding after the Catastrophe of 587." In *I Am Yahweh.* Ed. W. Brueggemann; tr. D. W. Stott. Atlanta: John Knox, 1982, 111-33, 156-60. Translated from "Planungen für Wiederaufbau nach der Katastrophe von 587." *VT* 18 (1968) 229-55.

This final section of the book is organized around a series of visionary narratives. In chaps. 40-42 the prophet is transported to the area of Jerusalem and taken by a supernatural guide on a tour of a restored, holy temple. The temple area stands empty and unused until in 43:1-5 it is energized by Yahweh's glory, returning to take up permanent royal residence. The divine coming enables the temple to come to life, so that the text can move from an anatomical description to a physiological one. The altar is dedicated as the hub of atonement and worship (43:13-27). Now the clock of temple ritual can start ticking again so as to reflect and to maintain the holiness of Israel's God. The flow of the visionary narrative is then diverted to a series of divine revelations as to the running of the temple (44:5-46:18). First, temple personnel are described, in a two-tier system of priests and Levites (44:6-16). The text concentrates upon the priests as prime representatives of the divine holiness, and outlines their holy lifestyle (44:17-31). The practical matters of the support of the priests and of the regular provision of sacrifices for the temple are dealt with (45:1-17). Finally within chaps 43-46, rulings are laid down for temple procedure, in terms of annual, monthly, weekly and daily rites and of the participation of people and head of state (45:18-46:15).

In the last part of the overall vision, chaps. 47-48, the temple is set within a larger perspective. The vision of 47:1-12 draws upon older Zion symbolism to describe in apocalyptic-like vein the blessing that flows from the temple graced by God's presence. Life and healing are brought by a powerful river of blessing. Then in 47:13-48:29 the relation of temple and land is revealed in a new geographical configuration of tribal territories. Concentric bands are arranged around a reservation that itself has at its heart the temple. Within this buffer zone there are also areas for the temple staff, the new Jerusalem and crown property. The city receives added recognition in 48:30-35.

The whole section is oriented toward the theme of the temple. It thus reflects priestly concerns already evident earlier in the book. The prophetic thinking of Ezekiel and of his immediate literary successors moved within a strongly religious orbit, and the trait reappears in this literary complex. This common concern enables the section to function as a reversal of earlier temple-oriented material. The vision of chaps. 8-11 in which temple and city are destroyed in reprisal for cultic aberrations finds here a positive counterpart. Moreover, the motif of the departing glory of God that not only pervades chaps. 8-11 but spills into chap. 1 is brought to a happy conclusion in the return of the divine presence. Thereby a frame is provided for the book. This literary polarization also serves as a reflection of the pattern of judgment and salvation in the book as a whole, and enables the section to function as a satisfying finale.

A similar note of contrast is struck by the deliberate mention of changes in temple layout and organization. There is a new emphasis on divine transcendence that results in a conscious endeavor to reflect it in the areas of topography and personnel. What was good enough for the old temple would no longer do (cf. 43:10, 11). Its role as a royal chapel, overshadowed by a complex of palace buildings, must end (43:7-8). The policing of the temple area by the "Swiss guards" who patrolled the palace grounds was no longer permissible (44:7, 9). Instead, a double system of temple staff, priests and Levites, must be inaugurated on lines already laid down in priestly literature (Num 18). The holiness of God was to be a paramount principle, and its outworking was to permeate both the structure and the procedure of the temple.

Functioning as an extended oracle of salvation, the section continues the message of chaps. 34-39 and belongs with them as the conclusion of an overall complex. Perhaps in this connection its most important role is to serve as a direct outworking of 37:24-28, which at an earlier stage probably immediately preceded chaps. 40-48, before the redactional insertion of chaps. 38-39. The four motifs of new temple, covenant, king and land find here a practical grounding and a detailed development. Although this role for the section does seem to be the redactional intent, there is a little tension between the two sets of material. Chaps. 40-48 have their own temple-oriented agenda, and although they embrace the other motifs to a greater or lesser extent, its prime motif tends to obscure the rest. Notably the motif of the future king could not be developed as fully as 34:23-24 and 37:24-25 (cf. 17:22-24) might lead one to expect. However, the hints within this section are consonant with the earlier representations. Especially the contrast in 34:1-16, 23-34 between the pre-exilic monarchy and its future counterpart corresponds well with 45:8-9; 46:16-18, although the first of these latter passages has its own part to play in a context of economic support for the temple. It is possible that their presence reflects a redactional concern to link with the material earlier in the book. There seems to be a conscious desire to ensure that pre-exilic royal abuses would never be repeated, just as tribal inequities (47:14) and the plight of the landless resident alien (47:21-23) are addressed. This concern for human rights obviously reflects fears among the exiles that return to the land would mean the resumption of the bad old status quo. So a pastoral concern, already seen in earlier chapters, is here shining out afresh. Especially in the issue of monarchy there is a pastoral sensitivity both to earlier prophetic ideals (cf. e.g., Isa 9:1-6[2-7]) that must still have had their advocates (cf. 2 Kgs 25:27-30) and to a popular disenchantment with the monarchy as totalitarian and not reflecting the people's best interests, let alone the will of the divine King. The result of this sensitivity is a remarkably realistic presentation that limits royal power, even as it invests the head of state with privilege. Was this pastoral sensitivity responsible for the restricted perspective of the monarchy in this section, which majors in its religious role and leaves much else unsaid? If in 34:24 the future Davidic king was to function as upholder of the laws of the Sinai covenant, here his ability to interfere with Yahweh's will for his covenant people is expressly checked (cf. "my people," 45:8, 9; 46:18).

There is also ample room for the motif of the covenant people to surface in 47:13-48:35. The blessing of the people with fertility promised in 34:26-27; 36:8, 11, 30, 34-35 is crowned by the vision of blessing in 47:1-12. Insistence on their traditional completeness as twelve tribes, found in 37:16-22, recurs in the twelvefold tribal division of the land and in the twelve gates of the city. It expresses the same sense of tragic loss that the united kingdom had ever been divided and reduced to a shadow in the kingdom of Judah. Such a truncated torso was not worthy of the kingdom of God. The contours of the restored land and its distribution in 47:13-48:29 dramatically develops the promise of return to the land that punctuates the book, at 20:42; 28:25-26; 34:27; 36:24, 28; 37:12, 14, 25; 39:28 (cf. 38:8, 12). The old theological triangle of Yahweh, people and land which summed up the covenant would be reestablished.

Supremely the divine promise of renewal of worship in the climactic 20:40-41 and in the equally climactic 37:26b-27 is developed in this final part of the book. The new sanctuary would again be Yahweh's dwelling place, the sign that he dwelt or presenced himself among his people (43:7). The divine initiative with respect to the temple in 37:26b ("I will put my sanctuary among them") seems also to underlie the present section. Significantly there is no call to rebuild the temple, only to observe the regulations for rites and offerings (43:11; cf. 44:5). The new temple was to be Yahweh's creation built for rather than by his people (cf. Zimmerli, *I Am Yahweh* 115-16), as a model of his own being and of his relationship with them. "The temple that Ezekiel saw is a house not made with hands" (Skinner 392).

Readers will find themselves embarrassed by these chapters (cf. Roberts' helpful facing up to this problem in *Int* 33 [1979] 245-53). To some extent at least they were presumably presented as normative for the future. Yet the post-exilic community, even when adoption of their rulings was within its power, found other models for its worship, while the different orientation of the Christian faith has left these chapters outdated. Must one relegate them to a drawer of lost hopes and disappointed dreams, like faded photographs? To resort to dispensationalism and postpone them to a literal fulfillment in a yet future time strikes the author as a desperate expedient that sincerely attempts to preserve belief in an inerrant prophecy. The canon of scriptures, Jewish and Christian, took unfulfillment in its stride, ever commending the reading of them as the very word of God to each believing generation. Essentially they spoke first to their own generation, and one must overhear them before hearing them for oneself. It may be that, just as the book of Revelation gives up its treasures to a persecuted church, these chapters along with the other oracles of salvation speak loudest to those in a state of disorientation, who can catch their note of pastoral concern and reassurance. Land and temple become symbols of solid hope for the renewal of social identity, for full fellowship with God and for "a kingdom that cannot be shaken" (Heb 12:22-24). The concern with correction of pre-exilic abuses becomes God's call for the translation of theology into the stuff of worship and of daily life, so that, "as he who calls you is holy," you may "yourselves be holy in all your conduct" (1 Pet 1:15; cf. Ezek 43:10-11).

The New Temple (40:1-42:20)

Bibliography

Busink, T. A. *Der Tempel von Jerusalem von Salomo bis Herodes.* Vol. 2. *Von Ezechiel bis Middot.* Leiden: Brill, 1980, 701-75. **Elliger, K.** "Die grossen Tempelsakristeien im Verfassungsentwurf des Ezechiel (42, 1ff.)." *Geschichte und Altes Testament.* FS. A. Alt. BHS 16. Tübingen: Mohr, 1953, 79-103. **Jeremias, J.** "Hesekieltempel und Serubbabeltempel." *ZAW* 11 (1934) 109-12. **Maier, J.** "Die Hofanlagen in Tempel-Entwurf des Ezechiel im Licht der 'Tempelrolle' von Qumran." *Prophecy.* FS. G. Fohrer, ed. J. A. Emerton. BZAW 150. Berlin: de Gruyter, 1980, 55-67. _____. *The Temple Scroll.* JSOTSup 34. Sheffield: JSOT Press, 1985. **Molin, G.** "Halonoth 'aṭumoth bei Ezechiel." *BZ* N.F. 15 (1971) 250-53. **Noth, M.** *Könige.* BKAT. Neukirchen-Vluyn: Neukirchener Verlag, 1968. **Scott, R. B. Y.** "The Hebrew Cubit." *JBL* 77 (1958) 205-14. **Vincent, L.-H.,** and **Steve, A. M.** *Jérusalem de l'Ancient Testament.* Vols. 2-3. Paris: Gabalda, 1956, 471-95.

Translation

[1]*In the twenty-fifth year of our exile, thirteen years after the capture of the city, at the new year, on the tenth of the month — that was the very day I felt Yahweh's hand on me, and that was where*[a] *he brought me.* [2]*In a divine vision he brought me to the land of Israel and set me down*[a] *on*[b] *a very high mountain, on which there was a group of buildings that looked like a city, to the south.*[c] [3]*When he brought me there, I found standing by a gatehouse a man who glistened like copper. He had in his hand a linen tape and a measuring rod.* [4]*The man told me, "Human one, use your eyes to look and your eyes to listen, and pay attention to everything I show you, because the purpose of your having been brought*[a] *here is that I should show it to you. Tell the community of Israel everything you see."* [5]*I found*[a] *a wall marking the outer perimeter of the temple area,*[b] *and the man measured the thickness of the structure,*[c] *using the measuring rod in his hand, which was 6 cubits*[d] *long — 1 cubit being reckoned as 1 cubit plus 1 handbreadth. It was 1 rod thick and 1 rod high.* [6]*Then he approached the*[a] *gatehouse, which faced east, and, going up its steps,*[b] *measured the threshold of the gatehouse: it was 1 rod deep.*[c] [7]*Then the alcoves, each of which was 1 rod long by 1 rod deep. The alcoves were set 5 cubits apart,*[a] *while next to the porch of the gatehouse was its inner threshold, which was 1 rod deep.* [8]*He measured the porch of the gatehouse*[a] [9]*on the inner side of the gate structure, and it was 8 cubits (deep), while its jambs were 2 cubits (thick).* [10]*There were three alcoves on either side of the east-facing gatehouse. The alcoves were all the same size, and so were the jambs that stood on either side of the passage.* [11]*Then he measured the width of the gatehouse entrance, and it was 10 cubits, while the width*[a] *of the gate was 13 cubits.* [12]*There were barriers across the front of the alcoves, 1 cubit deep on either side of the passage. The alcoves on either side measured 6 cubits.* [13]*He measured the gate structure at roof height*[a] *to find the distance between the far walls of the alcoves through their parallel openings, and it was 25 cubits.*[b] [15]*The measurement from*[a] *the front of the gatehouse at its point of entry*[b] *to*[c] *the front of the porch on the inner side*[d] *of the gatehouse was 50 cubits.* [16]*All along its inner length the gatehouse had recessed*[a] *windows in*[b] *its alcoves.*[c] *Likewise its porch*[d] *had windows round its interior. There were palm trees on the jambs of the gatehouse.*[e] [17]*Then he took me into the outer court, where I found rooms*

and a pavement constructed[a] *all round the court; there were thirty rooms fronting on the pavement.* [18]*The pavement (that is, the lower pavement) abutted*[a] *the gatehouses; it extended to the same depth as the gatehouses themselves did.* [19]*He measured the distance from the inner front of the lower gatehouse to*[a] *the outer front of the inner gatehouse,*[b] *and it was 100 cubits.*[c] [20]*Then he measured*[a] *the north-facing gatehouse of the outer court, its length and breadth.* [21]*Its alcoves, three on either side, jambs and porch*[a] *all had*[b] *the same proportions as those of the first gatehouse. It was 50 cubits long and 25 cubits*[c] *wide.* [22]*Its porch windows*[a] *and palms were the same*[b] *as those of the east-oriented gatehouse. There were seven steps by which one climbed up to it, and its porch was at the inner end.*[c] [23]*A gatehouse leading to the inner court faced the north gatehouse, as in the case of the east gatehouse.*[a] *He measured the distance between the two gatehouses, and it was 100 cubits.* [24]*Then he led me to the south, and I found a gatehouse facing south. He measured its jambs and vestibule, and the dimensions were the same as before.* [25]*Both it and its porch had windows all round their interior just like the windows of the other gatehouses. It was 50 cubits long and 25 cubits wide.* [26]*It had a stairway of seven steps*[a] *and its porch was at the inner end;*[b] *it had palm trees on its jambs, one on each opposite jamb.* [27]*The inner court had a gatehouse facing south: he measured the distance between the south-facing gatehouses, and it was 100 cubits.*

[28]*Then he led me through the south gatehouse into the*[a] *inner court and measured the gatehouse,*[b] *and it had the same dimensions as the others.* [29]*Its alcoves, jambs and porches measured the same as before, and both it and its porch had windows round them. It was 50 cubits long by 25 cubits wide.*[a] [31]*Its porch faced the outer court, and it had palm trees on its jambs, and its stairway*[a] *had eight steps.* [32]*He brought me east into the inner court and measured the gatehouse, which had the same dimensions as the others.* [33]*Its alcoves, jambs and porch were also the same size as before, and both it and its porch had windows round them. It was 50 cubits long by 25 cubits wide.* [34]*Its porch faced*[a] *the outer court, and its opposing jambs had palms on them, while its stairway had eight steps.* [35]*He led me into the north gatehouse and measured it, finding the same dimensions for it* [36]*and its alcoves, jambs and porch. It had windows round it. It was 50 cubits long by 25 cubits wide.* [37]*Its porch*[a] *faced the outer court, and there were palm trees on its opposite jambs, and its stairway had eight steps.*

[38]*There was a room opening into the porch of the gatehouse,*[a] *where the holocausts were to be washed.* [39]*In the vestibule itself stood tables, two on each side, on which to slaughter the holocausts,*[a] *sin offerings*[b] *and reparation offerings,* [40]*while two more tables stood outside by either sidewall of the porch,*[a] *at the entrance to the north*[b] *gatehouse.* [41]*So there were four tables inside the sidewalls of the gatehouse and four outside, a total of eight tables on which slaughtering was to take place.* [42A]*The*[a] *four tables for the holocausts were made of stone blocks: they were 1½ cubits long and wide, and 1 cubit high.*[b] [43A]*Shelves*[a] *1 handbreadth wide were fixed all round the inside walls:* [42B]*on them were to be put*[a] *the instruments for slaughtering the holocausts and the sacrificial offerings.* [43B]*The meat for the oblations was to be placed on the tables.*[a]

[44]*Outside the inner gatehouse*[a] *there were two rooms*[b] *in the inner court, one*[c] *facing*[d] *south and the other*[e] *on the sidewall of the south*[f] *gatehouse facing*[g] *north.* [45]*He told me, "This room*[a] *that faces south is meant for the priests responsible for the temple area,* [46]*while the room that faces north is for the priests responsible for the altar. The latter are the Zadokites, those descendants of Levi who may approach Yahweh to serve him."*

[47]*Then he measured the court: it was a square, 100 cubits long and wide, with the altar standing in front of the temple.* [48]*He led me into the temple porch and measured its*

pair of jambs[a]*: they were each 5 cubits (thick). The doorway was 14 cubits wide and its sidewalls*[b] *were each 3 cubits.* [49]*The breadth*[a] *of the porch was 20 cubits and the length*[a] *12*[b] *cubits. There were ten*[c] *steps by which one went up to it, and a pillar stood by each of the jambs.* [41:1]*He led me into the nave and measured the pair of jambs: they were each 6 cubits (thick).*[a] [2]*The entrance was 10 cubits wide, and the sidewalls at the entrance were each 5 cubits. Next he measured its*[a] *depth, which was 40 cubits, and its breadth, 20 cubits.* [3]*Then he went inside*[a] *and measured the jambs at the (next) entrance: they were each 2 cubits (thick), while the entrance itself was 6 cubits (wide). The sidewalls*[b] *next to the entrance were each*[b] *7 cubits wide.* [4]*He measured its depth and its width across the nave: it was 20 cubits deep and wide. "This is the holy of holies," he told me.*

[5]*Then he measured the wall of the temple, which was 6 cubits (thick), and the width of the annex that surrounded the temple, which was 4 cubits.* [6]*The annex rooms*[a] *consisted of three stories of thirty rooms.*[b] *There were offsets*[c] *in the temple wall for the annex rooms that surrounded it; their purpose was to allow supports*[d] *but not of a kind that penetrated the temple wall.* [7]*The annex rooms had a wider portion in the form of an ascending ramp:*[a] *the sides of the temple were enclosed*[b] *up to the top. Consequently the temple had extra breadth from bottom to top, with ascent being made from*[c] *the lowest story up to the highest one, as well as*[d] *the middle one.* [8]*The temple had a raised foundation (?),*[a] *an elevated area*[b] *that extended all round it, which provided a base*[c] *for the annex rooms; its substructure*[d] *measured a full*[e] *rod or 6 cubits.* [9]*The thickness of the external wall of the annex was 5 cubits. There was an area left open*[a] *between*[b] *the annex rooms of the temple* [10]*and the (other) rooms: it surrounded the temple to a width of 20 cubits.* [11]*The annex had a door*[a] *to the open area, in fact one door on the north side and another on the south. The wall*[b] *around the open area was 5 cubits thick.* [12]*The building fronting a restricted area on the west was 70 cubits wide; there was a wall round it 5 cubits thick, while its length was 90 cubits.* [13]*Next he measured the temple, which was 100 cubits long, and the restricted area plus the building, including its walls, which in all were 100 cubits deep.* [14]*The breadth of the front of the temple plus the restricted area to the east was 100 cubits.* [15]*He then measured the length of the building that lay alongside, i.e., behind, the (other) restricted area,*[a] *and it was 100 cubits.*

The inside of the nave and its outer porch[b] [16]*were paneled.*[a] *The recessed windows and the gradations with their three layers had a wooden trim*[b] *round them, excluding the sills.*[c] *From*[d] *the floor up to the windows there was a facing,*[e] [17]*up to*[a] *the area of the wall above the entrance. Inside*[b] *the temple room and in the outer section,*[c] *covering all the walls inside and in the outer section,* [18]*there was a design*[a] *depicting*[b] *cherubs and palm trees in an alternating pattern. Every cherub had two faces,* [19]*one human and the other a lion's, which looked in different directions, toward the palms beside them. The temple room had this same design on all its walls:* [20]*the design of cherubs and palm trees covered them from the floor to an area above the entrance. The wall*[a] *of the nave*[b] [21]*had doorposts*[a] *with quadruple gradations. In front of*[b] *the holy place there was an object that looked like* [22]*a wooden altar:*[a] *its*[b] *height was 3 cubits, its length 2 cubits and its breadth 2 cubits.*[c] *It had corners,*[d] *and its base*[e] *and sides were made of wood. "This," he told me, "is the table that stands in front of Yahweh."* [23]*The nave had a pair of double doors, and the holy place*[24]*also had a pair of double doors.*[a] *Each double door had leaves that opened right back,*[b] *two leaves to each door.* [25]*On them, or at least on the doors of the nave, there was a design*[a] *of cherubs and palm trees, the same design as on the walls. There was a wooden railing(?)*[b] *outside, in front of the porch.* [26]*There were recessed windows and palm trees on both sidewalls of the porch. The temple annex rooms also had railings.*[a]

42:1 *Then he took me out northwards*[a] *into the outer*[b] *court, and led me to a set of rooms*[c] *situated opposite the restricted area and also opposite the building, north of them.* [2]*Its length was 100 cubits*[a] *on the north side,*[b] *and the width was 50 cubits.* [3]*It lay between*[a] *the 20 cubits belonging to the inner court and the pavement that was part of the outer court; it was built tier upon tier*[b] *in three levels.*[c] [4]*In front of the rooms there was a walkway 10 cubits wide, giving access to the interior,*[a] *and a wall 1 cubit thick,*[b] *and their doors were on the north.* [5]*The top rooms did not extend the full breadth,*[a] *since the tiers that consisted of lower and middle rooms limited them.*[b] [6]*This was because the rooms were built on three levels, instead of having pillars like those elsewhere in the courts;*[a] *so it was reduced*[b] *from the bottom, as it rose from the lower and middle rooms.* [7]*The wall outside was parallel to the rooms and in front of them, beside the outer court; its length was 50 cubits,* [8]*since that was the length of the rooms as they related to the outer court, facing it,*[a] *although the total length*[b] *was 100 cubits.* [9]*At the base*[a] *of these rooms there was an entry*[b] *from the east, leading in from the outer court,* [10]*at the start*[a] *of the wall blocking the court. On the south*[b] *side, alongside the restricted area and the building, there were (other) rooms,* [11]*with a path in front of them. They looked the same as the rooms on the north side: the same length, breadth,*[a] *exits,*[b] *design and doors* [12]*pertained to the rooms*[a] *on the south side. There was an entrance at the open end of a path*[b] *beside the protective*[c] *wall, which afforded entry to them*[d] *at the east end.* [13]*He told me, "The northern and*[a] *southern rooms adjoining the restricted area are the sacred rooms where the priests who have access to Yahweh are to eat the most sacred offerings. It is there that they are to put the most sacred offerings, namely the cereal offerings, sin offerings and reparation offerings, because the place is sacred.* [14]*Once the priests have entered*[a] *the sanctuary, they are not to go out to the outer court without leaving*[b] *there the clothing they wear for their official duties, because it is sacred. They are to put on other clothing before they approach the people's area."*

[15]*Having completed the measurements inside the temple area,*[a] *he took me out through the gatehouse that faced east, and measured its perimeter.* [16]*He used the measuring rod to measure the east side:*[a] *it was 500 (cubits)*[b] *by the measuring rod. He changed direction,*[c] [17]*measured the north side: it was 500 (cubits) by the measuring rod. He changed direction* [18]*to*[a] *the south side, measured it: it was 500 (cubits) by the measuring rod.* [19]*Then he changed direction to the west side, measured it: it was 500 (cubits) by the measuring rod.* [20]*On the four sides he measured it: it had a perimeter wall whose dimensions were 500 (cubits) long and wide. Its purpose was to separate the sacred area from the profane.*

Notes

1. a. Heb. שמה "there" does not anticipate the venue of v 2 (Cooke 429 et al.), but refers back to the city of Jerusalem mentioned in v 1a, so that there is a double emphasis on time and place. But the allusiveness of the description in v 2 may favor its absence from LXX* and suggest an addition assimilating to v 3aα. Then the verbal form הביאני "he brought me" in v 2aα must also be deleted with LXX* (Cornill 433; Zimmerli 331 et al.). However, a contrast of destruction and implicit restoration is impressive, and there may well have been a deliberate echo of 8:3 "and it brought me to Jerusalem."

2. a. For the unusual verbal form cf. 37:1.

2. b. Repeatedly in the vision description אל "to" is used in the sense of על "on."

2. c. MT מנגב "in the south" may be an early gloss that wrongly finds reference to the city of Jerusalem south of the temple; "south" is דרום in chaps. 40-42, not נגב (Gese, *Verfassungsentwurf* 10, et al.). However, it may simply represent the prophet's position vis-a-vis the temple: in 8:3 he also landed to the north of the temple (Vogt, *Untersuchungen* 134). For the use of נגב see 47:1 and Zimmerli 511. LXX presupposes an adaptation to מנגד "opposite," which seems to be a paraphrase.

4. a. LXX represents "your coming" and Syr "my coming," but the hoph reflects the hiph forms of vv 1-3 (Zimmerli 332).

5. a. Lit. "behold," also in v 17.

5. b. Lit. "house, temple," here, as elsewhere, used in a wider sense.

5. c. Cf. Driver, *Bib* 35 (1954) 304-5.

5. d. The Heb. adds באמה "by the cubit": see GKC 134n; S. J. DeVries, *1 Kings* (WBC. Waco, TX: Word, 1985) 90-93.

6. a. For MT שער "a gate" השער "the gate" is expected after the reference in v 3. But the anarthrous form (cf. 43:1) seems to be idiomatic, representing the constr before a relative clause (GKC 130c).

6. b. The defectively written form in K, whereby ו, is written for יו,, is legion in chaps. 40-48. It represents an orthographical style that is not to be "corrected" (see Gese, *Verfassungsentwurf* 133; Zimmerli 333). It represents an older convention of writing: see Andersen and Forbes, *Spelling in the Hebrew Bible* 323-28.

6. c. Heb. רחב, normally "breadth," can also indicate a horizontal distance away from an observer or starting point. MT adds "the threshold one, one rod in depth," of which the foregoing is a correction. A copyist's eye and hand leapt to אחד "one," omitting קנה השער "the gate rod"; then the error was partially corrected by inserting קנה אחד "one rod." The muddle has been corrected in v 6bα, but the error has been retained. LXX presupposes only v 6bα, but fails to represent רחב: presumably in its underlying Heb. text the conflated text of MT had suffered hypercorrection by the deletion of one word too many. Busink's attempt to retain MT (*Tempel* 715) is unconvincing: he finds reference to a landing at the top of the steps in v 6bα and to the threshold proper in v 6bβ, reading אחר "another" with Syr for אחד².

7. a. For the addition in LXX see Gese, *Verfassungsentwurf* 130-32.

8. a. Many MSS LXX Syr Vg lack the dittograph of MT, which repeats מהבית . . . השער "inner . . . gatehouse" in vv 8-9.

11. a. Heb. ארך, usually "length," here refers to the longer dimension and רחב "width" to the shorter one (Gese, *Verfassungsentwurf* 125). Hence an emendation of ארך to דרך "way, passage" (*BHK*; Galling in Fohrer 223; see Cooke 433, 442) is unnecessary.

13. a. Galling (in Bertholet 136 and Fohrer 223) emended מגג . . . לגגו "from the roof . . . to its roof" to מגו . . . לגוו "from the back . . . to its back," taking גו as "back wall" on the basis of LXX τοῖχος "wall"; RSV, NEB AND (N)JB have adopted the emendation. But there is no evidence that גו was used architecturally (Cooke 442; Gese, *Verfassungsentwurf* 139).

13. b. MT adds v 14 "And he made (the) jambs 60 cubits and to the jamb of the gate, the court, around." Gese (*Verfassungsentwurf* 146-47; cf. *BHS*) has observed that there is no room for material between v 13 and v 15, which move logically from overall width of the gatehouse to its overall depth. He has explained v 14a as a variant of v 15ayδ-b with the omission of הפנימי "inner," and v 14b as corresponding to v 16aα without the first four words and with לפנימי omitted. He rightly rejected ויעש את-אילים"and he made (the) jambs" in favor of an earlier ועל-פני אלם השער "across the front of the porch of the gate," which LXX attests. A complex series of adaptations to the text seems to have occurred. First, double parablepsis took place: the copyist's eye jumped from ועל-פני in v 15aα to אלם השער (. . . פני) in v 15aβ to סביב סביב (לשער) in v 16aα. Then this truncated text had incorporated into it (between אלם and השער) two glosses from the account of Solomon's building of the temple in 1 Kgs 6: (i) ששים אמה "60 cubits" from 1 Kgs 6:2, the length of the temple (cf. "20 cubits" underlying LXX, which read תאים "alcoves" in error for אמות "cubits": it appears to refer to its width), and (ii) ויעש "and he made (recessed windows)" from 1 Kgs 6:4. The latter gloss displaced ועל-פני "and in front of," and the object sign was subsequently added. These comparative annotations properly related to 41:13-16, but they seem to have been misplaced here because this and the other gatehouses also had recessed windows (v 16). A third incorporation, missing from LXX's *Vorlage*, was ואל-איל החצר "and to the jamb of the court," which, it may be suggested, represents אל החצר ואלמו (= ואל) "and its porch faced the court," a correction of חצר "court" in v 31 preceded by cue words. The marginal correction was related to the wrong column, and אל was miswritten איל under the influence of ואל-איל"and on jamb" in v 16. The original text of vv 15-16aα has been added in MT without deletion of the truncated and annotated version in v 14.

15. a, c. MT על-פני "to the front" represents an early correction of על-לפני "to, before" (cf. Gese, *Verfassungsentwurf* 141), which suffered dittography of *lamed*. The reading has some support in the masoretic tradition (see *BHK*). The marginal correction was wrongly taken as a replacement for the first prepositional phrase: v 19 suggests that it was מלפני (ו) "(and) from before." The fact that

the sequences מלפני and על-פני have four out of five consonants in common encouraged the substitution; this factor and the demands of the context confirm the conjectural emendation.

15. b. K היאתון and Q האיתון may be errors for a *hapax legomenon* אתיון (ה), an adjectival form from אתי / אתה "come" referring to the part of the gate at which one enters (cf. Cornill 440; Gese, *Verfassungsentwurf* 145). A nominal phrase "the entry of the gate" would be a more natural expression. But it may function as a counterpart to השער הפנימי "the inner gate," which seems to refer to the inner part or western end of the (outer!) east gate (cf. Zimmerli 336). LXX ἔξωθεν "outside" is an intelligent guess or correct paraphrase suggested by the contrasting phrase that follows.

15. d. See the preceding note.

16. a. The term אטמות, lit. "closed," occurs also in 1 Kgs 6:4 and Ezek 41:16, 26. G. Molin (*BZ* N.F. 15 [1971] 250-53) took it literally with reference to blocked imitation windows, but usually it is interpreted in terms of partial closure. Driver (*Bib* 35 [1954] 305) compared Arab. *'atama* "contract, narrow." Then it may refer to embrasured windows, narrowing toward the inside, as Driver urged. However, the further definition in 41:16 seems to indicate a recessed, gradated framing, which narrowed toward the outside, as Syr interpreted here and in 1 Kgs 6:4 (Galling in Fohrer 226; Zimmerli 351 and note 35; cf. too 41:21 and *Note*). LXX^L at 1 Kgs 6:4 and LXX in Ezek 41:16 rendered "latticed," with reference to a grating filling the window opening (see Busink, *Tempel* 1, 195-96).

16. b. Heb. אל is used loosely for ל with the sense "belonging to," as in 45:2.

16. c. MT adds ואל אליהמה "and belonging to their jambs." The long form of the suffix, found in Qumran documents (see Gese, *Verfassungsentwurf* 148), occurs only here in Ezek: cf. fem יהנה - in 1:11 (GKC 911). It is difficult to conceive of windows set in the jambs. The phrase seems to have originated as an explanatory note on the suffixless ואל איל "and on jamb" in v 16bβ, relating the jambs to the alcoves next to them; the expedient caused the gloss to enter the text alongside התאים "the alcoves."

16. d. For MT לאלמות וחלונות "to the porches and windows" must be read חלונות לאלמו "belonging to its porch (were) windows," with partial support from LXX (Gese, *Verfassungsentwurf* 149). There was only one porch in each gatehouse: plurals also wrongly occur in suffixed forms at v 21 and following verses. For the form of the noun see *BHS*. Here mechanical assimilation to the ending of the next noun seems to have occurred, which then necessitated the insertion of the copula. The *'athnach* needs to be written on סביב² (Gese, ibid.).

16. e. MT איל "(and on) jamb" requires correction to אלו (=אליו) "its jambs" (Gese, ibid.).

17. a. Heb. עשוי "constructed" lacks grammatical agreement here and in 41:18-19. For suggested explanations see Zimmerli 337.

18. a. Lit. "(was) along the side of." Heb. כתף means here the long sides of the gatehouse, not the short projecting walls beside the porch entrances of the gatehouses and temple, as elsewhere in chaps. 40-42.

19. a. For MT התחתונה לפני "the lower (fem!) before" LXX implies התחתון אל-פני "the lower to the front of." Gese (*Verfassungsentwurf* 141) may be correct in assuming wrong word division as the basic error.

19. b. LXX correctly implies השער "the gateway" for MT החצר "the court." MT reflects the influence of vv 23 and 27, where the inner court is mentioned together with the same measurement.

19. c. MT adds הקדים והצפון "the east and the north," which seems to reflect marginal rubric glosses relating to the topics of the previous (vv 16-19) and following (vv 20-23) material (Herrmann 256; cf. in principle Zimmerli 337; Freedy, *VT* 20 [1970] 141-44, 151-52). LXX has a guidance formula at this point, harmonizing with v 24 (Gese, *Verfassungsentwurf* 153; Zimmerli 337; contra *BHS*, RSV, NEB).

20. a. For the pf and *w^eqatal* forms here and in vv 24 and 35, in place of the consec impf forms of vv 6-19 Gese (*Verfassungsentwurf* 19) finds a stylistic tendency evident too in 41:13-15; 42:15-20.

21. a. See note 16. d. above.

21. b. The sg vb may be agreeing with the nearest of its subjects (Zimmerli 338).

21. c. See note 5. d.

22. a. In place of MT "its windows and its porches," where the copula cannot stand since the porch was already mentioned in v 21, it is better to read חלונות אלמו "the windows of its porch": cf. vv 25, 29, 33 (Zimmerli 339).

22. b. MT כמדת "the same dimensions as" labors under the difficulty that no measurements were ever given for the windows or palms. Cornill (443), with appeal to the LXX, suggested the graphically close כמו "the same as" (cf. 16:57). Then the phrase in v 21 influenced MT (Jahn 281).

22. c. One must read here and in v 26 לפנימה "inside," as LXX implies for MT לפניהם "before them," which has suffered metathesis. The porch and the steps were at opposite ends of each outer gatehouse (cf. vv 7, 9).

23. a. Heb. ולקדים "and in respect to the east" appears to bear this meaning (Zimmerli, ibid.). Cornill, ibid., et al. consider that LXX implies כשער לקדים "like the east gate"; NEB and (N)JB so read. Gese (*Verfassungsentwurf* 18 note 5) regarded as a gloss, comparing v 19b.

26. a. MT שבעה עלותו "seven its stairway (?)" presents difficulties: Heb. idiom requires a masc numeral, and עלה nowhere else occurs with this sense. One should probably read שבע מעלו (cf. vv 31, 34, 37): MT basically reflects a ה/מ error.

26. b. See note 22. c.

28. a. For the dispensability of the article see GKC 126w.

28. b. MT adds הדרום "the south," not expressed in LXX* Vg. The abs השער "the gate" (contrast v 28a) militates against it. It may have been copied mechanically from v 28a; see further in note 44. f.

29. a. MT adds v 30 which is very similar to v 29 and is missing in some Heb. MSS and in LXX*. It seems to represent a corrupted text, to which a corrected text has been prefixed in v 29. Parablepsis was responsible for the loss of כמדות . . . ולאלמו "like the dimensions . . . and to its porches" (cf. v 16). Next חמשים אמה "50 cubits" and ורחב "and width" were overlooked and the measurement of 25 cubits was given in the form in which it was supplied in vv 25, 33, 36 (contrast v 13). Then the missing ורחב "and width" was supplied. The pl אמות "cubits" seems to be a correction of the sg אמה. Finally חמש אמות "5 cubits," intended as "50 cubits" (חמש for חמשים) attempted to supply the missing length (for the pl noun cf. 42:2).

31. a. Here and in v 34 K מעלו intended מעלו "its stairway," rather than a defectively written pl as Q interpreted it.

34. a. Here and in v 37 ל is used for אל (v 31) in the sense of facing toward.

37. a. MT "and its jambs" is a false anticipation of the term later in the verse. LXX Vg imply ואלמו "and its porch," as in vv 31, 34.

38. a. For MT באילים השערים "into the jambs, the gatehouses" should be read באלם השער "into the porch of the gatehouse" with Syr in line with v 39. Assimilation to האילים "the jambs" in the next column at 40:49; 41:1 was probably to blame. In LXX parablepsis has led to the omission of v 38aβb, which Gese (*Verfassungsentwurf* 154) and Zimmerli (363) failed to recognize: ἔκρυσις "outpouring" is its rendering of a partly illegible שלחנות "tables" in v 39aα (Cornill 446, following F. Field).

39. a. LXX's omission of the holocaust was probably on rationalizing grounds: see Zimmerli 367.

39. b. See *Comment* on 43:19.

40. a. MT לעולה "to him who goes up" is generally emended conjecturally to לאולם "in respect of the porch," by comparison with v 40b. LXX Syr interpret as לעולה "for the holocaust." In fact the outside tables of v 40 were not for the holocaust in view of v 42b, but their understanding may supply a clue to the origin of the reading. It was probably intended as a rubric gloss drawing attention to the sacrificial content of vv 38-43. It was taken as a correction of לאולם, with which it has three letters in common, and displaced it.

40. b. Heb. הצפונה "northern" qualifies not the sidewall, which is too far away, but the gatehouse, so that the north gate rather than the east one is in view (Gese, *Verfassungsentwurf*, 156-57, followed by Zimmerli 363).

42A. a. To MT שלחנות "tables" a he, lost by haplography, is probably to be prefixed.

42A. b. In vv 42-43 as arranged in MT the massive tables are the repository for both the sacrificial meat and the knives, while the narrow שפתים (see note on 43A) are mentioned without a statement of their purpose. It is logical to posit an order vv 42a, 43a, 42b, 43b, so that object and purpose are distributed in an ABB'A' order (Herrmann 267 et al.; cf. Cornill 450). Why was the order changed? In v 39 the slaughter of the holocausts was related to the tables. Accordingly אליהם "upon them," which referred to the tables in v 39, was interpreted in the same way here, and this necessitated the placing of v 42b in its present position in MT.

43A. a. MT שפתים is a dual form of a term derived from "set on." It appears to mean "places on which to set down things" (KB 1006b; cf. *HALAT* 616a). LXX Syr Vg 'ΑΣΘ all related to שפה "lip," while Tg rendered ענקלין "hooks," with a feature of the slaughter chamber of the Herodian temple in mind (Levey, *Targum of Ezekiel* 113 note 19, with reference to the Mishnah, *Mid.* 3:5). A rendering "ledges" (NEB) or "shelves" (Eichrodt 534) would suit the context. The relevance of a dual vocalization is hard to discern, and a pl pointing (*BHS*) is expected.

42B. a. The ancient versions imply יניחו "they were to put" for MT ויניחו "and . . ." MT is more emphatic: "it was upon them that . . ." (Cooke 444; cf. Exod 16:6, 7). But extant examples refer to expressions of time rather than place; and one would expect a consec pf form.

43B. a. In LXX v 43b has been replaced with mention of a protective cover or awning over the tables. MT is preferable: see Gese, *Verfassungsentwurf* 160.

44. a. MT "gate" is to be preferred to LXX "court": see Zimmerli 368. The variant may be linked to the guidance formula introduced in LXX (cf. v 28).

44. b. LXX presupposes שְׁתַּיִם לְשָׁכוֹת "two rooms" for MT "singers' rooms," which is at odds with the purpose stated in vv 45-46. Mechanical assimilation to the שר sequence before (בשר) and after (אשר) may be to blame. The context favors the LXX reading.

44. c. For MT אשר "which," relating to both rooms, LXX presupposes אחת "one," required by the parallelism in v 44bα and the differentiation in vv 45-46. A copyist looked ahead to the two occurrences of אשר in vv 45-46 and wrongly anticipated them here.

44. d. MT ופניהם "and their face" is a logical consequence of the former error: ופניה "and its face" is generally restored.

44. e. The fem form אחת "one" is expected: the masc form in v 43a may have been thoughtlessly repeated.

44. f. LXX implies הדרום "the south" for MT הקדים "the east." The directional orientation of the two rooms suggests their antithetical location. Was the otiose הדרום "the south" at v 28 originally a marginal correction that was related to the wrong column?

44. g. MT פני "face of" needs to be adapted to פניה "its face" for symmetry. Probably an abbreviated form was misunderstood.

45. a. For the construction see GKC 136d note 1.

48. a. MT's anarthrous אלם "porch" is more grammatically represented as האלם by LXX (but see note 6. a above); אל "jamb" is defectively written for איל, which LXX αιλ implies. Mechanical assimilation to the earlier אל-אלם "to (the) porch" seems to have occurred.

48. b. MT has lost by homoeoteleuton five words represented in LXX: וכהפות השער ארבע עשרה אמה "14 cubits and the sidewalls of the gatehouse" (cf. Gese, *Verfassungsentwurf* 23 note 2).

49. a. See note 11. a. above.

49. b. MT "11" does not accord with the total length of 100 cubits; LXX "12" does. For the שתי / עשתי error see the next note.

49. c. MT ובמעלות אשר "and by the steps which" must be corrected to ובמעלות עֶשֶׂר "and by ten steps" with LXX, as even Barthélemy et al., *Preliminary Report on the Hebrew OT*, vol 5, 148, acknowledge. LXX has preserved a superior reading: a main clause is required and a number is expected. The extra *'ayin* earlier (see note 49. b.) probably originated as a correction of the *'aleph*.

41:1. a. MT adds רחב האהל "the width of the tent," evidently an early comparative gloss on v 2. It seems to refer to the width of the tabernacle, which by deduction was 10 cubits (Exod 36:21, 27-28; cf. D. W. Gooding, *Illustrated Bible Dictionary* 3, 1508). LXX's αιλαμ = אולם "porch" is a contextually harmonized reading; its earlier placing of the phrase also represents contextual integration.

2. a. I.e. of the nave (v 1a).

3. a. I.e. into the inner room.

3. b. LXX implies וכהפות "and the sidewalls" for MT ורחב "and the width," and has a longer text מפה ושבע אמות מפה "on this side and 7 cubits on that side." Expected parallelism with v 2a favors the LXX readings. In MT assimilation to הפתח ורחב "and the width of the entrance" in v 2 may have occurred (Cornill 452) and/or to the sequence שש אמות ורחב "6 cubits and the width" in v 5. The loss of the later four words may be a subsequent dropping of now meaningless words (Zimmerli 342) or represent oversight of a 14-letter line (cf. Allen, *Greek Chronicles* 2, 134-36).

6. a. The Heb. pl seems to refer to the annex rooms. Alternatively the sg would relate to the annex on a ground plan, and the pl to its vertical aspect as a series of stories.

6. b. MT "annex (room?) upon annex (room?) three and thirty times" appears to signify thirty-three stories. The easiest and most feasible reconstruction, with some support from LXX Vg, is to reverse the numbers and omit the copula: ". . . thirty (rooms), three times" (Cornill 454 et al.). Others delete ושלשים "and thirty" as a gloss (Herrmann 258, 269 et al.).

6. c. Heb. באות "insets" correspond to מגרעות "recesses" in 1 Kgs 6:6, referring (from different perspectives) to spaces let into or out of the wall (Driver, *Bib* 35 [1954] 305). LXX copies the Kgs translation with διάστημα "interval, dimension." Gese (*Verfassungsentwurf* 164), has maligned the Gk. translator by regarding it as a stopgap word betraying ignorance.

6. d. This is a noun, not a participial adj, since it would then be fem: for the form see GKC 84ᵃm (Herrmann, ibid.).

7. a. MT ורחבה ונסבה "and it was wide and went round" can hardly have the annex as subj: Cooke (453) viewed its fem sg as impersonal. Tg presupposes וְרֹחַב הַמְּסִבָּה "and the width of the surrounding path," with support from LXX Vg for the first word. This emendation is now widely read: (i) the contextual series of nouns or nominal clauses (vv 5b, 6aα, 6aβb) is then continued (Gese,

*Verfassungsentwurf*165), and (ii) v 7aγb functions in accord with its stated intent as a logical deduction from v 7aαb. Heb. רחב is here used in a concrete sense (Driver, *Bib* 35 [1954] 307).

7. b. MT's noun form מוסב "surrounding" is more naturally pointed as a hoph ptcp מוסָב (Gese, *Verfassungsentwurf* 167 note 4).

7. c. C reads and LXX Syr presuppose an expected ומן "and from" for MT וכן "and so," which has suffered assimilation to כן earlier.

7. d. Heb. ל seems to signify "in addition to" (cf. BDB 511b).

8. a. MT וראיתי "and I saw" introduces a verb alien to the vision report of chaps. 40-42 and breaks the sequence of nominal clauses (Gese, *Verfassungsentwurf* 169). LXX θραελ implies a technical term תראל which from the context appears to have some such meaning (Zimmerli 371-72; cf. Jahn 291): evidently in MT an unknown term has been rendered intelligible, via haplography of *lamed* and metathesis.

8. b. MT גבה "height" may have a concrete sense (cf. note 7. a. above). A popular repointing is גַּבָּה "back, elevation": cf. Γαββαθα in John 19:13 (Herrmann 259, following C. Siegfried, et al.).

8. c. Reading Q; LXX διάστημα "dimension" implies a misreading מדות "measurements."

8. d. Heb. אצילה is evidently a technical building term, with reference to a terrace according to Elliger (*Geschichte* 92), followed by Zimmerli (372), who related it to נאצל in 42:6: see the note there. In fact it does not seem to have formed a projecting terrace (Gese, *Verfassungsentwurf* 170; Busink, *Tempel* 750). LXX διάστημα "intervening space," followed by Vg *spatio*, reflects an exegetical tradition shared by Tg רוח "wide space." Busink (*Tempel* 752) plausibly renders "Grundlage," relating to Arab. *'asula* "be deep rooted" (cf. *HALAT* 79b).

8. e. For the form cf. GKC 23f.

9. a. Lit. "that which was left." In v 11 the verbal form is used as a noun.

9. b. The continuation in v 10 requires בין ה(צלעות) "between the (annex rooms)," as LXX presupposes, for MT בית "house of," which may have suffered assimilation to בית later.

11. a. The Heb. sg form, often emended to a pl with the seeming support of LXX, may stand as a harder reading (Zimmerli 373).

11. b. Instead of MT מקום "place" LXX has φὸς "window," which is the standard interpretation of גדר "wall" in 42:7, 10, 12 and does not imply a misreading as אור "light" (Zimmerli 394; cf. Cooke 461). Evidently in MT a gloss המנח מקום "a place which was left open," intended to explain the phrase in v 9b (cf. Tg אתר "place" for אשר "that which"), was taken as a correction of גדר המנח "the wall of the open space" and displaced it.

15. a. MT adds מפו ומפו (Q ואתיקיהא) ואתוקיהא "and its ledges on either side," using a type of suffix found at Qumran (see Zimmerli 374). The term is used in v 16 of a window design and in 42:3, 5 of a feature of a building. It seems to be derived from נתק "take away," with a prosthetic *'aleph* (Elliger, *Geschichte* 85). Here it appears with reference to quite a different building than that in 42:3, 5. It may well have originated as an early explanatory gloss (cf. Gese, *Verfassungsentwurf* 173-74; Zimmerli, ibid.) on the term in v 16, indicating that the recessed frames of each window were stepped in lateral ridges.

15. b. For the anomalous ואלמי החצר "and the porches of the court" in MT, LXX presupposes והאלם החצון "and the outer porch." A feasible reading graphically closer to MT is ואלמו החצון "and its outer porch," which 2 MSS^Ken read (Cornill 461, following Ewald, et al.).

16. a. For MT הספים "the thresholds" LXX implies סְפֻנִים "paneled" and takes with v 15, as the context requires. In MT "porches" earlier seems to have suggested "thresholds" by word association (cf. 40:7).

16. b. Driver (*Bib* 35 [1954] 305-6) compared Syr. *shp'* "course (of wood, stone)" and *shpt'* "covering" and Talm.-Aram. סחף "cover" to elucidate the *hapax legomenon* שׂחיף, which Vg Syr Tg interpreted on similar lines.

16. c. Lit. "opposite the sill," with reference to the three sides of the window frame. LXX Syr omit, perhaps because of the difficulty of grappling with a complex text. Gese (*Verfassungsentwurf* 175) et al. have regarded it as a gloss.

16. d. LXX (in a doublet) and comparison with v 20 suggest ומהארץ "and from the floor" in place of MT והארץ "and the floor."

16. e. MT has "and the windows were covered," taking מכסות "coverings" as a verbal form, but the context requires a nominal reference to the covering of the walls. Hence והחלנות "and the windows," already presupposed by LXX, is to be omitted (Galling in Bertholet 144, et al.).

17. a, b. MT על "on" and עד "up to" seem to have been reversed. Either עד (ו) "(and) up to" was the initial error by assimilation and a correcting note על "on" was taken as a correction of the earlier

עד or vice versa.

17. a. I.e. on the inner surfaces of the walls of the porch (Gese, *Verfassungsentwurf* 178 note 2).

18. a. For MT see the note on 40:17; cf. vv 18, 25 and contrast the normal form in v 20.

18. b. MT has מדות "measurements" (cf. 42:15; 43:13) at the end of v 17, which LXX does not represent. Zimmerli (384) has urged the unique sense of a measured area. Perhaps an original reading דְּמוּת "likeness" (cf. *BHK*) earlier followed וְעָשׂוּי "and there was made" (Brockington, *Hebrew Text* 237; cf. Driver, *Bib* 35 [1954] 306).

20. a. MT is abrupt and disjointed: for וקיר "and the wall" it may have earlier had ולקיר "and to the wall" (*BHK*) or לקיר "to the wall." Wrong verse division in vv 20-21 may have encouraged the change.

20. b. MT repeats ההיכל "the nave": its use of "extraordinary points" over the first instance reflects its own query. LXX Syr Vg have only one representation.

21. a. MT מזוזת "doorpost" is better pointed as pl.

21. b. MT ופני "and the front of" is again staccato, giving an awkward listing of disconnected items in vv 20b-22; ולפני "and before" is often read (*BHK* et al.).

22. a. LXX Syr imply כמראה מזבח "like the appearance of a (wooden) altar": wrong verse division and dittography underlie MT.

22. b. For MT גבה "high" the context requires גבהו "its height," as LXX Syr Tg presuppose: haplography of *waw* is to blame.

22. c. MT lacks the last clause, presupposed in LXX* and lost by homoeoteleuton: see *BHS*.

22. d. MT ומקצעותיו "and its corners" may be a case of mechanical assimilation to the following suffixed nouns: LXX Syr Tg do not represent the suffix.

22. e. MT וארכו "and its length" has been assimilated to the earlier form: LXX attests וַאֲדָנָו "and its base," the Heb. noun being regularly used in the pl (Cornill 465 et al.).

24. a. For the need to change the phrasing in MT see especially Gese, *Verfassungsentwurf* 180-83. The copula in ושתים "and two" should be deleted, as LXX attests.

24. b. Heb. מוסבות has a gerundive force "capable of being turned" (cf. GKC 116e). Heb. דלת means here both "door" and "door leaf."

25. a. The fem seems to have a neuter sense: cf. Ps 37:31b (Cooke 455).

25. b. See Zimmerli (390) for this and other suggested meanings. In v 26b this interpretation would suit the ramp of v 7 (Busink, *Tempel* 763).

26. a. J. P. Peters' suggestion (*JBL* 12 [1893] 48) that v 26b "and the temple annex rooms and the railings(?)" was a rubric gloss defining the topics of vv 5-7 and v 25 and so of vv 5-26 does not carry conviction. Zimmerli (390) considers that a longer account has been broken off. Perhaps a coordinated listing has once more replaced subordination (cf. vv 16a, b, 20, 21), and עבים ... ולצלעות "and the annex rooms ... had railings(?)" should be read.

42:1. a. MT הדרך דרך "the way, way of" constitutes a conflated text: the second term corrected the first, which arose by dittography of *he* and mechanical continuation of a series of words preceded by the article. Syr omits the first term.

1. b. LXX has "inner," read by Cornill (468), *BHK*, RSV et al. It represents a change that takes seriously the description of the temple in 41:15b-26. Strictly the prophet was last perceived to be in the inner court (41:15a). What follows is written from the perspective of the outer court.

1. c. The Heb. has a collective sg and thereafter pl forms.

2. a. MT and perhaps the *Vorlage* of LXX* (see Zimmerli 392) begin with an intrusive אל-פני "adjoining": it seems to be a comparative gloss relating to the phrase נגד הגזרה "before the restricted area" in v lb and comparing אל-פני הגזרה "adjoining the restricted area" in v 13. In MT's ארך אמות המאה "length of cubits the 100," transposition and wrong word division appear to have disfigured an original ארכה מאה אמות "its length was 100 cubits" (cf. 40:27): in the description of length and breadth a suffix accompanies the length in 40:21; 41:2, 4, 12 (Elliger, *Geschichte* 84 note 1).

2. b. For MT פתח "door, entrance" LXX rightly implies פאת "side." Was פתח הצפון "the north door" an explanatory note on פתח "door" in 41:11, which was taken as a correction of פאת הצפון "the north side" in the next column?

3. a. Lit. "in front of . . . and in front of."

3. b. For אתיק "ledge, tier" see the note on 41:15.

3. c. Lit. "in the thirds," i.e., in an area divided into three. Scholars tend to assimilate to the participial form in v 6, with some apparent ancient support (see *BHS*), but stylistic variation and the principle of the harder reading are adequate arguments for MT.

4. a. Elliger (*Geschichte* 87) relates to the inner court (= NEB): see *Comment*.

4. b. MT has דרך אמה אחת "a passage 1 cubit," presumably wide, but this is an impracticable di-

mension. Standard recourses are (a) to read with the support of LXX Syr מאה אמה וארך "and length 100 cubits" (Smend 346 et al.), which suits the context (see Zimmerli 393; even Keil [259] so reads) and is generally adopted by modern versions; and (b) to emend conjecturally to ונדר (אמה אחת) "and a wall (1 cubit thick)" (Galling in Bertholet 146, 148; Elliger, ibid.; *BHS*). The second expedient better explains the present text of MT: דרך "passage" may have originated as a comparative gloss, noting דרך in v 11 instead of מהלך "walkway." Then an original ונדר "and a wall" was displaced by the similar-looking gloss. The wall is further described in v 7.

5. a. Lit. "were shortened." Brockington (*Hebrew Text* 237 = NEB) prefers a pointing קצרות "short," since the verb is intransitive (cf. Ehrlich, *Randglossen* 146).

5. b. The double usage מן of "from/consisting of" is awkward, but the text can hardly be understood otherwise. MT construes the verbal form from אכל "eat," with the derived sense "take away space," as in postbiblical Heb. (Ehrlich, ibid.; *HALAT* 44b, 45a; cf. Tg "took away"). However, an impf is unexpected in a descriptive context (cf. v 6b) and LXX "projected" points to the stem יכל "be able" with the sense "predominate (over)": cf. Job 31:23 (Elliger, *Geschichte* 89). Then a vocalization יָכְלוֹ is necessary (*BHS*). MT adds בנין "building," already in the *Vorlage* of LXX, which cannot be construed, unless with Zimmerli (394) one takes the final three words as a separate clause, in which case it awkwardly relates not to the west building, as in the context (vv 1, 10), but to the vestries themselves. Probably it was a gloss that supplied a subject to the sg נאצל in v 6 (cf. Zimmerli's translation "so [the building] was terraced"), but became attached to the phrase מהתחתנות ומהתכנות "from the lower and middle rooms" in v 5 instead of v 6.

6. a. Cornill (471) and Zimmerli (394) prefer LXX's *Vorlage* החיצנות "the outer (rooms)" to MT החצרות "the courts"; the latter finds reference to 40:17-18 or 40:38-46.

6. b. Elliger (*Geschichte* 92) related to אציל(ה) in 41:8, which he took as "terrace," finding here a verb "was terraced"; but see the note there. Driver (*Bib* 19 [1938] 185) explained the stem as a byform of נצל "take away."

8. a. For MT והנה על-פני ההיכל "and behold, facing the temple" it is preferable to read וְהֵנָּה עַל-פָּנֶיהָ הַכֹּל "and they were facing it; the whole" (= LXX). The visionary particle הנה "behold" does not suit this context, where no new object is revealed (Cornill, ibid.; Zimmerli, ibid.). The term היכל refers in chaps. 40-42 to the nave, not to the temple, for which בית "house" is used (Cornill, ibid.; Elliger, *Geschichte* 95 note 3). Wrong word division introduced the term (cf. Driver, *Bib* 35 [1954] 306-7). The suffix relates to the court; LXX implies על-פניהם "in front of them," mistakenly differentiating the rooms of v 8a from those of v 7.

8. b. See the previous note.

9. a. Q is to be followed. LXX found a reference to the "doors" (פתחי), as in v 12, which Zimmerli (395) prefers, but it was probably due to assimilation.

9. b. K is to be followed.

10. a. MT ברחב "in breadth" is difficult to explain in text-critical or exegetical terms. Driver's recourse to a ramp, as in 41:7 (*Bib* 35 [1954] 305), hardly fits here. LXX implies בראש "at the head," probably as a comparative gloss from v 12, as its order of words implies, but ultimately this reading must underlie the text. Did רחב originate as an explanatory gloss ("thickness") on the single cubit of v 4, and be rendered wrongly related to גדר "wall" in v 10? If so, גדר must have been the older reading in v 4, as argued earlier.

10. b. LXX presupposes הדרום "the south," which the context requires (see esp. v 13) and so which most scholars (even Keil 264) and modern versions read. MT דרך הקדים "in an easterly direction," it may be suggested, originated as a comparative gloss on מהקדים "from the east" in v 9bα, referring to דרך הקדים in v 12bα. The gloss was wrongly taken as a correction of the original directional phrase here, which also uses דרך.

11. a. LXX presupposes וכרחבן "and like their width" for MT כן רחבן "so (was) their width"; the context so requires. Was abbreviation (כ for כן) wrongly assumed?

11. b. MT וכל מוצאיהן "and all their exits" surprisingly accentuates this element. Generally וכמוצאיהן "and like their exits" is read: cf. the conflated וכלל-מ "and like all . . ." implied by LXX. Did כל "all" originate as a correction of v 8b?

12. a. MT in vv 11-12 has a seemingly conflated text וכפתחיהן וכפתחי "and like their doors and like the doors of." The second term, not represented by LXX, was evidently an error caused by homoeoarcton of *he*, which the first term corrected. In the *Vorlage* of the LXX פתח "door" later in v 12 was displaced by וכפתחי "and like the doors of," an annotation approximating to MT earlier. *BHS* and RSV, following Galling (in Fohrer 235) and Elliger (*Geschichte* 98 note 4), emend in accordance with v 9a, but see the note there.

12. b. MT's repetition of דרך "path" is generally taken as a dittograph (see *BHS*). Zimmerli (396) proposes a new clause.

12. c. See Elliger (*Geschichte* 101), who points הַגִּינָה and relates to the stem גנן "protect," comparing גִינָה for גֶּדָה in Lam 1:8 for the form (cf. GKC 20n). LXX presupposes הבינה "intervening"; within the Greek tradition the translation was glossed "a distance of 1 rod," with reference to the outer wall of 40:5.

12. d. The Heb. implies an objective suffix: cf. 32:11. One expects בבואו "as one enters," in line with v 9bα.

13. a. The copula appears necessary, as LXX Syr Vg suggest.

14. a. For the proleptic suffix see Joüon 146e; Driver, *L'Ancien Testament et l'Orient* 135 note 37.

14. b. Lit. "they are not to go (straight) out, but leave . . ."

15. a. Heb. הבית "the house" so signifies here, as in 40:5.

16. a. Heb. רוח "wind" so signifies here.

16. b. MT קנים (Q) חמש מאות "500 rods" is inconceivable since the dimensions given hitherto favor a square of 500 x 500 cubits (cf. Busink, *Tempel* 709-10); v 20 appears so to state and 45:2 does more clearly. A rod was 6 cubits (40:5), which gives a square of 3000 x 3000 cubits. To claim that only in this passage it is equivalent to a cubit (Barthélemy et al., *Preliminary Report*, vol. 5, 165) is willfully to perpetuate an erroneous reading. Here and in vv 17-19 קנים "rods" has been added in MT, presumably as a result of misunderstanding בקנה המדה "by the measuring rod" in vv 16b, 17b, 18b and 19b as an expression of the unit, like באמה "by the cubit" in 40:21; 47:3. It is not represented in LXX. For the ellipse of אמות "cubits" compare v 20; 43:16-17; 45:1; 46:22 (Cooke 462): K אמות "cubits" makes the unit explicit in a conflated text, perhaps as a correction of קנים "rods." In MT it has displaced the necessary מאות "100." The LXX specifies "cubits" once, in v 17 (and also in v 20aγ).

16. c. V 19 and LXX suggest that MT סביב "around" should be read as סבב "he turned" (the copula is not required in this asyndetic passage: see Gese, *Verfassungsentwurf* 29) and taken with v 17. The same applies to v 17b. The error arose by assimilation to the end of v 15.

18. a. LXX presupposes אל "to," as in v 19, for the object sign in MT. The error at the end of v 17 necessitated a change in MT.

Form/Structure/Setting

This long visionary account of the new temple complex is uneven in content, style and perspective. Basically it appears to fall into five sections: (i) 40:1-5, introduction and description of the perimeter wall; (ii) 40:6-37, the gate structures of the outer and inner courts; (iii) 40:47-41:4, the inner court and the temple; (iv) 41:5-15a, the buildings in the immediate area of the temple structure; and (v) 42:15-20, conclusion and dimension of the perimeter wall. The first and last sections obviously correspond and are of the same length (7 and 7½ lines in *BHS*); both feature a measuring rod. The third section (12 lines) is central and has an importance that often attaches to the middle portion of a Hebrew composition. One may speak of a loose chiasmus, ABCB'A', with the looseness relating to the second and fourth sections, which are quite unequal in size (44½ lines and 16½ lines) and diverse in content, but do lead the reader architecturally toward and away from the center respectively. Parunak (*Structural Studies* 510) with different divisions envisages a chiastic structure for 40:1-42:16 (ABCB'A'), but mistakenly links 42:1-14 with the outer court.

This basic account seems to have been supplemented at three points. 40:38-46 supplements 40:6-37 (B) by referring to rooms adjacent to certain of the gatehouses, while 42:1-14 supplements 41:5-15a (B') by mentioning two sets of rooms in the particular area; both are united in specifying a feature not found in the basic sections, the priestly use to which the respective rooms were to be put. Also, 41:15b-26 is concerned mainly with the woodwork of the temple: this passage obviously relates to the temple-oriented material of 40:47-41:4 (C) and separates 41:5-15a from the related supplementary material in 42:1-14. One expects to find it after 41:4, as a supplement to the C section, which in content it really is. The ultimate intent in chaps. 40-42 seems to have been to present an A/B+/C+/B'+/A' structure, but it has been flawed by the positioning of 41:15b-26. All three supplements echo the direct speech of the prophet's supernatural guide (41:4b), in 40:45-46; 41:22b and 42:13-14. However, there are differences: (a) while priestly functions are communicated in what one may call the B and B' supplements, a sacred element is identified in the C supplement, as in the C section; (b) in the B and B' supplements the direct speech comes at the end, as in the C section, while in the C supplement it comes in the middle; and (c) in the B and B' supplements the direct speech is extensive and prescriptive, while in the C supplement it is brief and descriptive, as in the C section. It is clear that the C supplement of 41:15b-26 stands somewhat apart from the other two.

Chaps. 40-42 are similar to chaps. 8-11 in consisting of the description of a visionary experience involving transportation to the Jerusalem area and guidance through the temple precincts. This vision majors in careful measurements of the constituent parts of the precincts. Insofar as the dimensions concern length and breadth but rarely height, it has generally been concluded that the account depends on an architectural ground plan, which may be true (for ancient parallels see *ANEP* 749 and cf. Isa 49:16; cf. Talmon and Fishbane, *ASTI* 10 [1975-76] 139, 142), but the measurements given may reflect what could be ascertained by someone walking, measuring rod in hand. Certainly the format was intended to be conducive to the construction of a ground plan, according to 43:11. But Busink (*Tempel* 773) has adduced the references to height in 41:6-8 (cf. 42:3)—one might mention too the wall height of 40:5 and the steps of 40:6, etc.—as evidence for a vertical perspective that belies a ground plan.

A full style with verbs of guidance and measuring appears in the main descriptive passages of 40:1-19, which after the introduction describes the outer east gate, and 40:47-41:4, which describes the inner court and the temple. As for 40:20-37, which describes the other outer gates and the inner gates, there is frequent use of a weak perfect with copula ומדד "and he measured" instead of the regular consecutive imperfect וימד used earlier. In the rest of what has been termed the basic account, 41:5-15a lacks guidance formulas; it falls into a cataloguing style in vv 5-12, with a series of nominal clauses, while vv 13-15a again exhibit the ומדד version of the measurement formula. In 42:15-20 the latter phenomenon also appears, at v 15, and is followed by a series of asyndetic verbs (cf. 40:20) in a weighty climax.

Of the supplementary passages, 40:38-46 lacks both guidance and measurement formulas, and so does 41:15b-26, while 42:1-14 has no measurement formulas and only an initial guidance formula. When one weighs up the evidence of style and content, the supplementary passages, which read like extended footnotes to the main sections, appear to be redactional additions to a primary account. Zimmerli (397) has observed on the one hand the similarity of 40:38-46 (or at least 44-46) and 42:1-14, and on the other hand the later insertion of 41:15b-26, in that it interrupts 41:5-15a and its continuation in 42:1-14. As so often in the literary units of this book, there is evidence of three strata: a basic layer, an added layer with related theme, and a third one that stands at a noticeable distance from the previous layers in its perspective. We have tended to credit the second stage to Ezekiel himself, and the third to later hands within the exilic period. Accordingly it is feasible that the triple layering of chaps. 40-42 reflects the same compositional process. The amplification in 41:15b-26, which is marked by different terminology (see Zimmerli 386), has then emanated from the priestly school of Ezekiel (cf. Zimmerli 387, 553). Mention should be made here of 40:46b, which appears secondarily to relate v 46a to 44:6-31 (see *Form/Structure/Setting* of chaps. 43-46).

Comment

1 The reference to "the new year" is ambiguous. Does it refer to the spring and so to 19 April 573 B.C. (Parker and Dubberstein, *Babylonian Chronology* 28) or to the autumn, to 22 October? The latter would link well with Lev 25:9: on that date the year of jubilee was proclaimed (cf. Lev 25:10; Ezek 46:17). Zimmerli (345-46) has noted that the particular year of exile lends support to a symbolic interpretation of the jubilee, the 50th year, with reference to the end of exile (cf. Lev 26:34): the 25th year marks a significant stage toward release. Moreover, in the ensuing dimensions the number twenty-five and its multiples predominate (Zimmerli 347; Greenberg, *Int* 38 [1984] 190; Levenson, *Theology* 24 note 56, interestingly compares the midpoint theme in Dante's *Divine Comedy*).

If one date points forward, the other points back, to the fall of Jerusalem. As a historical fact the language recalls 33:21, but in prophetic terms it is reminiscent of chaps. 8-11, where in another temple vision destruction was forecast. Compare הכתה העיר "the city was captured" with והכו . . . בעיר "in the city. . . and smite," 9:5. For the hand of Yahweh and Ezekiel's metaphysical transportation see 33:22; 37:1 and *Comment*.

2-5 The "very high mountain" represents theological geography and points to Yahweh's supremacy: cf. Isa 2:2. Mount Zion is in view (cf. 17:22; 20:40). The city-like appearance of the temple complex was doubtless prompted by its gate structures (Galling in Fohrer 223). The ostensibly human figure is a supernatural being, as his radiance indicates (cf. 1:7; Rev 21:17): his role will be to guide, measure and interpret. His equipment is a rod (lit. "reed") for short measurements and a tape for longer ones (cf. 47:3). The vision is explicitly related to the exiles: its purpose was to crystallize Yahweh's promises of restoration given through Ezekiel. The unit of measurement is defined as a long cubit. Scott has related the Hebrew common cubit to the Egyptian cubit of 6 palms or 24 fingers, close to 17.5 inches, and the long cubit to the Egyptian royal cubit of 7 palms or 28 fingers, about 20.6 inches; the extra palm or handbreadth amounts to 4 fingers (*JBL* 77 [1958] 205-14). The account will revert to the wall and state its purpose in 42:15-20. The height of the wall reflects its external measurement. The higher level of the ground in the outer court (vv 6, 22) meant that from the inside the wall was only about 2 cubits high.

6-16 The outer east gatehouse (see fig. 1) is treated as representative of the others. It is singled out in anticipation of its key role in 43:1-4. It is presupposed that the prophet followed his guide and watched him. Comparison with vv 22, 26 shows that there were seven steps: the outer court and its gatehouses were built about 4 cubits or 7 feet (cf. 40:49; 41:8) higher than the surrounding area. The gatehouse measured internally 50 cubits x 25 cubits (about 86 x 43 feet). Through the middle of the gatehouse ran a passage, with three alcoves on each side, doubtless meant as guardrooms, as in the case of Solomon's temple (1 Kgs 14:28).

The alcoves were separated by internal walls. At both ends of the passage were thresholds, with a porch at the inner end. The gate seems to have been set at the inner end of the outer threshold, so that it spanned the 13 cubits wide passage and overlapped the sidewalls of the 10 cubits wide threshold (Busink, *Tempel* 716-17). We are not told whether there was also a gate at the inner end of the gatehouse. Access to the alcoves was barred by a railing or the like. Light was provided by the window openings in the alcoves and porch. Mention is made of palm tree decoration on the ends of the walls between the alcoves (see further v 26; 41:18; cf. *ANEP* 654). The overall design of the gatehouse, with its three alcoves beside a corridor, is typical of pre-exilic Palestinian city gates, such as have been found at the sites of Megiddo, Hazor and Gezer (see Zimmerli 352-53; Busink, *Tempel* 714-15, 720; see *ANEP* 721).

17-19 A brief description is given of the outer court. The gatehouses projected into the court beyond the wall; on either side of them and extending to the same distance from the wall (i.e., 50 cubits) was a paved area. The thirty rooms, probably porticoes (cf. 42:6) and used by small groups of worshipers as meeting and eating places, seem to have been divided into eight on the east, north and south sides, 50 cubits wide and 25 cubits deep, and six on the west side, 25 cubits wide and 50 cubits deep (42:8; Vincent, *Jérusalem* 475; see Busink's diagram of the temple plan [fig. 2]). The area left unpaved was 100 cubits wide.

20-27 Now first the northern and then the southern inner gates are summarily described, together with the distance from the corresponding inner gates. There was no gate on the west side.

28-37 The three inner gates are measured from the inner court. The dimensions are the same, but they are mirror images of the outer gates in that their porches are placed at their outer ends and so face the (inner) porches of those gates. The design of the inner gates is the expected one, and exposes the unusual nature of the design of the outer ones. The effect is to make a demarcation between the two courts: properly entry into the sanctuary occurs only at the point of passing into the inner court (cf. Busink, *Tempel* 720-21). One receives the impression of the greater holiness of the inner court (cf. 42:14; 44:19; 46:1-3, 20). Eight steps led up to the inner gatehouses: thus the inner court formed a terrace nearly 5 cubits or 8 feet above the outer court. There was no west gate: the large building of 41:12 took its place.

38-46 The first supplement to the basic account falls into two parts. It begins with extra information about the north gatehouse just mentioned (vv 38-43; see *Note* 40. b.) and then has more to say in connection with the north and south inner gate structures (vv 44-46). Both parts are interested in cultic functions. Washing of the sacrificial victim took place after the slaughter (cf. Lev 1:9, 13). The holocaust was completely burned on the altar hearth; parts of the other sacrifices were eaten by priests. Sin offerings restored to a state of purity; reparation offerings accompanied fines for damage done to persons or property. In the case of the outside tables we are to envisage a landing 25 cubits wide at the top of the steps, alongside walls 7½ cubits wide on either side of a 10 cubit wide porch (Busink, *Tempel* 727-28). In v 42 "the holocaust" seems to be mentioned as shorthand for the three offerings of v 39 (Gese, *Verfassungsentwurf* 158). The outside tables were presumably used for the slaughter of the "sacrificial offerings" (זבח, v 42b), otherwise known as "shared (or peace) offerings" (cf. 43:27; 46:2). There

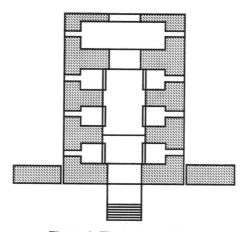

Figure 1. The outer gatehouse

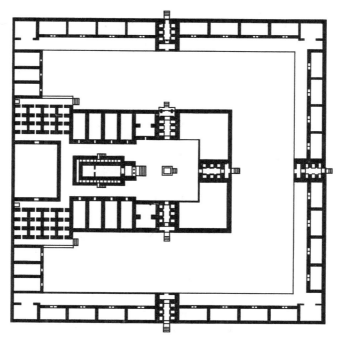

Figure 2. The temple plan

was a distinction in holiness between the two types of offerings in that only the latter were shared by the people in a sacrificial meal (Gese, *Verfassungsentwurf* 159; cf. 46:19-20).

In vv 44-46 the topic of the room of v 38 is expanded in a seemingly independent way: the two passages may have originated separately (see Zimmerli 365-66, 549). Busink (*Tempel* 729-30) finds difficulty in squaring the purpose of the room beside the north gatehouse with v 38: should not altar personnel occupy it? But in the light of information supplied in later chapters the temple personnel align with the Levites responsible for slaughtering the animals (44:11) and assigned to general temple duties (44:11, 14; 46:24). V 46b (see *Form/Structure/Setting*) identifies the second group with the Zadokite priests who are differentiated from the Levites in 44:15-16 and perform the actual sacrifices. In the present representation, however, both groups are described as priests .

47 This verse concludes the information about the inner gates (vv 28-37), as vv 17-19 concluded vv 6-16, and vv 23 and 27 concluded vv 20-22 and vv 24-26 respectively. The "court" seems to refer to the inner, unpaved area between the gates and to the east of the temple: on its southeast and northeast was probably a pavement corresponding to the lower pavement of v 18. There is strangely no mention of a wall around the court. The altar is described in 43:13-17.

40:48-41:4 The temple building, set on a raised foundation 6 cubits or 10 feet high (cf. 41:8) is divided into three rooms, the porch, the nave and the holy of holies. The pillars beside the porch are generally identified with the freestanding pillars named Jachin and Boaz in Solomon's temple (1 Kgs 7:15-22; contra Busink, *Tempel* 752; cf. vol. 1, 174). In increasing sacred privacy the openings into the rooms contract from 14 cubits, to 10 cubits, to 6 cubits, although their internal width is the same, 20 cubits. Although Ezekiel, with his priestly rank, is taken into the first two rooms, his angelic guide goes alone into the third. By such means is exemplified the absolute degree of holiness revealed in the declaration that breaks the silence of the basic account.

5-15a This section is concerned with the temple complex formed by the two annexes, and with the areas to its north, south and west. In vv 5-12 it supplies individual measurements and in vv 13-15a overall ones corresponding to the areas described in 40:48-41:12. First, attached to the south, west and north sides of the temple were annex rooms. As in Solomon's temple (1 Kgs 6:6, 10), they were structurally differentiated from the holy temple itself, by building the temple wall in a vertically narrowing design so that wooden beams, resting on the resultant ledges, supported the two upper stories. If each story contained thirty rooms, the distribution was doubtless twelve on each side and six at the rear. The total dimensions of the temple complex on its raised foundation (v 8) add up to 100 cubits long by 50 cubits wide (cf. v 13). The width evidently has to be increased by the "ramp" of v 7, if such it is, which Busink (*Tempel* 763) has compared to the outer stairing of the Babylonian ziggurat.

The open area on the north and south sides of the complex extended 20 cubits each way to a wall, beyond which were other rooms that are left undescribed (v 10). The walls and open areas, together with the complex, made up a total width of 100 cubits. The resultant square of 100 x 100 cubits was bounded by one of the same size on the west: it was broken up into another open area —significantly called "the restricted area" (lit. "cut off place": cf. Gk. τέμενος "sacred precinct" [Vogt, *Untersuchungen* 144]) since it was next to the holy of holies—100 cubits by 20 cubits, and a structure called simply "the building" whose external area was 100 (=5 + 90 + 5) cubits by 80 (= 5 + 70 + 5) cubits. Over on the east side of the temple the two rectangles of open space on either side of the porch were also called a "restricted area." The open spaces around the temple complex obviously made it into a structural island of holiness, while the building on the west served similarly to seal off the back of the holy of holies.

15b-26 This appendix to 40:48-41:4 is concerned with the internal design and decoration of the temple porch and nave, with respect to its woodwork. The wooden framing of the windows corresponds to the triple rabbeted design in the Lady at the Window carving found at Nimrud (*ANEP* 131). The windows must have been set high in the walls, above the level of the annex rooms, as evidently in Solomon's temple (1 Kgs 6:4-5). The reliefs on the paneling complement the palms seen in the gatehouses with two-headed cherubim, but omit the flowers added in the Solomonic temple (1 Kgs 6:29, 32, 35). The two heads are a two-dimensional version of the four heads of 1:10; 10:14 (Wevers 213; Haran, *Temples* 258 note 17). The all-seeing cherubim or sphinxes are vigilant guardians of God's sovereign holiness, while the palms, as often in ancient Near Eastern art, represent the tree of life (cf. 47:1-12). The door frames, as in Solomon's temple, had quadruple rabbeting (cf. Noth, *Könige* 127; Zimmerli 388). A wooden piece of furniture is specified, an altar-like table, which evidently refers to the table for the showbread (lit. "bread of the presence [פנים]," 1 Kgs 7:48; cf. לפני "before," v 22). The "corners" seem to refer to the "horns" on top of an altar (cf. 43:15). The description in terms of an altar is presumably meant to discourage any notion of food being eaten by the deity (cf. Ps 50:12-13). For the design of the doors of the nave and the rear room ("holy place," vv 21, 23) see Gese's sketch reproduced here (fig. 3; cf. Zimmerli 389).

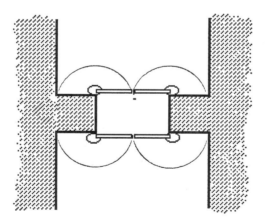

Figure 3. The inner doors of the temple

42:1-14 This second main supplement wants to amplify the description of 41:5-15a, which at an earlier stage it doubtless followed, by reference to two identical structures on the north and south sides of the building behind the temple. Earlier commentators located them on either side of the temple, but Elliger (*Geschichte*

80-84, 93-94) established their location further west, by comparison with 40:17-18; 41:12, 15. First, a northern set of rooms is described in vv 1-10a, and then the southern counterpart briefly in vv 10b-12. The prophet is taken from the temple area of 41:5-15a, presumably out through the north inner gate and in a westerly direction, to view the north rooms from the outer court. There is a pointed avoidance of the alternative possibility, to linger behind the temple. Seemingly, there is a gap between the building and the rooms: נֶגֶד "opposite" implies some intervening space. On their south side they were 100 cubits long, parallel to both the 20 cubits of the restricted area and the 80 (= 5 + 70 + 5) cubits of the exterior of the building. Access was via doors in the north wall and a path 10 cubits wide running parallel with the set of rooms. The path on its north side was bounded by a wall that separated it from the outer court for a length of 50 cubits. This path, which was open to the outer court at its eastern end, was 100 cubits long, corresponding to the length of the set of rooms; the other 50 cubits were protected by other rooms built on the pavement alongside the northwest perimeter wall of the whole temple complex. Vv 4 and 7-10a refer to this path and wall. It is customary to relate v 4 to a path on the other (south) side, but they can hardly be localized there in view of the prepositional phrase "in front of" with relation to the prophet's perspective.

The construction of the rooms is not clear. The roof was built on three levels. Was this to accommodate the difference in level between the outer court and the inner court (cf. Galling's design reproduced here [fig. 4]) or was it purely an artistic feature?

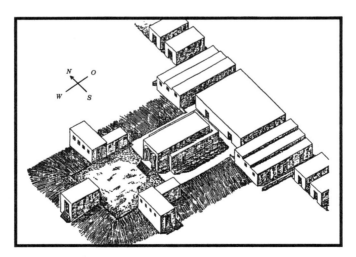

Figure 4. Galling's reconstruction of the inner temple area

A related issue is whether each level had one series of rooms (cf. Busink, *Tempel* 741) or whether the highest level encompassed three stories. The reference to the absence of pillars is not clear: are they envisaged as forming a substructure, as the rooms of 40:44 may have had? In vv 10b-12 the southern rooms are briefly described. The reference to exits must be to access on the far side adjoining the western building (cf. Elliger, *Geschichte* 99). The statements of vv 13-14 ascribe two functions to the rooms. First, they were to serve as a refectory for the priests, with reference to the offerings used as their food (cf. 44:29 *Comment*; Num 18:9-10). The rooms would have this sacred function because of their position at the rear of the temple, on the level of the inner court, which was reserved for priests. Second, they were to be vestries or changing rooms, where sacred clothing used while performing duties in the inner court and nave would be left. Different clothing was to be worn in the outer court accessible to the people.

15-20 This explicit conclusion rounds off the account with further reference to the perimeter wall of 40:5 and with fresh mention of the measuring rod of 40:5-8. It originally stood after 41:15a, and it follows the directional order of 40:6-41:15a as it related to areas near the outer wall: east, north, south and west. In staccato sentences suitable for a finale the collective area is surveyed. The dimension of 500 cubits accords with details given in 40:6-41:15a. From south to north along the orientation of the gatehouses there stretches a total of four gatehouses (4 x 50 cubits), two outer courts (2 x 100 cubits) and the inner court (100 cubits). From east to west the area embraces two gatehouses (2 x 50 cubits), the outer and inner courts (100 + 100 cubits), the temple including the rear annex (100 cubits), the restricted area (20 cubits) and the rear building (80 cubits).

There is a lack of clarity concerning the relation of the perimeter wall to the back walls of the rooms and of the rear building. Were they the same, with the back wall of the building narrowing to 5 cubits (41:12; cf. 40:6)? Or was the perimeter wall a supporting structure outside them, as the LXX appears to have envisaged (cf. Busink, *Tempel* 711-12)? The latter solution would exceed the dimension of 500 cubits. Either the former expedient is correct or there is a slight inconsistency here.

The statement of the purpose of the wall in v 20b reveals the sanctity of the temple area as the domain of God. This sphere of the divine was set aside, in the world and yet not of the world, as a colony of heaven.

Explanation

Chaps. 40-42 are a celebration. They harness the wagon of contemporary reality to a star of hope. The prophet and his constituency are stuck fast in exile. For Ezekiel and those of the exiles who had been his fellow hostages, twenty-five weary years have elapsed since they were deported in 597 B.C. Yet on this Rosh ha-Shanah or New Year's Day, when the vision is experienced, he is looking forward to the completion of a calendar process, the year of Jubilee at the end of forty-nine years (cf. Lev 25:9-10; Ezek 46:17). He views it as a metaphor for God's new work of liberation and restoration for his people. At this spiritual midpoint he celebrates in advance the "salvation that is nearer than" ever before (Rom 13:11). Present time and the eschatological future are blended in a series of geometrical shapes, squares and half-squares, whose dimensions are made up of twenty-fives and fifties and their multiples. Even the total number of steps from outside the temple area to the temple itself amounts to twenty-five (7 + 8 + 10 [40:22, 34, 49]). The account is an architectural symphony, an intricate composition that counterpoints the predicament of exile and the promise of restoration in a grand celebration of God's sure purposes. This theological stylization is presented both as an assurance and as a challenge to the exiles; it ministers pastorally to their needs (40:4; cf. 43:10-11).

Along with chaps. 43-46, the vision stands as a positive counterpart to the negative temple vision of chaps. 8-11. Parunak (*Structural Studies* 508-9) has observed that 40:1-2 echoes the phraseology of 8:1-3, while 43:2-5 picks up motifs found in 8:3-4. In stark contrast to the cultic aberrations and consequent judgment stands an edifice whose symmetry spells decent order and which brings only glory to the holy God, keeping at bay all that is profane. No abominable illustrations besmirched these walls (8:10; cf. 43:10)!

Moreover, Ezek 37:26-28 (cf. 20:40) serves to pave the way for the vision, with the promise that God would set his sanctuary among his people. The vision, unfolded by the supernatural guide and portraying the temple as already built, is a concrete outworking of the promise, in terms of feet and inches. It fleshes out the promise with gates and courts, with pavements and pillars. It is true to the heart of the promise, although the term "sanctuary" is not used in these initial chapters: "sanctuary" (מקדש) relates to holiness (קדש), and above all the temple area is a monument to the holiness of God. The perimeter wall demarcates the sacred square. The massive gatehouses, as forbidding as those at the entrance to any city, warn all who come to worship of the awesome solemnity of the areas beyond. Access should not lightly be undertaken. "Who can go up to the mount of Yahweh and who can stand in his holy place? The one who has clean hands and a pure heart" (Ps 24:3-4; cf. Ps 15; Isa 33:14-15). There is a sliding scale of holiness. The temple area stands out from its surroundings like a three-tiered wedding cake, with a series of elevations marking first the outer court, where the people worshiped, then the inner court, where only the priests might go, and finally the temple with its innermost shrine, over which a veil of reticence is drawn.

This symbolic stylization, along with the geometric symmetry, contrasts with the pre-exilic temple, where the outer court enclosed the palace complex as well as the temple, and both courts were open to the laity (cf. Isa 1:12; Ps 100:4; see Haran, *Temples* 192-93. On the detailed relation between the pre-exilic temple and Ezekiel's see Zimmerli 358-60, 379-80, 400-401).

The ministry of the prophet and his literary successors was to their own generation. We twentieth-century believers may only overhear the message of theological hope and extrapolate its spirit in terms of 1 Cor 3:16-17; 2 Cor 6:16-7:1; Heb 3:6; 6:19-20; 12:22-24. In Rev 21:22 there is no temple! Even the post-exilic community who rebuilt the temple found only peripheral value in the vision (Jeremias, *ZAW* 11 [1934] 109-12, critiqued by Noth, *Könige* 107). The Qumran sect in their Temple Scroll developed from this vision their ideals for the temple, in terms of a quadratic layout and gradations of holiness (see Maier, *Temple Scroll* 58-65, 90-96). The modern reader is called, like the exiles, to glean from the vision a reflection of divine reality that challenges present living and invests the future with hope.

The New Temple in Action (43:1-46:24)

Bibliography

Abba, R. "Priests and Levites in Deuteronomy." *VT* 27 (1977) 257-67. _____. "Priests and Levites in Ezekiel." *VT* 28 (1978) 1-9. **Allan, N.** "The Identity of the Jerusalem Priesthood During the Exile." *Heythrop Journal* 23 (1982) 259-69. **Baltzer, D.** *Ezechiel und Deuterojesaja.* BZAW 121. Berlin: de Gruyter, 1971, 49-58. **Baudissin, W. W. Graf.** *Die Geschichte des alttestamentlichen Priestertums.* Osnabrück: Otto Zeller, 1889 (reprinted 1967), 105-34. _____. "Priests and Levites." *Dictionary of the Bible.* Ed. J. Hastings. Vol. 4. Edinburgh: T. & T. Clark, 1902, 67-97. **Botterweck, G. J.** "Textkritische Bemerkungen zu Ez xliv 3a." *VT* 1 (1951) 145-46. **Cody, A.** *A History of Old Testament Priesthood.* AnBib 34. Rome: Pontifical Biblical Institute, 1969. **Cross, F. M.** *Canaanite Myth and Hebrew Epic.* Cambridge, MA: Harvard University Press, 1973, 207-15. **Duke, R. K.** "Punishment or Restoration? Another Look at the Levites of Ezekiel 44:6-16." *JSOT* 40 (1988) 61-81. **Ebach, J. H.** "*Pgr* = (Toten-) Opfer? Ein Vorschlag zum Verständnis von Ez. 43.7, 9." *UF* 3 (1971) 365-68. **Eissfeldt, O.** *Erstlinge und Zehnten in Alten Testament.* Beiträge zur Wissenschaft vom AT 22. Leipzig: Hinrich, 1917. **Emerton, J. A.** "Priests and Levites in Deuteronomy." *VT* 12 (1962) 129-38. **Galling, K.** "Erwägungen zum Säulenheiligtum von Hazor." *ZDPV* 75 (1959) 1-13. **Greenberg, M.** "A New Approach to the History of the Israelite Priesthood." *JAOS* 70 (1950) 41-47. **Gunneweg, A. H. J.** *Leviten und Priester.* FRLANT 89. Göttingen: Vandenhoeck und Ruprecht, 1965, 188-203. **Koch, K.** *Die Priesterschrift von Exodus 25 bis Leviticus 16.* FRLANT 71. Göttingen: Vandenhoeck und Ruprecht, 1959, 104-8. **McConville, J. G.** "Priests and Levites in Ezekiel: A Crux in the Interpretation of Israel's History." *TynBul* 34 (1983) 3-31. _____. *Law and Theology in Deuteronomy.* JSOTSup 33. Sheffield: Dept. of Biblical Studies, University of Sheffield, 1984. **Mettinger, T.N.D.** *The Dethronement of Sabaoth. Studies in the Shem and Kabod Theologies.* ConB OT 18. Lund: Gleerup, 1982. **Milgrom, J.** "Atonement in the OT." *IDBSup* 78-82. _____. *Studies in Levitical Terminology,* 1. Berkeley: University of California Press, 1970. _____. "Sin-Offering or Purification-Offering?" *VT* 21 (1971) 237-39. _____. "Two Kinds of *hattat.*" *VT* 26 (1976) 333-37. _____. "Profane Slaughter and a Formulaic Key to the Composition of Deuteronomy." *HUCA* 47 (1976) 1-17. **Neiman, D.** "*Pgr*: A Canaanite Cult-Object in the Old Testament." *JBL* 67 (1948) 55-60. **Parunak, H. van D.** "Transitional Techniques in the Bible." *JBL* 102 (1983) 525-48. **Talmon, S.**, and **Fishbane, M.** "The Structuring of Biblical Books: Studies in the Book of Ezekiel." *ASTI* 10 (1975/76) 129-53. **Talmon, S.** "The Textual Study of the Bible—A New Outlook." In Cross, F. M., and Talmon, S., *Qumran and the History of the Biblical Text.* Cambridge, MA: Harvard University Press, 1975, 321-400. **Wellhausen, J.** *Prolegomena to the History of Israel.* E.T. Edinburgh: Black, 1885 (reprinted New York: Meridian Books, 1957). **Wright, D. P.** *The Disposal of Impurity.* SBL Dissertation Series 101. Atlanta: Scholars Press, 1987, 149-55. **Zohar, N.** "Repentance and Purification: The Significance and Semantics of חטאת in the Pentateuch." *JBL* 107 (1988) 609-18.

Translation

[1] *Then he brought me to the east-facing[a] gate.[b]* [2] *My attention was drawn to the glory of the God of Israel coming from the east. The noise it made was as loud as floodwaters, and the land was lit up by its brightness.* [3] *The manifestation[a] was comparable to the one I had seen when Yahweh came[b] to destroy[c] the city, and to the one[d] I had seen by the river Chebar, and I fell on my face.* [4] *The glory of Yahweh approached the temple via the east-*

facing gate.[a] [5]*The spirit lifted me up and brought me into the inner court, and I observed the glory of Yahweh filling the temple.*[a] [6] *I heard someone speaking*[a] *to me from the temple—the*[b] *man was standing next to me at the time.* [7]*"Human one," he said to me, "The*[a] *place of my throne, the*[a] *place for the soles of my feet, where I will live among the Israelites for ever—never again will the community of Israel or their kings sully my holy name with their debauchery or with the memorials*[b] *of their kings erected at their death.*[c] [8]*When they set*[a] *their threshold beside my threshold and their doorposts next to my doorposts, with only a wall separating them from me, they used to sully my holy name with the shocking practices they committed, and so in my anger I destroyed them.* [9]*From now on they must cease to associate me with*[a] *their debauchery and their royal memorials, and I will live among them for ever.* [10]*You, human one, are to describe the temple to the community of Israel, to make them ashamed of their iniquities. They are to measure its layout,*[a] [11]*and then they themselves*[a] *will be ashamed of all they have done. Inform them of the design*[b] *of the temple and its layout, its exits and its entrances,*[c] *and all the instructions*[d] *and regulations for it. Draw it for them to see, so that they may duly follow all the instructions and regulations for it*[e] *and carry them out.* [12]*This is the instruction for the temple area on the top of the mountain: the whole territory surrounding it is particularly holy.*[a]

[13]*"These are the dimensions of the altar, in cubits increased by a handbreadth. Its gutter*[a] *is 1 cubit (deep) and 1 cubit wide, while its*[b] *ridge all round the edge is 1*[c] *span (high). The protruding base*[d] *of the altar is constructed as follows:* [14]*the distance from*[a] *the gutter in the ground up to the ledge of the lower plinth*[b] *is 2 cubits, and the width (of the ledge) is 1 cubit. The distance from the ledge of the shorter plinth to that of the taller one is 4 cubits, and its width*[c] *is 1 cubit.* [15]*The hearth*[a] *is 4 cubits (high), and from the hearth project horns, four in number.*[b] [16]*The hearth is 12 cubits long by*[a] *12 cubits wide, a square with four equal sides.* [17]*The plinth is 14 (cubits) long by 14 wide with four equal sides,*[a] *and the ridge surrounding it*[b] *is ½ cubit*[c] *(wide), while the related*[d] *gutter extends 1 cubit all round. Its*[e] *steps face*[f] *east."*

[18]*He said to me, "Human one, here is the message of the Lord*[a] *Yahweh. These are the regulations for the altar, when it has been constructed, to permit the sacrificing of holocausts on it and the splashing of blood against it.* [19]*You are to give a young bull as a sin offering to the levitical priests of Zadokite lineage, who have access to me in my service—the Lord Yahweh is speaking.* [20]*You are to take*[a] *some of its blood and put it on its four horns, the four corners of the plinth and all round the ridge, and so decontaminate*[b] *it and make expiation for it.* [21]*Then take the sin offering bull*[a] *and get it burned*[b] *outside the sanctuary area*[c] *at the place designated*[d] *in the temple area.* [22]*On the second day you are to offer an unblemished young goat as the sin offering and they are to decontaminate the altar, as they did with the bull.* [23]*When you have finished the decontamination, you are to offer an unblemished young bull and an unblemished young ram,* [24]*offering them in Yahweh's presence, and the priests are to throw salt on them and sacrifice them to Yahweh as a holocaust.* [25]*Every day for seven days you are to prepare a goat as a sin offering. They must also prepare a young bull and a young ram, both unblemished.* [26]*Over a period of seven days they are to make expiation for the altar and so cleanse it and dedicate*[a] *it,* [27]*and they are to complete this period. On the eighth day and afterwards the priests will sacrifice your*[a] *holocausts and shared offerings*[b] *on the altar, and I will accept you. So runs the oracle of the Lord Yahweh."*

[44:1]*He brought me back to the east-facing outer gate of the sanctuary area, but it was closed.* [2]*He*[a] *said to me, "This gate is to be kept closed. It is not to be opened and no human beings are to come in through it, because Yahweh, the God of Israel, has come through it and so it is to be kept closed.* [3]*The head of state*[a] *is to sit in it, eating a meal in Yahweh's presence. He is to enter from the side of the gate porch and leave from the same side."*

[4]*Then he brought me in through the north gate to the front of the temple. There I saw the glory of Yahweh filling Yahweh's temple, and I fell on my face.* [5]*He*[a] *said to me, "Pay attention, human one, use your eyes to see and your ears to hear everything I tell you about all the regulations for Yahweh's temple and all the instructions for it.*[b] *Pay attention to all*[c] *the procedures for entering*[d] *the temple and to all*[e] *those for exiting the sanctuary.*

[6]*"Tell that rebellious community,*[a] *the community of Israel, the following message from the Lord Yahweh: You went too far in all your shocking practices, community of Israel,* [7]*when you introduced foreigners*[a] *uncircumcised in heart and body to function in my sanctuary, profaning it*[b] *when you offered my food,*[c] *the fat and the blood. They*[d] *caused my covenant to be broken because of*[e] *all such shocking practices of yours.* [8]*You failed to undertake the duties*[a] *pertaining to what I hold sacred.*[b] *Instead, you appointed them*[c] *to undertake those duties for me. Therefore*[d] [9]*the Lord Yahweh's message is as follows: No foreigner uncircumcised in heart and body is to enter my sanctuary, not one*[a] *of the foreigners living among the Israelites.* [10]*Rather, the Levites will do so,*[a] *who absconded from me when Israel*[b] *went astray from me in pursuit of their idols. They will suffer punishment for their iniquity:*[c] [11]*they will function in my sanctuary, carrying out security*[a] *service at the temple gates and other services in the temple area. They it is who will slaughter the holocausts and sacrifices for the people, and they it is who will be in attendance on them to serve them.* [12]*Because*[a] *they used to serve*[b] *them in the presence of their idols and caused the community of Israel to fall into iniquity, for that reason I swear*[c] *with uplifted hand an oath against them, runs the Lord Yahweh's oracle, that they will suffer punishment for their own iniquity.*[d] [13]*They will have no access to me by acting as my priests or by having access to anything I hold sacred or most sacred. They are to suffer the shame they deserve and the consequences of the shocking practices they have perpetrated.* [14]*I will make them responsible for duties that pertain to all the labor*[a] *of the temple area and to all the work that has to be done in it.*

[15]*"The levitical priests of Zadokite lineage, however, who discharged the duties of my sanctuary when the Israelites went astray from me, are to be the ones who have access to me in serving me. They will be in attendance on me, offering me the fat and the blood, runs the Lord Yahweh's oracle.* [16]*They it is who will enter my sanctuary, and they it is who will carry out duties on my personal behalf.*

[17]*"When they come through the gates of the inner court, they are to put on linen clothes: they are to wear nothing woolen when they serve in the gates of the inner court and further inside.* [18]*They are to wear on their heads linen caps and on their loins linen breeches, and nothing round their waists that causes sweat.* [19]*When they go out to the people in the outer court,*[a] *they are to take off the clothes they wore while serving and leave them in the sacred rooms. They must put on other clothing, to prevent them transmitting holiness to the people from their clothes.* [20]*They should neither shave their heads nor wear long locks, but keep their hair quite short.* [21]*None of the priests is to drink wine when he enters the inner court.* [22]*They are not to marry widows or divorcees, but only virgins of Israelite stock; however, they may marry widows provided that they are widows of priests.* [23]*They are to teach my people the difference between what is sacred and what is profane, and to make them knowledgeable in distinguishing cleanness and uncleanness.* [24]*In*

disputes they should pass formal judgment,[a] using my rulings as the basis of their verdicts.[b] They are to follow my instructions and regulations relating to all my public services, and to keep my sabbaths holy. [25] They must not defile themselves by contact[a] with a dead person; they may only get defiled in the case of a father or mother, a son or daughter, a brother[b] or unmarried sister. [26] After purification each one should let a week elapse,[a] [27] and on the day he comes to the sanctuary,[a] entering the inner court for service in the sanctuary, he is to offer up a sin offering for himself. So runs the Lord Yahweh's oracle.

[28] "They are not to own any tenured land:[a] I am their basis of tenure. You are to give them no property in Israel: I represent their property. [29] The cereal offerings, sin offerings and reparation offerings are to be their food, and they are to have everything devoted[a] by Israel. [30] The best of all the firstfruits of all kinds[a] and each contribution of every kind selected from your total contributions are to belong to the priests. You must give to the priest the best of your dough[b] and in this way make a blessing rest on your home.[c] [31] The priests cannot eat any bird or beast that has died from natural causes or from predators.

[45:1] "When you allot the country for tenure,[a] you must set aside a reservation for Yahweh as a sacred area of the country 25,000 (cubits) long[b] and 20,000[c] wide, and it is[d] to be sacred throughout its entire extent. ([2] Of this area a square of 500 by[a] 500 [cubits] is to belong to[b] the sanctuary, surrounded by 50 cubits of open land.) From this measured area you[a] should measure off a section 25,000[b] (cubits) long and 10,000 wide, containing the sanctuary. It will be the most sacred part [4] of the country.[a] It will belong to the priests that serve in the sanctuary, who have access to Yahweh in his service, and will furnish room for their houses (as well as open land[b] for the sanctuary). [5] A section 25,000 (cubits) long and 10,000 wide is to be assigned[a] to the Levites who serve in the temple area as their property, with cities to live in.[b] [6] Alongside the sacred reservation you must provide an area 5,000 (cubits) wide and 25,000 long as the city's property; it will belong to the whole community of Israel. [7] The territory on each side of the sacred reservation and the city property, adjoining both of them, will belong to the head of state. On the west side it will extend westwards and on the east[a] side eastwards. In length it will correspond to[b] one of the (tribal) tracts,[c] being bounded by the west[d] and east frontiers [8] of the country. That will be[a] his property in Israel. Never again will my heads of state[b] oppress my people: they will let the community of Israel have[c] the country, tribe by tribe.

[9] "This is the Lord Yahweh's message: You heads of the state of Israel, you have gone too far. Have done with violence and mayhem, and practice what is just and fair. Give my people respite from your evictions. So runs the Lord Yahweh's oracle.

[10] "Have standard weights and a standard ephah and bath. [11] The ephah and bath are to have the same capacity: the bath is to contain 1/10th homer and the ephah 1/10th homer, the capacity of each being determined by the homer. [12] The shekel is to be 20 gerahs. 5 shekels are to be really 5; 10 shekels are to be 10. There must be 50 shekels to your mina.[a]

[13] "These are the contributions you should give: 1/6th ephah out of every homer of wheat and 1/6th[a] ephah out of every homer of barley; [14] the set amount of oil, oil being measured by the bath,[a] 1/10th bath out of each kor, at the rate of 10 baths to the kor[b]; [15] 1 sheep out of a flock of 200 from Israel's watered land (?)[a] for the cereal offerings, holocausts and shared offerings that will be used to make expiation for them (so runs the Lord Yahweh's oracle). [16] All the people[a] will be liable for[b] these contributions to the head of state in Israel. [17] The head of state will be responsible for the holocausts[a] and cereal offerings and the libations at the festivals, new moons and sabbaths—all the public services[b] of the community of Israel. He is to provide the sin offerings, cereal offerings, holocausts and shared offerings given that expiation may be made on behalf of the community of Israel.

[18] "The Lord Yahweh's message is as follows: On the first of the first month you[a] are to take an unblemished young bull and decontaminate the sanctuary. [19]The priest will take some of the blood from this sin offering and put it on the doorposts[a] of the temple, the four corners of the altar plinth and the doorposts[a] of the gate to the inner court. [20]You are to do likewise on the seventh of the month,[a] for[b] anyone who sins inadvertently or through ignorance. In this way you are to make expiation for the temple.[c] [21]On the fourteenth day of the first month you should hold the passover, after which unleavened bread is to be eaten[a] for seven[b] days. [22]The head of state is to provide on that day a bull as a sin offering for himself and all the people in the land. [23]During the seven days of the festival he is to provide as a holocaust to Yahweh seven bulls and seven rams, unblemished beasts, on each of the seven days; also a young goat for a sin offering each day. [24]For every bull and ram he is to provide an ephah as a cereal offering, with a hin of oil to every ephah. [25]At the festival that begins on the fifteeenth day of the seventh month he is to make the same provision for seven days, the same sin offerings, holocausts,[a] cereal offerings and oil.

[46:1] "The Lord Yahweh's message is as follows: The east-facing gate to the inner court is to be kept closed on the six working days, but on the sabbath it shall be opened, and also on the new moon day. [2]The head of state is to enter through the porch on the outer side of the gatehouse and to take his stand by its doorpost, while the priests present his holocaust and shared offering. He is to kowtow in worship on the threshold[a] of the gatehouse and then leave, but the gate is not to be closed till the evening. [3]On sabbaths and new moons the people in the land are to kowtow worshipfully in Yahweh's presence by the entrance to the same gate. [4]On the sabbath the holocaust brought to Yahweh by the head of state is to consist of six unblemished lambs and an unblemished ram, [5]while the cereal offering is to be an ephah with the ram and as much as he cares to give with the lambs, together with a hin of oil to every ephah. [6]On the new moon day it is to consist of an unblemished[a] young bull and six lambs and a ram, which are also to be unblemished; [7]and an ephah with the bull and a further one with the ram are what he must present as a cereal offering, and as much as he can afford with the lambs, and a hin of oil to every ephah. [8]When the head of state enters, he is to do so through the porch of the gatehouse and to leave the same way. [9]But when the people in the land come into Yahweh's presence for the public services, those who enter through the north gate to kowtow in worship should leave by the south gate, while those who enter through the south gate are to leave by the north gate. They are not to go back through the gate of entry, but leave[a] by the opposite[b] one. [10]The head of state is to join them, entering as they do and leaving[a] as they do. [11]At festivals and other public services the cereal offering should be an ephah with each bull and a further one with each ram, and as much as he cares to give with the lambs, together with a hin of oil to every ephah. [12]Whenever the head of state presents a voluntary sacrifice, whether a holocaust or shared offering as a voluntary sacrifice to Yahweh, the east-facing gate should be opened for him, and he is to present his holocaust or shared offering just as he does on the sabbath. Then he should leave, and the gate is to be closed after he has done so.

[13] "You[a] are to present an unblemished yearling lamb as a daily holocaust to Yahweh, presenting it every morning. [14]In addition to it you are to present every morning a cereal offering consisting of 1/6th ephah and 1/3rd hin of oil to moisten the flour. This cereal offering for Yahweh is a permanent ruling.[a] [15]The lamb, together with the cereal offering and the oil, is to be presented[a] every morning as the regular holocaust.

[16] "The Lord Yahweh's message is as follows: If the head of state makes a gift to any of his sons, it will become the latter's tenured possession[a] and, passing on to his sons, become

their tenured property. [17] *But if he makes a gift out of his tenured possessions to anyone in his service, it will belong to that person till the year of release and then revert*[a] *to the head of state. After all, it is his tenured possession; it must pass to his sons.*[b] [18] *The head of state must not seize any part of the people's tenured land by ousting them from*[a] *their property oppressively. He must settle his own property on his sons, to avoid my people becoming displaced from their personal property.*"

[19] *Then he brought me through the entrance adjacent to the gatehouse that leads to the north-facing sacred rooms*[a] *of the priests.*[b] *There I found a place at the west end,*[c] [20] *about which he told me, "This is the place where*[a] *the priests are to boil the meat of the reparation offerings and sin offerings, and where they are to bake the cereal offerings. Then they will not have to bring them out into the outer court and so transmit holiness to the people.*" [21] *Next he took me out into the outer court and led me over to the four corners of the court. I found an enclosure in each*[a] *of the corners:* [22] *in the court's four corners there were integrated(?)*[a] *enclosures, each the same size,*[b] *40 (cubits) long by 30 wide.* [23] *Each of the four had as a constituent part*[a] *a low wall*[b] *around it. All round the bottom of the walls were constructed*[c] *fireplaces for cooking.* [24] "*These,*" *he told me, "are the kitchens*[a] *where those who serve in the temple area are to boil the sacrifices offered by the people.*"

Notes

1. a. For MT פנה "(which) faces" פניו "its face" is expected. The usual formulation is אשר פניו "whose face" (e.g., v 4; 42:15); less common is הפנה "which faces," as in 44:1. Did a comparative gloss פנה displace פניו? In LXX an added τῆς βλεπούσης "which faces" in v 2 may represent a misplacement of the same gloss.

1. b. In MT שער "gate" introduces an appositional definition of השער "the gate," but LXX Syr Vg do not represent it. The text is conflated with alternative formulations, that of 42:15 and that of 40:6; 43:4.

3. a. MT has "And like the manifestation, the manifestation which I saw": LXX is generally followed in its nonrepresentation of "like the manifestation" (see *BHS*). MT has anticipated subsequent terms. Zimmerli (407-8) may be right in regarding MT's "which I saw" as a similar anticipation: cf. for the resultant text 8:4; 41:21.

3. b. MT has "when I came to destroy" or, since Ezekiel took no part in the destruction, not even by prophecy, "when I came in connection with destruction" (cf. GKC 114o). Generally preferred is a minority reading בבואו "when he came," supported by a few MSS ϴ Vg. A conjectured source for both readings may be found in בבוא יהוה "when Yahweh came," via an abbreviation יʹ (cf. Cooke 474; cf. LXX 38:20).

3. c. LXX του χρῖσαι "to anoint" in place of "to destroy" represents למשחית "for destruction," perhaps a comparative gloss from 9:6 that displaced לשחת; it was wrongly linked with the stem משח "anoint."

3. d. MT adds מראות "visions," which Syr does not represent. It was probably a comparative gloss from 1:1 (cf. 8:3).

4. a. See 40:6 *Note*.

5. a. For the construction see Ehrlich, *Randglossen* 148; BDB 570a and cf. 44:4.

6. a. For the form cf. 2:2 and Zimmerli 408.

6. b. For MT איש "a man" one expects האיש "the man," as the ancient versions represent and as in 40:4.

7. a. Heb. את has been ascribed an emphatic value, e.g., by Cooke (474) with reference to Mishnaic Heb., but the non-integration of the following nouns militates against this explanation. More naturally this is a case of anacoluthon, with את functioning as an object sign relating to the object of יטמאו "they sully" later; but the stream of thought was diverted (Muraoka, *Emphasis* 133). LXX* supplied a verb "you have seen": it is unlikely that a verb הראית "have you seen?" fell out by homoeoteleuton before את (Cornill 478 et al.; cf. NEB), since the Gk. verb occurs before "son of man." Tg paraphrased "this is …, this is …"

7. b. See *Comment*.

7. c. MT בָּמוֹתָם, usually "their high places," may here mean "funeral shrines" and be short for בְּבָמוֹתָם "in ..." (Albright, VTSup 4, 247). But some MSS Θ Tg^{ed} represent a pointing בְּמוֹתָם "at their death," which is generally preferred.

8. a. The use of an inf suggests that the phrase is not coordinate with the noun phrases of v 7b, but starts a fresh sentence as a subordinate clause (cf. GKC 11200; Cooke, ibid.).

9. a. Lit. "keep away from me."

10. a. The Heb. noun occurs in 28:12, but תכונתו in v 11 and the identical renderings for both in Tg Vg (see *BHS*) suggest that it be read here too (Gese, *Verfassungsentwurf* 40). For an evaluation of suggested emendations of the preceding verb see Gese, ibid.; Zimmerli 410. In place of the preceding verb ומדדו "and they will measure" RSV and NEB ("and its appearance" = מראהו) follow the LXX with some scholars, including Cornill (480).

11. a. MT ואם נכלמו "and if they shall have become ashamed" is logically inferior to והם יכלמו "and they will be ashamed," represented by LXX Vg. A condition for communication does not accord with v 10 (Gese, ibid.).

11. b. LXX presupposes a verb וצרת "and depict," which has often been preferred (cf. *BHK*; BDB 849a; RSV; NEB), but it was the factual basis for the noun-related errors partially perpetrated by the LXX later in the verse (Cooke, ibid.).

11. c. For the Heb. assonance see Zimmerli, ibid.

11. d. Herrmann's explanation of MT in terms of a cue gloss correcting an error (263) accords with the evident formulation of three pairs of terms (Gese, *Verfassungsentwurf* 40-41): וכל־צורתו "and all its shape" was an assimilating error for וכל־תורתו "and all its instructions," while in v 11b וכל־צורתו וכל־תורתו "and all its shape and all its instructions," which LXX* does not represent, was a marginal correcting note that was subsequently swept into the text. In *BHS* צורתי is a printing error for צורתו (cf. *BHK*). For the K/Q variants see in principle the note on 40:6.

11. e. LXX represents first person suffixes, which are sometimes preferred (see *BHS*), but they represent assimilation to a common deuteronomistic formulation. In this case LXX's underlying תורתי suggests an original תורתו "instructions for it."

12. a. MT adds a superfluous "Behold, this is the instruction for the temple," not represented in LXX* Syr. It seems to have arisen from a grammatical note הֵנָּה "these (fem)," which, used as object as in Aram. (cf. GKC 135a note 1), observed that אותם at the end of v 11 referred to fem antecedents; it was wrongly understood as הִנֵּה "behold" and related to v 12a. Talmon and Fishbane (*ASTI* 10 [1975/76] 140-42) defend the clause in terms of a concluding inclusion, comparing Lev 14:54-57; Num 7:84-88. Their explanation is closely tied to their structural interpretation of v 12 (see *Form/Structure/Setting*).

13. a. MT has "and gutter the cubit": the consonantal text would be more naturally divided as וחיקה אמה "and its gutter (is) a cubit," as Syr Vg imply. Heb. חיק, usually "bosom, fold of garment at the chest," has the sense of a hollow space: it is used figuratively for the bottom of a chariot in 1 Kgs 22:35 and here for an area hollowed out of the ground.

13. b. The fem suffixes here and on the next noun (also לה, v 17) indicate that the antecedent, חיק "gutter," is regarded as fem: see Zimmerli 423.

13. c. For MT האחד "the one (masc)," a fem and anarthrous form אחת "one" is expected, agreeing with זרת "span."

13. d. Most emend גב to גֻּבָה "height" on the evidence of LXX: an error of haplography is easily assumed. But MT is to be retained as the harder reading: גב "bulge, protuberance, mound" here refers to the squat, lower block of the altar, half below ground (Galling in Bertholet 153-54; Vincent, *Jérusalem* 491; Gese, *Verfassungsentwurf* 44; Zimmerli 424 ; they compare the usage in 16:24).

14. a. MT ומחיק)ו("and (from the gutter)" is a consequence of taking v 13bβ to relate to the gutter and rim. More probably it refers to the dimensions of v 14a, and the copula, unrepresented in LXX, is to be omitted.

14. b. Driver (*Bib* 35 [1954] 307-8) related עזרה "ledge" to Arab. ^c*dr* "protect, screen," and so here surrounding ledge or stone framework around the earthen core of the altar.

14. c. MT's ורחב האמה "and width (is) the cubit" is more naturally divided as ורחבה אמה "and its width (is) a cubit" (Ehrlich, *Randglossen* 149; *BHK*). Cf. ארכו "its length" in 40:21; 41:12; 42:7.

15. a. The form of the noun is variously represented in vv 15-16. In v 15a MT takes as "mountain of God" (הראל). Q אריאל in vv 15b, 16 aligns with Isa 29:1-2 and construes as "lion of God." Both are popular etymologies. The term seems to mean "hearth" from a presumed stem ארה "burn" cognate with Arab. *'ry*, whence *'iratun* "hearth" (BDB 72a; *HALAT* 82a; the ending is developed from an affixed *lamed* [cf. GKC 85s]).

15. b. For the construction see Zimmerli, ibid.

16. a. The preposition *beth* here and in v 17; 45:2; 48:20 finds parallel usage in its Arab. cognate (Ehrlich, ibid.).

17. a. One expects reference to the lower block of 16 x 16 cubits, not least as a referent for the surrounding ridge in v 17bα. Loss by homoeoteleuton, often predicated, is feasible, although an adj הגדולה "taller" is also required with והעזרה "and the ledge" in v 17a (see *BHS*). More probably incomplete writing from the outset is to blame: the text concentrates on the upper, vertically larger plinth, as in v 20.

17. b. MT is ungrammatical: either (a) סובב אותה "surrounding it" (cf. Driver, *Bib* 35 [1954] 308) or (b) סביבותיה "around it" is required. LXX κυκλόθεν κυκλούμενον αὐτῷ "around, surrounding it" is a doublet that may go back to its Heb. *Vorlage* in a form סובב אותה סביב and attest the first alternative, which is closer to MT than the latter. MT is easily explained as assimilated to the form later in v 17 (cf. v 20). In MT one alternative, סביב, may have displaced סובב.

17. c. The article in האמה "the cubit" is unexpected: see Cooke 476.

17. d. For the construction see Cooke, ibid.

17. e. For the form of the suffix see GKC 911. Driver, ibid., regarded MT as a mixed form attesting sg ("ramp" = Tg) and pl ("stairs" = LXX Syr Vg) nouns.

17. f. MT vocalizes as inf construct; a ptcp פנות "facing" is required, as the ancient versions imply.

18. a. For אדני "Lord" here and in vv 19, 27; 44:6, 9, 12, 15, 27; 45:9, 15; 46:1, 16 see the note on 20:3.

20. a. For the variants in LXX harmonizing difference of person here and elsewhere in the section see *BHS* and Zimmerli 431.

20. b. For the privative piel, "de-sin," see GKC 52h.

21. a. The construction is appositional instead of genitival; to read a construct פר "bull of (the sin offering)" (cf. *BHS*) is to surrender to an obvious correction (Cooke, ibid.), in line with v 25. The second term may have been added (Herrmann 276 et al.) to differentiate from the holocaust bull of vv 23-24. Or was it a comparative gloss from Lev 8:14(-17)?

21. b. The verb has an indefinite sg subject: Zimmerli (434) aptly compared Lev 16:27-28.

21. c. Heb. מקדש "sanctuary" is here used in the sense of the temple area, as in 44:5, etc., according to Gese (*Verfassungsentwurf* 126-27), but Milgrom may well be right in relating it to the inner court, as in 45:4, etc. (*VT* 26 [1976] 335).

21. d. Heb. מפקד is of uncertain meaning. It has been linked topographically with the Muster (מפקד) Gate of Jerusalem in Neh 3:31 to the northeast of the temple area. Tg interprets as "proper, prepared place." LXX Vg "separated place" is a paraphrase.

26. a. Lit. "fill its hand" (K sg ידו "its hand" is idiomatic [Cornill 484]). The phrase primarily relates to the ordination of a priest, but is here used in a developed sense. It may have originally referred to the priest's inauguratory sacrifice. Here it signifies the dedication of a sacred object. See further *HALAT* 552b, 553a.

27. a. The pronouns in v 27b are pl.

27. b. Heb. שלמים, here rendered "shared offerings," has defied any certain interpretation. The options are outlined by Milgrom, *IDBSup* 769, to which should be added "final offerings" (Rendtorff, *Studien* 133, following Köhler).

44:2. a. MT יהוה "Yahweh," although supported in the general tradition, is usually deleted as a gloss influenced by 43:5-6 (cf. 46:1): Ezekiel is no longer in that special situation (Rautenberg, *ZAW* 33 [1913] 102). In the speech Yahweh is mentioned in the third person. Zimmerli (437) has noted that the word order does not conform with the normal sequence found in 9:4; 23:36.

3. a. It is difficult to avoid the conclusion that the preceding particle את emphasizes the subject (J. Blau, *VT* 4 [1954] 7 note 3; Driver, *Bib* 35 [1954] 308, et al.). The emendation אך "however" (Toy 80 et al.) does not commend itself nor does אל "concerning," introducing a gloss (Botterweck, *VT* 1 [1951] 146, claiming some versional support). MT repeats נשיא "head of state," unlike LXX* Syr, and it is generally taken as a dittograph or an incorporation of a marginal note (Zimmerli 438). Driver, ibid., interpreted MT as "*qua* prince" (= NEB "when he is here as prince").

5. a. MT and ancient versions add יהוה "Yahweh," which appears to be an early explanation misled by the following בן־אדם "son of man," usually in divine address (but see 40:4), and by finding wrong cues in the messenger formula of v 6. The addition probably occurred earlier than the same one in v 2 (Ehrlich, *Randglossen* 150).

5. b. For the suffix forms in K/Q see the note on 40:6.

5. c. One expects כל "all" in the context. Did בכ drop out by haplography from לבך בכל "(set) your mind on all" (Vogt, *Untersuchungen* 161)? The preposition *beth* introduces the object of the verbal phrase: cf. Job 23:6. Note בכל following. Later in the verse LXX ἐν πᾶσι τοῖς ἁγίοις in all the

holy places" (=בכל־המקדש "in the sanctuary") for המקדש "the sanctuary" probably attests a misplaced correction.

5. d. Analogy with both the parallel noun and the basic 43:11 suggests that MT's sg מבוא "entrance" be simply emended to מבאי "entrances," as Syr Vg Tg may imply: see Zimmerli 443. Haran (*HUCA* 50 [1979] 56 note 22; also Vogt, *Untersuchungen* 161-62) feasibly suggested that in this context the nouns have a verbal force.

5. e. Before MT לכל "to all" one expects the copula (cf. Syr), probably dropped as a consequence of textual damage earlier. The emendation ולכל מוּצָאֵי ... לְמוּבָאֵי (Bertholet 156 et al.; cf. Ehrlich, ibid.) "those who may be admitted . . . and all who are to be excluded" (RSV, cf. [N]JB) is not cogent: the present text looks back to 43:11 and forward to 46:8-10 (Gese, *Verfassungsentwurf* 52 note 2, 57 note 1), and such a sense for the second verb is unparalleled.

6. a. MT מרי "rebellion," presumably regarded as abstract for concrete ("rebels"), stands in place of the expected בית המרי "the house of rebellion," the normal phrase in Ezek, which is represented in LXX and apparently in Tg, unless it is paraphrasing. MT is partly paralleled in a predicative use at 2:7, but even that is textually uncertain. Probably בית "house" was overlooked in view of its occurrence in the next phrase.

7. a. Elsewhere in the book זרים "aliens" is used for foreigners, not the term נכר. It may have been avoided here because in a cultic context P uses זר in the particular sense of a person unauthorized to perform a cultic act, a layperson.

7. b. MT adds את־ביתי "my house, temple area," unrepresented in LXX*, apparently to clarify the suffix. Probably it was originally intended as a correct exegetical gloss on מקדשי "my sanctuary," explaining that it referred to the temple area, like בית "house, temple area" in vv 11, 14. For את used to introduce a gloss see Driver, *L'Ancien Testament et l'Orient* 127.

7. c. Rather than "bread": see Driver, *Bib* 35 (1954) 309, and also BDB 537a.

7. d. LXX Syr Vg presuppose ותפרו "and you broke," which is often read, but it smacks of an easier reading. Driver, ibid., has explained the Heb. in terms of causing a covenant to which one is not a partner to be broken, citing Jer 33:20-21 (cf. NEB).

7. e. Or "in addition to" (Cooke 491; BDB 755b).

8. a. Milgrom (*Studies* 8-16, esp. 11 note 41) has restricted the meaning of שמר משמרת to "perform guard duty" and, with Yahweh as object, "guard the taboos." The former technical sense fits some OT passages well, but it is uncertain whether it is so widespread as Milgrom urges.

8. b. LXX* omits, "undoubtedly in error" (Zimmerli 448). Perhaps a 17-letter line was omitted from its *Vorlage* (cf. Allen, *The Greek Chronicles* 2, 134-36).

8. c, d. MT ותשימון "and you made them (fem, with reference to abominations?)," in place of the expected ותשימום "and you made them (masc)," and לכם "to you," in place of לכן "therefore," attested by LXX and taken with v 9, seem to be related errors (Cornill 485). Did לכם after the messenger formula in v 6 influence MT and was a correcting *nun* related to the wrong word?

9. a. For the emphatic particle *lamed* see GKC 143e, Driver, ibid., and *HALAT* 485b, 486a.

10. a. The force of the previous verb carries over (Duke, *JSOT* 40 [1988] 65).

10. b. MT adds אשר תעו "who went astray," not represented in LXX* Syr. It seems to have been intended as a variant of אשר רחקו "who went far away," assimilating to 48:11, which was inserted into the text before the wrong מעלי "from me."

10. c. Duke's interpretation in terms of the technical phrase of Num 18:1, etc. (*JSOT* 40 [1988] 65-66) fails to take into account the accusatory usage of עון "iniquity" in v 12aβ.

11. a. Heb. פקדה signifies guard duty in 2 Kgs 11:18 and here (*HALAT* 902b).

12. a. Duke (*JSOT* 40 [1988] 68) subordinates v 12a to v 11. But vv 12-14 appear to elaborate vv 10-11. A double movement from accusation to punishment so suggests. The repetition of vocabulary points in this direction: שרת "serve," functioning as a hinge in vv 11b, 12aα, גלוליהם "their idols" (vv 10aβ, 12aα), ונשאו עונם "and they will bear their iniquity" (vv 10b, 12bβ) and הבית "the temple area" (vv 11aβ, γ, 14aβ).

12. b. The imperfect may be frequentative (Cooke 481).

12. c. As in 36:7, the pf is performative.

12. d. The lack of representation of v 12bß in LXX* is probably for non-repetitive conciseness. The stylistic scheme observed above supports its presence. The unusual construction with *waw* is dictated by a rhetorical motive, to repeat the clause of v 10b.

14. a. For this sense see Milgrom, *Studies* 60-87, esp. 83-86.

19. a. MT repeats this phrase by dittography, as even Barthélemy et al. (*Preliminary Report* 5, 176) grant: it is absent from some MSS and LXX Syr Vg.

24. a. Heb. "stand to judge" (= K, supported by LXX Syr Tg; Q "for judgment" is clumsy in the context) refers to the formal posture of a judge delivering his verdict: cf. Isa 3:13 and de Vaux, *Ancient Israel* 156.

24. b. Q is generally preferred with many MSS LXX Syr Tg.

25. a. MT's sg יבוא "he shall come" appears to be a case of metathesis, as often in the book: see 36:20 *Note.*

25. b. The context favors insertion of the copula read by some MSS and presupposed in LXX Syr Vg.

26. a. MT's pl verb seems to reflect harmonization with v 25: יספר "he shall count off" is attested by one MS and LXX Syr (cf. Lev 15:13, 28). In this verse RSV and in part NEB follow Cornill (488) in adopting the variants of Syr, but see Cooke (493); Wevers (222).

27. a. LXX* omits אל הקדש "to the sanctuary" as redundant, but it may be retained as emphatic (see *Comment*).

28. a. LXX[967] Vg have preserved the correct reading (cf. *BHS*), required by the parallelism. MT probably arose as a comparative gloss on 45:8bβ from 36:12 והיית להם לנחלה "and you (the land) will become their possession." It was taken with the wrong column and displaced the original text. The verb was adapted to והיתה "and it (fem) will be" and related to the sin offering of v 27.

29. a. And so not redeemable: cf. Num 18:14.

30. a. See Cooke, ibid.; Driver, *Bib* 35 (1954) 310.

30. b. Heb. עריסה is of uncertain meaning; it occurs in Num 15:20; Neh 10:38. The LXX in Num renders "dough." See the discussion in Eissfeldt, *Erstlinge* 62.

30. c. For ביתך "your (sg) house" LXX Syr presuppose בתיכם "your (pl) houses" in accordance with the earlier pl verb.

45:1. a. For the construction see Cooke 505.

1. b. MT has a conflated text: ארך "length" occurs both at the head of the phrase (= Syr Vg), as in v 3 and very often, and at the end (= LXX), as in v 5.

1. c. MT אלף עשרה "10,000" is a revision of "20,000" (= ... עשרים) attested by LXX*, which is generally preferred, even by Keil (320), since it aligns with vv 3, 5. "10,000" would be עשרת אלפים, as in vv 3, 5; 48:9 (MT), 10, 13, 18. MT secondarily restricts the sacred reservation to its priestly half (cf. 48:9).

1. d. Heb. הוא "it" is attracted to the masc predicate (Cooke, ibid.; Jöuon 149c).

2. a. See the note on 43:16.

2. b. For this use of אל see 40:16.

3. a. In the pl context of vv 1, 6 תמוד "you (sg) will measure" is generally emended to a pl תמדו, assuming metathesis. In fact it turns up in this pre-corrupted form as a misplaced comparative gloss in 47:18.

3. b. Q is the expected form: K probably suffered assimilation to the forms in v 2.

4. a. MT קדש "(It will be) a sacred area (of the country)" harks back to v 1 in accord with MT's reference to the priestly half of the total area (Gese, *Verfassungsentwurf* 103 note 1; Eichrodt 568). Its omission in LXX* supports its secondary nature. Originally v 4aα as far as הוא "it" completed v 3 (Zimmerli 466).

4. b. MT ומקדש (למקדש) "and sanctuary/ a sacred area (?) (for the sanctuary)" seems to be a dittographic error for ומגרש "and open land," attested by LXX (cf. Lev 25:34) Tg; it refers to v 2b (cf. Smend 371). A further, conjectural emendation למקנה "(and grazing land) for cattle" (*BHK* et al.) is speculative and unwarranted.

5. a. K is generally preferred, in line with vv 4, 6.

5. b. MT עשרים לשכת "twenty rooms" does not suit the context: ערים לשבת "cities to live in," presupposed by LXX, is generally read, even by Barthélemy et al., *Preliminary Report* 5, 178-79, via a ב/כ error in the second case (cf. Num 35:2; Josh 14:4; 21:1). Did the numeral originate as a correction relating to v 1 or was it assimilated mechanically to the number "20" earlier in v 5? Did the second term fall under the influence of the noun adjacent in the previous column at 44:19?

7. a. In place of קדמה with a meaningless *he* of place (cf. 48:21) analogy with the previous phrase leads one to expect קדים "east." Did קדמה, intended as a variant of קדימה "eastwards," displace קדים?

7. b. Elsewhere the form is sg, as in v 6: see *BHS*.

7. c. Cf. chap. 48.

7. d. Comparison with the parallel 48:21 and consistency with the coordinated phrase suggest ימה "west," as presupposed by LXX, with a meaningless *he* of place. Perhaps MT was influenced by מפאת־ים "on the west side" earlier.

8. a. LXX is generally followed in taking the awkward לארץ "in relation to the country" with v 7 and reading והיה "and it will be" for יהיה "it will be," a consequence of the wrong division (cf. K/Q in v 5).

8. b. One MS and LXX imply נשיאי ישראל "heads of state of Israel" for נשיאי "my heads of state." Obviously scribal abbreviation underlies the variants (Driver, *Textus* 1 [1960] 121 = NEB; cf. נשיש "we will rejoice" in 21:15[10]). The longer reading is often preferred, but MT can stand (Cooke 496).

8. c. Bertholet (159) referred to 1 Kgs 18:26 for נתן "give" in this sense.

12. a. MT construes v 12b as a single clause: "20 shekels, 25 shekels, 15 shekels shall be your mina," apparently meaning that a 60-shekel mina is to be represented by three weights, weighing respectively 20, 25 and 15 shekels. However, (a) the form of the numeral 15 is unique (cf. GKC 97d, e) and (b) in the third case "shekels" switches to a sg form, which suggests that its clause is not coordinated with the foregoing (Smend 373). Accordingly the reading of LXX adopted in the translation (cf. RSV), with the numerals 5/5, 10/10, 50, is generally preferred. Perhaps the root of the problem lies in the second numeral in MT, חמשה ועשרים "5 and 20." Did it originate as a marginal variant or correcting gloss on the number in K at v 3 in the previous column, and then displace חמשה ועשרה "5 and 10"? Then in the case of the other numbers, 20 and 15, the elements עשרים "20" and חמשה "5" were subsequent assimilations to the central figures. In v 13 the extra *mem* on ושתים (see next note) may represent a correction for the *he* of the final חמשה "5," indicating חמשם (י) ם "50."

13. a. MT ושתים "and you shall give a sixth part" invents a denominative verb. The parallelism leads one to expect וששית "and a sixth," as the ancient versions attest. Ehrlich (*Randglossen* 153) suggested wrong word division, וששית מהאיפה "and a sixth from/of the ephah" (cf. 2 Kgs 11:5), but again the parallelism is broken. See the previous note.

14. a. Lit. an appositional phrase, "the oil (being in terms of) the bath": cf. Cooke 506. Cf. the paraphrase in Tg, and Zimmerli 474. It is often taken as a gloss, even by Barthélemy et al, *Preliminary Report* 5, 180.

14. b. MT has "the 10 baths are a homer, for the 10 baths (are) a homer." In the second clause Vg attests הכר "(for) the kor (is 10 baths)" for חמר "a homer"; it suits the context better. MT could have arisen by assimilation to the other term, used frequently earlier, through ה/ח, כ/מ similarities. Then the first clause, unrepresented in LXX*, rather than being a dittograph of MT, as it is usually taken to be, may have originated as a variant חמר "homer" preceded by cue words, which entered the text and caused the assimilation of הכר "the kor" to חמר. Conceivably the clauses are parallel, equating a homer and a kor (cf. RSV, GNB, NJPS); yet the article would then be required with חמר "homer," and כי "for" is unexpected.

15. a. Heb. משקה (מ) is literally "irrigation, drink," here conceivably "watered land" (cf. Gen 13:10; Wevers 225; cf. 47:1-12; cf. KJV "fat pastures," NJB "pastures"). LXX may imply משפחות "families" (Cornill 494 et al.; cf. RSV, NEB), unless it is a guess (Zimmerli 475). Gese (*Verfassungsentwurf* 70 note 1) et al., following Grätz, emended to מקנה "cattle."

16. a. MT adds ungrammatically הארץ "the land," unattested by LXX*. It was probably a comparative gloss with reference to עם הארץ "the people of the land" in v 22; 46:3 (cf. Gese, *Verfassungsentwurf* 72).

16. b. For היה אל "be obliged to" see Gese, *Verfassungsentwurf* 71 note 2; Zimmerli, ibid., with reference to GB 179a. An emendation יתנו את "will give" (Ehrlich, *Randglossen* 154; Cooke 507, claiming the support of LXX Syr) is unnecessary.

17. a. MT has a pl העולות "the holocausts," for which a sg העולה, read by many MSS, is expected. Did the pl form come in from the margin, originally clarifying the sg form at 46:4 in the next column, where it has a pl predicate?

17. b. The prefacing of a copula, with much support (see *BHS*), is unnecessary for this summarizing phrase. Cornill (495) takes it with v 17b.

18. a. The second person references are sg in vv 18-20a, but pl in vv 20b and 21.

19. a. LXX Syr Vg have pl forms: probably the sg forms in MT have been influenced by 46:2.

20. a. Instead of בחדש "in the month" one expects לחדש "of the month" (see Cooke 507), and a few MSS so read. For the variant in LXX, which many adopt, see Gese, *Verfassungsentwurf* 77-78 and Zimmerli 480, 483.

20. b. Heb. מן here signifies "because of, on account of" (BDB 580a).

20. c. The clause functions as a final summary: cf. 47:17a and the analogous use of a consec pf (cf. GKC lllk).

21. a. For the construction of an impersonal pass with a retained acc cf. GKC 121a, b.

21. b. MT חג שבעות "a feast, weeks" is hardly original. The latter term appears as "seven" שׁבְעַת) in a few MSS and the ancient versions, which suits the context. MT appears to have originated in an

annotation that referred to the missing festival of weeks; the annotation displaced שבעת "seven." Heb. חג "feast," which is pointed as abs in MT, can hardly qualify הפסח "the passover" in v 21a. It may have been an early note paving the way for the "feast" of unleavened bread in v 23 (Zimmerli 481).

25. a. LXX Syr, along with a few MSS, prefix a copula; but noun lists follow various patterns and even the asyndeton here is possible: cf. Jer 2:26 and GKC 154a note 1.

46:2. a. In 40:6-7; 43:8 the term for "threshold" is סף; here and in 47:1 it is מפתן. See Zimmerli 490.

6. a. The pl תמימם "unblemished" is anomalous with a sg noun. Generally a sg תמים is read with much ancient support (see BHS). MT could be a case of dittography (Zimmerli 487) or of assimilation to the form in v 6b (Gese, Verfassungsentwurf 82 note 4).

9. a. For pl יצאו (K) "they will leave" one expects a sg יצא (Q etc.: see BHS). Hitzig (359) defended K as the harder reading, explaining the preceding sg as distributive (cf. GKC 145m). The waw may be simply a dittograph. A similar case occurs in v 10 (see BHS). Were the two instances originally meant as marginal notes on יצא[1,2] in v 9a, indicating that the subjects were collective?

9. b. The suffix more probably refers to the gate (LXX Vg; Smend 381) than to the subj (cf. v 10bβ).

10. a. See note 9. a.

13. a. There is ancient evidence for a third sg verb here and in v 14 (see BHS), with reference to the head of state, which some older scholars and RSV and NJB follow, but it smacks of an easier and so inferior reading (Gese, Verfassungsentwurf 84).

14. a. There is overwhelming ancient support (see BHS) for a sg חקת "ruling" in place of the pl form in MT. The pl seems to have arisen from a desire to include the daily holocaust with the cereal offering. The same desire may have encouraged the early overloading with תמיד "regular" in the ancient tradition: the term refers primarily to the holocaust (v 15; Num 28:6, etc.). Gese (Verfassungsentwurf 85 note 2) et al. regard תמיד simply as an intrusion from v 15. However, more probably it represents an independent annotation to the effect that not only the daily holocaust (v 15) but also the daily cereal offering could be termed תמיד, as in Lev 6:13 (20); Num 4:16; Neh 10:34 (33). Seemingly LXX* attests a text in which תמיד had displaced עולם "permanent." The expression חקת עולם "permanent ruling (sg)" is common in the priestly literature.

15. a. K is usually followed. The pl has priests in view.

16. a. Generally LXX is followed in reading מנחלתו "out of his inheritance," as in v 17, and taking with the preceding. But (a) LXX* omits the term in v 17 and in its Vorlage it may well have been displaced here, and (b) there is awkwardness in a switch from "one of the sons" to sons in general. MT may be retained, and the suffix related to "one of the sons": cf. the contrasting v 17aβγ (Keil 346).

17. a. For the old form of verbal ending see GKC 44f, 72o.

17. b. Generally נחלת "the inheritance of (his sons, it will become theirs)" is read with LXX Syr, but MT (= Vg Tg) has the merit of being the harder reading. The particle אך is asseverative, "surely"; for בניו "his sons" as casus pendens with a retrospective suffix cf. GKC 143b.

18. a. For the pregnant use of מן "from" cf. GKC 119ff.

19. a. The article is anomalous before a noun pointed as constr: an anarthrous לשכות "rooms" is expected, as in 42:13. Was there assimilation to the sequence אל ה־ later in the sentence?

19. b. MT אל הכהנים "to the priests" is strange on three counts: (a) elsewhere in the vision account the only person the prophet encounters is the supernatural guide; (b) in LXX Syr Tg the priests function as users of the rooms, as in 42:13-14; and (c) the phrase must be subordinate to the rooms, since the following phrase in the Heb., "north-facing," refers back to the rooms (Zimmerli 498). Cooke (516), following a cue from Herrmann (286), plausibly suggested that אל arose from an abbreviation אשר ל = א ל "which belong to" (cf. Driver, Textus 1 [1960] 123).

19. c. K בירכתם "at their far side" envisages a sg noun with suffix (= Syr Tg), as only in Gen 49:13. Q is preferable: it accords with the usage of P in Exod 26:27; 36:32, where the abs dual is combined with ימה "westward" (Zimmerli, ibid., who reasonably explained LXX*'s nonrepresentation of ימה in terms of haplography).

20. a. MT's staccato and loose relative conjunction is not impossible (Herrmann, ibid.). LXX Syr may imply ושם "and there," which is often read, but the harder reading is to be preferred. Wevers (228) took the lack of coordination as evidence that the clause is secondary.

21. a. For the Heb. distributive repetition cf. GKC 123d.

22. a. MT קטרות is most uncertain: see the discussions in Cooke, ibid., and Zimmerli 499. The most plausible rendering in terms of etymology and context is "joined, attached" (Tg Σ), with reference to the overall structure of the outer wall and bordering rooms (Busink, Tempel 723 and note 26; cf. Driver, Bib 35 [1954] 311). LXX Syr appear to presuppose קטנות "small," which is generally read; but, being an easier reading, it does not commend itself (Cooke 514).

22. b. MT adds מהקצעות pointed as a denominative hoph ptcp, "set in corners," but the special points over it (cf. GKC 5n) indicate the Masoretes' suspicions. It is not represented in LXX Syr Vg; it may have originated as מקצעות "corners," intended as a grammatical note on the unusual masc form in v 21.

23. a. Lit. "in them." Contra *BHK* and *BHS*, Ehrlich (*Randglossen* 156) and Zimmerli, ibid., have defended MT.

23. b. Lit. "a course (of masonry)."

23. c. The uninflected form עשוי "constructed" is paralleled in 40:17; 41:18.

24. a. For the representation of the pl see GKC 124r.

Form/Structure/Setting

The next major literary unit of the book in its present form should probably be demarcated as chaps. 43-46 (Parunak, *Structural Studies* 506-9; cf. Gese, *Verfassungsentwurf* 2, 6, 36, 54; Zimmerli 406; Vogt, *Untersuchungen* 132, 146, 165). Talmon and Fishbane (*ASTI* 10 [1975-76] 138-53) have impressively argued for 40:1-43:12 as a redactional unit. They were followed by Greenberg (*Int* 38 [1984] 189, 193-4), who regarded the next main division as 44:1-46:24, with 43:13-27 functioning as a transitional passage. Talmon and Fishbane might have come to a different conclusion, if they had conducted a wider study that embraced chaps. 40-46. They interpret 43:12 as a concluding formula, but it could equally be an initial formula, such as occurs in Lev 6:2, 7, 18 (9, 14, 25); 7:1, 11, as they observe. In fact, the reference to "the most holy" may be influenced by the convention followed in Lev 6:18(25); 7:1. Their interpretation of תורה "law, instruction" as "instruction-plan" is given without elucidation. Does it not more naturally refer to instructions for cultic procedure, in line with the plural usage in 43:11; 44:5, 24 (cf. Eichrodt 556)? The parallels with the early verses of chap. 40 seem to represent not an inclusion (A...A'), but matching beginnings (A.../A'...). In v 12b גבול "territory/boundary" may well look forward structurally to the sacred "territory" of the reservation described in 45:1-4, rather than back to the wall of 40:20.

Haran (*HUCA* 50 [1979] 53, 55-56), examining chaps. 40-48 as a whole, found three parts, of which the first comprises 40:1-44:3 and concerns the form of the temple, while the second in 44:4-46:24 deals with temple procedures. He too took 43:12 as a conclusion. He rightly noted that the largely parallel 40:4 and 44:5 have different references to material layout and to rules of procedure. He did not take into account the role of 43:11 in relation to 40:4 and 44:5 nor the structural role of the visionary scenes. He played down the fact that procedure seems already to be in view in 43:18-27; 44:1-3 (cf. 43:11-12).

Rautenberg (*ZAW* 33 [1913] 114-15), stripping chaps. 40-46 down to a shorter, pre-redactional entity, analyzed 40:4-42:20 and 44:5-46:14 as main parts, with 43:1-11 functioning as a middle portion and 44:1-4 as a bridge to the second main part. It is clear that chap. 43 and the early verses of chap. 44 have posed problems for structural analysts.

Parunak (*Structural Studies* 522-23; *JBL* 102 [1983] 542) has found within 43:1-46:24 a compositional block made up of three units, 44:5-31; 45:1-8 and 45:9-46:18. The first and third he takes as parallel treatments of the worship of the priests and of the head of state, dealing with past offenses (44:5-8; 45:9-12), future ministry (44:9-27; 45:13-46:15) and inheritance (44:28-31; 46:16-18). The middle section is a hinge concerned with the allotment of land, dealing with priests (vv 1-5) and head of state (vv 7-8), as well as people (v 6). The advantages of Parunak's scheme are that he does nicely integrate the otherwise difficult 46:16-18 and that he can find structural highlighting for the two occurrences of רב־לכם "you went too far" in 44:6; 45:9 (cf. Rautenberg, ZAW 33 [1913] 103). However, he ignores the catchword תרומה "contribution" in chap. 45, overlooks that not only the head of state is in view in 45:9-46:18 (see 45:13-16, 18-21; 46:9, 13-15) and in general does not perceive how intimately the material is related to temple concerns.

Gese (Verfassungsentwurf 6, 8) drew attention to the conglomeration of individual passages that confront the reader in chaps. 43-48 and the difficulty of discerning their coherence. What follows is an attempt to see a structural wood in those different trees. 43:1-44:5 appears to function as an extended introduction. Then there are three main sections. (1) 44:6-31 is concerned with cultic personnel. Vv 28-30 form a bridge over to the next section, (2) 45:1-17, which features the maintenance of the cult by means of the people's contributions. (3) 45:18-46:15 explores the theme of ritual offerings. A framework is provided by the narratives of visionary guidance in 43:1-5; 44:1-5 and 46:19-24: they provide an inclusion both for the introduction and for the whole, in an A...A/...A pattern. 46:16-18 provides an intersectional link between a concern of its longer section, expressed in 45:1-8, and that of the next, the issue of property rights in the land. The three sections vary in length: the first is 26 verses long (41 lines in BHS), the second 17 verses (30 lines) and the third 23 verses (34 lines). It is clear that most weight rests on the first section with its theme of cultic personnel; moreover its theme spills over into the other sections and even into the preceding and following units.

The overall literary unit starts with a vision narrative introduced by a formula of guidance and a double communication from Yahweh (43:1-12). The guide soon retires to the background, to be replaced by the transporting spirit and by Yahweh's own voice. As elements of 8:1-3 were echoed in 40:1-3, so here motifs of 8:3-4 are resumed in 43:2-5: the divine glory that now returns, explicit reminiscence of the visions of chap. 1 as well as of chap. 8, and the spirit's work. The introduction to chap. 8 has been split into two, to preface the visionary counterparts in chaps. 40-42 and 43-46 (Parunak, Structural Studies 509). The divine communication falls into two parts, both headed by the address בן־אדם "human one." Vv 6-9 are a carefully constructed statement (see Comment) of a necessary change from pre-exilic conditions to be instituted. Vv 10-11 serve to recapitulate chaps. 40-42 and look forward to what follows, in instructing the prophet to report the design and procedures of the temple. V 12, which may be redactional, forms the conclusion of the divine speech and serves as a heading for what follows. It is structurally significant that the vocabulary of vv 10-11 is developed in the תורה "instruction," מדות "measurements" and חקות "regulations" of v 12, 13 and 18.

The regulation for dedicating the altar which appears in vv 18-27 would more naturally appear next. It is introduced by divine address of the prophet, with the customary title, as in v 6, and a messenger formula, before a brief description that announces the topic. It is typical of chaps. 43-46 that ritual regulations are introduced in terms of a prophetic oracle (cf. F. Baumgärtel, ZAW 73 [1961] 286): priestly and prophetic concerns are here united. Vv 13-17, which begin with their own superscription, are prefixed in order to explain the design of the altar, which is done in verbless terms, and so prepare for the technical vocabulary used in the dedicatory regulation. In the latter the second person verbs indicate that Ezekiel was to be assigned a key role in the rite. In this respect and in the representation of a ritual regulation as divine communication, there are formal echoes of the usage in P (cf. Exod 25-29; Num 19 [Zimmerli 430-31]). In v 19 there appears to be a redactional expansion like that of 40:46b, which will be considered later.

44:1-5 is at first sight very similar to 43:1-11 in respect of form. It certainly contains vision narrative featuring guidance formulas and the motif of Yahweh's glory, and in v 5 the prophet is addressed as בן־אדם "son of man" and exhorted in terms close to those of 43:11. Closer examination shows that there are two vision narratives, in vv 1-3 and 4-5. The first case includes an explanation relating to cultic procedure, which is reminiscent of material in chaps. 40-42. V 3 introduces the reader to the נשיא "head of state," who plays a prominent role in chaps. 43-46: it will require discussion below. V 5 deliberately echoes both 40:4 and 43:11. The former factor suggests that the overall unit is parallel with the previous one of chaps. 40-42, 40:4/44:5 serving as parallel introductions. The verse also functions as a recapitulation, after the intervening material of 43:13-27 (Gese, *Verfassungsentwurf* 57). The double echoing confirms the role of 44:5 within an extended introduction. The exhortation looks forward as well as back. It serves as a structural heading for the rest of the unit or at least up to 46:18 (Gese, *Verfassungsentwurf* 56).

44:6-16 constitutes the first half of the first main section concerning temple personnel. Introduced by a commission to address the exiled community and a messenger formula, in form it is reminiscent of the complex oracles of judgment/salvation that occurred earlier in 34:2-16, 17-22. It is strongly influenced by the style of the priestly ordinance: only the accusation of vv 6b-8 employs direct address (to Israel). Israel's punishment is expressed in legal terms from v 9, after לכן "therefore" and a messenger formula. V 10a introduces the complication of a fresh accusation relating to a particular group, the Levites, whose new subordinate role is punitively laid down in the regulations of vv 10b-11. Accusation and punishment of the Levites are emphatically reasserted in vv 12-14. After an oath formula qualified by a divine saying formula (v 12bα) the same legal terminology as in v 10b introduces the punishment, ונשאו עונם "and they will bear their punishment" (v 12bβ; cf. 14:10 and Zimmerli, *Ezekiel* 1, 305). Vv 15-16 provide the legal equivalent of a promise of salvation: a further group, the Zadokite priests, as a reward for their loyalty (v 15aα), are assigned an exclusive, prime role (vv 15aβ-16). The reinforcing divine saying formula in v 15bβ corresponds to the one in v 12.

Despite the complexity of the piece, it is bound together with strong structural ties. A framework is provided by the threefold use of the phrase שמר משמרת "carry out (cultic) duties" in vv 8, 14 and 16 in relation to the three groups of Israel, the Levites and the priests. Levitical and priestly roles are polarized in the respective service of Israel and Yahweh (vv 11, 15), the contrasting right or denial of special access (vv 13, 15) and the matching המה ... והמה "they ... and they" (vv 11, 16). A negative wordplay pervades the piece, the תע combination in תעבות "abominations" and the stem תעה "go astray," in vv 6, 7, 10, 13, 15. An inclusion is supplied by reference to "the fat and the blood" in vv 7 and 15.

44:17-31 is an appendage to vv 15-16 that comprises a selection of regulations for the cultic and social behavior of priests. It is dominated by a keyword, forms of קדש "holiness" in vv 19, 23, 24 and 27. The motif of entry to the inner court in vv 17, 21 and 27 provides a framework. This factor, together with the divine saying formula of v 27b, seems to suggest that vv 28-31 were added subsequently. In fact, as noted earlier, they build a bridge to the next section. Not only תרומה "contribution" (v 30), but נחלה "tenured land" and אחזה "property" (v 28) link them to 45:1-8 (cf. 45:1, 5-8). Vv 28-30ba stand out as addressed to Israel; thus they provide a structural tie with the beginning of the section, vv 6-8.

The next section, concerning maintenance of the cult, falls into three parts, 45:1-8, 9-12 and 13-17. It is dominated by an initial key phrase, תרימה תרומה "you are to give a contribution," in vv 1 and 13; it is ironically echoed by הרימו "remove" in v 9. The first part, or at least vv 1-8a, has evidently been borrowed from 47:13-48:29, specifically 48:8-22 (see Zimmerli 467, 542). Vv 1-8a are addressed to Israel. The promise of v 8b in its first clause echoes the לא . . . עוד "no longer" formulations of earlier chapters, while its second clause is reminiscent of 47:21. It not only rounds off this first part, but is formulated to prepare for the beginning of the second, v 9.

V 9 appears to be an originally independent prophetic oracle that rhetorically addresses the oppressive rulers of pre-exilic times (cf. 34:2-10). It begins with a messenger formula and ends with a divine saying formula, and is artistically constructed. Its accusation, vigorously introduced like that of 44:6, constitutes an implicit promise to God's people. Vv 10-12 comprise regulation concerning weights and measures, addressed to Israel. An inclusion is provided by יהי(ה) לכם "let there be/it will be for you" (cf. the intermediate יהיה "will be" twice in v 11). V 9 is rhetorically woven in by its own use of לכם "to you" and by the presence of צדק(ה) "righteousness" in vv 9 and 10.

The regulations of vv 13-17 fall into two parts, vv 13-15, with a heading in v 13a addressed to Israel (but note v 15ba) and a final divine saying formula, and the appended vv 16-17, which speak of the people in the third person. The two parts are integrated by parallel endings, vv 15b and v 17bβ.

The third part, 45:18-46:15, is concerned with rites and offerings. The comprehensive vocabulary of v 17aβ-ba serves admirably to introduce it. It subdivides into two unequal halves, 45:18-25 and 46:1-15, both demarcated by messenger formulas. The regulations of vv 18-25, dealing with annual rites, fall into two parts, vv 18-20 and 21-25. The former concerns the cleansing of the temple and is seemingly addressed to Ezekiel; the second plural statement in v 20b appears to be a summarizing postscript that links with the plural address to Israel in v 21. Vv 21-25 major in the role of the head of state at the spring and autumn festivals. 46:1-15 discuss other cultic offerings and gate procedures. Vv 1-12 are bound together by the key figure of the head of state and by an inclusion relating to the inner east gate of the temple (vv 1-3, 12). The piece about daily offerings in vv 13-15 is evidently addressed to Ezekiel in vv 13-14.

The three related regulations of vv 16-18 are differentiated from what precedes by an initial messenger formula. The casuistic (כי "when") formulations in vv 16 and 17 link with the one in v 12 and may indicate that at an earlier stage this piece, which continues to highlight the head of state, was joined with vv 1-15 (Zimmerli 495, 551-52). However, with its emphasis on property, its present placing serves to prepare for the topic of the next unit.

46:19-24 provides a vision narrative that has a concluding function. It has two halves, vv 19-20, 21-24, each opening with a guidance formula and closing with an explanation of cultic procedure for cooking sacrifices. Its topic of separate kitchens for priests and people makes it a fitting finale to the sectional emphasis on offerings and also to the pervasive issue of the two groups of temple personnel and the related motif of holiness.

So much for the form and structure of the various pieces and their role in an overall scheme. The question of setting raises redactional issues. The impression conveyed by the previous survey is surely that the very real coherence of chaps. 43-46 is contrived rather than natural (cf. Craigie 291). Greenberg has conceded that the composition of chaps. 43-46 took place in stages (*Int* 38 [1984] 199). Its unevenness may be illustrated from the juxtaposition of 45:10-12 with vv 13-17: they prepare the way for most of the measures mentioned in vv 13-14 but lack reference to the kor (v 14) and include the shekel, which finds no place in what follows. Clearly pre-existing material has been re-used in a new context. McConville, who presupposes a basic, authorial unity for chaps. 40-48, has claimed structural evidence for it in a centripetal and centrifugal movement within chaps. 40-46 (*TynBul* 34 [1983] 20-21). This movement reaches its midpoint not in the holy of holies (41:4) but in the altar of 43:13; and then an outward flow veers to the temple (44:5) and on to the holy reservation (chap. 45) and the tribal areas. If this structural analysis were correct, it would not remove the necessity of taking into account other phenomena that point away from a primary unity; but McConville has overlooked the presence of the altar in 40:47, where it has a minor role within the static blueprint of the holy temple in chaps. 40-42. It leaps to prominence, however, in the presentation of a dynamically functioning temple, in which the issue of maintaining the intrinsic holiness of the temple arises.

A good case has been made by Gese (*Verfassungsentwurf* 85) and refined by Zimmerli (550) that an underlying unit of chaps. 43-46 was a stratum concerned with the נשׂיא "head of state"; its characteristics are (1) a positive attitude, (2) parallel mention of עם הארץ "the people of the land," and (3) singular mention of the נשׂיא "head of state." This hypothetical stratum would have consisted of 44:3 (cf. Rautenberg, *ZAW* 13 [1933] 102 note 1); 45:21-25 and 46:1-12. It may early have attracted 46:16-18 (cf. Zimmerli 552) and the related 45:16-17, and even 45:8 and 45:9. If, as seems likely, this expanded stratum lies behind our chapters, it is striking how its components have been divided among the various sections of chaps. 43-46 and creatively integrated into new contexts with their own agendas.

Evidence of redactional development appears in connection with what Gese called a Zadokite stratum (*Verfassungsentwurf* 67), but which Gunneweg more justly defined as a Zadokite section in 44:6-16 and "metastases" or corresponding sporadic amplifications in 40:46b; 43:19 and 48:11aβb (*Leviten* 188). A quadruple series may be discerned. First, in 40:45-46a are mentioned two types of priest, those with duties in the temple area and those with altar duties. The former are clearly subordinate to the latter, in a sacerdotal hierarchy. The latter are qualified as levitical Zadokites in 40:46b, while no corresponding qualification is added to the former. This lopsidedness suggests redactional supplementation from 44:15. Duke (*JSOT* 40 [1988] 75, following Milgrom, *Studies* 13-14 note 47; cf. Smend 333; Hitzig 324; Allan, *Heythrop Journal* 23 [1982] 260 note 4) has urged that the qualification applies to both types, since בית in v 45 means not "temple area" but "temple building." This interpretation would create unnecessary tension within chaps. 40-48, in which only the inner circle who serve at the altar or in the sanctuary (cf. Num 18:5) are called Zadokites and are differentiated from other cultic staff responsible for the temple area (see 44:14; 45:5; 46:24; cf. Baudissin, *Geschichte* 114; *HDB* 4, 78). It has generally been overlooked that the subordinate priests are assigned to a room next to the inner north gate, where according to v 41 slaughtering took place. A similar phenomenon occurs in 43:19, where originally only priests were mentioned and again the reference to levitical priests of Zadokite descent appears to be a secondary comment derived from 44:15, to which a divine saying formula has been added by way of emphasis. In fact the context requires a reference to or inclusion of slaughtering; as in 40:45, this seems to have been the role of the priests originally in view here. Already then these priests have a role like that of the Levites to be mentioned in 44:11.

A second category of texts is represented in 46:19-20, 24, where "priests" and "those who serve in the temple area" are polarized, but the latter group is not expressly identified with the Levites. Gese (*Verfassungsentwurf* 89 note 2) found here the influence of 44:11 (cf. 45:5), where the latter terminology is used of the Levites, but more probably an older formula has been used there, as the similar language of 40:45 suggests. One should consider in this category 42:13-14, which Gunneweg (*Leviten* 189-90, 196) rightly brought into the discussion of texts relevant to the general issue. In this passage "the priests who have access to Yahweh" (cf. 45:4) or "the priests" are mentioned. It is clear that they are a privileged, exclusive group, which implies an unnamed subordinate group. One cannot deduce with Gunneweg (*Leviten* 189) that mention of two sets of rooms in the west building involves two groups of priests who are defined in the same way (cf. Zimmerli 400).

A third category distinguishes explicitly between priests and Levites. It appears in the basic text of 48:8-26, where the most holy territory of the priests is differentiated from that of the Levites in the holy reservation. It is evidently this basic text that is reflected in 45:4-5, which lacks a reference to Zadokite ancestry and simply distinguishes between "the priests who serve in the sanctuary and have access to serve Yahweh" and "the Levites who serve in the temple area." Gese (*Verfassungsentwurf* 66) saw here the influence of chap. 44 because of overlapping terminology, but the precedents in 40:45 deserve consideration. The reference to Levites is the only new factor.

The fourth category explicitly refers to Zadokite priests. It receives fullest expression in 44:15-16, over against reference to Levites with duties in the temple area, including responsibility for slaughtering, gate security and menial tasks (vv 11-14). There was a quite thorough endeavor to incorporate this final development elsewhere, into 48:11, as the aberrant first person reference to Yahweh suggests, 40:46 and 43:19.

There are thus a series of texts that reflect development in the conception of temple personnel, although they are not necessarily to be assigned to four separate historical stages. The series begins with a hierarchy of two priestly classes, the lower of which already has the task of slaughtering. It progresses to separate classes of priests and Levites, and reaches an extreme form in the categorization of the priests as Zadokite in descent, together with an insistence that the Levites have no priestly role (44:13). Such development must run counter to a unitary approach to the text.

The dating of the diverse material in chaps. 43-46 can only be treated in a tentative and partial way. One must listen to McConville's caution (*TynBul* 34

[1983] 10-15, 18), underlined by Duke (*JSOT* 40 [1988] 73-74), against importing a rigid distinction between a prophetic gospel and cultic law or between visionary material and legislation (Eichrodt 555-56, 564; Zimmerli 431-33; cf. 20:40). It is another aspect of a common confusion between form-critical and redactional issues, noted in connection with earlier chapters. However, the caution has to be held in tension with the evidence of compositional unevenness and development that these chapters indubitably contain, unless one adopts a purely canonical approach.

A suitable beginning is with Zimmerli's minimal acceptance of the visionary 43:1-11 (12) and 44:1-2 as historically very close to the 573 B.C. date of the basic stratum of chaps. 40-42 (548, 552). At the other extreme, 45:1-8, having been borrowed from chap. 48, must fall outside present consideration. The little oracle in 45:9 has an original ring in light of 34:1-16, although its insertion seems to be redactional. Its striking introductory רב־לכם "enough of your . . ." seems to have been imitated in 44:6. The final vision in 46:19-24 has close links with 42:1-14, which was assigned to an early redactional layer that very possibly goes back to the prophet himself. A group of legislative sections seem to address the prophet as cultic founder (43:18-27; 45:18-20a; 46:13-14 [15]), and it is most natural to credit these to Ezekiel. If so, the closely related 43:13-17 cannot be far removed. The נשיא ("head of state") stratum, if such it is, invites comparison with 34:24 and 37:25, where the term occurred. In both cases the immediate contexts were judged to reflect a relatively late redactional stage.

The review of the material relating to temple personnel undertaken above seems to show that 44:6-16 stands at the end of a process of development. Its starting point, in the pre-redacted texts of 40:38-46 and 43:18-27, with their references to subordinate priests, interestingly accords with the deuteronomistic 2 Sam 2:35-36 (cf. 2 Kgs 2:27). There the house of Eli seems to represent those who claimed priestly authority outside Jerusalem, and its rejection points to their reduction to a minor priestly role (see McCarter, *1 Samuel* [AB; Garden City, NY: Doubleday, 1980] 91-93). Accordingly, both passages, as already suggested on other grounds, can be credited to the period of Ezekiel. The development to the perspective of 44:6-16 was not so radical as is often thought. Even the Deuteronomist had Zadokites in view as the main priestly authority, while even the earliest texts in Ezek 40 and 43 envisage the subordinate cultic personnel as slaughterers.

The Zadokite reference which in 1 Samuel reflects the priesthood of the Jerusalem temple is certainly perpetuated in the last stage of the literary sequence. It is usually attributed to the postexilic period (e.g., P. Hanson, *The Dawn of Apocalyptic* [Philadelphia: Fortress Press, 1975] 238-40). Gese (*Verfassungsentwurf* 122), following Procksch, assigned it to the earliest period, prior to Zerubbabel's governorship, and Zimmerli (553) has followed him. Should it be pushed back earlier? Fishbane (*Biblical Interpretation* 138-42), developing work done by Milgrom (*Studies* 83-86; cf. Gunneweg, *Leviten* 199-202), has shown that 44:6-16 is an "exegetical" oracle that closely follows the terminology of Num 18:1-7, 22-23. Although he too assigns the oracle to a post-exilic date, the phenomenon is comparable with the verbal echoing of Lev 26:4-13 in Ezek 34 and 37. Both later passages were credited to a late redactional stage, but they are evidently exilic, inasmuch as they look forward to a return from exile. Perhaps the echoing of Num 18 has the same setting. Certainly the relative closeness between Ezek 40:45-46a and the Zadokite overlay, which was noted earlier, suggests that a long period of development is not necessary (cf. Levenson, *Theology* 131, 153 note 13: he envisages an exilic dating for 44:6-16). It is noteworthy that the redacted text claims full prophetic authority (44:6) and refuses to distinguish between the authorially "authentic" and the "inauthentic." The fact that the oracle is given pride of place as the keynote passage of the first main section is significant. It is a pointer to the redactional shaping that underlies the present text of chaps. 43-46.

Comment

43:1-5 This visionary experience may have formed the climax of the temple vision at an earlier literary stage, but in the present form of the text it forms an introduction to the promise of chaps. 43-46 that worship would be restored. The luminous presence of Yahweh, which had departed in the vision of chaps. 8-11 and had followed the first Judean exiles to Babylonia according to chap. 1, was to return from there. In v 3 the text explicitly makes the connection with the earlier motif and brings it to a grand conclusion. The outer east gate, where the tour had begun in 40:6 and to which Ezekiel had been brought back in 42:15 before he followed his celestial guide around the walls, features once more. Now it is the closest point of entry for Yahweh's return to take up residence in the new, east-facing temple—just as it had been the way he had earlier left the old temple (10:18-19; 11:23). The noise and light that bombard Ezekiel's senses recall the flapping wings of the living creatures that transported the chariot throne in 1:24, and the theophanic appearing of 1:28. "Glory" here refers to "the complete manifestation of divine majesty, both to the chariot throne and to God himself" (Mettinger, *Dethronement* 107). The prophet again reacts with the body language of shocked submission (1:28). In a deliberate counterpart to 8:3 and in an expression of the climactic point the present vision has reached, he is transported by the spirit above the route taken by the divine apparition. He witnesses its occupation of the temple building that till now had been but a shell.

6-9 Hitherto the angelic guide has explained significant features of what the prophet saw. Now in a conscious differentiation his voice is superseded by what is recognized from its source as a greater one. "When the sun rises, the stars grow pale. When the king enters and begins to speak, the courtiers . . . fall back" (Zimmerli 415). The first of two communications is strikingly given in vv 7-9 in a rhetorical scheme of alternating parallelism (ABC/ABC) set in a framing inclusion (Parunak, *Structural Studies* 520; cf. Talmon, *Qumran* 365). The framework, in vv 7aβ and 9b, interprets the vision in terms of Yahweh's immanence among his people, never to leave again. The verb שׁכן "live" recalls the tabernacle (משׁכן) of P: the sovereign God, who moved where he willed, was graciously to settle in the new temple, his wanderings over. In language derived from the ark tradition, the temple is initially described as the exclusive royal residence of Yahweh (cf. Isa 6:1; 60:13; Ps 99:5). The footstool is no longer the ark itself, as originally in the tradition, but the temple: the ark never features in the new temple (cf. Jer 3:16-17).

In pre-exilic times a cultic offense had been committed against the divine immanence, which is now graced with the term Yahweh's "holy name" (A/A: vv 7bα, 8bα; cf. 20:39; 36:21-23). The offense is described in strong terms as "debauchery" or infidelity to the covenant (B/B: vv 7bα, 9a), before it is at last defined first as "memorials of their kings" (C/C: vv 7bβ, 9a) and then as insufficient differentiation between Yahweh's and Israel's zones (v 8a). The first accusation of lese majesty significantly cites prerogatives claimed by the kings of Israel. The implication is that their kingship was markedly inferior to Yahweh's and that its exercise spelled an encroachment upon his own. The Hebrew term פגרים seems here to mean not "corpses" but royal stelae, in the light of Ugaritic usage (see Neiman, *JBL* 67 [1948] 58-59; Galling, *ZDPV* 75 [1959] 11-12; however, Ebach, *UF* 3 [1971] 365-68, has argued for a meaning "offerings for the dead"), set up in memory of deceased kings. The second charge relates to the duplex-like layout of palace and temple since Solomon's period, the latter forming a part of the larger royal complex (see the sketch in Hasting's *Dictionary of the Bible* 4, 695). Henceforth, in line with the holiness zones built into the new temple of chaps. 40-42, such closeness between Yahweh and Israel in the persons of their kings or their representations could no longer be tolerated. Inevitably the immanence of a transcendent ("holy") God could only be realized by a corresponding separateness. A God so near to them ("among") had nevertheless to be so far from them, if his revelation was not to be impugned.

10-11 The second communication flows smoothly from the first (see Gese, *Verfassungsentwurf* 41-42). If such wrong practices had resulted in exile (v 8bβ; cf. 22:31), a prerequisite for return from exile was a change of heart that took seriously their shamefulness. Proclamation of Yahweh's new work of salvation was to stimulate a realization of how far the people stood from God and from his will (cf. 16:54, 61; 36:31-32). This end was to be served first by study of the temple plan, to be drawn by the prophet, with its massive gatehouses that warned of the awesomeness of the one who resided there, and with its gradations in holiness from periphery to center. Second, the temple procedures that promoted and protected Yahweh's holiness, which were also revealed to the prophet (and presented in the course of what follows) would bring a challenging message. The architectural plan was itself to serve as an inducement for inaugurating and maintaining the procedures.

12 In the present compositional structure this verse is a headline for the overall unit. It forms a bridge with the foregoing oracle by echoing its theme, the holiness of the temple as Yahweh's abode. Not only the temple complex built on the mountain top (cf. 40:2) but also the surrounding reservation (see 45:1-3) partook of this holiness. So far did its aura spread. The superlative expression grandiosely differentiates the area from the rest of the land (cf. 45:3-4: "the most sacred part of the country").

13-17 This section represents a preliminary footnote to the next one about the dedication of the altar (cf. 1 Sam 9:9 in relation to 9:11). It explains the technical vocabulary used in v 20 by presenting the design of the altar and its dimensions. The altar was mentioned in passing in 40:47 as standing in the inner court, but now it leaps into prominence as a major element in the operation of the temple. The reminder of the larger unit from 40:5, together with the echo of 40:2 in v 12, gives the impression of a fresh beginning and so of the continuance of introductory material within a new unit. For a reconstruction of the design see Fig. 5. After the heading in v 13a, vv 13b-15 describe the parts of the altar from bottom to top and in terms of its lateral tapering, while vv 16-17 supply its respective widths from top to bottom and the access by steps from its east side. The circular gutter, deepened by its raised edging, was a sump for sacrificial blood to drain into (cf. v 18bβ), so that the inner court was kept clean and dry. Above it rose the altar to a height of 10 cubits above the bottom of the gutter, and 9 above ground level. It apparently consisted of three square blocks of diminishing lateral size: a "lower plinth," also called a "protruding base," a vertically larger "upper plinth" and a "hearth." However, Milgrom (*EncJud* 2, 763), followed by Wright (*Disposal* 151-53), envisages four tiers, with the base set below the lower plinth and of the same width, and the "ridge" of v 17 constructed at the outer, upper edge of the lower plinth and bordering a separate gutter. The width of the altar ranged from 12 x 12 cubits at the level of the hearth, widening to 14 x 14, then to 16 x 16 at the level of the lower plinth, with the gutter measuring 18 x 18 externally. The overall dimensions compare with the Chronicler's figures for the temple altar: 20 cubits long, 20 wide and 10 high (2 Chr 4:1). The Herodian altar consisted of four blocks that increased from 24 x 24 cubits at the top to a base of 32 x 32, according to the Mishnah (*Mid.* 3:1). The "horns" were projections rising from the corners of the hearth, a regular feature of ancient altars (cf. 1 Kgs 2:28). The steps, which have no number given, permitted access to the hearth (cf. Cooke 469; the ban in Exod 20:26 was impracticable with so high an altar): the orientation meant that the officiating priest faced the temple and so Yahweh's symbolic presence. It is often urged that the altar's design was modeled on a Babylonian ziggurat (Galling in Fohrer 238; Wevers 313; de Vaux, *Ancient Israel* 412; Fishbane, *Biblical Interpretation* 370 note 132); Zimmerli (425-27) has vigorously countered the arguments adduced.

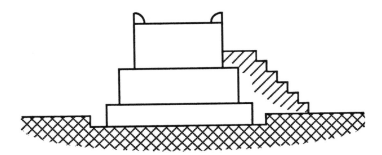

Figure 5. The altar

18-24 If the presence of Yahweh is the sine qua non for the temple to function, another essential premise is a properly dedicated altar, on which the regular rites of worship and expiation may be carried out (v 18b; cf. v 27b). The implication of the dedication is that the altar would be consecrated or made holy for such use, as all of P's specifications for the dedication of the tabernacle altar expressly state (Exod 29:37; 40:10; Lev 8:11; cf. 16:19). The directions are presented as a further communication of Yahweh to the prophet (cf. vv 7, 10; the third-person references to Yahweh in v 24 are formulaic). The prophet functions as a second Moses in inaugurating the new cult (cf. Exod 29:36b-37). The ceremony described here is especially close to part of P's Day of Atonement rites (Lev 16:18-19). The sin offering, or more strictly decontamination offering, since its function reflects the privative use of the verb that actually appears in v 20 (cf. Milgrom, *VT* 21 [1971] 237-39; G. Wenham, *Leviticus* [NICOT; Grand Rapids: Eerdmans, 1979] 88-89), plays a crucial part, in purifying the inherently profane material used to construct the altar. There is no mention of the necessary slaughter of the young bull or of the sacrifice of its fat, liver and kidneys on the altar (cf. Lev 4:8-10). The text rushes on to the smearing of key parts of the altar with some of the blood drained from the animal, as a means of expiation. The flesh was not to be eaten by the priests (cf. 42:13; 44:29), but the carcass was to be disposed of outside the sacred area, as in the case of an initiatory sin offering or in a ceremony of consecration of priests according to P (Exod 29:14; Lev 8:17; 9:11; cf. Milgrom, *VT* 26 [1976] 333-37). How the blood ceremony was deemed to achieve expiation we are not told. The Hebrew verb כפר, rendered "make expiation," may function as a denominative verb, "function as a ransom (כֹּפֶר)," so that death is averted (cf. Wenham, *Leviticus* 28, 59-61). However, Milgrom (*VT* 26 [1976] 336-37), although he allows this sense in a number of cases (e.g., Lev 17:11), in the context of the sin offering works from a primary meaning "wipe off." He envisages a purging effect upon the contaminated part of the sanctuary (cf. Lev 15:31; 16:19): the blood is applied as a neutralizing cathartic. Zohar (*JBL* 107 [1988] 614-15), while concurring with Milgrom's view of the magnetic contamination of the sanctuary by sin, conceives of the transfer of impurity to another medium, the blood that is presented to God by the smearing of the altar.

The ceremonies of a second day begin in the same way as those of the first, but involve a young goat (cf. Lev 16:11, 15, 18). Then follow holocausts, with an expiatory intent (cf. Lev 16:24). Here the rite unusually includes salt, as in later Jewish ritual (see Cooke 472 and note the textual gloss in Mark 9:49). Salt is specifically mentioned in P only in connection with the cereal offering (Lev 2:13) and incense (Exod 30:35); it alludes to the covenant relationship according to Lev 2:13; Num 18:19 (cf. 2 Chron 13:5). The parallel with Lev 16:24 suggests that in vv 23-24 expiation of the people's sins is in view (cf. 2 Chron 29:21-24). The contextual references to Israel's pre-exilic cultic sins in 43:7-9, 10-11 are significant. They required formal expiation before the cult could function properly again. The altar, polluted by the people's sins, needed to be cleansed (v 26).

25-27 The second day's double ceremony was to provide a model for the ceremonies of a week (strictly, six days of rites, including the second day). Zimmerli (431, 435), following Rautenberg's lead (*ZAW* 33 [1913] 102), regards vv 25-27 as secondary (cf. Rendtorff, *Studien* 28) with the purpose of harmonizing with later P regulations (cf. Exod 29:36b-37; Lev 8:33, 35); but v 27b provides an expected conclusion, which moreover supplies a partial inclusion with v 18b. The orientation of the ritual description veers elliptically from the prophet (v 25a) to Israel. The double sacrificial system of holocausts and shared offerings (see 40:42 *Comment*) could only be initiated after the dedication of the altar. It was the only way to ensure right, acceptable cultic activity (cf. 20:40-41; Lev 1:3-4; Amos 5:22; Rom 12:1; see Rendtorff, *Studien* 253-58).

44:1, 2 A further visionary experience is related, which presupposes the vision of 43:1-5, especially in v 2aβ. The old pattern of the guide's leading the prophet to a new phenomenon and then explaining it, which is found in chaps. 40-42, is now resumed. From the inner court Ezekiel is taken to the outer court, near its east gateway. He is able to glimpse its closed doors at the far end of the long corridor of the gatehouse (cf. 40:6-16 *Comment*). The shut doors, defying their natural purpose, were to commemorate the initial point of the divine re-entry into the temple area. Though in a public place, the east gate thus shared the special sanctity of the temple itself and was off limits to the people.

3 The theme of the head of state in his ritual capacity is broached here (see 45:21-25 *Comment*). It apparently formed part of the נשׂיא ("head of state") layer (see *Form/Structure/Setting*). Entering the outer court through the outer north or south gate, he was to have access from the outer court to the porch of the east gate, which opened into the outer court. There in the roomy porch, which measured 20 x 8 cubits, he would have the privilege of eating his sacrificial meal that was associated with the shared offering (cf. 46:2). The privilege is reminiscent of the place reserved for the worshiping king in the pre-exilic temple (2 Kgs 11:14; 23:3).

4, 5 The complex introduction of 43:1-44:5 is drawn to a close by this further vision, which includes an explanation that serves to point forward to the main body of the unit. Ezekiel is taken into the inner court via the north gate, presumably because of the closure of the inner east gate to be mentioned in 46:1. The visionary experience is a reprise of 43:3b, 5b, and functions as a reminder of the basic message of the presence of Yahweh as motivation for temple procedure. The methods of worship are dictated by the nature of the God to whom it is directed and who graces the place of worship with his presence. The explanation seeks to express this link. It couples the esoteric vision of Yahweh's glory ("saw/see," vv 4, 5) with practical instructions for operating the temple. There is a focus on access, which refers not only to the use of gates (vv 3, 11; 46:1-3, 8-10, 12) but also to the gradations of holiness expressed in the system of outer and inner courts (cf. vv 16, 17, 19, 21; 45:4, 19; 46:19-24). V 5 echoes 40:4, as a parallel element of introduction; the focus on showing there changes to one on speaking here, in line with the change in theme from temple plan to temple procedure. V 5 more closely echoes 43:11, in an indication that the long introduction is drawing to a close. The four plural nouns are reversed (ABCD/DCBA), a standard technique in recapitulation (cf. Talmon, *Qumran* 359-62, who calls the phenomenon "distant chiastic parallelism").

6-16 The topic of temple personnel, which occupies 44:6-31, is dominated by this oracle addressed to the exiles as a "rebellious community," an accusatory phrase often found in Ezekiel's judgment oracles. The emphasis on pre-exilic cultic aberration in the charges of vv 6-8 is reminiscent of chaps. 6 and 8. As in 43:7-9, the references to the cultic past imply a summons to a radical break and the need for religious reformation in a particular area. The underlying fault in both passages appears to be similar. Another facet of anti-secularization is in view. The foreigners of v 7 are generally related to the Nethinim or temple slaves, who seem to have originated as prisoners of war. This group is included in the list of returning exiles that is found in both Ezra 2:43-58 and Neh 7:46-60 and probably reflects the early decades of the post-exilic era (see H. G. M. Williamson, *Ezra and Nehemiah* [WBC; Waco, TX: Word, 1985] 31-32). Accordingly, it is difficult to imagine that the group was not fully integrated into Yahwism by the exilic period (cf. Greenberg, *JAOS* 70 [1950] 44 note 9). If we are to take literally the appositional phrase "uncircumcised in heart and body," which is emphatically repeated in v 9, the reference must be sought elsewhere. A more likely identification is with the Carian royal guards of 2 Kgs 11, from southwest Asia Minor. Although they were palace guards, their regular sphere of duty also covered the temple, within the complex of royal buildings (2 Kgs 11:6-7; Hitzig 348; Skinner 427-28). That gate duty is in view is suggested by v 11 below.

Such an arrangement would clearly conflict with the categorical holiness of the new temple. Interestingly the Chronicler's version of 2 Kgs 11 replaces the Carians with Levites for the express reason of cultic holiness (see esp. 2 Chr 23:4-7). Here the term מקדש "sanctuary, holy place" in vv 7, 9 (cf. קדשׁי "my holy things," v 8) is eloquent on this very point. The pagan intrusion cast a cloud of profanation over the central act of altar worship, where the sacrificial fat burned on its hearth and the blood splashed on its sides constituted Yahweh's "food" brought to the altar table (cf. v 16). More generally it caused a rift in the covenant relationship. Israel had neglected its cultic responsibilities as the covenant people by entrusting them to pagans (contra Levenson, *Theology* 146-47, who finds a reference to Yahweh's covenant with Levi [Jer 33:17-26; Mal 2:4-9]; cf. the association of "shocking practices" and "covenant" in 16:58, 59).

10-14 Their place as temple guards was to be taken by the Levites, who feature here as a non-priestly group of temple attendants, as in P. Seemingly by way of punishing Israel (Milgrom, *Studies* 84), they were also to take over Israel's role of slaughtering sacrificial victims (cf. Lev 1:5, etc.) and to be generally responsible for the outer area (cf. 40:45; 45:5; 46:24 and also Ezra 8:17). The Levites are introduced with a new factor of accusation: they had been abettors of Israel in its worship of idols. Thus the punishment of Israel becomes overshadowed by that of the Levites. Vv 10-14 fall into two parts, vv 10-11 and the parallel but fuller vv 12-14. Much of the terminology of accusation and punishment seems to be derived from 14:1-11 concerning the idolatrous exilic elders, but here it is overlaid by the concept of different degrees of cultic holiness, which prescribed separate roles for people, Levites and priests (vv 11, 13, 14). In the new order of the cultic relationship between Israel and Yahweh, the Levites were to represent the interests of the former, while the priests represented those of the latter (v 11, cf. v 15). For the range of "holy things" and "most holy things" (v 13) in priestly writings see Haran, *Temples* 172 note 50.

15-16 The role of the priests is duly spelled out. They are strikingly demarcated as "levitical" and "Zadokite," that is, members of the same tribe as the Levites but descended only from Zadok. While the Levites' role is tinged with a vehement expression of disgrace, that of the priests is antithetically expressed in terms of honor. Theirs were to be the privileges of the central task of altar duty and of access into the inner court, to which, together with the temple, the term "sanctuary" now refers, over against the "temple area" of v 14 (cf. Gese, *Verfassungsentwurf* 127).

This passionate oracle, which is most heated in the middle section concerning the Levites, vv 10-14, clearly reflects a situation of controversy. Fishbane (*Biblical Interpretation* 138-43) has observed an appeal to Num 18, reflected in the overlap of key vocabulary between Num 18:1-7, 22-23 and Ezek 44:9-16. In the former passage Israel, Levites and Aaronide priests are similarly polarized in a pecking order. Here, by means of both citation and reinterpretation, implicit justification seems to be claimed for the roles now assigned to them. New factors that appear in the present passage are the religious unorthodoxy of the Levites, stated doubly for emphasis in vv 10 and 15, and the orthodoxy of the "Zadokite" priests. Both factors evidently mean to hark back to the pre-exilic period.

Commonly the Levites are identified with the priests of the high places of Judah—presumably of levitical descent—who were displaced by Josiah's reform and were maintained at the Jerusalem temple but not permitted to officiate in altar service (2 Kgs 23:8-9). If these same priests are called כמרים "pagan, idolatrous priests" in 2 Kgs 23:5 (Abba, VT 28 [1978] 4; but cf. Gunneweg, *Leviten* 122 note 2), there would be an alignment with the charges made here. The present context suggests that earlier the Levites had carried out priestly duties (vv 9-11, not foreigners but Levites; vv 12-16, not Levites but Zadokites). Accordingly the Zadokite priests would represent the priests of the Jerusalem temple, where the leading priests were descended from Zadok, whom Cross has argued was an Aaronide priest of the sanctuary at Hebron (*Canaanite Myth* 207-15). Then the use of Num 18 in Ezek 44 was intended to equate the sons of Aaron with the descendants of Zadok, the shift of name being dictated simply by historical circumstances. It is often objected that the alleged orthodoxy of the Jerusalem priesthood ill accords with Ezekiel's own representations in 7:26; 22:26. Certainly one may allow for some argumentative hyperbole here; Baudissin (*Geschichte* 107 note 1) observed that at least they were not accused of idolatry there. Some blame must accrue to the temple priests for tolerating the religious deviations in the temple attested in Ezek 8, but it is noteworthy that the perpetrators are not specified as priests (McConville, *TynBul* 34 [1983] 17, who also refers to 9:6b). Zimmerli himself raised the question as to whether the lamenting pious of 9:4 included Zadokite priests who lacked influence (*Ezekiel 1* 248). Fundamentally the passage seems to argue for one religious group as preferable to another in the all-important practicality of the staffing of the post-exilic temple, probably to settle controversial debate among the exiles. "The judgment is only a relative one, as all class judgments necessarily are" (Skinner 433). If it be urged that elsewhere in the book forgiveness was to be the order of a new day of grace, it is expected in 20:33-38 (cf. 34:17-22) that the new Exodus would be accompanied by an act of judgment and here a more lenient punishment is envisaged. Indeed, a purpose in citing Num 18, which follows the cultic aberration of Num 16-17, may have been to claim a typological warrant for the cultic differentiation, like that of the wilderness judgment in chap. 20.

The passage raises a much larger question. Wellhausen superimposed the (post-exilic) priestly writing (P) on a pre-existing tripod whose legs were Ezek 44:6-16; 2 Kgs 23:8-9 and Deut 18:6-8 (*Prolegomena* 121-24): P's Levites developed solely from the late pre-exilic disfranchised priests of the high places, for whom D claimed priestly privileges. There have been some countertrends since Wellhausen's time. There is a tendency to recognize that P consists of a series of strata from different periods, rather than being a monolithic entity. And difficulty has been seen in relating 2 Kgs 23:9 too quickly to Deut 18:6-8 (see A. D. H. Mayes, *Deuteronomy* [NCB; London: Oliphants, 1979] 278-79; McConville, *TynBul* 34 [1983] 6-9). Certainly the present passage gives the impression of dependence on a written source known to us as Num 18. Milgrom has argued that D at times explicitly depends on portions of P (*HUCA* 47 [1976] 9-13). In the formula כאשר דבר "as he promised" in Deut 18:2 he urges that a written priestly source is being echoed, which must be Num 18:20. Whereas the P passage grants to priests the right to food offerings, D claims that all members of the tribe of Levi had the right to officiate at the central sanctuary and to receive the sacrificial stipend. D polemically advocates that "the levitical priests, the whole tribe of Levi" were so privileged (Deut 18:1; cf. 17: 9, 18; 21:5; 24:8 etc.). If Milgrom is right, it is possible to view the present passage as a further development, a statement of arbitration between D and P that finds grounds to come firmly down on P's side, yet acknowledges its awareness of D's claims by the use of the phrase "levitical priests" (v 15; 43:19). As to the pre-existence of Levites as a cultic subgroup, it is difficult to draw incontrovertible conclusions; but at least Ezek 44 seems to hark back to an earlier claim that the non-Aaronide members of the tribe of Levi at some point had such a role, and finds a precedent in the claim. However, for D the whole tribe of Levi had priestly rank and privilege (see Emerton, *VT* 12 [1962] 129-38; Abba's tentative claim that in Deut 18:7 "fellow Levites" means not priests but subordinate Levites already serving at the central sanctuary [*VT* 27 (1977) 264-65] is invalid: in the context only tribal affinity is in view, the priest of v 3 being the antecedent of the tribal "him" of v 5 [see Cody, *History* 131 note 17]). D may well have had its own theological ax to grind in its distinctive presentation (cf. McConville, *Law* 147-53).

17-31 To the clarification of vv 15-16 has been smoothly appended a potpourri of regulations concerning priests. They are essentially a selection designed to illustrate how cultic holiness was to be translated into the priestly lifestyle. Holiness is their explicit (see *Form/Structure/Setting*) or implicit motif. The priests' right of access to the inner court (vv 17, 21, 27) made them stewards of a scrupulously guarded holiness.

17-19 Vv 17 and 19 are closely related to the explanation in 42:13-14 concerning the use of the rooms on either side of the west building as changing rooms. They were to form a sort of air lock between the inner court and the outer court accessible to the people. Holiness is here regarded as a dangerous, contagious element from which nonpriestly mortals needed to be protected (cf. Exod 19:12-13; Lev 10:1-2; 2 Sam 6:7). Linen, although the particular word used here is different from that used elsewhere in the Old Testament, was the traditional material for the priest's ritual uniform. V 18 supplies information about part of this uniform: the cap and breeches accord with Exod 28:40-42; 39:28. The ban on wool in v 17 is explained as a way of preventing perspiration, which was probably regarded as unclean.

20-27 Clusters of regulations from Lev 10 and 21 have provided the basis for this group (Fishbane, *Biblical Interpretation* 294-95). Lev 10:6 and 21:5, 10 underlie the ruling about hair style in v 20, which thus links the two clusters. The prohibition of v 21 depends on Lev. 10:9, while the job description of vv 23-24 depends on Lev 10:10-11. Lev 21:1-3 has supplied the family death regulation of v 25, while the marriage ruling of v 22 has drawn on Lev 21:7, 13-14. The holiness motif in the Lev 10 cluster appears at v 23 (= Lev 10:10). The group from Lev 21 contains it abundantly in its source (Lev 21:6-9, 12-15), and presumably this is the implicit reason for their citation here.

There are a few variations. One factor is the absence of the high priest from the present material (cf. Levenson, *Theology* 141-44; Fishbane, *Biblical Interpretation* 295). The permission in v 22bβ is not found in Lev 21. V 24 takes v 23 further in several respects, beyond the Lev 10 parallel. The judicial responsibility of the priests may have been inspired by Deut 17:9; 21:5, where their cultic closeness to Yahweh is stressed. The reference to sabbath holiness and to public services reflects Ezekielian concerns: see 22:26; 45:17; 46:9-11. The purificatory ritual of vv 26-27 has been added to v 25: so the switch to a singular subject suggests. It may be based on the lay regulation of Num 19:11-19, with extra demands in view of a priestly status. The emphatic references to the sanctuary (קדש) in v 27 reveal the necessity for these demands, as well as carrying forward the overall motif of holiness.

28-30 These verses anticipate the next section on the material support of priests. They closely reflect Num 18:8-20; but, unlike that passage, are addressed to Israel as a statement of their obligations, just as vv 6-8 were a statement of their cultic irresponsibility. Accordingly vv 28-30 may have been an earlier continuation of vv 6-16 (Cooke 488; Gese, *Verfassungsentwurf* 64). In favor of this reconstruction is the dependence of vv 28-30 on Num 18, in line with vv 9-16. The priests' income was to be derived from the land allocated to the laity indirectly, by way of offerings. The contextual relevance of this provision, in relation to the motif of holiness, is that it had the quality of קדש קדשים "most holy things" (Num 18:9; cf. Lev 27:28; Ezek 42:13), inasmuch as it was consumed by the priests alone. A tenth part of the tithe (here called "contributions": cf. Num 18:26-29; Eissfeldt, *Erstlinge* 65-67) presented to the Levites was forwarded to them. Implicitly these dues were "holy" in that they were to be eaten by priests' families (cf. Num 18:11-13, 29; Lev 23:20; 27:30). Also counted as their perquisite is the "best of the firstfruits," a possible interpretation of the Hebrew of Num 18:12 (cf. Budd, *Numbers* 199) and one that was doubtless influenced by Exod 23:19 (E); 34:26 (J). In this context it may envisage a partial priestly due from among a larger due assigned to the Levites. As in vv 6-16, there appears to be a deliberate conflation of older traditions. The last emolument includes a singular reference to the priest, which may indicate a later expansion, especially as Num 18 no longer lies in the background. Instead, Num 15:20-21 appears to be in view. That passage has a link with Num 18 in the use of the phrase הרים תרומה "make a contribution," besides having ראשית "best" in common. The final clause of v 30, with its switch to a second person singular pronoun, seems to be a further amplification. The incentive may loosely echo Deut 14:29b, which shares a second singular and is set in a context of giving tithes to the landless Levite. The motivating postscript reveals a knowledge of human nature!

31 Now Lev 22:8 appears to be the basis, in a prohibition of eating carrion that has priests in mind, unlike the general ban of Exod 22:30 (31), etc. Lev 22 is organically linked with Lev 21, which was echoed earlier in the passage. As before, there seems to be an implicit awareness of a literary context of holiness: Lev 22:9 speaks of Yahweh as the sanctifier of priests. There is a further relevance in that Lev 22:2-9 is mainly a discussion of access to "holy things" assigned as food to the priests, the very topic of vv 29-30. Thus this final injunction serves to reinforce the role of the priests as mirrors of divine holiness.

45:1-8 This summary of 48:8-22 opens a new section on the maintenance of the cult (45:1-17). Its significance in its original context and consideration of its detailed content may be left till later in the commentary. At this point the use to which it is put in its present setting requires brief examination. The theme of the תרומה "contribution," broached in 44:30, is developed. Now it is used in the sense of "reservation," a contribution of land to Yahweh. What is called "the sacred reservation" was to be divided into two strips, each 25,000 x 10,000 cubits. One was to possess the highest degree of sanctity: it would contain the temple area and also provide habitation for the priests. In the other strip the Levites were to reside. This allocation of land creates some tension with the lack of land mentioned in 44:28, but it was a tension that already existed with the older system of levitical cities (cf. "cities," v 5; cf. Budd, *Numbers* 376), which this plan replaces. Essentially the priests and Levites were "grace and favor" (to use a British royal idiom) tenants of religious property, while the laity occupied their own tribal areas and had rights of disposal (contrast 48:14). Strictly only the priests were involved in the full scheme (cf. 44:28). The Levites' territory had an intermediate status in that it was termed their "property." This territorial system, along with the explicit degrees of holiness, is obviously an extension of what pertained within the temple area, in relation to holiness and the related differentiated staffing, as vv 4-5 suggest. Again the motif of holiness is looming large in the text. V 2, which breaks the continuity of vv 1 and 3 and has a slightly different word for "sanctuary," appears to be an afterthought, along with the related v 4bβ. It supplies the dimensions of 42:15-20 and specifies an insulating circle of no man's land.

The passage majors in the allocation of part of Israel's land for the needs of the temple personnel. The remaining material earmarking land for the city and for the head of state in part serves the holiness motif: both entities were to be kept at a certain distance from the temple (contrast 43:8). In the latter case temptation to upset the economic stability of his subjects is averted: adequate provision is made for his support. In turn—and this is the contextual point—the material upkeep of the temple staff was thereby safeguarded. The underlying thought of the people's freedom from royal landgrabbing comes to the fore in the appended v 8b, in which the peremptory voice of Yahweh is heard as advocate for his covenant people so pained by memories of the pre-exilic monarchy. It was an indispensable premise of the smooth running of the temple.

9-12 V 8b has paved the way for the incorporation of a curt oracle that now rhetorically serves to proclaim a new era of economic justice in which private land would be protected from royal confiscation (cf. 1 Kgs 21:1-16; Jer 22:1-5, 13-17; Ezek 22:25). It would mean the realization at long last of a royal ideal: cf. 2 Sam 8:15; Ps 72:1-2; Jer 22:3 and the eschatological Isa 9:6(7). The ironic wordplay of הרימו "remove" on הרים תרומה "make a contribution" reminds the reader of the overall theme. V 9 ministers to this theme by providing circumstances that permitted sufficient giving to the religious cause. The economic welfare of the temple was intertwined with that of the state. Vv 10-11 elaborate these conditions by particularizing the fair play (צדקה) of v 9 with fair, "standard" (צדק) weights and measures. Vv 10-11 also look forward to the contributions of vv 13-14, and thus indicate the subservience of economic matters to religious. As for dry measures, the ephah was about ½ bushel, and the homer about 5 bushels; as for liquid measures, the bath was about 5½ gallons and the homer (or kor, v 14) about 55 gallons (see *IDB* 4, 834-35). As for weights, in v 12 the MT wrongly accords with the Babylonian sexagesimal system of 60 shekels to the mina, rather than the regular one of 50 shekels. The shekel has been estimated as 11.424 grams (*IDB* 4, 832). Evidently weights of 5 and 10 shekels were in common use.

13-17 The theme becomes explicit once more in the heading. A tax in kind, separate from the tithe, was to be imposed. It amounted to ¹⁄₆₀th in the case of wheat and barley, 1% in the case of oil, and ½% in the case of sheep or goats. These contributions would go toward cereal and animal offerings, which actually became the perquisites of the priests who achieved expiation for the people by ritually offering them. Vv 16-17 add supplementary material relating to the head of state. Evidently the religious tax was to be channeled through him as representive of the cultic community. In vv 16, 17a and 17b emphasis is laid on his role. Libations are probably specified not as consisting of wine but of oil, aligning with the oil of v 14 (cf. vv 24-25; 46:5, 7, 11). The ritual occasions are enumerated. For comprehensiveness the sin offering is added to a fresh list in v 17b, and the expiatory function of the sacrificial work of the priests is again stressed. Significantly both the priests and the head of state were to strive for the restoration of right relations with Yahweh and so for the community to accord with the holiness of Yahweh.

18-25 V 17 serves to introduce the final section, 45:18-46:15, concerning the rites of offerings to be enacted in the new temple. In the present unit, which deals with annual ceremonies, the first part, vv 18-20, announces an annual ritual of decontaminating the inner sanctuary area. It is reminiscent of the dedication of the altar in 43:13-17. It is a counterpart of P's great Day of Atonement ceremony in Lev 16, but here the rite takes place in the spring, at the start of the year. As there, the blood of the sin offering has the function of bringing about the regular decontamination of the sanctuary from the accumulation of past sins that had a polluting effect upon it (cf. Lev 16:19 ". . . sanctify it from the impurities of the people of Israel"). Probably major sins were covered by this rite (cf. Milgrom, *IDBSup* 767, with regard to Lev 16), but there was a minor ceremony on the seventh day to cope with lesser sins (for the concept of inadvertency see Milgrom, *JQR* 58 [1967/68] 115-25). However, it is possible that the specification of such sins was intended to refer to both ceremonies, if it is significant that the holy of holies is not included in the places daubed with blood (cf. Milgrom, ibid.). V 20b may want to relate this second ceremony to the whole temple area (Gese, *Verfassungsentwurf* 79; Koch, *Priesterschrift* 107).

In vv 21-25, which are part of the נשיא ("head of state") layer (see *Form/Structure/Setting*), the sacrificial requirements for two annual festivals are sketchily featured, the combined passover and festival of unleavened bread in the spring and the autumn festival (of booths). The sequencing for the former two-part celebration in vv 21/22/23-24 represents an AB/A'/B' structure. In each case there is some emphasis upon the sin offering. In particular, the passover sin offering has no parallel in the Pentateuch. This emphasis aligns with v 17b and implies the regular need to purify the sanctuary and so protect its holiness from the people's sins. For the relationship of the sacrifices to those in the comparable Num 28-29 see Zimmerli 485-86. The missing reference to the traditional third festival of weeks or harvest or firstfruits (Exod 23:14, 16; 34:22-23; Deut 16:16; Num 28:26) may be linked with the fact that in H (Lev 23:16-21) and P (Num 28:26) it is not called a חג "pilgrimage festival" and so does not necessitate pilgrimage to the temple (Haran, *Temples* 297). Oil was regularly mixed into the cereal offering; a hin, 1/16th of a bath, amounted to about a gallon (*IDB* 4, 835).

A further emphasis in this passage (and also in 46:1-12; cf. 43:3; 45:16-17) is the cultic role of the head of state both in his own right and as representative of "the people of the land." He is described largely from a cultic perspective. He is given a position of privilege over against the people (43:1; 46:2, 8) and functions as the representative of the people in presenting sacrifices (45:16-17, 22-25). He is assigned his own tract of land (45:7; 48:21-22) and is not to usurp that of other

Israelites (46:16-18). In the last reference there is obviously a restrictive note that reflects the excesses of the pre-exilic monarchy (cf. 45:8-9). The same attitude seems to underlie the other references. In the temple area he may go so far and no further. Crown property no longer adjoins the temple (cf. 43:8). An impression is given of a future constitutional monarchy that seeks to do justice to two factors. The first is the messianic hope inherited from other prophetic thinking. The second is the pain that lingered in the hearts of the Judean exiles after experiencing the imperiousness of late pre-exilic kings with regard to the cult and to the property rights of their subjects. Moreover, human kingship must never again be a threat to the kingship of Yahweh himself (43:7-9).

46:1-15 This second part of the section dealing with ritual procedure continues the series adumbrated in the listing of 45:17a. After the annual rites of 45:18-25, there is a majoring in those of the sabbath and new moon day (vv 1-3, 4-8). Vv 13-15 will round off the cultic survey by featuring the daily offerings.

1-12 This material continues the נשׂיא ("head of state") layer from 45:21-25 (see *Form/Structure/Setting*). It is framed by references to the inner east gate (vv 1-3, 12); gates also feature in vv 8-10. One might consider this element contextually subordinate to the theme of sacrificial occasions, but its importance is revealed by the attention drawn to it in the introductory 44:5. Access and limits were regulated so that the holiness of the temple should not be infringed. The two motifs of access and sacrifice are given a role to play in the structure. On the sabbath and new moon day the access of the head of state (vv 1-2) and the people (v 3) is regulated before the offerings of those days are discussed (vv 4-7). Then at the public services the access of people (v 9) and head of state (v 10) is again broached before their offerings are mentioned (v 11). A reverting to the gate in the first case, at v 8, has as a corresponding feature in the second case, in v 12, a gate regulation for a separate occasion; here a sacrificial component is included as a minor element, as indeed it is in v 2.

Closure and limited access to the head of state are predicated of both the outer (44:1-3) and inner east gates. Since the outer east gate could be approached via the other outer gates, it was kept permanently closed. However, in the case of the inner east gate, it had to be opened, if the head of state was to have access, since there was no other point of entry, the inner court being off limits to all but priests (cf. v 8). The closure of both gates was to commemorate Yahweh's entry through them when he came to take up permanent residence in the new temple. The head of state had the privilege of passing through the porch at the outer end of the gatehouse (cf. 40:31, 34) and standing at the inner end, at the point to which 45:19b refers, in order to witness the priests' sacrificing his offerings and to perform there a gesture of obeisance, kneeling with head pressed to the ground. Leaving the gate open allowed the people to look from the other side of the gateway in the outer court, as they chose to come during the holiday to perform their act of worship (cf. Ps 5:8[7]). Even if for most the outer steps and the 75 foot long corridor blocked their vision, the open door would provide at least a token of intimacy each week and month. The content of the holocaust mentioned in v 2 is spelled out in vv 4-7, along with the accompanying cereal offerings, which were moistened with oil (cf. Num 28:9-15).

The public services evidently excluded the sabbath and new moon services, but were wider than the festivals. Since attendance was mandatory, a system of traffic control within the outer court had to be set up, creating two orderly streams in procession (cf. Ps 42:5[4]; 68:25-28 [24-27]), with no U-turns permitted. On these occasions the head of state had no special privilege, although he may have headed a procession. V 11, although structurally relevant, as we argued above, is strangely incomplete in its concentration on the cereal offering (cf. Num 15:1-16). The missing holocaust might be explained as superfluous after 45:24, were it not for the fact that the lambs are an extra (cf. v 47; Num 28:19; 29:13-36). The sabbath (and new moon day) privilege of the head of state is extended to his voluntary sacrificing, but there was no need to keep the gate open longer at such times.

13-15 The daily offerings were to consist of a holocaust (v 13) and a cereal offering made from semolina ("fine flour," v 14). The injunction is repeated in v 15 to emphasize both its timing, in the morning, and the major role of the holocaust. There was probably an awareness of (an)other tradition(s), double morning and evening offerings (P: Exod 29:38-42; Num 28:3-8) and/or an animal offering in the morning and a cereal offering in the evening (2 Kgs 16:15; cf. 1 Kgs 18:29, 36) and/or only a cereal offering in the morning (2 Kgs 3:20).

16-18 This unit reads like a belated footnote to the land-oriented 45:1-9. V 18 is close to 45:8 in tone. One could almost regard the unit as an economic counterpart of the cultic v 10: privilege remained within certain limits, beyond which it must not trespass. There may be a subtle wordplay contrasting what the head of state gives to God (מתת ידו "gift of his hand," vv 5, 11) and what he gives to others (מתנה "gift," vv 16-17). In ownership of the land the head of state was bound up in a vertical and horizontal solidarity of human relationships. Vertical, inasmuch as he owed it to his descendants to preserve crown property within the family. Horizontal, insofar as property rights were guaranteed for commoners as well as for royalty, by divine sanction (cf. 1 Kgs 21:18-19). In these respects the passage lets the reader look ahead to the territorial material of chaps. 47-48. V 17 makes an interesting reference to the institution of the fiftieth year of release or jubilee (cf. 40:1 *Comment*; Lev 25:8-13).

19-24 This is the final part of the visionary framework for the whole unit, chaps. 43-46. Its references to cultic procedure and sacrifices make it a fitting conclusion to the section 45:18-46:15, which has been concerned with this very topic. Two sets of outdoor kitchens are described. The first is situated beside the rooms on the north side of the west building, at the far end of the access path leading from the outer court (cf. 42:9). To get there the prophet is taken out of the inner court (44:4) through the north gate into the outer court, and then left to the entrance to the path, which was built up on the higher level of the inner court and was regarded as an extension of it. As such, it was priestly ground, and so the other end of the path formed a suitable location for cooking the most holy offerings, which were the priests' dues (cf. 42:13; 44:29; cf. the rulings of P in Exod 29:32-33; Lev 10:12-13, etc.). Confining these offerings to the inner court meant that the people, who had access to the outer court, were protected from contagious holiness (cf. 44:19 and *Comment*).

Ezekiel is made to retrace his steps, back into the outer court, and is taken over to each of the four corners, where outdoor kitchens were demarcated by a low wall. There the laity's sacred meals associated with the shared offerings were to be prepared by the lower order of temple personnel (cf. 44:11; 45:5). The demarcation is typical of the temple vision; it reinforces the concept of a scale of holiness that peaked at the center.

Explanation

The theme of the temple as a material embodiment of divine holiness continues in this complex unit. The palace could not stand next door to the temple any longer nor could the city include it in its limits. It must stand in isolated splendor (43:12). Pagans might no more do guard duty at the temple gates, as if the temple were an annex to the palace. Rather, within its walls the two-tier system of holiness that pertained to the buildings and courts must find expression in the human sphere. The inner court was to be reserved for the priests, while the outer one was to be where the people worshiped, serviced by a lower order. The priests were to reflect both in their work and in a different lifestyle the very holiness of God (cf. 1 Pet 1:15; 2:5).

The empty temple complex of chaps. 40-42 now comes alive. Supremely Yahweh takes possession of his new home. Earlier threads in the book which have traced the departure of his glory are now drawn together in a positive finale. The traditional phrase "in the presence of Yahweh" may now be meaningfully used again (44:3; 46:3, 9; cf. 41:22). It is Yahweh's taking up residence in the temple that starts the wheels of worship turning and energizes the temple area into a concourse of bustling activity. Thereupon, staffing with temple personnel, the question of their economic support, and temple procedures become the relevant topics of this unit.

Now that a working temple is in view, another aspect of holiness comes into consideration, alongside the former one. The altar, an item mentioned in passing in the earlier unit, now leaps into prominence. If the divinely occupied temple building is a throbbing heart, the altar represents lungs that maintain the spiritual life of the community of faith. Accordingly the visionary narrative of Yahweh's return is followed by the description of the altar and its dedication (43:13-17, 18-27). In both the latter acount and in the delineation of annual rites (46:18-25) the sin offering plays a key role. It was the means by which the infringement of cultic holiness by human sinning could be repaired. There was constant need to remove the pollution by daubing the blood of the sin offering and indeed of other sacrifices (45:15, 17; cf. the christological application in Heb 9:21-26; 10:19-22). The weekly and monthly rites are presented as an everflowing stream of worship that consisted of sacrifice, body language (46:3, 9) and sacrificial meals (44:3; cf. 46:23, 24).

Most space, however, and prior place are devoted to the personnel of the temple, who in their twofold grouping not only reflect gradations of holiness but also, one might say, cultically embody the two-sided covenant relationship, one group representing the people and the other Yahweh himself (44:11, 15). Yet the priests also directly reveal God's will to his people (44:23-24). There are at least two attempts to work out the relationship between the two cultic groups (cf. esp. 40:45; 44:13). In part at least these attempts correspond to the difficulties of translating theology into human actuality (cf. 37:5-10!) and of adequately reforming a system that had become corrupt.

Theology has ever to embrace social and economic factors if it is to be worthy of the name. Here there is concern for the maintenance of especially the upper order of the temple staff. The people paid sacred dues that went to support the priesthood; their sacrifices too in many cases were so allocated, on the principle that "those who serve at the altar share in the altar offerings" (1 Cor 9:13). There were to be no hindrances in the steady flow of the people's contributions. Especially the head of state was not to follow the precedent of his pre-exilic counterparts and by his unjust demands upset this rhythm. The messianic hope of earlier prophets, although tempered by political realism, is preserved; even in the mainly cultic orientation of these chapters the head of state comes over as a key figure.

Overall these chapters present sketches of the working temple, often taking over earlier cultic traditions and sometimes evidently creating new details of cultic expression. The unit gives the practical outworking of a theology of an overwhelmingly transcendent God immanent among his covenant people. It presents a challenge still relevant to modern believers. Worship that is done decently and in order (1 Cor 14:40; cf. Ezek 46:9), the constant reconciliation of an imperfect people (cf. 1 John 1:8-2:2), and viable back-up systems of administration and economic support are issues that still confront the people of God.

Temple and Land (47:1-48:35)

Bibliography

Aharoni, Y. *The Land of the Bible: A Historical Geography.* 2nd ed. Philadelphia: Westminster, 1979, 68-77. **Auld, A. G.** *Joshua, Moses and the Land.* Edinburgh: T. & T. Clark, 1980, 72-87. **Barr, J.** "*Migraš* in the Old Testament." *JSS* 29 (1984) 15-31. **Clements, R. E.** *God and Temple.* Oxford: Blackwell, 1965. **Darr, K. P.** "The Wall around Paradise: Ezekielian Ideas about the Future." *VT* 37 (1987) 271-79. **Farmer, W. R.** "The Geography of Ezekiel's River of Life." *BA* 19 (1956) 17-22. **Greenberg, M.** "Idealism and Practicality in Numbers 35:3-4 and Ezekiel 48." *JAOS* 88 (1969) 59-66. **Kallai, Z.** "The Boundaries of Canaan and the Land of Israel in the Bible" (Heb.). *Eretz-Israel* 12 (1975) 27-34. **Macholz, G. Ch.** "Noch einmal: Planungen für den Wiederaufbau nach der Katastrophe von 587. Erwägungen zum Schlussteil des sog. 'Verfassungsentwurf des Hesekiel'." *VT* 19 (1969) 322-52. **Mackay, C.** "The North Boundary of Palestine." *JTS* 35 (1934) 22-40. **North, R.** "Phoenician-Canaan Frontier L^ebô' of Hama." *Mélanges de l'Université Saint-Joseph* 46 (1970) 71-103. **de Vaux, R.** "Le pays de Canaan." *JAOS* 88 (1968) 23-30.

Translation

[1]*He brought me back to the entrance to the temple, and there I found water issuing from under the temple threshold and flowing east, the direction the temple faced. The water ran along[a] the southern sidewall of the temple, then to the south of the altar.* [2]*He led me out through the north[a] gate and took me round the outside to the outer[b] gate that faces [c] east, where I found the water[d] gurgling[e] out on the south side.* [3]*As the man went on eastward with the measuring line in his hand, he measured 1000 cubits[a] and led me through the water, which came up to the ankles.[b]* [4]*He measured a further 1000 and led me on through the water, which[a] was now up to the knees. Then he measured another 1000 and led me through[b]—it came up to the waist.* [5]*He measured 1000 more: it became a river I could not wade through because the water came so high. It was deep enough to swim in, an unfordable river.* [6]*He asked me, "Do you see, human one?" Then he led me back to the river bank.* [7]*When I got back,[a] I found a great number of trees on both banks of the river.* [8]*"This water," he told me, "flows out to the region in the east and then it will go down into the Arabah and reach the sea, which is polluted water,[a] and that water will become pure.[b]* [9]*All the living things that surge wherever the river formed by it[a] reaches will thrive. There will be fish aplenty once this water has reached there.[b]* [10]*Fishermen will stand[a] on its[b] shores; nets will be[c] spread out to dry from En-gedi to En-eglaim.[d] It will match the Mediterranean[e] in the variety[f] and quantity of its[g] fish.* [11]*But its marshes and pools will be left impure and used to supply salt.* [12]*Along the river, on either bank, will grow fruit trees of every kind, with leaves that never wither and fruit that never stops cropping. They will produce new fruit every month, because the water for them issues from the sanctuary. Their fruit will be used[a] for food and their leaves for healing."*

[13]*The following message comes from the Lord[a] Yahweh: "Here[b] is a description of the frontiers[c] of the land you are to share as tenured property among Israel's twelves tribes.[d]* [14]*You are to receive in equal shares tenure of this land I promised with raised hand to give to your ancestors and which now you will have allotted to you as tenured property.*

[15]*Here then are its frontiers: on the north a line from the Mediterranean through*[a] *Hethlon and the Hamath*[b] *Pass to Zedad,* [16]*then through Berothah and Sibraim, situated between the territories of Damascus and Hamath, to Hazar-enon,*[a] [17]*So the frontier*[a] *runs from the sea to*[b] *Hazar-enon, where the territory of Damascus lies to the north*[c] *and likewise that of Hamath. Such*[d] *will be its northern border.* [18]*East border: it runs from that point between*[a] *Hauran and Damascus, and then the Jordan forms the frontier*[b] *between Gilead and the land of Israel down to*[c] *the eastern sea as far as Tamar*[d]—*such will be its eastern border.* [19]*South*[a] *border: it extends from Tamar and runs to Lake Meribah*[b] *at Kadesh and to the Wady and on to the Mediterranean—such will be the southern border.* [20]*West border: the Mediterranean forms the frontier up to a point level with the Hamath Pass—such will be the western border.* [21]*You are to make a distribution of this land among yourselves on the basis of Israel's tribes,* [22]*allotting it as tenured property to yourselves and to the aliens who reside with you and have produced families there. You must treat them the same as native Israelites: they are to share the allotment*[a] *of tenured land with Israel's tribes.* [23]*The land you give each alien to hold by tenure is to be located in the tribal area where he resides. So runs the oracle of the Lord Yahweh.*

48:1 *"Here is a list of the denominated tribal areas.*[a] *(1)*[b] *At the northern end, next to*[c] *the line made by Hethlon, the Hamath Pass and Hazar-enan, south of the territory of Damascus and adjacent to Hamath, with an allocation*[d] *from east*[e] *to*[f] *west: Dan.* [2]*(2) Bordering Dan's territory, from east to west: Asher.* [3]*(3) Bordering Asher's territory, from east to west: Naphtali.* [4]*(4) Bordering Naphtali's territory, from east to west: Manasseh.* [5]*(5) Bordering Manasseh's territory, from east to west: Ephraim.* [6]*(6) Bordering Ephraim's territory, from east to west: Reuben.* [7]*(7) Bordering Reuben's territory, from east to west: Judah.* [8]*Bordering Judah's territory, from east to west, will be situated the reservation that you are to set apart, 25,000 (cubits) wide and as long as each of the allocations extending from east to west; it will have the sanctuary within it.*[a] [9]*The reservation you set apart as Yahweh's is to be 25,000 (cubits) long and 20,000*[a] *wide.* [10]*The following groups will have the sacred reservation assigned to them: an area with north and south dimensions of 25,000 (cubits) in length*[a] *and west and east dimensions of 10,000 in breadth,*[a] *at the center of which Yahweh's sanctuary will be situated, is to be assigned to the priests,* [11]*the consecrated*[a] *priests, descendants*[b] *of Zadok, who discharged their duties for me, refraining from going astray when the Israelites did—unlike the Levites!* [12]*They will have a special area set apart*[a] *from the reservation that is set apart from the land, a particularly sacred area adjoining the Levites' territory.* [13]*Assigned to the Levites*[a] *will be a section adjacent to the priests' territory, 25,000 (cubits) long and 10,000 in breadth. The whole of it*[b] *will be 25,000 long and 20,000*[c] *wide.* [14]*None of this prime land is to be sold or exchanged*[a] *by the holders or transferred*[b] *to others, because it is sacred to Yahweh.* [15]*The extra strip 5,000 cubits wide, broadside to the dimension of 25,000, is unconsecrated: it will belong to the city for residence and as open land,*[a] *and will have the city at its center.* [16]*The latter's dimensions are as follows: the north, south, east and west limits will each be 4,500*[a] *cubits.* [17]*The city's open land will extend 250 (cubits) to the north, south, east and west.* [18]*As for the remaining area that lengthwise runs alongside the sacred reservation and measures 10,000 (cubits) on the east and west edges,*[a] *its produce will be the food supply of the city workers.* [19]*The city's workforce, drawn from all the tribes of Israel, is to farm it.*[a] [20]*So the entire reservation will be 25,000 by 25,000 (cubits). You are to set aside this square*[a] *sacred reservation, including*[b] *the city property.* [21]*The remaining sections on each side of the sacred reservation and of the city's property are to be assigned to the head of state. The section on the east*[a] *will abut the area of 25,000 (cu-*

bits) and stretch to the eastern frontier, while the western section will also abut the area of 25,000 (cubits) and will extend to[b] the western frontier. These sections, which are parallel to the other allocations,[c] are to be assigned to the head of state. The sacred reservation, within which[d] lies the temple sanctuary [22] and which is bounded by[a] the Levites' property and by[a] the city's property and is flanked by the land that belongs to the head of state, is to be situated between the territories of Judah and Benjamin.[b] [23] The rest of the tribal areas, (8) from east to west: Benjamin. [24] (9) Bordering Benjamin's territory, from east to west: Simeon. [25] (10) Bordering Simeon's territory, from east to west: Issachar. [26] (11) Bordering Issachar's territory, from east to west: Zebulun. [27] (12) Bordering Zebulun's territory, from east to west: Gad. [28] The southern border of Gad's territory will coincide with the frontier[a] running from Tamar, through[b] Lake Meribah at Kadesh and through the Wady to the Mediterranean. [29] That is the specification of the land you are to allocate as tenured property[a] to the tribes of Israel, and those are to be their allocations. So runs the oracle of the Lord Yahweh."

[30] Here is a description of the city's exterior.[a] On[b] the north side 4,500 (cubits) are to be measured[c] [31] and there will be three of the city gates, which are to be named after Israel's tribes,[a] in the north: (1)[b] Reuben Gate, (2) Judah Gate, (3) Levi Gate. [32] On the east side there will be 4,5000 (cubits) and three gates: (1) Joseph Gate,[a] (2) Benjamin Gate, (3) Dan Gate. [33] The south side is to measure 4,500 (cubits) and there are to be three gates: (1) Simeon Gate, (2) Issachar Gate, (3) Zebulun Gate. [34] The west side[a] will be 4,500 (cubits) and there are to be three gates[b]: (1) Gad Gate, (2) Asher Gate, (3) Naphtali Gate. [35] The perimeter will be 18,000 (cubits), and from that time on the city will be named "Yahweh-is-there."

Notes

1. a. MT prefixes מתחת which, if correct, is locative "at the foot." Yet in v 1a it has been used literally "from beneath." This awkwardness and its absence from LXX* Syr Vg suggest that it has been wrongly copied from v 1a (Toy 201; Cooke 522).

2. a. For the form of the Heb. cf. 46:9; 47:15.

2. b. Cf. 44:1, although there the term is adjectival.

2. c. An error of metathesis is generally assumed, so that one reads הפונה דרך "that faces toward" (cf. 43:1).

2. d. Since the water has already been mentioned, המים "the water" is generally read, as LXX implies, assuming haplography.

2. e. The Heb. is onomatopoeic.

3. a. For the Heb. idiom see 40:5 and note.

3. b. For the genitive see GKC 128n.

4. a. The abs form מים "waters" implies apposition, but constr מי "waters of" is generally read with C, many Heb. MSS, LXX and Tg. MT probably suffered assimilation to the preceding במים "through the waters" (Cooke 523).

4. b. For consistency's sake במים "through the waters" is often inserted, with ancient support (see BHS), but significantly LXX supports MT's shorter text.

7. a. The objective suffix is anomalous and doubtless assimilation to וישבני "and he brought me back" in v 6 has occurred (GKC 91e). The regular form would be בשוב׳ (cf. Driver, Bib 35 [1954] 312).

8. a. MT אל־הימה המוצאים "to the sea, those which had been brought out" is problematic. The first term with its otiose ending is generally emended to אל־המים "to the waters," with the support of LXX Syr, assuming assimilation to the preceding הימה "to the sea." Then the following pl term qualifies it. In this case MT's consonants are supported by LXX (cf. 48:30). Accordingly Driver (Bib 19 [1938] 186-87), followed by NEB ("foul"), suggested a hoph ptcp from the stem צוא "be filthy, polluted" (cf. Syr "stagnant"). He judged that the Gk. translation "salty" cited in LXX^Qmg, which inspired Field's popular suggestion החמוצים "seasoned, salty" (cf. Isa 30:24), was a guess.

8. b. For Q cf. GKG 75oo.

9. a. MT's dual נְחָלִים "two rivers" is strange. LXX Vg (cf. Syr Tg "the waters of the river") imply הנחל "the river," as in v 9b (see the next note). Ehrlich (*Randglossen* 158) plausibly revocalized נחלם "their river, the river formed by them (= "waters" of v 8)," comparing "rivers of water" in Deut 8:7; 10:7; Jer 31:9; Syr Tg may reflect such an understanding. MT may have been influenced by the two rivers of Zech 14:8 (Cooke 520, with reference to Jewish tradition; cf. Clements' suggestion that it echoes the two rivers at the source of which El lived in Ugaritic mythology [*God and Temple* 107 note 2]).

9. b. MT and the ancient versions add "and it (lit. pl with reference to the waters) will become pure and it (sg) will live, everywhere that the river reaches," with a violent change of subject in the first case to the polluted water of v 8b. The material adds nothing to the content and is best explained as a collection of textual variants. The first verb is a variant of ונרפאו "and they will become pure" in v 8b. What follows is another form of the latter part of v 9aα, incorporating the variants שמה "thither" for שם "there" and הנחל "the river" for נחלים (see preceding note).

10. a. L reads ועמדו "and they will stand" according to *BHK.* For a discussion of the various Heb. forms see Gese, *Verfassungsentwurf* 90 note 1.

10. b. The suffix naturally relates to the river of v 9a, via שמה "thither" of v 9bα (contra Zimmerli 507).

10. c. The pl verb relates to the pl notion suggested by the two places.

10. d. Probably to be identified with Ain el-Feshkah, just to the south of Khirbet Qumran.

10. e. Lit. "the great sea"; also vv 15, 19, 20; 48:28.

10. f. See GKC 91e for the form.

10. g. Lit. "their," relating to the pl earlier.

12. a. For the K/Q variants cf. GKC 146f.

13. a. For the formulaic אדני "Lord" here and in v 23; 48:29 see the note on 20:3.

13. b. MT גה, pointed as if (א)גֵּי "valley" (=Syr), is generally taken, even by Barthélemy et al, *Preliminary Report* 5, 188, as a textual error for זה "this," attested by MSS LXX Tg Vg (cf. Num 34:6, 13): *gimel* was written in anticipation of (ג(בול "frontier."

13. c. MT גבול "frontier" requires the article, lost by haplography.

13. d. MT, supported by the ancient versions, adds חבלים יוסף "Joseph: (two) portions": the noun requires pointing as a dual on the evidence of Tg Vg. It would be possible to integrate it into the text by reading ליוסף "for Joseph," assuming haplography (Ehrlich, ibid.); however, its ungrammatical nature (Driver, *L'Ancien Testament et l'Orient* 144) and use of חבל instead of חלק "portion" (Cooke 530: cf. 45:7; 48:8, 21) brand it as an early harmonizing gloss that contrasted the reckoning of the twelve tribes here (excluding Levi) and in 48:30-34 (Rautenberg, *ZAW* 33 [1913] 112 note 1).

15. a. In MT הדרך "the way of" the article is otiose (cf. *BHS*). See the note on v 16.

15. b. In MT צדדה "to Zedad" and חמת "Hamath" (v 16) are out of order: cf. LXX; 48:1; Num 34:8. Probably a copyist's omission was restored at the wrong place.

16. a. MT חצר התיכון "the central court" was probably part of an annotation that together with the cue phrase דרך ה' (= דרך החון "outer, toward") now in v 15 belongs with v 2. It was connected with the reading החצר "the court" presupposed by LXX Syr for החון "the outside." It was referred to the wrong column: הדרך was taken as a correction of דרך, and the next phrase as a correction of the similar-looking חצרה עינון "to Hazar-enon" that underlies LXX (cf. v 17; 48:1; Num 34:9). The form of the second noun is עינן חצר in 48:1, as in Num 34:9-10, and LXX so standardizes.

17. a. As in v 13, the article lost by haplography needs to be restored: see *BHS.*

17. b. For חצר the context seems to require חצרה ("to . . ."), as originally in v 16. Was the form assimilated to that in 48:1 or to MT in v 16?

17. c. MT וצפונה צפון "and north northwards" is attested by the ancient versions (cf. Zimmerli 519), but probably originated as an early note that displaced צפונה "northwards" (cf. 48:1). It recorded the variants צפונה/צפון (tap) "north (side)" in vv 15, 17.

17. d. The copula and object sign ואת in MT here and in vv 18, 19 are an error for זאת "this" (cf. v 20): see *BHS.*

18. a. Heb. מבין[1,2] here signifies "from the place between" (see Zimmerli 519; Wevers 231; cf. 2 Kgs 16:14). The insertion of חצר-enon (Cornill 506 et al.; RSV) is unnecessary. However, the form seems to have contaminated מבין[3,4]: the latter replaced בין "between," which is generally read.

18. b. For MT מגבול "from a boundary" a verb מגביל "bounds" is implied by LXX Syr Vg here and by LXX Syr in v 20. MT was assimilated to the noun form that dominates the context.

18. c. Heb. על is used, as often, in the sense of אל "to" (Fohrer 257). Another instance occurs in 48:28.

18. d. MT תמדו "you shall measure" is generally judged, even by Barthélemy et al., *Preliminary Report* 5, 192-93, a reading inferior to תמרה "to Tamar" that underlies LXX Syr and is corroborated by

v 19; 48:28. Doubtless MT originated as a comparative gloss on 48:10, inspired by the parallel 45:3. The note was related to the wrong side of the margin and taken as a correction of the look-alike חמרה.

19. a. For the double representation in this verse and 48:28 see Zimmerli 520.

19. b. MT מריבות "Meriboth" is supported only by LXX; in 48:28; Deut 32:51 a sg form appears.

22. a. As in v 22a, a hiph form is expected: see *BHS*. MT יפלו "they shall be allotted" can hardly be used of people. Strictly the hiph signifies not "acquire by lot" (Zimmerli 521) but that the aliens were to join the Israelites in distributing the land (Cooke 530; cf. Ehrlich, *Randglossen* 159).

48:1. a. Lit. "the names of tribes." The language may have been influenced by Num 34:17, 19, which immediately follows the underlying literary model for Ezek 47:13-23.

1. b. The Heb. adds "one" (i.e., allocation, חלק, v 8) to each of the tribal statements of vv 1-7, 23-27. As in Josh 12:9-24, it is a primitive method of counting, like the strokes a prisoner traditionally puts on the cell wall.

1. c. For justification of the Heb. see Zimmerli, ibid.

1. d. Lit. "and they shall be (assigned) to him": the pronoun anticipates Dan; the pl verb envisages a compound subj (Cooke 539).

1. e. For MT פאת "(east) side" מפאת "from . . ." is required in the context (cf. vv 2-8) and underlies LXX. The opposite occurs in v 16 (see *BHS*). Undoubtedly this is an inter-column phenomenon: perhaps corrections of errors were misplaced (cf. 44:8).

1. f. MT הים "the sea" has suffered metathesis: in the context ימה "to the sea" is necessary and is supported by LXX (see Zimmerli, ibid.). Was it a comparative note relating v 1 to 47:15?

8. a. The same Heb. occurs in v 10; contrast K in v 21. The fem antecedent is not always remembered (Cooke 539).

9. a. See the relevant note on 45:1. LXX* (=LXX⁹⁶⁷) has preserved the original, adapted to "10,000" in MT. Cornill (508-9) shrewdly deduced the pristine form of LXX.

10. a. Heb. רחב¹,² "breadth" and ארך "length" occur here only: ארך is expected in the northern phrase, as in Vg. LXX*(⁻⁹⁶⁷) represents MT, except in the case of רחב²; Syr presupposes only רחב¹. For a similar inconsistency in the Heb. cf. מדה "measurement" in vv 30, 33.

11. a, b. MT המקדש מבני "the consecrated (place) from the sons" is generally redivided as המקדשם בני "consecrated, sons," supported by LXX and partially by Syr Tg: cf. 44:15; 2 Chr 26:18.

12. a. For the Heb. form see BDB 929a; Zimmerli 522-23.

13. a. LXX Vg rightly imply וללוים "and to the Levites" for MT והלוים "and the Levites," which has been assimilated to the end of v 12 (Hitzig 375).

13. b. For MT כל־ארך "whole length" LXX attests כל־הארך "the whole length," which is surely an error for כלה ארך "the whole of it (in) length" presupposed by Syr (cf. Driver, *Bib* 19 [1938] 187, who emended to כלו): for the form see 11:15; 20:40; 36:10.

13. c. As in v 9, LXX* again preserved the correct number: see *BHS*.

14. a. MT's indefinite sg ימר "one shall exchange" is supported by LXX, which also represents a sg verb in the first case. A pl form ימרו, presupposed by Syr Vg, was probably distorted by dittography.

14. b. Q aligns with the preceding verb. Probably K is to be followed, the masc being used as the simplest form of the verb (Ehrlich, *Randglossen* 160).

15. a. For מגרש "open land" see Barr, *JSS* 29 (1984) 22-27. Comparison with Num 35:2-3 suggests that here it was to be used as grazing land, while the land of v 18 below was to be used for crops.

16. a. In the southern dimension חמש "five" has been accidentally repeated in MT, as the Masoretes recognized.

18. a. MT, supported by the ancient versions, adds "and it will be alongside the sacred reservation," seemingly an early case of vertical dittography eased into place by the verb (Ehrlich, ibid.).

19. a. The syntax of v 19b is not clear: see Macholz, *VT* 19 (1969) 344 note 1.

20. a. The form of MT רביעית usually connotes a fraction, "a fourth." For a meaning "square" either רבועה (cf. 41:21; 43:16) or מרבעת (cf. 40:47; 45:2) is expected. The 'athnach needs to be moved to this word.

20. b. Lit. "together with," אל being used in the sense of על.

21. a. In place of MT תרומה "reservation," which is uncoordinated and which LXX Syr do not represent, the parallelism requires קדימה "east" (Smend 396-97 et al.). Did MT originate as a marginal note recording a variant, which a few MSS do read, for תרומיה in v 12? If so, it was related to the wrong column and taken as a correction of the similar-looking קדימה.

21. b. Heb. על is presumably used in the sense of אל. Strict parallelism is not necessary, contra *BHS* et al.

21. c. The article is contextually necessary (cf. v 8): *he* fell out by pseudohaplography between *taw* and *heth.*

21. d. The suffix relates to the reservation (K) rather than to the remaining area of v 21a (Q).

22. a. Lit. "and (it [= the reservation] extends) from . . . and from," specifying the northern and southern purlieus after the reservation's central nucleus (cf. Keil 377-78). The oft counseled deletion of the prepositions, initiated by Toy (89), is not justifiable. For the repeated prepositions cf. מזה ומזה "on this side and on that," 47:7, etc.

22. b. MT לנשיא יהיה "it will belong to the head of state," omitted by Syr, seems to be another case of vertical dittography. It spoils the thrust of vv 21b-22 (Zimmerli 525).

28. a. Haplography of *he* is suggested by LXX Syr Tg: הגבול "the frontier," as some MSS read, is required, as in 47:13, 17.

28. b. Lit. "up to," if עד is read with some ancient support (see *BHS*) and in line with 47:19. Oversight by homoeoteleuton may be assumed.

29. a. Generally בנחלה "as an inheritance" is read with the ancient versions and 45:1; 47:14, 22. Unless it was simply a common ב/מ error, MT מנחלה "from inheritance" may have originated as a note on נחלה "to the Wady" in v 28, in which it was misunderstood as "inheritance" like the ancient versions, attempting to integrate it into the context. If so, it was wrongly taken as a correction of בנחלה here, which it displaced.

30. a. Heb. תוצאה refers to the extremity of a boundary in Num 34; here the following references to walls and gates suggest "exterior parts, outer limits" (cf. BDB 426a; Cooke 537). The meaning in Num 34 may well have influenced the present usage.

30. b. The preposition is local in sense.

30. c. Inconsistently the Heb. uses מדה "measurement" again only for the south side. LXX adds in v 34, while Syr typically represents it in all four cases. Zimmerli's refusal to "restore" a uniform text here and in other cases (544) is commendable.

31. a. The Heb. places this clause first, in v 31aα. Its original position is often judged to be after v 30a (e.g., *BHK*), while Zimmerli (ibid.) considers it a gloss. It may simply be a case of clumsy writing, which matches the lack of symmetry in vv 30-35.

31. b. The Heb. adds "one" to each gate: see the relevant note on v 1.

32. a. Surprisingly MT prefixes the copula, which is generally removed, with much ancient support (see *BHS*). Doubtless assimilation to ושער(ים) "and gates" is to blame.

34. a. The parallels in vv 32, 33 have a copula: should it be restored, as is often counseled, e.g. by *BHS*?

34. b. MT, in place of the expected ושערים "and . . . gates," implied by LXX* Syr and read by one MS, has שעריהם "their gates," with no clear antecedent. Was it originally a marginal comment or variant referring to שערים "gates" in v 31, the suffix relating to the tribes? If so, it eventually displaced ושערים later in the list.

Form/Structure/Setting

The final redactional unit of the series of temple-related visionary descriptions and legislative prescriptions in chaps. 40-48 is found in these last two chapters. It falls into two unequal parts, a short visionary account of the stream that flows from the temple in 47:1-12, and a long description of the boundaries and tribal divisions of the land in 47:13-48:35. As in the second unit (chaps. 43-48), a visionary description forms the introduction to other relevant and related material. Structurally these quite different sections are tied together by several factors. The first is a wordplay formed by the terms that dominate each section: נחל "river" and נחלה "inheritance" (and the verb [הת]נחל "inherit"). The second is a shared reference to the Dead Sea in the east (47:8, 18) and to the Mediterranean (47:10, 20). The third and most important is the source in the first section and the center in the second: the בית "house" (47:1) and מקדש "sanctuary" (47:12), which find echoes, the latter term reappearing in 48:8, 10 and both terms in 48:21. The common theme is the essential bond between temple and land.

47:1-12 is the first primary unit. Its elements of guidance, measurement and explanation accord with the earlier visions of chaps. 40-46, especially those of chaps. 40-42, although its vocabulary diverges slightly (cf. Gese, *Verfassungsentwurf* 94-95, but see also Zimmerli 511). The explanation, which here plays a major role, functions as a means of communicating the miraculous effects of the river. However, the tone of the narrative is much more apocalyptic than any of the other visionary accounts in chaps. 40-48 (cf. Zech 14:8). The water that issues from the temple or sanctuary (vv 1, 12) provides a framework for the whole piece. Moreover, the "water" (מים) dominates it throughout; from v 5 onwards it shares its prevalence with "river" (נחל). The explanation of vv 8-12 has a double healing as its inclusion, the water's healing or purification (ונרפאו, v 8) of the Dead Sea, and the healing effect (תרופה, v 12) of the trees growing beside the river. The reference to the trees lining the river (vv 7, 12) provides a common conclusion for the visionary narrative (vv 1-7) and the explanation. The first part of the framework of the explanation, in v 8, is expanded by a double elaboration, in terms of fish (vv 9-10) and residual salt (v 11). The elaboration is rhetorically tied to v 8 by an initial echo of "these waters" (המים האלה, vv 8, 9) and a closing echo of the earlier verb of healing or purification (ונרפאו, v 8; ירפאו, v 11). The block of vv 8-11 and the statement of v 12 both culminate in cases of *lamed* of purpose ("for salt"/"for food . . . for healing").

Within the visionary description והנה "and behold" (translated "and I found") has the role of introducing a series of disclosures, in vv 1aα, 2b and 7. This feature is varied by the attention-seeking question of v 6, which highlights the phenomenon of v 5abβ. These stylistic elements suggest that the narrative moves in four stages, vv 1/2/3-6a/6b-7. Each stage is introduced by the prophet's being led to a fresh location. In the third case the leading is slightly delayed: it develops into a series of its own, each phase prefaced by mention of measuring—until the prophet cannot follow. Indeed, from v 4 till the end of the unit hyperbole is a marked stylistic trait. It is evidenced by repetition within vv 5 and 9, רב מאד "very many" (vv 7, 9), כל "all" (vv 9, 12) and by the comparison of v 10 and the miraculous monthly cropping of v 12. Exception has been taken to vv 6b-8aα (Gese, *Verfassungsentwurf* 92-93 et al.) on account of the repetition of ויאמר אלי "and he said to me" and the anticipation of the material of v 12. It has been hailed as a typical case of *Wiederaufnahme*, or redactional insertion, that repeats an earlier element as a tie back into an older narrative. However, repetition is not necessarily to be so explained (cf. other cases where *Wiederaufnahme* has been questionably assumed: in 21:14 by B. Lang [*VT* 29, 1979, 40] and in 40:2, 4-5a by Talmon and Fishbane [*ASTI* 10, 1975/76, 144-45]). In this case there seems to be an intention in v 6a to borrow a feature from the vision in chap. 8, where an alternating sequence of such questioning and narrative of guidance and discovery occurs (see especially 8:6-13) as a device both to draw attention to something remarkable and to refer to further surprises in store. V 11 too has been even more widely regarded as a secondary amplification, but stylistically it does nestle comfortably in its context, as noted above.

47:13-48:29, to which 48:30-35 has been appended, forms an integral unit, as Gese (*Verfassungsentwurf* 100) confirmed from its stylistically homogeneous series of passages framed with headings and summaries. The unit falls into two parts, 47:13-23, which describes the frontiers of the land to be distributed to the tribes, and 48:1-29, which outlines its actual tribal distribution. 48:29 seems to resume both 47:13-23, with its reference to the allotting (תפּ[י]לו) of "this land" (הָאָרֶץ הַזֹּאת) as "tenured property" (בנחלה), and 48:1-28, by echoing "and these" (ואלה) from 48:1. Basically the unit combines geographical and demographical lists (47:15-20; 48:1-28), with their own headings in 47:15a and 48:1a, and sets them in an oracular framework addressed with second plural references to Israel. The framework is bounded by a messenger formula and by two divine saying formulas, which appear to demarcate the two halves of the unit (A . . . A'/ . . . A': 47:13-14, 21-23; 48:29. Cf. too the framing 48:8b-9a, 20b). The divine speaking of 47:14 nominally conflicts with the third person references of 48:9, 10, 14 (for v 11 see *Comment*), but each fits its own form-critical context. The mixed composition is reminiscent of the deliberate presentation of cultic regulations as prophetic revelation within chaps. 43-46.

There is a tendency to regard 47:22-23 as redactional: their reference to resident aliens is taken as a correction of v 14 (see Gese, *Verfassungsentwurf* 98-99; Zimmerli 526, 532). Certainly these verses go beyond v 14, but their content seems to function both as a parallel to vv 13-14 and as a climactic advance. There is a nice correspondence between כם . . . לאבתיכם אִישׁ כּאָחִיו "each like his brother . . . to your fathers" and כּאֶזְרָח בבני ישׂראל "like a native among the sons of Israel."

The tribal list in 48:1-28 interlocks with the frontier lists of 47:15-20 in that the initial reference to the north frontier and the final reference to the south border are brief echoes of the earlier list (47:15b-17//48:1bα; 47:19//48:28b). This latter list divides into vv 1-7, 8-22, 23-29 in an ABA pattern, with proportions of seven, fifteen and seven lines respectively. The second, largest section concerning the central reservation is carefully interwoven into the other two. V 8a dovetails into v 7, while vv 21b-22 elaborately tie into vv 7 and 23-29; v 23a glances back at vv 1-7.

48:30-35 is a supplement that develops v 16 by giving details of its gates and wall. It is modeled on the tribal list of 48:1-29 in its initial heading . . . ואלה "and these . . ." in v 30a and in its numerical system of a repeated אֶחָד "one." The order of the compass points does not correspond exactly to that of v 16, but echoes that of the frontier description in 47:15-20. The structure of the piece is a framing of the description of the external parts of the city (vv 30b-34) with material concerning the whole (vv 30a, 35).

The three pieces of this redactional unit, behind a facade of compositional coherence, mirror on a smaller scale the unevenness of the previous unit in chaps. 43-46. The spiritual fantasy of the vision in 47:1-12 gives way to the down-to-earth geographical and demographical details of 47:13-48:29. As for 48:30-35, although it is obviously written with the previous piece in view, a skewing of emphasis from sanctuary to city represents a different perspective. 47:1-12 is widely accepted as the high-flown, climactic conclusion to a series of primary vision accounts, which reflects the phenomenon of the closed east gate (43:1-11; 44:1-2, 4; cf. Zimmerli 549-50). Within 47:13-48:29, 47:15-20 demonstrates a close dependence on Num 33-34 that is reminiscent of the echoes of Num 18 in the late 44:4-16 and of Lev 26 in the parts of chaps. 34 and 37 that were the fruit of late, though still exilic, redaction. 48:30-35, which leans heavily on 47:13-48:29, but has its own counter emphasis, is later still. Redaction is as alive and well in this unit as in any of the previous ones; so too is its sense of divine authority, evidenced in the prophetic formulas of 47:13, 23; 48:29.

Comment

47:1-2 This visionary experience portrays and proclaims the temple as source of blessing for the land. Redactionally the prophet returns from inspecting kitchens in the outer court (46:21). Ezekiel evidently stands at the entrance to the nave of the temple (cf. 41:2; Busink, *Tempel* 767, contra Zimmerli 511, who envisages a position in front of the temple building). The "threshold" (מפתן, cf. 46:2) seemingly equates with the סף ("threshold") of 41:16. A trickle of water ran down the steps in the direction of the east gate. However, since the altar stood in the way of a direct flow, the water first flowed down the right side of the steps and along the south sidewall of the temple before crossing the inner court in a course to the south of the altar. That course was apparently maintained across the outer court and beyond the outer east gate, as the prophet discovered after a necessary detour through the north gate(s), since the east gates were closed. There is an implicit reminder that this was the route that Yahweh had traveled in his return to the temple (43:1-5). The stream, virtually retracing his path, was flowing from the very presence of God.

3-6a The two discoveries made in quick succession in vv 1-2 are followed by a third, which is described at greater length as a focus of interest. The description is heightened by a series of stops and starts. Probes undertaken by the supernatural guide, who in this final appearance is introduced in a way similar to his first appearance in 40:3, record the amazing progress of the stream. Clearly the measuring has a different function than in chaps. 40-42. In just over a mile the stream increases to a deep river. Normally one would envisage tributaries and drainage as the cause of such a phenomenon. Here, however, a miracle is at work, somewhat like the unspent jar of meal and unfailing cruse of oil in 1 Kgs 8:12-16, or like the growth of the kingdom of God from mustard seed to spreading tree (Mark 4:31-32; cf. Dan 4:8[11]) or like the stone that became a great mountain (Dan 2:35). Still more surprises are in store. As the question implies, Ezekiel has seen nothing yet!

6b-7 The climax in the narrative, as in the ensuing explanation (v 12), comes with the discovery of an oasis of trees growing in the barren Wilderness of Judah between Jerusalem and the Dead Sea. Do they find an echo in Second Isaiah's trees in the desert (Isa 41:19; cf. 35:1-2)?

8-12 The habitual visionary element of explanation here serves to describe first the further course of the river, although the topography is left unclear (cf. Zimmerli 513), and then another miraculous effect, both of which lie beyond the prophet's sight. At the end, in v 12, a more usual type of explanation is devoted to the orchard of trees that line the river in v 7. First, however, the healing effect of the river upon the Dead Sea is described in vv 8-10. It was to become a freshwater lake, able to sustain an enormous abundance of fish. The upper half of the west shore of the Dead Sea (cf. Farmer, *BA* 19 [1956] 19-20) is portrayed as a fisherman's paradise. In its backwaters, however, would be left salt water to provide salt for cultic (43:24) and presumably for human needs, although the verse seems primarily to reflect the cultic concern evident throughout chaps. 40-48. The Dead Sea is cursed with its deadly minerals, which make up 25% of its water over against a 5% salt content of sea water (Cooke 520). Moreover, simply as a mass of water it is a symbol of chaos, that which is hostile to the purposes of God for his people (cf. Rev 21:2). The explanation reverts in v 12 to the trees. Barren land was to be transformed into a scene of sustenance and herbal healing, a perennial antidote to pain and need. Rev 22:2, drawing on a slightly different tradition, firmly equates this blessing with the tree of life. The source of such blessing, v 12 wants to remind us, is the sanctuary (cf. Ps 133:3; 134:3; Mal 3:10-12).

Behind the vision stands the cultic concept of blessing, as the power of God which, crowning the worship of his pilgrim people, returns home with them and enriches their lives. Here it appears appropriately, after the regulations for temple upkeep and worship have been revealed in chaps. 43-46. The particular imagery is drawn from a motif in the Songs of Zion tradition, the "river whose streams delight the city of God, the holy habitation of the Most High" (Ps 46:5[4]). The river was a religious metamorphosis of the little Gihon spring, which was itself of some cultic significance (1 Kgs 1:33, 45; cf. Ps 110:7) or possibly of the Shiloh canal (Isa 8:6). The rivers of Eden (Gen 2:10-14) may have also been a contributing tradition, as is often claimed (see e.g. Baltzer, *Ezechiel* 155; Levenson, *Theology* 28-29, 32; Fishbane, *Biblical Interpretation* 370 note 131).

13-23 This passage functions as an introduction to 48:1-29, where the allocation of the land is described. V 14 lays down a theological premise, the revival of the theme of the land promised to the patriarchs, which runs through the pentateuchal sources. Once more a landless people stood on tiptoe, to use the language of Rom 8:19, awaiting God's promise. Like the Second Exodus, a second possession of the land was typologically theirs. A geographical premise to be clarified is the total extent of the land to be severally allocated, and to this question the present passage addresses itself. The answer is again expressed in a traditional form, inspired by the material of Num 33:50-34:15, of which this is a briefer version apart from the description of the northern boundary. Only in Num 33:54; 34:13 and Ezek 47:13 is התנחל "take as one's inheritance" used with the land as object, while 47:14b is close to Num 34:2bα (Auld, *Joshua* 74-75). However, the land is no longer to be distributed by lot but by the sovereign decree of Yahweh. Essentially both in Numbers and here the promised land is described as the land of Canaan, as regularly in P. This was a recognized political entity that included Palestine and southern Syria in the fourteenth and thirteenth centuries B.C. It is these ancient limits that are echoed (Aharoni, *Land* 68-69; M. Weippert, *IDBSup* 126). The emphasis on equal shares intentionally seems to run counter to the disparate portions of Num 33:54 (cf. Num 26:52-56), which depended on tribal size. The motif of equality anticipates the tribal strips of chap. 48.

15-17 A heading and summary box in the description of each frontier. While the order is south/west/north/east in Num 34, here the order north/east/south/west is intended to accord more closely with the order of chap. 48, where there is a longitudinal progression, from north to south, of strips on a lateral east/west plane. The crucial identification for the northern frontier is that of לבוא חמת, which occurs in a number of Old Testament texts as Israel's most northerly point. Is it "Lebo (of) Hamath" or "entrance to Hamath"? The controverted identification of this place drastically affects the placing of the north border. It is perhaps best interpreted as the approach road that leads north to Hamath, and specifically the southern end, near the modern Merj ʿUyun (see North, *Mélanges* 46 [1970] esp. 97-99; cf. the discussion in Zimmerli 528-30). Then the western end, which is left undefined, may begin just north of Tyre, at the mouth of the Litani river perhaps. De Vaux (*JAOS* 88 [1968] 29) has put forward the attractive suggestion that in vv 16-18 reference is made to the Assyrian provinces of Hamath, Damascus and Hauran, established between 733 and 720 B.C. One may add "Israel" in v 18, corresponding to the province of Samerina. The northwest border of the province of Hauran seems to have come to a northerly limit parallel with a point just to the north of Tyre (see J. M. Miller and J. H. Hayes, *A History of Ancient Israel and Judah* [Philadelphia: Westminster, 1986] 333, map 24). The mention of Hamath creates some difficulty: even as a province it lies too far to the north. However, if it was governed jointly with the province of Manṣuate (see J. D. Hawkins, *CAH* [revised] 3:1, 417), the name may be used loosely to cover both areas; there would be consistency with a line running horizontally from the vicinity of Tyre. The other place names are no longer identifiable.

18 The description of the east frontier pinpoints its northerly end, then seemingly runs down the eastern boundary of the province of Hauran, then along the boundary between the provinces of Qarnini (Karnaim) and Gal'azu (Gilead) till it reaches the Jordan. It follows the Jordan and the west bank of the Dead Sea as far as Tamar at the southwest end of the Dead Sea (cf. J. T. Butler, *ISBE* 4, 724-25). As consistently in P, the promised land, coinciding with the land of Canaan, excludes the Transjordan, which is regarded as unclean (Josh 22:19, 25, 27; cf. Haran, *Temples* 39, 41). Did Tolkien have this conception in mind when he wrote of the outlandish Buckland hobbits who lived to the east of the river Brandywine?

19-20 The south border makes a wide sweep to the southwest, to the oasis of Kadesh-barnea, as Num 34:4 terms it (cf. Num 20:1-13; 27:14), before linking with the Wady el- ᶜArish, the standard frontier with Egypt (cf. Josh 15:4, 47; 1 Kgs 8:65). The west frontier, which skirts the Mediterranean, is an ideal limit never attained by Israel in the Old Testament period.

21-23 Num 34:13-15, like 33:54, is deliberately transformed: mention of the 9½ cisjordanian tribes and of the 2½ tribes in the Transjordan is replaced by citation of two other categories, native Israelites and resident aliens. Elsewhere in the Old Testament the latter are represented as incapable of owning land. Their underprivileged status left them open to oppression (cf. 22:7, 29). The injunction to treat them like nationals did indeed form part of the legal traditions in H and P, in moralistic (but lacking teeth) and religious exhortations (e.g. Lev 19:33-34; Num 15:29), but here it is given a radically new application in terms of naturalization and integration into tribal communities.

48:1-29 There follows a schematic representation of the tribal allocation of the land, in which the equality of 47:14 is expressed in latitudinal strips of equal size (cf. v 8), each just over eight miles from north to south. The tribal areas (vv 1-7, 23-29) are augmented by a further one that is designated a territorial "contribution" or "reservation" set aside as a token that the whole land belonged to Yahweh (vv 8-22; cf. Lev 25:23). In literary terms this reservation has the lion's share of the elaboration, in keeping with the primarily cultic interests of chaps. 40-48.

1-7, 23-29 The tribal allocations to the north of the reservation are prefaced with a recapitulation of the northern frontier. Correspondingly those to the south will conclude with a repetition of the southern border (v 28). The assignment of seven tribes to the north of the reservation and five to the south accords with the fixed position of Jerusalem and the temple in Hebrew tradition, and analogously with the larger size of the northern kingdom. The traditional number of twelve

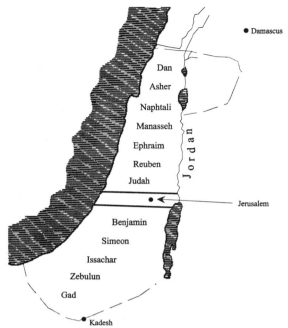

Figure 6. The division of the land

tribes is attained by the division of Joseph into the tribal groups Ephraim and Manasseh, after the omission of the landless Levi.

Historical tradition is also followed in the ordering of Dan, Asher, Naphtali, Manasseh and Ephraim and in their allocation to the north, and also in the placing of Simeon in the south. With the Jordan as the eastern frontier, Reuben and Gad had to be moved west. A further, major principle at work in the distribution was a genealogical one, derived from Gen 29-30; 35 (Fohrer 262). The sons of Jacob's two wives, Leah and Rachel, who included Levi, are given the privilege of proximity to the reservation and so to the temple. The sons of his two concubines Bilhah and Zilpah are set at a distance. Accordingly the geographical placing of the top three tribes nicely combine historical tradition and a stepson status; for balance the (transjordanian) stepson Gad had to be set in the far south. The eight full sons are placed four and four, to the immediate north and south of the reservation. The placing of Manasseh and Ephraim is also true to both history and the family principle; for balance Issachar and Zebulun had to be displaced to the south. The transjordanian Reuben, as the firstborn full son and part of the old northern kingdom, fits well below Ephraim. A surprising feature is the placement of Judah and Benjamin. Although their juxtaposition to the reservation is expected in view of their long history of support of the temple, one expects them to be reversed. The juxtaposition of Reuben, Judah and Levi as north gates of the city (v 31) suggests that in both cases common roles as sons of Leah may have been a determining factor (Zimmerli 541, who also notes that the meaning of Benjamin's name, "son of the right [= south]," also suits the southern location of this tribe).

8-22 The tribal units provide an outer framework for the main, cultic concern of this passage, which lies at the center: the literary and geographical structures nicely correspond. The reservation is defined in fluctuating terms. It can be the whole strip (v 8) or the central square including the city and its land (v 20). But, most often, as "the sacred reservation," it consists of the oblong made up by the priests' and Levites' territories (vv 9, 10). The priests' territory, which includes the sanctuary (v 10), is regarded as the most sacred area (v 12). The definition of the priests in v 11 represents a scrupulous revision in terms of the book's final ruling in 44:4-16 (see *Form/Structure/Setting* of chaps. 43-46). The two levels of holiness in the sacred reservation obviously extend the gradation that was a key feature of the sanctuary itself. As in their work, so in their living quarters the temple personnel reflect their respective standing. In principle the sacred reservation obviously corresponds to the older system of levitical cities advocated in P (Num 35:1-8), which is generally held to go back to pre-exilic times (see Budd, *Numbers* 372-75). The phrase "cities to live in" at 45:5 is a clear echo of terminology associated with that system (cf. Num 35:2; Josh 14:4; 31:2). A difference is that, whereas the tribe of Levi was landless in tribal terms and had the cities for residence and their surrounding land for grazing (rather than for crops), here the priests have that corresponding privilege, while according to the transitional summary in v 22 (=45:5; contrast the priests' lack of property in 44:28) the Levites are in an intermediate position. They own their land and evidently use it for crops (see Haran, *Temples* 116-17, 127), although it is inalienable, like that of the priests (v 14). The distinction reflects the midway position of the Levites observed in other portions of chaps. 40-48. In certain respects they are aligned with the people, as their representatives (44:11; 46:24). Accordingly the term "property" is used both of the city (vv 20-22) and of the Levites' holding.

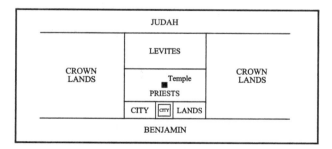

Figure 7. The reservation

The inclusion of the city and of crown land in the reservation is a reflex of older traditions: king, capital and temple had been interconnected for centuries. Although these bonds are noticeably loosened—palace and temple no longer adjoin (43:7-8) and the city is kept at a respectful distance from the temple—the influence of their unity is not allowed to fade into oblivion. The city, open to the members of every tribe (v 19; cf. 45:6), like some federal district, functions as a microcosm of the whole nation of tribes, representing them in the focal part of the land, next to the divine dwelling place.

The order of the three areas in the middle square of the reservation is not categorically stated. Does the order of mention imply a north-south order, priests/Levites/city (Macholz, *VT* 19 [1969] 335; Greenberg, *Int* 38 [1984] 202 note 37; Busink, *Tempel* 770)? Probably not. It is appropriate to conceive of the temple as in the center of the priests' territory and so of the whole reservation laterally and, less literally, vertically. It is not possible, however, to render בתוך consistently as "in the center": although it fits the priests' territory (v 10, cf. v 15), it obviously would not suit the rectangle of the sacred reservation (vv 8, 21b). The positioning of the Levites' and city's areas on either side of the priests' area is indicated by the closing v 22, if it has been interpreted aright. Most probably the city was envisaged as on the south side of the temple, in keeping with the pre-exilic tradition of the topography of city and temple. The tribe of Judah has a slightly more honorable position than Benjamin, next to the sacred reservation (cf. Macholz, ibid.)

The estates of the head of state extend in two large blocks on either side of the sacred reservation and city land. The size of this property and its positioning reflect the pre-exilic links with temple and city. The distancing from the temple, like that of the city, symbolizes a loosening of the dangerous old bonds, in order to accentuate the holiness of the temple. Yet in the clustering of all three elements within the reservation there is a clear echo of the theological significance that the two "secular" elements had in Judah's traditions. The reservation "in its various parts, not all of them equally sacred, keeps alive the memory of God's way with his people" (Zimmerli 543). In social and doubtless by implication political terms there is also a statement of the prestige, status and power possessed by the head of state. Quietly but firmly a negative note is also being sounded, as explicitly in 45:8, 9: the head of state, already richly endowed, was not to trespass upon tribal property.

30-35 This final section is a commentary on v 16: the "measurements" (מדות) of the latter are echoed in the "measurement" (מדה) of vv 30 and 33. In changing the order of the compass points from that of v 16 to that of 47:15-20, was there an intent to portray the city as a microcosm of the land? The twelve tribes are listed differently than in vv 1-29: reasonably so, because there a purely territorial tradition was being echoed, which excluded Levi, while here the genealogical tradition is resumed, in which Levi had a normative place, with Joseph replacing Ephraim and Manasseh to keep the number down to twelve. The city walls, which are nowhere mentioned but must be in view, are punctuated by gates named after the tribes. Perhaps the idea was suggested by the Ephraim and Benjamin gates of pre-exilic Jerusalem (2 Kgs 14:13; Jer 37:13); they, however, were named solely for reasons of geographical orientation.

The west side is regarded as the least significant, being allocated to three of the concubines' children. The south side is represented by three of Leah's sons: there may be an echo of the geographical placing of these tribes, to the south of the city, as indeed in the case of the north side. The east side is shared by Rachel's two children, while Dan, a concubine's son, is promoted to join them. The genealogical factor has clearly influenced the ordering, but not in the same way as in vv 1-29. The main point is that, as in the case of the city's population at v 19, all the traditional tribes are represented in the capital.

If the names of the gates represent the tribes' stake in the city, the eschatological name of the city symbolizes Yahweh's own stake in it. Although the temple where Yahweh had come to dwell in 43:1-9 was now separate from the city, his presence is firmly claimed here too. The new name "Yahweh-is-there" (יהוה־שׁמה) may reflect a wordplay on the old name "Jerusalem" (ירושׁלם). The aura of sacred privilege that in earlier verses pervaded the city by its position within the central reservation, here extends to an enjoyment of full fellowship with Yahweh. The city thus symbolizes the covenant bond between the whole people, portrayed in its gates, and their God, who was present within. These final verses seek to rehabilitate the old Zion traditions and claim them for the new Jerusalem as "the city of our God" (Ps 48:2[1]) and the city "to which the tribes go up" (Ps 122:4). One can hear a pastoral response to the spiritual longings of the exiles here, and an endorsement of their fervent prayer for Yahweh to "build up Zion, appearing in his glory" (Ps 102:17[16]).

Explanation

These closing chapters trace the relation of the temple to the land of Israel. There is a tradition deeply embedded in Israel's faith that inextricably linked together the fortunes of temple and land. To worship in the temple carried with it the privilege of dwelling in the land and enjoying God's blessing there (cf. Exod 15:17; Ps 78:54; Isa 57:13; Obad 17; cf. Clements, *Temple* 73). That tradition finds reaffirmation in this representation of Israel's future. It is used in conjunction with a further cultic tradition, expressed in a Song of Zion, Ps 46:5(4), of the mythological river that enhanced the city of God. In Ps 36:9-10 (8-9) the river is spiritualized as "a fountain of life" in the temple, which God gives his worshiping people to drink. That life is a blessing that enriches their future after they leave the temple courts (cf. Ps 133:3; 121). Correspondingly, here the river overflows its cultic bounds and spreads out into the Wilderness of Judah and down to the Dead Sea, to transform wherever it reaches and to bring life (v 9). God's abundant power to bless is affirmed by the increasing depth of what originated as a bubbling spring and by its instrumentality in creating entities that were "very many" (vv 7, 9, 10; cf. Eph 1:19; 2:7; 3:20). His dominion over the powers of chaos and death is clearly sounded in the healing brought about by the water and by the trees it nourishes (vv 8, 11). The seer in Revelation later borrowed from this vision. For him the leaves were for the healing of the nations (Rev 22:2). Ezekiel does not go that far: he makes a necessary pastoral start in the healing of the people of God, disoriented by the trauma of exile (cf. Darr, *VT* 37 [1987] 271-79, contra Eichrodt 585-86).

If chaps. 40-48 begin with theological architecture, they end with theological geography. The destruction of the old people of God gave an opportunity for a new beginning on sounder principles that took theology seriously. The tradition of the promised land and its distribution in Num 34 is re-used, so that Yahweh's ancient promise may eventually find a fulfillment that will supersede the old history of tragic self-will, with which the earlier chapters of this book are concerned. Land and people are closely connected throughout the Old Testament and not least in the book of Ezekiel. Expulsion from the land was the people's judgment; restoration to it was to be their salvation. Indeed, the repeated phrase עם הארץ "people of the land" in the previous section (45:22; 46:3, 9) may be considered a

seminal concept that entails as its corollary a literary progression to the renewed
gift of the land.

At the heart of the land stands the temple, its holiness suitably insulated from
the tribal territories by the sacred lands assigned to the priests and Levites. There
is respect for the otherness of the immanent God, a respect that is also evident in
the removal of the crown land and the city from close proximity to the temple.
Gone for good is a feature of the old Jerusalem, where the temple had been too
often subordinated to fallible, human concerns. Yet, in an echo of the positive
traditions that bound temple, palace and city together in holy concord, the city's
territory and the crown estates still lie in a demarcated cluster, within the strip of
land reserved for Yahweh.

The reservation, a material token that the whole land belongs to Yahweh, is
sandwiched between two groupings of tribal strips. The twelve strips serve to
recall the exiles from the narrowness of pre-exilic Judah and to widen their vision
to the ecumenical ideal of an association of twelve tribes. Indeed, this liberating
spirit goes further than ever before, embracing within its range of tribal privilege
the resident alien (47:22-23). If there was no longer room in the temple for
pagan staff who cared nothing for Yahweh (44:7, 9), there was room aplenty in
the land and so in the covenant for non-Israelites who were committed to him in
faith. The covenant clearly has implications for human relations. The tribal territories are differentiated from the portion of the head of state: by implication, as
46:18 stated, there was to be no more exploitation of human power through the
seizing of subjects' land. Moreover, the tribal strips were to be equal longitudi-
nally (contrast Num 33:54). Each strip included a slice of coastal plain, high-
lands and the Jordan valley, as far as it goes (Greenberg, *JAOS* 88 [1968] 64-66).
The message was that large tribes were never again to swamp the interests of smaller
ones. Lessons from the recent past have been well learned in this representation
of a new Israel.

There is an absence of a sterile egalitarianism. The head of state still has an
exalted role, as the large estates assigned to the royal family attest. The grouping
of the tribes in proximity to or at a distance from the temple presumes a tradition
of ancestral rank within the family of Jacob. This latter feature aligns with the
importance that the priestly school found in patriarchal narratives as archetypal
for the faith of Israel.

The postscript in 48:30-35 wants to highlight the positive role assigned to the
city in vv 16-17, rather than the negative implication. In so doing it seeks to give
greater prominence to the Zion tradition, in which the city shared in the aura of
divine presence that emanated from the temple (Ps 46:6[5]) and in which the
people found their basic oneness with God (Ps. 48:13-15 [12-14]). Also in these
verses a conspicuous loose end of the book is tied up. The city that Yahweh had
abandoned to destruction (9:5-8; 11:23; cf. 33:21; 40:1) would once more rejoice
in the nearness of its Lord, in line with the positive message of 16:53, 55 (cf. Isa
1:21-26).

The two parts of this final literary unit give expression to a biblical tension, the
paradox of an immanent God who blesses his covenant people in lavish abundance, and of a transcendent God who, however immanent, must remain apart
in his holiness of being. The tension finds its implicit resolution in the fact that
the people who worship and pay tribute to him by their contribution/ reserva-

tion receive from him a rich quality of life and the healing of their hurts. One can go on to envisage a perennial cycle, in which a second stage is the further bringing of worshipful contributions. Strictly it is this second stage that the present unit has in view, in which the initiative lies with the divine blessing (cf. 2 Chr 31:5-10; Joel 2:14).

The symbolism of theology translated into the stuff of an imaginative vision and more mundane cartography challenges believers to new efforts in the communication and outworking of their faith. The faithfulness and grace of God, the covenant bond of fellowship with him, social implications for church and state—in these lies inspiration for our dreams and endeavors.

Index of Authors Cited

Index of Principal Subjects

Index of Biblical Texts

A.   The Old Testament

B. Apocrypha

C. New Testament